TEST BANK FOR

BIOLOGY

Campbell • Reece

SIXTH EDITION

William Barstow, Editor
University of Georgia

CONTRIBUTORS
Michael Dini, Texas Tech University
Eugene Fenster, Longview Community College
Conrad Firling, University of Minnesota, Duluth
Kurt Redborg, Coe College
Marshall Sundberg, Emporia State University
Catherine Wilcoxson Ueckert, Northern Arizona University
Robert Yost, Indiana University/Purdue University, Indianapolis

Benjamin Cummings

San Francisco   Boston   New York
Cape Town   Hong Kong   London   Madrid   Mexico City
Montreal   Munich   Paris   Singapore   Sydney   Tokyo   Toronto

Project Editor: Evelyn Dahlgren
Production Editor: Steven Anderson
Publishing Assistant: David DeRouen
Production Service: Matrix Productions
Compositor: Tamarack Software
Cover Designer: Roy Neuhaus

On the cover: Photograph of an agave plant, Hawaii, © 1991 by Brett Weston.
Courtesy of the Brett Weston Archive.

ISBN 0-8053-6637-7

2 3 4 5 6 7 8 9 10—VG—05 04 03 02

www.aw.com/bc

Benjamin
Cummings

CONTENTS

PREFACE

The test bank for the Sixth Edition of Campbell and Reece's *Biology* is a thorough revision based on the solid foundation established by the five previous editions. Each test bank contributor reviewed every question carefully to ensure that the content and terminology of that question accurately reflects the material in the new edition of *Biology*. The contributors also wrote an average of fifteen new questions per chapter. Every attempt has been made to order the questions in the same sequence as the presentation of topics in the sixth edition text.

In this edition, two new sections of questions are included. The Media Activity questions are five additional questions per chapter that test material from the student media activities provided with the textbook. The Self-Quiz questions found at the end of each text chapter have also been added to the test bank. It should be noted that the answers to these Self-Quiz questions are in the textbook.

The classification scheme for the questions in the Sixth Edition has also been revised. We have tried to classify each question according to the complexity of the mental processes involved. The model we used is modified from Bloom, Benjamin *et al.*, *Taxonomy of Educational Objectives: The Classification of Educational Goals, Handbook I: Cognitive Domain.* New York, Longmans, Green, 1956. The categories in the cognitive domain that we use to classify questions are:

1. **Knowledge**: recognizing or recalling information.
2. **Comprehension**: grasping (understanding) the meaning of informational materials.
3. **Application**: applying previously-learned information in new situations to solve problems that have single or best answers.
4. **Analysis**: analyzing higher order questions that require students to think critically and in depth.

We recognize that you may interpret our classifications differently; therefore, these classifications should be considered only as a rough guide to the abilities required to answer each question.

The editing of prior questions and the writing of new questions was accomplished by the following group of biologists:

Unit 1	**Conrad Firling**, University of Minnesota, Duluth, MN
Unit 2	**William Barstow**, University of Georgia, Athens, GA
Unit 3	**Catherine Wilcoxson Ueckert**, Northern Arizona University. Flagstaff, AZ
Units 4-5	**Michael Dini**, Texas Tech University, Lubbock, TX
Unit 6	**Marshall Sundberg**, Emporia State University, Emporia, KS
Unit 7	**Robert Yost**, Indiana University Purdue University at Indianapolis, Indianapolis, IN
Unit 8	**Kurt Redborg**, Coe College, Cedar Rapids, IA

Chapter 1 and the Student Media Questions were provided by **Eugene Fenster**, Longview Community College, Lee's Summit, MO

The questions in the Sixth Edition Test bank are built upon questions authored by others. I am grateful to the following biologists who have contributed questions to previous editions of the test bank (edition numbers are shown in parentheses): William Barstow, University of Georgia (2, 3, 6); Neil Campbell, UC Riverside (3); Angela Cunningham, Baylor University (5); Richard Duhrkopf, Baylor University (4, 5); Gary Fabris, Red Deer College, Alberta Canada (4); Frank Heppner, University of Rhode Island (1); Walter MacDonald, Trenton State University (2); Rebecca Pyles, East Tennessee State University (4); Kurt Redborg, Coe College (4, 5, 6); Marc Snyder, The Colorado College (5); Richard Storey, The Colorado College (4, 5); Martha Taylor, Cornell University (3); Margaret Waterman, Harvard Medical School (3); Dan Wivagg, Baylor University (3, 4, 5); Catherine Wilcoxson Ueckert, Northern Arizona University (5, 6); Betty Ann Wonderly, J.J. Pearce High School, Richardson, TX (3).

Acknowledgments

I want to thank Evelyn Dahlgren, Developmental Editor at Benjamin Cummings, for asking me to edit the questions and for her immense help in coordinating the entire project. I thank, too, Steven Anderson, Production Editor at Benjamin Cummings, and Merrill Peterson and his staff at Matrix Productions for their expertise and hard work in copyediting and then translating our computer files to the printed page and to the cross-platform CD-ROM. I appreciate the sharp eyes and attention to detail of freelancers Susan Holt, who checked the copyedited manuscript, and Richard Morel, who checked many of the questions against the manuscript. Richard also added new questions to the test bank. A special thanks to Tameka Allison who worked nights and weekends to word process all the questions into our test generation program files. Thanks Evelyn, Steve, Merrill, Susan, Dick, and Tameka.

I recognize that the questions in the test bank may have errors. Since I edited all the questions, I take full responsibility for any mistakes. If you find errors, I would appreciate hearing from you.

William Barstow
Associate Biology Division Chairman and
   Director of Undergraduate Biology Majors
University of Georgia
Athens, GA 30602
Phone (706) 542-1688
Fax: (706) 542-1695
E-mail: barstow@dogwood.botany.uga.edu

Chapter 1   Introduction: Ten Themes in the Study of Life

1) Which of these is the *best* description of the science of biology?
   A) the study of life
   B) the study of rocks
   C) the study of humans
   D) the study of biodiversity
   E) the study of the way humans interact with their environment

   Answer: A
   Skill: Knowledge

2) A maple leaf is at which level in the hierarchical organization of life?
   A) tissue
   B) organ
   C) organelle
   D) population
   E) organism

   Answer: B
   Skill: Knowledge

3) Which of these is an example of an organelle?
   A) amoeba
   B) muscle
   C) stomach
   D) digestive system
   E) chloroplast

   Answer: E
   Skill: Knowledge

4) Which of the following are molecules?
   A) carbon
   B) water
   C) chlorophyll
   D) A and B
   E) B and C

   Answer: E
   Skill: Knowledge

5) What is a localized group of organisms that belong to the same species?
   A) network
   B) community
   C) population
   D) ecosystem
   E) collection

   Answer: B
   Skill: Knowledge

6) In terms of the hierarchical organization of life, an amoeba is _____ level of organization, whereas a dog is at the _____ level of organization.
   A) at the cell and organism ... multicellular organism
   B) only at the cell ... organism
   C) only at the organelle ... cell and multicellular organism
   D) only at the tissue ... multicellular organism
   E) only at the organelle ... unicellular organism

   Answer: A
   Skill: Knowledge

7) Which of these is a correct representation of the hierarchical organization of life from least to most complex?
   A) hydrogen, water, heart muscle cell, nucleus, heart muscle tissue, heart, human
   B) hydrogen, water, nucleus, heart muscle cell, heart muscle tissue, heart, human
   C) hydrogen, water, nucleus, heart muscle cell, heart, heart muscle tissue, human
   D) water, hydrogen, nucleus, heart muscle cell, heart muscle tissue, heart, human
   E) nucleus, hydrogen, water, heart muscle cell, heart, heart muscle tissue, human

   Answer: B
   Skill: Comprehension

8) Which of the following is reflective of the phrase "the whole is greater than the sum of its parts"?

A) the cell theory

B) emergent properties

C) homeostasis

D) reductionism

E) evolution

Answer: B
Skill: Knowledge

9) In order to understand the chemical basis of inheritance, one must understand the molecular structure of DNA. This is an example of the application of _____ to the study of biology.

A) evolution

B) emergent properties

C) the cell theory

D) reductionism

E) natural selection

Answer: D
Skill: Knowledge

10) Who first named and described cells in 1665?

A) Robert Hooke

B) Anton van Leeuwenhoek

C) Matthias Schleiden

D) Theodor Schwann

E) Charles Darwin

Answer: A
Skill: Knowledge

11) Which of these statements is one of the generalizations of the cell theory?

A) Life is extraterrestrial in origin.

B) All cells contain a nucleus.

C) DNA is the genetic material of all cells.

D) Cells have homeostatic mechanisms that maintain their internal environment.

E) New cells arise from preexisting cells.

Answer: E
Skill: Knowledge

12) One of the key distinctions between prokaryotic and eukaryotic cells is the presence of _____ cells, which is lacking in _____ cells.

A) a nucleus in eukaryotic ... prokaryotic

B) a nucleus in prokaryotic ... eukaryotic

C) DNA in prokaryotic ... eukaryotic

D) DNA in eukaryotic ... prokaryotic

E) a cytoplasmic organelle in prokaryotic ... eukaryotic

Answer: A
Skill: Comprehension

13) What are the basic "building blocks" of DNA?

A) protein

B) carbohydrates and lipids

C) 20 amino acids

D) 26 nucleotides

E) four nucleotides

Answer: E
Skill: Knowledge

14) Which of the following utilize DNA as their genetic material?

A) prokaryotes

B) eukaryotes

C) archaea

D) A and C only

E) A, B, and C

Answer: E
Skill: Comprehension

15) For most ecosystems _____ is (are) the ultimate source of energy and energy leaves the ecosystem in the form of _____.

   A) light ... heat

   B) heat ... light

   C) plants ... animals

   D) plants ... heat

   E) producers ... consumers

   Answer: A
   Skill: Knowledge

16) Which of the following is the main source of energy for producers such as plants?

   A) light

   B) carbon dioxide

   C) minerals

   D) heat

   E) chemicals

   Answer: A
   Skill: Knowledge

17) As a result of photosynthesis, plants release _____ into the atmosphere.

   A) methane

   B) carbon dioxide

   C) sugar

   D) minerals

   E) oxygen

   Answer: E
   Skill: Knowledge

18) Plants convert the energy of sunlight into

   A) the energy of motion.

   B) carbon dioxide and water.

   C) the potential energy of chemical bonds.

   D) minerals.

   E) kinetic energy.

   Answer: C
   Skill: Knowledge

19) A rock rolling down a hill is exhibiting

   A) photosynthesis.

   B) kinetic energy.

   C) chemical energy.

   D) decomposition.

   E) potential energy.

   Answer: B
   Skill: Comprehension

20) If a population of plants contains 10,000 kilocalories, what would be a reasonable estimate of the number of kilocalories found in a population of animals that feed on nothing but that population of plants?

   A) 1,000 kilocalories

   B) 10,000 kilocalories

   C) 20,000 kilocalories

   D) 50,000 kilocalories

   E) 100,000 kilocalories

   Answer: A
   Skill: Comprehension

21) Chemical reactions of metabolism within cells are regulated by organic catalysts. What are these catalysts called?

   A) kinetic transformers

   B) enzymes

   C) feedback inhibitors

   D) analogs

   E) nutrients

   Answer: B
   Skill: Knowledge

22) Once labor begins in childbirth, contractions increase in intensity and frequency until delivery. Therefore, the increasing labor contractions of childbirth are an example of

A) a feedforward mechanism.

B) positive feedback.

C) negative feedback.

D) feedback inhibition.

E) both C and D.

Answer: B
Skill: Comprehension

23) When blood glucose levels rise, the pancreas secretes insulin and as a result blood glucose levels decline. When blood glucose levels are low, the pancreas secretes glucagon and as a result blood glucose levels rise. Such regulation of blood glucose levels is an example of

A) a feedforward mechanism.

B) positive feedback.

C) negative feedback.

D) feedback inhibition.

E) both C and D.

Answer: E
Skill: Comprehension

24) The maintenance of a relatively stable internal environment is referred to as

A) taxonomy.

B) natural selection.

C) evolution.

D) cell theory.

E) homeostasis.

Answer: E
Skill: Knowledge

25) There are approximately _____ identified and named species.

A) 1,500

B) 150,000

C) 1,500,000

D) 15,000,000

E) 150,000,000

Answer: C
Skill: Knowledge

26) Which branch of biology is concerned with the naming and classifying of organisms?

A) genetics

B) physiology

C) genomics

D) taxonomy

E) evolution

Answer: D
Skill: Knowledge

27) Species that are in the same _____ are more closely related than species that are only in the same _____.

A) phylum ... class

B) family ... order

C) class ... order

D) family ... genus

E) kingdom ... phylum

Answer: B
Skill: Comprehension

28) Which of these is reflective of the hierarchical organization of life from most to least inclusive?

A) kingdom, phylum, class, order, family, genus, species

B) phylum, class, order, kingdom, family, genus, species

C) kingdom, order, family, phylum, class, genus, species

D) genus, species, kingdom, phylum, class, order, family

E) class, order, kingdom, phylum, family, genus, species

Answer: A
Skill: Knowledge

29) Which of the following are characteristics shared by members of both Domain Bacteria and Domain Archaea?

A) cytosol

B) nucleus

C) DNA

D) A and C only

E) A, B, and C

Answer: D
Skill: Knowledge

30) What are the two classifications of prokaryotes?

A) Domain Bacteria and Domain Eukarya

B) Domain Archaea and Kingdom Monera

C) Domain Eukarya and Domain Archaea

D) Domain Bacteria and Kingdom Monera

E) Domain Bacteria and Domain Archaea

Answer: E
Skill: Knowledge

31) A water sample from a hot thermal vent contained a single–celled organism that lacked a nucleus. What is its most likely classification?

A) Domain Eukarya

B) Domain Archaea

C) Domain Bacteria

D) Kingdom Protista

E) Kingdom Fungi

Answer: B
Skill: Comprehension

32) A rose bush is classified into Domain _____ and Kingdom _____.

A) Eukarya ... Animalia

B) Eukarya ... Fungi

C) Eukarya ... Plantae

D) Eukarya .... Protista

E) Bacteria ... Archaea

Answer: C
Skill: Knowledge

33) A new species was discovered. Individuals of this species are multicellular eukaryotes that obtain nutrients from decomposing organic matter. How should this species be classified?

A) Eukarya, Archaea

B) Eukarya, Bacteria

C) Eukarya, Plantae

D) Eukarya, Protista

E) Eukarya, Fungi

Answer: E
Skill: Comprehension

34) How are most unicellular eukaryotes classified?

A) Monera

B) Protista

C) Bacteria

D) Archaea

E) Eukarya

Answer: B
Skill: Knowledge

35) A new species has been discovered. Individuals of this species are multicellular eukaryotes that obtain nutrients by ingesting other organisms. How should this species be classified?

A) Domain Bacteria

B) Kingdom Protista

C) Kingdom Plantae

D) Kingdom Animalia

E) Domain Archaea

Answer: D
Skill: Comprehension

36) You have just discovered a new species that has starch, rather than DNA, as its genetic material. You are elated because you may have just discovered a new

A) member of Kingdom Protista.

B) member of Domain Bacteria.

C) member of Domain Archaea.

D) member of Domain Eukarya.

E) domain of life.

Answer: E
Skill: Comprehension

37) The fact that there is strong genetic similarity among species is strong evidence in support of

A) multiple independent origins of life.

B) the extraterrestrial origin of life.

C) creationism.

D) evolution.

E) intelligent design.

Answer: D
Skill: Comprehension

38) Which of these provides evidence of the common ancestry of *all* life?

A) the ubiquitous use of catalysts by living systems

B) the universality of the genetic code

C) the structure of the nucleus

D) the structure of cilia

E) the structure of chloroplasts

Answer: B
Skill: Comprehension

39) Which of these individuals is *most* likely to be successful in an evolutionary sense?

A) a reproductively sterile individual who never falls ill

B) an individual who dies after 5 days of life but leaves 10 offspring, all of whom survive to reproduce

C) a male who mates with 20 females and fathers 1 offspring

D) an individual who lives 100 years and leaves 2 offspring, both of whom survive to reproduce

E) a female who mates with 20 males and produces 1 offspring

Answer: B
Skill: Comprehension

40) Natural selection

A) does not require genetic variation.

B) does not require inheritance.

C) is differential reproductive success.

D) is not descent with modification.

E) requires a small population size.

Answer: C
Skill: Knowledge

41) In a hypothetical world, every 50 years people over 6 feet tall are eliminated from the population. Based on your knowledge of natural selection, you would predict that the average height of the human population will

A) remain unchanged.

B) gradually decline.

C) rapidly decline.

D) gradually increase.

E) rapidly increase.

Answer: B
Skill: Comprehension

42) Through time, the lineage that led to modern whales shows a change from four-limbed land animals to aquatic animals with two limbs that function as flippers. This change is best explained by

A) the cell theory.

B) creationism.

C) the hierarchical organization of life.

D) natural selection.

E) homeostasis.

Answer: D
Skill: Comprehension

43) Which of the following questions is outside the realm of science?

A) How did humans arise?

B) Why do humans have a finite life span?

C) How do red blood cells carry oxygen?

D) What is the basis of heredity?

E) Does God exist?

Answer: E
Skill: Comprehension

44) Collecting data based on observation is an example of _____; analyzing this data to reach a conclusion is an example of _____ reasoning.

A) discovery science ... inductive

B) the process of science ... deductive

C) hypothesis testing ... deductive

D) descriptive science ... deductive

E) hypothesis generation ... deductive

Answer: A
Skill: Comprehension

45) What is a hypothesis?

A) the same thing as a theory

B) an untestable idea

C) a verifiable observation

D) a tentative explanation

E) a fact

Answer: D
Skill: Knowledge

46) Which of these is a deduction?

A) My car won't start.

B) My car's battery is dead.

C) If I turn the key in the ignition while stepping on the gas pedal, then my car will start.

D) I lost my car key.

E) My car is out of gas.

Answer: C
Skill: Comprehension

47) When applying the process of science, which of these is tested?

A) a question

B) a result

C) an observation

D) a prediction

E) a hypothesis

Answer: D
Skill: Comprehension

48) The statement "If you show your dog affection then your dog will seek your company" is an example of

A) a statement that can be tested.

B) a statement derived from a hypothesis.

C) a prediction.

D) deductive reasoning.

E) all of the above.

Answer: E
Skill: Comprehension

49) A controlled experiment is one in which

A) the experiment is repeated many times to ensure that the results are accurate.

B) the experiment proceeds at a slow pace to guarantee that the scientist can carefully observe all reactions and process all experimental data.

C) there are at least two groups, one of which does not receive the experimental treatment.

D) there are at least two groups, one differing from the other by two or more variables.

E) there is one group for which the scientist controls all variables.

Answer: C
Skill: Comprehension

50) Why is it important that an experiment include a control group?

A) The control group is the group that the reseacher is in control of; it is the group in which the researcher predetermines the nature of the results.

B) The control group provides a reserve of experimental subjects.

C) A control group is required for the development of an "if ... then" statement.

D) A control group assures that an experiment will be repeatable.

E) Without a control group, there is no basis for knowing if a particular result is due to the variable being tested or to some other factor.

Answer: E
Skill: Comprehension

Media Activity Questions

1) What is the difference between a tissue and an organ system?

   A) The tissue level of organization is more inclusive than the organ system level.

   B) Tissues are not composed of cells; organ systems are composed of cells.

   C) A tissue cannot exist unless it is a component of an organ system, whereas an organ system can exist independently of tissues.

   D) An organ system includes tissues.

   E) Tissues are not considered to be living; organ systems are considered to be living.

   Answer: D
   Topic: Web/CD Activity 1A

2) Which of the following correctly matches a cell type with its primary function?

   A) nerve cell ... protection

   B) muscle cell ... absorption of nutrients

   C) intestinal cell ... contraction

   D) nerve cell ... transmission of signals

   E) skin cell ... absorption of nutrients

   Answer: D
   Topic: Web/CD Activity 1D

3) Energy enters *most* ecosystems as

   A) light.

   B) chemical energy.

   C) heat and chemical energy.

   D) heat.

   E) light and chemical energy.

   Answer: A
   Topic: Web/CD Activity 1E

4) What name is given to the process by which plants convert the energy of light to chemical energy?

   A) metabolism

   B) evolution

   C) photosynthesis

   D) homeostasis

   E) cellular respiration

   Answer: C
   Topic: Web/CD Activity 1E

5) What feature is common to prokaryotes, fungi, and plants?

   A) a nucleus

   B) single cells

   C) at one time, membership in the kingdom Monera

   D) cell walls

   E) photosynthesis

   Answer: D
   Topic: Web/CD Activity 1G

Chapter 2   The Chemical Context of Life

1) Which of the following best explains the distinction between biology and chemistry?
   A) Biologists study living things, whereas chemists study nonliving things.
   B) Biology has a hierarchy of structural levels, whereas chemistry does not.
   C) Chemists study molecules, whereas biologists do not.
   D) Chemical systems have emergent properties; biological systems do not.
   E) There is no clear distinction because the two sciences are parts of the same whole.

   Answer: E
   Skill: Comprehension

2) Which four elements make up approximately 96% of living matter?
   A) carbon, hydrogen, nitrogen, oxygen
   B) carbon, sulfur, phosphorus, hydrogen
   C) oxygen, hydrogen, calcium, sodium
   D) carbon, sodium, chlorine, magnesium
   E) carbon, oxygen, sulfur, calcium

   Answer: A
   Skill: Knowledge

3) Which of the following is a trace element that is essential to humans?
   A) nitrogen
   B) calcium
   C) iodine
   D) carbon
   E) oxygen

   Answer: C
   Skill: Knowledge

4) Which of the following is a trace element that is essential to humans and other living organisms?
   A) carbon
   B) nitrogen
   C) hydrogen
   D) iron
   E) oxygen

   Answer: D
   Skill: Knowledge

5) Each element is unique and different from other elements because of its
   A) atomic weight.
   B) atomic number.
   C) mass number.
   D) Only A and B are correct.
   E) A, B, and C are correct.

   Answer: B
   Skill: Knowledge

6) The mass number of an element can be easily approximated by adding together the number of
   A) protons and neutrons.
   B) electron orbitals in each energy level.
   C) protons and electrons.
   D) neutrons and electrons.
   E) isotopes of the atom.

   Answer: A
   Skill: Knowledge

7) Oxygen has an atomic number of 8. Therefore, it must have
   A) 8 protons.
   B) 8 electrons.
   C) 16 neutrons.
   D) Only A and B are correct.
   E) A, B, and C are correct.

   Answer: D
   Skill: Comprehension

8) The atomic number of neon is 10. Therefore, it

   A) has 8 electrons in the outer electron shell.

   B) is inert.

   C) has an atomic mass of 10.

   D) Only A and B are correct.

   E) A, B, and C are correct.

   Answer: D
   Skill: Comprehension

9) From its atomic number of 15, it is possible to predict that the phosphorus atom has

   A) 15 neutrons.

   B) 15 protons.

   C) 15 electrons.

   D) Only B and C are correct.

   E) A, B, and C are correct.

   Answer: D
   Skill: Comprehension

10) How does one refer to an atomic form of an element containing the same number of protons but a different number of neutrons?

    A) ion

    B) isotope

    C) polar atom

    D) isomer

    E) radioactive

    Answer: B
    Skill: Knowledge

11) How do isotopes differ from each other?

    A) number of protons

    B) number of electrons

    C) number of neutrons

    D) valence electron distribution

    E) ability to form ions

    Answer: C
    Skill: Knowledge

12) Which of the following best describes the relationship between the atoms described below?

Atom 1	Atom 2
$^{1}_{1}H$	$^{3}_{1}H$

    A) They are isomers.

    B) They are polymers.

    C) They are isotopes.

    D) They are ions.

    E) They are both radioactive.

    Answer: C
    Skill: Comprehension

13) Which of the following best describes the relationship between the atoms described below?

Atom 1	Atom 2
$^{31}_{15}P$	$^{32}_{15}P$

    A) They are both radioactive.

    B) They are both phosphorous cations.

    C) They are both phosphorous anions.

    D) They are both isotopes of phosphorous.

    E) They contain 31 and 32 protons respectively.

    Answer: D
    Skill: Comprehension

14) One difference between carbon–12 $\left(^{12}_{6}C \right)$ and carbon–14 ($^{14}_{6}C$) is that carbon–14 has

    A) 2 more protons than carbon–12.

    B) 2 more electrons than carbon–12.

    C) 2 more neutrons than carbon–12.

    D) Only A and C are correct.

    E) A, B, and C are correct.

    Answer: C
    Skill: Comprehension

15) ^{3}H is a radioactive isotope of hydrogen. One difference between hydrogen–1 ($^1_1$H) and hydrogen–3 ($^3_1$H) is that hydrogen–3 has

A) one more neutron and one more proton than hydrogen–1.

B) one more proton and one more electron than hydrogen–1.

C) one more electron and one more neutron than hydrogen–1.

D) two more neutrons than hydrogen–1.

E) two more protons than hydrogen–1.

Answer: D
Skill: Comprehension

16) The atomic number of carbon is 6. ^{14}C is heavier than ^{12}C because the atomic nucleus of ^{14}C contains

A) six protons and six neutrons.

B) six protons and seven neutrons.

C) six protons and eight neutrons.

D) seven protons and seven neutrons.

E) eight protons and six neutrons.

Answer: C
Skill: Comprehension

17) Electrons exist only at fixed levels of potential energy. However, if an atom absorbs sufficient energy, a possible result is that

A) an electron may move to an electron shell farther out from the nucleus.

B) the atom may become a radioactive isotope.

C) an electron may move to an electron shell closer to the nucleus.

D) the atom would become a positively charged ion.

E) the atom would become a negatively charged ion.

Answer: A
Skill: Knowledge

The following questions refer to Figure 2.1.

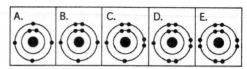

Figure 2.1

18) Which drawing depicts the electron configuration of neon ($^{20}_{10}$Ne)?

Answer: E
Skill: Knowledge

19) Which drawing depicts the electron configuration of oxygen ($^{16}_{8}$O)?

Answer: C
Skill: Knowledge

20) Which drawing depicts the electron configuration of carbon ($^{12}_{6}$C)?

Answer: A
Skill: Knowledge

21) Which drawing is of an atom with the atomic number of 8?

Answer: C
Skill: Comprehension

22) Which drawing depicts an atom that is inert or chemically unreactive?

Answer: E
Skill: Comprehension

23) Which drawing depicts an atom with a valence of 3?

Answer: B
Skill: Knowledge

24) Which drawing depicts an atom with a valence of 2?

Answer: C
Skill: Knowledge

25) The reactive properties or chemical behavior of an atom depend on the number of

A) valence shells in the atom.

B) orbitals found in the atom.

C) electrons in each orbital in the atom.

D) electrons in the outer valence shell in the atom.

E) hybridized orbitals in the atom.

Answer: D
Skill: Knowledge

26) Atoms whose outer electron shells contain eight electrons tend to

A) form ionic bonds in aqueous solutions.

B) form covalent bonds in aqueous solutions.

C) be stable and nonreactive.

D) be unstable and very reactive.

E) be biologically important because they are present in organic molecules.

Answer: C
Skill: Knowledge

27) What are the chemical properties of atoms whose valence shells are filled with electrons?

A) They form ionic bonds in aqueous solutions.

B) They form covalent bonds in aqueous solutions.

C) They are stable and unreactive.

D) They exhibit similar chemical behaviors.

E) Both C and D are correct.

Answer: E
Skill: Knowledge

Use the information extracted from the periodic table in Figure 2.2 to answer the following questions.

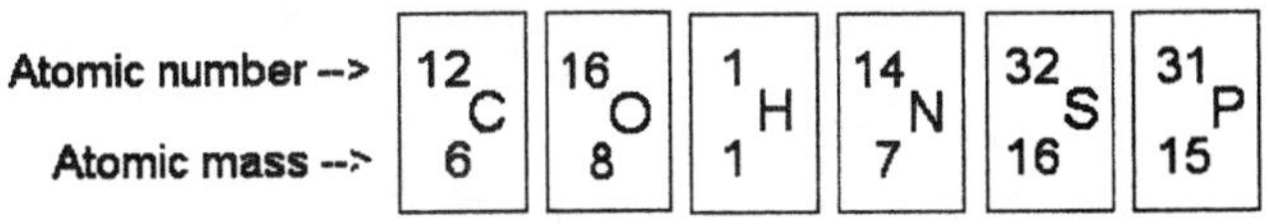

Atomic number --> | 12 C 6 | 16 O 8 | 1 H 1 | 14 N 7 | 32 S 16 | 31 P 15 |
Atomic mass -->

Figure 2.2

28) How many electrons does carbon have in its valence shell?

A) 4   B) 8   C) 7   D) 5   E) 2

Answer: A
Skill: Comprehension

29) How many electrons does sulfur have in its valence shell?

A) 1   B) 2   C) 4   D) 6   E) 8

Answer: D
Skill: Comprehension

30) How many neutrons does the nucleus of sulfur contain?

A) 16

B) 19

C) 32

D) 35

E) 51

Answer: A
Skill: Comprehension

31) How many neutrons does the nucleus of a nitrogen atom contain?

A) 2

B) 7

C) 8

D) 14

E) 21

Answer: B
Skill: Comprehension

32) Based on electron configuration, which of these elements would exhibit chemical behavior most like that of oxygen?

A) C

B) H

C) N

D) S

E) P

Answer: D
Skill: Application

33) How many electrons would be expected in the outermost electron shell of an atom with atomic number 17?

A) 2

B) 5

C) 7

D) 8

E) 17

Answer: C
Skill: Comprehension

34) The atomic number of each atom is given to the left of each of the elements below. Which of the atoms has the same valence as carbon ($_6^{12}C$) ?

A) 7nitrogen

B) 9fluorine

C) 10neon

D) 12magnesium

E) 14silicon

Answer: E
Skill: Application

35) What is the valence of an atom with seven electrons in its outer electron shell?

A) 1   B) 2   C) 3   D) 4   E) 5

Answer: A
Skill: Comprehension

36) How many additional electrons are needed to complete the valence shell of hydrogen?

A) 1   B) 2   C) 3   D) 4   E) 5

Answer: A
Skill: Comprehension

37) How many protons are in an atom with the atomic number of 5?

A) 1   B) 2   C) 3   D) 4   E) 5

Answer: E
Skill: Comprehension

38) What is the maximum number of electrons in the 1_s orbital?

A) 1   B) 2   C) 3   D) 4   E) 5

Answer: B
Skill: Knowledge

39) What are the maximum number of electrons in the 2_p orbital of an atom?

A) 1   B) 2   C) 3   D) 4   E) 5

Answer: B
Skill: Knowledge

40) A covalent chemical bond is one in which

A) electrons are removed from one atom and transferred to another atom so that the two atoms become oppositely charged.

B) protons or neutrons are shared by two atoms so as to satisfy the requirements of both.

C) outer-shell electrons are shared by two atoms so as to satisfactorily fill the outer electron shells of both.

D) outer-shell electrons of one atom are transferred to the inner electron shells of another atom.

E) the inner-shell electrons of one atom are transferred to the outer shell of another atom.

Answer: C
Skill: Knowledge

41) What do atoms form when they share electron pairs?

A) elements

B) ions

C) aggregates

D) isotopes

E) molecules

Answer: E
Skill: Knowledge

42) If atom ^{6}X(atomic number 6) were allowed to react with hydrogen, the molecule formed would be

A) X-H

B) H-X-H

C) H-X-H
        |
        H

D)   H
       |
   H-X-H
       |
       H

E) H=X=H

Answer: D
Skill: Application

43) What are the maximum number of covalent bonds an element with atomic number 16 can make with hydrogen?

A) 1   B) 2   C) 3   D) 4   E) 5

Answer: B
Skill: Comprehension

44) What do the four elements most abundant in life--carbon, oxygen, hydrogen, and nitrogen--have in common?

A) They all have the same number of valence electrons.

B) Each element exists in only one isotopic form.

C) They are equal in electronegativity.

D) They are elements produced only by living cells.

E) They all have unpaired electrons in their valence shells.

Answer: E
Skill: Comprehension

45) When two atoms are equally electronegative, they will interact to form

A) equal numbers of isotopes.

B) ions.

C) polar covalent bonds.

D) nonpolar covalent bonds.

E) ionic bonds.

Answer: D
Skill: Comprehension

46) A covalent bond is likely to be polar when

A) one of the atoms sharing electrons is much more electronegative than the other atom.

B) the two atoms sharing electrons are equally electronegative.

C) the two atoms sharing electrons are of the same element.

D) it is between two atoms that are both very strong electron acceptors.

E) the two atoms sharing electrons are different elements.

Answer: A
Skill: Comprehension

47) Which of the following represents a polar covalent bond?

  A) H–H

  B) C–C

  C) H–O

  D) C–H

  E) O–O

Answer: C
Skill: Comprehension

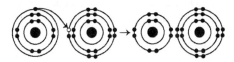

Figure 2.3

48) What results from the chemical reaction illustrated in Figure 2.3?

  A) a cation with a net charge of +1

  B) a cation with a net charge of –1

  C) an anion with a net charge of +1

  D) an anion with a net charge of –1

  E) Both A and D are correct.

Answer: E
Skill: Knowledge

49) The ionic bond of sodium chloride is formed when

  A) chlorine gains an electron from sodium.

  B) sodium and chlorine share an electron pair.

  C) sodium and chlorine both lose electrons from their outer valence shells.

  D) sodium gains an electron from chlorine.

  E) chlorine gains a proton from sodium.

Answer: A
Skill: Knowledge

50) What bond does NH_4 form with Cl to make ammonium chloride salt?

  A) nonpolar covalent bond

  B) polar covalent bond

  C) ionic bond

  D) hydrogen bond

  E) covalent bond

Answer: C
Skill: Knowledge

51) What is the formula for ammonium chloride salt?

  A) NHCl

  B) NH_4Cl

  C) NH_4Cl_2

  D) $NHCl_2$

  E) ClNH

Answer: B
Skill: Comprehension

52) Which atom is the cation in ammonium chloride salt?

  A) NH_4

  B) Cl

  C) H

  D) N

  E) NH_4Cl

Answer: A
Skill: Comprehension

Use these choices to answer the following questions.

  A. nonpolar covalent bond
  B. polar covalent bond
  C. ionic bond
  D. hydrogen bond
  E. hydrophobic interaction

53) Results from a transfer of electron(s) between atoms.

Answer: C
Skill: Knowledge

54) Results from an unequal sharing of electrons between atoms.

Answer: B
Skill: Knowledge

55) Explains most specifically the attraction of water molecules to one another.

Answer: D
Skill: Knowledge

56) Nitrogen (N) is much more electronegative than hydrogen (H). Which of the following statements is *correct* about the atoms in ammonia (NH_3)?

A) Each hydrogen atom has a partial positive charge.

B) The nitrogen atom has a strong positive charge.

C) Each hydrogen atom has a slight negative charge.

D) The nitrogen atom has a partial positive charge.

E) There are covalent bonds between the hydrogen atoms.

Answer: A
Skill: Comprehension

57) Van der Waals interactions result when

A) hybrid orbitals overlap.

B) electrons are not symmetrically distributed in a molecule.

C) molecules held by ionic bonds react with water.

D) two polar covalent bonds react.

E) a hydrogen atom loses an electron.

Answer: B
Skill: Knowledge

58) Which of the following is *not* considered to be a weak molecular interaction?

A) covalent bond

B) van der Waals interactions

C) ionic bond in the presence of water

D) hydrogen bond

E) Both A and B are correct.

Answer: A
Skill: Knowledge

59) $3H_2 + N_2 \Leftrightarrow 2NH_3$

Which of the following is *true* for the above reaction?

A) The reaction is nonreversible.

B) Acid is being formed.

C) Concentrations of reactants are higher than those of products.

D) Ammonia is being formed and decomposed.

E) Hydrogen and nitrogen are being decomposed.

Answer: D
Skill: Comprehension

60) Which of the following best describes chemical equilibrium?

A) Reactions continue with no effect on the concentrations of reactants and products.

B) Concentrations of products are high.

C) Reactions have stopped.

D) Reactions stop only when all reactants have been converted to products.

E) There are equal concentrations of reactants and products.

Answer: A
Skill: Comprehension

Media Activity Questions

1) What is the atomic mass of an atom that has 6 protons, 6 neutrons, and 6 electrons?

   A) 6

   B) 8

   C) +1

   D) 12

   E) 18

   Answer: D
   Topic: Web/CD Activity 2B

2) An uncharged atom of boron has an atomic number of 5 and an atomic mass of 11. How many electrons does boron have?

   A) 11

   B) 15

   C) 0

   D) 5

   E) 2

   Answer: D
   Topic: Web/CD Activity 2C

3) A hydrogen atom has 1 electron. How many bonds can hydrogen form?

   A) 1

   B) 4

   C) 2 covalent bonds

   D) 2 ionic bonds

   Answer: A
   Topic: Web/CD Activity 2E

4) In a water molecule, hydrogen and oxygen are held together by a(an) _____ bond.

   A) double covalent

   B) ionic

   C) nonpolar covalent

   D) hydrogen

   E) polar covalent

   Answer: E
   Topic: Web/CD Activity 2F

Self–Quiz Questions

Answers to these questions also appear in the textbook.

1) An element is to a(an) _____ as a tissue is to a(an) _____.

A) atom; organism

B) compound; organ

C) molecule; cell

D) atom; organ

E) compound; organelle

Answer: B

2) In the term *trace element*, the modifier *trace* means

A) the element is required in very small amounts.

B) the element can be used as a label to trace atoms through an organism's metabolism.

C) the element is very rare on Earth.

D) the element enhances health but is not essential for the organism's long–term survival.

E) the element passes rapidly through the organism.

Answer: A

3) Compared to ^{31}P, the radioactive isotope ^{32}P has

A) a different atomic number.

B) one more neutron.

C) one more proton.

D) one more electron.

E) a different charge.

Answer: B

4) Atoms can be represented by simply listing the number of protons, neutrons, and electrons--for example, $2p^+$; $2n^0$; $2e^-$ for helium. Which atom represents the ^{18}O isotope of oxygen?

A) $6p^+$; $8n^0$; $6e^-$

B) $8p^+$; $10n^0$; $8e^-$

C) $9p^+$; $9n^0$; $9e^-$

D) $7p^+$; $2n^0$; $9e^-$

E) $10p^+$; $8n^0$; $10e^-$

Answer: B

5) The atomic number of sulfur is 16. Sulfur combines with hydrogen by covalent bonding to form a compound, hydrogen sulfide. Based on the electron configuration of sulfur, we can predict that the molecular formula of the compound will be

A) HS

B) HS_2

C) H_2S

D) H_3S_2

E) H_4S

Answer: C

6) Review the valences of carbon, oxygen, hydrogen, and nitrogen, and then determine which of the following molecules is most likely to exist.

A) O = C-H

B)
```
        H   H
        |   |
H – O – C – C = O
            |
            H
```

C)
```
    H       H
    |       |
H – C – H – C = O
    |
    H
```

D)
```
    O
    |
H – N – H
```

Answer: B

7) The reactivity of an atom arises from

A) the average distance of the outermost electron shell from the nucleus.

B) the existence of unpaired electrons in the valence shell.

C) the sum of the potential energies of all the electron shells.

D) the potential energy of the valence shell.

E) the energy difference between the s and p orbitals.

Answer: B

8) Which of these statements is true of all anionic atoms?

A) The atom has more electrons than protons.

B) The atom has more protons than electrons.

C) The atom has fewer protons than does a neutral atom of the same element.

D) The atom has more neutrons than protons.

E) The net charge is minus 1.

Answer: A

9) What coefficients must be placed in the blanks to balance this chemical reaction?

$$C_6H_{12}O_6 \rightarrow \_\_C_2H_6O + \_\_CO_2$$

A) 1; 2

B) 2; 2

C) 1; 3

D) 1; 1

E) 3; 1

Answer: B

10) Which of the following statements correctly describes any chemical reaction that has reached equilibrium?

A) The concentration of products equals the concentration of reactants.

B) The rate of the forward reaction equals the rate of the reverse reaction.

C) Both forward and reverse reactions have halted.

D) The reaction is now irreversible.

E) No reactants remain.

Answer: B

Chapter 3   Water and the Fitness of the Environment

1) In a single molecule of water, the two hydrogen atoms are bonded to a single oxygen atom by
   A) hydrogen bonds.
   B) nonpolar covalent bonds.
   C) polar covalent bonds.
   D) ionic bonds.
   E) van der Waals interactions.

   Answer: C
   Skill: Knowledge

2) The partial negative charge at one end of a water molecule is attracted to the partial positive charge of another water molecule. What is this attraction called?
   A) a covalent bond
   B) a hydrogen bond
   C) an ionic bond
   D) a hydrophilic bond
   E) a hydrophobic bond

   Answer: B
   Skill: Knowledge

3) Which of the following is an example of a hydrogen bond?
   A) the bond between C and H in methane
   B) the bond between the H of one water molecule and the O of another water molecule
   C) the bond between Na and Cl in salt
   D) the bond between two hydrogen atoms
   E) the bond between Mg and Cl in MgCl$_2$

   Answer: B
   Skill: Knowledge

4) Water is able to form hydrogen bonds because
   A) oxygen has a valence of 2.
   B) the water molecule is shaped like a tetrahedron.
   C) the water molecule is polar.
   D) the oxygen atom in a water molecule has a strong positive charge.
   E) the hydrogen atoms in a water molecule are weakly negative in charge.

   Answer: C
   Skill: Knowledge

5) What is the maximum number of hydrogen bonds a water molecule can form with neighboring water molecules?
   A) one
   B) two
   C) three
   D) four
   E) five

   Answer: D
   Skill: Knowledge

6) What determines the cohesiveness of water molecules?
   A) hydrophobic interactions
   B) high specific heat
   C) covalent bonds
   D) hydrogen bonds
   E) ionic bonds

   Answer: D
   Skill: Knowledge

7) What do cohesion, surface tension, and adhesion have in common with reference to water?

A) All increase when temperature increases.

B) All are produced by covalent bonding.

C) All are properties related to hydrogen bonding.

D) All have to do with nonpolar covalent bonds.

E) Both A and C are correct.

Answer: C
Skill: Knowledge

8) Water is transported in plant tissues against gravity due to which of the following properties?

A) cohesion

B) adhesion

C) hydrogen bonding

D) two of the above

E) all of the above

Answer: E
Skill: Comprehension

9) Which of the following is possible due to the surface tension of water?

A) Lakes don't freeze solid in the winter, despite low temperatures.

B) A waterstrider can walk across a small pond.

C) Organisms resist temperature changes although they give off heat due to chemical reactions.

D) Water can act as a solvent.

E) The pH remains neutral.

Answer: B
Skill: Comprehension

10) When an ice cube cools a drink 1°C, which of the following is *true*?

A) Molecule collisions in the drink increase.

B) Kinetic energy in the drink decreases.

C) A kilocalorie of heat is transferred to the water.

D) A kilocalorie of heat is transferred to the ice.

E) Evaporation of the water increases.

Answer: B
Skill: Comprehension

11) Which of the following is a *correct* definition of a kilocalorie?

A) The amount of heat energy required to raise 1 g of water by 1°F.

B) The amount of heat energy required to raise 1 g of water by 1°C.

C) The amount of heat energy required to raise 1 kg of water by 1°C.

D) A measure of the average kinetic energy of 1 L of water.

E) The amount of energy in 1 kg of glucose.

Answer: C
Skill: Knowledge

12) The nutritional information on a cereal box shows that one serving of dry cereal has 90 calories (actually kilocalories). If one were to burn a serving of cereal, the amount of heat given off would be sufficient to raise the temperature of 1 kg of water how many degrees Celsius?

A) 0.9°C

B) 9.0°C

C) 90.0°C

D) 900.0°C

E) 9000.0°C

Answer: C
Skill: Application

13) Water's high specific heat is mainly a consequence of the

    A) small size of the water molecules.

    B) high specific heat of oxygen and hydrogen atoms.

    C) absorption and release of heat when hydrogen bonds break and form.

    D) fact that water is a poor heat conductor.

    E) inability of water to dissipate heat into dry air.

Answer: C
Skill: Comprehension

14) Which bonds must be broken for water to vaporize?

    A) ionic bonds

    B) nonpolar covalent bonds

    C) polar covalent bonds

    D) hydrogen bonds

    E) Both C and D are correct.

Answer: D
Skill: Knowledge

15) The formation of ice during colder weather helps temper the seasonal transition to winter. This is mainly because

    A) the formation of hydrogen bonds releases heat.

    B) the formation of hydrogen bonds absorbs heat.

    C) there is less evaporative cooling of lakes.

    D) ice melts each autumn afternoon.

    E) ice is warmer than the winter air.

Answer: A
Skill: Comprehension

16) Temperature usually increases when water condenses. Which behavior of water is most directly responsible for this phenomenon?

    A) change in density when it condenses to form a liquid or solid

    B) reactions with other atmospheric compounds

    C) release of heat by the formation of hydrogen bonds

    D) release of heat by the breaking of hydrogen bonds

    E) high surface tension

Answer: C
Skill: Comprehension

17) Desert rabbits are adapted to the warm climate because their large ears aid in the removal of heat by

    A) the high surface tension of water.

    B) the high heat of vaporization of water.

    C) the high specific heat of water.

    D) the buffering capacity of water.

    E) the dissociation of water molecules.

Answer: B
Skill: Comprehension

18) At what temperature is water at its densest?

    A) $0°C$

    B) $4°C$

    C) $32°C$

    D) $100°C$

    E) $212°C$

Answer: B
Skill: Knowledge

19) Ice is lighter and floats in water because it is a crystalline structure held together by

   A) ionic bonds only.

   B) hydrogen bonds only.

   C) covalent bonds only.

   D) Both A and C are correct.

   E) A, B, and C are correct.

   Answer: B
   Skill: Knowledge

20) Why does ice float in liquid water?

   A) The liquid water molecules have more energy and can push up the ice.

   B) The ionic bonds between the molecules in ice prevent the ice from sinking.

   C) Ice always has air bubbles that keep it afloat.

   D) Hydrogen bonds keep the molecules of ice farther apart than in liquid water.

   E) The crystalline lattice of ice causes it to be denser than liquid water.

   Answer: D
   Skill: Comprehension

21) Life on Earth is dependent on all the properties of water as well as the abundance of water. Which property of water is probably *most* important for the functioning of organisms at the molecular level?

   A) cohesion and high surface tension

   B) high specific heat

   C) high heat of vaporization

   D) expansion upon freezing

   E) versatility as a solvent

   Answer: E
   Skill: Comprehension

The following question is based on Figure 3.1: solute molecules surrounded by a hydration shell of water.

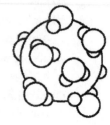

Figure 3.1

22) Based on your knowledge of the polarity of water, the solute molecule is most likely

   A) positively charged.

   B) negatively charged.

   C) neutral in charge.

   D) hydrophobic.

   E) nonpolar.

   Answer: B
   Skill: Application

23) Hydrophobic substances like vegetable oil are

   A) non–ionic or nonpolar substances that repel water.

   B) non–ionic or nonpolar substances that have an affinity for water.

   C) ionic or polar substances that repel water.

   D) ionic or polar substances that have an affinity for water.

   E) ionic substances that readily dissolve in water.

   Answer: A
   Skill: Knowledge

24) One mole (mol) of a substance is equal to

   A) 6.02×10^{23} molecules of the substance.

   B) 1 g of the substance dissolved in 1 L of solution.

   C) the largest amount of the substance that can be dissolved in 1 L of solution.

   D) the molecular weight of the substance expressed in grams. One mol of glucose ($C_6H_{12}O_6$) is equivalent to 180 g of glucose.

   E) Answers A and D are correct.

   Answer: E
   Skill: Knowledge

25) How many molecules of sucrose ($C_{12}H_{22}O_{11}$) molecular weight, 342, would be present in one mole of sucrose?

   A) 45 molecules

   B) 342 molecules

   C) 1×10^{14} molecules

   D) 6.02×10^{14} molecules

   E) 6.02×10^{23} molecules

   Answer: E
   Skill: Comprehension

26) How many molecules of glycerol ($C_3H_8O_3$) would be present in 1 L of a 1 M glycerol solution?

   A) 1

   B) 14

   C) 92

   D) 1×10^7

   E) 6.02×10^{23}

   Answer: E
   Skill: Knowledge

27) Recall that when sodium chloride (NaCl) is placed in water the component atoms of the NaCl crystal dissociate into individual sodium ions (Na+) and chloride ions (Cl–). In contrast, the atoms of covalently bonded molecules (for example: glucose, sucrose, glycerol) do not generally dissociate when placed in aqueous solution. Which of the following solutions would be expected to contain the greatest number of particles (molecules or ions)?

   A) 0.5 M NaCl

   B) 0.5 M glucose

   C) 1.0 M NaCl

   D) 1.0 M glucose

   E) 1.0 M $MgCl_2$

   Answer: E
   Skill: Comprehension

28) The molecular weight of glucose is 180 g. To make a 1 M solution of glucose, you should do which of the following?

   A) Dissolve 1 g of glucose in 1 L of water.

   B) Dissolve 100 g of glucose in 1 L of water.

   C) Dissolve 180 g of glucose in 100 g of water.

   D) Dissolve 180 mg (milligrams) of glucose in 1 L of water.

   E) Dissolve 180 g of glucose in water, and then add more water until the total volume of the solution is 1 L.

   Answer: E
   Skill: Application

29) The molecular weight of glucose ($C_6H_{12}O_6$) is 180 g. To make a 0.5 M solution of glucose, you should

    A) dissolve 0.5 g of glucose in 1 L of water.

    B) dissolve 12 g of glucose in 1 L of water.

    C) dissolve 24 g of glucose in 1 L of water.

    D) dissolve 90 g of glucose in a small volume of water and then add more water until the total volume of solution is 1 L.

    E) dissolve 180 g of glucose in a small volume of water, and then add more water until the total volume of the solution is 1 L.

Answer: D
Skill: Application

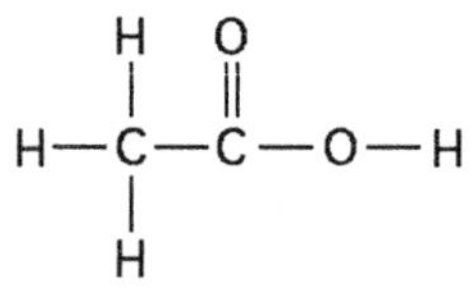

Figure 3.2

30) How many grams of the molecule in Figure 3.2 would be required to make 1 L of a 0.2 M solution of the molecule?
(Carbon = 12, Oxygen = 16, Hydrogen = 1)

    A) 8

    B) 12

    C) 24

    D) 32

    E) 60

Answer: B
Skill: Application

31) How many grams of the molecule in Figure 3.2 would be required to make 1 L of a 1.5 M solution of the molecule?
(Carbon = 12, Oxygen = 16, Hydrogen = 1)

    A) 37

    B) 55

    C) 60

    D) 74

    E) 90

Answer: E
Skill: Application

32) A given solution is found to contain 0.0001 mol of hydrogen ions (H^+) per liter. Which of the following best describes this solution?

    A) acidic: H^+ acceptor

    B) basic: H^+ acceptor

    C) acidic: H^+ donor

    D) basic: H^+ donor

    E) neutral

Answer: C
Skill: Comprehension

33) A solution is found to contain 0.000001 mol of hydroxide ions (OH^-) per liter. Which of the following best describes this solution?

    A) acidic: H^+ acceptor

    B) basic: H^+ acceptor

    C) acidic: H^+ donor

    D) basic: H^+ donor

    E) neutral

Answer: B
Skill: Comprehension

34) Which of the following ionizes completely in solution and is therefore a strong acid?

A) NaOH

B) H_2CO_3

C) CH_3COOH

D) NH_2

E) HCl

Answer: E
Skill: Knowledge

35) Which of the following ionizes completely in solution and is therefore a strong base?

A) NaOH

B) HCl

C) NH_3

D) H_2CO_3

E) NaCl

Answer: A
Skill: Knowledge

36) Which of the following statements is *completely* correct?

A) H_2CO_3 is a weak acid, and NaOH is a weak base.

B) H_2CO_3 is a strong acid, and NaOH is a strong base.

C) NH_3 is a weak base, and H_2CO_3 is a strong acid.

D) NH_3 is a strong base, and HCl is a weak acid.

E) NH_3 is a weak base, and HCl is a strong acid.

Answer: E
Skill: Knowledge

37) Assume that acid rain has lowered the pH of a particular lake to pH 5.0. What is the hydroxide ion concentration of this lake?

A) 1×10^{-5} mol of hydroxide ion per liter of lake water

B) 1×10^{-9} mol of hydroxide ion per liter of lake water

C) 5.0 *M* with regard to hydroxide ion concentration

D) 9.0 *M* with regard to hydroxide ion concentration

E) Both B and D are correct.

Answer: B
Skill: Application

38) What would be the pH of a solution with a hydroxide ion concentration [OH⁻] of 10^{-10} *M*?

A) 2

B) 4

C) 8

D) 10

E) 14

Answer: B
Skill: Comprehension

39) What would be the pH of a solution with a hydrogen ion concentration [H⁺] of 10^{-8} *M*?

A) pH 2

B) pH 4

C) pH 6

D) pH 8

E) pH 10

Answer: D
Skill: Comprehension

40) Which of the following solutions has the greatest concentration of hydrogen ions [H^+]?

A) gastric juice at pH 2

B) vinegar at pH 3

C) tomato juice at pH 4

D) black coffee at pH 5

E) household bleach at pH 12

Answer: A
Skill: Knowledge

41) Which of the following solutions has the greatest concentration of hydroxide ions [OH^-]?

A) lemon juice at pH 2

B) vinegar at pH 3

C) tomato juice at pH 4

D) urine at pH 6

E) seawater at pH 8

Answer: E
Skill: Knowledge

42) If the pH of a solution is decreased from 7 to 6, it means that the

A) concentration of H^+ has decreased to 10 times of what it was at pH 7.

B) concentration of H^+ has increased to 10 times what it was at pH 7.

C) concentration of OH^- has increased to 10 times what it was at pH 7.

D) concentration of OH^- has decreased 10 times what it was at pH 7.

E) Both B and D are correct.

Answer: E
Skill: Comprehension

43) If the pH of a solution is increased from pH 8 to pH 9, it means that the

A) concentration of H^+ is 10 times greater than what it was at pH 8.

B) concentration of H^+ is 100 times less than what it was at pH 8.

C) concentration of OH^- is 10 times greater than what it was at pH 8.

D) concentration of OH^- is 100 times less than what it was at pH 8.

E) concentration of H^+ is greater and the concentration of OH^- is less than at pH 8.

Answer: C
Skill: Comprehension

44) One liter of a solution with a pH of 3 has how many more H^+ than 1 L of a solution with a pH of 6?

A) 3 times more

B) 10 times more

C) 100 times more

D) 300 times more

E) 1,000 times more

Answer: E
Skill: Comprehension

45) One liter of a solution with a pH of 11 has how many more OH^- than 1 L of a solution with a pH of 6?

A) 5 times more

B) 10 times more

C) 50 times more

D) 10,000 times more

E) 100,000 times more

Answer: E
Skill: Comprehension

46) Which of the following statements is *true* about buffer solutions? They

   A) will always have a pH of 7.

   B) tend to maintain a relatively constant pH.

   C) maintain a constant pH when bases are added to them but not when acids are added to them.

   D) cause a lowering of pH when acids are added to them.

   E) are rarely found in living systems.

   Answer: B
   Skill: Knowledge

47) Buffers are substances that help resist shifts in pH by

   A) releasing H^+ in acidic solutions.

   B) releasing H^+ in basic solutions.

   C) releasing OH^- in basic solutions.

   D) combining with OH^- in acidic solutions.

   E) combining with H^+ in basic solutions.

   Answer: B
   Skill: Knowledge

48) One of the buffers that contribute to pH stability in human blood is carbonic acid (H_2CO_3). Carbonic acid is a weak acid that dissociates into a bicarbonate ion (HCO_3^-) and a hydrogen ion (H^+). Thus,

$$H_2CO_3 \Leftrightarrow HCO_3^- + H^+$$

If the pH of the blood drops, one would expect

   A) a decrease in the concentration of H_2CO_3 and an increase in the concentration of HCO_3^-.

   B) the concentration of hydroxide ion (OH^-) to increase.

   C) the concentration of bicarbonate ion (HCO_3^-) to increase.

   D) the HCO_3^- to act as a base and remove excess H+ with the formation of H_2CO_3.

   E) the HCO_3^- to act as an acid and remove excess H+ with the formation of H_2CO_3.

   Answer: D
   Skill: Application

49) One of the buffers that contribute to pH stability in human blood is carbonic acid (H_2CO_3). Carbonic acid is a weak acid that when placed in an aqueous solution dissociates into a bicarbonate ion (HCO_3^-) and a hydrogen ion (H^+). Thus,

$$H_2CO_3 \Leftrightarrow HCO_3^- + H^+$$

If the pH of the blood increases, one would expect:

A) a decrease in the concentration of H_2CO_3 and an increase in the concentration of H_2O.

B) an increase in the concentration of H_2CO_3 and a decrease in the concentration of H_2O.

C) a decrease in the concentration of HCO_3^- and an increase in the concentration of H_2O.

D) an increase in the concentration of HCO_3^- and a decrease in the concentration of H_2O.

E) a decrease in the concentration of HCO_3^- and an increase in the concentration of both H_2CO_3 and H_2O.

Answer: A
Skill: Application

The following questions refer to the terms below.

A. calorie
B. temperature
C. heat of vaporization
D. buffer
E. mole

50) A measure of the average kinetic energy of the molecules in a body of matter

Answer: B
Skill: Knowledge

51) The number of grams of a substance that equals its molecular mass in daltons

Answer: E
Skill: Knowledge

52) A weak acid or base that combines reversibly with hydrogen ions

Answer: D
Skill: Knowledge

53) Recent research indicates that acid precipitation can damage life by

A) buffering aquatic systems such as lakes and streams.

B) decreasing the H^+ concentration of lakes and streams.

C) changing the solubility of soil minerals.

D) altering the structures of biological molecules required for essential life processes.

E) Both C and D are true.

Answer: E
Skill: Knowledge

Media Activity Questions

1) Water's surface tension and heat storage capacity is accounted for by its

   A) orbitals.

   B) weight.

   C) hydrogen bonds.

   D) mass.

   E) size.

   Answer: C
   Topic: Web/CD Activity 3A

2) The tendency of water molecules to stick together is referred to as

   A) adhesion.

   B) polarity.

   C) cohesion.

   D) transpiration.

   E) evaporation.

   Answer: C
   Topic: Web/CD Activity 3B

3) When water dissociates, what is transferred from one water molecule to form a hydronium ion?

   A) H_3O^+

   B) hydrogen atom

   C) a hydrogen ion

   D) H_2O

   E) OH^-

   Answer: C
   Topic: Web/CD Activity 3D

4) Which of these is a synonymous pair of terms?

   A) hydrogen ion—hydroxide ion

   B) hydrogen ion—proton

   C) hydroxide ion—hydronium ion

   D) water—hydronium

   E) hydrogen ion—hydronium ion

   Answer: B
   Topic: Web/CD Activity 3E

5) A pH of 9 is _____ times more _____ than a pH of 5.

   A) 10,000; acidic

   B) 4; acidic

   C) 45; basic

   D) 4; basic

   E) 10,000; basic

   Answer: E
   Topic: Web/CD Activity 3E

Self-Quiz Questions

1) What is the main thesis of Lawrence Henderson's *The Fitness of the Environment*?

   A) Earth's environment is constant.

   B) It is the physical environment, not life, that has evolved.

   C) The environment of Earth has adapted to life.

   D) Life as we know it depends on certain environmental qualities on Earth.

   E) Water and other aspects of Earth's environment exist because they make the planet more suitable for life.

   Answer: D

2) Air temperature often increases slightly as clouds begin to drop rain or snow. Which behavior of water is *most directly* responsible for this phenomenon?

   A) water's change in density when it condenses

   B) water's reactions with other atmospheric compounds

   C) release of heat by the formation of hydrogen bonds

   D) release of heat by the breaking of hydrogen bonds

   E) water's high surface tension

   Answer: C

3) For two bodies of matter in contact, heat always flows from

   A) the body with greater heat to the one with less heat.

   B) the body of higher temperature to the one of lower temperature.

   C) the denser body to the less dense body.

   D) the body with more water to the one with less water.

   E) the larger body to the smaller body.

   Answer: B

4) A slice of pizza has 500 kcal. If we could burn the pizza and use all the heat to warm a 50-L container of cold water, what would be the approximate increase in temperature of the water? (*Note:* A liter of cold water weighs about 1 kg.)

   A) 50°C

   B) 5°C

   C) 10°C

   D) 100°C

   E) 1°C

   Answer: C

5) The bonds that are broken when water vaporizes are

   A) ionic bonds.

   B) bonds between water molecules.

   C) bonds between atoms within individual water molecules.

   D) polar covalent bonds.

   E) nonpolar covalent bonds.

   Answer: B

6) Which of the following is an example of a hydrophobic material?

   A) paper

   B) table salt

   C) wax

   D) sugar

   E) pasta

   Answer: C

7) We can be sure that a mole of table sugar and a mole of vitamin C are equal in their

   A) weight in daltons.

   B) weight in grams.

   C) number of molecules.

   D) number of atoms.

   E) volume.

   Answer: C

8) How many grams of acetic acid ($C_2H_4O_2$) would you use to make 10 L of a 0.1 M aqueous solution of acetic acid?

(*Note:* The atomic weights, in daltons, are approximately 12 for carbon, 1 for hydrogen, and 16 for oxygen.)

A) 10 g

B) 0.1 g

C) 6 g

D) 60 g

E) 0.6 g

Answer: D

9) Acid precipitation has lowered the pH of a particular lake to 4.0. What is the *hydrogen* ion concentration of the lake?

A) 4.0 M

B) 10^{10} M

C) 10^{-4} M

D) 10^4 M

E) 4%

Answer: C

10) Acid precipitation has lowered the pH of a particular lake to 4.0. What is the *hydroxide* ion concentration of the lake?

A) 10^{-7} M

B) 10^{-4} M

C) 10^{-10} M

D) 10^{-14} M

E) 10 M

Answer: C

Chapter 4　Carbon and the Molecular Diversity of Life

1) Which type of molecule would be most abundant in a typical prokaryotic or eukaryotic cell?

A) hydrocarbon

B) protein

C) water

D) lipid

E) carbohydrate

Answer: C
Skill: Knowledge

2) Organic chemistry is a science based on the study of

A) functional groups.

B) vital forces interacting with matter.

C) carbon compounds.

D) water and its interaction with other kinds of molecules.

E) the properties of oxygen.

Answer: C
Skill: Knowledge

3) Early 19th–century scientists believed that living organisms differed from nonliving things as a result of possessing a "life force" that could create organic molecules from inorganic matter. The term given to this belief is

A) materialism.

B) vitalism.

C) mechanism.

D) organic evolution.

E) inorganic synthesis.

Answer: B
Skill: Knowledge

4) The concept of vitalism is based on a belief in a life force outside the jurisdiction of physical and chemical laws. According to this belief, organic compounds can arise only within living organisms. Which of the following did the most to refute the concept of vitalism?

A) Wohler's synthesis of urea

B) Berzelius's definition of organic molecules

C) Miller's experiments with ancient atmospheres

D) Rodriguez's studies of phytochemicals

E) Kolbe's synthesis of acetic acid

Answer: C
Skill: Knowledge

5) The experimental approach taken in current biological investigation presumes that

A) simple organic compounds can be synthesized in the laboratory from inorganic precursors, but complex organic compounds like carbohydrates and proteins can only be synthesized by living organisms.

B) a life force ultimately controls the activities of living organisms and this life force cannot be studied by physical or chemical methods.

C) although a life force, or vitalism, exists in living organisms, this life force cannot be studied by physical or chemical methods.

D) living organisms are composed of the same elements present in nonliving things, plus a few special trace elements found in only living organisms or their products.

E) organisms can be understood in terms of the same physical and chemical laws that can be used to explain nonliving things.

Answer: E
Skill: Comprehension

6) Which property of the carbon atom gives it compatibility with a greater number of different elements than any other type of atom?

A) Carbon has six to eight neutrons.

B) Carbon has a valence of 4.

C) Carbon forms ionic bonds.

D) Only A and C are correct.

E) A, B, and C are correct.

Answer: B
Skill: Knowledge

7) How many electron pairs does carbon share in order to complete its valence shell?

A) 1   B) 2   C) 3   D) 4   E) 5

Answer: D
Skill: Knowledge

8) What type of bonds does carbon have a tendency to form?

A) ionic

B) hydrogen

C) covalent

D) Only A and B are correct.

E) A, B, and C are correct.

Answer: C
Skill: Knowledge

9) The carbon present in all organic molecules

A) is incorporated into organic molecules by plants.

B) is processed into sugars through photosynthesis.

C) is derived from carbon dioxide.

D) two of the above.

E) all of the above.

Answer: E
Skill: Comprehension

10) What is the reason why hydrocarbons are not soluble in water?

A) They are hydrophilic.

B) The C–H bond is nonpolar.

C) The C–H bond is polar.

D) They are large molecules.

E) They are lighter than water.

Answer: B
Skill: Knowledge

11) How many structural isomers are possible for butane having the molecular formula C_4H_{10}?

A) 1   B) 2   C) 4   D) 5   E) 8

Answer: B
Skill: Application

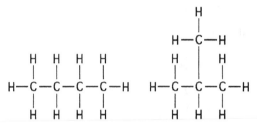

Figure 4.1

12) The two molecules shown in Figure 4.1 are best described as

A) optical isomers.

B) radioactive isotopes.

C) structural isomers.

D) positive ions.

E) geometric isomers.

Answer: C
Skill: Comprehension

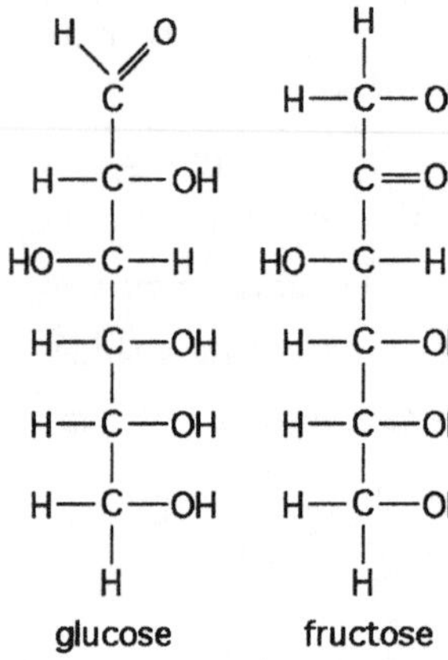

Figure 4.2

13) Observe the structures of glucose and fructose in Figure 4.2. These two molecules differ in the

   A) number of carbon, hydrogen, and oxygen atoms.

   B) types of carbon, hydrogen, and oxygen atoms.

   C) arrangement of carbon, hydrogen, and oxygen atoms.

   D) Only A and B are correct.

   E) A, B, and C are correct.

   Answer: C
   Skill: Comprehension

14) Observe the structures of glucose and fructose in Figure 4.2. These two molecules are

   A) geometric isotopes.

   B) enantiomers.

   C) geometric isomers.

   D) structural isomers.

   E) nonisotopic isomers.

   Answer: D
   Skill: Comprehension

15) Which of the following is *true* of geometric isomers?

   A) They have variations in arrangement around a double bond.

   B) They have an asymmetric carbon that makes them mirror images.

   C) They have the same chemical properties.

   D) They have different molecular formulas.

   E) Their atoms and bonds are arranged in different sequences.

   Answer: A
   Skill: Knowledge

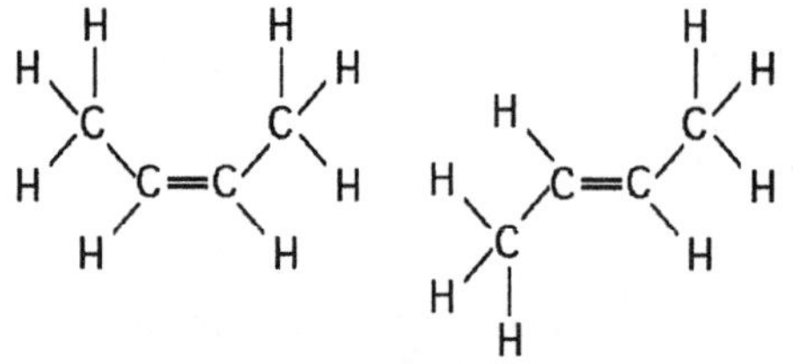

Figure 4.3

16) The two molecules shown in Figure 4.3 are best described as

   A) enantiomers.

   B) radioactive isotopes.

   C) structural isomers.

   D) nonisotopic isomers.

   E) geometric isomers.

   Answer: E
   Skill: Comprehension

17) Recent research suggests that side effects from Ritalin, the drug used to treat attention deficit disorder, may be caused by contamination of enantiomers, or molecules that

A) have identical three-dimensional shapes.

B) are mirror images of one another.

C) lack an asymmetric carbon.

D) differ in the location of their double bonds.

E) differ in their electrical charge.

Answer: B
Skill: Knowledge

18) A compound contains hydroxyl groups as its predominant functional group. Which of the following statements is *true* concerning this compound?

A) It is probably a lipid.

B) It should dissolve in water.

C) It should dissolve in a nonpolar solvent.

D) It won't form hydrogen bonds with water.

E) It is hydrophobic.

Answer: B
Skill: Comprehension

19) Which is the best description of a carbonyl group?

A) a carbon and hydrogen atom

B) an oxygen double-bonded to a carbon and a hydroxyl group

C) a nitrogen and a hydrogen bonded to a carbon atom

D) a sulfur and a hydrogen bonded to a carbon atom

E) a carbon atom joined to an oxygen atom by a double bond

Answer: E
Skill: Knowledge

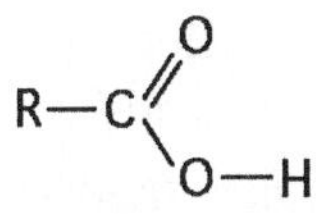

Figure 4.4

20) What is the name of the functional group shown in Figure 4.4?

A) carbonyl

B) methyl

C) dehydroxyl

D) carboxyl

E) acetyl

Answer: D
Skill: Knowledge

21) Which of the following contains nitrogen in addition to carbon, oxygen, and hydrogen?

A) an alcohol such as ethanol

B) a monosaccharide such as starch

C) a steroid such as testosterone

D) an amino acid such as glycine

E) a hydrocarbon such as benzene

Answer: D
Skill: Comprehension

22) Which of the following is a *false* statement concerning amino groups?

A) They are basic in pH.

B) They are found in amino acids.

C) They contain nitrogen.

D) They are nonpolar.

E) They are components of urea.

Answer: D
Skill: Comprehension

23) Which two functional groups are *always* found in amino acids?

A) amine and sulfhydryl

B) carbonyl and carboxyl

C) carboxyl and amine

D) alcohol and aldehyde

E) ketone and amine

Answer: C
Skill: Knowledge

24) Amino acids are acids because they possess which functional group?

A) amino

B) alcohol

C) carboxyl

D) sulfhydryl

E) aldehyde

Answer: C
Skill: Knowledge

25) A carbon skeleton is covalently bonded to both an amino group and a carboxyl group. When placed in water,

A) it would function only as an acid because of the carboxyl group.

B) it would function only as a base because of the amino group.

C) it would function as neither an acid nor a base.

D) it would function as both an acid and a base.

E) it is impossible to determine how it would function.

Answer: D
Skill: Application

26) A chemist wishes to make an organic molecule less acidic. Which of the following functional groups should be added to the molecule?

A) carboxyl

B) sulfhydryl

C) hydroxyl

D) amino

E) phosphate

Answer: D
Skill: Application

27) Which functional groups can act as acids?

A) amine and sulfhydryl

B) carbonyl and carboxyl

C) carboxyl and phosphate

D) alcohol and aldehyde

E) ketone and amino

Answer: C
Skill: Comprehension

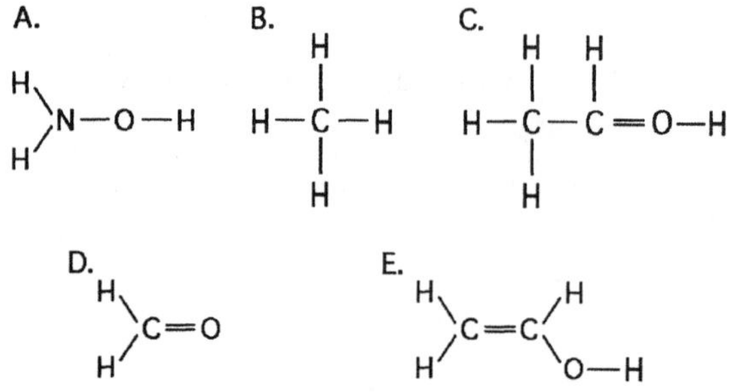

Figure 4.5

28) Which of the structures in Figure 4.5 is an impossible covalently bonded molecule?

Answer: C
Skill: Comprehension

The following questions refer to the functional groups shown in Figure 4.6.

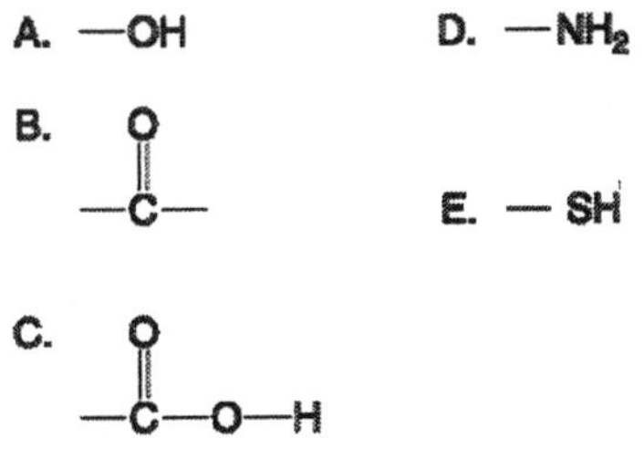

Figure 4.6

29) Which is an alcohol group?

Answer: A
Skill: Knowledge

30) Which is an amino group?

Answer: D
Skill: Knowledge

31) Which is a carbonyl group?

Answer: B
Skill: Knowledge

32) Which is a carboxyl group?

Answer: C
Skill: Knowledge

33) Acidic, can dissociate and release H^+

Answer: C
Skill: Knowledge

34) Basic, accepts H^+ and becomes positively charged

Answer: D
Skill: Knowledge

35) Helps stabilize proteins by forming covalent cross–links within or between protein molecules.

Answer: E
Skill: Knowledge

The following questions refer to the molecules shown in Figure 4.7.

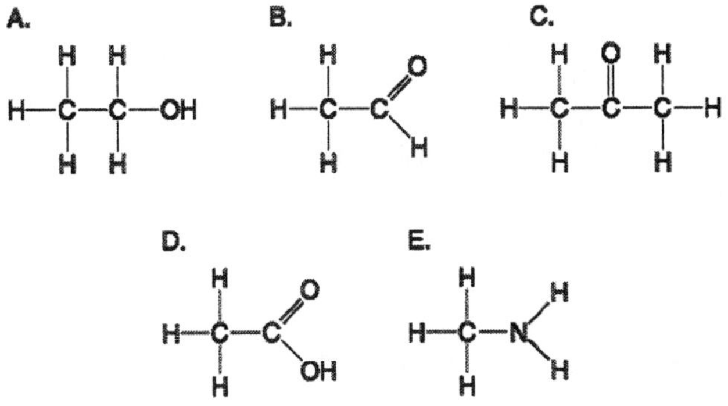

Figure 4.7

36) Which molecule is water–soluble because it has a functional group that is an alcohol?

Answer: A
Skill: Knowledge

37) Which two molecules contain a carbonyl group?
  A) A and B
  B) B and C
  C) C and D
  D) D and E
  E) A and E

Answer: B
Skill: Knowledge

38) Which molecule has a carbonyl group in the form of a ketone?

Answer: C
Skill: Knowledge

39) Which molecule has a carbonyl functional group in the form of an aldehyde?

Answer: B
Skill: Knowledge

40) Which molecule contains a carboxyl group?

Answer: D
Skill: Knowledge

41) Which molecule increases the concentration of hydrogen ions in a solution and is therefore an organic acid?

Answer: D
Skill: Comprehension

The following questions refer to the molecules shown in Figure 4.8.

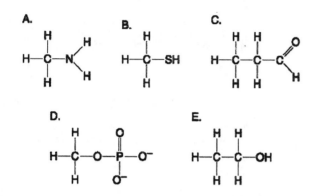

Figure 4.8

42) Which molecule contains a sulfhydryl group?

Answer: B
Skill: Knowledge

43) Which molecule contains a group that functions to transfer energy between organic molecules?

Answer: D
Skill: Knowledge

44) Which molecule contains a functional group known as an amino group?

Answer: A
Skill: Knowledge

45) Which molecule is a thiol?

Answer: B
Skill: Knowledge

46) Which molecule is an organic phosphate?

Answer: D
Skill: Knowledge

47) Which molecule can function as a base?

Answer: A
Skill: Comprehension

Media Activity Questions

1) Hydrocarbons

A) are polar.

B) are held together by ionic bonds.

C) contain nitrogen.

D) contain only hydrogen and carbon atoms.

E) are held together by hydrogen bonds.

Answer: D
Topic: Web/CD Activity 4A

2) What is the definition of the term *isomer*?

A) active and inactive versions of a molecule

B) molecules made up of the same elements

C) molecules with different structures but similar functions

D) molecules with the same molecular formula but different structures

E) molecules with the same structure but different molecular formulas

Answer: D
Topic: Web/CD Activity 4B

3) Structural isomers are molecules that

A) are enantiomers.

B) are hydrocarbons.

C) have a ring structure.

D) are mirror images.

E) differ in the covalent arrangements of their atoms.

Answer: E
Topic: Web/CD Activity 4B

4) Which of these functional groups does *not* contain oxygen?

A) carboxyl

B) sulfhydryl

C) hydroxyl

D) carbonyl

E) phosphate

Answer: B
Topic: Web/CD Activity 4C

5) Which of these functional groups is characteristic of ketones?

A) amino

B) sulfhydryl

C) carbonyl

D) phosphate

E) hydroxyl

Answer: C
Topic: Web/CD Activity 4C

Self-Quiz Questions

Answers to these questions also appear in the textbook.

1) Organic chemistry is currently defined as
   A) the study of compounds that can be made only by living cells.
   B) the study of carbon compounds.
   C) the study of vital forces.
   D) the study of natural (as opposed to synthetic) compounds.
   E) the study of hydrocarbons.

   Answer: B

2) Choose the pair of terms that correctly completes this sentence: Hydroxyl is to _____ as _____ is to aldehyde.
   A) carbonyl; ketone
   B) oxygen; carbon
   C) alcohol; carbonyl
   D) amine; carboxyl
   E) alcohol; ketone

   Answer: C

3) Which of the following hydrocarbons has a double bond in its carbon skeleton?
   A) C_3H_8
   B) C_2H_6
   C) CH_4
   D) C_2H_4
   E) C_2H_2

   Answer: D

4) The gasoline consumed by an automobile is a fossil fuel consisting mostly of
   A) aldehydes.
   B) amino acids.
   C) alcohols.
   D) hydrocarbons.
   E) thiols.

   Answer: D

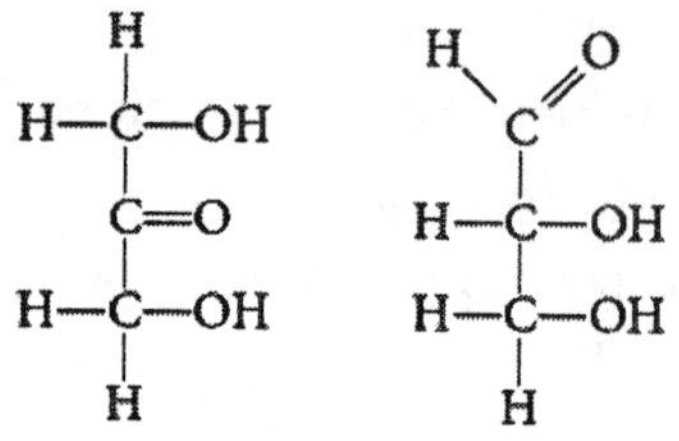

Figure 4.9

5) Choose the term that correctly describes the relationship between the two sugar molecules shown in Figure 4.9.
   A) structural isomers
   B) geometric isomers
   C) enantiomers
   D) isotopes

   Answer: A

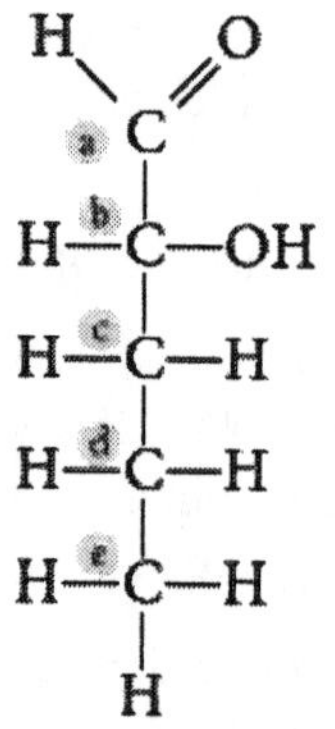

Figure 4.10

6) Identify the asymmetric carbon in the molecule shown in Figure 4.10.

   Answer: B

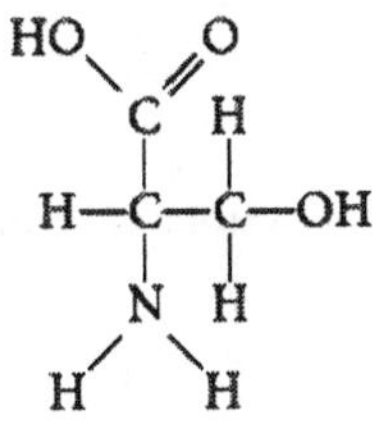

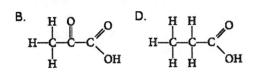

Figure 4.11

Figure 4.12

7) Which functional group is *not* present in the molecule shown in Figure 4.11?

    A) carboxyl   B) sulfhydryl

    C) hydroxyl   D) amino

    Answer: B

8) Which action could produce a carbonyl group?

    A) the removal of the hydroxyl from a carboxyl

    B) the addition of a thiol to a hydroxyl

    C) the addition of a hydroxyl to a phosphate

    D) the replacement of the nitrogen of an amine with oxygen

    E) the addition of a sulfhydryl to a carboxyl

    Answer: A

9) Which functional group is most likely to be responsible for an organic molecule behaving as a base?

    A) hydroxyl

    B) carbonyl

    C) carboxyl

    D) amino

    E) phosphate

    Answer: D

10) Which of the molecules shown in Figure 4.12 would be the strongest acid?

    Answer: B

Chapter 5   The Structure and Function of Macromolecules

1) A molecule inside a cell consists of over 3,500 covalently linked atoms weighing about 105,000 daltons. From this description, the molecule can most specifically be described as a

A) protein.

B) macromolecule.

C) polysaccharide.

D) lipid.

E) polypeptide.

Answer: B
Skill: Knowledge

2) Polymers of polysaccharides, fats, and proteins are all synthesized from monomers by

A) connecting monosaccharides together.

B) the addition of water to each monomer.

C) the removal of water (dehydration reactions).

D) ionic bonding of the monomers.

E) the formation of disulfide bridges between monomers.

Answer: C
Skill: Comprehension

3) Which of the following best summarizes the relationship between dehydration reactions and hydrolysis?

A) Dehydration reactions assemble polymers, and hydrolysis breaks them down.

B) Hydrolysis occurs during the day, and dehydration reactions happen at night.

C) Dehydration reactions can occur only after hydrolysis.

D) Hydrolysis creates monomers, and dehydration reactions destroy them.

E) Dehydration reactions occur in plants, and hydrolysis happens in animals.

Answer: A
Skill: Comprehension

4) Carbohydrates normally function in animals as

A) the functional units of lipids.

B) enzymes in the regulation of metabolic processes.

C) a component of triglycerides.

D) energy–storage molecules.

E) sites of protein synthesis.

Answer: D
Skill: Knowledge

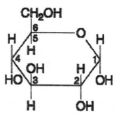

Figure 5.1

5) If 100 molecules of the general type shown in Figure 5.1 were covalently joined together in sequence, the single molecule that would result would be a

A) polysaccharide.

B) polypeptide.

C) polyunsaturated lipid.

D) nucleic acid.

E) fatty acid.

Answer: A
Skill: Comprehension

6) Consider a polysaccharide consisting of 828 glucose molecules. The total hydrolysis of the polysaccharide would result in the production of

A) 827 glucose molecules.

B) 827 water molecules.

C) 827 glucose molecules and 827 water molecules.

D) 828 glucose molecules and 828 water molecules.

E) 828 glucose molecules and no water molecules.

Answer: E
Skill: Comprehension

7) Which of the following are polysaccharides?

A) RNA and DNA

B) glucose and sucrose

C) cholesterol and triacylglycerol

D) glycogen and starch

E) uracil and thymine

Answer: D
Skill: Knowledge

8) Which of the following is *true* of both starch and cellulose?

A) They are both polymers of glucose.

B) They are geometric isomers of each other.

C) They can both be digested by humans.

D) They are both used for energy storage in plants.

E) They are both structural components of the plant cell wall.

Answer: A
Skill: Knowledge

9) What is a fat or triacylglycerol?

A) a protein with tertiary structure

B) a lipid made of three fatty acids and glycerol

C) a kind of lipid that makes up much of the plasma membrane

D) a molecule formed from three alcohols

E) a carbohydrate with three sugars

Answer: B
Skill: Knowledge

10) Which of the following is *true* concerning saturated fatty acids?

A) They are the predominant fatty acid in corn oil.

B) They have double bonds between the carbon atoms of the fatty acids.

C) They have a higher ratio of hydrogen to carbon than do unsaturated fatty acids.

D) They are usually liquid at room temperature.

E) They are usually produced by plants.

Answer: C
Skill: Knowledge

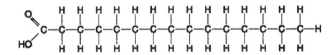

Figure 5.2

11) What is the molecule illustrated in Figure 5.2?

A) a saturated fatty acid

B) an unsaturated fatty acid

C) a polyunsaturated triglyceride

D) a common component of plant oils

E) similar in structure to a steroid

Answer: A
Skill: Knowledge

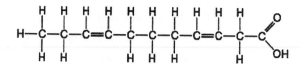

Figure 5.3

12) The molecule shown in Figure 5.3 is a

A) polysaccharide.

B) polypeptide.

C) saturated fatty acid.

D) nucleic acid.

E) unsaturated fatty acid.

Answer: E
Skill: Knowledge

13) The hydrogenation of vegetable oil would result in

A) a decrease in the number of carbon–carbon double bonds in the oil molecules.

B) an increase in the number of hydrogen atoms in the oil molecule.

C) the oil being a solid at room temperature.

D) two of the above.

E) all of the above.

Answer: E
Skill: Knowledge

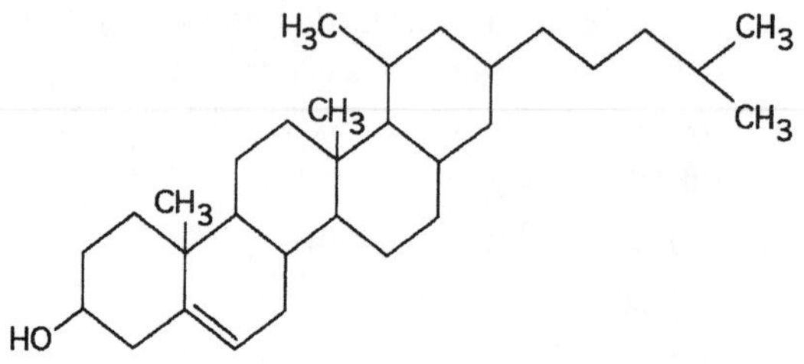

Figure 5.4

14) What is the structure shown in Figure 5.4?

A) a starch molecule

B) a steroid

C) a protein

D) a cellulose molecule

E) a nucleic acid polymer

Answer: B
Skill: Knowledge

15) Which type of lipid is most important in biological membranes?

A) fat

B) wax

C) phospholipid

D) oil

E) triglyceride

Answer: C
Skill: Knowledge

16) The 20 different amino acids found in polypeptides exhibit different chemical and physical properties because of different

A) carboxyl groups.

B) amino groups.

C) side chains (R groups).

D) tertiary structure.

E) Both A and B are correct.

Answer: C
Skill: Knowledge

17) The bonding of two amino acid molecules to form a larger molecule requires the

A) release of a water molecule.

B) release of a carbon dioxide molecule.

C) addition of a nitrogen atom.

D) addition of a water molecule.

E) Both C and D are correct.

Answer: A
Skill: Knowledge

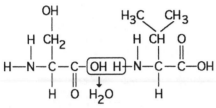

Figure 5.5

18) The chemical reactions illustrated in Figure 5.5 result in the formation of

A) peptide bonds.

B) ionic bonds.

C) glycosidic bonds.

D) hydrogen bonds.

E) an isotope.

Answer: A
Skill: Knowledge

19) Upon chemical analysis, a particular protein was found to contain 438 amino acids. How many peptide bonds are present in this protein?

A) 20

B) 437

C) 438

D) 439

E) 876

Answer: B
Skill: Comprehension

Refer to Figure 5.6 to answer the following questions.

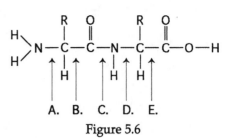

Figure 5.6

20) At which bond would water need to be added to achieve hydrolysis of the dipeptide shown, back to its component amino acids?

A) A

B) B

C) C

D) D

E) E

Answer: C
Skill: Comprehension

21) Which bond is closest to the N–terminus of the dipeptide?

A) A

B) B

C) C

D) D

E) E

Answer: A
Skill: Comprehension

22) Which bond is closest to the C-terminus of the dipeptide?

A) A

B) B

C) C

D) D

E) E

Answer: E
Skill: Comprehension

23) Which bonds are created during the formation of the primary structure of a protein?

A) peptide bonds

B) hydrogen bonds

C) disulfide bonds

D) Only A and C are correct.

E) A, B, and C are correct.

Answer: A
Skill: Knowledge

24) How many different kinds of polypeptides, each composed of 5 amino acids, could be synthesized using the 20 common amino acids?

A) 5

B) 20

C) 5^5

D) 20^5

E) 20^{10}

Answer: D
Skill: Application

25) What maintains the secondary structure of a protein?

A) peptide bonds

B) hydrogen bonds

C) disulfide bridges

D) ionic bonds

E) electrostatic charges

Answer: B
Skill: Knowledge

26) Which type of interaction stabilizes the α–helix structure of proteins?

A) hydrophobic interactions

B) nonpolar covalent bonds

C) ionic interactions

D) hydrogen bonds

E) polar covalent bonds

Answer: D
Skill: Knowledge

27) The α–helix and the β–pleated sheet are both common forms found in which level of protein structure?

A) primary   B) secondary

C) tertiary   D) quaternary

Answer: B
Skill: Knowledge

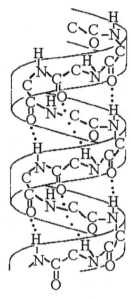

Figure 5.7

28) Figure 5.7 shows

A) the linear form of glucose.

B) the α–helix of starch.

C) the α–helix of DNA.

D) a polynucleotide folding into a double helix.

E) an α–helix of a polypeptide.

Answer: E
Skill: Comprehension

29) Figure 5.7 best illustrates

A) the primary structure of a protein.

B) β 1–4 linkages in cellulose.

C) the double helix of DNA.

D) the secondary structure of a protein.

E) the twisting of a fatty acid chain.

Answer: D
Skill: Comprehension

30) The tertiary structure of a protein is the

A) bonding together of several polypeptide chains by weak bonds.

B) order in which amino acids are joined in a peptide chain.

C) bonding of two amino acids together to form a dipeptide.

D) twisting of a peptide chain into an α–helix.

E) three–dimensional shape.

Answer: E
Skill: Knowledge

31) What would be an expected consequence of changing one amino acid in a particular protein?

A) The primary structure would be changed.

B) The tertiary structure might be changed.

C) The biological activity of this protein might be altered.

D) Only A and C are correct.

E) A, B, and C are correct.

Answer: E
Skill: Comprehension

32) Altering which of the following levels of structural organization could change the function of a protein?

A) primary

B) secondary

C) tertiary

D) Only A and B are correct.

E) A, B, and C are correct.

Answer: E
Skill: Comprehension

33) At which level of protein structure are interactions between R groups *most* important?

A) primary

B) secondary

C) tertiary

D) quaternary

E) They are equally important at all levels.

Answer: C
Skill: Knowledge

34) The R group or side chain of the amino acid serine is $-CH_2-OH$. The R group or side chain of the amino acid alanine is $-CH_3$. Where would you expect to find these amino acids in globular protein in aqueous solution?

A) Serine would be in the interior, and alanine would be on the exterior of the globular protein.

B) Alanine would be in the interior, and serine would be on the exterior of the globular protein.

C) Both serine and alanine would be in the interior of the globular protein.

D) Both serine and alanine would be on the exterior of the globular protein.

E) Both serine and alanine would be in the interior and on the exterior of the globular protein.

Answer: B
Skill: Application

35) A change in a protein's three–dimensional shape or conformation due to disruption of hydrogen bonds, disulfide bridges, and ionic bonds is termed

A) hydrolysis.

B) stabilization.

C) destabilization.

D) renaturation.

E) denaturation.

Answer: E
Skill: Knowledge

36) Of the following functions, the major purpose of RNA is to
   A) transmit genetic information to offspring.
   B) function in the synthesis of proteins.
   C) make a copy of itself, thus ensuring genetic continuity.
   D) act as a pattern to form DNA.
   E) form the genes of an organism.

   Answer: B
   Skill: Comprehension

37) Which of the following *best* describes the relationship between proteins, RNA, DNA, and genes in humans?
   A) DNA → genes → RNA → proteins
   B) RNA → DNA → genes → proteins
   C) proteins → RNA → DNA → genes
   D) genes → RNA → DNA → proteins
   E) genes → proteins → RNA → DNA

   Answer: A
   Skill: Comprehension

38) Which of the following descriptions *best* fits the class of molecules known as nucleotides?
   A) a nitrogen base and a phosphate group
   B) a nitrogen base and a five-carbon sugar
   C) a nitrogen base, a phosphate group, and a five-carbon sugar
   D) a five-carbon sugar and adenine or uracil
   E) a five-carbon sugar and a purine or pyrimidine

   Answer: C
   Skill: Knowledge

39) Which of the following are nitrogen bases of the pyrimidine type?
   A) guanine and glucose
   B) cystine and sucrose
   C) thymine and cytosine
   D) ribose and deoxyribose
   E) glycerol and glycogen

   Answer: C
   Skill: Knowledge

40) Which of the following are nitrogen bases of the purine type?
   A) cytosine and guanine
   B) guanine and adenine
   C) adenine and thyamine
   D) thyamine and uridine
   E) uridine and cytosine

   Answer: B
   Skill: Knowledge

41) All of the following bases are found in DNA *except*
   A) thymine.
   B) adenine.
   C) uracil.
   D) guanine.
   E) cytosine.

   Answer: C
   Skill: Knowledge

42) A sequence of a DNA polymer consisting of 80 purines and 80 pyrimidines could have
   A) 160 cytosine and 160 thymine molecules.
   B) 80 uracil and 80 adenine molecules.
   C) 80 adenine and 80 thymine molecules.
   D) 80 adenine and 80 guanine molecules.
   E) both B and C.

   Answer: C
   Skill: Comprehension

43) The difference between the sugar in DNA and the sugar in RNA is that the sugar in DNA

A) contains less oxygen.

B) can form a double–stranded molecule.

C) has a six-membered ring of carbon and nitrogen atoms.

D) can attach to a phosphate, unlike the sugar in RNA.

E) is a six-carbon sugar and the sugar in RNA is a five-carbon sugar.

Answer: A
Skill: Knowledge

44) Which of the following statements *best* summarizes structural differences between DNA and RNA?

A) RNA is a protein, whereas DNA is a nucleic acid.

B) DNA is not a polymer, but RNA is.

C) DNA contains a different sugar from RNA.

D) RNA is a double helix, but DNA is not.

E) DNA has different purine bases from RNA.

Answer: C
Skill: Knowledge

45) In the double–helix structure of nucleic acids, cytosine hydrogen bonds to

A) deoxyribose.

B) ribose.

C) adenine.

D) thymine.

E) guanine.

Answer: E
Skill: Knowledge

46) The two strands making up the DNA molecule

A) cannot be separated.

B) contain ribose and deoxyribose in opposite strands.

C) are held together by hydrogen bonds and van der Waals forces.

D) are attached through a phosphate to hold the strands together.

E) contain uridine but not thymine.

Answer: C
Skill: Knowledge

47) If one strand of a DNA molecule has the sequence of bases ATTGCA, the other complementary strand would have the sequence

A) TAACGT.

B) UAACGU.

C) TUUCGU.

D) TAAGCT.

E) TUUGCT.

Answer: A
Skill: Knowledge

48) The structural feature that allows DNA to replicate itself is the

A) sugar–phosphate backbone.

B) complementary pairing of the bases.

C) phosphodiester bonding of the helices.

D) twisting of the molecule to form an α–helix.

E) three-part structure of the nucleotides.

Answer: B
Skill: Knowledge

49) A new organism is discovered in the deserts of New Mexico. Scientists there determine that the polypeptide sequence of hemoglobin from the new organism has 68 amino acid differences from humans, 62 differences from a gibbon, 24 differences from a rat, and 6 differences from a frog. These data

A) were collected to determine the type of blood in the new organism.

B) indicate that the new organism may be closely related to frogs.

C) suggest that the new organism evolved from gibbons but not rats and mice.

D) suggest that the new organism is closely related to humans.

E) show that the new organism is best adapted to an aquatic habitat.

Answer: B
Skill: Application

50) Dehydration reactions are used in forming which of the following compounds?

A) triglycerides

B) polysaccharides

C) proteins

D) Only A and C are correct.

E) A, B, and C are correct.

Answer: E
Skill: Knowledge

51) Polysaccharides, lipids, and proteins are similar in that they

A) are synthesized from monomers by the process of hydrolysis.

B) are synthesized from monomers by the process of dehydration reactions.

C) are synthesized by peptide bonding between monomers.

D) are decomposed into their subunits by the process of dehydration reactions.

E) all contain nitrogen in their monomers.

Answer: B
Skill: Knowledge

52) Which of the following illustrates hydrolysis?

A) the reaction of two monosaccharides to form a disaccharide with the release of water

B) the synthesis of two amino acids to form a dipeptide with the utilization of water

C) the reaction of a fat to form glycerol and fatty acids with the release of water

D) the reaction of a fat to form glycerol and fatty acids with the utilization of water

E) the synthesis of a nucleotide from a phosphate, a ribose sugar, and a nitrogen base with the production of a molecule of water

Answer: D
Skill: Comprehension

53) Large organic molecules are usually assembled by polymerization of a few kinds of simple subunits. Which of the following is an *exception* to the above statement?

A) a steroid

B) cellulose

C) DNA

D) an enzyme

E) a contractile protein

Answer: A
Skill: Comprehension

54) The element nitrogen is present in all of the following *except*

A) proteins.

B) nucleic acids.

C) amino acids.

D) DNA.

E) monosaccharides.

Answer: E
Skill: Knowledge

55) All of the following molecules are proteins *except*

A) hemoglobin.

B) antibodies.

C) collagen.

D) lysozyme.

E) cellulose.

Answer: E
Skill: Knowledge

56) All of the following molecules are carbohydrates *except*

A) lactose.

B) cellulose.

C) hemoglobin.

D) glycogen.

E) starch.

Answer: C
Skill: Knowledge

The following questions are based on the 15 molecules illustrated in Figure 5.8. Each molecule may be used once, more than once, or not at all.

(Figure 5.8 appears on page 56.)

57) Which of the following molecules are structural isomers?

A) 1 and 4

B) 6 and 7

C) 8 and 9

D) 12 and 13

E) 14 and 15

Answer: A
Skill: Comprehension

58) Which of the following combinations could be linked together to form a nucleotide?

A) 1 and 4

B) 2, 7, and 8

C) 5, 9, and 10

D) 11, 12, and 13

E) 14 and 15

Answer: D
Skill: Comprehension

59) Which of the following molecules contains a ketone–type of carbonyl functional group?

A) 1

B) 4

C) 8

D) 9

E) none of the above

Answer: E
Skill: Knowledge

60) Which of the following molecules contains an aldehyde–type of carbonyl functional group?

A) 1

B) 4

C) 9

D) 10

E) Answers A and B are correct.

Answer: E
Skill: Knowledge

61) Which of the following molecules is a carbohydrate?

A) 1

B) 6

C) 14

D) 15

E) all of the above

Answer: E
Skill: Knowledge

62) Which of the following molecules is a saturated fatty acid?

   A) 5

   B) 7

   C) 9

   D) 10

   E) 14

   Answer: C
   Skill: Knowledge

63) Which of the following molecules is a purine type of nitrogen base?

   A) 5

   B) 7

   C) 8

   D) 12

   E) 13

   Answer: E
   Skill: Knowledge

64) Which of the following molecules acts as building blocks of polypeptides?

   A) 1, 4, and 6

   B) 2, 7, and 8

   C) 9 and 10

   D) 11 , 12, and 13

   E) 14 and 15

   Answer: B
   Skill: Knowledge

65) Which of the following molecules is an amino acid with a hydrophobic R group or side chain?

   A) 4   B) 5   C) 6   D) 7   E) 9

   Answer: D
   Skill: Knowledge

66) Which of the following molecules could form a peptide bond as a result of a dehydration reaction?

   A) 2 and 3

   B) 3 and 7

   C) 7 and 8

   D) 8 and 9

   E) 12 and 13

   Answer: C
   Skill: Comprehension

67) Which of the following molecules could form a fat (or triacylglycerol) as a result of a dehydration reaction?

   A) 1 and 2

   B) 3 and 5

   C) 7 and 8

   D) 9 and 10

   E) 12 and 13

   Answer: D
   Skill: Knowledge

68) Which of the following molecules could be joined together by an ester linkage type of covalent bond?

   A) 1 and 4

   B) 5 and 6

   C) 7 and 8

   D) 9 and 10

   E) 11 and 13

   Answer: D
   Skill: Knowledge

69) Which of the following molecules contains several glycosidic linkage covalent bonds?

   A) 1

   B) 6

   C) 12

   D) 14

   E) 15

   Answer: D
   Skill: Comprehension

70) Which of the following molecules is the sugar found in RNA?

A) 1

B) 6

C) 12

D) 14

E) 15

Answer: C
Skill: Knowledge

71) Which of the following is a disaccharide form of carbohydrate?

A) 1

B) 6

C) 13

D) 14

E) 15

Answer: E
Skill: Knowledge

72) Which of the following molecules has a functional group that frequently is involved in maintaining the tertiary structure of a protein?

A) 2

B) 3

C) 8

D) 10

E) 13

Answer: A
Skill: Knowledge

73) Which of the following molecules consists of a hydrophilic "head" region and a hydrophobic "tail" region?

A) 3

B) 5

C) 7

D) 9

E) 11

Answer: B
Skill: Knowledge

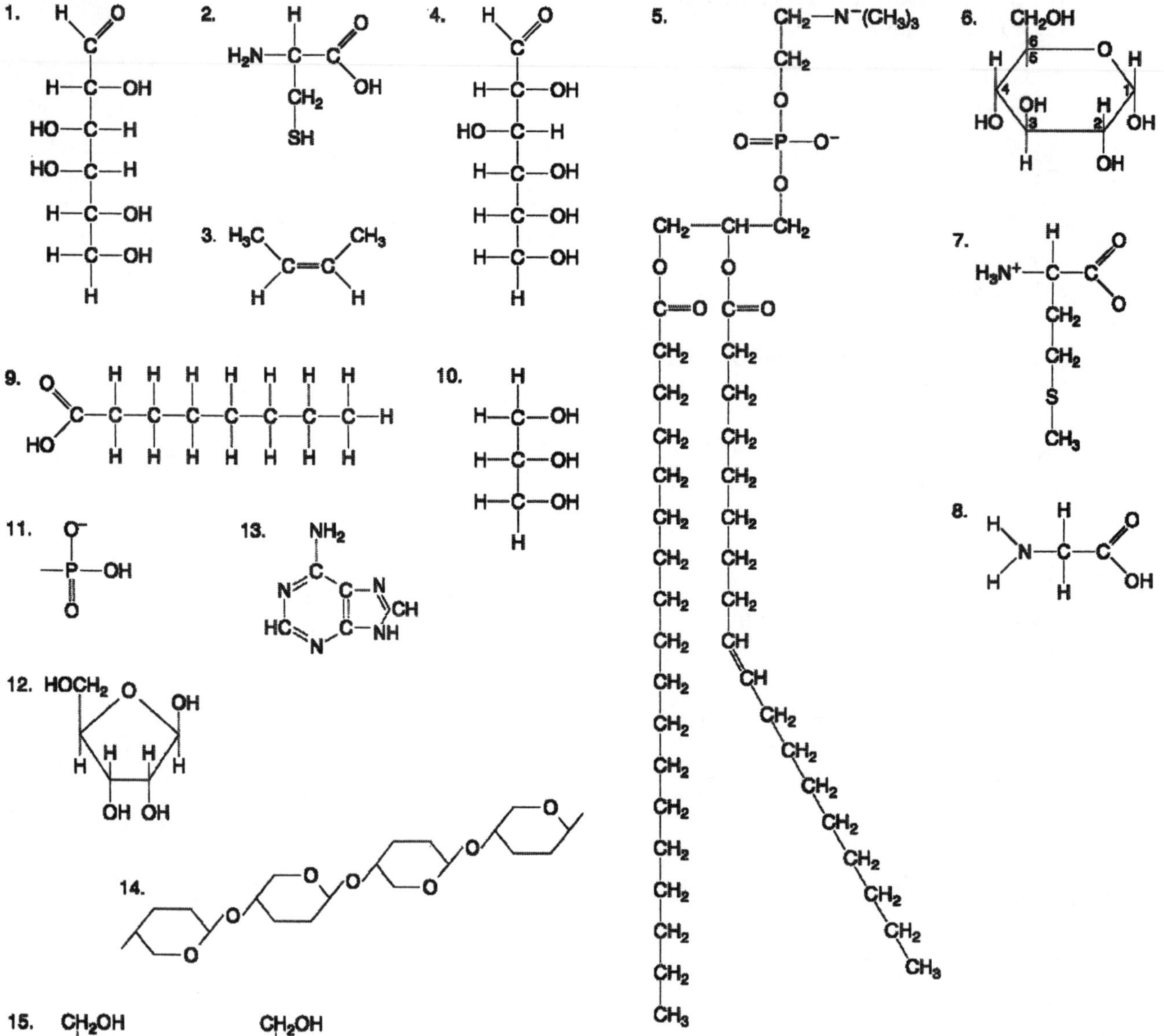

1.

2.

H₂N

3. H₃C — CH₃

4.

5. CH₂—N⁻(CH₃)₃

6. CH₂OH

7. H₃N⁺

8.

9.

10.

11.

13.

12. HOCH₂

14.

15. CH₂OH   CH₂OH

Figure 5.8

Media Activity Questions

1) Carbohydrates generally have a molecular formula

   A) that includes a –SH group.

   B) in which carbon, hydrogen, and oxygen are present in a ratio of 1:2:1.

   C) that includes a –NH$_2$ group.

   D) that includes at least one hydrocarbon tail.

   E) in which carbon, hydrogen, and oxygen are present in a 2:1:2 ratio.

   Answer: B
   Topic: Web/CD Activity 5C

2) Fatty acids are

   A) composed of carbon, hydrogen, and oxygen in a 1:2:1 ratio.

   B) composed of carbon, hydrogen, glycerol, and a phosphate group.

   C) hydrophobic.

   D) composed of four linked rings.

   E) components of DNA.

   Answer: C
   Topic: Web/CD Activity 5D

3) Structural proteins

   A) include receptor molecules.

   B) respond to environmental changes.

   C) include hemoglobin.

   D) anchor cell parts.

   E) bond to hormones.

   Answer: D
   Topic: Web/CD Activity 5E

4) The primary structure of a protein is

   A) an α–helix or a pleated sheet.

   B) the amino acid sequence of the polypeptide chain.

   C) composed of two or more polypeptide chains.

   D) maintained by hydrogen bonds.

   E) irregular folding.

   Answer: B
   Topic: Web/CD Activity 5F

5) Which of these is a difference between DNA and RNA?

   A) RNA is double–stranded; DNA is single–stranded.

   B) DNA is found in the nucleus; RNA is never found in the nucleus.

   C) In DNA, adenine pairs with guanine; in RNA, adenine pairs with thymine.

   D) DNA contains thymine; RNA contains uracil.

   E) DNA consists of five different nucleotides; RNA consists of four different nucleotides.

   Answer: D
   Topic: Web/CD Activity 5H

Self–Quiz Questions

Answers to these questions also appear in the textbook.

1) Which of the following terms includes all others in the list?

   A) monosaccharide

   B) disaccharide

   C) starch

   D) carbohydrate

   E) polysaccharide

   Answer: D

2) The molecular formula for glucose is $C_6H_{12}O_6$. What would be the molecular formula for a polymer made by linking ten glucose molecules together by dehydration reactions?

   A) $C_{60}H_{120}O_{60}$

   B) $C_6H_{12}O_6$

   C) $C_{60}H_{102}O_{51}$

   D) $C_{60}H_{100}O_{50}$

   E) $C_{60}H_{111}O_{51}$

   Answer: C

3) The two ring forms of glucose (α and β)

   A) are made from different structural isomers of glucose.

   B) arise from different linear (nonring) glucose molecules.

   C) arise when different carbons of the linear structure join to form the rings.

   D) arise because the hydroxyl group at the point of ring closure can be trapped in either one of two possible positions.

   E) include an aldose and a ketose.

   Answer: D

4) Choose the pair of terms that correctly completes this sentence:
   Nucleotides are to _____ as _____ are to proteins.

   A) nucleic acids; amino acids

   B) amino acids; polypeptides

   C) glycosidic linkages; polypeptide linkages

   D) genes; enzymes

   E) polymers; polypeptides

   Answer: A

5) Which of the following statements concerning *unsaturated* fats is correct?

   A) They are more common in animals than in plants.

   B) They have double bonds in the carbon chains of their fatty acids.

   C) They generally solidify at room temperature.

   D) They contain more hydrogen than saturated fats having the same number of carbon atoms.

   E) They have fewer fatty acid molecules per fat molecule.

   Answer: B

6) The structural level of a protein least affected by a disruption in hydrogen bonding is the

   A) primary level.

   B) secondary level.

   C) tertiary level.

   D) quaternary level.

   E) All structural levels are equally affected.

   Answer: A

7) To convert a nucleoside to a nucleotide, it would be necessary to

   A) combine two nucleosides using dehydration synthesis.
   B) remove the pentose from the nucleoside.
   C) replace the purine with a pyrimidine.
   D) add phosphate to the nucleoside.
   E) replace ribose with deoxyribose.

   Answer: D

8) Which of the following is *not* a protein?

   A) hemoglobin
   B) cholesterol
   C) an antibody
   D) an enzyme
   E) insulin

   Answer: B

Chapter 6   An Introduction to Metabolism

1) Metabolism is best described as

   A) synthesis of macromolecules.

   B) breakdown of macromolecules.

   C) control of enzyme activity.

   D) A and B.

   E) A, B, and C.

   Answer: E
   Skill: Knowledge

2) Which term most precisely describes the general process of breaking down large molecules into smaller ones?

   A) catalysis

   B) metabolism

   C) anabolism

   D) dehydration

   E) catabolism

   Answer: E
   Skill: Knowledge

3) Which of the following is true regarding catabolic pathways?

   A) They do not depend on enzymes.

   B) They consume energy to build up polymers from monomers.

   C) They release energy as they degrade polymers to monomers.

   D) They lead to the synthesis of catabolic compounds.

   E) Both A and B are correct.

   Answer: C
   Skill: Knowledge

4) Anabolic pathways

   A) do not depend on enzymes.

   B) depend on enzymes.

   C) consume energy to build up polymers from monomers.

   D) release energy as they degrade polymers to monomers.

   E) Both B and C are correct.

   Answer: E
   Skill: Knowledge

5) The transfer of free energy from catabolic pathways to anabolic pathways is best called

   A) feedback regulation.

   B) bioenergetics.

   C) energy coupling.

   D) entropy.

   E) cooperativity.

   Answer: C
   Skill: Knowledge

6) Which of the following is part of the first law of thermodynamics?

   A) Energy cannot be created or destroyed.

   B) The entropy of the universe is decreasing.

   C) The entropy of the universe is constant.

   D) Kinetic energy is stored energy that results from the specific arrangement of matter.

   E) Energy cannot be transferred or transformed.

   Answer: A
   Skill: Knowledge

7) Of the following, the structure of ATP is most closely related to

 A) an anabolic steroid.

 B) a double helix.

 C) RNA nucleotides.

 D) an amino acid with three phosphate groups attached.

 E) a phospholipid.

Answer: C
Skill: Application

8) According to the first law of thermodynamics,

 A) matter can be neither created nor destroyed.

 B) energy is neither created nor destroyed.

 C) all processes increase the entropy of the universe.

 D) systems rich in energy are intrinsically unstable.

 E) the universe loses energy because of friction.

Answer: B
Skill: Knowledge

9) Whenever energy is transformed, there is always an increase in the

 A) free energy of the system.

 B) free energy of the universe.

 C) entropy of the system.

 D) entropy of the universe.

 E) enthalpy of the universe.

Answer: D
Skill: Comprehension

10) According to the second law of thermodynamics,

 A) the entropy of the universe is constantly increasing.

 B) for every action there is an equal and opposite reaction.

 C) every energy transfer requires activation energy from the environment.

 D) the total amount of energy in the universe is conserved or constant.

 E) energy can be transferred or transformed, but it can be neither created nor destroyed.

Answer: A
Skill: Application

11) All of the following statements are representative of the second law of thermodynamics *except*

 A) energy transfers are always accompanied by some loss.

 B) heat energy represents lost energy to most systems.

 C) systems tend to rearrange themselves toward greater entropy.

 D) highly organized systems require energy for their maintenance.

 E) every time energy changes form, there is a decrease in entropy.

Answer: E
Skill: Comprehension

12) Which of the following is the most randomized form of energy?

 A) light energy

 B) electrical energy

 C) thermal (heat) energy

 D) mechanical energy

 E) chemical potential energy

Answer: C
Skill: Knowledge

13) Which of the following would decrease the entropy within a system?

   A) dehydration reactions

   B) hydrolysis

   C) respiration

   D) digestion

   E) catabolism

Answer: A
Skill: Comprehension

14) According to the second law of thermodynamics, all of the following statements are true *except* that

   A) the synthesis of large molecules from small molecules is exergonic.

   B) the Earth is an open system.

   C) life exists at the expense of greater energy than it contains.

   D) entropy increases in a closed system.

   E) every chemical transformed represents a loss of free energy.

Answer: A
Skill: Comprehension

15) Evolution of biological order

   A) is consistent with the second law of thermodynamics.

   B) was based on organisms as closed systems.

   C) violates both the first and second law of thermodynamics.

   D) can be seen in individual organisms but not in the ancestry of plant and animal kingdoms.

   E) Both C and D are correct.

Answer: A
Skill: Comprehension

16) In an organism, the energy available to do work is called free energy because

   A) it can be obtained with no cost to the system.

   B) it can be spent with no cost to the universe.

   C) the organism can live free of it if necessary.

   D) it is available to do work.

   E) it is equivalent to the system's total energy.

Answer: D
Skill: Knowledge

17) The mathematical expression for the change in free energy of a system is: $\Delta G = \Delta H - T\Delta S$. Which of the following is incorrect?

   A) ΔS is the change in entropy.

   B) ΔH is the change in heat.

   C) ΔG is the change in free energy.

   D) T is the absolute temperature.

   E) Both A and B are incorrect.

Answer: B
Skill: Knowledge

18) What is the change in free energy at chemical equilibrium?

   A) slightly increasing

   B) greatly increasing

   C) slightly decreasing

   D) greatly decreasing

   E) There is no net change.

Answer: E
Skill: Comprehension

19) Which of the following is *true* for exergonic reactions?

A) The products have more free energy than the reactants.

B) The products have less free energy than the reactants.

C) Reactants will always be completely converted to products.

D) A net input of energy from the surroundings is required for the reactions to proceed.

E) The reactions upgrade the free energy in the products at the expense of energy from the surroundings.

Answer: B
Skill: Knowledge

20) When a protein forms from amino acids, the following changes apply:

A) $+\Delta H, -\Delta S, +\Delta G$

B) $+\Delta H, -\Delta S, -\Delta G$

C) $+\Delta H, +\Delta S, +\Delta G$

D) $-\Delta H, -\Delta S, +\Delta G$

E) $-\Delta H, +\Delta S, +\Delta G$

Answer: A
Skill: Comprehension

21) When glucose monomers are joined together by glycosidic linkages to form a cellulose polymer, the changes in free energy, total energy, and entrophy are as follows:

A) $+\Delta G, +\Delta H, +\Delta S$

B) $+\Delta G, +\Delta H, -\Delta S$

C) $+\Delta G, -\Delta H, -\Delta S$

D) $-\Delta G, +\Delta H, +\Delta S$

E) $-\Delta G, -\Delta H, -\Delta S$

Answer: B
Skill: Comprehension

22) A chemical reaction that has a positive ΔG is correctly described as

A) endergonic.

B) exergonic.

C) enthalpic.

D) spontaneous.

E) exothermic.

Answer: A
Skill: Knowledge

23) Why is ATP an important molecule in metabolism?

A) It energizes other molecules by transferring phosphate groups.

B) Its phosphate bonds are easily formed and broken.

C) Hydrolysis of its phosphate groups is endergonic.

D) Two of the above.

E) All of the above.

Answer: D
Skill: Comprehension

24) The hydrolysis of ATP into ADP and inorganic phosphate
$(ATP + H_2O \rightarrow ADP + P_i)$

A) has a ΔG of –7.3 kcal/mol under standard conditions.

B) involves hydrolysis of a terminal phosphate bond of ATP.

C) is a nonspontaneous reaction.

D) two of the above.

E) all of the above.

Answer: D
Skill: Knowledge

25) ATP generally energizes a cellular process by

A) releasing heat upon hydrolysis.

B) acting as a catalyst.

C) direct chemical transfer of a phosphate group.

D) releasing ribose electrons to drive reactions.

E) emitting light flashes.

Answer: C
Skill: Comprehension

26) Which of the following reactions could be coupled to the reaction ATP + $H_2O \rightarrow$ ADP + P_i(–7.3 kcal/mol)?

A) A + P_i → AP (+10 kcal/mol)

B) B + P_i → BP (+8 kcal/mol)

C) CP → C + P_i (–4 kcal/mol)

D) DP → D + P_i (–10 kcal/mol)

E) E + P_i → EP (+5 kcal/mol)

Answer: E
Skill: Application

27) Which of the following statements is *true* concerning catabolic pathways?

A) They combine molecules into more complex and energy–rich molecules.

B) They are usually coupled with anabolic pathways to which they supply energy in the form of ATP.

C) They involve endergonic reactions that break complex molecules into simpler ones.

D) They are spontaneous and do not need enzyme catalysis.

E) They build up complex molecules such as protein from simpler compounds.

Answer: B
Skill: Comprehension

28) Correct statements regarding ATP include:
   I. ATP serves as a main energy shuttle inside cells.
   II. ATP drives endergonic reaction in the cell by the enzymatic transfer of the phosphate group to specific reactants.
   III. The regeneration of ATP from ADP and phosphate is an endergonic reaction.

A) I only

B) II only

C) III only

D) I and III only

E) I, II, and III

Answer: E
Skill: Comprehension

29) How can one increase the rate of a chemical reaction?

A) Increase the activation energy needed.

B) Cool the reactants.

C) Decrease the concentration of reactants.

D) Add a catalyst.

E) Increase the entropy of reactants.

Answer: D
Skill: Comprehension

30) The hydrolysis of sucrose by the enzyme sucrase results in

A) bringing glucose and fructose together to form sucrose.

B) the release of free water from sucrose as the glycosidic linkage between glucose and fructose is broken.

C) breaking the glycosidic bond between glucose and fructose and forming new bonds from water.

D) production of water from the sugar as bonds are broken between the glucose monomers.

E) utilization of water as a glycosidic linkage is formed between glucose and fructose to form sucrase.

Answer: C
Skill: Comprehension

31) Molecules capable of interacting must first overcome a thermodynamic barrier known as the reaction's

A) entropy.

B) activation energy.

C) endothermic level.

D) heat content.

E) free-energy content.

Answer: B
Skill: Knowledge

32) A solution of starch at room temperature does not decompose rapidly to a sugar solution because

A) the starch solution has less free energy than the sugar solution.

B) the hydrolysis of starch to sugar is endergonic.

C) the activation energy barrier cannot be surmounted in most of the starch molecules.

D) starch cannot be hydrolyzed in the presence of so much water.

E) starch hydrolysis is nonspontaneous.

Answer: C
Skill: Comprehension

33) Which of the following statements regarding enzymes is *true*?

A) Enzymes decrease the rate of a reaction.

B) Enzymes increase the rate of reaction.

C) Enzymes change the direction of chemical reactions.

D) Enzymes are permanently altered by the reactions they catalyze.

E) Enzymes prevent changes in substrate concentrations.

Answer: B
Skill: Knowledge

34) How does an enzyme catalyze a reaction?

A) by supplying the energy to speed up a reaction

B) by lowering the energy of activation of a reaction

C) by lowering the ΔG of a reaction

D) by changing the equilibrium of a spontaneous reaction

E) by increasing the amount of free energy of a reaction

Answer: B
Skill: Knowledge

35) Which of these statements regarding enzymes is *false*?

A) Enzymes are proteins that function as catalysts.

B) Enzymes display specificity for certain molecules to which they attach.

C) Enzymes provide activation energy for the reactions they catalyze.

D) The activity of enzymes can be regulated by factors in their immediate environment.

E) An enzyme may be used many times over for a specific reaction.

Answer: C
Skill: Knowledge

36) All of the following are true of enzymes *except*

A) Enzyme function is dependent on the pH and temperature of the reaction environment.

B) Enzyme function is dependent on the three-dimensional structure or conformation of the enzyme.

C) Enzymes provide activation energy for the reaction they catalyze.

D) Enzymes are essentially protein in their chemical compound.

E) Enzyme activity can be inhibited if their allosteric site is bound with a noncompetitive inhibitor.

Answer: C
Skill: Knowledge

37) During a laboratory experiment, you discover that an enzyme–catalyzed reaction has a ΔG of –20 kcal/mol. You double the amount of enzyme in the reaction, and the ΔG now equals

A) –40 kcal/mol.

B) –20 kcal/mol.

C) 0 kcal/mol.

D) +20 kcal/mol.

E) +40 kcal/mol.

Answer: B
Skill: Comprehension

38) The active site of an enzyme is the region that

A) binds with the allosteric site.

B) binds with the substrate.

C) binds with allosteric inhibitors.

D) is inhibited by a coenzyme or a cofactor.

E) none of the above

Answer: B
Skill: Knowledge

39) According to the induced fit hypothesis of enzyme function, which of the following is *correct*?

A) The binding of the substrate depends on the shape of the active site.

B) Some enzymes become denatured when activators bind to the substrate.

C) A competitive inhibitor can outcompete the substrate for the active site.

D) The binding of the substrate changes the shape of the enzyme slightly.

E) The active site creates a microenvironment ideal for the reaction.

Answer: D
Skill: Knowledge

Refer to Figure 6.1 to answer the following questions.

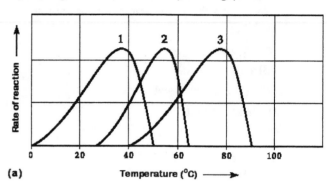

(a)

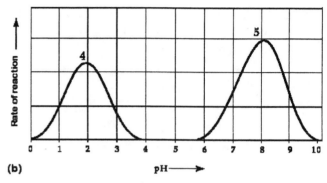

(b)

Figure 6.1

40) Which curve was generated using an enzyme taken from a bacterium that lives in hot springs at temperatures of 70°C or higher?

A) curve 1

B) curve 2

C) curve 3

D) curve 4

E) curve 5

Answer: C
Skill: Comprehension

41) The optimum temperature for enzyme 1 (curve 1) is approximately

A) 0°C.

B) 35°C.

C) 45°C.

D) 75°C.

E) The temperature optimum cannot be determined from these data.

Answer: B
Skill: Comprehension

42) Which curve was most likely generated from analysis of an enzyme from a human stomach where conditions are strongly acid?

A) curve 1

B) curve 2

C) curve 3

D) curve 4

E) curve 5

Answer: D
Skill: Comprehension

43) Which curve was most likely generated from an enzyme that requires a cofactor?

A) curve 1

B) curve 2

C) curve 4

D) curve 5

E) It is not possible to determine if an enzyme requires a cofactor from these data.

Answer: E
Skill: Comprehension

44) Increasing the substrate concentration in an enzymatic reaction could overcome which of the following?

A) denaturization of the enzyme

B) allosteric inhibition

C) competitive inhibition

D) noncompetitive inhibition

E) insufficient cofactors

Answer: C
Skill: Comprehension

45) What is an organic, nonprotein component of an enzyme molecule called?

A) accessory enzyme

B) allosteric group

C) coenzyme

D) functional group

E) active cofactor

Answer: C
Skill: Knowledge

46) Which of the following is true of enzymes?

A) Enzymes may require a nonprotein cofactor or ion for catalysis to take place.

B) Enzyme function is reduced if the three-dimensional structure or conformation of an enzyme is altered.

C) Enzyme function is influenced by physical and chemical environment factors such as pH and temperature.

D) Enzymes increase the rate of chemical reaction by lowering activation energy barriers.

E) All of the above are true of enzymes.

Answer: E
Skill: Knowledge

47) Zinc, an essential trace element, is presented in the active site of the enzyme carboxypeptidase. The zinc most likely functions as a(n)

A) competitive inhibitor of the enzyme.

B) noncompetitive inhibitor of the enzyme.

C) allosteric activator of the enzyme.

D) cofactor necessary for enzyme activity.

E) coenzyme derived from a vitamin.

Answer: D
Skill: Knowledge

48) Consider the following: Succinic acid dehydrogenase catalyzes the reaction of succinic acid to fumaric acid. The reaction is inhibited by malonic acid, which resembles succinic acid but cannot be catalyzed by succinic dehydrogenase. Increasing the ratio of succinic acid to malonic acid reduces the inhibitory effect of malonic acid. Which of the following is correct?

A) Succinic acid dehydrogenase is the enzyme, and fumaric acid is the substrate.

B) Succinic acid dehydrogenase is the enzyme, and malonic acid is the substrate.

C) Succinic acid is the substrate, and fumaric acid is the product.

D) Fumaric acid is the product, and malonic acid is a noncompetitive inhibitor.

E) Malonic acid is the product, and fumaric acid is a competitive inhibitor.

Answer: E
Skill: Comprehension

The next questions are based on the following information. A series of enzymes catalyze the reaction X→Y→Z→A. Product A binds to the enzyme that converts X to Y at a position remote from its active site. This binding decreases the activity of the enzyme.

49) Substance X is

A) a coenzyme.

B) an allosteric inhibitor.

C) a substrate.

D) an intermediate.

E) the product.

Answer: C
Skill: Comprehension

50) Substance A functions as

A) a coenzyme.

B) an allosteric inhibitor.

C) the substrate.

D) an intermediate.

E) a competitive inhibitor.

Answer: B
Skill: Comprehension

51) The mechanism in which the end product of a metabolic pathway inhibits an earlier step in the pathway is known as

A) metabolic inhibition.

B) feedback inhibition.

C) allosteric inhibition.

D) noncooperative inhibition.

E) reversible inhibition.

Answer: B
Skill: Knowledge

52) The regulation of enzyme function is an important aspect of cell metabolism. Which of the following is *least* likely to be a mechanism for enzyme regulation?

A) allosteric regulation

B) cooperativity

C) feedback inhibition

D) removing cofactors

E) reversible inhibition

Answer: D
Skill: Comprehension

53) Which of the following statements is *true* regarding enzyme cooperativity?

A) A multi–enzyme complex contains all the enzymes of a metabolic pathway.

B) A product of a pathway serves as a competitive inhibitor of an early enzyme in the pathway.

C) A substrate molecule bound to an active site affects the active site of several subunits.

D) Several substrate molecules can be catalyzed by the same enzyme.

E) A substrate binds to an active site and inhibits cooperation between enzymes in a pathway.

Answer: C
Skill: Knowledge

54) Location of an enzyme within a specific membrane–enclosed organelle

A) allows the use of ATP and cofactors by the enzyme.

B) brings order and promotes efficiency within eukaryotic cells.

C) allows cells to evolve by violating the second law of thermodynamics.

D) protects the enzyme from feedback inhibition.

E) is restricted to allosteric enzymes because it allows two polypeptide subunits to join efficiently.

Answer: B
Skill: Comprehension

The following questions are based on the reaction A + B → C + D shown in Figure 6.2

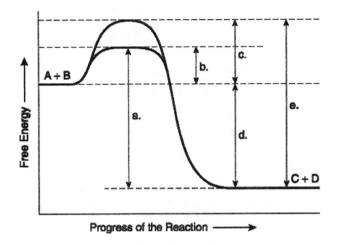

Figure 6.2

55) Which of the following terms best describes the reaction?

A) endergonic

B) exergonic

C) anabolic

D) allosteric

E) nonspontaneous

Answer: B
Skill: Knowledge

56) Which of the following represents the ΔG of the reaction?

A) a   B) b   C) c   D) d   E) e

Answer: D
Skill: Knowledge

57) Which of the following would be the same in an enzyme–catalyzed or –uncatalyzed reaction?

A) a   B) b   C) c   D) d   E) e

Answer: D
Skill: Comprehension

58) Which of the following bests describes the reaction?

    A) negative ΔG, spontaneous

    B) positive ΔG, nonspontaneous

    C) positive ΔG, exergonic

    D) negative ΔG, endergonic

    E) ΔG of zero, chemical equilibrium

Answer: A
Skill: Comprehension

59) Which of the following represents the difference between the free-energy content of the reaction and the free-energy content of the products?

    A) a   B) b   C) c   D) d   E) e

Answer: D
Skill: Knowledge

60) Which of the following represents the activation energy required for the enzyme-catalyzed reaction?

    A) a   B) b   C) c   D) d   E) e

Answer: B
Skill: Comprehension

61) Which of the following represents the activation energy required for a noncatalyzed reaction?

    A) a   B) b   C) c   D) d   E) e

Answer: C
Skill: Knowledge

62) Which *best* describes the reaction?

    A) The amount of free energy initially presented in the reactants is indicated by "a."

    B) The amount of free energy present in the products is indicated by "e."

    C) The amount of free energy released as a result of the noncatalyzed reaction is indicated by "c."

    D) The amount of free energy released as a result of the catalyzed reaction is indicated by "d."

    E) Both C and D are correct.

Answer: D
Skill: Comprehension

63) Assume that the reaction has a ΔG of -5.6 kcal/mol. Which of the following would be true?

    A) The reaction could be coupled to power an endergonic reaction with a ΔG of $+6.2$ kcal/mol.

    B) The reaction could be coupled to power an exergonic reaction with a ΔG of $+8.8$ kcal/mol.

    C) The reaction would result in a decrease in entropy (S) and an increase in the total energy content (H) of the system.

    D) The reaction would result in an increase in entropy (S) and a decrease in the total energy content (H) of the system.

    E) The reaction would result in products (C + D) with a greater free-energy content than in the initial reactants (A + B).

Answer: D
Skill: Comprehension

Media Activity Questions

1) The more heat released by a reaction, the

A) greater the increase in entropy.

B) less the conservation of energy.

C) greater the amount of potential energy in the products of the reaction.

D) greater the conservation of energy.

E) less the increase in entropy.

Answer: A
Topic: Web/CD Activity 6A

2) What type of bond joins the phosphates of the ATP?

A) hydrophobic

B) hydrogen

C) covalent

D) hydrophilic

E) ionic

Answer: C
Topic: Web/CD Activity 6B

3) In the reaction A → B + C + heat,

A) there is a net input of energy.

B) the potential energy of the products is greater than that of the reactant.

C) the potential energy of the products is the same as that of the reactant.

D) the potential energy of the products is less than that of the reactant.

E) entropy has decreased.

Answer: D
Topic: Web/CD Activity 6C

4) The energy required to initiate an exergonic reaction is called the

A) exergonic energy.

B) endergonic energy.

C) nothing: spontaneous reactions do not require an input of energy.

D) hydrolytic energy.

E) energy of activation.

Answer: E
Topic: Web/CD Activity 6D

5) Substrates bind to an enzyme's _____ site.

A) reactant

B) allosteric

C) regulatory

D) phosphate

E) active

Answer: E
Topic: Web/CD Activity 6D

Self–Quiz Questions

Answers to these questions also appear in the textbook.

1) Choose the pair of terms that correctly completes this sentence: Catabolism is to anabolism as _____ is to _____.

   A) exergonic; spontaneous

   B) exergonic; endergonic

   C) free energy; entropy

   D) work; energy

   E) entropy; order

   Answer: B

2) Most cells cannot harness heat to perform work because

   A) heat is not a form of energy.

   B) cells do not have much heat; they are relatively cool.

   C) temperature is usually uniform throughout a cell.

   D) heat cannot be used to do work.

   E) heat denatures enzymes.

   Answer: C

3) According to the first law of thermodynamics,

   A) matter can be neither created nor destroyed.

   B) energy is conserved in all processes.

   C) all processes increase the order of the universe.

   D) systems rich in energy are intrinsically stable.

   E) the universe constantly loses energy because of friction.

   Answer: B

4) Which of the following metabolic processes can occur without a net influx of energy from some other process?

   A) $ADP + P_i \rightarrow ATP + H_2O$

   B) $C_6H_{12}O_6 + 6\ O_2 \rightarrow 6\ CO_2 + 6\ H_2O$

   C) $6\ CO_2 + 6\ H_2O \rightarrow C_6H_{12}O_6 + 6\ O_2$

   D) amino acids $\rightarrow$ protein

   E) glucose + fructose $\rightarrow$ sucrose

   Answer: B

5) If an enzyme has been noncompetitively inhibited,

   A) the DG for the reaction it catalyzes will always be negative.

   B) the active site will be occupied by the inhibitor molecule.

   C) increasing the substrate concentration will increase the inhibition.

   D) a higher activation energy will be necessary to initiate the reaction.

   E) the inhibitor molecule may be chemically unrelated to the substrate.

   Answer: E

6) If an enzyme solution is saturated with substrate, the most effective way to obtain an even faster yield of products is to

   A) add more of the enzyme.

   B) heat the solution to 90°C.

   C) add more substrate.

   D) add an allosteric inhibitor.

   E) add a noncompetitive inhibitor.

   Answer: A

7) An enzyme accelerates a metabolic reaction by

   A) altering the overall free–energy change for the reaction.

   B) making an endergonic reaction occur spontaneously.

   C) lowering the activation energy.

   D) pushing the reaction away from equilibrium.

   E) making the substrate molecule more stable.

   Answer: C

8) Some bacteria are metabolically active in hot springs because

   A) they are able to maintain an internal temperature much cooler than that of the surrounding water.

   B) the high temperatures facilitate active metabolism without the need of catalysis.

   C) their enzymes have high optimal temperatures.

   D) their enzymes are insensitive to temperature.

   E) they use molecules other than proteins as their main catalysts.

   Answer: C

9) Which of the following characteristics is not associated with allosteric regulation of an enzyme's activity?

   A) A molecule mimics the substrate and competes for the active site.

   B) A naturally occurring molecule stabilizes a catalytically active conformation.

   C) Regulatory molecules bind to a site remote from the active site.

   D) Inhibitor and activator molecules may compete with one another.

   E) The enzyme usually has a quaternary structure.

   Answer: A

10) In the following branched metabolic pathway, a dotted arrow with a minus sign symbolizes inhibition of a metabolic step by an end product:

Which reaction would prevail if both Q and S were present in the cell in high concentrations?

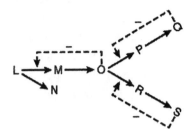

   A) L → M

   B) M → O

   C) L → N

   D) O → P

   E) R → S

   Answer: C

Chapter 7   A Tour of the Cell

1) What limits the resolving power of a light microscope?

   A) the type of lens used to magnify the object under study

   B) the shortest wavelength of light used to illuminate the specimen

   C) the type of lens that focuses a beam of electrons through the specimen

   D) the type of heavy metal or dye that is used to stain the specimen

   E) the ratio of an object's image to its real size

   Answer: B
   Skill: Knowledge

2) When biologists wish to study the internal ultrastructure of cells, they most likely would use

   A) a light microscope.

   B) a scanning electron microscope.

   C) a transmission electronic microscope.

   D) both A and C.

   E) A, B, and C.

   Answer: C
   Skill: Comprehension

3) A primary objective of cell fractionation is

   A) to view the structure of cell membranes.

   B) to identify the enzymes outside the organelles.

   C) to determine the size of various organelles.

   D) to separate the major organelles so their particular functions can be determined.

   E) to crack the cell wall so the cytoplasmic contents can be released.

   Answer: D
   Skill: Knowledge

(Figure 7.1 appears on page 81.)

Cell fractionation can be accomplished by a series of increasingly rapid spins in a centrifuge. The figure above shows the results of such a series of spins. Match the letter of the cell fractions that would be obtained by the numbered steps.

   A. ribosomes
   B. microsomes
   C. supernatant
   D. nuclei
   E. mitochondria

4) fraction number 1

   Answer: D
   Skill: Comprehension

5) fraction number 2

   Answer: E
   Skill: Comprehension

6) fraction number 3

   Answer: B
   Skill: Comprehension

7) fraction number 4

   Answer: A
   Skill: Comprehension

8) fraction number 5

   Answer: C
   Skill: Comprehension

9) Which of the following are prokaryotic cells?

   A) plants

   B) fungi

   C) bacteria

   D) animals

   E) both B and C

   Answer: C
   Skill: Knowledge

10) Which of the following is *not* found in a prokaryotic cell?

A) DNA

B) cell wall

C) plasma membrane

D) ribosomes

E) endoplasmic reticulum

Answer: E
Skill: Knowledge

For the following questions, use the lettered answers to match the structure to its proper cell type. Choose the most inclusive category. Each answer may be used once, more than once, or not at all.

A. *a feature of all cells*
B. *found in prokaryotic cells only*
C. *found in eukaryotic cells only*
D. *found in plant cells only*
E. *found in animal cells only*

11) plasma membrane

Answer: A
Skill: Knowledge

12) tonoplast

Answer: D
Skill: Knowledge

13) nucleoid

Answer: B
Skill: Knowledge

14) Large numbers of ribosomes are present in cells that specialize in producing which of the following molecules?

A) lipids

B) starches

C) proteins

D) steroids

E) glucose

Answer: C
Skill: Knowledge

15) Which of the following does *not* contain functional ribosomes?

A) a prokaryotic cell

B) a plant mitochondrion

C) a chloroplast

D) an animal mitochondrion

E) a nucleolus

Answer: E
Skill: Knowledge

16) Which of the following is *not* a part of the endomembrane system?

A) mitochondria

B) Golgi apparatus

C) rough endoplasmic reticulum

D) lysosomes

E) smooth endoplasmic reticulum

Answer: A
Skill: Comprehension

17) Which type of organelle is primarily involved in the synthesis of oils, phospholipids, and steroids?

A) ribosomes

B) lysosomes

C) smooth endoplasmic reticulum

D) mitochondria

E) contractile vacuoles

Answer: C
Skill: Knowledge

18) Which structure is the site of the synthesis of proteins that may be exported from the cell?

A) rough ER

B) lysosomes

C) plasmodesmata

D) Golgi vesicles

E) tight junctions

Answer: A
Skill: Knowledge

19) To which structure would you assign the function of secretion activities leading, for example, to the formation of a new cell wall in plants?

A) smooth ER

B) lysosomes

C) plasmodesmata

D) Golgi vesicles

E) tight junctions

Answer: D
Skill: Knowledge

20) Of the following, which is probably the most common route for membrane flow in the endomembrane system?

A) Golgi → lysosome → ER → plasma membrane

B) tonoplast → plasma membrane → nuclear envelope → smooth ER

C) nuclear envelope → lysosome → Golgi → plasma membrane

D) rough ER → vesicles → Golgi → plasma membrane

E) ER → chloroplasts → mitochondrion → cell membrane

Answer: D
Skill: Knowledge

21) Which of the following pairs is mismatched?

A) nucleolus–ribosomal RNA

B) nucleus–DNA replication

C) lysosome–protein synthesis

D) cell membrane–lipid bilayer

E) cytoskeleton–microtubules

Answer: C
Skill: Comprehension

22) Which of the following cell components is *not* directly involved in synthesis or secretion?

A) ribosomes

B) rough endoplasmic reticulum

C) Golgi bodies

D) smooth endoplasmic reticulum

E) lysosome

Answer: E
Skill: Comprehension

Refer to the following five terms to answer the following questions. Choose the most appropriate term for each phrase. Each term may be used once, more than once, or not at all.

A. *lysosome*

B. *tonoplast*

C. *mitochondrion*

D. *Golgi apparatus*

E. *peroxisome*

23) secretes many polysaccharides

Answer: D
Skill: Knowledge

24) contains hydrolytic enzymes

Answer: A
Skill: Knowledge

25) helps to recycle the cell's organic material

Answer: A
Skill: Knowledge

26) one of the main energy transformers of cells

Answer: C
Skill: Knowledge

27) involved in Pompe's disease, in which the liver is damaged by an accumulation of glycogen due to the absence of an enzyme needed to break down glycogen

Answer: A
Skill: Knowledge

28) contains its own DNA and ribosomes

Answer: C
Skill: Knowledge

29) detoxifies alcohol in the liver

Answer: E
Skill: Knowledge

30) contains enzymes that transfer hydrogen from various substrates to oxygen, producing H_2O_2

Answer: E
Skill: Knowledge

31) a membrane that encloses a versatile plant compartment that may hold reserves of organic compounds or inorganic ions

Answer: B
Skill: Knowledge

32) Of the following, what do both mitochondria and chloroplasts have in common?
   A) ATP is produced.
   B) DNA is present.
   C) Ribosomes are present.
   D) Only B and C are correct.
   E) A, B, and C are correct.

Answer: E
Skill: Knowledge

33) Grana, thylakoids, and stroma are all components found in
   A) cilia and flagella.
   B) chloroplasts.
   C) mitochondria.
   D) lysosomes.
   E) nuclei.

Answer: B
Skill: Knowledge

34) Organelles that contain DNA include
   A) ribosomes.
   B) mitochondria.
   C) chloroplasts.
   D) Only B and C are correct.
   E) A, B, and C are correct.

Answer: D
Skill: Knowledge

35) An animal secretory cell and a photosynthetic leaf cell are similar in all of the following ways *except:*
   A) They both have a Golgi apparatus.
   B) They both have mitochondria.
   C) They both have transport proteins for active transport of ions.
   D) They both have chloroplasts.
   E) They both have a cell membrane.

Answer: D
Skill: Knowledge

36) Which of the following is capable of converting light energy to chemical energy?
   A) chloroplasts
   B) mitochondria
   C) leucoplasts
   D) peroxisomes
   E) Golgi bodies

Answer: A
Skill: Knowledge

37) A biologist ground up some plant cells and then centrifuged the mixture. She obtained some organelles from the sediment in the test tube. The organelles took up CO_2 and gave off O_2. The organelles are most likely

A) chloroplasts.

B) ribosomes.

C) nuclei.

D) mitochondria.

E) Golgi apparatuses.

Answer: A
Skill: Knowledge

38) Which of the following relationships between cell structures and their respective functions is *not* correct?

A) cell wall: support, protection

B) chloroplasts: chief site of cellular respiration

C) chromosomes: genetic control information

D) ribosomes: site of protein synthesis

E) mitochondria: formation of ATP

Answer: B
Skill: Comprehension

39) Of the following, which cell structure would most likely be visible with a light microscope that had been manufactured to the maximum resolving power possible?

A) mitochondrion

B) microtubule

C) ribosome

D) largest microfilament

E) nuclear pore

Answer: A
Skill: Comprehension

40) In animal cells, hydrolytic enzymes are packaged to prevent general destruction of cellular components. Which of the following organelles functions in this compartmentalization?

A) chloroplast

B) lysosome

C) central vacuole

D) peroxisome

E) glyoxysome

Answer: B
Skill: Knowledge

41) Cells can be described as having a cytoskeleton of internal structures that contribute to the shape, organization, and movement of the cell. All of the following are part of the cytoskeleton *except*

A) the cell wall.

B) microtubules.

C) microfilaments.

D) intermediate filaments.

E) actin.

Answer: A
Skill: Knowledge

42) Which of the following is *not* a known function of the cytoskeleton?

A) to maintain a critical limit on cell size

B) to provide mechanical support to the cell

C) to maintain characteristic shape of the cell

D) to hold mitochondria and other organelles in place within the cytosol

E) to assist in cell motility by interacting with specialized motor proteins

Answer: A
Skill: Knowledge

43) Which of the following possesses a microtubular structure similar in form to a basal body?

A) centriole

B) lysosome

C) nucleolus

D) peroxisome

E) ribosome

Answer: A
Skill: Knowledge

44) What structure is often deposited in several laminated layers and has a strong and durable matrix that affords the cells protection and support?

A) primary cell wall

B) secondary cell wall

C) middle lamella

D) glycocalyx

E) tonoplast

Answer: B
Skill: Knowledge

45) Microfilaments are well known for their role in which of the following?

A) ameboid movement

B) formation of cleavage furrows

C) contracting of muscle cells

D) A and B only

E) A, B, and C

Answer: E
Skill: Comprehension

46) All of the structures listed below are associated with movement in cells or by cells *except*

A) cilia.

B) dynein.

C) myosin.

D) flagella.

E) peroxisomes.

Answer: E
Skill: Comprehension

47) When a potassium ion (K^+) passes from the soil into the vacuole of a root cell, it encounters some cellular barriers. Which of the following is the most direct path the K^+ would take through these barriers?

A) secondary cell wall → plasma membrane → thylakoid

B) primary cell wall → secondary cell wall → tonoplast

C) primary cell wall → plasma membrane → tonoplast

D) cell wall → plasma membrane → tonoplast → grana

E) cell wall → plasma membrane → grana

Answer: C
Skill: Comprehension

48) Plasmodesmata in plant cells are *most* similar in function to which of the following structures in animal cells?

A) peroxisomes

B) desmosomes

C) gap junctions

D) glycocalyx

E) tight junctions

Answer: C
Skill: Comprehension

49) A cell has the following molecules and structures: enzymes, DNA, ribosomes, plasma membrane, and mitochondria. It could be a cell from

A) a bacterium.

B) an animal, but not a plant.

C) a plant, but not an animal.

D) a plant or an animal.

E) any kind of organism.

Answer: D
Skill: Comprehension

50) Which of the following contain the 9 + 2 arrangement of microtubules?
   A) cilia
   B) centrioles
   C) flagella
   D) A and C only
   E) A, B, and C

   Answer: D
   Skill: Comprehension

51) A cell lacking the ability to make and secrete glycoproteins would most likely be deficient in its
   A) nuclear DNA.
   B) extracellular matrix.
   C) Golgi apparatus.
   D) B and C only.
   E) A, B, and C.

   Answer: D
   Skill: Comprehension

52) The extracellular matrix is thought to participate in regulation of animal cell behavior by communicating via
   A) lipoproteins in the membrane.
   B) the nucleus.
   C) DNA and RNA.
   D) integrins.
   E) plasmodesmata.

   Answer: D
   Skill: Knowledge

53) Ions can travel directly from the cytoplasm of one animal cell to the cytoplasm of an adjacent cell through
   A) plasmodesmata.
   B) intermediate filaments.
   C) tight junctions.
   D) desmosomes.
   E) gap junctions.

   Answer: E
   Skill: Knowledge

54) All of the following are associated with the extracellular matrix of animal cells *except*
   A) collagen.
   B) cellulose.
   C) fibronectins.
   D) integrins.
   E) proteoglucans.

   Answer: B
   Skill: Knowledge

55) Cells would be unable to form cilia or flagella if they do not have
   A) ribosomes.
   B) chloroplasts.
   C) centrioles.
   D) plastids.
   E) actin.

   Answer: C
   Skill: Comprehension

56) Which of the following intercellular junctions are common in epithelial tissue?
   A) tight junctions
   B) desmosomes
   C) gap junctions
   D) both A and B
   E) A, B, and C

   Answer: E
   Skill: Knowledge

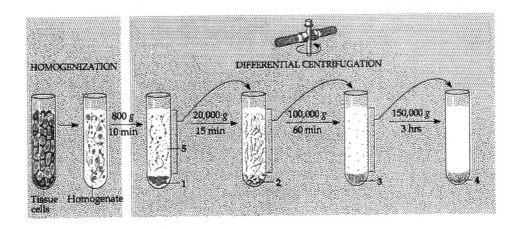

Figure 7.1

Media Activity Questions

1) A bacterial cell's DNA is found in its
   - A) ribosomes.
   - B) nucleus.
   - C) peroxisome.
   - D) nucleoid region.
   - E) capsule.

   Answer: D
   Topic: Web/CD Activity 7B

2) Which of these is *not* a component of the endomembrane system?
   - A) endoplasmic reticulum
   - B) transport vesicles
   - C) mitochondria
   - D) nuclear envelope
   - E) Golgi apparatus

   Answer: C
   Topic: Web/CD Activity 7H

3) The types of cell junctions found in plant cells are called
   - A) tight junctions.
   - B) plasmodesmata.
   - C) communicating junctions.
   - D) anchoring junctions.
   - E) desmosomes.

   Answer: B
   Topic: Web/CD Activity 7L

4) Most of a eukaryotic cell's genes are found in the
   - A) nucleus.
   - B) peroxisome.
   - C) mitochondrion.
   - D) flagellum.
   - E) lysosome.

   Answer: A
   Topic: Web/CD Activity 7M

5) Which of these structures is unique to plant cells?
   - A) mitochondrion
   - B) peroxisome
   - C) flagellum
   - D) central vacuole
   - E) nucleoid region

   Answer: D
   Topic: Web/CD Activity 7N

Self–Quiz Questions

Answers to these questions also appear in the textbook.

1) The symptoms of a certain inherited disorder in humans include respiratory problems and, in males, sterility. Which of the following is a reasonable hypothesis for the molecular basis of this disorder?

   A) a defective enzyme in the mitochondria

   B) defective actin molecules in cellular microfilaments

   C) defective dynein molecules in cilia and flagella

   D) abnormal hydrolytic enzymes in the lysosomes

   E) a defective secretory protein

   Answer: C

2) Choose the statement that correctly characterizes bound ribosomes.

   A) Bound ribosomes are enclosed in their own membrane.

   B) Bound ribosomes are structurally different from free ribosomes.

   C) Bound ribosomes generally synthesize membrane proteins and secretory proteins.

   D) The most common location for bound ribosomes is the cytoplasmic surface of the plasma membrane.

   E) Bound ribosomes are concentrated in the cisternal space of rough ER.

   Answer: C

3) Which of the following organelles is *least* closely associated with the endomembrane system?

   A) nuclear envelope

   B) chloroplast

   C) Golgi apparatus

   D) plasma membrane

   E) ER

   Answer: B

4) Cells of the pancreas will incorporate radioactively labeled amino acids into proteins. This "tagging" of newly synthesized proteins enables a researcher to track the location of these proteins in a cell. In this case, we are tracking an enzyme that is eventually secreted by pancreatic cells. Which of the following is the most likely pathway for movement of this protein in the cell?

   A) ER → Golgi → nucleus

   B) Golgi → ER → lysosome

   C) nucleus → ER → Golgi

   D) ER → Golgi → vesicles that fuse with plasma membrane

   E) ER → lysosomes → vesicles that fuse with plasma membrane

   Answer: D

5) Which of the following organelles is common to plant *and* animal cells?

   A) chloroplasts

   B) wall made of cellulose

   C) tonoplast

   D) mitochondria

   E) centrioles

   Answer: D

6) Which of the following components is present in a prokaryotic cell?

   A) mitochondria

   B) ribosomes

   C) nuclear envelope

   D) chloroplasts

   E) ER

   Answer: B

7) Which type of cell would probably provide the best opportunity to study lysosomes?

A) muscle cell

B) nerve cell

C) phagocytic white blood cell

D) leaf cell of a plant

E) bacterial cell

Answer: C

8) Which of the following statements is a correct distinction between prokaryotic and eukaryotic cells attributable to the absence of a prokaryotic cytoskeleton?

A) Compartmentalized organelles are found only in eukaryotic cells.

B) Cytoplasmic streaming is not observed in prokaryotes.

C) Only eukaryotic cells are capable of movement.

D) Prokaryotic cells are usually 10 mm or less in diameter.

E) Only the eukaryotic cell concentrates its genetic material in a region separate from the rest of the cell.

Answer: B

9) Which of the following structure–function pairs is *mismatched*?

A) nucleolus; ribosome production

B) lysosome; intracellular digestion

C) ribosome; protein synthesis

D) Golgi; secretion of cell products

E) microtubules; muscle contraction

Answer: E

10) Cyanide binds with at least one of the molecules involved in the production of ATP. Following exposure of a cell to cyanide, most of the cyanide could be expected to be found within the

A) mitochondria.

B) ribosomes.

C) peroxisomes.

D) lysosomes.

E) endoplasmic reticulum.

Answer: A

Chapter 8 Membrane Structure and Function

For the following questions, match the membrane model or description with the scientist(s) who proposed the model. Each choice may be used once, more than once, or not at all.

    A. H. Davson and J. Danielli
    B. I. Langmuir
    C. C. Overton
    D. S. Singer and G. Nicolson
    E. E. Gorter and F. Grendel

1) Membranes are made of lipids because substances that dissolve in lipids enter cells more rapidly than lipid–insoluble substances.

    Answer: C
    Skill: Knowledge

2) Made artificial membranes by adding phospholipids dissolved in benzene to water.

    Answer: B
    Skill: Knowledge

3) The first to propose that cell membranes are phospholipid bilayers.

    Answer: E
    Skill: Knowledge

4) Membranes are a phospholipid bilayer between two layers of globular protein.

    Answer: A
    Skill: Knowledge

5) The membrane is a mosaic of protein molecules bobbing in a fluid layer of phospholipids.

    Answer: D
    Skill: Knowledge

6) Which of the following types of molecules are the major structural components of the cell membrane?

    A) phospholipids and cellulose
    B) nucleic acids and proteins
    C) phospholipids and proteins
    D) proteins and cellulose
    E) glycoproteins and cholesterol

    Answer: C
    Skill: Knowledge

For the following questions, match the labeled component of the cell membrane (Figure 8.1) with its description.

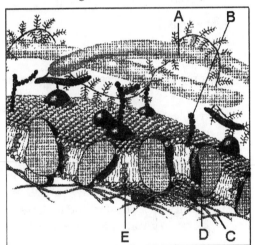

Figure 8.1

7) peripheral protein

    Answer: D
    Skill: Knowledge

8) cholesterol

    Answer: E
    Skill: Knowledge

9) fiber of the extracellular matrix

    Answer: A
    Skill: Knowledge

10) filament of the cytoskeleton

Answer: C
Skill: Knowledge

11) glycolipid

Answer: B
Skill: Knowledge

12) All of the following molecules are part of the cell membrane *except*

A) lipid.

B) nucleic acids.

C) protein.

D) phosphate group.

E) steroid.

Answer: B
Skill: Knowledge

13) The presence of cholesterol in the plasma membranes of some animals

A) enables the membrane to stay fluid more easily when cell temperature drops.

B) enables the animal to remove hydrogen atoms from saturated phospholipids.

C) enables the animal to add hydrogen atoms to unsaturated phospholipids.

D) makes the membrane less flexible, so it can sustain greater pressure from within the cell.

E) makes the animal more susceptible to circulatory disorders.

Answer: A
Skill: Comprehension

14) According to the fluid mosaic model of cell membranes, which of the following is a *true* statement about membrane phospholipids?

A) They can move laterally along the plane of the membrane.

B) They frequently flip-flop from one side of the membrane to the other.

C) They occur in an uninterrupted bilayer, with membrane proteins restricted to the surface of the membrane.

D) They are free to depart from the membrane and dissolve in the surrounding solution.

E) They have hydrophilic tails in the interior of the membrane.

Answer: A
Skill: Knowledge

15) What is one of the ways that the membranes of winter wheat are able to remain fluid when it is extremely cold?

A) by increasing the percentage of unsaturated phospholipids in the membrane

B) by increasing the percentage of cholesterol molecules in the membrane

C) by decreasing the number of hydrophobic proteins in the membrane

D) A and B

E) A, B, and C

Answer: A
Skill: Comprehension

16) What are the elevated regions (particles) seen in electron micrographs of split freeze-fractured membranes?

A) peripheral proteins

B) phospholipids

C) carbohydrates

D) integral proteins

E) cholesterol molecules

Answer: D
Skill: Knowledge

17) All of the following are functions of integral membrane proteins *except*

A) enzyme synthesis.

B) active transport.

C) hormone reception.

D) cell adhesion.

E) cytoskeleton attachment.

Answer: A
Skill: Knowledge

18) All of the following statements about membrane structure and function are true *except:*

A) Diffusion of gases is faster in air than across membranes.

B) Diffusion, osmosis, and facilitated diffusion do not require any energy input from the cell.

C) Both sides of a membrane are identical in structure and function.

D) Voltage across the membrane depends on an unequal distribution of ions across the plasma membrane.

E) Special membrane proteins can cotransport two solutes by coupling diffusion with active transport.

Answer: C
Skill: Comprehension

19) Integral proteins

A) lack tertiary structure.

B) are loosely bound to the bilayer.

C) are usually transmembrane proteins.

D) are not mobile within the bilayer.

E) have no known functions in membranes.

Answer: C
Skill: Application

20) All of the following are functions of membrane proteins *except*

A) cell–cell recognition.

B) protein synthesis.

C) signal transduction.

D) intercellular joining.

E) transport.

Answer: B
Skill: Knowledge

21) Of the following functions, the glycoproteins and glycolipids of animal cell membranes are most important for

A) facilitated diffusion of molecules down their concentration gradients.

B) active transport of molecules against their concentration gradients.

C) maintaining the integrity of a fluid mosaic membrane.

D) maintaining membrane fluidity at low temperatures.

E) the ability of cells to recognize like and different cells.

Answer: E
Skill: Comprehension

22) One of the functions of cholesterol in animal cell membranes is to

A) facilitate transport of ions.

B) store energy.

C) maintain membrane fluidity.

D) speed diffusion.

E) phosphorylate ADP.

Answer: C
Skill: Knowledge

23) What membrane-surface molecules are thought to be most important as cells recognize each other?

A) phospholipids

B) integral proteins

C) peripheral proteins

D) cholesterol

E) glycoproteins

Answer: E
Skill: Knowledge

24) A cell lacking oligosaccharides on the external surface of its plasma membrane would likely be inefficient in

A) transporting ions against an electrochemical gradient.

B) cell-cell recognition.

C) maintaining fluidity of the phospholipid bilayer.

D) attaching to the cytoskeleton.

E) establishing the diffusion barrier to charged molecules.

Answer: B
Skill: Application

25) Which of the following adheres to the extracellular surface of animal cell plasma membranes?

A) fibers of the extracellular matrix

B) fibers of the cytoskeleton

C) the phospholipid bilayer

D) cholesterol

E) carrier proteins

Answer: A
Skill: Knowledge

26) According to the endomembrane model for the formation of cell membranes, what components of the membrane of an animal cell will be at the extracellular surface exposed directly to the cytosol?

A) phospholipids

B) peripheral proteins

C) membrane carbohydrates

D) A and C

E) A, B, and C

Answer: D
Skill: Comprehension

27) The kinds of molecules that pass through a cell membrane most easily are

A) large and hydrophobic.

B) small and hydrophobic.

C) large polar molecules.

D) ionic.

E) monosaccharides such as glucose.

Answer: B
Skill: Comprehension

28) Which of the following is a characteristic feature of a carrier protein in a plasma membrane?

A) It is a peripheral membrane protein.

B) It exhibits a specificity for a particular type of molecule.

C) It requires energy to function.

D) It works against diffusion.

E) It has few, if any, hydrophobic amino acids.

Answer: B
Skill: Comprehension

29) All of the following cellular activities require ATP energy *except*

A) movement of O_2 into the cell.

B) protein synthesis.

C) Na^+ ions moving out of the cell.

D) cytoplasmic streaming.

E) exocytosis.

Answer: A
Skill: Knowledge

30) Which of the following would likely move through the lipid bilayer of a plasma membrane most rapidly?

A) CO_2

B) an amino acid

C) glucose

D) K^+

E) starch

Answer: A
Skill: Comprehension

31) Which of the following statements is *correct* about diffusion?

A) It is very rapid over long distances.

B) It requires an expenditure of energy by the cell.

C) It is a passive process in which molecules move from a region of higher concentration to a region of lower concentration.

D) It is an active process in which molecules move from a region of lower concentration to one of higher concentration.

E) It requires integral proteins in the cell membrane.

Answer: C
Skill: Knowledge

Use the diagram of the U–tube setup below to answer the questions that follow. The solutions in the two arms of this U–tube are separated by a membrane that is permeable to water and glucose but not to sucrose. Side A is half filled with a solution of 2 M sucrose and 1 M glucose. Side B is half filled with 1 M sucrose and 2 M glucose. Initially the liquid levels on both sides are equal.

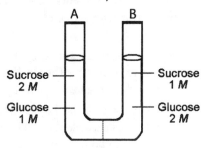

Figure 8.2

32) Initially, in terms of molarity, the solution in side A with respect to that in side B is

A) hypotonic.

B) plasmolyzed.

C) isotonic.

D) saturated.

E) hypertonic.

Answer: C
Skill: Knowledge

33) After the system reaches equilibrium, what changes are observed?

A) The molarity of sucrose and glucose are equal on both sides.

B) The molarity of glucose is higher in side A than in side B.

C) The water level is higher in side A than in side B.

D) The water level is unchanged.

E) The water level is higher in side B than in side A.

Answer: E
Skill: Comprehension

34) A patient has had a serious accident and lost a lot of blood. In an attempt to replenish body fluids, a large amount of distilled water was transferred directly into one of his veins. What will be the most probable result of this transfusion?

A) It will have no unfavorable effect as long as the water is free of viruses and bacteria.

B) It will have serious, perhaps fatal, consequences because there will be too much fluid for the heart to pump.

C) It will have serious, perhaps fatal, consequences because the red blood cells will be hypotonic relative to the body fluids and the cells will shrivel.

D) It will have serious, perhaps fatal, consequences because the red blood cells will be hypertonic relative to the body fluids and the cells will burst.

E) It will have no serious effect because the kidneys would quickly eliminate the excess water.

Answer: D
Skill: Comprehension

35) Celery stalks that are immersed in fresh water for several hours become stiff and hard. Similar stalks left in a salt solution become limp and soft. From this we can deduce that the cells of the celery stalks are

A) hypotonic to both fresh water and the salt solution.

B) hypertonic to both fresh water and the salt solution.

C) hypertonic to fresh water but hypotonic to the salt solution.

D) hypotonic to fresh water but hypertonic to the salt solution.

E) isotonic with fresh water but hypotonic to the salt solution.

Answer: C
Skill: Comprehension

36) A cell with an internal concentration of 0.02 molar glucose is placed in a test tube containing 0.02 molar glucose solution. Assuming that glucose is not actively transported into the cell, which of the following terms describes the internal concentration of the cell relative to its environment?

A) isotonic

B) hypertonic

C) hypotonic

D) flaccid

E) A or B, depending on the temperature

Answer: A
Skill: Application

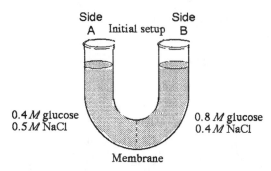

Figure 8.3

Refer to Figure 8.3 to answer the following questions. The solutions in the arms of a U-tube are separated at the bottom of the tube by a selectively permeable membrane. The membrane is permeable to sodium chloride but not to glucose. Side A is filled with a solution of 0.4 molar glucose and 0.5 molar sodium chloride (NaCl) and side B is filled with a solution containing 0.8 molar glucose and 0.4 molar sodium chloride. Initially, the volume in both arms is the same.

37) At the beginning of the experiment,

A) side A is hypertonic to side B.

B) side A is hypotonic to side B.

C) side A is isotonic to side B.

D) side A is hypertonic to side B with respect to glucose.

E) side A is hypotonic to side B with respect to sodium chloride.

Answer: B
Skill: Application

38) If you examine side A after 3 days, you should find

A) a decrease in the concentration of NaCl and glucose and an increase in the water level.

B) a decrease in the concentration of NaCl, an increase in water level, and no change in the concentration of glucose.

C) no net change in the system.

D) a decrease in the concentration of NaCl and a decrease in the water level.

E) no change in the concentration of NaCl and glucose and an increase in the water level.

Answer: D
Skill: Application

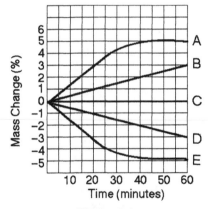

Figure 8.4

Read the following information and refer to Figure 8.4 to answer the following questions. Five dialysis bags, impermeable to sucrose, were filled with various concentrations of sucrose and then placed in separate beakers containing an initial concentration of 0.6 M sucrose solution. At 10-minute intervals, the bags were massed (weighed) and the percent change in mass of each bag was graphed.

39) Which line represents the bag that contained a solution isotonic to the 0.6 molar solution at the beginning of the experiment?

Answer: C
Skill: Application

40) Which line represents the bag with the highest initial concentration of sucrose?

Answer: A
Skill: Application

41) Which line or lines represent(s) bags that contain a solution that is hypertonic at the end of 60 minutes?

A) A and B

B) B

C) C

D) D

E) D and E

Answer: B
Skill: Application

42) What is the best explanation for the shape of line E after 50 minutes?

A) Water is no longer leaving the bag.

B) Water is no longer entering the bag.

C) Water is leaving and entering the bag at the same rate.

D) Water is entering the bag at the same rate that sucrose is leaving the bag.

E) Water is entering and leaving the bag at the same rate.

Answer: C
Skill: Application

43) All of the following membrane activities require ATP energy *except*

A) facilitated diffusion.

B) active transport.

C) Na$^+$ ions moving out of the cell.

D) proton pumps.

E) translocation of potassium into a cell.

Answer: A
Skill: Knowledge

44) Which of the following would indicate that facilitated diffusion was taking place?

A) Substances were moving against the diffusion gradient.

B) A substance was diffusing much faster than the physical condition indicated it should.

C) ATP was being rapidly consumed as the substance moved.

D) A substance was slowing as it moved down its concentration gradient.

E) A substance was moving from a region of low concentration into a region of higher concentration.

Answer: B
Skill: Comprehension

45) What are the membrane structures that function in active transport?

A) peripheral proteins

B) carbohydrates

C) cholesterol

D) cytoskeleton filaments

E) integral proteins

Answer: E
Skill: Knowledge

46) The movement of a substance across a biological membrane against its concentration gradient with the help of energy input is which of the following?

A) diffusion

B) active transport

C) osmosis

D) facilitated diffusion

E) exocytosis

Answer: B
Skill: Knowledge

47) Carrier molecules in the membrane and metabolic energy are required for

A) osmosis.

B) facilitated diffusion.

C) active transport.

D) B and C.

E) A, B, and C.

Answer: C
Skill: Knowledge

48) Glucose diffuses slowly through artificial phospholipid bilayers. The cells lining the small intestine, however, rapidly move large quantities of glucose from the glucose-rich food into their glucose-poor cytoplasm. Using this information, which transport mechanism is most probably functioning in the intestinal cells?

A) simple diffusion

B) phagocytosis

C) active transport pumps

D) exocytosis

E) facilitated diffusion

Answer: E
Skill: Comprehension

49) All of the following situations are consistent with active transport *except*

A) the conversion of ATP to ADP accompanies the movement of molecules.

B) the rate of oxygen consumption by the cell increases when molecules move.

C) molecules move in or out of a cell against the osmotic gradient.

D) cells accumulate diffusible molecules in greater quantity than was found outside.

E) the rate of movement of molecules across the cell membrane increases in an anaerobic environment.

Answer: E
Skill: Comprehension

50) You are conducting research on nerve cells. During an experiment, you administer an electrical stimulation to the cells. The probable result of this stimulation will be to

A) start the membrane water pump.

B) cause increased saturation of phospholipid tails.

C) increase membrane fluidity and asymmetry.

D) activate the active transport system.

E) open gated channels.

Answer: E
Skill: Application

51) Water passes quickly through cell membranes because

A) the bilayer is hydrophilic.

B) it moves through hydrophobic channels.

C) water movement is tied to ATP hydrolysis.

D) it is a small, polar, charged molecule.

E) it moves through aquaporins in the membrane.

Answer: E
Skill: Knowledge

52) What is the voltage across cell membranes called?

A) water potential

B) chemical gradient

C) membrane potential

D) osmotic potential

E) electrochemical gradient

Answer: C
Skill: Knowledge

53) The sodium–potassium pump is called an electrogenic pump because it

A) pumps equal quantities of Na$^+$ and K$^+$ across the membrane.

B) pumps hydrogen ions into the cell.

C) contributes to the membrane potential.

D) ionizes sodium and potassium.

E) pumps hydrogen ions into the cell.

Answer: C
Skill: Knowledge

54) The movement of potassium into or out of an animal cell requires

A) low cellular concentrations of sodium.

B) high cellular concentrations of potassium.

C) an energy source such as ATP or a proton gradient.

D) glucose for binding and releasing ions.

E) plant hormones embedded in the cell membrane.

Answer: C
Skill: Comprehension

55) The cotransport protein that allows two different substances to pass through a membrane in the same direction is

A) usually also a uniport.

B) usually also a biport.

C) usually associated with a proton pump.

D) insensitive to temperature.

E) usually associated with an antiport.

Answer: C
Skill: Knowledge

56) Ions diffuse across membranes down their

A) chemical gradients.

B) concentration gradients.

C) electrical gradients.

D) electrochemical gradients.

E) Both A and B are correct.

Answer: D
Skill: Knowledge

57) Which of the following characterizes the sodium–potassium pump?

   A) Sodium ions are pumped out of a cell against their gradient.

   B) Potassium ions are pumped into a cell against their gradient.

   C) A carrier protein undergoes conformational change.

   D) A and B

   E) A, B, and C

   Answer: A
   Skill: Knowledge

58) What mechanisms do plants use to load sucrose produced by photosynthesis into specialized cells in the veins of leaves?

   A) an electrogenic pump

   B) a protein pump

   C) membrane contransport proteins

   D) A and C

   E) A, B, and C

   Answer: E
   Skill: Comprehension

59) All of the following processes take material into cells *except*

   A) pinocytosis.

   B) endocytosis.

   C) exocytosis.

   D) active transport.

   E) carrier–facilitated diffusion.

   Answer: C
   Skill: Knowledge

60) An organism with a cell wall would have the most difficulty doing which process?

   A) diffusion

   B) osmosis

   C) active transport

   D) phagocytosis

   E) exocytosis

   Answer: D
   Skill: Comprehension

61) The membrane activity most nearly opposite to exocytosis is

   A) plasmolysis.

   B) osmosis.

   C) facilitated diffusion.

   D) phagocytosis.

   E) active transport.

   Answer: D
   Skill: Comprehension

62) White blood cells engulf bacteria through what process?

   A) exocytosis

   B) phagocytosis

   C) pinocytosis

   D) osmosis

   E) receptor–mediated exocytosis

   Answer: B
   Skill: Knowledge

63) Of the following, which is the most important role of exocytosis?

   A) to move away from danger

   B) to release substances from the cell

   C) to incorporate nutrients

   D) to pump protons

   E) to create new cells

   Answer: B
   Skill: Knowledge

64) Mutant cells lacking coated pits would most likely be

   A) deficient in receptor–mediated endocytosis.

   B) unable to adapt to the cold.

   C) characterized by a smooth surface on both sides of the bilayer.

   D) unable to actively transport ions into the cell.

   E) involved in steroid synthesis.

   Answer: A
   Skill: Application

65) What is the cause of familial hypercholesterolemia?

   A) defective LDL receptors on the membranes of liver cells

   B) poor attachment of the cholesterol to the extracellular matrix of liver cells

   C) a poorly formed lipid bilayer that cannot incorporate cholesterol into the membranes of liver cells

   D) inhibition of the cholesterol active transport system in red blood cells

   E) a general lack of glycolipids in the blood cell membranes

Answer: A
Skill: Knowledge

Media Activity Questions

1) The interior of the phospholipid bilayer is
    A) composed of fatty acids.
    B) hydrophobic.
    C) composed of cholesterol.
    D) hydrophilic.
    E) water.

    Answer: B
    Topic: Web/CD Activity 8B

2) Oxygen crosses a plasma membrane by
    A) osmosis.
    B) phagocytosis.
    C) active transport.
    D) pinocytosis.
    E) passive transport.

    Answer: E
    Topic: Web/CD Activity 8C

3) In a hypotonic solution an animal cell will
    A) lyse.
    B) experience turgor.
    C) neither gain nor lose water.
    D) shrivel.
    E) lose water.

    Answer: A
    Topic: Web/CD Activity 8D

4) Which of these processes can move a
   solute against its concentration gradient?
    A) osmosis
    B) passive transport
    C) diffusion
    D) facilitated diffusion
    E) active transport

    Answer: E
    Topic: Web/CD Activity 8G

5) Cholesterol enters cells via
    A) phagocytosis.
    B) osmosis.
    C) receptor-mediated endocytosis.
    D) exocytosis.
    E) pinocytosis.

    Answer: C
    Topic: Web/CD Activity 8H

Self-Quiz Questions

Answers to these questions also appear in the textbook.

1) In what way do the various membranes of a eukaryotic cell differ?
   A) Phospholipids are found only in certain membranes.
   B) Certain proteins are unique to each membrane.
   C) Only certain membranes of the cell are selectively permeable.
   D) Only certain membranes are constructed from amphipathic molecules.
   E) Some membranes have hydrophobic surfaces exposed to the cytosol, while others have hydrophilic surfaces facing the cytosol.

   Answer: B

2) According to the fluid mosaic model of membrane structure, proteins of the membrane are mostly
   A) spread in a continuous layer over the inner and outer surfaces of the membrane.
   B) confined to the hydrophobic core of the membrane.
   C) embedded in a lipid bilayer.
   D) randomly oriented in the membrane, with no fixed inside–outside polarity.
   E) free to depart from the fluid membrane and dissolve in the surrounding solution.

   Answer: C

3) Which of the following factors would tend to increase membrane fluidity?
   A) a greater proportion of unsaturated phospholipids
   B) a lower temperature
   C) a relatively high protein content in the membrane
   D) a greater proportion of relatively large glycolipids compared to lipids having smaller molecular weights
   E) a high membrane potential

   Answer: A

4) Which of the following processes includes all others?
   A) osmosis
   B) diffusion of a solute across a membrane
   C) facilitated diffusion
   D) passive transport
   E) transport of an ion down its electrochemical gradient

   Answer: D

5) Based on the model of sucrose uptake in Figure 8.18 in the textbook, which of the following experimental treatments would increase the rate of sucrose transport into the cell?
   A) decreasing extracellular sucrose concentration
   B) decreasing extracellular pH
   C) decreasing cytoplasmic pH
   D) adding an inhibitor that blocks the regeneration of ATP
   E) adding a substance that makes the membrane more permeable to hydrogen ions

   Answer: B

Chapter 9   Cellular Respiration: Harvesting Chemical Energy

1) Which of the following statements concerning the breakdown of glucose to CO_2 and water is (are) *true*?

   A) The breakdown of glucose is exergonic.

   B) Adding electrons to another substance is known as reduction.

   C) An electron acceptor is called the reducing agent.

   D) A and B only are correct.

   E) A, B, and C are correct.

   Answer: D
   Skill: Knowledge

2) The oxygen consumed during cellular respiration is directly involved in .

   A) glycolysis.

   B) accepting electrons at the end of the electron transport chain.

   C) the citric acid cycle.

   D) the oxidation of pyruvate to acetyl CoA.

   E) the phosphorylation of ADP.

   Answer: B
   Skill: Knowledge

3) All of the following statements about NAD^+ are true *except*:

   A) NAD^+ is reduced to NADH during both glycolysis and the Krebs cycle.

   B) NAD^+ has more chemical energy than NADH.

   C) NAD^+ is reduced by the action of dehydrogenases.

   D) NAD^+ can receive electrons for use in oxidative phosphorylation.

   E) In the absence of NAD^+, glycolysis cannot function.

   Answer: B
   Skill: Comprehension

4) Glycolysis is believed to be one of the most ancient of metabolic processes. Which statement below *least* supports this idea?

   A) If run in reverse, glycolysis will build glucose molecules.

   B) Glycolysis neither uses nor needs O_2.

   C) Glycolysis is found in all eukaryotic cells.

   D) The enzymes of glycolysis are found in the cytosol rather than in a membrane–enclosed organelle.

   E) Bacteria, the most primitive of cells, make extensive use of glycolysis.

   Answer: A
   Skill: Comprehension

5) Which kind of metabolic poison would most directly interfere with glycolysis?

   A) an agent that reacts with oxygen and depletes its concentration in the cell

   B) an agent that binds to pyruvate and inactivates it

   C) an agent that closely mimics the structure of glucose but is not metabolized

   D) an agent that reacts with NADH and oxidizes it to NAD^+

   E) an agent that inhibits the formation of acetyl coenzyme A

   Answer: C
   Skill: Application

6) Which process in eukaryotic cells will normally proceed whether O_2 is present or absent?

   A) electron transport

   B) glycolysis

   C) the Krebs cycle

   D) oxidative phosphorylation

   E) fermentation

   Answer: B
   Skill: Knowledge

7) All of the following statements about glycolysis are true *except:*

   A) Glycolysis has steps involving oxidation–reduction reactions.

   B) The enzymes of glycolysis are located in the cytosol of the cell.

   C) Glycolysis can operate in the complete absence of O_2.

   D) The end products of glycolysis are CO_2 and H_2O.

   E) Glycolysis makes ATP exclusively through substrate–level phosphorylation.

   Answer: D
   Skill: Knowledge

8) All of the following substances are produced in a muscle cell under anaerobic conditions *except*

   A) ATP.

   B) pyruvate.

   C) lactate.

   D) acetyl CoA.

   E) NADH.

   Answer: D
   Skill: Comprehension

9) In addition to ATP, what are the end products of glycolysis?

   A) CO_2 and H_2O

   B) CO_2 and ethyl alcohol

   C) NADH and pyruvate

   D) CO_2 and NADH

   E) H_2O and ethyl alcohol

   Answer: C
   Skill: Knowledge

10) All of the following are products or intermediaries in glycolysis *except*

    A) ATP.

    B) NADH.

    C) $FADH_2$.

    D) pyruvate.

    E) phosphoenolpyruvate.

    Answer: C
    Skill: Application

11) All of the following are functions of the Krebs cycle *except*

    A) production of ATP.

    B) production of NADH.

    C) production of $FADH_2$.

    D) release of carbon dioxide.

    E) adding electrons and protons to oxygen to form water.

    Answer: E
    Skill: Application

Refer to Figure 9.1 to answer the following questions. In Figure 9.1 there are some reactions of glycolysis in their proper sequence. Each reaction is lettered. Use these letters to answer the questions.

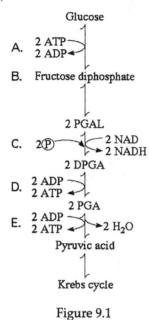

Figure 9.1

12) Which reaction shows a split of one molecule into two smaller molecules?

Answer: B
Skill: Comprehension

13) In which reaction is an inorganic phosphate added to the reactant?

Answer: C
Skill: Comprehension

14) In which reaction is a net gain of ATP finally realized from glycolysis?

Answer: E
Skill: Comprehension

15) Which step requires ATP to occur?

Answer: A
Skill: Comprehension

16) Which step is the first to produce an acid?

Answer: D
Skill: Comprehension

17) The Krebs cycle produces which of the following molecules that then transfer energy to the electron transport system?
   A) ATP and CO_2
   B) CO_2 and FAD
   C) $FADH_2$ and NADH
   D) NADH and ATP
   E) NADH, $FADH_2$, and ATP

Answer: C
Skill: Knowledge

18) Which of the following intermediary metabolites enters the Krebs cycle and is formed, in part, by the removal of CO_2 from a molecule of pyruvate?
   A) lactate
   B) glyceraldehyde phosphate
   C) oxaloacetic acid
   D) acetyl CoA
   E) citric acid

Answer: D
Skill: Knowledge

19) A young relative of yours has never had much energy. He goes to a doctor for help and is sent to the hospital for some tests. There they discover his mitochondria can use only fatty acids and amino acids for respiration, and his cells produce more lactate than normal. Of the following, which is the best explanation of his condition?

A) His mitochondria lack the transport protein that moves pyruvate across the outer mitochondrial membrane.

B) His cells cannot move NADH from glycolysis into the mitochondria.

C) His cells contain something that inhibits oxygen use in his mitochondria.

D) His cells lack the enzyme in glycolysis that forms pyruvate.

E) His cells have a defective electron transport chain, so glucose goes to lactate instead of to acetyl CoA.

Answer: A
Skill: Application

20) Each time a molecule of glucose is completely oxidized via aerobic respiration, how many oxygen (O_2) molecules are required?

A) 1

B) 2

C) 6

D) 12

E) 38

Answer: C
Skill: Application

Refer to Figure 9.2 as a guide to answer the following questions.

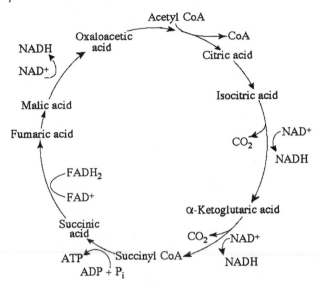

Figure 9.2

21) Starting with fumaric acid and ending with α–ketoglutaric acid in Figure 9.2, what is the maximum number of ATP molecules that could be made through substrate–level phosphorylation?

A) 1

B) 2

C) 11

D) 12

E) more than 20

Answer: A
Skill: Comprehension

22) Refer to Figure 9.2. Carbon skeletons for amino acid biosynthesis are supplied by intermediates of the Krebs cycle. Which intermediate would supply the carbon skeleton for synthesis of a 5–carbon amino acid?

A) citric acid

B) α–ketoglutaric acid

C) succinic acid

D) malic acid

E) isocitric acid

Answer: B
Skill: Comprehension

23) Refer to Figure 9.2. Starting with citric acid and ending with oxaloacetic acid, how many ATP molecules can be formed from oxidative phosphorylation?

   A) 1

   B) 5

   C) 11

   D) 15

   E) 38

   Answer: C
   Skill: Comprehension

24) Refer to Figure 9.2. Where do the catabolism products of fatty acid breakdown enter into the Krebs cycle?

   A) pyruvate

   B) glyceraldehyde phosphate

   C) acetyl CoA

   D) α–ketoglutaric acid

   E) succinyl CoA

   Answer: A
   Skill: Comprehension

25) Refer to Figure 9.2. How many ATP molecules can be made through substrate-level phosphorylation and oxidative phosphorylation if you started with succinyl CoA and ended with oxaloacetate?

   A) 5

   B) 6

   C) 7

   D) 9

   E) 15

   Answer: B
   Skill: Comprehension

26) During oxidative phosphorylation, H_2O is formed. Where do the oxygen atoms in the H_2O come from?

   A) carbon dioxide

   B) glucose

   C) molecular oxygen

   D) pyruvate

   E) lactate

   Answer: C
   Skill: Knowledge

27) Cellular respiration harvests the most chemical energy from which process?

   A) substrate–level phosphorylation

   B) forming lactate from pyruvate

   C) converting oxygen to ATP

   D) transferring electrons from organic molecules to oxygen

   E) generating carbon dioxide and oxygen in the electron transport chain

   Answer: D
   Skill: Knowledge

28) During aerobic respiration, electrons travel downhill in which sequence?

   A) food → Krebs cycle → ATP→ NAD^+

   B) food → NADH → electron transport chain → oxygen

   C) glucose → ATP→ oxygen

   D) glucose → ATP → electron transport chain → NADH

   E) food → glycolysis → Krebs cycle → NADH → ATP

   Answer: B
   Skill: Application

29) During aerobic respiration, which of the following directly donates electrons to the electron transport chain at the lowest energy level?

A) NAD$^+$

B) NADH

C) ATP

D) ADP + P$_i$

E) FADH$_2$

Answer: E
Skill: Knowledge

30) Which metabolic process is most closely associated with intracellular membranes?

A) substrate–level phosphorylation

B) oxidative phosphorylation

C) glycolysis

D) the Krebs cycle

E) ethanolic fermentation

Answer: B
Skill: Comprehension

31) In chemiosmotic phosphorylation, what is the most direct source of energy that is used to convert ADP + P$_i$ to ATP?

A) energy released as electrons flow through the electron transport system

B) energy released from substrate–level phosphorylation

C) energy released from ATP synthase pumping hydrogen ions against their concentration gradient

D) energy released from movement of protons through ATP synthase

E) No external source of energy is required because the reaction is exergonic.

Answer: D
Skill: Knowledge

32) Hydrogen ions flowing through a cylinder causing the cylinder and attached rod to rotate like rushing steam turns a water wheel is an analogy that best describes

A) the Krebs cycle.

B) ATP synthase activity.

C) formation of NADH in glycolysis.

D) oxidative phosphorylation.

E) the electron transport system.

Answer: B
Skill: Application

33) During aerobic cellular respiration, a proton gradient in mitochondria will be generated by _____ and used primarily for _____.

A) the electron transport chain ... ATP synthesis

B) the electron transport chain ... substrate–level phosphorylation

C) glycolysis ... production of H$_2$O

D) fermentation ... NAD reduction

E) diffusion of protons ... ATP synthesis

Answer: A
Skill: Comprehension

34) The direct energy source that drives ATP synthesis during respiratory oxidative phosphorylation is

A) oxidation of glucose to CO$_2$ and water.

B) the thermodynamically favorable flow of electrons from NADH to the mitochondrial electron transport carriers.

C) the final transfer of electrons to oxygen.

D) the difference in H$^+$ concentrations on opposite sides of the inner mitochondrial membrane.

E) the thermodynamically favorable transfer of phosphate from glycolysis and the Krebs cycle intermediate molecules of ADP.

Answer: D
Skill: Comprehension

35) A major function of the mitochondrial inner membrane is the conversion of energy from electrons to the stored energy of the phosphate bond in ATP. To accomplish this function, this membrane must have all of the following features *except*

A) proteins to accept electrons from NADH.

B) integral, transverse ATP synthase.

C) proton pumps embedded in the membrane.

D) the electron transport chain of proteins.

E) high permeability to protons.

Answer: E
Skill: Knowledge

36) When hydrogen ions are pumped from the mitochondrial matrix across the inner membrane and into the intermembrane space, the result is

A) the formation of ATP.

B) the reduction of NAD^+.

C) the restoration of the Na^+-K^+ balance across the membrane.

D) the creation of a proton gradient.

E) the lowering of pH in the mitochondrial matrix.

Answer: D
Skill: Knowledge

37) Where is ATP synthase located in the mitochondrion?

A) ribosomes

B) cytochrome system

C) outer membrane

D) inner membrane

E) matrix

Answer: D
Skill: Knowledge

38) The primary role of oxygen in respiration is to

A) yield energy in the form of ATP as it is passed down the respiratory chain.

B) act as an acceptor for electrons and hydrogen, forming water.

C) combine with carbon, forming CO_2.

D) combine with lactic acid to form pyruvic acid.

E) catalyze the glycolysis reaction.

Answer: B
Skill: Knowledge

39) It is possible to prepare vesicles from portions of the inner membrane of the mitochondrial components. Which one of the following processes could still be carried on by this isolated inner membrane?

A) the Krebs cycle

B) oxidative phosphorylation

C) glycolysis and fermentation

D) reduction of NAD

E) both the Krebs cycle and oxidative phosphorylation

Answer: B
Skill: Comprehension

40) The primary function of the mitochondrion is the production of ATP. To carry out this function, the mitochondrion must have all of the following *except*

A) the membrane–bound electron transport chain.

B) proton pumps embedded in the inner membrane.

C) enzymes for glycolysis.

D) enzymes for the Krebs cycle.

E) mitochondrial ATP synthase.

Answer: C
Skill: Knowledge

41) How many moles of ATP are produced from the complete oxidation of a mole of glucose in cellular respiration?

A) 12
B) 15
C) 20
D) 30
E) 36

Answer: E
Skill: Application

42) How many carbon atoms feed into the Krebs cycle?

A) 2
B) 4
C) 6
D) 8
E) 10

Answer: A
Skill: Knowledge

43) Inside an active mitochondrion, most electrons follow which pathway?

A) glycolysis → NADH → oxidative phosphorylation → ATP → oxygen
B) Krebs cycle → $FADH_2$ → electron transport chain → ATP
C) electron transport chain → Krebs cycle → ATP
D) pyruvate → Krebs cycle → ATP → NADH → oxygen
E) Krebs cycle → NADH → electron transport chain → oxygen

Answer: E
Skill: Application

44) How many molecules of CO_2 would be released from the complete aerobic respiration of a molecule of sucrose, a disaccharide?

A) 2
B) 3
C) 6
D) 12
E) 38

Answer: D
Skill: Comprehension

The questions below are based on the stages of glucose oxidation listed below.

    A. *stage I: glycolysis*
    B. *stage II: oxidation of pyruvate to acetyl CoA*
    C. *stage III: Krebs cycle*
    D. *stage IV: oxidative phosphorylation (chemiosmosis)*

45) Which one of the stages produces the most ATP when glucose is completely oxidized to carbon dioxide and water?

Answer: D
Skill: Knowledge

46) Which one of the stages normally occurs whether or not oxygen is present?

Answer: A
Skill: Knowledge

47) Which one of the stages occurs in the cytosol of the cell?

Answer: A
Skill: Knowledge

48) Carbon dioxide is released during which stage(s)?

A) stage III only

B) stages II and III

C) stages III and IV

D) stages I, II, and III

E) stages II, III, and IV

Answer: B
Skill: Knowledge

The questions below will use the following key:

A. cytosol
B. mitochondrial outer membrane
C. mitochondrial inner membrane
D. mitochondrial intermembrane space
E. mitochondrial matrix

49) The electron transport chain energy is used to pump H^+ ions into which location?

Answer: D
Skill: Knowledge

50) Glycolysis takes place in which location?

Answer: A
Skill: Knowledge

51) Where are the proteins of the electron transport chain located?

Answer: C
Skill: Knowledge

52) Electron shuttle across the membrane begins in which location?

Answer: B
Skill: Application

53) Acetyl CoA accumulates in which location?

Answer: E
Skill: Application

54) Which of the following statements is true of fermentation?

A) It produces a net gain of ATP.

B) It produces a net gain of NADH.

C) It is an aerobic process.

D) It can be performed only by bacteria.

E) It produces more energy per glucose molecule than does aerobic respiration.

Answer: A
Skill: Knowledge

55) Muscle cells in oxygen deprivation convert pyruvate to _____ and in this step gain _____.

A) lactate ... ATP

B) alcohol ... CO_2

C) alcohol ... ATP

D) ATP ... NAD^+

E) lactate ... NAD^+

Answer: E
Skill: Application

56) The ATP made during fermentation is generated by which of the following?

A) substrate–level phosphorylation

B) electron transport

C) photophosphorylation

D) chemiosmosis

E) oxidation of NADH

Answer: A
Skill: Knowledge

57) What must a muscle cell do to keep contracting?

A) regenerate ATP at a very fast rate

B) receive sufficient oxygen for glycolysis

C) store sufficient ATP as a raw material for oxidative phosphorylation

D) rapidly replace the enzymes of respiration

E) effectively transport NADH into the mitochondria

Answer: A
Skill: Application

58) Which of the following is *not* true concerning the cellular compartmentation of the steps of respiration or fermentation?

A) Acetyl CoA is produced only in the mitochondria.

B) Lactate is produced only in the cytosol.

C) NADH is produced only in the mitochondria.

D) $FADH_2$ is produced only in the mitochondria.

E) ATP is produced in the cytosol and the mitochondria.

Answer: C
Skill: Application

59) An organism is discovered that consumes a considerable amount of sugar, yet does not gain much weight when denied air. Curiously, the consumption of sugar increases as air is removed from the organism's environment, but the organism seems to thrive even in the absence of air. When returned to normal air, the organism does fine. Which of the following best describes the organism?

A) It must use a molecule other than oxygen to accept electrons from the electron transport chain.

B) It is a normal eukaryotic organism.

C) The organism obviously lacks the Krebs cycle and electron transport chain.

D) It is an anaerobic organism.

E) It is a facultative anaerobe.

Answer: E
Skill: Application

60) Catabolism of proteins, lipids, and carbohydrates can result in a 2–carbon molecule that enters the Krebs cycle. What is the molecule?

A) glucose

B) acetic acid or acetyl CoA

C) a fatty acid

D) an amino acid

E) pyruvate

Answer: B
Skill: Comprehension

61) Carbon skeletons to be broken down during cellular respiration can be obtained from

A) polysaccharides.

B) proteins.

C) lipids.

D) A and B.

E) A, B, and C.

Answer: E
Skill: Knowledge

62) Which of the following does *not* participate in glycolysis?

A) fatty acids

B) sucrose

C) glucose

D) glycerol

E) starch

Answer: A
Skill: Knowledge

63) You have a friend who lost 15 pounds of fat on a diet. Where did the fat go (how was it lost)?

A) It was released as CO_2 and H_2O.

B) Chemical energy was converted to heat and then released.

C) It was converted to ATP, which weighs much less than fat.

D) It was broken down to amino acids and eliminated from the body.

E) It was converted to urine and eliminated from the body.

Answer: A
Skill: Application

64) Phosphofructokinase is an important control enzyme. All of the following statements concerning this enzyme are true *except:*

A) It is activated by citrate.

B) It is inhibited by ATP.

C) It is activated by ADP.

D) It is a coordinator of the processes of glycolysis and the Krebs cycle.

E) It is an allosteric enzyme.

Answer: A
Skill: Knowledge

Media Activity Questions

1) How many ATP molecules are produced by glycolysis?

   A) 1   B) 2   C) 3   D) 4   E) 5

Answer: D
Topic: Web/CD Activity 9C

2) Glycolysis is a(n) _____ reaction.

   A) exergonic

   B) endothermic

   C) unregulated

   D) endergonic

   E) abnormal

Answer: A
Topic: Web/CD Activity 9C

3) Pyruvate is formed

   A) on the inner mitochondrial membrane.

   B) in the mitochondrial matrix.

   C) on the outer mitochondrial membrane.

   D) in the nucleus.

   E) in the cytosol.

Answer: E
Topic: Web/CD Activity 9D

4) Most of the energy that enters electron transport enters as

   A) ATP.

   B) acetyl CoA.

   C) glucose.

   D) CO_2.

   E) $FADH_2$ and NADH.

Answer: E
Topic: Web/CD Activity 9E

5) In fermentation, _____ is _____.

   A) NADH ... reduced

   B) NAD^+ ... oxidized

   C) NADH ... oxidized

   D) pyruvate ... oxidized

   E) ethanol ... oxidized

Answer: C
Topic: Web/CD Activity 9F

Self–Quiz Questions

Answers to these questions also appear in the textbook.

1) What is the reducing agent in the following reaction?

   Pyruvate + NADH + H$^+$ → Lactate + NAD$^+$

   A) oxygen

   B) NADH

   C) NAD$^+$

   D) lactate

   E) pyruvate

   Answer: B

2) The *immediate* energy source that drives ATP synthesis during oxidative phosphorylation is

   A) the oxidation of glucose and other organic compounds.

   B) the flow of electrons down the electron transport chain.

   C) the affinity of oxygen for electrons.

   D) a difference of H$^+$ concentration on opposite sides of the inner mitochondrial membrane.

   E) the transfer of phosphate from Krebs cycle intermediates to ADP.

   Answer: D

3) Which metabolic pathway is common to both fermentation and cellular respiration?

   A) the Krebs cycle

   B) the electron transport chain

   C) glycolysis

   D) synthesis of acetyl CoA from pyruvate

   E) reduction of pyruvate to lactate

   Answer: C

4) In mitochondria, exergonic redox reactions

   A) are the source of energy driving prokaryotic ATP synthesis.

   B) are directly coupled to substrate–level phosphorylation.

   C) provide the energy to establish the proton gradient.

   D) reduce carbon atoms to carbon dioxide.

   E) are coupled via phosphorylated intermediates to endergonic processes.

   Answer: C

5) The final electron acceptor of the electron transport chain that functions in oxidative phosphorylation is

   A) oxygen.

   B) water.

   C) NAD$^+$.

   D) pyruvate.

   E) ADP.

   Answer: A

6) When electrons flow along the electron transport chains of mitochondria, which of the following changes occurs?

   A) The pH of the matrix increases.

   B) ATP synthase pumps protons by active transport.

   C) The electrons gain free energy.

   D) The cytochromes of the chain phosphorylate ADP to form ATP.

   E) NAD$^+$ is oxidized.

   Answer: A

7) In the presence of a metabolic poison that specifically and completely inhibits the function of mitochondrial ATP synthase, which of the following would you expect?

A) a decrease in the pH difference across the inner mitochondrial membrane

B) an increase in the pH difference across the inner mitochondrial membrane

C) increased synthesis of ATP

D) oxygen consumption to cease

E) proton pumping by the electron transport chain to cease

Answer: B

8) Cells do not catabolize carbon dioxide because

A) its double bonds are too stable to be broken.

B) CO_2 has fewer bonding electrons than other organic compounds.

C) the carbon atom is already completely reduced.

D) most of the available electron energy was released by the time the CO_2 was formed.

E) the molecule has too few atoms.

Answer: D

9) Which of the following is a true distinction between fermentation and cellular respiration?

A) Only respiration oxidizes glucose.

B) NADH is oxidized by the electron transport chain only in respiration.

C) Fermentation, but not respiration, is an example of a catabolic pathway.

D) Substrate-level phosphorylation is unique to fermentation.

E) NAD^+ functions as an oxidizing agent only in respiration.

Answer: B

10) Most CO_2 from catabolism is released during

A) glycolysis.

B) the Krebs cycle.

C) lactate fermentation.

D) electron transport.

E) oxidative phosphorylation.

Answer: B

Chapter 10   Photosynthesis

Use the following information to answer the questions below. Thomas Engelmann illuminated a filament of algae with light that passed through a prism, thus exposing different segments of algae to different wavelengths of light. He added aerobic bacteria and then noted in which areas the bacteria congregated. He noted that the largest groups were found in the areas illuminated by the red and blue light.

1) What did he conclude about the congregation of bacteria in the red and blue areas?

   A) Bacteria released excess carbon dioxide in these areas.

   B) Bacteria congregated in these areas due to an increase in the temperature of the red and blue light.

   C) Bacteria congregated in these areas because these areas had the most oxygen being released.

   D) Bacteria are attracted to red and blue light and thus these wavelengths are more reactive than other wavelengths.

   E) Bacteria congregated in these areas due to an increase in the temperature caused by an increase in photosynthesis.

   Answer: C
   Skill: Knowledge

2) An outcome of this experiment was to help determine

   A) the relationship between heterotrophic and autotrophic organisms.

   B) the relationship between wavelengths of light and the rate of aerobic respiration.

   C) the relationship between wavelengths of light and the amount of heat released.

   D) the relationship between wavelengths of light and the oxygen released during photosynthesis.

   E) the relationship between the concentration of carbon dioxide and the rate of photosynthesis.

   Answer: D
   Skill: Knowledge

3) If you ran the same experiment without passing light through a prism, what would you predict?

   A) There would be no difference in results.

   B) The bacteria would be relatively evenly distributed along the algal filaments.

   C) The number of bacteria present would decrease due to an increase in the carbon dioxide concentration.

   D) The number of bacteria present would increase due to an increase in the carbon dioxide concentration.

   E) The number of bacteria would decrease due to a decrease in the temperature of the water.

   Answer: B
   Skill: Application

4) Organisms that can exist on light and an inorganic form of carbon and other raw materials

A) are called photoautotrophs.

B) do not exist in nature.

C) are called heterotrophs.

D) are best classified as decomposers.

E) are both C and D.

Answer: A
Skill: Knowledge

5) Organisms that metabolize organic molecules produced by other organisms

A) are autotrophs.

B) are heterotrophs.

C) are decomposers.

D) are B and C.

E) are A, B, and C.

Answer: E
Skill: Knowledge

6) The early suggestion that the oxygen (O_2) liberated from plants during photosynthesis comes from water was

A) first published by Melvin Calvin, who also discovered the Calvin cycle.

B) confirmed by experiments using oxygen–18 (^{18}O).

C) made following the discovery of photorespiration because of rubisco's sensitivity to oxygen.

D) A and B.

E) A, B, and C.

Answer: B
Skill: Application

7) Which of the following are products of the light reactions of photosynthesis that are utilized in the Calvin cycle?

A) CO_2 and glucose

B) H_2O and O_2

C) ADP, P_i, and $NADP^+$

D) electrons and H^+

E) ATP and NADP

Answer: E
Skill: Comprehension

8) A new flower species has a unique photosynthetic pigment. The leaves of this plant appear to be reddish yellow. What wavelengths of visible light are *not* being absorbed by this pigment?

A) red and yellow

B) blue and violet

C) green and yellow

D) blue, green, and red

E) green, blue, and violet

Answer: A
Skill: Comprehension

9) The color of light *least* effective in driving photosynthesis is

A) blue.

B) red.

C) orange.

D) green.

E) yellow.

Answer: D
Skill: Knowledge

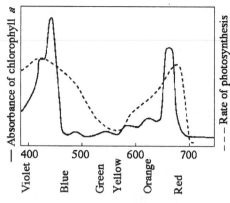

Figure 10.1

10) Figure 10.1 shows the absorption spectrum for chlorophyll *a* and the action spectrum for photosynthesis. Why are they different?

A) Green and yellow wavelengths inhibit the absorption of red and blue wavelengths.

B) Bright sunlight destroys photosynthetic pigments.

C) The two lines are probably the result of inaccurate measurements.

D) Other pigments absorb light in addition to chlorophyll *a*.

E) Anaerobic bacteria probably interfered with light absorption.

Answer: D
Skill: Comprehension

11) The reaction–center chlorophyll of photosystem I is known as P700 because

A) there are 700 chlorophyll molecules in the center.

B) this pigment is best at absorbing light with a wavelength of 700 nm.

C) there are 700 photosystem I components to each chloroplast.

D) it absorbs 700 photons per minute.

Answer: B
Skill: Application

12) All of the events listed below occur in the energy-capturing light reactions of photosynthesis *except*

A) oxygen is produced.

B) $NADP^+$ is reduced to NADPH.

C) carbon dioxide is incorporated into PGA.

D) ADP is phosphorylated to yield ATP.

E) light is absorbed and funneled to reaction–center chlorophyll *a*.

Answer: C
Skill: Knowledge

13) In the thylakoid membranes, what is the main role of the antenna pigment molecules?

A) to split water and release oxygen to the reaction–center chlorophyll

B) to harvest photons and transfer light energy to the reaction–center chlorophyll

C) to synthesize ATP from ADP and P_i

D) to pass electrons to ferredoxin and then NADPH

E) to concentrate photons inside the stroma

Answer: B
Skill: Knowledge

14) The following statements about the light reactions of photosynthesis are all true *except:*

A) The splitting of water molecules provides a source of electrons.

B) Chlorophyll (and other pigments) absorb light energy, which excites electrons.

C) ATP is generated by photophosphorylation.

D) RUBP carboxylase is activated by photons.

E) Electrons are transferred from water to $NADP^+$.

Answer: D
Skill: Comprehension

15) What is the primary function of the light reactions of photosynthesis?

   A) to produce energy-rich glucose from carbon dioxide and water

   B) to produce ATP and NADPH

   C) to produce NADPH used in respiration

   D) to convert light energy to the chemical energy of PGAL

   E) to use ATP to make glucose

Answer: B
Skill: Comprehension

16) Because bundle-sheath cells are relatively protected from atmospheric oxygen, the level of _____ is held to a minimum in C$_4$ plants.

   A) glycolysis

   B) photosynthesis

   C) oxidative phosphorylation

   D) photorespiration

   E) decarboxylation of malic acid

Answer: D
Skill: Knowledge

17) Which of the following statements regarding events in the functioning of photosystem II is *false*?

   A) Light energy excites electrons in an antenna pigment in a photosynthetic unit.

   B) The excitation is passed along to a molecule of P680 chlorophyll in the photosynthetic unit.

   C) The P680 chlorophyll donates a pair of protons to NADPH, which is thus converted to NADP$^+$.

   D) The electron vacancies in P680 are filled by electrons derived from water.

   E) The splitting of water yields molecular oxygen as a by-product.

Answer: C
Skill: Comprehension

18) All of the following are directly associated with photosystem II *except*

   A) photolysis.

   B) release of oxygen.

   C) harvesting of light energy by chlorophyll.

   D) photophosphorylation.

   E) P680.

Answer: D
Skill: Application

19) All of the following are directly associated with photosystem I *except*

   A) harvesting of light energy by chlorophyll.

   B) receiving electrons from plastocyanin.

   C) P700.

   D) photolysis.

   E) passing electrons to ferredoxin.

Answer: D
Skill: Comprehension

20) What are the products of the light reactions that are subsequently used by the Calvin cycle?

   A) oxygen and carbon dioxide

   B) carbon dioxide and RuBP

   C) water and carbon

   D) electrons and photons

   E) ATP and NADPH

Answer: E
Skill: Knowledge

21) Some photosynthetic organisms contain chloroplasts that lack photosystem II, yet are able to survive. The best way to detect the lack of photosystem II in these organisms would be

A) to determine if they have thylakoids in the chloroplasts.

B) to test for liberation of O_2 in the light.

C) to test for CO_2 fixation in the dark.

D) to do experiments to generate an action spectrum.

E) to test for production of either sucrose or starch.

Answer: B
Skill: Application

22) Cyclic electron flow in the chloroplast produces

A) ATP.

B) NADPH.

C) glucose.

D) A and B.

E) A, B, and C.

Answer: A
Skill: Knowledge

23) As a research scientist, you measure the amount of ATP and NADPH consumed by the Calvin cycle in 1 hour. You find 30,000 molecules of ATP consumed, but only 20,000 molecules of NADPH. Where did the extra ATP molecules come from?

A) photosystem II

B) photosystem I

C) cyclic electron flow

D) noncyclic electron flow

E) chlorophyll

Answer: C
Skill: Comprehension

24) Assume a thylakoid is somehow punctured so that the interior of the thylakoid is no longer separated from the stroma. This damage will have the most direct effect on which of the following processes?

A) the splitting of water

B) the absorption of light energy by chlorophyll

C) the flow of electrons from photosystem II to photosystem I

D) the synthesis of ATP

E) the reduction of $NADP^+$

Answer: D
Skill: Application

25) In plant cells, ATP is made in response to light. An electron transport chain is involved. This electron transport chain is found in the

A) thylakoid membranes of chloroplasts.

B) stroma of chloroplasts.

C) inner membrane of mitochondria.

D) matrix of mitochondria.

E) cytoplasm.

Answer: A
Skill: Knowledge

26) Which of the following statements *best* describes the relationship between photosynthesis and respiration?

A) Respiration is the exact reversal of the biochemical pathways of photosynthesis.

B) Photosynthesis stores energy in complex organic molecules, while respiration releases it.

C) Photosynthesis occurs only in plants and respiration occurs only in animals.

D) ATP molecules are produced in photosynthesis and used up in respiration.

E) Respiration is anabolic and photosynthesis is catabolic.

Answer: B
Skill: Comprehension

27) The chemiosomotic process in chloroplasts involves the

A) establishment of a proton gradient.

B) diffusion of electrons through the thylakoid membrane.

C) oxidation of water to produce ATP energy.

D) movement of water by osmosis into the thylakoid space from the stroma.

E) reduction of carbon dioxide to glucose by NADPH and ATP.

Answer: A
Skill: Knowledge

28) Noncyclic photophosphorylation uses light energy to synthesize

A) ADP and ATP.

B) ATP and P700.

C) ATP and NADPH.

D) ADP and NADP.

E) P700 and P680.

Answer: C
Skill: Knowledge

29) In a plant cell, where is ATP synthase located?

A) thylakoid membrane

B) plasma membrane

C) inner mitochondrial membrane

D) A and C

E) A, B, and C

Answer: D
Skill: Comprehension

30) Which of the following statements best represents the relationships between the light reactions and the Calvin cycle?

A) The light reactions provide ATP and NADPH to the Calvin cycle, and the cycle returns ADP, P_i, and $NADP^+$ to the light reactions.

B) The light reactions provide ATP and NADPH to the carbon fixation step of the Calvin cycle, and the cycle provides water and electrons to the light reactions.

C) The light reactions supply the Calvin cycle with CO_2 to produce sugars, and the Calvin cycle supplies the light reactions with sugars to produce ATP.

D) The light reactions provide the Calvin cycle with oxygen for electron flow, and the Calvin cycle provides the light reactions with water to split.

E) There is no relationship between the light reactions and the Calvin cycle.

Answer: A
Skill: Comprehension

31) In mitochondria, chemiosmosis translocates protons from the matrix into the intermembrane space, whereas in chloroplasts, chemiosmosis translocates protons from

A) the stroma to the chlorophyll.

B) the matrix to the stroma.

C) the stroma into the thylakoid compartment.

D) the intermembrane space to the matrix.

E) the light reactions to the Calvin cycle.

Answer: C
Skill: Comprehension

32) The Calvin cycle requires all of the following molecules *except*

   A) CO_2.

   B) ATP.

   C) RuBP.

   D) glucose.

   E) NADPH.

Answer: D
Skill: Knowledge

33) All of the following statements are true *except*:

   A) Thylakoid membranes contain the photosynthetic pigments.

   B) The O_2 released during photosynthesis comes from water.

   C) Glyceraldehyde phosphate is produced only in the light reactions of photosynthesis.

   D) The light reactions of photosynthesis provide the energy for the Calvin cycle.

   E) When chlorophyll is reduced, it gains electrons.

Answer: C
Skill: Comprehension

34) Which of the following is (are) true of the enzyme ribulose bisphosphate carboxylase?

   A) It participates in the Calvin cycle.

   B) It catalyzes a phosphorylation reaction.

   C) It has an affinity for both O_2 and CO_2.

   D) A and C are true.

   E) A, B, and C are true.

Answer: D
Skill: Comprehension

35) All of the following statements are correct regarding the Calvin cycle of photosynthesis *except*:

   A) The energy source utilized is the ATP and NADPH obtained through the light reaction.

   B) These reactions begin soon after sundown and end before sunrise.

   C) The 5–carbon sugar RuBP is constantly being regenerated.

   D) One of the end products is glyceraldehyde phosphate.

Answer: B
Skill: Comprehension

36) If photosynthesizing green algae are provided with CO_2 synthesized with heavy oxygen (^{18}O), later analysis will show that all but one of the following compounds produced by the algae contain the ^{18}O label. That one exception is

   A) PGA.

   B) PGAL.

   C) glucose.

   D) RuBP.

   E) O_2.

Answer: E
Skill: Comprehension

Refer to the following choices to answer the following questions. Each choice may be used once, more than once, or not at all. Indicate whether the following events occur during

   A. *photosynthesis*
   B. *respiration*
   C. *both photosynthesis and respiration*
   D. *neither photosynthesis nor respiration*

37) synthesis of ATP by the chemiosmotic mechanism

Answer: C
Skill: Comprehension

38) oxidation of water

Answer: A
Skill: Comprehension

39) reduction of NADP+

   Answer: A
   Skill: Knowledge

40) CO_2 fixation

   Answer: A
   Skill: Knowledge

41) electron flow along a cytochrome chain

   Answer: B
   Skill: Knowledge

42) oxidative phosphorylation

   Answer: B
   Skill: Knowledge

43) generation of proton gradients across membranes

   Answer: C
   Skill: Comprehension

44) In green plants, the primary function of the Calvin cycle is to

   A) use ATP to release carbon dioxide.

   B) use NADPH to release carbon dioxide.

   C) split water and release oxygen.

   D) transport RuBP out of the chloroplast.

   E) construct simple sugars from carbon dioxide.

   Answer: E
   Skill: Comprehension

For the following questions, compare the light reactions with the Calvin cycle of photosynthesis in plants.
Use the following key:

   A. light reactions alone
   B. the Calvin cycle alone
   C. both the light reactions and the Calvin cycle
   D. neither the light reactions nor the Calvin cycle
   E. occurs in the chloroplast but is not part of photosynthesis

45) produces molecular oxygen (O_2)

   Answer: A
   Skill: Knowledge

46) forms a proton gradient

   Answer: B
   Skill: Knowledge

47) requires ATP

   Answer: B
   Skill: Knowledge

48) requires ADP

   Answer: A
   Skill: Knowledge

49) produces NADH

   Answer: D
   Skill: Knowledge

50) produces NADPH

   Answer: A
   Skill: Knowledge

51) produces triose sugars

   Answer: B
   Skill: Knowledge

52) inactive in the dark

   Answer: C
   Skill: Knowledge

53) requires CO_2

Answer: B
Skill: Knowledge

54) requires glucose

Answer: D
Skill: Knowledge

55) The three substrates (normal reactants) for the enzyme RuBP carboxylase/oxidase (rubisco) are

A) CO_2, O_2, and RuBP.

B) CO_2, glucose, and RuBP.

C) RuBP, ATP, and NADPH.

D) triose-P, glucose, and CO_2.

E) RuBP, CO_2, and ATP.

Answer: A
Skill: Application

56) Photorespiration lowers the efficiency of photosynthesis by removing which of the following from the Calvin cycle?

A) carbon dioxide molecules

B) glyceraldehyde phosphate molecules

C) ATP molecules

D) ribulose bisphosphate molecules

E) RuBP carboxylase molecules

Answer: D
Skill: Knowledge

57) Why are C_4 plants able to photosynthesize with no apparent photorespiration?

A) They do not participate in the Calvin cycle.

B) They use PEP carboxylase to initially fix CO_2.

C) They are adapted to cold, wet climates.

D) They conserve water more efficiently.

E) They exclude oxygen from their tissues.

Answer: B
Skill: Comprehension

58) In C_4 photosynthesis, carbon fixation takes place in the _____ cells, and then is transferred as malic or aspartic acid to _____ cells, where carbon dioxide is released for entry into the Calvin cycle.

A) mesophyll ... bundle–sheath

B) stomatal ... mesophyll

C) bundle–sheath ... epidermal

D) epidermal ... mesophyll

E) stomatal ... epidermal

Answer: A
Skill: Knowledge

59) CAM plants can keep stomates closed in daytime, thus reducing loss of water. They can do this because they

A) fix CO_2 into organic acids during the night.

B) fix CO_2 into sugars in the bundle–sheath cells.

C) fix CO_2 into pyruvic acid in the mesophyll cells.

D) use the enzyme phosphofructokinase, which outcompetes rubisco for CO_2.

E) use photosystems I and II at night.

Answer: A
Skill: Knowledge

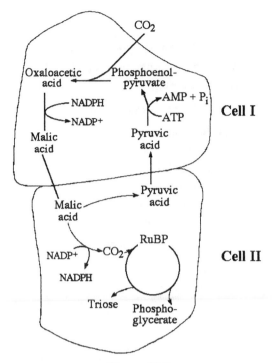

Figure 10.2

60) Which of the following statements is *true* concerning the diagram in Figure 10.2?

A) It represents some of the events of C_4 photosynthesis.

B) It represents the type of photosynthesis found in most aquatic plants.

C) It represents the kinds of cells found in conifers from cold, wet climates.

D) Two of the above statements are true.

E) All of the above statements are true.

Answer: A
Skill: Knowledge

61) Referring to Figure 10.2, oxygen would inhibit the CO_2 fixation reactions in

A) cell I only.

B) cell II only.

C) neither cell I nor cell II.

D) both cell I and cell II.

E) cell I during the night and cell II during the day.

Answer: B
Skill: Comprehension

62) In an experiment studying photosynthesis performed during the day, you provide a plant with radioactive carbon (^{14}C) dioxide as a metabolic tracer. The ^{14}C is incorporated first into oxaloacetic acid. The plant is best characterized as a

A) C_4 plant.

B) C_3 plant.

C) CAM plant.

D) heterotroph.

E) chemoautotroph.

Answer: A
Skill: Application

63) Plants that fix CO_2 into organic acids at night when the stoma are open and carry out the Calvin cycle during the day when the stoma are closed are called

A) C_3 plants.

B) C_4 plants.

C) CAM plants.

D) A and B.

E) A, B, and C.

Answer: C
Skill: Knowledge

64) Where does the Calvin cycle of photosynthesis take place?

A) stroma of the chloroplast

B) thylakoid membrane

C) cytoplasm surrounding the chloroplast

D) chlorophyll molecule

E) outer membrane of the chloroplast

Answer: A
Skill: Knowledge

Media Activity Questions

1) _____ cells in leaves are specialized for photosynthesis.
   A) Companion
   B) Mesophyll
   C) Sclerenchyma
   D) Tracheid
   E) Collenchyma

   Answer: B
   Topic: Web/CD Activity 10A

2) A redox reaction involves the transfer of a(n)
   A) hydrogen ion.
   B) oxygen.
   C) water.
   D) electron.
   E) carbon dioxide.

   Answer: D
   Topic: Web/CD Activity 10B

3) Which of these colors contributes the *least* energy to photosynthesis?
   A) blue
   B) red
   C) violet
   D) orange
   E) green

   Answer: E
   Topic: Web/CD Activity 10C

4) A concentration gradient is a form of
   A) kinetic energy.
   B) life.
   C) an exergonic reaction.
   D) potential energy.
   E) entropy.

   Answer: D
   Topic: Web/CD Activity 10D

5) Under arid conditions C_4 plants fix carbon dioxide more efficiently than C_3 plants because C_4 plants
   A) use ATP to fix carbon dioxide.
   B) utilize rubisco.
   C) decrease the rate at which carbon dioxide diffuses into the plant from the atmosphere.
   D) have chloroplasts concentrated in mesophyll cells.
   E) are larger than C_3 plants.

   Answer: A
   Topic: Web/CD Activity 10F

Self-Quiz Questions

Answers to these questions also appear in the textbook.

1) The light reactions of photosynthesis supply the Calvin cycle with

   A) light energy.

   B) CO_2 and ATP.

   C) H_2O and NADPH.

   D) ATP and NADPH.

   E) sugar and O_2.

   Answer: D

2) Which of the following sequences correctly represents the flow of electrons during photosynthesis?

   A) NADPH → O_2 → CO_2

   B) H_2O → NADPH → Calvin cycle

   C) NADPH → chlorophyll → Calvin cycle

   D) H_2O → photosystem I → photosystem II

   E) NADPH → electron transport chain → O_2

   Answer: B

3) Which of the following conclusions does *not* follow from studying the absorption spectrum for chlorophyll *a* and the action spectrum for photosynthesis?

   A) Not all wavelengths are equally effective for photosynthesis.

   B) There must be accessory pigments that broaden the spectrum of light that contributes energy for photosynthesis.

   C) The red and blue areas of the spectrum are most effective in driving photosynthesis.

   D) Chlorophyll owes its color to the absorption of green light.

   E) Chlorophyll *a* has two absorption peaks.

   Answer: D

4) Cooperation of the *two* photosystems of the chloroplast is required for

   A) ATP synthesis.

   B) reduction of $NADP^+$.

   C) cyclic photophosphorylation.

   D) oxidation of the reaction center of photosystem I.

   E) generation of a proton–motive force.

   Answer: B

5) In *mechanism*, photophosphorylation is most similar to

   A) substrate-level phosphorylation in glycolysis.

   B) oxidative phosphorylation in cellular respiration.

   C) the Calvin cycle.

   D) carbon fixation.

   E) reduction of $NADP^+$.

   Answer: B

6) In what respect are the photosynthetic adaptations of C_4 plants and CAM plants similar?

   A) In both cases, the stomata normally close during the day.

   B) Both types of plants make their sugar without the Calvin cycle.

   C) In both cases, an enzyme other than rubisco carries out the first step in carbon fixation.

   D) Both types of plants make most of their sugar in the dark.

   E) Neither C_4 plants nor CAM plants have grana in their chloroplasts.

   Answer: C

7) Which of the following processes is most directly driven by light energy?

A) creation of a pH gradient by pumping protons across the thylakoid membrane

B) carbon fixation in the stroma

C) reduction of NADP molecules

D) removal of electrons from membrane-bound chlorophyll molecules

E) ATP synthesis

Answer: D

8) Which of the following statements is a correct distinction between cyclic and noncyclic photophosphorylation?

A) Only noncyclic photophosphorylation produces ATP.

B) In addition to ATP, cyclic photophosphorylation also produces O_2 and NADPH.

C) Only cyclic photophosphorylation utilizes light at 700 nm.

D) Chemiosmosis is unique to noncyclic photophosphorylation.

E) Only cyclic photophosphorylation can operate in the absence of photosystem II.

Answer: E

9) Which of the following statements is a correct distinction between autotrophs and heterotrophs?

A) Only heterotrophs require chemical compounds from the environment.

B) Cellular respiration is unique to heterotrophs.

C) Only heterotrophs have mitochondria.

D) Autotrophs, but not heterotrophs, can nourish themselves beginning with CO_2 and other nutrients that are entirely inorganic.

E) Only heterotrophs require oxygen.

Answer: D

10) Which of the following processes could still occur in a chloroplast in the presence of an inhibitor that prevents H^+ from passing through ATP synthase complexes?

A) sugar synthesis

B) generation of a proton–motive force

C) photophosphorylation

D) the Calvin cycle

E) oxidation of NADPH

Answer: B

Chapter 11   Cell Communication

1) In yeast (*Saccharomyces cerevisiae*), the two sexes are called

   A) S plus and S minus.

   B) a and α.

   C) a and b.

   D) b and β.

   E) male and female.

   Answer: B
   Skill: Knowledge

2) In the yeast signal-transduction pathway, after both types of mating cells have released the mating factors and the factors have bound to specific receptors on the correct cells,

   A) binding induces changes in the cells that lead to cell fusion.

   B) the cells then produce the **a** factor and the α factor.

   C) one cell nucleus binds the mating factors and produces a new nucleus in the opposite cell.

   D) the cell membranes fall apart, releasing the mating factors that lead to new yeast cells.

   Answer: A
   Skill: Comprehension

3) Which of the following is *true* of the mating signal-transduction pathway in yeast?

   A) The pathway carries an electrical signal between mating cell types.

   B) Mating type **a** secretes a signal called **a** factor.

   C) The molecular details of the pathway in yeast and in animals are very different.

   D) Scientists think the pathway evolved long after multicellular creatures appeared on Earth.

   Answer: B
   Skill: Knowledge

4) Which of the following responses would be expected in myxobacteria when nutrients are scarce?

   A) Cells would cannibalize each other unless they secrete a chemical signal telling the other myxobacteria they are alike.

   B) Cells secrete an **a**-factor and an α-factor signal that releases new nutrients.

   C) Starving cells secrete a chemical signal that simulates other cells to aggregate in the soil and form spores.

   D) The starved cells secrete a signal to other cells that it is time to move to another environment.

   E) Both C and D are expected responses.

   Answer: C
   Skill: Comprehension

5) What could happen to target cells in an animal that lack receptors for local regulators?

   A) They could compensate by receiving nutrients via an **a** factor.

   B) They could develop normally in response to neurotransmitters instead.

   C) They would divide but could never reach full size.

   D) They would not be expected to multiply in response to growth factors from nearby cells.

   E) Hormones would not be able to interact with target cells.

   Answer: D
   Skill: Comprehension

6) Paracrine signaling

A) involves secreting cells acting on nearby target cells by discharging a local regulator into the extracellular fluid.

B) requires nerve cells to release a neurotransmitter into synapse.

C) occurs only in paracrine yeast cells.

D) has been found in plants but not animals.

E) involves mating factors attaching to target cells and causing production of new paracrine cells.

Answer: A
Skill: Knowledge

7) Which of the following is *true* of synaptic signaling and hormone signaling?

A) Hormone signaling occurs in animals only.

B) Hormone signaling is important between cells that are at greater distances apart than in synaptic signaling.

C) Both use neurotransmitters, but hormone signaling is for adjacent cells in animals only.

D) Both are forms of paracrine signaling.

Answer: B
Skill: Comprehension

8) The old saying "one rotten apple spoils the whole barrel" comes from chemical signaling in plants

A) via an increased uptake of carbon dioxide during respiration in target cells.

B) via a local regulator for apple development.

C) via release of ethylene gas, a plant hormone for ripening.

D) via an a/α cell signal system in the rotten apple.

E) None of these explains the saying.

Answer: C
Skill: Comprehension

9) From the perspective of the cell receiving the message, the three stages of cell signaling are

A) the paracrine, local, and synaptic stages.

B) signal reception, signal transduction, and cellular response.

C) signal reception, nucleus disintegration, and new cell generation.

D) the alpha, beta, and gamma stages.

E) signal reception, cellular response, and cell division.

Answer: B
Skill: Knowledge

10) A small molecule that specifically binds to a larger one

A) is called a signal transducer.

B) is a ligand.

C) is a polymer.

D) seldom is involved in hormone signaling.

E) usually terminates a signal reception.

Answer: B
Skill: Knowledge

11) Ligand–gated ion channels

A) are important in the nervous system.

B) lead to changes in sodium and calcium concentrations in cells.

C) open or close in response to a chemical signal.

D) involve A and B.

E) involve A, B, and C.

Answer: E
Skill: Knowledge

12) Of the following, a receptor protein in a membrane that recognizes a chemical signal is most similar to
   A) a specific catalytic site of an enzyme binding to a substrate.
   B) DNA encoding a message into RNA.
   C) a particular metabolic pathway operating within a specific organelle.
   D) an enzyme with an optimum pH and temperature for activity.
   E) genes making up a chromosome.

   Answer: A
   Skill: Comprehension

13) Most signal molecules
   A) bind to specific sites on receptor proteins in a membrane.
   B) are water soluble.
   C) are able to pass through the plasma membrane by active transport.
   D) A and B.
   E) A, B, and C.

   Answer: D
   Skill: Comprehension

14) Which of the following signal systems use(s) G-protein-linked receptors?
   A) yeast mating factors
   B) epinephrine
   C) neurotransmitters
   D) A and C
   E) A, B, and C

   Answer: E
   Skill: Comprehension

15) The signaling system in an animal cell lacking the ability to produce GTP
   A) would not be able to activate and inactivate the G protein on the cytoplasmic side of the plasma membrane.
   B) could activate only the epinephrine system.
   C) was discovered by Sutherland, who won the Nobel Prize for this work.
   D) would be able to carry out reception and transduction, but would not be able to respond to a signal.

   Answer: A
   Skill: Comprehension

16) G proteins and G-protein receptors
   A) are found only in animal cells.
   B) are found only in bacterial cells.
   C) are thought to have evolved very early, possibly as sensory receptors in ancient bacteria.
   D) probably evolved from an adaptation of the Krebs cycle.
   E) are not widespread in nature and were unimportant in the evolution of eukaryotes.

   Answer: C
   Skill: Knowledge

17) The ability of a single ligand binding to a receptor protein to trigger several pathways
   A) is characteristic of the synaptic signal system.
   B) is unique to the yeast mating system.
   C) does not occur in animals, but is common in bacteria.
   D) is a key difference between the tyrosine-kinase and G-protein-linked receptor systems.
   E) is common to all plasma membrane receptor proteins.

   Answer: D
   Skill: Knowledge

18) Membrane receptors that attach phosphates to specific animo acids in proteins are

A) not found in humans.

B) called tyrosine–kinase receptors.

C) a class of GTP G–protein signal receptors.

D) associated with several bacterial diseases in humans.

E) important in yeast mating factors that contain amino acids.

Answer: B
Skill: Knowledge

19) The general name for an enzyme that transfers phosphate groups from ATP to a protein is

A) phosphorylase.

B) phosphatase.

C) protein kinase.

D) ATPase.

E) protease.

Answer: C
Skill: Knowledge

20) Up to 60% of all medicines used today exert their effects by influencing what structure in the cell membrane?

A) tyrosine–kinase receptors

B) gated ion–channel receptors

C) growth factors

D) G proteins

E) cholesterol

Answer: D
Skill: Knowledge

21) The plasma membrane receptor for a growth factor is often a

A) ligand–gated ion channel.

B) G–protein–linked receptor.

C) cyclic AMP.

D) tyrosine–kinase receptor.

E) neurotransmitter.

Answer: D
Skill: Knowledge

22) Which of the following are hydrophobic chemical messengers that pass through the cell's plasma membrane and have receptor molecules in the cytosol?

A) insulin

B) nitric oxide

C) testosterone

D) B and C

E) A, B, and C

Answer: D
Skill: Knowledge

23) Testosterone functions inside a cell by

A) acting as a signal receptor that activates ion–channel proteins.

B) binding with a receptor protein that enters the nucleus and activates specific genes.

C) acting as a steroid signal receptor that activates ion–channel proteins.

D) becoming a second messenger that inhibits adenylyl cyclase.

E) coordinating a phosphorylation cascade that increases glycogen metabolism.

Answer: B
Skill: Comprehension

24) Chemical signal pathways

    A) operate in animals, but not in plants.

    B) are absent in bacteria, but are plentiful in yeast.

    C) involve the release of hormones into the blood.

    D) usually involve signal molecules binding to a target cell surface protein.

    E) use hydrophilic molecules to activate enzymes.

Answer: D
Skill: Knowledge

25) A selective advantage of cell signaling is

    A) that it allowed some organisms to evolve without having a nervous system.

    B) to ensure proper timing of communication between cells in different parts of an organism.

    C) to ensure that crucial activities occur in the right cells at the right time.

    D) A and C.

    E) A, B, and C.

Answer: E
Skill: Comprehension

26) In general, a signal transmitted via phosphorylation of a series of proteins

    A) brings a conformational change to each protein.

    B) requires binding of a hormone to a cytosol receptor.

    C) cannot occur in yeasts because they lack protein phosphatases.

    D) always results in enzyme activation inside the target cell.

    E) allows target cells to change their shape and therefore their activity.

Answer: A
Skill: Comprehension

27) The activity of a protein regulated by phosphorylation

    A) depends mostly on the concentration of inorganic phosphate inside the cell.

    B) depends on the balance in the cell between active kinase and active phosphatase enzymes.

    C) is dependent on the site of attachment of the protein to the plasma membrane.

    D) is independent of kinase activity, but directly dependent on phosphatase activity inside the cell.

Answer: B
Skill: Comprehension

28) The process of transduction usually begins

    A) when the chemical signal is released from the alpha cell.

    B) when the signal molecule changes the receptor protein in some way.

    C) after the target cell divides.

    D) after the third stage of cell signaling is completed.

    E) when the hormone is released from the gland into the blood.

Answer: B
Skill: Knowledge

29) Which of the following are widely used second messengers in signal-transduction pathways?

    A) calcium ions

    B) cyclic AMP

    C) nitric oxide

    D) A and B

    E) A, B, and C

Answer: D
Skill: Knowledge

30) The signal–transduction pathway in animals that use epinephrine

A) involves activation of glycogen breakdown in liver and skeletal muscle cells.

B) is a classic example of synaptic signaling.

C) is a classic example of paracrine signaling.

D) operates independently of hormone receptors on target cells.

E) None of these describes the epinephrine system.

Answer: A
Skill: Knowledge

31) Sutherland discovered that epinephrine

A) signals bypass the plasma membrane of cells.

B) lowers blood glucose by binding to liver cells.

C) interacts with insulin inside muscle cells.

D) interacts directly with glycogen phosphorylase.

E) elevates the cytosolic concentration of cyclic AMP.

Answer: E
Skill: Knowledge

32) A plant deficient in calcium could experience several problems, including

A) poor response to signals of stress, drought, or cold.

B) decreased response to epinephrine.

C) overactive cyclic AMP responses.

D) B and C.

E) A, B, and C.

Answer: A
Skill: Comprehension

33) An animal deficient in adenylyl cyclase

A) would not be able to transmit nerve impulses via a synapse.

B) could not convert GTP to ATP.

C) would lack plasma membrane-bound receptors.

D) would not respond properly to epinephrine.

E) would be unable to carry out all of the above activities.

Answer: D
Skill: Comprehension

34) Which of the following is *not* considered a secondary messenger?

A) cAMP

B) GTP

C) calcium ions

D) diacylglycerol

E) inositol triphosphate

Answer: B
Skill: Knowledge

35) Transcription factors

A) regulate the synthesis of DNA in response to a signal.

B) transcribe ATP into cAMP.

C) initiate the epinephrine response in animal cells.

D) control which genes are turned on to form mRNA.

E) are needed to regulate the synthesis of protein in the cytoplasm.

Answer: D
Skill: Knowledge

36) The response of a particular cell to a specific chemical signal depends on its particular collection of

A) receptor proteins.

B) relay proteins.

C) proteins needed to carry out the response.

D) A and C.

E) A, B, and C.

Answer: D
Skill: Knowledge

37) Which of the following is the best explanation for the inability of an animal cell to reduce the Ca^{2+} concentration in its cytosol compared to the extracellular fluid?

A) blockage of the synaptic signal

B) loss of transcription factors

C) a plasma membrane impervious to calcium ions

D) low oxygen concentration around the cell

E) low levels of protein kinase in the cell

Answer: D
Skill: Comprehension

38) All of the following are true of cell communication systems *except:*

A) Cell signaling was an early event in the evolution of life.

B) Communicating cells may be far apart or close together.

C) Most signal receptors are bound to the outer membrane of the nuclear envelope.

D) Protein phosphorylation is a major mechanism of signal transduction.

E) In response to a signal, the cell may alter activities by changes in cytosol activity or in transcription of RNA.

Answer: C
Skill: Comprehension

39) The toxin of *Vibrio cholerae* causes profuse diarrhea because it

A) modifies a G protein involved in regulating salt and water secretion.

B) decreases the cytosolic concentration of calcium ions, which makes the cells hypotonic to the intestinal cells.

C) binds with adenyl cyclase and triggers the formation of cAMP.

D) signals inositol triphosphate to become a second messenger for the release of calcium.

E) modifies calmodulin and activates a cascade of protein kinases.

Answer: A
Skill: Comprehension

40) All of the following are part of the phosphorylation cascade model *except:*

A) A signal molecule binds to a membrane receptor protein.

B) Protein kinase is activated.

C) GTP donates a phosphate group to an inactive protein kinase.

D) A specific protein is activated via phosphorylation.

E) A cellular response is initiated.

Answer: C
Skill: Knowledge

41) Which of the following is *least* related to the others?

A) protein kinase

B) scaffolding proteins

C) signal transduction

D) messenger RNA

E) signal–relay proteins

Answer: D
Skill: Knowledge

Media Activity Questions

1) The correct sequence of events in the cell–signaling process is
   A) reception, response, transduction.
   B) transduction, reception, response.
   C) transduction, response, reception.
   D) reception, transduction, response.
   E) response, transduction, reception.

   Answer: D
   Topic: Web/CD Activity 11A

2) G protein is inactivated when
   A) its two parts join.
   B) GTP displaces GDP on the G protein.
   C) it phosphorylates its steroid signal molecule.
   D) it hydrolyzes its GTP to GDP.
   E) a signal molecule changes its shape, closing its ion channel.

   Answer: D
   Topic: Web/CD Activity 11B

3) G protein is activated when _____ attaches to it.
   A) cyclic AMP
   B) ATP
   C) GDP
   D) protein kinase
   E) GTP

   Answer: E
   Topic: Web/CD Activity 11B

4) ATP is converted to cyclic AMP by the direct action of
   A) protein kinase.
   B) G protein.
   C) phospholipase C.
   D) tyrosine–kinase receptor molecules.
   E) adenylyl cyclase.

   Answer: E
   Topic: Web/CD Activity 11C

5) The enzyme glycogen phosphorylase is directly activated by
   A) cyclic AMP.
   B) GTP.
   C) IP_3.
   D) calcium ions.
   E) protein kinases.

   Answer: E
   Topic: Web/CD Activity 11D

Self-Quiz Questions

Answers to these questions also appear in the textbook.

1) Phosphorylation cascades involving a series of protein kinases are useful for cellular signal transduction because
   A) they are species specific.
   B) they always lead to the same cellular response.
   C) they amplify the original signal many fold.
   D) they counter the harmful effects of phosphatases.
   E) the number of molecules used is small and fixed.

   Answer: C

2) Binding of a signal molecule to which type of receptor leads to a change in membrane potential?
   A) tyrosine–kinase receptor
   B) G-protein-linked receptor
   C) phosphorylated tyrosine–kinase dimer
   D) ligand-gated ion channel
   E) intracellular receptor

   Answer: D

3) The activation of tyrosine–kinase receptors is characterized by
   A) aggregation and phosphorylation.
   B) IP₃ binding.
   C) calmodulin formation.
   D) GTP hydrolysis.
   E) channel protein conformational change.

   Answer: A

4) Cell signaling is believed to have evolved early in the history of life because
   A) it is seen in "primitive" organisms such as bacteria.
   B) yeast cells of different mating types signal one another.
   C) signal-transduction molecules found in distantly related organisms are similar.
   D) signaling can operate over large distances, a function required before the development of multicellular life.
   E) signal molecules typically interact with the outer surface of the plasma membrane.

   Answer: C

5) Which observation suggested to Sutherland the involvement of a second messenger in epinephrine's effect on liver cells?
   A) Enzymatic activity was proportional to the amount of calcium added to a cell-free extract.
   B) Receptor studies indicated epinephrine was a ligand.
   C) Glycogen depolymerization was observed only when epinephrine was administered to intact cells.
   D) Glycogen depolymerization was observed when epinephrine and glycogen phosphorylase were combined.
   E) Epinephrine was known to have different effects on different types of cells.

   Answer: C

6) Protein phosphorylation is commonly involved with all of the following *except*

A) regulation of transcription by extracellular signal molecules.

B) enzyme activation.

C) activation of G-protein-linked receptors.

D) activation of tyrosine-kinase receptors.

E) activation of protein-kinase molecules.

Answer: C

7) Amplification of a chemical signal occurs when

A) a receptor in the plasma membrane activates several G-protein molecules while a signal molecule is bound to it.

B) a cAMP molecule activates one protein-kinase molecule before being converted to AMP.

C) phosphorylase and phosphatase activities are balanced.

D) numerous calcium ions flow through an open ligand-gated calcium channel.

E) both A and D occur.

Answer: A

8) Lipid-soluble signal molecules, such as testosterone, cross the membranes of all cells but affect only target cells because

A) only target cells retain the appropriate DNA segments.

B) intracellular receptors are present only in target cells.

C) most cells lack the Y chromosome required.

D) only target cells possess the cytosolic enzymes that transduce the testosterone.

E) only in target cells is testosterone able to initiate the phosphorylation cascade leading to activated transcription factor.

Answer: B

9) Signal-transduction pathways benefit cells for all of the following reasons *except* that

A) they help cells respond to signal molecules that are too large or too polar to cross the plasma membrane.

B) they enable different cells to respond appropriately to the same signal.

C) they help cells use up phosphate generated by ATP breakdown.

D) they can amplify a signal.

E) variations in the signal-transduction pathways can enhance response specificity.

Answer: C

10) Consider this pathway: epinephrine → G-protein-linked receptor → G protein → adenylyl cyclase → cAMP. Identify the "second messenger."

A) cAMP

B) G protein

C) GTP

D) adenylyl cyclase

E) G-protein-linked receptor

Answer: A

Chapter 12   The Cell Cycle

1) All of the following statements are true *except:*

A) Mitosis produces new nuclei with exactly the same chromosomal endowment as the parent nucleus.

B) Mitosis may occur without cytokinesis.

C) Mitosis and cytokinesis are required for asexual reproduction.

D) All cells come from a preexisting cell.

E) The mitotic spindles in prokaryotic cells are composed of microtubules.

Answer: E
Skill: Knowledge

2) The centromere is a region in which

A) chromatids are attached to one another.

B) metaphase chromosomes become aligned.

C) chromosomes are grouped during telophase.

D) the nucleus is located prior to mitosis.

E) new spindle microtubules form.

Answer: A
Skill: Knowledge

Use the following information to answer the questions below. Figure 12.1 shows a diploid cell with four chromosomes. There are two types of chromosomes, one long and the other short. One haploid set is symbolized by unbroken lines, while the other haploid set is represented by dotted lines. At this time, the chromosomes have not yet replicated. Now, choose the correct chromosomal conditions for the following stages:

Figure 12.1

3) at metaphase of mitosis

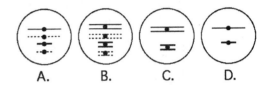

Answer: B
Skill: Knowledge

4) a possible daughter cell of mitosis

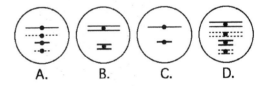

Answer: A
Skill: Knowledge

The questions below refer to the following terms. Each term may be used once, more than once, or not at all.

A. telophase
B. anaphase
C. prometaphase
D. metaphase
E. prophase

5) Two centrosomes are arranged at opposite poles of the cell.

Answer: C
Skill: Knowledge

6) Centrioles begin to move apart in animal cells.

Answer: E
Skill: Knowledge

7) This is the longest of the mitotic stages.

Answer: E
Skill: Knowledge

8) Centromeres uncouple, sister chromatids are separated, and the two new chromosomes move to opposite poles of the cell.

Answer: B
Skill: Knowledge

9) If cells in the process of dividing are subjected to colchicine, a drug that interferes with the functioning of the spindle apparatus, at which stage will mitosis be arrested?

A) anaphase

B) prophase

C) telophase

D) metaphase

E) interphase

Answer: D
Skill: Application

10) A cell containing 92 chromatids at metaphase of mitosis would, at its completion, produce two nuclei containing how many chromosomes?

A) 12

B) 16

C) 23

D) 46

E) 92

Answer: D
Skill: Comprehension

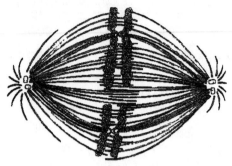

Figure 12.2

11) If the cell whose nuclear material is shown in Figure 12.2 continues toward completion of mitosis, which of the following events would occur next?

A) cell membrane synthesis

B) spindle fiber formation

C) nuclear envelope breakdown

D) formation of telophase nuclei

E) synthesis of chromatids

Answer: D
Skill: Knowledge

12) All of the following occur during prometaphase of mitosis in animal cells *except*

A) the centrioles move toward opposite poles.

B) the nucleolus can no longer be seen.

C) the nuclear envelope disappears.

D) chromosomes are duplicated.

E) the spindle is organized.

Answer: D
Skill: Comprehension

13) If there are 20 centromeres in a cell, how many chromosomes are there?

A) 10

B) 20

C) 30

D) 40

E) 80

Answer: B
Skill: Application

Use the data in Table 12.1 to answer the following questions. The data below were obtained from a study of the length of time spent in each phase of the cell cycle by cells of three eukaryotic organisms, designated beta, delta, and gamma.

Table 12.1: Minutes Spent in Cell Cycle Phases

Cell Type	G_1	S	G_2	M
Beta	18	24	12	16
Delta	100	0	0	0
Gamma	18	48	14	20

14) Of the following, the best conclusion concerning the difference between the S phases for beta and gamma is that

A) gamma contains more DNA than beta.

B) beta and gamma contain the same amount of DNA.

C) beta contains more RNA than gamma.

D) gamma contains 48 times more DNA and RNA than beta.

E) beta is a plant cell and gamma is an animal cell.

Answer: A
Skill: Application

15) The best conclusion concerning delta is that the cells

A) contain no DNA.

B) contain no RNA.

C) contain only one chromosome that is very short.

D) are actually in the G_0 phase.

E) divide in the G_1 phase.

Answer: D
Skill: Application

16) The S phase was measured by

A) counting the number of cells.

B) determining the start and stop of increased DNA in the cells.

C) synthesis versus breakdown of S protein.

D) synthesis of the S chromosome.

E) stopping G_1.

Answer: B
Skill: Application

17) Where do the microtubules of the spindle originate during mitosis in both plant and animal cells?

A) centromere

B) centrosome

C) centriole

D) chromatid

E) kinetochore

Answer: B
Skill: Knowledge

18) All of the following occur during mitosis *except*

A) the condensing of chromosomes.

B) the uncoupling of chromatids at the centromere.

C) the formation of a spindle.

D) the synthesis of DNA.

E) the disappearance of the nucleolus.

Answer: D
Skill: Knowledge

19) If a cell has 8 chromosomes at metaphase of mitosis, how many chromosomes will it have during anaphase?

A) 1

B) 2

C) 4

D) 8

E) 16

Answer: E
Skill: Comprehension

20) Cytokinesis usually, but not always, follows mitosis. If a cell completed mitosis but not cytokinesis, what would be the result?

A) a cell with a single large nucleus

B) a cell with high concentrations of actin and myosin

C) a cell with two abnormally small nuclei

D) a cell with two nuclei

E) a cell with two nuclei but with half the amount of DNA

Answer: D
Skill: Knowledge

21) Regarding mitosis and cytokinesis, one difference between higher plants and animals is that in plants

A) the spindles contain microfibrils in addition to microtubules, whereas animal spindles do not contain microfibrils.

B) sister chromatids are identical, but they differ from one another in animals.

C) a cell plate begins to form at telophase, whereas in animals a cleavage furrow is initiated at that stage.

D) chromosomes become attached to the spindle at prophase, whereas in animals chromosomes do not become attached until anaphase.

E) spindle poles contain centrioles, whereas spindle poles in animals do not.

Answer: C
Skill: Knowledge

22) How do the daughter cells at the end of mitosis and cytokinesis compare with their parent cell when it was in G_1 of the cell cycle?

A) The daughter cells have half the amount of cytoplasm and half the amount of DNA.

B) The daughter cells have half the number of chromosomes and half the amount of DNA.

C) The daughter cells have the same number of chromosomes and half the amount of DNA.

D) The daughter cells have the same number of chromosomes and the same amount of DNA.

E) The daughter cells have the same number of chromosomes and twice the amount of DNA.

Answer: D
Skill: Comprehension

23) The formation of a cell plate is beginning across the middle of a cell and nuclei are re-forming at opposite ends of the cell. What kind of cell is this?

A) an animal cell in metaphase

B) an animal cell in telophase

C) an animal cell undergoing cytokinesis

D) a plant cell in metaphase

E) a plant cell undergoing cytokinesis

Answer: E
Skill: Knowledge

24) Taxol is an anticancer drug extracted from the Pacific yew tree. In animal cells, taxol disrupts microtubule formation by binding to microtubules and accelerating their assembly from the protein precursor, tubulin. Surprisingly, this stops mitosis. Specifically, taxol must affect

A) the fibers of the mitotic spindle.

B) anaphase.

C) formation of the centrioles.

D) chromatid assembly.

E) the S phase of the cell cycle.

Answer: A
Skill: Application

25) Which of the following is (are) primarily responsible for cytokinesis in plant cells?

A) kinetochores

B) Golgi–derived vesicles

C) actin and myosin

D) centrioles and basal bodies

E) cyclin-dependent kinases

Answer: B
Skill: Knowledge

26) Which of the following organisms does *not* reproduce cells by mitosis and cytokinesis?

A) cow

B) bacterium

C) mushroom

D) cockroach

E) banana tree

Answer: B
Skill: Knowledge

27) During which phase(s) of mitosis do we find chromosomes composed of two chromatids?

A) from interphase through anaphase

B) from G_1 of interphase through metaphase

C) from metaphase through telophase

D) from anaphase through telophase

E) from G_2 of interphase through metaphase

Answer: E
Skill: Comprehension

28) Which of the following is *not* true of the bacterial chromosome?

A) It consists of a single, circular DNA molecule.

B) DNA replication begins at the origin of replication.

C) Its centromeres uncouple during replication.

D) It is highly folded within the cell.

E) It has genes that control binary fission.

Answer: C
Skill: Knowledge

29) In which group of eukaryotic organisms does the nuclear envelope remain intact during mitosis?

A) seedless plants

B) dinoflagellates

C) diatoms

D) B and C

E) A, B, and C

Answer: D
Skill: Knowledge

30) Movement of the chromosomes during anaphase would be *most* affected by a drug that

A) reduced cyclin concentrations.

B) increased cyclin concentrations.

C) prevented elongation of microtubules.

D) prevented shortening of microtubules.

E) prevented attachment of the microtubules to the kinetochore.

Answer: D
Skill: Application

31) If mammalian cells receive a go–ahead signal at at the G_1 checkpoint, they will

A) move directly into telophase.

B) complete the cycle and divide.

C) exit the cycle and switch to a nondividing state.

D) show a drop in MPF concentration.

E) complete cytokinesis and form new cell walls.

Answer: B
Skill: Knowledge

32) Cells that are in a nondividing state are in which phase?

A) G_0

B) G_2

C) G_1

D) S

E) M

Answer: A
Skill: Knowledge

33) Measurements of the amount of DNA per nucleus were taken on a large number of cells from a growing fungus. The measured DNA levels ranged from 3 to 6 picograms per nucleus. In which stage of the cell cycle was the nucleus with 6 picograms of DNA?

A) G_0

B) G_1

C) S

D) G_2

E) M

Answer: D
Skill: Application

34) What causes the rhythmic change in cyclin concentration in the cell cycle?

A) an increase in production once the restriction point is passed

B) the cascade of increased production once its protein is phosphorylated by Cdk

C) the changing ratio of cytoplasm to genome

D) its destruction by an enzyme phosphorylated by MPF

E) the binding of PDGF to receptors on the cell surface

Answer: D
Skill: Knowledge

The following questions consist of five phrases or sentences related to the control of cell division. For each one, select the term from below that is most closely related to it. Each term may be used once, more than once, or not at all.

A. *PDGF*
B. *MPF*
C. *protein kinase*
D. *cyclin*
E. *Cdk*

35) released by platelets in the vicinity of an injury

Answer: A
Skill: Knowledge

36) enzymes that activate or inactivate other proteins by phosphorylating them

Answer: C
Skill: Knowledge

37) fibroblasts have receptors for this substance on their plasma membranes

Answer: A
Skill: Knowledge

38) a protein synthesized through the cell cycle that associates with a kinase to form active enzymes

Answer: D
Skill: Knowledge

39) triggers the cell's passage past the G_2 checkpoint into mitosis

Answer: B
Skill: Knowledge

The questions below consist of five phrases or sentences concerned with the cell cycle. For each phrase or sentence, select the answer letter from below that is most closely related to it. Each answer may be used once, more than once, or not at all.

A. G_0
B. G_1
C. S
D. G_2
E. M

40) The "restriction point" occurs here.

Answer: B
Skill: Knowledge

41) Nerve and muscle cells are in this phase.

Answer: A
Skill: Knowledge

42) the shortest part of the cell cycle

Answer: E
Skill: Knowledge

43) DNA is replicated at this time of the cell cycle.

Answer: C
Skill: Knowledge

44) Cyclin is destroyed toward the end of this phase.

Answer: E
Skill: Knowledge

The following questions are based on Figure 12.3.

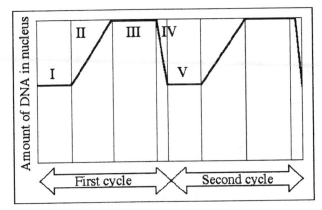

Figure 12.3

45) In the figure above, mitosis is represented by which number?
A) I
B) II
C) III
D) IV
E) V

Answer: D
Skill: Comprehension

46) MPF reaches its threshold concentration at the end of this stage.
A) I
B) II
C) III
D) IV
E) V

Answer: C
Skill: Comprehension

47) Which number represents G1?

A) I and V

B) II and IV

C) III

D) IV

E) V

Answer: A
Skill: Comprehension

48) Which number represents DNA synthesis?

A) I

B) II

C) III

D) IV

E) V

Answer: B
Skill: Comprehension

49) What are enzymes called that control the activities of other proteins by phosphorylating them?

A) ATPases

B) kinases

C) cyclins

D) chromatin

E) protein kinases

Answer: B
Skill: Knowledge

50) A group of cells is assayed for DNA content immediately following mitosis and is found to have an average of 8 picograms of DNA per nucleus. Those cells would have _____ picograms at the end of the S phase and _____ picograms at the end of G2.

A) 8 ... 8

B) 8 ... 16

C) 16 ... 8

D) 16 ... 16

E) 12 ... 16

Answer: D
Skill: Application

51) As the cell progresses through prophase and into metaphase, what happens to the active anaphase–promoting complex proteins?

A) They increase gradually during telophase.

B) They decrease gradually until it is depleted at metaphase.

C) They increase sharply once all the chromosomes are lined up in metaphase.

D) They are initially high, but drop precipitously when all the chromosomes are lined up in metaphase.

E) They remain constant from prophase through metaphase.

Answer: C
Skill: Knowledge

52) What triggers the separation of chromatids during mitosis?

A) internal signals originating at the centromere

B) the activation of proteins holding sister chromatids together

C) the buildup of cyclin near the kinetochores

D) activation of an anaphase–promoting complex (APC)

E) the release of platelet–derived growth factor from the Golgi

Answer: D
Skill: Comprehension

53) Proteins that are involved in the regulation of the cell cycle, and that show fluctuations in concentration during the cell cycle, are called

A) ATPases.

B) kinetochores.

C) centrioles.

D) proton pumps.

E) cyclins.

Answer: E
Skill: Knowledge

54) The MPF protein complex turns itself off by

A) activating an enzyme that destroys cyclin.

B) activating an enzyme that stimulates cyclin.

C) binding to chromatin.

D) exiting the cell.

E) activating the anaphase–promoting complex.

Answer: A
Skill: Knowledge

55) Recent research has indicated that cancer cells

A) transform normal cells by altering genes involved in the control of mitosis.

B) always develop into a tumor.

C) contain more than the normal number of chromosomes.

D) are unable to complete the cell cycle after the S phase.

E) enter and exit the G_0 phase three times before they divide.

Answer: A
Skill: Knowledge

56) A mutation results in a cell that no longer produces a normal protein kinase for the M phase checkpoint. Which of the following would likely be the immediate result of this mutation?

A) The cell would prematurely enter anaphase.

B) The cell would never leave metaphase.

C) The cell would never enter metaphase.

D) The cell would never enter prophase.

E) The cell would undergo normal mitosis, but fail to enter the next G_1.

Answer: E
Skill: Comprehension

57) "Density-dependent inhibition" is explained by which of the following?

A) As cells become more numerous, they begin to squeeze against each other, restricting their size and ability to produce control factors.

B) As cells become more numerous, the amount of required growth factors and nutrients per cell becomes insufficient to allow for cell growth.

C) As cells become more numerous, the protein kinases they produce begin to compete with each other, such that the proteins produced by one cell essentially cancel those produced by its neighbor.

D) As cells become more numerous, more and more of them enter the S phase of the cell cycle.

E) As cells become more numerous, the level of waste products increases, eventually slowing down metabolism.

Answer: B
Skill: Knowledge

58) Which of the following is *true* concerning cancer cells?

A) They do not exhibit density-dependent inhibition when growing in culture.

B) When they stop dividing they do so at random points in the cell cycle.

C) They have escaped from cell cycle controls.

D) B and C are true.

E) A, B, and C are true.

Answer: E
Skill: Knowledge

Media Activity Questions

1) Asexual reproduction requires _____ individual(s).

A) 0   B) 1   C) 2   D) 3   E) 4

Answer: B
Topic: Web/CD Activity 12A

2) The genetic material is duplicated during

A) the mitotic phase.

B) G_1.

C) the S phase.

D) G_2.

E) mitosis.

Answer: C
Topic: Web/CD Activity 12B

3) Chromosomes are aligned along the cell's equator during

A) interphase.

B) anaphase.

C) prophase.

D) metaphase.

E) prometaphase.

Answer: D
Topic: Web/CD Activity 12C

4) The absence of _____ would result in a single cell with two nuclei.

A) interphase

B) prophase

C) anaphase

D) prometaphase

E) cytokinesis

Answer: E
Topic: Web/CD Activity 12C

5) _____ is a carcinogen that may promote colon cancer.

A) Fat

B) UV light

C) Estrogen

D) A virus

E) Testosterone

Answer: A
Topic: Web/CD Activity 12E

Self–Quiz Questions

Answers to these questions also appear in the textbook.

1) During the cell cycle, increases in the enzymatic activity of protein kinases are due to
   A) kinase synthesis by ribosomes.
   B) activation of inactive kinase by binding to cyclin.
   C) conversion of inactive cyclin to the active kinase by means of phosphorylation.
   D) cleavage of the inactive kinase molecules by cytoplasmic proteases.
   E) a decline in external growth factors to a concentration below the inhibitory threshold.

   Answer: B

2) Through a microscope, you can see a cell plate beginning to develop across the middle of the cell and nuclei re–forming at opposite poles of the cell. This cell is most likely
   A) an animal cell in the process of cytokinesis.
   B) a plant cell in the process of cytokinesis.
   C) an animal cell in the S phase of the cell cycle.
   D) a bacterial cell dividing.
   E) a plant cell in metaphase.

   Answer: B

3) Vinblastine is a standard chemotherapeutic drug used to treat cancer. Since it interferes with the assembly of microtubules, its effectiveness must be related to
   A) disruption of mitotic spindle formation.
   B) inhibition of regulatory protein phosphorylation.
   C) suppression of cyclin production.
   D) myosin denaturation and inhibition of cleavage furrow formation.
   E) inhibition of DNA synthesis.

   Answer: A

4) A particular cell has half as much DNA as some of the other cells in a mitotically active tissue. The cell in question is most likely in
   A) G_1.
   B) G_2.
   C) prophase.
   D) metaphase.
   E) anaphase.

   Answer: A

5) One difference between a cancer cell and a normal cell is that
   A) the cancer cell is unable to synthesize DNA.
   B) the cell cycle of the cancer cell is arrested at the S phase.
   C) cancer cells continue to divide even when they are tightly packed together.
   D) cancer cells cannot function properly because they suffer from density–dependent inhibition.
   E) cancer cells are always in the M phase of the cell cycle.

   Answer: C

6) The decline of MPF at the end of mitosis is caused by

A) the destruction of the protein kinase (Cdk).

B) decreased synthesis of cyclin.

C) the enzymatic destruction of cyclin.

D) synthesis of DNA.

E) an increase in the cell's volume-to-genome ratio.

Answer: C

7) A red blood cell (RBC) has a 120-day life span. If an average adult has 5 L (5,000 cm^3) of blood and each cubic millimeter contains 5 million RBCs, how many new cells must be produced each second to replace the entire RBC population?

A) 30,000

B) 2,400

C) 2,400,000

D) 18,000

E) 30,000,000

Answer: C

8) In function, the plant cell structure that is analogous to an animal cell's cleavage furrow is the

A) chromosome.

B) cell plate.

C) nucleus.

D) centrosome.

E) spindle apparatus.

Answer: B

9) In some organisms, mitosis occurs without cytokinesis occurring. This will result in

A) cells with more than one nucleus.

B) cells that are unusually small.

C) cells lacking nuclei.

D) destruction of chromosomes.

E) cell cycles lacking an S phase.

Answer: A

10) Which of the following does *not* occur during mitosis?

A) packaging of the chromosomes

B) replication of the DNA

C) separation of sister chromatids

D) spindle formation

E) separation of the centrosomes

Answer: B

Chapter 13   Meiosis and Sexual Life Cycles

1) What is a genome?
    A) the complete complement of an organism's genes
    B) a specific sequence of polypeptides within each cell
    C) a specialized polymer of four different kinds of monomers
    D) a specific segment of DNA that is found within a prokaryotic chromosome
    E) an arrangement of our chromosomes from largest to smallest

    Answer: A
    Skill: Knowledge

2) If the liver cells of an animal have 24 chromosomes, its sperm cells would have how many chromosomes?
    A) 6   B) 12   C) 24   D) 48

    Answer: B
    Skill: Comprehension

3) Which of the following is *true* of a species that has a chromosome number of 2n = 16?
    A) The species is diploid with 32 chromosomes.
    B) The species has 16 sets of chromosomes.
    C) There are 16 homologous pairs.
    D) During the S phase of the cell cycle there will be 32 separate chromosomes.
    E) A gamete from this species has 8 chromosomes.

    Answer: E
    Skill: Knowledge

4) What is a karyotype?
    A) the phenotype of an individual
    B) the genotype of an individual
    C) a unique combination of chromosomes found in a gamete
    D) a system of classifying cell nuclei
    E) a display of homologous chromosomes of a cell organized in relation to their number, size, and type

    Answer: E
    Skill: Knowledge

5) Which of the following is the term for a human cell that contains 22 pairs of autosomes and two X chromosomes?
    A) an unfertilized egg cell
    B) a sperm cell
    C) a male somatic cell
    D) a female somatic cell
    E) Both A and D are correct.

    Answer: D
    Skill: Knowledge

6) In animals, meiosis results in gametes, and fertilization results in
    A) spores.
    B) somatic cells.
    C) zygotes.
    D) sporophytes.
    E) clones.

    Answer: C
    Skill: Knowledge

7) The X and the Y chromosomes are called sex chromosomes because

A) the number of Y chromosomes determines the sex of the individual.

B) females have X chromosomes and males have Y chromosomes.

C) they are present only when cells undergo meiosis.

D) genes located on these chromosomes play a role in determining the sex of the individual.

E) they are formed only as a result of fertilization.

Answer: D
Skill: Knowledge

8) Syngamy occurs between

A) karyotypes.

B) autosomes.

C) gametes.

D) homologous chromosomes.

E) one haploid and one diploid cell.

Answer: C
Skill: Knowledge

9) At which stage of mitosis are chromosomes photographed in the preparation of a karyotype?

A) prophase

B) metaphase

C) anaphase

D) telophase

E) interphase

Answer: B
Skill: Knowledge

10) Referring to a plant sexual life cycle, which of the following terms describes the process that leads directly to the formation of gametes?

A) sporophyte meiosis

B) gametophyte mitosis

C) gametophyte meiosis

D) sporophyte mitosis

Answer: B
Skill: Knowledge

11) All of the following are functions of meiosis in plants *except*

A) production of spores.

B) reduction of chromosome number by half.

C) independent assortment of chromosomes.

D) crossing over and recombination of homologous chromosomes.

E) production of identical daughter cells.

Answer: E
Skill: Knowledge

12) Eukaryotic sexual life cycles show tremendous variation. Of the following elements, which do *all* sexual life cycles have in common?
I.   *alternation of generations*
II. *meiosis*
III. *fertilization*
IV. *gametes*
V.   *spores*

A) I, IV, and V

B) I, II, and IV

C) II, III, and IV

D) II, IV, and V

E) all of the above

Answer: C
Skill: Comprehension

13) Which of these statements is *false*?

A) In humans, each of the 22 maternal autosomes has a homologous paternal chromosome.

B) In humans, the 23rd pair, the sex chromosomes, determines whether the person is female (XX) or male (XY).

C) Single, haploid (*n*) sets of chromosomes in ovum and sperm unite during fertilization, forming a diploid (2*n*) single-celled zygote.

D) At sexual maturity, ovaries and testes produce diploid gametes by meiosis.

E) Sexual life cycles differ in the timing of meiosis in relation to fertilization.

Answer: D
Skill: Knowledge

Refer to the life cycles illustrated in Figure 13.1 to answer the following questions.

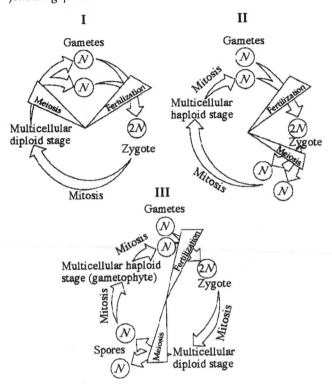

Figure 13.1

14) Which of the life cycles is typical for animals?

A) I only

B) II only

C) III only

D) I and II

E) I and III

Answer: A
Skill: Knowledge

15) Which of the life cycles is typical for plants and some algae?

A) I only

B) II only

C) III only

D) I and II

E) I and III

Answer: E
Skill: Knowledge

16) Which of the life cycles is typical for many fungi and some protists?

A) I only

B) II only

C) III only

D) I and II

E) I and III

Answer: B
Skill: Knowledge

17) In which group of organisms does alternation of generations occur?

A) mammals

B) plants

C) fungi

D) spores

E) humans

Answer: B
Skill: Knowledge

18) How do cells at the completion of meiosis compare with cells that have replicated their DNA and are just about to begin meiosis?

A) They have twice the amount of cytoplasm and half the amount of DNA.

B) They have half the number of chromosomes and half the amount of DNA.

C) They have the same number of chromosomes and half the amount of DNA.

D) They have half the number of chromosomes and one–fourth the amount of DNA.

E) They have half the amount of cytoplasm and twice the amount of DNA.

Answer: D
Skill: Application

19) Which of the following is missing from the life cycle listed below?

zygote-sporophyte-spore-gametophyte-gametes– _____ –zygote

A) meiosis

B) mitosis

C) synapsis

D) karyotype

E) fertilization

Answer: E
Skill: Knowledge

20) In animals, somatic cells result from mitosis and _____ result from meiosis.

A) gametes

B) clones

C) zygotes

D) spores

E) diploid cells

Answer: A
Skill: Knowledge

21) When does the synaptonemal complex disappear?

A) late prophase of meiosis I

B) during fertilization or fusion of gametes

C) metaphase of meiosis I

D) prophase of meiosis II

E) metaphase of meiosis II

Answer: A
Skill: Knowledge

22) The phases of meiosis that produce the most genetic variation from crossing-over and independent assortment are

   A) prophase I and telophase II.

   B) prophase II and anaphase II.

   C) metaphase I and telophase II.

   D) anaphase I and prophase II.

   E) prophase I and anaphase I.

Answer: E
Skill: Comprehension

23) Which of the following terms belongs *least* suitably with the others?

   A) fertilization

   B) spore

   C) gamete

   D) zygote

   E) chiasmata

Answer: E
Skill: Comprehension

24) Which of the following terms belongs *least* suitably with the others?

   A) synapsis

   B) karyotype

   C) tetrad

   D) chiasmata

   E) crossing over

Answer: B
Skill: Knowledge

25) Recombinant chromosomes are the result of

   A) crossing-over.

   B) environmental factors such as radiation and carcinogenic chemicals.

   C) mutations.

   D) separation of homologous chromosomes in metaphase I of meiosis.

   E) incorrect pairings of DNA nucleotides.

Answer: A
Skill: Knowledge

26) Which of the following happens at the conclusion of meiosis I?

   A) Homologous chromosomes are separated.

   B) The chromosome number is conserved.

   C) Sister chromatids are separated.

   D) Four daughter cells are formed.

   E) The sperm cells elongate to form a head and a tail end.

Answer: A
Skill: Knowledge

27) Which of the following is *true* of the process of meiosis?

   A) Two diploid cells result.

   B) Four diploid cells result.

   C) Four haploid cells result.

   D) Four autosomes result.

   E) Four chiasmata result.

Answer: C
Skill: Knowledge

28) Crossing-over occurs during which phase of meiosis?

   A) prophase I

   B) anaphase I

   C) telophase I

   D) prophase II

   E) metaphase II

Answer: A
Skill: Knowledge

29) What is the end result of meiosis?

   A) one diploid cell

   B) two diploid cells identical to the parent cell

   C) an unlimited number of cells identical to the parent cell

   D) new cells for growth and tissue repair

   E) four haploid cells

Answer: E
Skill: Knowledge

Refer to the drawings in Figure 13.2 of a single pair of homologous chromosomes as they might appear during various stages of either mitosis or meiosis and answer the following questions.

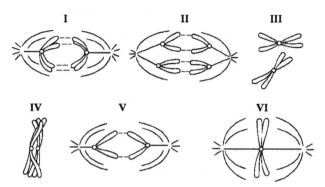

Figure 13.2

30) Which diagram represents late prophase I of meiosis?

   A) I
   B) II
   C) III
   D) IV
   E) V

   Answer: D
   Skill: Comprehension

31) Which drawing represents anaphase of mitosis?

   A) II
   B) III
   C) IV
   D) V
   E) VI

   Answer: A
   Skill: Comprehension

32) Which drawing represents metaphase II of meiosis?

   A) I
   B) II
   C) IV
   D) V
   E) VI

   Answer: E
   Skill: Comprehension

33) Which drawing represents a stage of meiosis where independent assortment might occur if there were more than one pair of chromosomes represented?

   A) I
   B) II
   C) IV
   D) V
   E) VI

   Answer: A
   Skill: Application

Use the following key to answer the following questions. Each answer may be used once, more than once, or not at all.

   A. *The statement is true for mitosis only.*
   B. *The statement is true for meiosis I only.*
   C. *The statement is true for meiosis II only.*
   D. *The statement is true for mitosis and meiosis I.*
   E. *The statement is true for mitosis and meiosis II.*

34) This occurs when a cell divides to form two nuclei that are genetically identical.

   Answer: A
   Skill: Comprehension

35) Homologous chromosomes synapse and crossing over occurs.

   Answer: B
   Skill: Comprehension

36) Centromeres uncouple and chromatids are separated from each other.

   Answer: E
   Skill: Comprehension

37) Independent assortment of chromosomes occurs.

Answer: B
Skill: Comprehension

38) The events during this process cause the majority of genetic recombinations.

Answer: B
Skill: Comprehension

39) The process(es) is (are) preceded by a copying (replication) of the DNA.

Answer: D
Skill: Comprehension

For the following questions, match the key event of meiosis with the stages listed below.

I. *prophase I*
II. *metaphase I*
III. *anaphase I*
IV. *telophase I*
V. *interkinesis or Interphase*

VI. *prophase II*
VII. *metaphase II*
VIII. *anaphase II*
IX. *telophase II*

40) Tetrads of chromosomes are aligned at the center of the cell; independent assortment soon follows.

A) I
B) II
C) IV
D) VII
E) IX

Answer: B
Skill: Knowledge

41) Synapsis of homologous pairs occurs; crossing over may occur.

A) I
B) II
C) IV
D) VI
E) VII

Answer: A
Skill: Knowledge

42) Nuclear envelopes may form; no replication of chromosomes takes place.

A) III
B) V
C) VI
D) VII
E) VIII

Answer: B
Skill: Knowledge

43) Centromeres of sister chromatids uncouple and chromatids separate.

A) II
B) III
C) VI
D) VII
E) VIII

Answer: E
Skill: Knowledge

The following questions refer to the essential steps in meiosis described below.

1. *formation of four new nuclei, each with half the chromosomes present in the parental nucleus*
2. *alignment of tetrads at the metaphase plate*
3. *separation of sister chromatids*
4. *separation of the homologs; no uncoupling of the centromere*
5. *synapsis; chromosomes moving to the middle of the cell in pairs*

44) From the descriptions above, which of the following is the order that most logically illustrates a sequence of meiosis?

A) 1, 2, 3, 4, 5
B) 5, 4, 2, 1, 3
C) 5, 3, 2, 4, 1
D) 4, 5, 2, 1, 3
E) 5, 2, 4, 3, 1

Answer: E
Skill: Knowledge

45) After telophase I of meiosis, what is the chromosomal makeup of each daughter cell?

A) diploid, and the chromosomes are composed of single chromatid chromosomes

B) diploid, and the chromosomes are composed of two chromatids

C) haploid, and the chromosomes are composed of single chromatid chromosomes

D) haploid, and the chromosomes are composed of two chromatids

E) tetraploid, and the chromosomes are composed of two chromatids

Answer: D
Skill: Knowledge

Refer to the diagram of a meiotic process in Figure 13.3 to answer the following questions.

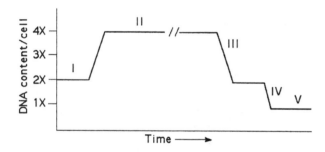

Figure 13.3

46) Which number represents G₂?

A) I

B) II

C) III

D) IV

E) V

Answer: B
Skill: Comprehension

47) Which number represents the DNA content of a sperm cell?

A) I

B) II

C) III

D) IV

E) V

Answer: E
Skill: Comprehension

48) Which number represents the separation of homologous pairs of chromosomes?

A) I

B) II

C) III

D) IV

E) V

Answer: C
Skill: Application

49) Where would you place crossing over in this diagram?

A) I

B) between I and II

C) II

D) III

E) IV

Answer: C
Skill: Comprehension

Figure 13.4 shows a diploid cell with four chromosomes. There are two pairs of homologous chromosomes, one long and the other short. One haploid set is symbolized by unbroken lines, while the other haploid set is represented by dotted lines. At this time, the chromosomes have not yet replicated.

Centromere

Figure 13.4

Now, choose the correct answers for the following stages:

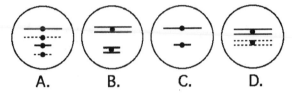

A.　B.　C.　D.

50) the chromosome makeup of a daughter cell at the completion of meiosis I

Answer: B
Skill: Application

51) the chromosome makeup of a daughter cell at the completion of meiosis II

Answer: C
Skill: Application

52) When comparing prophase I of meiosis with prophase of mitosis, which of the following occurs only in meiosis?
A) the chromosomes condense
B) tetrads form
C) the nuclear envelope disassembles
D) a spindle forms
E) each chromosome is composed of two chromatids

Answer: B
Skill: Knowledge

53) Which of the following occurs in meiosis but not in mitosis?
A) chromosome replication
B) synapsis
C) daughter cells are produced
D) tetrads align at metaphase plate
E) B and D above

Answer: E
Skill: Comprehension

54) How does the sexual life cycle increase the genetic variation in a species?
A) by allowing independent assortment of chromosomes
B) by allowing random fertilization
C) by allowing crossing over
D) Both A and B are correct.
E) A, B, and C are correct.

Answer: E
Skill: Comprehension

55) Which of the following events occurs during prophase I of meiosis?
A) reduction in chromosome number
B) segregation of alleles of unlinked genes
C) synapsis and crossing over
D) DNA replication
E) the homologous chromosome pairs separate because linked genes haven't been introduced

Answer: C
Skill: Knowledge

56) Which of the following terms belongs with the words synapsis, tetrads, and chiasmata?
A) haploid
B) crossing over
C) autosomes
D) prophase II
E) fertilization

Answer: B
Skill: Knowledge

57) For a species with a haploid number of 23 chromosomes, how many different combinations of maternal and paternal chromosomes are possible for the gametes?

A) 23

B) 46

C) 460

D) 920

E) about 8 million

Answer: E
Skill: Knowledge

58) The significance of a synaptonemal complex is that it

A) holds homologous chromosomes tightly together.

B) allows the centromeres of sister chromatids to separate.

C) stimulates cytokinesis.

D) ensures the development of two genetically identical chromosomes.

E) is needed for the separation of homologous chromosome pairs.

Answer: A
Skill: Comprehension

59) You are genetically unique. This is at least in part a result of

A) random fertilization.

B) genetic recombination.

C) independent assortment of chromosomes.

D) both A and C.

E) A, B, and C.

Answer: E
Skill: Comprehension

60) What are the sources of genetic variation in sexual life cycles of animals?

A) independent assortment of chromosomes during meiosis

B) crossing over during meiosis

C) random fertilization

D) B and C

E) A, B, and C

Answer: E
Skill: Comprehension

Media Activity Questions

1) What name is given to the process that restores the diploid number of chromosomes?

   A) fertilization

   B) asexual reproduction

   C) meiosis

   D) mitosis

   E) the cell cycle

   Answer: A
   Topic: Web/CD Activity 13A

2) During meiosis, tetrads align along the metaphase plate during

   A) metaphase.

   B) metaphase II.

   C) prometaphase.

   D) metaphase I.

   E) megaphase.

   Answer: D
   Topic: Web/CD Activity 13B

3) Both mitosis and meiosis are preceded by

   A) prometaphase.

   B) interphase.

   C) prophase.

   D) telophase.

   E) anaphase.

   Answer: B
   Topic: Web/CD Activity 13C

4) In sexually reproducing organisms, the events of _____ do *not* contribute to an increase in genetic variation.

   A) prophase I

   B) metaphase I

   C) random fertilization

   D) prophase II

   E) all of these

   Answer: D
   Topic: Web/CD Activity 13D

5) In a cell in which $2n = 6$, the independent assortment of chromosomes during meiosis can by itself give rise to _____ genetically different gametes.

   A) two

   B) four

   C) five

   D) six

   E) eight

   Answer: E
   Topic: Web/CD Activity 13D

Self–Quiz Questions

Answers to these questions also appear in the textbook.

1) A human cell containing 22 autosomes and a Y chromosome is

A) a somatic cell of a male.

B) a zygote.

C) a somatic cell of a female.

D) a sperm cell.

E) an ovum.

Answer: D

2) Homologous chromosomes move to opposite poles of a dividing cell during

A) mitosis.

B) meiosis I.

C) meiosis II.

D) fertilization.

E) binary fission.

Answer: B

3) Meiosis II is similar to mitosis in that

A) homologous chromosomes synapse.

B) DNA replicates before the division.

C) the daughter cells are diploid.

D) sister chromatids separate during anaphase.

E) the chromosome number is reduced.

Answer: D

4) The DNA content of a diploid cell in the G_1 phase of the cell cycle is measured (see Chapter 12 in the textbook). If the DNA content is x, then the DNA content of the same cell at metaphase of meiosis I would be

A) $0.25x$

B) $0.5x$

C) x.

D) $2x$.

E) $4x$.

Answer: D

5) If we continued to follow the cell lineage from question 4, then the DNA content at metaphase of meiosis II would be

A) $0.25x$.

B) $0.5x$.

C) x.

D) $2x$.

E) $4x$.

Answer: C

6) How many different combinations of maternal and paternal chromosomes can be packaged in gametes made by an organism with a diploid number of 8 ($2n = 8$)?

A) 2

B) 4

C) 8

D) 16

E) 32

Answer: D

7) The immediate product of meiosis in a plant is a

A) spore.

B) gamete.

C) zygote.

D) sporophyte.

E) gametophyte.

Answer: A

8) Multicellular haploid organisms

A) are typically called sporophytes.

B) produce new cells for growth by meiosis.

C) produce gametes by mitosis.

D) are found only in aquatic environments.

E) are the direct result of syngamy.

Answer: C

9) Crossing over usually contributes to genetic variation by exchanging chromosomal segments between

   A) sister chromatids of a chromosome.

   B) chromatids of nonhomologues.

   C) nonsister chromatids of homologues.

   D) nonhomologous loci of the genome.

   E) autosomes and sex chromosomes.

   Answer: C

10) In comparing the typical life cycles of plants and animals, a stage found in plants but not in animals is a

   A) gamete.

   B) zygote.

   C) multicellular diploid.

   D) multicellular haploid.

   Answer: D

Chapter 14   Mendel and the Gene Idea

1) A plant with purple flowers is allowed to self-pollinate. Generation after generation, it produces purple flowers. This is an example of

A) hybridization.

B) incomplete dominance.

C) true-breeding.

D) the law of segregation.

E) polygenetics.

Answer: C
Skill: Knowledge

2) A cross between homozygous purple-flowered and homozygous white-flowered pea plants results in offspring with purple flowers. This demonstrates

A) the blending model of genetics.

B) true-breeding.

C) dominance.

D) a dihybrid cross.

E) the mistakes made by Mendel.

Answer: C
Skill: Comprehension

3) What was the most significant result Gregor Mendel drew from his experiments with pea plants?

A) There is considerable genetic variation in garden peas.

B) Traits are inherited in discrete units, and are not the results of "blending."

C) Recessive genes occur more frequently in the F_1 than do dominant ones.

D) Genes are composed of DNA.

E) An organism that is homozygous for many recessive traits is at a disadvantage.

Answer: B
Skill: Knowledge

4) Alleles

A) are the result of hybridization.

B) are present only in the F_1 generation.

C) occur in a 3:1 ratio.

D) are alternative forms of a gene.

E) don't affect the phenotypes until the F_2 generation.

Answer: D
Skill: Knowledge

5) Mendel's law of segregation was nearly impossible for most biologists to understand until there was a general understanding of

A) dominance.

B) meiosis.

C) mitosis.

D) pleiotropy.

E) epistasis.

Answer: B
Skill: Comprehension

6) A couple who are both carriers of the gene for cystic fibrosis have two children who have cystic fibrosis. What is the probability that their next child will have cystic fibrosis?

A) 0%

B) 25%

C) 50%

D) 75%

E) 100%

Answer: B
Skill: Application

7) A couple who are both carriers of the gene for cystic fibrosis have two children who have cystic fibrosis. What is the probability that their next child will be phenotypically normal?

A) 0%

B) 25%

C) 50%

D) 75%

E) 100%

Answer: D
Skill: Application

8) In crossing a homozygous recessive with a heterozygote, what is the chance of getting an offspring with the homozygous recessive phenotype?

A) 0%

B) 25%

C) 50%

D) 75%

E) 100%

Answer: C
Skill: Application

9) In snapdragons, heterozygotes have pink flowers, whereas the two homozygotes have red flowers or white flowers. When plants with red flowers are crossed with plants with white flowers, what proportion of the offspring will have pink flowers?

A) 0%

B) 25%

C) 50%

D) 75%

E) 100%

Answer: E
Skill: Application

10) In cattle, roan coat color (mixed red and white hairs) occurs in the heterozygous (Rr) offspring of red (RR) and white (rr) homozygotes. When two roan cattle are crossed, the phenotypes of the progeny are found to be in the ratio of 1 red:2 roan:1 white. Which of the following crosses could produce the highest percentage of roan cattle?

A) red × white

B) roan × roan

C) white × roan

D) red × roan

E) All of the above crosses would give the same percentage of roan.

Answer: A
Skill: Comprehension

11) Roan color in cattle is the result of incomplete dominance between red and white color genes (Rr). How would one produce a herd of pure-breeding roan-colored cattle?

A) cross roan with roan

B) cross red with white

C) cross roan with red

D) cross roan with white

E) It cannot be done.

Answer: E
Skill: Application

12) Huntington's disease is caused by a dominant allele. If one of your parents has the disease, what is the probability that you, too, will have the disease?

A) 1

B) 3/4

C) 1/2

D) 1/4

E) 0

Answer: C
Skill: Knowledge

13) P = purple, pp = white. The offspring of a cross of two heterozygous purple–flowering plants (*Pp* × *Pp*) results in

   A) all purple-flowered plants.

   B) purple-flowered plants and white-flowered plants.

   C) two types of white-flowered plants: *PP* and *Pp*.

   D) all white-flowered plants.

   E) all pink-flowered plants.

Answer: B
Skill: Comprehension

Use the following information to answer the question below. Albinism (lack of skin pigmentation) is caused by a recessive autosomal allele. A man and woman, both normally pigmented, have an albino child together.

14) For this trait, what is the genotype of the albino child?

   A) homozygous dominant

   B) homozygous recessive

   C) heterozygous

   D) hemizygous

   E) unknown, because not enough information is provided

Answer: B
Skill: Application

15) The couple decides to have a second child. What is the probability that this child will be albino?

   A) 0

   B) 1/4

   C) 1/2

   D) 3/4

   E) 1

Answer: B
Skill: Application

16) The mother is now pregnant for a third time, and her doctor tells her she is carrying fraternal twins. What is the probability that both children will have normal pigmentation?

   A) 3/4

   B) 1/4

   C) 1/16

   D) 9/16

   E) 16/16

Answer: D
Skill: Application

The following questions refer to the pedigree chart in Figure 14.1 for a family, some of whose members exhibit the recessive trait, wooly hair. Affected individuals are indicated by an open square or circle.

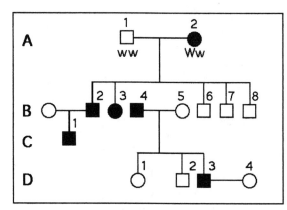

Figure 14.1

17) What is the genotype of individual B-5?

   A) *WW* only

   B) *Ww* only

   C) *ww* only

   D) *WW* or *ww*

   E) *ww* or *Ww*

Answer: C
Skill: Application

18) What is the genotype of individual D–3?

 A) *WW* only

 B) *Ww* only

 C) *ww* only

 D) *WW* or *ww*

 E) *ww* or *Ww*

Answer: B
Skill: Application

19) What is the probability that individual C–1 is *Ww*?

 A) 3/4

 B) 1/4

 C) 2/4

 D) 2/3

 E) 1

Answer: E
Skill: Application

20) What is a genetic cross called between an individual of unknown genotype and a homozygous recessive?

 A) a self–cross

 B) a testcross

 C) a hybrid cross

 D) an F₁ cross

 E) a dihybrid cross

Answer: B
Skill: Knowledge

21) A sexually reproducing animal has two unlinked genes, one for head shape (*H*) and one for tail length (*T*). Its genotype is *HhTt*. Which of the following genotypes is possible in a gamete from this organism?

 A) *HT*

 B) *Hh*

 C) *HhTt*

 D) *T*

 E) *tt*

Answer: A
Skill: Comprehension

22) Which of the following terms is *least* related to the others?

 A) homozygous

 B) tetrad

 C) recessive

 D) heterozygous

 E) dominant

Answer: B
Skill: Comprehension

23) Two plants are crossed, resulting in offspring with a 3:1 ratio for a particular trait. This indicates

 A) that the parents were true–breeding for contrasting traits.

 B) incomplete dominance.

 C) that a blending of traits has occurred.

 D) that the parents were both heterozygous.

 E) that each offspring has the same alleles.

Answer: D
Skill: Knowledge

Use the following information to answer the questions below. A woman and her spouse both show the normal phenotype for pigmentation, but both had one parent who was an albino. Albinism is an autosomal recessive trait.

24) What is the probability that their first child will be an albino?

 A) 0

 B) 1/4

 C) 1/2

 D) 3/4

 E) 1

Answer: B
Skill: Application

25) If their first two children have normal pigmentation, what is the probability that their third child will be an albino?
A) 0
B) 1/4
C) 1/2
D) 3/4
E) 1

Answer: B
Skill: Application

26) What is the probability that their fourth child will have a homozygous genotype?
A) 0
B) 1/4
C) 1/2
D) 3/4
E) 1

Answer: C
Skill: Application

27) Black fur in mice (*B*) is dominant to brown fur (*b*). Short tails (*T*) is dominant to long tails (*t*). What fraction of the progeny of the cross *BbTt* × *BBtt* will have black fur and long tails?
A) 1/16
B) 3/16
C) 3/8
D) 1/2
E) 9/16

Answer: D
Skill: Application

28) A couple has three children, all of whom have brown eyes and blond hair. Both parents are homozygous for brown eyes (*BB*), but one is a blond (*rr*) and the other is a redhead (*Rr*). What is the probability that their next child will be a brown-eyed redhead?
A) 1/16
B) 1/8
C) 1/4
D) 1/2
E) 1

Answer: D
Skill: Application

29) Two true-breeding stocks of garden peas are crossed. One parent had red, axial flowers and the other had white, terminal flowers; all F_1 individuals had red, axial flowers. If 1,000 F_2 offspring resulted from the cross, how many of them would you expect to have red, terminal flowers? (Assume independent assortment.)
A) 65
B) 190
C) 250
D) 565
E) 750

Answer: B
Skill: Application

30) Tallness (*T*) is dominant to dwarfness (*t*), while red (*R*) flower color is dominant to white (*r*). The heterozygous condition results in pink (*Rr*) flower color. A dwarf, homozygous red snapdragon is crossed with a plant homozygous for tallness and white flowers. What are the genotype and phenotype of the F$_1$ individuals?

A) *ttRr*—dwarf and pink

B) *ttrr*—dwarf and white

C) *TtRr*—tall and red

D) *TtRr*—tall and pink

E) *TTRR*—tall and red

Answer: D
Skill: Comprehension

31) In a dihybrid cross, the expected proportion of offspring showing both recessive traits is

A) 1/16.

B) 3/16.

C) 9/16.

D) 1/4.

E) 1/32.

Answer: A
Skill: Application

32) In a cross between parents who both exhibit the dominant curly- and dark-haired traits, one child has straight, light-colored hair. What are the hair genotypes of the parents?

A) *CCdd* × *ccDd*

B) *CcDd* × *CcDd*

C) *CcDd* × *ccdd*

D) *Ccdd* × *CcDd*

E) *CCDD* × *CcDd*

Answer: B
Skill: Application

33) In a cross *AaBbCc* × *AaBbCc*, what is the probability of producing the genotype *AABBCC*?

A) 1/4

B) 1/8

C) 1/16

D) 1/32

E) 1/64

Answer: E
Skill: Application

34) Skin color in a fish is inherited via a single gene with four different alleles. How many different genotypes would be possible in this system?

A) 3

B) 6

C) 8

D) 10

E) 16

Answer: D
Skill: Comprehension

Use the information given here to answer the following questions. Feather color in budgies is determined by two different genes that affect the pigmentation of the outer feather and its core. Y_B_ is green; yyB_ is blue; Y_bb is yellow; and yybb is white.

35) A green budgie is crossed with a blue budgie. Which of the following results is *not* possible?

A) all green offspring

B) all blue offspring

C) all white offspring

D) all yellow offspring

E) All of the above are possible, but with different probabilities.

Answer: E
Skill: Application

36) Two blue budgies were crossed. Over the years, they produced 22 offspring, 5 of which were white. What are the most likely genotypes for the two blue budgies?

A) *yyBB* and *yyBB*

B) *yyBB* and *yyBb*

C) *yyBb* and *yyBb*

D) *yyBB* and *yybb*

E) *yyBb* and *yybb*

Answer: C
Skill: Comprehension

37) The fact that all seven of the garden pea traits studied by Mendel obeyed the principle of independent assortment means that the

A) haploid number of garden peas is 7.

B) diploid number of garden peas is 7.

C) seven pairs of alleles determining these traits are on the same pair of homologous chromosomes.

D) seven pairs of alleles determining these traits behave as if they are on different chromosomes.

E) formation of gametes in plants is by mitosis only.

Answer: D
Skill: Comprehension

38) A 9:3:3:1 phenotypic ratio is characteristic of

A) a monohybrid cross.

B) a dihybrid cross.

C) a trihybrid cross.

D) linked genes.

E) C and D.

Answer: B
Skill: Comprehension

39) The probability that four coins will come up heads when flipped simultaneously is

A) 1/4 (0.25).

B) 1/2 (0.5).

C) 1/8 (0.125).

D) 1/16 (0.063).

E) 1/64 (0.016).

Answer: D
Skill: Application

40) Mendel's law of independent assortment was nearly impossible for most biologists to understand until there was a general understanding of

A) dominance.

B) meiosis.

C) mitosis.

D) pleiotropy.

E) epistasis.

Answer: B
Skill: Comprehension

41) A woman has six sons. The chance that her next child will be a daughter is

A) 1.

B) 0.

C) 1/2.

D) 1/6.

E) 5/6.

Answer: C
Skill: Comprehension

42) Given the parents *AABBCc* × *AabbCc*, assume simple dominance and independent assortment. What proportion of the progeny will be expected to phenotypically resemble the first parent?

A) 1/4

B) 1/8

C) 3/4

D) 3/8

E) 1

Answer: C
Skill: Application

43) How many unique gametes could be produced through independent assortment by an individual with the genotype *AaBbCCDdEE*?

A) 4

B) 8

C) 16

D) 32

E) 1/64

Answer: B
Skill: Application

44) A 1:2:1 phenotypic ratio in the F$_2$ generation of a monohybrid cross is a sign of

A) complete dominance.

B) multiple alleles.

C) incomplete dominance.

D) polygenic inheritance.

E) pleiotropy.

Answer: C
Skill: Comprehension

45) The F$_1$ offspring of Mendel's classic pea cross always looked like one of the two parental varieties because

A) one allele was completely dominant over another.

B) each allele affected phenotypic expression.

C) the traits blended together during fertilization.

D) no genes interacted to produce the parental phenotype.

E) different genes interacted to produce the parental phenotype.

Answer: A
Skill: Knowledge

46) In certain plants, tall is dominant to short. If a heterozygous plant is crossed with a homozygous tall plant, what is the probability that the offspring will be short?

A) 1/2

B) 1/4

C) 0

D) 1

E) 1/6

Answer: C
Skill: Comprehension

Use the information given here to answer the following questions. Feather color in budgies is determined by two different genes that affect the pigmentation of the outer feather and its core. Y_B_ is green; yyB_ is blue; Y_bb is yellow; and yybb is white.

47) The inheritance of color in budgies is an example of what genetic phenomenon?

A) pleiotropy

B) penetrance

C) polygenic inheritance

D) dominance

E) epistasis

Answer: E
Skill: Knowledge

48) A 9 purple to 7 white phenotype in sweet peas in the F$_2$ generation is most likely due to

A) linkage.

B) trisomy 21.

C) epistasis.

D) crossing over.

E) pleiotropy.

Answer: C
Skill: Comprehension

49) Three babies were recently mixed up in a hospital. After consideration of the data below, which of the following represent the correct baby/parent combinations?

Couple #	I	II	III
Blood groups	A and A	A and B	B and O

Baby #	1	2	3
Blood groups	B	O	AB

A) I–3, II–1, III–2

B) I–1, II–3, III–2

C) I–2, II–3, III–1

D) I–2, II–1, III–3

E) I–3, II–2, III–1

Answer: C
Skill: Application

50) Which of the following terms is *least* related to the others?

A) segregation

B) independent assortment

C) homologous chromosomes

D) pleiotropy

E) random recombination

Answer: D
Skill: Comprehension

51) A Punnett square

A) is useful in predicting the result of genetic crosses between organisms of unknown genotypes.

B) computes the probable genotype of future offspring.

C) identifies the gene locus where allelic variations are possible.

D) tests for the presence of the allele responsible for Huntington's disease.

E) directly examines a fetus for genetic abnormalities.

Answer: A
Skill: Knowledge

Use the following information to answer the questions below. A woman who belongs to blood group A and is Rh positive has a daughter who is O positive and a son who is B negative. Rh positive is a simple dominant over Rh negative.

52) Which of the following is a possible genotype for the son?

A) $I^B I^B rr$

B) $I^B I^B RR$

C) $I^B i Rr$

D) $I^B i rr$

E) $I^B I^B Rr$

Answer: D
Skill: Application

53) Which of the following is a possible genotype for the mother?

A) $I^A I^A RR$

B) $I^A I^A Rr$

C) $I^A i rr$

D) $I^A i Rr$

E) $I^A i RR$

Answer: D
Skill: Application

54) Which of the following is a possible phenotype for the father?

A) A negative

B) O negative

C) B positive

D) A positive

E) O positive

Answer: C
Skill: Application

The questions below refer to the following terms. Each term may be used once, more than once, or not at all.

    A. *incomplete dominance*
    B. *multiple alleles*
    C. *pleiotrophy*
    D. *epistasis*
    E. *penetrance*

55) the ability of a single gene to have multiple phenotype effects

Answer: C
Skill: Knowledge

56) One example is the ABO blood group system.

Answer: B
Skill: Knowledge

57) The phenotype of the heterozygote differs from the phenotypes of both homozygotes.

Answer: A
Skill: Knowledge

Use the following information to answer the questions below. A man is brought to court in a paternity case. He has blood type B, Rh positive. The mother has blood type B, Rh negative.

58) Which blood type of a child would exclude the accused from paternity?

A) AB, Rh negative

B) B, Rh negative

C) O, Rh negative

D) B, Rh positive

E) None of these choices will exclude.

Answer: A
Skill: Application

59) The child's blood type is A, Rh negative. What can you say about the man's chances of being the father?

A) He is the father.

B) He might be the father.

C) He is not the father.

D) He might not be the father.

E) There is not enough information to make a decision.

Answer: C
Skill: Application

60) The child's blood type is A, Rh negative. What can you say about the chances of a male with A, Rh positive blood being the father?

A) He is the father.

B) He might be the father.

C) He is not the father.

D) He is almost certainly the father.

E) There is not enough information to make a decision.

Answer: B
Skill: Application

61) Which of the following is an example of polygenic inheritance?

A) pink flowers in snapdragons

B) the ABO blood groups in humans

C) sex linkage in humans

D) white and purple color in sweet peas

E) skin pigmentation in humans

Answer: E
Skill: Knowledge

62) Hydrangea plants of the same genotype are planted in a large flower garden. Some of the plants produce blue flowers and others pink flowers. This can be best explained by

A) environmental factors such as soil pH.

B) the allele for blue violet being completely dominant.

C) the alleles being codominant.

D) the fact that a mutation has occurred.

E) acknowledging that multiple alleles are involved.

Answer: A
Skill: Knowledge

63) People with sickle–cell trait

A) are heterozygous for the sickle–cell allele.

B) are usually healthy.

C) have increased resistance to malaria.

D) produce normal and abnormal hemoglobin.

E) All of the above are true.

Answer: E
Skill: Knowledge

64) Which of the following terms is *least* related to the others?

A) pedigree

B) karyotype

C) amniocentesis

D) chorionic villus sampling

E) epistasis

Answer: E
Skill: Comprehension

65) Below are three major discoveries that led to our understanding of genetics.
I.   an understanding of mitosis and meiosis
II. an understanding of DNA structure and function
III. Mendel's realization of the particulate nature of heredity

Which of the following is a *correct* historical progression of these three events, from first to last?

A) I, II, III

B) II, III, I

C) I, III, II

D) III, II, I

E) III, I, II

Answer: E
Skill: Knowledge

The questions below will use the following answers. Each answer may be used once, more than once, or not at all.

A. *Huntington's disease*
B. *Tay–Sachs disease*
C. *phenylketonuria*
D. *cystic fibrosis*
E. *sickle–cell disease*

66) Substitution of the "wrong" amino acid in the hemoglobin protein results in this disorder.

Answer: E
Skill: Knowledge

67) Individuals with this disorder are unable to metabolize gangliosides, which affects proper brain development. Affected individuals die in early infancy.

Answer: B
Skill: Knowledge

68) This is caused by a dominant single gene defect and generally does not appear until the individual is 30–40 years of age.

Answer: A
Skill: Knowledge

69) Effects of this recessive single gene can be completely overcome by regulating the diet of the affected individual.

Answer: C
Skill: Knowledge

70) This results from having defective membrane proteins that normally function in chloride ion transplant.

Answer: D
Skill: Knowledge

Media Activity Questions

1) All the offspring of a cross between a black–eyed MendAlien and an orange–eyed MendAlien have black eyes. This means that the allele for black eyes is _____ the allele for orange eyes.

   A) codominant to

   B) recessive to

   C) more aggressive than

   D) dominant to

   E) better than

   Answer: D
   Topic: Web/CD Activity 14A

2) What is the expected phenotypic ratio of a cross between two orange–eyed MendAliens?

   A) 3 black–eyed:1 orange–eyed

   B) 0 black–eyed:1 orange–eyed

   C) 1 black–eyed:3 orange–eyed

   D) 1 black–eyed:0 orange–eyed

   E) 1 black–eyed:1 orange–eyed

   Answer: B
   Topic: Web/CD Activity 14A

3) What is the expected phenotypic ratio of the following cross: *AaBb* × *AaBb*? In this example *A* is dominant to *a* and *B* is dominant to *b*.

   A) 16:0:0:0

   B) 8:4:2:2

   C) 4:4:4:4

   D) 1:1:1:1

   E) 9:3:3:1

   Answer: E
   Topic: Web/CD Activity 14B

4) Mendel conducted his most memorable experiments on

   A) peas.

   B) roses.

   C) guinea pigs.

   D) fruit flies.

   E) clones.

   Answer: A
   Topic: Web/CD Activity 14C

5) All the offspring of a cross between a red–flowered plant and a white–flowered plant have pink flowers. This means that the allele for red flowers is _____ to the allele for white flowers.

   A) dominant

   B) codominant

   C) pleiotropic

   D) incompletely dominant

   E) recessive

   Answer: D
   Topic: Web/CD Activity 14D

Self-Quiz Questions

Answers to these questions also appear in the textbook.

Note: The following Self-Quiz questions are not in multiple choice format.

1) A rooster with gray feathers is mated with a hen of the same phenotype. Among their offspring, 15 chicks are gray, 6 are black, and 8 are white. What is the simplest explanation for the inheritance of these colors in chickens? What offspring would you predict from the mating of a gray rooster and a black hen?

   Answer: Incomplete dominance, with heterozygotes being gray in color. Mating a gray rooster with a black hen should yield approximately equal numbers of gray and black offspring.

2) In some plants, a true-breeding, red-flowered strain gives all pink flowers when crossed with a white-flowered strain: RR (red) × rr (white) → Rr (pink). If flower position (axial or terminal) is inherited as it is in peas (see Table 14.1, p. 250 in the textbook), what will be the ratios of genotypes and phenotypes of the F_1 generation resulting from the following cross: axial-red (true-breeding) × terminal-white? What will be the ratios in the F_2 generation?

   Answer: Parental cross is $AARR$ × $aarr$. Genotype of F_1 is $AaRr$, phenotype is all axial-pink. Genotypes of F_2 are 4 $AaRr$: 2 $AaRR$: 2 $AARr$: 2 $aaRr$: 2 $Aarr$: 1 $AARR$: 1 $aaRR$: 1 $AArr$: 1 $aarr$; phenotypes are 6 axial-pink : 3 axial-red : 3 axial-white : 2 terminal-pink : 1 terminal-white : 1 terminal-red.

3) Flower position, stem length, and seed shape were three characters that Mendel studied. Each is controlled by an independently assorting gene and has dominant and recessive expression as follows:

Character	Dominant	Recessive
Flower position	Axial (A)	Terminal (a)
Stem length	Tall (L)	Dwarf (l)
Seed shape	Round (R)	Wrinkled (r)

   If a plant that is heterozygous for all three characters is allowed to self-fertilize, what proportion of the offspring would you expect to be as follows? (*Note*: Use the rules of probability instead of a huge Punnett square.)
   A) homozygous for the three dominant traits
   B) homozygous for the three recessive traits
   C) heterozygous
   D) homozygous for axial and tall, heterozygous for seed shape

   Answer: A) 1/64
   B) 1/64
   C) 1/8
   D) 1/32

4) A black guinea pig crossed with an albino guinea pig produces 12 black offspring. When the albino is crossed with a second black one, 7 blacks and 5 albinos are obtained. What is the best explanation for this genetic situation? Write genotypes for the parents, gametes, and offspring.

   Answer: Albino is a recessive trait; black is dominant.
   First cross: parents BB × bb; gametes B and b; offspring all Bb.
   Second cross: parents bb × Bb; gametes b and 1/2 B, 1/2 b; offspring 1/2 Bb, 1/2 bb.

5) In sesame plants, the one-pod condition (P) is dominant to the three-pod condition (p), and normal leaf (L) is dominant to wrinkled leaf (l). Pod type and leaf type are inherited independently. Determine the genotypes for the two parents for all possible matings producing the following offspring:
A) 318 one-pod normal, 98 one-pod wrinkled
B) 323 three-pod normal, 106 three-pod wrinkled
C) 401 one-pod normal
D) 150 one-pod normal, 147 one-pod wrinkled, 51 three-pod normal, 48 three-pod wrinkled
E) 223 one-pod normal, 72 one-pod wrinkled, 76 three-pod normal, 27 three-pod wrinkled

Answer: A) *PPLl* × *PPLl*, *PpLl*, or *ppLl*
B) *ppLl* × *ppLl*
C) *PPLL* × any of the 9 possible genotypes or *PPll* × *ppLL*
D) *PpLl* × *Ppll*
E) *PpLl* × *PpLl*

6) A man with group A blood marries a woman with group B blood. Their child has group O blood. What are the genotypes of these individuals? What other genotypes, and in what frequencies, would you expect in offspring from this marriage?

Answer: Man I^Ai; woman I^Bi; child *ii*. Other genotypes for children are $1/4$ I^AI^B, $1/4$ I^Ai, $1/4$ I^Bi

7) Color pattern in a species of duck is determined by one gene with three alleles. Alleles *H* and *I* are codominant, and allele *i* is recessive to both. How many phenotypes are possible in a flock of ducks that contains all the possible combinations of these three alleles?

Answer: Four

8) Phenylketonuria (PKU) is an inherited disease caused by a recessive allele. If a woman and her husband are both carriers, what is the probability of each of the following?
A) All three of their children will be of normal phenotype.
B) One or more of the three children will have the disease.
C) All three children will have the disease.
D) At least one child will be phenotypically normal.
(*Note*: Remember that the probabilities of all possible outcomes always add up to 1.)

Answer: A) $3/4 \times 3/4 \times 3/4 = 27/64$
B) $1 - 27/64 = 37/64$
C) $1/4 \times 1/4 \times 1/4 = 1/64$
D) $1 - 1/64 = 63/64$

9) The genotype of F_1 individuals in a tetrahybrid cross is *AaBbCcDd*. Assuming independent assortment of these four genes, what are the probabilities that F_2 offspring will have the following genotypes?
A) *aabbccdd*
B) *AaBbCcDd*
C) *AABBCCDD*
D) *AaBBccDd*
E) *AaBBCCdd*

Answer: A) 1/256
B) 1/16
C) 1/256
D) 1/64
E) 1/128

10) What is the probability that each of the following pairs of parents will produce the indicated offspring? (Assume independent assortment of all gene pairs.)
A) *AABBCC* × *aabbcc* → *AaBbCc*
B) *AABbCc* × *AaBbCc* → *AAbbCC*
C) *AaBbCc* × *AaBbCc* → *AaBbCc*
D) *aaBbCC* × *AABbcc* → *AaBbCc*

Answer: A) 1
B) 1/32
C) 1/8
D) 1/2

Chapter 15   The Chromosomal Basis of Inheritance

1) There is good evidence for linkage when
   A) two genes occur together in the same gamete.
   B) a gene is associated with a specific phenotype.
   C) two genes work together to control a specific characteristic.
   D) genes do not segregate independently during meiosis.
   E) two characteristics are caused by a single gene.

Answer: D
Skill: Comprehension

2) People who have red hair usually have freckles. This can best be explained by
   A) linkage.
   B) reciprocal translocation.
   C) independent assortment.
   D) sex-influenced inheritance.
   E) nondisjunction.

Answer: A
Skill: Comprehension

3) Vermilion eyes is a sex-linked recessive characteristic in fruit flies. If a female having vermilion eyes is crossed with a wild-type male, what percentage of the F_1 males will have vermilion eyes?
   A) 0%
   B) 25%
   C) 50%
   D) 75%
   E) 100%

Answer: E
Skill: Application

4) The following is a map of four genes on a chromosome:

A   W   E   G
| 5 | 3 | 12 |

Between which two genes would you expect the highest frequency of recombination?
   A) *A* and *W*
   B) *W* and *E*
   C) *E* and *G*
   D) *A* and *E*
   E) *A* and *G*

Answer: E
Skill: Comprehension

5) A 0.1% frequency of recombination is observed
   A) only in sex chromosomes.
   B) on genetic maps of viral chromosomes.
   C) on unlinked chromosomes.
   D) for any two genes on different chromosomes.
   E) in genes located very close to one another on the same chromosome.

Answer: E
Skill: Knowledge

6) A cassette tape or compact disk contains a series of distinct pieces of electrical or physical information that are interpreted by a tape player or compact disk player, resulting in music or video. If the information that produces a song is analogous to a gene, and the tape or compact disk is analogous to a chromosome, then the linkage of genes is analogous to

A) the length of the songs on the tape or disk.

B) the sequence of songs on the tape or disk.

C) the volume of the music on the tape or disk.

D) the tempo of the music on the tape or disk.

E) the informational content of the songs on the tape or disk.

Answer: B
Skill: Comprehension

7) New combinations of linked genes are due to

A) nondisjunction.

B) crossing over.

C) independent assortment.

D) mixing of sperm and egg.

E) environmental changes such as temperature extremes.

Answer: B
Skill: Comprehension

8) A 50% frequency of recombination means that

A) the two genes are located on different chromosomes.

B) the offspring have combinations of traits that match one of the two parents.

C) the genes are located on sex chromosomes.

D) abnormal meiosis occurred.

E) independent assortment is hindered.

Answer: A
Skill: Knowledge

The following questions refer to the data below and to Figures 15.1 and 15.2.

CROSS I. Purebred lines of wild-type fruit flies (gray body and normal wings) are mated to flies with black bodies and vestigial wings.

Figure 15.1

F₁ offspring all have a normal phenotype.

Figure 15.2

CROSS II. F₁ flies are crossed with flies recessive for both traits (a testcross).

Resulting Offspring	Normal	Percent
Gray body; normal wings	575	25.1
Black body; vestigial wings	571	24.9
Black body; normal wings	577	25.2
Gray body; vestigial wings	568	24.8

KEY:
A. CROSS I results give evidence supporting the statement.
B. CROSS I results give evidence against the statement.
C. CROSS II results give evidence supporting the statement.
D. CROSS II results give evidence against the statement.
E. Neither CROSS I nor CROSS II results support the statement.

9) Vestigial wings is a recessive trait.

Answer: A
Skill: Application

10) The genes for body color and wing shape are linked.

Answer: C
Skill: Application

11) An F_1 cross should produce flies that will fall into a Mendelian 9:3:3:1 ratio.

Answer: C
Skill: Application

12) There are 25 centimorgans (map units) between the genes for body color and wing shape.

Answer: D
Skill: Application

13) In the following list, which term is *least* related to the others?

A) genetic recombination

B) karyotype

C) parental types

D) linkage map

E) recombinants

Answer: B
Skill: Comprehension

14) The reason that linked genes are inherited together is

A) that they are located on the same chromosome.

B) that the number of genes in a cell is greater than the number of chromosomes.

C) that chromosomes are unbreakable.

D) tha alleles are paired.

E) due to gene alignment during metaphase I.

Answer: A
Skill: Knowledge

15) Genetic recombinants are produced by

A) X inactivation.

B) methylation of cytosine.

C) crossing over and independent assortment.

D) nondisjunction.

E) deletions and duplications during meiosis.

Answer: C
Skill: Knowledge

16) A linkage map

A) always has a total of 100 map units.

B) can pinpoint actual loci of genes.

C) is a genetic map based on recombination frequencies.

D) requires preparation of karyotypes.

E) reflects the frequency of crossing over between X and Y sex chromosomes.

Answer: C
Skill: Knowledge

17) The frequency of crossing over between any two linked genes is

A) higher if they are recessive.

B) difficult to predict.

C) determined by their relative dominance.

D) the same as if they were not linked.

E) proportional to the distance between them.

Answer: E
Skill: Knowledge

18) When does crossing over occur during meiosis?

A) metaphase I

B) anaphase II

C) prophase I

D) prophase II

E) anaphase I

Answer: C
Skill: Knowledge

19) How do geneticists map a chromosome's genetic locus?

A) by analysis of recombination data

B) by analysis of genomic imprinting

C) by studying the frequency rate of nondisjunction

D) by analyzing pictures of chromosomes

E) by using specialized staining techniques

Answer: A
Skill: Knowledge

20) In birds, sex is determined by a ZW chromosome scheme. Males are ZZ and females are ZW. A lethal recessive allele that causes death of the embryo occurs on the Z chromosome in pigeons. What would be the sex ratio in the offspring of a cross between a male heterozygous for the lethal allele and a normal female?

A) 2:1 male to female

B) 1:2 male to female

C) 1:1 male to female

D) 4:3 male to female

E) 3:1 male to female

Answer: A
Skill: Application

21) Barring in chickens is due to a sex-linked dominant gene (*B*). The sex of chicks at hatching is difficult to determine, but barred chicks can be distinguished from nonbarred at that time. To use this trait so that at hatching all chicks of one sex are barred, what cross would you make?

A) barred males × barred females

B) barred males × nonbarred females

C) nonbarred males × barred females

D) nonbarred males × nonbarred females

Answer: B
Skill: Comprehension

22) Cytological maps

A) are used to prepare karyotypes.

B) locate genes using microscopically visible chromosomal features.

C) can be used for determining sex-linked human disorders.

D) if accurate should show the same spacing between genes as linkage maps.

E) are based on recombination frequencies.

Answer: B
Skill: Knowledge

Use the list of chromosomal systems below to answer the following questions.

A. *haploid–diploid*
B. *X–O*
C. *X–X*
D. *X–Y*
E. *Z–W*

23) What is the chromosomal system for determining sex in mammals?

Answer: D
Skill: Knowledge

24) What is the chromosomal system for sex determination in grasshoppers and certain other insects?

Answer: B
Skill: Knowledge

25) What is the chromosomal system for sex determination in birds?

Answer: E
Skill: Knowledge

26) In most species of ants and bees, the chromosomal system of sex determination is _____.

Answer: A
Skill: Knowledge

Refer to Figure 15.3 to answer the following questions.

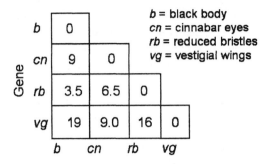

b = black body
cn = cinnabar eyes
rb = reduced bristles
vg = vestigial wings

The numbers in the boxes are the recombination frequencies in between the genes (in percent).

Figure 15.3

27) In a series of mapping experiments, the recombination frequencies for four different linked genes of *Drosophila* were determined as shown above. What is the order of these genes on a chromosome map?

A) *rb–cn–vg–b*
B) *vg–b–rb–cn*
C) *cn–rb–b–vg*
D) *b–rb–cn–vg*
E) *vg–cn–b–rb*

Answer: D
Skill: Application

28) Which of the following two genes are closest on a genetic map of *Drosophila*?

A) *b* and *vg*
B) *vg* and *cn*
C) *rb* and *cn*
D) *cn* and *b*
E) *b* and *rb*

Answer: E
Skill: Application

29) A recessive allele on the X chromosome is responsible for red-green color blindness in humans. A woman with normal vision whose father is color-blind marries a color-blind male. What is the probability that this couple's son will be color-blind?

A) 0

B) 1/4

C) 1/2

D) 3/4

E) 1

Answer: C
Skill: Application

30) A man who carries an X-linked allele will pass it on to

A) all of his daughters.

B) half of his daughters.

C) all of his sons.

D) half of his sons.

E) all of his children.

Answer: A
Skill: Comprehension

31) The statement "The X and Y chromosomes determine sex" is inaccurate and misleading. Which of the following statements is *most* accurate?

A) Genes on the X and Y chromosomes determine sex.

B) Genes on the X chromosome that are not present on the Y determine sex.

C) Genes on the Y chromosome that are not present on the X determine sex.

D) A variety of genes on other chromosomes play various roles in determining sex, and the activity of those genes is controlled by a small number of genes on the X and/or Y chromosomes.

E) A variety of genes on the X and/or Y chromosomes play various roles in determining sex, and the activity of those genes is controlled by a small number of genes on other chromosomes.

Answer: D
Skill: Comprehension

Refer to the following information to answer the questions below. An achondroplastic dwarf man with normal vision marries a color-blind woman of normal height. The man's father was six feet tall, and both the woman's parents were of average height. Achondroplastic dwarfism is autosomal dominant, and red-green color blindness is X-linked recessive.

32) How many of their female children might be expected to be color-blind dwarfs?

A) all

B) none

C) half

D) one out of four

E) three out of four

Answer: B
Skill: Application

33) How many of their male children would be color-blind and normal height?

A) all

B) none

C) half

D) one out of four

E) three out of four

Answer: C
Skill: Application

34) They have a daughter who is a dwarf with normal color vision. What is the probability that she is heterozygous for both genes?

A) 0

B) 0.25

C) 0.50

D) 0.75

E) 1.00

Answer: E
Skill: Application

35) If inheritance of a human trait is sex-linked (on the X chromosome) and recessive, any of the following could result except that

A) expression of the trait might "skip" a generation.

B) the trait could be more common in females than males.

C) all females must be homozygous to express the trait.

D) the gene for the trait might mutate to a dominant allele.

E) females could be a mosaic of two cell types.

Answer: B
Skill: Comprehension

36) To what does independent assortment refer?

A) the separation of alleles in anaphase I

B) the random arrangement of chromosomal tetrads at metaphase I

C) the separation of chromatids at anaphase II

D) the random arrangement of gene loci on a chromosome

E) the fact that any pair of chromatids in a tetrad can cross over

Answer: A
Skill: Comprehension

37) A Barr body is normally found in the nucleus of which kind of human cell?

A) unfertilized egg cells only

B) sperm cells only

C) somatic cells of a female only

D) somatic cells of a male only

E) both male and female somatic cells

Answer: C
Skill: Knowledge

38) In cats, black color is caused by an X-linked allele; the other allele at this locus causes orange color. The heterozygote is tortoiseshell. What kinds of offspring would you expect from the cross of a black female and an orange male?

A) tortoiseshell female; tortoiseshell male

B) black female; orange male

C) orange female; orange male

D) tortoiseshell female; black male

E) orange female; black male

Answer: D
Skill: Application

39) If a human interphase nucleus of a person contained three Barr bodies, it can be assumed that the person

    A) is a hemophiliac.

    B) is a male.

    C) has 4 X chromosomes.

    D) has Turner syndrome.

    E) has Down syndrome.

Answer: C
Skill: Comprehension

40) Which of these syndromes afflicts males only?

    A) Turner syndrome

    B) Down syndrome

    C) Duchenne muscular dystrophy

    D) Cry of the Cat syndrome

    E) Prader-Willi syndrome

Answer: C
Skill: Knowledge

41) Male calico cats are the result of

    A) sex-linked inheritance.

    B) nondisjunction, where the male calico presumably has two X chromosomes.

    C) incomplete dominance of multiple alleles.

    D) recessive alleles retaining their fundamental natures even when expressed.

    E) a reciprocal translocation.

Answer: B
Skill: Application

42) In the following list, which term is *least* related to the others?

    A) Duchenne muscular dystrophy

    B) wild type

    C) sex-linked genes

    D) color blindness

    E) hemophilia

Answer: B
Skill: Comprehension

43) Red-green color blindness is a sex-linked recessive trait in humans. Two people with normal color vision have a color-blind son. What are the genotypes of the parents?

    A) *XcXc* and *XcY*

    B) *XcXc* and *XCY*

    C) *XCXC* and *XcY*

    D) *XCXC* and *XCY*

    E) *XCXc* and *XCY*

Answer: E
Skill: Application

44) If nondisjunction occurs in meiosis II during gametogenesis, what will be the result at the completion of meiosis?

    A) All the gametes will be diploid.

    B) Two gametes will be $n + 1$ and two will be $n - 1$.

    C) One gamete will be $n + 1$, one will be $n - 1$, and two will be n.

    D) There will be three extra gametes.

    E) Two of the four gametes will be haploid and two will be diploid.

Answer: C
Skill: Comprehension

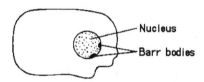

Figure 15.4

45) Figure 15.4 represents the stained nucleus from a cheek epithelial cell of an individual whose genotype would probably be

    A) XX.

    B) XY.

    C) XYY.

    D) XXX.

    E) XXY.

Answer: D
Skill: Comprehension

46) If a pair of homologous chromosomes fails to separate during anaphase of meiosis I, what will be the chromosome number (n) of the four resulting gametes?

A) $n + 1; n + 1; n - 1; n - 1$

B) $n + 1; n - 1; n; n$

C) $n + 1; n - 1; n - 1; n - 1$

D) $n + 1; n + 1; n; n$

E) $n - 1; n - 1; n; n$

Answer: A
Skill: Comprehension

47) Most calico cats are females because

A) a male inherits only one of the two X-linked genes controlling hair color.

B) the males die during embryonic development.

C) the Y chromosome has a gene blocking orange coloration.

D) only females have Barr bodies.

E) multiple crossovers on the Y chromosome prevent orange pigment production.

Answer: A
Skill: Comprehension

48) A cell that has $2n + 1$ chromosomes

A) is trisomic.

B) is monosomic.

C) is aneuploid.

D) is polyploid.

E) is both A and C.

Answer: E
Skill: Knowledge

49) If a chromosome lacks certain genes, what has most likely occurred?

A) disjunction

B) an inversion

C) a deletion

D) a translocation

E) a nonduplication

Answer: C
Skill: Knowledge

50) One possible result of chromosomal breakage is for a fragment to join a nonhomologous chromosome. This is called

A) a deletion.

B) a disjunction.

C) an inversion.

D) a translocation.

E) a duplication.

Answer: D
Skill: Knowledge

51) In the following list, which term is *least* related to the others?

A) trisomic

B) monosomic

C) aneuploid

D) triploid

E) nondisjunction

Answer: D
Skill: Comprehension

52) The following is a list of chromosomal alterations. Which one of these would automatically cause two of the others?

A) deletion

B) duplication

C) inversion

D) reciprocal translocation

E) nonreciprocal translocation

Answer: E
Skill: Comprehension

53) In the following list, which term is *least* related to the others?

A) nondisjunction

B) duplication

C) inversion

D) translocation

E) deletion

Answer: A
Skill: Comprehension

54) One possible result of chromosome breakage can be that a fragment reattaches to the original chromosome in a reverse orientation. This is called

A) disjunction.

B) translocation.

C) deletion.

D) inversion.

E) aneuploidy.

Answer: D
Skill: Knowledge

55) Which of the following statements is *true* regarding genomic imprinting?

A) It explains cases where the gender of the parent from whom an allele is inherited affects the expression of that allele.

B) It is greatest in females because of the larger maternal contribution of cytoplasm.

C) It may explain the transmission of Duchenne muscular dystrophy.

D) It explains sex-linked inheritance in which the sex of the parent carrying the mutant allele determines whether male or female offspring will be affected.

E) It is found in X inactivation in human females during early embryonic development.

Answer: A
Skill: Knowledge

56) A human individual is phenotypically female but her interphase somatic nuclei do not show the presence of sex chromatin (Barr bodies). Which of the following statements concerning her is probably *true*?

A) She has Klinefelter syndrome.

B) She has an extra X chromosome.

C) She has Turner syndrome.

D) She has the normal number of sex chromosomes.

E) She has two Y chromosomes.

Answer: C
Skill: Comprehension

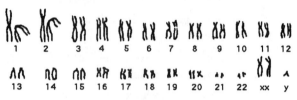

Figure 15.5

57) The karyotype shown in Figure 15.5 is associated with which of the following genetic disorders?

A) Turner syndrome

B) Down syndrome

C) Klinefelter syndrome

D) hemophilia

E) male–pattern baldness

Answer: C
Skill: Knowledge

58) The finding that defective genes behave differently in offspring depending on whether they belong to the maternal or paternal chromosome is implicated in which of the following?

A) Prader-Willi syndrome

B) fragile X syndrome

C) Angelman syndrome

D) A and C

E) A, B, and C

Answer: E
Skill: Knowledge

59) Fragile X syndrome is more common in males than in females. One explanation for this is

A) genomic imprinting by the mother.

B) sex–linked inheritance.

C) the age of the mother.

D) Only A and C are correct.

E) A, B, and C are correct.

Answer: A
Skill: Knowledge

60) In humans, male–pattern baldness is controlled by a gene that occurs in two allelic forms. Allele *Hn* determines nonbaldness and allele *Hb* determines pattern baldness. The interaction of these two alleles in the heterozygote condition is of special interest because in the presence of male hormone, allele *Hn* is dominant over *Hb*. If a man and woman both with genotype *HnHb* have many children, approximately what percentage of their male children would be expected eventually to be bald?

A) 0%

B) 25%

C) 33%

D) 50%

E) 75%

Answer: E
Skill: Application

61) In the following list, which term is *least* related to the others?

A) fragile X syndrome

B) X inactivation

C) Mary Lyon

D) tortoiseshell coat pattern in cats

E) Barr body

Answer: A
Skill: Comprehension

62) What do all human males inherit from their mother?

A) mitochondrial DNA

B) an X chromosome

C) the gene for normal gonad development (SRY)

D) A and B

E) A, B, and C

Answer: D
Skill: Knowledge

Media Activity Questions

1) You conduct a dihybrid cross and then testcross the F_1 generation. A _____ ratio would make you suspect that the genes are linked.

A) 3:1

B) 1:2:1

C) 1:1:1:1

D) 7:7:1:1

E) 9:3:3:1

Answer: D
Topic: Web/CD Activity 15A

2) Linked genes are an exception to

A) Boyle's law.

B) Hopkins's bioclimatic law.

C) Mendel's law of independent assortment.

D) Cope's law.

E) Mendel's law of segregation.

Answer: C
Topic: Web/CD Activity 15A

3) A color–blind woman mates with a man who is not color–blind. All of the sons and none of the daughters are color–blind. What is the best explanation of this result?

A) The gene for color vision is incompletely dominant to the gene for sex determination.

B) The gene for color vision is completely dominant to the gene for sex determination.

C) The gene for color vision is codominant with the gene for sex determination.

D) The gene for color vision is linked to the X chromosome.

E) The gene for color vision is linked to the Y chromosome.

Answer: D
Topic: Web/CD Activity 15B

4) The sex chromosome complements of both normal human and normal MendAlien males is

A) XO.

B) XX.

C) XY.

D) YY.

E) YO.

Answer: C
Topic: Web/CD Activity 15B

5) A tetraploid individual has _____ sets of chromosomes.

A) 1   B) 2   C) 3   D) 4   E) 5

Answer: D
Topic: Web/CD Activity 15C

Self-Quiz Questions

Answers to these questions also appear in the textbook.

Note: The following Self-Quiz questions are not in multiple choice format.

1) A man with hemophilia (a recessive, sex-linked condition) has a daughter of normal phenotype. She marries a man who is normal for the trait. What is the probability that a daughter of this mating will be a hemophiliac? That a son will be a hemophiliac? If the couple has four sons, what is the probability that all four will be born with hemophilia?

   Answer: 0; 1/2, 1/16

2) Pseudohypertrophic muscular dystrophy is a disorder that causes gradual deterioration of the muscles. It is seen only in boys born to apparently normal parents and usually results in death in the early teens. Is this disorder caused by a dominant or a recessive allele? Is its inheritance sex-linked or autosomal? How do you know? Explain why this disorder is seen only in boys and never in girls.

   Answer: Recessive. If the disorder were dominant, it would affect at least one parent of a child born with the disorder. For a girl to have the disorder, she would have to inherit recessive alleles from *both* parents. This would be very rare, especially since males with the allele die in their early teens.

3) Red-green color blindness is caused by a sex-linked recessive allele. A color-blind man marries a woman with normal vision whose father was color-blind. What is the probability that they will have a color-blind daughter? What is the probability that their first son will be color-blind? (*Note:* The two questions are worded a bit differently.)

   Answer: 1/4 for each daughter (1/2 chance that child will be female × 1/2 chance of a homozygous recessive genotype); 1/2 for first son.

4) A wild-type fruit fly (heterozygous for gray body color and normal wings) is mated with a black fly with vestigial wings. The offspring have the following phenotypic distribution: wild type, 778; black-vestigial, 785; black-normal, 158; gray-vestigial, 162. What is the recombination frequency between these genes for body color and wing type?

   Answer: 17%

5) What pattern of inheritance would lead a geneticist to suspect that an inherited disorder of cell metabolism is due to a defective mitochondrial gene?

   Answer: The disorder would always be inherited from the mother.

6) An aneuploid person is obviously female, but her cells have two Barr bodies. What is the probable complement of sex chromosomes in this individual?

   Answer: *XXX*

7) Determine the sequence of genes along a chromosome based on the following recombination frequencies:
   A–B, 8 map units; *A–C*, 28 map units; *A–D*, 25 map units; *B–C*, 20 map units; *B–D*, 33 map units.

   Answer: *D–A–B–C*

8) About 5% of individuals with Down syndrome are the result of chromosomal translocation in which one copy of chromosome 21 becomes attached to chromosome 14. How does this translocation lead to Down syndrome?

Answer: In meiosis, the combined 14–21 chromosome will behave as one chromosome. If a gamete receives the combined 14–21 chromosome and a normal copy of chromosome 21, trisomy 21 will result when this gamete combines with a normal gamete.

9) More common than completely polyploid animals are mosaic polyploids, animals that are diploid except for patches of polyploid cells. How might a mosaic tetraploid—an animal with some cells containing four sets of chromosomes—arise from an error in *mitosis*?

Answer: At some point during development, one of the embryo's cells may have failed to carry out mitosis after duplicating its chromosomes. Subsequent normal cell cycles would produce genetic copies of this tetraploid cell.

10) Assume that genes *A* and *B* are linked and are 50 map units apart. An animal heterozygous at both loci is crossed with one that is homozygous recessive at both loci. What percentage of the offspring will show phenotypes resulting from crossovers? If you did not know that genes *A* and *B* were linked, how would you interpret the results of this cross?

Answer: Fifty percent of the offspring would show phenotypes that resulted from crossovers. These results would be the same as those from a cross where *A* and *B* were not linked. Further crosses involving other genes on the same chromosome would reveal the linkage and map distances.

Chapter 16   The Molecular Basis of Inheritance

1) For a couple of decades, biologists knew the nucleus contained DNA and proteins. The prevailing opinion was that proteins were the genetic material and not DNA. The reason for this belief was that proteins were more complex than DNA. This is because
   A) proteins have a greater variety of three–dimensional forms than does DNA.
   B) proteins have two different levels of structural organization; DNA has four.
   C) proteins are made of 20 amino acids and DNA is made of four nucleotides.
   D) A and C only are correct.
   E) A, B, and C are correct.

   Answer: D
   Skill: Comprehension

2) Which of the following is *least* related to the others in the list?
   A) transformation
   B) phage
   C) DNA
   D) Griffith
   E) Avery

   Answer: B
   Skill: Comprehension

3) What does transformation involve in bacteria?
   A) the creation of a strand of DNA from an RNA molecule
   B) the creation of a strand of RNA from a DNA molecule
   C) the infection of cells by a phage DNA molecule
   D) the type of semiconservative replication shown by DNA
   E) assimilation of external DNA into a cell

   Answer: E
   Skill: Knowledge

4) Tobacco mosaic virus has RNA rather than DNA as its genetic material. In a hypothetical situation where RNA from a tobacco mosaic virus is mixed with proteins from a related DNA virus, the result could be a hybrid virus. If that virus were to infect a cell and reproduce, what would the resulting "offspring" viruses be like?
   A) tobacco mosaic virus
   B) the related DNA virus
   C) a hybrid: tobacco mosaic virus RNA and protein from the DNA virus
   D) a hybrid: tobacco mosaic virus protein and nucleic acid from the DNA virus
   E) a virus with a double helix made up of one strand of DNA complementary to a strand of RNA surrounded by viral protein

   Answer: A
   Skill: Application

5) Which of the following names is *least* related to the others?
   A) Griffith
   B) Avery
   C) Meselson
   D) Watson
   E) Hershey

   Answer: A
   Skill: Knowledge

6) The following scientists made significant contributions to our understanding of the structure and functions of DNA:
    I.   Avery, McCarty, MacLeod
    II.   Chargaff
    III. Hershey and Chase
    IV. Meselson and Stahl
    V.   Watson and Crick
Place the scientists' names in the correct chronological order, starting with the oldest contribution.
    A) V, IV, II, I, III
    B) II, I, III, V, IV
    C) I, II, III, V, IV
    D) I, II, V, IV, III
    E) II, III, IV, V, I

Answer: C
Skill: Knowledge

7) All of the following elements are present in DNA *except*
    A) oxygen.
    B) nitrogen.
    C) carbon.
    D) sulfur.
    E) phosphorus.

Answer: D
Skill: Knowledge

8) In trying to determine whether DNA or protein was the genetic material, Al Hershey and Martha Chase made use of which of the following facts?
    A) DNA does not contain sulfur, whereas protein does.
    B) DNA contains phosphorus, but protein does not.
    C) DNA contains greater amounts of nitrogen than does protein.
    D) A and B only are correct.
    E) A, B, and C are correct.

Answer: D
Skill: Knowledge

9) If radioactive sulfur (^{35}S) is used in a culture medium of bacteria that contains phage viruses, it will later appear in the
    A) viral DNA.
    B) bacterial RNA.
    C) viral coats.
    D) viral RNA.
    E) bacterial cell wall.

Answer: C
Skill: Knowledge

10) For a science fair project, two students decided to repeat the Hershey and Chase experiment, with modifications. They decide that labeling the phosphates of the DNA wasn't good enough. Each nucleotide has only one phosphate, whereas each has two to five nitrogens. Thus, labeling the nitrogens would provide a stronger label than labeling the phosphates. This experiment will not work because
    A) there is no radioactive isotope of nitrogen.
    B) radioactive nitrogen has a half–life of 100,000 years and the material would be too dangerous for too long.
    C) Meselson and Stahl already did this experiment.
    D) although there are more nitrogens in a nucleotide, labeled phosphates actually have 16 extra neutrons, so they are more radioactive.
    E) amino acids (and thus proteins) also have nitrogen atoms, thus the radioactivity would not distinguish between DNA and proteins.

Answer: E
Skill: Comprehension

Refer to the following information to answer the following questions. For each of the important discoveries that led to our present knowledge of the nature of genes described below, select the investigator(s) associated with each.

A. *Griffith*
B. *Hershey and Chase*
C. *Avery, MacLeod, and McCarty*
D. *Chargaff*
E. *Meselson and Stahl*

11) Chemicals from heat–killed S cells were purified. The chemicals were tested for the ability to transform live R cells. The transforming agent was found to be DNA.

Answer: C
Skill: Knowledge

12) The DNA of a phage was injected into the bacterial host, but the protein coat stayed outside. The viral DNA directed the host to replicate new phage viruses.

Answer: B
Skill: Knowledge

13) In any DNA sample, the amount of adenine equals the amount of thymine and the amount of guanine equals the amount of cytosine.

Answer: D
Skill: Knowledge

14) What happens when T2 phages are grown in the presence of radioactive phosphorus?
A) Their DNA becomes radioactive.
B) Their proteins become radioactive.
C) Their DNA is found to be of medium density in a centrifuge tube.
D) They are no longer able to transform bacterial cells.
E) They transfer their radioactivity to *E. coli* chromosomes during infection.

Answer: A
Skill: Knowledge

15) When T2 phage viruses that infect bacteria make more viruses in the presence of radioactive sulfur, which of the following results?
A) The viral DNA is tagged by radioactivity.
B) The viral proteins are tagged by radioactivity.
C) The viral DNA is found to be of medium density in a centrifuge tube.
D) They transfer their radioactivity to *E. coli* DNA.
E) Both the viral DNA and the viral proteins are tagged by radioactivity.

Answer: B
Skill: Comprehension

16) Cytosine makes up 38% of the nucleotides in a sample of DNA from an organism. What percent of the nucleotides in this sample will be thymine?
A) 12
B) 24
C) 31
D) 38
E) It cannot be determined from the information provided.

Answer: A
Skill: Application

17) All of the following were determined directly from X-ray diffraction photographs of crystallized DNA *except*
A) the diameter of the double helix.
B) the helical shape of DNA.
C) the sequence of nucleotides.
D) the linear distance required for one full turn of the double helix.
E) the width of the helix.

Answer: C
Skill: Knowledge

18) What kind of chemical bonds are found between paired bases of the DNA double helix?

A) hydrogen

B) ionic

C) covalent

D) sulfhydryl

E) phosphate

Answer: A
Skill: Knowledge

19) All of the following statements apply to the Watson and Crick model of DNA *except:*

A) The two strands of the DNA form a double helix.

B) The distance between the strands of the helix is uniform.

C) The framework of the helix consists of sugar-phosphate units of the nucleotides.

D) The two strands of the helix are held together by covalent bonds.

E) The purines are attracted to pyrimidines.

Answer: D
Skill: Knowledge

20) It became apparent to Watson and Crick after completion of their model that the DNA molecule could carry a vast amount of hereditary information in its

A) sequence of bases.

B) phosphate–sugar backbones.

C) complementary pairing of bases.

D) side groups of nitrogenous bases.

E) different five–carbon sugars.

Answer: A
Skill: Knowledge

21) In an analysis of the nucleotide composition of DNA, which of the following is *true*?

A) A = C

B) A = G and C = T

C) A + C = G + T

D) A + T = G + C

E) Both B and C are true.

Answer: C
Skill: Application

22) Suppose one were provided with an actively dividing culture of *E. coli* bacteria to which radioactive thymine had been added. What would happen if a cell replicated once in the presence of this radioactive base?

A) One of the daughter cells, but not the other, would have radioactive DNA.

B) Neither of the two daughter cells would be radioactive.

C) All four bases of the DNA would be radioactive.

D) Radioactive thymine would pair with nonradioactive guanine.

E) DNA in both daughter cells would be radioactive.

Answer: E
Skill: Comprehension

Use Figure 16.1 to answer the following questions.

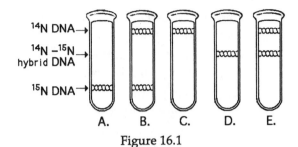

Figure 16.1

23) In the late 1950s Meselson and Stahl grew bacteria in a medium containing "heavy" nitrogen (^{15}N) and then transferred them to a medium containing ^{14}N. Which of the results in Figure 16.1 would be expected after one DNA replication in the presence of ^{14}N?

Answer: D
Skill: Comprehension

24) A space probe returns with a culture of a microorganism found on a distant planet. Analysis shows that it is a carbon–based life form that has DNA. You grow the cells in ^{15}N medium for several generations and then transfer it to ^{14}N medium. Which pattern in Figure 16.1 would you expect if the DNA was replicated in a conservative manner?

Answer: B
Skill: Comprehension

25) Which enzymes catalyze the elongation of a DNA strand in the 5' → 3' direction?
   A) primase
   B) DNA ligase
   C) DNA polymerases
   D) topoisomerase
   E) helicase

Answer: C
Skill: Knowledge

26) What is the function of DNA polymerase?
   A) to unwind the DNA helix during replication
   B) to seal together the broken ends of DNA strands
   C) to add nucleotides to the end of a growing DNA strand
   D) to degrade damaged DNA molecules
   E) to rejoin the two DNA strands (one new and one old) after replication

Answer: C
Skill: Knowledge

27) Which of the following is *least* related to the others in the list?
   A) Okazaki fragments
   B) replication fork
   C) telomerase
   D) DNA polymerases
   E) semiconservative

Answer: C
Skill: Comprehension

Refer to the following list of enzymes to answer the following questions. The answers may be used once, more than once, or not at all.

   A. *helicase*
   B. *nuclease*
   C. *ligase*
   D. *DNA polymerase*
   E. *primase*

28) catalyzes synthesis of a new strand of DNA

Answer: D
Skill: Knowledge

29) enhances separation of DNA strands during replication

Answer: A
Skill: Knowledge

30) covalently connects segments of DNA

Answer: C
Skill: Knowledge

31) synthesizes short segments of RNA

Answer: E
Skill: Knowledge

32) a DNA-cutting enzyme in the repair of damage to DNA

Answer: B
Skill: Knowledge

33) The difference between ATP and nucleoside triphosphate is that
   A) NTP has the sugar deoxyribose; ATP has the sugar ribose.
   B) NTP has 2 phosphate groups while ATP has 3 phosphate groups.
   C) ATP contains 3 high-energy bonds while NTP has 2.
   D) ATP is only found in human cells, while the other is negatively charged.
   E) triphosphate monomers are active in NTP but not ATP.

Answer: A
Skill: Knowledge

34) The strands that make up DNA are antiparallel. This means that
   A) the twisting nature of DNA creates nonparallel strands.
   B) the 5' to 3' direction of one strand runs counter to the 5' to 3' direction of the other strand.
   C) base pairings create unequal spacing between the two DNA strands.
   D) one strand is positively charged while the other is negatively charged.
   E) the chromosomes are circular in shape.

Answer: B
Skill: Knowledge

35) In DNA, the designations 3' and 5' refer to the
   A) carbon atoms of deoxyribose to which phosphate groups may bond.
   B) carbon or nitrogen atoms on the rings of purine or pyrimidine bases.
   C) cross-linking of the third and fifth carbon atoms of deoxyribose.
   D) bonding between purines and deoxyribose and between pyrimidines and deoxyribose.
   E) bonds that form between adenine and thymine and between guanine and cytosine.

Answer: A
Skill: Knowledge

36) The two strands of a DNA molecule run in opposite directions. The 3' and 5' ends of one strand are opposite the 5' and 3' ends of the complementary strand. This is analogous to
   A) a photograph and a photographic negative.
   B) one side of a divided highway.
   C) a baseball and a bat.
   D) an "up" escalator next to a "down" escalator.
   E) both A and C.

Answer: D
Skill: Comprehension

37) A new DNA strand only elongates in the 5' to 3' direction because

   A) DNA polymerase begins adding nucleotides at the 5' end.

   B) Okazaki fragments prevent elongation in the 3' to 5' direction.

   C) the polarity of the DNA molecule prevents addition of nucleotides at the 3' end.

   D) replication must progress toward the replication fork.

   E) DNA polymerase adds nucleotides only to the free 3' end.

Answer: E
Skill: Knowledge

38) The problem of replicating the lagging strand of DNA—that is, adding bases in the 3' → 5' direction—requires which of the following?

   A) DNA ligase

   B) RNA primers

   C) Okazaki fragments

   D) A and B only

   E) A, B, and C

Answer: E
Skill: Knowledge

39) Which of the following is *least* related to the others in the list?

   A) Okazaki fragment

   B) primer

   C) telomere

   D) leading strand

   E) lagging strand

Answer: C
Skill: Comprehension

40) What is the primer that is required to initiate the synthesis of a new DNA strand?

   A) RNA

   B) DNA

   C) protein

   D) ligase

   E) primase

Answer: A
Skill: Knowledge

41) What is the function of DNA ligase?

   A) covalent bonding of the 3' end of a new DNA fragment to the 5' end of a growing chain

   B) elongation of new DNA at a replication fork by addition of nucleotides to the existing chain

   C) the addition of methyl groups to bases of DNA

   D) unwinding of the double helix

   E) Both B and C are correct.

Answer: A
Skill: Application

42) What is the role of DNA ligase in the elongation of the lagging strand during DNA replication?

   A) synthesize RNA nucleotides to make a primer

   B) catalyze the lengthening of telomeres

   C) join Okazaki fragments together

   D) unwind the parental double helix

   E) stabilize the unwound parental DNA

Answer: C
Skill: Knowledge

43) All of the following are functions of DNA polymerase in DNA replication *except*

A) covalently adding nucleotides to the new strands.

B) proofreading each added nucleotide for correct base pairing.

C) replacing RNA primers with DNA.

D) initiating a polynucleotide strand.

Answer: D
Skill: Knowledge

44) Which of the following is *least* related to the others in the list?

A) nuclease

B) ligase

C) primase

D) helicase

E) DNA polymerase

Answer: A
Skill: Comprehension

45) Which of the following help to hold the DNA strands apart while they are being replicated?

A) helicase

B) ligase

C) DNA polymerase

D) single-stranded binding proteins

E) exonuclease

Answer: D
Skill: Knowledge

46) Which of these mechanisms ensures that DNA replication is accurate?

A) proofreading

B) mismatch repair

C) excision repair

D) complementary base pairing

E) all of the above

Answer: E
Skill: Knowledge

47) In making a movie, sometimes an editor will cut out one piece of film and insert another. This is analogous to which of the following?

A) mismatch repair

B) excision repair

C) transformation repair

D) recombinational repair

E) telomerase repair

Answer: B
Skill: Comprehension

48) In the following list of DNA properties, which relates to the disorder xeroderma pigmentosum?

A) replication

B) information storage

C) exchange with other organisms

D) repair of thymine dimers

E) mutation

Answer: D
Skill: Comprehension

49) Which of the following is analogous to telomeres?

A) the pull tab on a soft-drink can

B) the two ends of a shoe lace

C) the center spindle that a compact disk fits around while in the case

D) the mechanism of a zipper that allows the separated parts to be joined

E) the correct letters used to replace errors in a document after they have been deleted in a word processor

Answer: B
Skill: Application

50) With each replication of the DNA molecule, the DNA molecule becomes shorter.

A) This is best explained by the fact that DNA polymerase can only add nucleotides to a 3' end.

B) This problem is resolved by telomerase, which extends the 3' end of the DNA.

C) This is not a problem because the telomere is a nonessential repeating unit.

D) This is true only if the organism has been exposed to excessive amounts of ultraviolet rays of sunlight.

E) This is due to the fact that thymine dimers cause DNA to buckle and interfere with DNA replication.

Answer: B
Skill: Comprehension

51) A eukaryotic cell lacking telomerase would

A) have a high probability of becoming cancerous.

B) produce Okazaki fragments.

C) be unable to replicate.

D) undergo a reduction in chromosome length.

E) be highly sensitive to sunlight.

Answer: D
Skill: Comprehension

Media Activity Questions

1) One type of virus that infects bacteria is called a(n)

   A) phage.

   B) mage.

   C) rhinovirus.

   D) filovirus.

   E) Ebola.

   Answer: A
   Topic: Web/CD Activity 16A

2) DNA and RNA are polymers of

   A) fatty acids.

   B) nucleotides.

   C) monoglycerides.

   D) amino acids.

   E) monosaccharides.

   Answer: B
   Topic: Web/CD Activity 16B

3) Which of these is always true with regard to a DNA double helix?

   A) The amount of adenine is equal to the amount of uracil, and the amount of guanine is equal to the amount of cytosine.

   B) The amount of adenine is equal to the amount of thymine, and the amount of guanine is equal to the amount of uracil.

   C) The amount of adenine is equal to the amount of guanine, and the amount of thymine is equal to the amount of cytosine.

   D) The amount of adenine is equal to the amount of cytosine, and the amount of guanine is equal to the amount of thymine.

   E) The amount of adenine is equal to the amount of thymine, and the amount of guanine is equal to the amount of cytosine.

   Answer: E
   Topic: Web/CD Activities 16B, 16C

4) What enzyme catalyzes the elongation of a new DNA strand?

   A) helicase

   B) primase

   C) ligase

   D) single-stranded binding protein

   E) DNA polymerase

   Answer: E
   Topic: Web/CD Activities 16D, 16E, 16F

5) What enzyme catalyzes the unwinding of a DNA double helix?

   A) helicase

   B) primase

   C) ligase

   D) single-stranded binding protein

   E) DNA polymerase

   Answer: A
   Topic: Web/CD Activity 16E

Self–Quiz Questions

Answers to these questions also appear in the textbook.

1) In his work with pneumonia–causing bacteria and mice, Griffith found that
   A) the protein coat from pathogenic cells was able to transform nonpathogenic cells.
   B) heat–killed pathogenic cells caused pneumonia.
   C) some chemical from pathogenic cells was transferred to nonpathogenic cells, making them pathogenic.
   D) the polysaccharide coat of bacteria caused pneumonia.
   E) bacteriophages injected DNA into bacteria.

   Answer: C

2) *E. coli* cells grown on ^{15}N medium are transferred to ^{14}N medium and allowed to grow for two generations (two rounds of DNA replication). DNA extracted from these cells is centrifuged. What density distribution of DNA would you expect in this experiment?
   A) one high–density and one low–density band
   B) one intermediate–density band
   C) one high–density and one intermediate–density band
   D) one low–density and one intermediate–density band
   E) one low–density band

   Answer: D

3) A biochemist isolates and purifies various molecules needed for DNA replication. When she adds some DNA, replication occurs, but the DNA molecules formed are defective. Each consists of a normal DNA strand paired with numerous segments of DNA a few hundred nucleotides long. What has she probably left out of the mixture?
   A) DNA polymerase
   B) ligase
   C) nucleotides
   D) Okazaki fragments
   E) primers

   Answer: B

4) What is the basis for the difference in the synthesis of the leading and lagging strands of DNA molecules?
   A) The origins of replication occur only at the 5' end.
   B) Helicases and single–strand binding proteins work at the 5' end.
   C) DNA polymerase can join new nucleotides only to the 3' end of a growing strand.
   D) DNA ligase works only in the 3' → 5' direction.
   E) Polymerase can only work on one strand at a time.

   Answer: C

5) In analyzing the number of different bases in a DNA sample, which result would be consistent with the base–pairing rules?
   A) A = G
   B) A + G = C + T
   C) A + T = G + T
   D) A = C
   E) G = T

   Answer: B

6) The primer that initiates synthesis of a new DNA strand is usually
   A) RNA.
   B) DNA.
   C) an Okazaki fragment.
   D) a structural protein.
   E) a thymine dimer.

   Answer: A

7) A eukaryotic cell lacking telomerase would
   A) be unable to take up DNA from the surrounding solution.
   B) be unable to identify and correct mismatched nucleotides in its daughter DNA strands.
   C) experience a gradual reduction of chromosome length with each replication cycle.
   D) have a greater potential to become cancerous.
   E) incorporate one extraneous nucleotide for each Okazaki fragment added.

   Answer: C

8) The elongation of the *leading* strand during DNA synthesis
   A) progresses away from the replication fork.
   B) occurs in the 3' → 5' direction.
   C) produces Okazaki fragments.
   D) depends on the action of DNA polymerase.
   E) does not require a template strand.

   Answer: D

9) The spontaneous loss of amino groups from adenine results in hypoxanthine, an unnatural base, opposite thymine. What combination of molecules could the cell use to repair such damage?
   A) nuclease, DNA polymerase, DNA ligase
   B) telomerase, primase, DNA polymerase
   C) telomerase, helicase, single-strand binding protein
   D) DNA ligase, replication fork proteins, adenase
   E) nuclease, telomerase, primase

   Answer: A

10) Of the following, the most reasonable inference from the observation that defects in DNA repair enzymes contribute to some forms of cancer is that
   A) cancer is generally inherited.
   B) uncorrected changes in DNA can cause cancer.
   C) cancer cannot occur when DNA repair enzymes work properly.
   D) mutations generally lead to cancer.
   E) cancer is caused by environmental factors that damage DNA repair enzymes.

   Answer: B

Chapter 17   From Gene to Protein

1) Beadle and Tatum proposed the one gene–one enzyme concept. In its original form, this hypothesis could now be restated in which of the following ways?

   A) One DNA molecule contains the information to make one enzyme.

   B) A given sequence of DNA nucleotides contains the information to make one enzyme.

   C) Each gene contains the information to make one enzyme, one lipid, and one carbohydrate.

   D) Each gene is actually an enzyme that catalyzes the production of one protein.

   E) Each polypeptide is the result of the activity of one enzyme.

   Answer: B
   Skill: Application

The following questions refer to the following simple metabolic pathway:

enzyme a   enzyme b

A ———————→ B   ———————→ C

2) According to Beadle and Tatum's one gene–one enzyme hypothesis, how many gene(s) is (are) necessary for this pathway?

   A) 0

   B) 1

   C) 2

   D) 3

   E) It cannot be determined from the pathway.

   Answer: C
   Skill: Comprehension

3) A mutation results in a defective enzyme *a*. Which of the following would be a consequence of that mutation?

   A) an accumulation of A and no production of B and C

   B) an accumulation of A and B and no production of C

   C) an accumulation of B and no production of A and C

   D) an accumulation of B and C and no production of A

   E) an accumulation of C and no production of A and B

   Answer: A
   Skill: Comprehension

4) One strain of a diploid organism is homozygous for a recessive allele coding for a defective enzyme *a*. Another strain is homozygous for a recessive allele coding for a defective enzyme *b*. Crossing those two strains will result in a strain that would grow on which of the following?

   A) a minimal medium supplemented with A

   B) a minimal medium supplemented with B

   C) a minimal medium supplemented with both A and B

   D) All of the above will support the growth of the new strain.

   Answer: A
   Skill: Application

5) Which of the following represents a similarity between RNA and DNA?

A) the presence of a double–stranded helix

B) the presence of uracil

C) the presence of an OH group on the 3' carbon of the sugar

D) nucleotides consisting of a phosphate, sugar, and nitrogen base

E) repair systems that correct genetic code errors

Answer: D
Skill: Comprehension

6) The nitrogenous base adenine is found in all members of which of the following groups?

A) proteins, triglycerides, and testosterone

B) proteins, ATP, and DNA

C) ATP, RNA, and genes

D) alpha glucose, ATP, and DNA

E) proteins, carbohydrates, and ATP

Answer: C
Skill: Knowledge

7) RNA differs from DNA in that RNA

A) contains ribose as its sugar.

B) is found only in cytoplasm.

C) contains uracil instead of thymine.

D) Both A and C are correct.

E) A, B, and C are correct.

Answer: D
Skill: Knowledge

8) What is the primary transcript of eukaryotic genes?

A) hnRNA

B) tRNA

C) rRNA

D) mRNA

E) DNA

Answer: D
Skill: Knowledge

9) If proteins were composed of only 12 different kinds of amino acids, what would be the smallest possible codon size in a genetic system with four different nucleotides?

A) 1

B) 2

C) 3

D) 4

E) 12

Answer: B
Skill: Application

10) A new form of life is discovered. It has a genetic code much like that of organisms on Earth except that there are five different DNA bases instead of four and the base sequences are translated as doublets instead of triplets. How many different amino acids could be accommodated by this genetic code?

A) 5

B) 10

C) 25

D) 64

E) 32

Answer: C
Skill: Application

11) The enzyme polynucleotide phosphorylase randomly assembles a polymer of nucleotides. You add polynucleotide phosphorylase to a solution of adenosine triphosphate and guanosine triphosphate. The resulting artificial mRNA molecule would have _____ possible different codons if the code involved two-base sequences and _____ possible different codons if the code involved three-base sequences.

A) 2; 3

B) 2; 4

C) 4; 8

D) 4; 16

E) 16; 64

Answer: C
Skill: Comprehension

12) A particular triplet of bases in the coding sequence of DNA is AGT. The corresponding codon for the mRNA transcribed is

A) AGT.

B) UCA.

C) TCA.

D) AGU.

E) either UCA or TCA, depending on wobble in the first base.

Answer: B
Skill: Application

The following questions refer to Figure 17.1, a table of codons.

(Figure 17.1 appears on page 215.)

13) A possible sequence of nucleotides in DNA that would code for the polypeptide sequence phe–leu–ile–val would be

A) 5' TTG–CTA–CAG–TAG 3'.

B) 3' AAC–GAC–GUC–AUA 5'.

C) 5' AUG–CTG–CAG–TAT 3'.

D) 3' AAA–AAT–ATA–ACA 5'.

E) 3' AAA–GAA–TAA–CAA 5'.

Answer: E
Skill: Application

14) What amino acid sequence will be generated, based on the following mRNA codon sequence?
5'AUG–UCU–UCG–UUA–UCC–UUG

A) met–arg–glu–arg–glu–arg

B) met–glu–arg–arg–gln–leu

C) met–ser–leu–ser–leu–ser

D) met–ser–ser–leu–ser–leu

E) met–leu–phe–arg–glu–glu

Answer: D
Skill: Application

15) A peptide has the sequence NH$_2$–phe–pro–lys–gly–phe–pro–COOH. What is the sequence in DNA that codes for this peptide?

A) 3' UUU–CCC–AAA–GGG–UUU–CCC

B) 3' AUG–AAA–GGG–TTT–CCC–AAA–GGG

C) 3' AAA–GGG–TTT–CCC–AAA–GGG

D) 5' GGG–AAA–TTT–AAA–CCC–ACT–GGG

E) 5' ACT–TAC–CAT–AAA–CAT–TAC–UGA

Answer: C
Skill: Application

16) What is the sequence of a peptide based on the mRNA sequence
5' UUUUCUUAUUGUCUU?

A) leu–cys–tyr–ser–phe

B) cyc–phe–tyr–cys–leu

C) phe–leu–ile–met–val

D) leu–pro–asp–lys–gly

E) phe–ser–tyr–cys–leu

Answer: E
Skill: Application

17) Suppose the following DNA sequence was mutated from
AGAGAGAGAGAGAGAGAGA to
AGAAGAGAGATCGAGAGA.
What amino acid sequence will be generated based on this mutated DNA?

A) arg–glu–arg–glu–arg–glu

B) glu–arg–glu–leu–leu–leu

C) ser–leu–ser–leu–ser–leu

D) ser–ser–leu

E) leu–phe–arg–glu–glu–glu

Answer: D
Skill: Application

18) A particular eukaryotic protein is 300 amino acids long. Which of the following could be the maximum number of nucleotides in the DNA that codes for the amino acids in this protein?

A) 3

B) 100

C) 300

D) 900

E) 1,800

Answer: D
Skill: Application

19) A particular triplet of bases in the coding sequence of DNA is AGT. What is the corresponding triplet in the complementary strand of DNA?

A) AGT

B) UCA

C) TCA

D) GAC

E) TCA in eukaryotes, but UCA in prokaryotes

Answer: C
Skill: Application

20) A portion of the genetic code is UUU = phenylalanine, GCC = alanine, AAA = lysine, and CCC = proline. Assume the correct code places the amino acids phenylalanine, alanine, and lysine in a protein (in that order). Which of the following DNA sequences would substitute proline for alanine?

A) AAA–CGG–TTA

B) AAT–CGG–TTT

C) AAA–CCG–TTT

D) AAA–GGG–TTT

E) AAA–CCC–TTT

Answer: D
Skill: Application

21) Which of the following is correct about a codon? It

A) consists of two nucleotides.

B) may code for the same amino acid as another codon.

C) consists of discrete amino acid regions.

D) catalyzes RNA synthesis.

E) is the basic unit of the genetic code.

Answer: B
Skill: Knowledge

22) If the triplet UUU codes for the amino acid phenylalanine in bacteria, then in plants UUU should code for

A) leucine.

B) valine.

C) cystine.

D) phenylalanine.

E) proline.

Answer: D
Skill: Knowledge

23) The genetic code is essentially the same for all organisms. From this, one can logically assume all of the following *except*:

A) A gene from an organism could theoretically be expressed by any other organism.

B) All organisms have a common ancestor.

C) DNA was the first genetic material.

D) Codons usually translate into the same amino acids.

E) Related organisms have many similar genes.

Answer: C
Skill: Comprehension

24) Which of the following is *true* for both prokaryotic and eukaryotic gene expression?

A) After transcription, a 3' poly(A) tail and a 5' cap are added to mRNA.

B) Translation of mRNA can begin before transcription is complete.

C) RNA polymerase may recognize a promoter region and begin transcription.

D) mRNA is synthesized in the 3' → 5' direction.

E) The mRNA transcript is the exact complement of the gene from which it was copied.

Answer: C
Skill: Knowledge

25) Where is the attachment site for RNA polymerase?

A) structural gene region

B) initiation region

C) promoter region

D) operator region

E) regulator region

Answer: C
Skill: Knowledge

26) All of the following are transcribed from DNA *except*

A) protein.

B) exons.

C) rRNA.

D) tRNA.

E) mRNA.

Answer: A
Skill: Application

27) Which of the following is *not* involved in transcription?

A) initiation factors

B) RNA polymerase

C) TATA box

D) terminator

E) promoter

Answer: A
Skill: Comprehension

28) DNA has two functions: it can self–replicate and it can make non–DNA molecules. DNA is capable of these because

A) its two strands are held together by easily broken electrostatic interactions.

B) its nucleotides will form base pairs with both ribose and deoxyribose nucleotides.

C) both DNA and proteins can be synthesized directly at the DNA template.

D) its replication is semiconservative.

E) replication and expression are thermodynamically spontaneous and require no enzymes.

Answer: B
Skill: Application

29) Which of the following is *least* related to the other items?

A) translation

B) TATA box

C) transcription

D) template strand

E) RNA polymerase II

Answer: A
Skill: Comprehension

30) Which of the following helps to stabilize mRNA by inhibiting its degradation?

A) TATA box

B) spliceosomes

C) a modified guanosine triphosphate

D) snRNPs

E) poly(A) tail

Answer: E
Skill: Knowledge

31) What are the coding segments of a stretch of eukaryotic DNA called?

A) introns

B) exons

C) codons

D) replicons

E) transposons

Answer: B
Skill: Knowledge

32) All of the following are found in prokaryotic messenger RNA *except*

A) the AUG codon.

B) the UGA codon.

C) introns.

D) uracil.

E) cytosine.

Answer: C
Skill: Knowledge

33) A transcription unit that is 800 nucleotides long may use 1,200 nucleotides to make a protein consisting of 400 amino acids. This is best explained by the fact that

A) many noncoding nucleotides are present.

B) there is redundancy and ambiguity in the genetic code.

C) many nucleotides are needed to code for each amino acid.

D) nucleotides break off and are lost during the transcription process.

E) there are termination exons near the beginning of mRNA.

Answer: A
Skill: Application

34) Once transcribed, eukaryotic mRNA typically undergoes substantial alteration that includes

A) excision of introns.

B) fusion into circular forms known as plasmids.

C) linkage to histone molecules.

D) union with ribosomes.

E) fusion with other newly transcribed mRNA.

Answer: A
Skill: Knowledge

35) Which of the following is *least* related to the other items?

A) snRNP

B) triplet code

C) wobble

D) inosine

E) anticodon

Answer: A
Skill: Comprehension

36) Introns are significant to biological evolution because

A) their presence increases the frequency of recombination.

B) they protect the mRNA from degeneration.

C) they are translated into essential amino acids.

D) they maintain the genetic code by preventing incorrect DNA base pairings.

E) they correct enzymatic alterations of DNA bases.

Answer: A
Skill: Knowledge

37) All of the following are directly involved in translation *except*

A) mRNA.

B) tRNA.

C) ribosomes.

D) DNA.

E) amino acid–activating enzymes.

Answer: D
Skill: Knowledge

38) Which of the following is *false*?

A) Transcriptionally produced gene products are molecules of RNA.

B) Proteins are translated in the cytoplasm.

C) Steroid hormones may bind directly to DNA and regulate expression.

D) Histones are found only in eukaryotic chromosomes.

E) RNA polymerase attaches to DNA at the promoter sequence.

Answer: B
Skill: Comprehension

39) A particular triplet of bases in the coding sequence of DNA is AAA. The anticodon on the tRNA that binds the mRNA codon is

A) TTT.

B) UUA.

C) UUU.

D) AAA.

E) either UAA or TAA, depending on wobble in the first base.

Answer: D
Skill: Application

40) Accuracy in the translation of mRNA into the primary structure of a protein depends on specificity in the

A) binding of ribosomes to mRNA.

B) shape of the A and P sites of ribosomes.

C) bonding of the anticodon to the codon.

D) attachment of amino acids to tRNAs.

E) Both C and D are correct.

Answer: E
Skill: Comprehension

41) What is an anticodon part of?

A) DNA

B) tRNA

C) mRNA

D) a ribosome

E) an activating enzyme

Answer: B
Skill: Knowledge

42) A part of an mRNA molecule with the following sequence is being read by a ribosome: 5' CCG-ACG 3' (mRNA). The following activated transfer RNA molecules are available. Two of them can correctly match the mRNA so that a dipeptide can form.

tRNA Anticodon	Amino Acid
GGC	Proline
CGU	Alanine
UGC	Threonine
CCG	Glycine
ACG	Cysteine
CGG	Alanine

The dipeptide that will form will be

A) cysteine–alanine.

B) proline–threonine.

C) glycine–cysteine.

D) alanine–alanine.

E) threonine–glycine.

Answer: B
Skill: Application

43) What type of bonding is responsible for maintaining the shape of the tRNA molecule?

A) covalent bonding between sulfur atoms

B) ionic bonding between phosphates

C) hydrogen bonding between base pairs

D) van der Waals interactions between hydrogen atoms

E) peptide bonding between amino acids

Answer: C
Skill: Knowledge

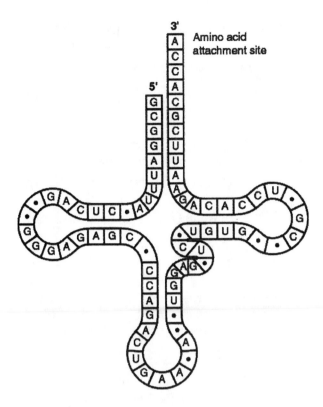

3'
Amino acid
attachment site

5'

Figure 17.2

44) Figure 17.2 represents tRNA that recognizes and binds a particular amino acid (in this instance, phenylalanine). Which of the following triplets of bases on the mRNA strand codes for this amino acid?

A) UGG

B) GUG

C) GUA

D) UUC

E) CAU

Answer: D
Skill: Application

45) Which of the following is *least* related to the other items?

A) elongation

B) termination

C) wobble

D) translation

E) initiation

Answer: C
Skill: Comprehension

46) There are 61 mRNA codons that specify an amino acid, but only 45 tRNAs. This is best explained by the fact that

A) some tRNAs have anticodons that recognize two or more different codons.

B) the rules for base pairing between the third base of a codon and tRNA are flexible.

C) inosine can hydrogen–bond with U, C, or A.

D) A and B are true.

E) A, B, and C are true.

Answer: E
Skill: Comprehension

47) What are ribosomes composed of?

A) two subunits, each consisting of rRNA only

B) two subunits, each consisting of several proteins only

C) both rRNA and protein

D) mRNA, rRNA, and protein

E) mRNA, tRNA, rRNA, and protein

Answer: C
Skill: Knowledge

48) Where is eukaryotic ribosomal RNA transcribed?

A) the Golgi apparatus

B) ribosomes

C) nucleoli

D) X chromosomes

E) prokaryotic cells only

Answer: C
Skill: Knowledge

49) What is the most abundant type of RNA?

A) mRNA

B) tRNA

C) rRNA

D) pre-mRNA

E) hnRNA

Answer: C
Skill: Knowledge

50) The function of the ribosome in polypeptide synthesis is to

A) hold mRNA and tRNAs together.

B) catalyze the addition of amino acids from the tRNAs to the growing polypeptide chain.

C) move tRNA and mRNA during the translocation process.

D) do A and B.

E) do A, B, and C.

Answer: E
Skill: Knowledge

51) From the following list, which is the first event in translation in eukaryotes?

A) elongation of the polypeptide

B) base pairing of activated methionine–tRNA to AUG of the messenger RNA

C) binding of the larger ribosomal subunit to smaller ribosome subunits

D) covalent bonding between the first two amino acids

E) Both B and D occur simultaneously.

Answer: B
Skill: Knowledge

52) Choose the answer that has these events of protein synthesis in the proper sequence.
1. An aminoacyl–tRNA binds to the A site.
2. A peptide bond forms between the new amino acid and a polypeptide chain.
3. tRNA leaves the P site and the P site remains vacant.
4. A small ribosomal subunit binds with mRNA.
5. tRNA translocates to the P site.

A) 1, 3, 2, 4, 5

B) 4, 1, 2, 5, 3

C) 5, 4, 3, 2, 1

D) 4, 1, 3, 2, 5

E) 2, 4, 5, 1, 3

Answer: B
Skill: Comprehension

53) The first event of translation in eukaryotes (starting with methionine) is the

A) joining of the ribosomal subunits.

B) base pairing of met–tRNA to AUG of the messenger RNA.

C) binding of the large ribosomal subunit to AUG of mRNA.

D) covalent bonding between the first two amino acids.

E) forming of polysomes.

Answer: B
Skill: Knowledge

54) Which of the following is *not* directly involved in the process of translation?

A) ligase

B) tRNA

C) rRNA

D) mRNA

E) aminoacyl–tRNA synthetase

Answer: A
Skill: Knowledge

55) When a ribosome first attaches to an mRNA molecule, one tRNA binds to the ribosome. The tRNA that recognizes the initiation codon binds to the

A) amino acid site (A site) of the ribosome only.

B) peptide site (P site) of the ribosome only.

C) large ribosomal subunit only.

D) second tRNA before attaching to the ribosome.

E) Both A and C are correct.

Answer: B
Skill: Knowledge

56) During translation, chain elongation continues until what happens?

A) No further amino acids are needed by the cell.

B) All tRNAs are empty.

C) The polypeptide is long enough.

D) Chain terminator codons occur.

E) The ribosomes run off the end of mRNA.

Answer: D
Skill: Knowledge

57) As a ribosome translocates along an mRNA molecule by one codon, which of the following occurs?

A) The tRNA that was in the A site moves into the P site.

B) The tRNA that was in the P site moves into the A site.

C) The tRNA that was in the P site moves to the E site and is released.

D) The tRNA that was in the A site departs from the ribosome.

E) Both A and C are correct.

Answer: E
Skill: Knowledge

58) Which of the following does *not* occur during the termination phase of translation?

A) A termination codon causes the A site to accept a release factor.

B) The newly formed polypeptide is released.

C) A tRNA with the next amino acid enters the P site.

D) The two ribosomal subunits separate.

E) Translation stops.

Answer: C
Skill: Knowledge

59) What are polyribosomes?

A) groups of ribosomes reading the same mRNA simultaneously

B) ribosomes containing more than two subunits

C) multiple copies of ribosomes found associated with giant chromosomes

D) aggregations of vesicles containing ribosomal RNA

E) ribosomes associated with more than one tRNA

Answer: A
Skill: Knowledge

60) What is one function of a signal peptide?

  A) to direct an mRNA molecule into the cisternal space of ER

  B) to bind RNA polymerase to DNA and initiate transcription

  C) to terminate translation of the messenger RNA

  D) to translocate polypeptide across the ER membrane

  E) to signal the initiation of transcription

Answer: D
Skill: Knowledge

61) According to the signal hypothesis, ribosomes are directed to the ER membrane

  A) by a specific characteristic of the ribosome itself, which distinguishes free ribosomes from bound ribosomes.

  B) by a signal-recognition particle that brings ribosomes to a receptor protein in the ER membrane.

  C) by moving through a specialized channel of the nucleus.

  D) by a chemical signal given off by the ER.

  E) by a signal sequence of RNA that precedes the start codon of the message.

Answer: B
Skill: Knowledge

62) Which of the following is *least* related to the other items?

  A) snRNP

  B) exons

  C) introns

  D) spliceosomes

  E) signal-recognition particles

Answer: E
Skill: Comprehension

63) Which of the following is *least* related to the other items?

  A) exons

  B) introns

  C) RNA splicing

  D) signal-recognition particles (SRPs)

  E) mRNA

Answer: D
Skill: Comprehension

64) When does translation begin in prokaryote cells?

  A) after a transcription initiation complex has been formed

  B) during transcription

  C) after the 5' caps are converted to mRNA

  D) once the pre-mRNA has been converted to mRNA

  E) as soon as the DNA introns are removed from the template

Answer: B
Skill: Knowledge

65) Which of these statements represents a common misconception regarding point mutations?

  A) They involve changes in one base pair.

  B) They can cause drastic changes in polypeptide structure.

  C) They always produce a change in the amino acid sequence of a protein.

  D) They can lead to the shortening of the mutated polypeptide.

  E) They could result in a frameshift mutation.

Answer: C
Skill: Knowledge

66) Of the following types of mutations, which one is likely to be the *most* common?

A) point mutation

B) missense mutation

C) base-pair substitution

D) nonsense mutation

E) frameshift mutation

Answer: A
Skill: Comprehension

67) Which of the following is *not* related to ribosomal activity?

A) A site

B) spliceosome

C) codon recognition

D) peptide bond formation

E) P site

Answer: B
Skill: Comprehension

For the following questions, each of the following is a modification of the sentence THECATATETHERAT.

A. THERATATETHECAT
B. THETACATETHERAT
C. THECATARETHERAT
D. THECATATTHERAT
E. CATATETHERAT

68) Which of the above is analogous to a frameshift mutation?

Answer: D
Skill: Application

69) Which of the above is analogous to a single substitution mutation?

Answer: C
Skill: Application

70) Sickle-cell disease is probably the result of which kind of mutation?

A) point only

B) frameshift only

C) nonsense only

D) nondisjunction only

E) both B and D

Answer: A
Skill: Application

71) A frameshift mutation could result from

A) a base insertion only.

B) a base deletion only.

C) a base substitution only.

D) deletion of three consecutive bases.

E) either an insertion or a deletion of a base.

Answer: E
Skill: Knowledge

72) Which of the following DNA mutations is the most potentially damaging to the protein it specifies?

A) a base-pair deletion

B) a codon substitution

C) a substitution in the last base of a codon

D) a codon deletion

E) a point mutation

Answer: A
Skill: Application

73) When a nucleotide pair is lost from the middle of a gene during the process of transcription, what happens?

A) snRNPs splice and then remove incorrect amino acids.

B) Normal termination does not occur; transcription continues indefinitely.

C) The reading frame is shifted, producing a nonfunctional polypeptide.

D) A signal–recognition particle moves in to correct coding errors.

E) There is little effect on the protein being synthesized due to redundancy of the genetic code.

Answer: C
Skill: Comprehension

74) Which point mutation would be most likely to have a catastrophic effect on the functioning of a protein?

A) a base substitution

B) a base deletion near the start of a gene

C) a base deletion near the end of the coding sequence, but not in the terminator codon

D) deletion of three bases near the start of the coding sequence, but not in the initiator codon

E) a base insertion near the end of the coding sequence, but not in the terminator codon

Answer: B
Skill: Comprehension

75) What is the relationship among DNA, a gene, and a chromosome?

A) A chromosome contains hundreds of genes, which are composed of protein.

B) A chromosome contains hundreds of genes, which are composed of DNA.

C) A gene contains hundreds of chromosomes, which are composed of protein.

D) A gene is composed of DNA, but there is no relationship to a chromosome.

E) A gene contains hundreds of chromosomes, which are composed of DNA.

Answer: B
Skill: Comprehension

76) A shrimp grower wants to create a new "green" shrimp. He plans on growing normal shrimp in green light because, he says, the green light will cause mutations that make the shrimp green. You tell him this is not a good idea because

A) if the green light is capable of causing such mutations, it will also turn him green.

B) mutations are random, and no agent (even green light) can cause a specific mutation like turning shrimp green.

C) it cannot work; everyone knows that water absorbs green light (that's why lakes and ponds are green).

D) the green shrimp would be mutagenic and anyone eating them would be in danger of turning green.

E) the color of a shrimp has nothing to do with its genes.

Answer: B
Skill: Comprehension

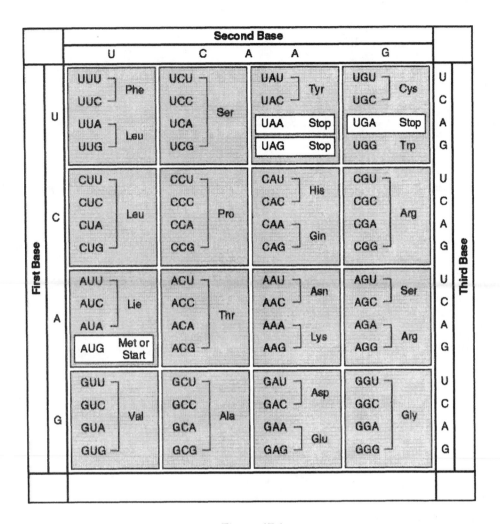

Figure 17.1

Media Activity Questions

1) Beadle and Tatum worked with

   A) zebrafish.

   B) bread mold.

   C) fruit flies.

   D) monkeys.

   E) guinea pigs.

   Answer: B
   Topic: Web/CD Activity 17A

2) _____ is the first of the three main steps of protein synthesis.

   A) RNA processing

   B) Polypeptide formation

   C) Translation

   D) Gene expression

   E) Transcription

   Answer: E
   Topic: Web/CD Activity 17B

3) Transcription of the DNA sequence AAGTTC will produce RNA with the sequence

   A) AAGTTC.

   B) TTGUUC.

   C) UUCAAG.

   D) TTCAAG.

   E) AAGUUC.

   Answer: C
   Topic: Web/CD Activity 17C

4) _____ are deleted portions of an RNA transcript.

   A) Tails

   B) Introns

   C) snRNPs

   D) Exons

   E) Caps

   Answer: B
   Topic: Web/CD Activity 17D

5) _____ are the site of translation.

   A) Peroxisomes

   B) Lysosomes

   C) Golgi apparatuses

   D) Ribosomes

   E) Centrioles

   Answer: D
   Topic: Web/CD Activity 17E

Self-Quiz Questions

Answers to these questions also appear in the textbook.

1) Base-pair substitutions involving the third base of a codon are unlikely to result in an error in the polypeptide. This is because
   A) base-pair substitutions are corrected before transcription begins.
   B) base-pair substitutions are restricted to introns, and these regions are later deleted from the mRNA.
   C) most tRNAs bind tightly to a codon with only the first two bases of the anticodon.
   D) a signal-recognition particle corrects coding errors before the mRNA reaches the ribosome.
   E) transcribed errors attract snRNPs, which then stimulate splicing and correction.

   Answer: C

2) In eukaryotic cells, transcription cannot begin until
   A) the two DNA strands have completely separated and exposed the promoter.
   B) the appropriate transcription factors have bound to the promoter.
   C) the 5' caps are removed from the mRNA.
   D) the DNA introns are removed from the template.
   E) DNA nucleases have isolated the transcription unit from the noncoding DNA.

   Answer: B

3) Which of the following is *not* true of a codon?
   A) It consists of three nucleotides.
   B) It may code for the same amino acid as another codon does.
   C) It never codes for more than one amino acid.
   D) It extends from one end of a tRNA molecule.
   E) It is the basic unit of the genetic code.

   Answer: D

4) Beadle and Tatum discovered several classes of *Neurospora* mutants that were able to grow on minimal medium with arginine added. Class I mutants were also able to grow on medium supplemented with either ornithine or citrulline, whereas class II mutants could grow on citrulline medium but not on ornithine medium. The metabolic pathway of arginine synthesis is as follows:

   $$\text{Precursor} \xrightarrow{\quad} \underset{A}{\text{Ornithine}} \xrightarrow{\quad} \underset{B}{\text{Citrulline}} \xrightarrow{\quad} \underset{C}{\text{Arginine}}$$

   From the behavior of their mutants, Beadle and Tatum could conclude that
   A) one gene codes for the entire metabolic pathway.
   B) the genetic code of DNA is a triplet code.
   C) class I mutants have their mutations later in the nucleotide chain than do class II mutants and thus have more functional enzymes.
   D) class I mutants have a nonfunctional enzyme at step A, and class II mutants have a nonfunctional enzyme at step B.
   E) class I mutants have a nonfunctional enzyme at step B, and class II mutants have a nonfunctional enzyme at step C.

   Answer: D

5) The anticodon of a particular tRNA molecule is

   A) complementary to the corresponding mRNA codon.

   B) complementary to the corresponding triplet in rRNA.

   C) the part of tRNA that bonds to a specific amino acid.

   D) changeable, depending on the amino acid that attaches to the tRNA.

   E) catalytic, making the tRNA a ribozyme.

   Answer: A

6) Which of the following is *not* true of RNA processing?

   A) Exons are excised and hydrolyzed before mRNA moves out of the nucleus.

   B) The presence of introns may facilitate crossing over between regions of a gene that code for polypeptide domains.

   C) Ribozymes may function in RNA splicing.

   D) RNA splicing may be catalyzed by spliceosomes.

   E) A primary transcript is often much longer than the final RNA molecule that leaves the nucleus.

   Answer: A

7) Which of the following is true of translation in both prokaryotes and eukaryotes?

   A) Translation occurs simultaneously with transcription.

   B) The product of transcription is directly translated.

   C) The codon UUU codes for phenylalanine.

   D) Ribosomes are affected by streptomycin.

   E) The signal–recognition particle (SRP) binds to the first 20 amino acids of certain polypeptides.

   Answer: C

The following questions refer to Figure 17.1, a table of codons.

(Figure 17.1 appears on page 215.)

8) Using the genetic code in Figure 17.1, identify a possible 5' → 3' sequence of nucleotides in the *DNA template strand* for an mRNA coding for the polypeptide sequence Phe-Pro-Lys.

   A) UUU-GGG-AAA

   B) GAA-CCC-CTT

   C) AAA-ACC-TTT

   D) CTT-CGG-GAA

   E) AAA-CCC-UUU

   Answer: D

9) Which of the following mutations would be *most* likely to have a harmful effect on an organism? Explain your answer.

   A) a base–pair substitution

   B) a deletion of three bases near the middle of a gene

   C) a single base deletion near the middle of an intron

   D) a single base deletion close to the end of the coding sequence

   E) a single base insertion near the start of the coding sequence

   Answer: E

10) Which component is *not directly* involved in the process known as translation?

   A) mRNA

   B) DNA

   C) tRNA

   D) ribosomes

   E) GTP

   Answer: B

Chapter 18 Microbial Models: The Genetics of Viruses and Bacteria

1) The simplest infectious biological systems are

   A) bacteria.

   B) viruses.

   C) viroids.

   D) A and B.

   E) B and C.

   Answer: C
   Skill: Knowledge

2) Which of the following is a *true* statement about viruses?

   A) Viruses are classified below the cellular level of biological organization.

   B) A single virus particle contains both DNA and RNA.

   C) Even small virus particles are visible with light microscopes.

   D) A and B only are true.

   E) A, B, and C are true.

   Answer: A
   Skill: Knowledge

3) A researcher lyses a cell that contains nucleic acid molecules and capsid units of tobacco mosaic virus (TMV). The cell contents are left in a covered test tube overnight. The next day this mixture is sprayed on tobacco plants. Which of the following would be expected to occur?

   A) The plants would develop some but not all of the symptoms of the TMV infection.

   B) The plants would develop symptoms typically produced by viroids.

   C) The plants would develop the typical symptoms of TMV infection.

   D) The plants would not show any disease symptoms.

   E) The plants would become infected, but the sap from these plants would be unable to infect other plants.

   Answer: C
   Skill: Comprehension

4) Which of the following is a characteristic of all viruses?

   A) nucleic acid genome

   B) a protein capsid

   C) glycoprotein cell wall

   D) A and B only

   E) A, B, and C

   Answer: D
   Skill: Knowledge

5) Viruses have some of the properties of living organisms. Which of the following is a characteristic of all organisms, but *not* of viruses?

A) genetic information stored as nucleic acid

B) ability to control metabolism

C) ability to reproduce

D) structure includes proteins

E) plasma membrane

Answer: E
Skill: Knowledge

6) The host range of a virus is determined by

A) the structure of the viral capsid.

B) whether the virus nucleic acid is DNA or RNA.

C) proteins on the surface of the cell.

D) enzymes produced by the virus before it infects the cell.

E) both A and C.

Answer: E
Skill: Knowledge

7) Viruses are referred to as obligate parasites because

A) they use the host cell's nucleotides and enzymes to reproduce.

B) viral DNA inserts itself into host DNA.

C) they reproduce and then exit the cell.

D) they are nonliving.

E) they use the host's energy to live.

Answer: A
Skill: Knowledge

8) The phage DNA is not hydrolyzed with the host DNA because

A) phage DNA contains an urecognizable form of cytosine.

B) phage DNA remains outside the host cell.

C) a protein sheath protects phage DNA.

D) the host cell ceases to function.

E) lysozyme releases phage particles before hydrolysis can occur.

Answer: A
Skill: Knowledge

9) Double–stranded viruses can reproduce the lytic cycle and the lysogenic cycle. Which of the following is characterstic of the lytic cycle?

A) Many bacterial cells containing viral DNA are produced.

B) Viral DNA is incorporated into the host chromosomes.

C) The viral genome replicates without destroying the host.

D) A large number of phages are released at a time.

E) The virus–host relationship usually lasts for generations.

Answer: D
Skill: Knowledge

10) Bacteriophage DNAs that have become integrated into the host cell chromosome are called

A) intemperate bacteriophages.

B) transposons.

C) prophages.

D) T–even bacteriophages.

E) plasmids.

Answer: C
Skill: Knowledge

11) Virulent phages undergo a(n) _____ life cycle, whereas temperate phages are capable of undergoing a(n) _____ cycle.

A) infective; retroviral

B) lysogenic; lytic

C) lytic; lysogenic

D) retroviral; infective

E) infective; benign

Answer: C
Skill: Knowledge

12) Viral envelopes are generally

A) composed of protein.

B) composed of a lipid bilayer.

C) composed of single–stranded RNA.

D) found between the viral protein coat and its DNA.

E) made of peptidoglycan cell wall material.

Answer: B
Skill: Knowledge

13) What is the function of reverse transcriptase in retroviruses?

A) hydrolyzes the host cell's DNA

B) uses viral RNA as a template for DNA synthesis

C) converts host cell RNA into viral DNA

D) translates viral RNA into proteins

E) uses viral RNA as a template for making complementary RNA strands

Answer: B
Skill: Knowledge

14) What is the function of the single–stranded RNA in certain animal viruses?

A) It becomes an mRNA.

B) It codes for an mRNA.

C) It is used as a template for the synthesis of DNA.

D) A and C only are correct.

E) A, B, and C are all correct.

Answer: D
Skill: Knowledge

15) Viruses that have a single strand of RNA that acts as a template for DNA synthesis are known as

A) retroviruses.

B) proviruses.

C) viroids.

D) bacteriophages.

E) lytic phages.

Answer: A
Skill: Knowledge

16) Which of the following is *true* of retroviruses? They

A) have the enzyme reverse transcriptase.

B) use their RNA as a template for mRNA.

C) use their RNA as a template for DNA.

D) A and C only are correct.

E) A, B, and C are correct.

Answer: D
Skill: Knowledge

17) Which of the following is a *true* statement?

A) Viruses are uncommon.

B) Viruses can cause diarrhea, colds, and measles.

C) All viruses have a common capsid and membranous envelope.

D) All viruses contain the nucleic acid RNA.

E) Viruses only invade animal cells.

Answer: B
Skill: Knowledge

18) For many bacteriophages, infections are self–limiting. Each phage that infects a cell produces hundreds of new phages, and eventually cells are infected by several phages at different times. This results in a competition for regulatory control over the cell, with the eventual result of the death of the cell without the production of new viruses. This phenomenon is called *superinfection*. Superinfection can be prevented by which of the following changes in the bacteriophage?

A) restricting the host range of the phage

B) slowing down the rate of the lytic infection

C) making larger numbers of new phages

D) the virus becoming a prophage in the cell

E) evolving a more complex protein coat

Answer: D
Skill: Comprehension

19) RNA viruses appear to have higher rates of mutation because

A) RNA nucleotides are more unstable than DNA nucleotides.

B) replication of their nucleic acid does not involve the proofreading steps of DNA replication.

C) RNA viruses replicate faster.

D) RNA viruses can incorporate a variety of nonstandard bases.

E) RNA viruses respond more to mutagens.

Answer: B
Skill: Knowledge

20) Which of the following does *not* contribute to the emergence of viral disease?

A) production of new strains of virus through mutation

B) spread of existing virus from one host to another

C) transformation from lytic to lysogenic activity

D) dissemination from a small, isolated host population

Answer: C
Skill: Knowledge

21) Which of the following is *true* of plant virus infections?

A) They can be controlled by the use of antibiotics.

B) They are spread throughout a plant by passing through the plasmodesmata.

C) They have little effect on plant growth.

D) A and B only are correct.

E) A, B, and C are correct.

Answer: C
Skill: Knowledge

22) Which of the following represents a difference between viruses and viroids?

A) Viruses infect many types of cells, while viroids infect only prokaryotic cells.

B) Viruses have capsids composed of protein, while viroids have no capsids.

C) Viruses contain introns; viroids have only exons.

D) Viruses have genomes composed of DNA, while viroids have genomes composed of RNA.

E) Viruses cannot pass through plasmodesmata; viroids can.

Answer: B
Skill: Knowledge

23) What are prions?

A) Misfolded versions of normal brain protein.

B) Tiny molecules of RNA that infect plants.

C) Viral DNA that has had to attach itself to the host genome.

D) Viruses that invade bacteria.

E) A mobile segment of DNA.

Answer: A
Skill: Knowledge

24) Of the following, which is *least* related to the others?

A) viral envelope

B) viroids

C) provirus

D) prophage

E) prions

Answer: A
Skill: Comprehension

25) Most molecular biologists believe that viruses originated from fragments of cellular nucleic acid. Which of the following observations supports this theory?

A) Viruses contain either DNA or RNA.

B) Viruses are enclosed in protein capsids rather than plasma membranes.

C) Viruses can reproduce only inside host cells.

D) Viruses can infect both prokaryotic and eukaryotic cells.

E) Viral genomes are usually more similar to the genome of the host cell than to the genome of other cells.

Answer: E
Skill: Knowledge

26) Reproduction in bacteria requires

A) the production of a mitotic spindle.

B) a plasmid.

C) cyclic AMP.

D) replication of DNA.

E) both B and D.

Answer: D
Skill: Comprehension

27) What is the most common source of genetic diversity in a bacterial colony?

A) transposons

B) plasmids

C) meiotic recombination

D) crossing over

E) mutation

Answer: E
Skill: Knowledge

28) In which of the following cases would a mutation have the most significant impact on the genetic diversity of a species?

A) The species reproduces only asexually.

B) The species reproduces only sexually.

C) The species usually reproduces asexually, but can reproduce sexually when conditions become unfavorable.

D) The species has a relatively long reproductive cycle.

E) The species' reproductive cycle is unpredictable.

Answer: A
Skill: Comprehension

29) The alteration of a cell's genotype by the uptake of naked, foreign DNA from surrounding environments is called

A) transduction.

B) conjunction.

C) prionization.

D) transformation.

E) horizontal transmission.

Answer: D
Skill: Comprehension

A. *transduction*
B. *transposition*
C. *translation*
D. *transformation*
E. *conjugation*

30) External DNA is assimilated by a cell.

Answer: D
Skill: Knowledge

31) DNA from pneumonia–causing bacteria is mixed with harmless bacteria. The bacteria are injected into mice. The mice develop pneumonia and die.

Answer: D
Skill: Knowledge

32) Bacteria have proteins on the surface that recognize and take in DNA from closely related species.

Answer: D
Skill: Knowledge

33) DNA is transferred from one bacterium to another by a virus.

Answer: A
Skill: Knowledge

34) Bacterial strains A and B are growing together in a colony that has been infected with viruses. After a short period of time, a new strain of bacteria is detected that is very similar to strain A but has a few characteristics of strain B.

Answer: A
Skill: Comprehension

35) A group of F⁺ bacteria is mixed with a group of F⁻ bacteria. After several days, all of the bacteria are F⁺.

Answer: E
Skill: Knowledge

36) A plasmid is exchanged between bacteria through a pilus.

Answer: E
Skill: Knowledge

37) Movement of a sequence of DNA to alternative locations in the DNA.

Answer: B
Skill: Comprehension

38) DNA is present that does not provide any known benefit to the cell, yet is replicated each time the genome replicates.

Answer: B
Skill: Knowledge

39) Antibiotic-resistant genes from different plasmids are found integrated into one large plasmid.

Answer: B
Skill: Knowledge

40) What does bacterial mating involve?
   A) exchange of egg and sperm
   B) formation of a conjugation tube for the transfer of male DNA
   C) sex pili that draw the cells together so mRNA can be inserted
   D) integration of male and female DNA into a conjugation tube
   E) binary fission of a bacterial cell

Answer: B
Skill: Knowledge

41) An Hfr bacterium is one that has

A) at least one plasmid present in the cytosol.

B) a special recognition site that will take up closely related DNA from its environment.

C) several insertion sequences scattered throughout its chromosome.

D) several copies of a single transposon repeated randomly throughout its chromosome.

E) a plasmid that has become integrated into its chromosome.

Answer: E
Skill: Knowledge

42) All of the following statements regarding transposons are true *except*:

A) Transposons are genes that encode sex pili and enable plasmid transfers between bacteria.

B) Transposons are found in both prokaryotes and eukaryotes.

C) Transposons can move from a plasmid to the bacterial circular chromosome.

D) Transposons may replicate at the original site and insert the copy at another site.

E) Transposons may carry only the genes necessary for insertion.

Answer: A
Skill: Knowledge

43) A composite transposon can

A) facilitate bacterial resistance to antibiotics.

B) adjust the rates of metabolic pathways.

C) repress gene expression.

D) convert an F+ to an F- bacterium.

E) reverse the direction of transcription.

Answer: A
Skill: Knowledge

44) Of the following, which is *least* related to the others?

A) prion

B) regulatory gene

C) promoter

D) operator

E) repressor

Answer: A
Skill: Comprehension

45) What does the operon model attempt to explain?

A) the control mechanism of gene expression in bacteria

B) bacterial resistance to antibiotics

C) how genes move between homologous regions of DNA

D) the mechanism of viral attachment to a host cell

E) horizontal transmission of plant viruses

Answer: A
Skill: Comprehension

46) All of the following consist of a sequence of nucleotide bases *except*

A) repressor.

B) structural gene.

C) promoter.

D) regulator gene.

E) operator.

Answer: A
Skill: Knowledge

47) The role of a metabolite that controls a repressible operon is to

A) bind to the promoter region and decrease the affinity of RNA polymerase for the promoter.

B) bind to the operator region and block the attachment of RNA polymerase to the promoter.

C) increase the production of inactive repressor proteins.

D) bind to the repressor protein and inactivate it.

E) bind to the repressor protein and activate it.

Answer: E
Skill: Comprehension

48) The tryptophan synthetase operon uses glucose to synthesize tryptophan. Repressible operons such as this one are

A) permanently turned on.

B) turned on only when tryptophan is present in the growth medium.

C) turned off only when glucose is present in the growth medium.

D) turned on only when glucose is present in the growth medium.

E) turned off whenever tryptophan is added to the growth medium.

Answer: E
Skill: Comprehension

For the following questions, match the following terms with the appropriate phrase or description below. Each term can be used once, more than once, or not at all.

A. *operon*
B. *operator*
C. *promoter*
D. *repressor*
E. *corepressor*

49) a protein that is produced by a regulatory gene

Answer: D
Skill: Knowledge

50) A mutation in this section of DNA could influence the binding of RNA polymerase to the DNA.

Answer: C
Skill: Comprehension

51) A lack of this nonprotein molecule would result in the inability of the cell to "turn off" genes.

Answer: E
Skill: Comprehension

52) A mutation that inactivates the regulator gene of a repressible operon in an *E. coli* cell would result in

A) continuous transcription of the structural gene controlled by that regulator.

B) complete inhibition of transcription of the structural gene controlled by that regulator.

C) irreversible binding of the repressor to the operator.

D) inactivation of RNA polymerase.

E) both B and C.

Answer: A
Skill: Application

53) When is the lactose operon likely to be transcribed? When

A) there is more glucose in the cell than lactose.

B) there is more lactose in the cell than glucose.

C) there is lactose but no glucose in the cell.

D) the cyclic AMP levels are high within the cell.

E) both C and D are correct.

Answer: E
Skill: Comprehension

54) Transcription of the structural genes in an inducible operon

A) occurs all the time.

B) starts when the pathway's substrate is present.

C) starts when the pathway's product is present.

D) stops when the pathway's product is present.

E) does not produce enzymes.

Answer: B
Skill: Comprehension

55) What is the function of the operator locus of the lactose operon?

A) terminate production of repressor molecules

B) identify the substrate allolactose

C) initiate production of mRNA

D) control the binding of RNA polymerase to the operator region

E) bind steroid hormones and control translation

Answer: D
Skill: Knowledge

56) For a repressible operon to be transcribed, which of the following must be *true*?

A) A corepressor must be present.

B) RNA polymerase and the active repressor must be present.

C) RNA polymerase must bind to the promoter and the repressor must be inactive.

D) RNA polymerase cannot be present and the repressor must be inactive.

E) RNA polymerase must not occupy the promoter and the repressor must be inactive.

Answer: C
Skill: Comprehension

57) Of the following, which is *least* related to the others?

A) corepressor

B) repressor

C) inducer

D) transposon

E) cAMP receptor protein

Answer: D
Skill: Comprehension

Media Activity Questions

1) A protein shell enclosing a viral genome is known as a(n)

   A) capsule.

   B) envelope.

   C) phage.

   D) capsid.

   E) prophage.

   Answer: D
   Topic: Web/CD Activity 18A

2) A phage is a

   A) virus that infects bacteria.

   B) virus–infected bacterium.

   C) protein shell enclosing a viral genome.

   D) lysed bacterium.

   E) viral genome.

   Answer: A
   Topic: Web/CD Activity 18B

3) Viral DNA incorporated into host cell DNA is known as a(n)

   A) capsid.

   B) prophage.

   C) envelope.

   D) phage.

   E) genome.

   Answer: B
   Topic: Web/CD Activity 18C

4) HIV is responsible for

   A) PKU.

   B) TB.

   C) STD.

   D) CPR.

   E) AIDS.

   Answer: E
   Topic: Web/CD Activity 18D

5) The *lac* operon governs the expression of genes concerned with

   A) prophage integration.

   B) provirus integration.

   C) lactate production.

   D) lactose production.

   E) lactose utilization.

   Answer: E
   Topic: Web/CD Activity 18F

Self–Quiz Questions

Answers to these questions also appear in the textbook.

1) Scientists have discovered how to put together a bacteriophage with the protein coat of phage T2 and the DNA of phage T4. If this composite phage were allowed to infect a bacterium, the phages produced in the host cell would have

A) the protein of T2 and the DNA of T4.

B) the protein of T4 and the DNA of T2.

C) a mixture of the DNA and proteins of both phages.

D) the protein and DNA of T2.

E) the protein and DNA of T4.

Answer: E

2) Horizontal transmission of a plant viral disease could be caused by

A) the movement of viral particles through plasmodesmata.

B) the inheritance of an infection from a parent plant.

C) the spread of an infection by vegetative (asexual) propagation.

D) insects as vectors carrying virus particles between plants.

E) the transmission of proviruses via cell division.

Answer: D

3) RNA viruses require their own supply of certain enzymes because

A) the viruses are rapidly destroyed by host cell defenses.

B) host cells do not have enzymes available that can replicate the viral genome.

C) the enzymes translate viral mRNA into proteins.

D) the viruses use these enzymes to penetrate host cell membranes.

E) these enzymes cannot be made in host cells.

Answer: B

4) Which of the following is descriptive of an R plasmid?

A) Its transfer converts an F⁻ cell into an F⁺ cell.

B) It contains genes for antibiotic resistance and for sex pili.

C) It is usually transferred between bacteria by transduction.

D) It is a good example of a composite transposon.

E) It makes bacteria resistant to phage.

Answer: B

5) Transposition differs from other mechanisms of genetic recombination because it

A) occurs only in bacteria.

B) moves genes between homologous regions of the DNA.

C) plays little or no role in evolution.

D) occurs only in eukaryotes.

E) scatters genes to new loci in the genome.

Answer: E

6) A particular operon encodes enzymes that together manufacture an essential amino acid. If the regulation of this operon is like that of the *trp* operon,

A) the amino acid inactivates the repressor.

B) the enzymes produced are called inducible enzymes.

C) the repressor binds to the operator in the absence of the amino acid.

D) the amino acid acts as a corepressor.

E) the amino acid turns on enzyme synthesis.

Answer: D

7) A mutation that makes the regulatory gene of an inducible operon nonfunctional would result in

A) continuous transcription of the operon's genes.

B) reduced transcription of the operon's genes.

C) accumulation of large quantities of a substrate for the catabolic pathway controlled by the operon.

D) irreversible binding of the repressor to the promoter.

E) overproduction of cAMP receptor protein.

Answer: A

8) Which of the following information transfers is catalyzed by reverse transcriptase?

A) RNA → RNA

B) DNA → RNA

C) RNA → DNA

D) protein → DNA

E) RNA → protein

Answer: C

9) Which of the following characteristics or processes is common to *both* bacteria *and* viruses?

A) nucleic acid as the genetic material

B) binary fission

C) mitosis

D) ribosomes in the cytoplasm

E) conjugation

Answer: A

10) Which of the following processes would *never* contribute to genetic variation within a bacterial population?

A) transduction

B) transformation

C) conjugation

D) mutation

E) meiosis

Answer: E

Chapter 19   The Organization and Control
of Eukaryotic Genomes

1) The compacted chromosomes observed in mitosis are due to
   A) DNA winding around histones.
   B) coiling of chromatin.
   C) looped domains.
   D) coiling, looping, and folding of DNA.
   E) tandemly repetitive DNA.

   Answer: D
   Skill: Knowledge

2) The fundamental form of chromatin is
   A) four "beads" consisting of DNA wrapped around eight histone molecules.
   B) successive levels of DNA packing.
   C) repeating, noncoding sequences of DNA.
   D) degradation of unnecessary proteins.
   E) cleavage.

   Answer: A
   Skill: Knowledge

3) In a nucleosome, what is the DNA wrapped around?
   A) polymerase molecules
   B) ribosomes
   C) mRNA
   D) histones
   E) nucleolus protein

   Answer: D
   Skill: Knowledge

4) All of the following statements concerning the eukaryotic chromosome are true *except* that
   A) it is composed of DNA and protein.
   B) the nucleosome is the structural subunit.
   C) gene expression is controlled by the histones.
   D) it consists of a single molecule of DNA wound around nucleosomes.
   E) active transcription occurs on euchromatin.

   Answer: C
   Skill: Comprehension

5) If a cell were unable to produce histone proteins, which of the following would be expected?
   A) There would be an increase in the amount of "satellite" DNA produced during centrifugation.
   B) The cell's DNA couldn't be packed into its nucleus.
   C) Spindle fibers would not form during prophase.
   D) The amplification of other protein genes would compensate for the lack of histones.
   E) Pseudogenes would be transcribed to compensate for the decreased protein in the cell.

   Answer: B
   Skill: Comprehension

6) Which of the following represents an order of increasingly higher levels of organization?

A) nucleosome, 30–nanometer chromatin fiber, looped domain

B) looped domain, 30–nanometer chromatin fiber, nucleosome

C) looped domain, nucleosome, 30–nanometer chromatin fiber

D) nucleosome, looped domain, 30–nanometer chromatin fiber

E) 30–nanometer chromatin fiber, nucleosome, looped domain

Answer: A
Skill: Knowledge

7) Which of the following statements is *true*?

A) Heterochromatin is composed of DNA, while euchromatin is made of DNA and RNA.

B) Both heterochromatin and euchromatin are found in the nucleus.

C) Heterochromatin is highly condensed, while euchromatin is less compact.

D) Euchromatin is *not* transcribed while heterochromatin is transcribed.

E) Only euchromatin is visible under the light microscope.

Answer: C
Skill: Knowledge

8) Approximately what proportion of the DNA in humans does *not* produce a protein or a functional RNA?

A) 17%

B) 54%

C) 68%

D) 87%

E) 97%

Answer: E
Skill: Knowledge

9) Most of the DNA in eukaryotic chromosomes is

A) organized into operons.

B) tandemly repetitive DNA.

C) moderately interspersed.

D) transposons.

E) Alu elements.

Answer: D
Skill: Knowledge

10) Which of the following is *not* a characteristic of triplet–repeat disorders like Huntington's disease?

A) The triplet is actually translated.

B) The resulting protein has a string of adjacent glutamines.

C) Extra repeat disorders have all been shown to operate by the same mechanism.

D) In general, these disorders affect the nervous system.

E) The number of repeats tends to correlate with the severity of the disease.

Answer: C
Skill: Knowledge

11) Artificial chromosomes have been made in the laboratory. A cell will be able to replicate these chromosomes if

A) an origin of replication is included.

B) the artificial chromosome has a centromere.

C) the artificial chromosome has two telomeres.

D) A and B are correct.

E) A, B, and C are correct.

Answer: E
Skill: Knowledge

12) Which of the following would you *not* expect to be part of a multigene family?

A) genes coding for the enzymes used in glycolysis

B) rRNA genes

C) tRNA genes

D) genes for histone proteins

E) genes for globin subunits

Answer: A
Skill: Knowledge

13) The numerous copies of rRNA genes in a salamander are an example of

A) eukaryotic multigene families.

B) prokaryotic multigene families.

C) a highly repetitive sequence.

D) enhanced promoter regions.

E) satellite DNA.

Answer: A
Skill: Knowledge

14) In humans, the embryonic and fetal forms of hemoglobin have a higher affinity for oxygen than that of adults. This is due to

A) nonidentical genes that produce different versions of globins during development.

B) identical genes that generate many copies of the ribosomes needed for fetal globin production.

C) pseudogenes, which interfere with gene expression in adults.

D) the attachment of methyl groups to cytosine following birth, which changes the type of hemoglobin produced.

E) histone proteins changing shape during embryonic development.

Answer: A
Skill: Knowledge

15) Which of the following is *least* related to the others?

A) 30 nm chromatin fiber

B) pseudogenes

C) nucleosomes

D) looped domains

E) histones

Answer: B
Skill: Comprehension

16) What do pseudogenes and introns have in common?

A) They code for RNA end products, rather than proteins.

B) They both contain uracil.

C) They have multiple promoter sites.

D) They both code for histones.

E) They are not expressed, nor do they code for functional proteins.

Answer: E
Skill: Comprehension

17) One of the best pieces of evidence for the process of gene duplication and mutation is the occurrence of

A) pseudogenes.

B) introns.

C) transposons.

D) oncogenes.

E) heterochromatin.

Answer: A
Skill: Knowledge

18) If a pseudogene were transposed between a functioning gene and its "upstream" regulatory components, which of the following would most likely occur?

A) The functioning gene would not be transcribed.

B) The pseudogene would not be transcribed.

C) The pseudogene would be transcribed.

D) Both genes would be transcribed.

E) Both A and C would probably occur.

Answer: E
Skill: Comprehension

19) Which of the following is *least* related to the others?

A) tandemly repetitive DNA

B) satellite DNA

C) gene amplification

D) interspersed repetitive DNA

E) microsatellite DNA

Answer: C
Skill: Comprehension

20) In which of the following cell types would you observe gene amplification?

A) white blood cells that produce antibodies

B) red blood cells that produce hemoglobin

C) cells of a developing fetus

D) cells that produce silk in silk worms

E) a developing amphibian ovum

Answer: E
Skill: Comprehension

21) Which of the following statements concerning transposons is *false*?

A) Transposons may increase the production of a particular protein.

B) Transposons may prevent the normal functioning of a gene.

C) Transposons may decrease the production of a particular protein.

D) Transposons may reduce the amount of DNA within certain cells.

E) Both A and C are false.

Answer: D
Skill: Knowledge

22) The fact that reverse transcriptase may be present in cells that have not been infected by a retrovirus is demonstrated by the presence of

A) immunoglobulins.

B) retrotransposons.

C) genomic imprinting.

D) proteasomes.

E) oncogenes.

Answer: B
Skill: Comprehension

23) Antibody diversity is due to

A) genetic recombination and combining of polypeptides.

B) the cell's ability to make rRNA.

C) the attachment of acetyl groups to histone proteins.

D) alternative splicing.

E) the presence of thousands of enhancers.

Answer: A
Skill: Knowledge

24) What percentage of the DNA in a typical eukaryotic cell is expressed at any given time?

A) 3–5%

B) 5–20%

C) 20–40%

D) 40–60%

E) 60–90%

Answer: A
Skill: Knowledge

25) Muscle cells and nerve cells in one species of animal owe their differences in structure to

A) having different genes.

B) having different chromosomes.

C) using different genetic codes.

D) expressing different genes.

E) having unique ribosomes.

Answer: D
Skill: Knowledge

26) Gene regulation in both prokaryotes and eukaryotes is achieved by controlling which process?

A) translation

B) histone coiling

C) transcription

D) cellular differentiation

E) RNA splicing

Answer: C
Skill: Comprehension

27) Which of the following statements is *true* about control mechanisms in eukaryotic cells?

A) Methylation of DNA may cause inactivity in part or all of a chromosome.

B) Cytoplasmic inductive influences act by altering what a particular gene makes.

C) Eukaryotic genes are organized in large operon systems.

D) Active gene transcription occurs in the heterochromatic regions of the nucleus.

E) Lampbrush chromosomes are areas of active tRNA synthesis.

Answer: A
Skill: Knowledge

28) In which of the following would you expect to find the most methylation of DNA?

A) tandem arrays for ribosomal genes

B) pseudogenes

C) inactivated mammalian X chromosomes

D) globin genes

E) transposons

Answer: C
Skill: Knowledge

29) If one were to observe the activity of methylated DNA, it would be expected that it would

A) be replicating.

B) be unwinding in preparation for protein synthesis.

C) have turned off or slowed down the process of transcription.

D) be very active in translation.

E) induce protein synthesis by not allowing repressors to bind with it.

Answer: C
Skill: Knowledge

The questions below refer to the following terms. Each term may be used once, more than once, or not at all.

> A. *tandemly repetitive DNA*
> B. *interspersed repetitive DNA*
> C. *multigene family*
> D. *methylated DNA*
> E. *pseudogenes*

30) When pieces of DNA are centrifuged a "satellite" band develops that is separate from the rest of the DNA. This layer is composed of _____.

Answer: A
Skill: Comprehension

31) Alpha and beta globins are classic examples of which type of DNA?

Answer: C
Skill: Comprehension

32) Many transposons fall into this class of DNA.

Answer: B
Skill: Knowledge

33) Hungtington's disease is an example of _____.

Answer: B
Skill: Application

34) This class of DNA codes for the three largest ribosomal RNA molecules.

Answer: C
Skill: Knowledge

35) This is most comonly found in inactivated DNA regions.

Answer: D
Skill: Knowledge

36) portions of the genome having sequences similar to functional genes but that lack control regions

Answer: E
Skill: Knowledge

37) Which of the following may explain genomic imprinting?

A) DNA methylation

B) oncogenes

C) retrotransposons

D) microsatellite DNA

E) post–translational modification of proteins

Answer: A
Skill: Knowledge

38) Two potential devices that eukaryotic cells use to regulate transcription are DNA _____ and histone _____.

A) methylation ... amplification

B) amplification ... methylation

C) acetylation ... methylation

D) methylation ... acetylation

E) amplification ... acetylation

Answer: D
Skill: Knowledge

39) In eukaryotes, transcription is generally associated with

A) euchromatin only.

B) heterochromatin only.

C) very tightly packed DNA only.

D) highly methylated DNA only.

E) both euchromatin and histone acetylation.

Answer: E
Skill: Comprehension

40) A significant difference between eukaryotes and prokaryotes is that

A) DNA is wound around proteins to form chromatin in eukaryotes, but not in prokaryotes.

B) gene expression is largely regulated by transcription in prokaryotes, but not in eukaryotes.

C) there is an absence of introns in prokaryotic genes.

D) noncoding DNA sequences are found on prokaryotes, but not in eukaryotes.

E) prokaryotes have less DNA but more noncoding segments than eukaryotes.

Answer: C
Skill: Knowledge

41) If the structure of a TV show is analogous to the structure of a gene, then the introns of a gene would be analogous to

A) the opening theme music.

B) the segments of the show.

C) the commercials between segments of the show.

D) the commercials between shows.

E) the closing credits.

Answer: C
Skill: Comprehension

42) A eukaryotic gene typically has all of the following features *except*

A) introns.

B) a promoter.

C) an operator.

D) control elements.

E) a terminator.

Answer: C
Skill: Knowledge

43) The processing of the RNA transcript involves

A) the removal of introns and the splicing together of exons.

B) the removal of exons and the splicing together of introns.

C) the addition of a guanine cap and a poly(A) tail.

D) the attachment of introns to ribosomal RNA.

E) both A and C.

Answer: E
Skill: Knowledge

44) Eukaryotes use all of the following as a means of controlling gene expression *except* the

A) binding of regulatory proteins to DNA.

B) degradation of mRNA molecules.

C) blockage of mRNA translation by certain proteins.

D) modification of the amino acid sequence of a protein after it has been translated.

E) modification of the RNA nucleotides to enhance transcription.

Answer: E
Skill: Knowledge

45) Which of the following is *least* related to the others?

A) proximal control elements

B) repressors

C) enhancers

D) operators

E) activators

Answer: D
Skill: Comprehension

46) Which of the following is an example of transcriptional control of gene expression?

A) mRNA is stored in the cytoplasm and needs a control signal to initiate translation.

B) mRNA exists for a specific time before it is degraded.

C) There is an amplification of genes for rRNA.

D) RNA processing occurs before mRNA exits the nucleus.

E) Transcription factors bind to the enhancer and promoter regions.

Answer: E
Skill: Comprehension

47) Gene expression in eukaryotes may depend upon

A) initiation complexes.

B) DNA binding domains.

C) transcription activation of silent genes.

D) A and C.

E) A, B, and C.

Answer: E
Skill: Knowledge

The questions below refer to the following terms. Each term may be used once, more than once, or not at all.

A. enhancers
B. promoter
C. activator
D. pseudogene
E. intron

48) helps position the initiation complex on the promoter

Answer: C
Skill: Knowledge

49) recognition sites for proteins that make the DNA more accessible to RNA polymerase, thereby boosting the activity of associated genes

Answer: A
Skill: Knowledge

50) site important for controlling the initiation of transcription in eukaryotic DNA

Answer: B
Skill: Knowledge

51) has sequences very similar to functional genes, but lacks the signals for gene expression

Answer: D
Skill: Knowledge

52) Steroid hormones produce their effects in cells by

A) activating key enzymes in metabolic pathways.

B) activating translation of certain mRNAs.

C) promoting the degradation of specific mRNAs.

D) binding to receptors and promoting transcription of certain regions of DNA.

E) promoting the formation of looped domains in certain regions of DNA.

Answer: D
Skill: Knowledge

53) Gene expression can be controlled by

A) alternative splicing.

B) mRNA degradation.

C) translation initiation.

D) protein processing and degradation.

E) all of the above.

Answer: E
Skill: Knowledge

54) All of the following are potential control mechanisms for regulation of gene expression in eukaryotic organisms *except*

A) the degradation of mRNA.

B) the transport of mRNA from the nucleus.

C) the lactose operon.

D) transcription.

E) gene amplification.

Answer: C
Skill: Knowledge

55) Which of the following statements concerning proto-oncogenes is *false*?

A) They code for proteins associated with cell growth.

B) They are similar to oncogenes found in retroviruses.

C) They are produced by somatic mutations induced by carcinogenic substances.

D) They are involved in producing proteins for cell adhesion.

E) They are genes that code for proteins involved in cell division.

Answer: C
Skill: Knowledge

56) Proto-oncogenes can be converted to oncogenes by various genetic changes. Which of these mechanisms does *not* contribute to an abnormal cell cycle?

A) Chromosomes break and fragments are translocated from one chromosome to another.

B) A gene is transposed to a more active promoter.

C) Extra copies of the gene are made, thereby enhancing expression.

D) Point mutations occur that result in a protein more resistant to degradation.

E) DNA methylation takes place.

Answer: E
Skill: Knowledge

57) Which of the following is *not* a mechanism whereby a proto-oncogene is converted to an oncogene?

A) methylation of bases

B) point mutation

C) gene transposition

D) gene amplification

E) chromosome translocation

Answer: A
Skill: Knowledge

58) Which of the following is *least* related to the others?

A) cyclins

B) ubiquitin

C) tumor suppression

D) protein degradation

E) proteasomes

Answer: C
Skill: Comprehension

59) The incidence of cancer increases dramatically with age because

A) the Ras protein is more likely to be hyperactive after age sixty.

B) proteasomes become more active with age.

C) as we age, normal cell division inhibitors cease to function.

D) the longer we live, the more mutations accumulate.

E) tumor–suppressor genes are no longer able to repair damaged DNA.

Answer: D
Skill: Knowledge

60) Which of the following is *not* a
characteristic of the product of the *p53*
gene? It

A) is a transcription factor for other genes.

B) slows down the cell cycle.

C) causes cell death.

D) prevents cells from passing on
mutations due to DNA damage.

E) slows down the rate of DNA
replication by interfering with the
binding of DNA polymerase.

Answer: E
Skill: Knowledge

61) Which of the following events is necessary
for the production of a malignant tumor?

A) activation of an oncogene in the cell

B) the inactivation of tumor-suppressor
genes within the cell

C) the presence of mutagenic substances
within the cell's environment

D) the presence of a retrovirus within the
cell

E) Both A and B are necessary.

Answer: E
Skill: Knowledge

Media Activity Questions

1) A _____ is composed of DNA wrapped around protein.

   A) ribosome

   B) peroxisome

   C) nucleosome

   D) chromosome

   E) polysome

   Answer: C
   Topic: Web/CD Activity 19A

2) The process of making multiple copies of a gene is called

   A) gene amplification.

   B) gene expression.

   C) genome rearrangement.

   D) DNA replication.

   E) multitasking.

   Answer: A
   Topic: Web/CD Activity 19B

3) RNA polymerase binds to the

   A) silencer.

   B) activator.

   C) operon.

   D) enhancer.

   E) promoter.

   Answer: E
   Topic: Web/CD Activity 19D

4) Which of these is *not* a component of RNA processing?

   A) the binding of translation factors to the RNA transcript

   B) the addition of a cap to the RNA transcript

   C) the removal of introns from the RNA transcript

   D) the addition of a tail to the RNA transcript

   E) the splicing together of the RNA transcript's exons

   Answer: A
   Topic: Web/CD Activity 19E

5) Which of these is *not* a carcinogen?

   A) testosterone

   B) cigarette smoke

   C) UV light

   D) fat

   E) all of the above are carcinogens

   Answer: E
   Topic: Web/CD Activity 19G

Self-Quiz Questions

Answers to these questions also appear in the textbook.

1) In a nucleosome, the DNA is wrapped around

   A) polymerase molecules.

   B) ribosomes.

   C) histones.

   D) the nucleolus.

   E) satellite DNA.

   Answer: C

2) Apparently, our muscle cells are different from our nerve cells mainly because

   A) they express different genes.

   B) they contain different genes.

   C) they use different genetic codes.

   D) they have unique ribosomes.

   E) they have different chromosomes.

   Answer: A

3) One of the unique characteristics of retrotransposons is that

   A) translation of their RNA transcript produces an enzyme that converts the RNA back to DNA.

   B) they are found only in animal cells.

   C) once removed from the DNA, the gene segments for an antibody variable region are rejoined to the constant region.

   D) they contribute a significant portion of the genetic variability seen within a population of gametes.

   E) their amplification is dependent on a concurrent retrovirus infection.

   Answer: A

4) The functioning of enhancers is an example of

   A) transcriptional control of gene expression.

   B) a post-transcriptional mechanism for editing mRNA.

   C) the stimulation of translation by initiation factors.

   D) post-translational control that activates certain proteins.

   E) a eukaryotic equivalent of prokaryotic promoter functioning.

   Answer: A

5) Multigene families are

   A) groups of enhancers that control transcription.

   B) usually clustered at the telomeres.

   C) equivalent to the operons of prokaryotes.

   D) collections of genes whose expression is controlled by the same regulatory proteins.

   E) identical or similar genes that have evolved by gene duplication.

   Answer: E

6) Which of the following statements about the DNA in one of your brain cells is *true*?

   A) Some DNA sequences are present in multiple copies.

   B) Most of the DNA codes for protein.

   C) The majority of genes are likely to be transcribed.

   D) Each gene lies immediately adjacent to an enhancer that helps control transcription.

   E) Many genes are grouped into operon-like clusters.

   Answer: A

7) Rearrangement of DNA segments is known to occur in genes coding for

A) ribosomal RNA.

B) most proteins in eukaryotes.

C) hemoglobin.

D) histone proteins.

E) antibodies.

Answer: E

8) Which of the following is an example of a possible step in the posttranscriptional control of gene expression?

A) the addition of methyl groups to cytosine bases of DNA

B) the binding of transcription factors to a promoter

C) the removal of introns and splicing together of exons

D) gene amplification during a stage in development

E) the folding of DNA to form heterochromatin

Answer: C

9) The amount of protein made from a given mRNA molecule depends partly on

A) the degree of DNA methylation.

B) the rate at which the mRNA is degraded.

C) the presence of certain transcription factors.

D) the number of introns present in the mRNA.

E) the types of ribosomes present in the cytoplasm.

Answer: B

10) All of our cells contain proto-oncogenes, which can change into oncogenes that cause cancer. Which of the following is the *best* explanation for the presence of these potential time bombs in our cells?

A) Proto-oncogenes first arose from viral infections.

B) Proto-oncogenes normally help regulate cell division.

C) Proto-oncogenes are genetic "junk."

D) Proto-oncogenes are mutant versions of normal genes.

E) Cells produce proto-oncogenes as a by-product of the aging process.

Answer: B

1) It is theoretically possible for a gene from any organism to function in any other organism. Why is this possible?

A) All organisms have the same genetic code.

B) All organisms are made up of cells.

C) All organisms have similar nuclei.

D) All organisms have ribosomes.

E) All organisms have transfer RNA.

Answer: A
Skill: Comprehension

2) One important approach to gene cloning uses

A) whole chromosomes.

B) plasmids.

C) noncoding nucleotide sequences.

D) bacteria.

E) B and D above.

Answer: E
Skill: Knowledge

3) Current applications of gene cloning include

A) cleaning up toxic waste.

B) instilling pest resistance in plants.

C) manufacturing human growth hormone.

D) A and C only.

E) A, B, and C.

Answer: E
Skill: Knowledge

4) Plasmids are important in biotechnology because they are

A) a vehicle for the insertion of recombinant DNA into bacteria.

B) recognition sites on recombinant DNA strands.

C) surfaces for protein synthesis in eukaryotic recombinants.

D) surfaces for respiratory processes in bacteria.

E) proviruses incorporated into the host DNA.

Answer: A
Skill: Knowledge

5) If you discovered a bacterial cell that contained no restriction enzymes, which of the following would you expect to happen?

A) The cell would be unable to replicate its DNA.

B) The cell would create incomplete plasmids.

C) The cell would be easily infected and lysed by bacteriophages.

D) The cell would become an obligate parasite.

E) Both A and D would occur.

Answer: C
Skill: Comprehension

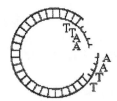

Figure 20.1

6) Which enzyme was used to produce the molecule in Figure 20.1?
   A) ligase
   B) transcriptase
   C) a restriction enzyme
   D) RNA polymerase
   E) DNA polymerase

Answer: C
Skill: Knowledge

7) Assume that you are trying to insert a gene into a plasmid and someone gives you a preparation of DNA cut with restriction enzyme X. The gene you wish to insert has sites on both ends for cutting by restriction enzyme Y. You have a plasmid with a single site for Y, but not for X. Your strategy should be to
   A) insert the fragments cut with X directly into the plasmid without cutting the plasmid.
   B) cut the plasmid with restriction enzyme X and insert the fragments cut with Y into the plasmid.
   C) cut the DNA again with restriction enzyme Y and insert these fragments into the plasmid cut with the same enzyme.
   D) cut the plasmid twice with restriction enzyme Y and ligate the two fragments onto the ends of the human DNA fragments cut with restriction enzyme X.
   E) cut the plasmid with enzyme X and then insert the gene into the plasmid.

Answer: C
Skill: Application

8) What is the genetic function of restriction enzyme?
   A) adds new nucleotides to the growing strand of DNA
   B) joins nucleotides during replication
   C) joins nucleotides during transcription
   D) cleaves nucleic acids at specific sites
   E) repairs breaks in sugar–phosphate backbones

Answer: D
Skill: Knowledge

9) The restriction enzyme used in constructing hybrid molecules of certain gene sequences and plasmid DNA acts by
   A) opening DNA molecules at specific sites, leaving sticky ends exposed.
   B) sealing plasmid DNA and foreign DNA into a closed circle.
   C) transcribing plasmid DNA into a transformed molecule.
   D) allowing a hybrid plasmid DNA into a transformed molecule.
   E) binding human genes to bacterial plasmids.

Answer: A
Skill: Knowledge

10) How does a bacterial cell protect its own DNA from restriction enzymes?
   A) by adding methyl groups to adenines and cytosines
   B) using DNA ligase to seal the bacterial DNA into a closed circle
   C) adding histones to protect the double–stranded DNA
   D) by forming "sticky ends" of bacterial DNA to prevent the enzyme from attaching
   E) by reinforcing bacterial DNA structure with covalent phosphodiester bonds

Answer: A
Skill: Knowledge

11) What two enzymes are needed to produce recombinant DNA?

   A) endonuclease, transcriptase

   B) restriction enzyme, ligase

   C) polymerase, ligase

   D) transcriptase, ligase

   E) DNA polymerase, topoisomerase

Answer: B
Skill: Knowledge

12) What is a cloning vector?

   A) the enzyme that cuts DNA into restriction fragments

   B) a DNA probe used to locate a particular gene in the genome

   C) an agent, such as a plasmid, used to transfer DNA from an *in vitro* solution into a living cell

   D) the laboratory apparatus used to clone genes

   E) the sticky end of a DNA fragment

Answer: C
Skill: Comprehension

13) What are the essential characteristics of a cloning vector?

   A) Bacterial cells cannot survive without it.

   B) Bacterial cells take it up.

   C) Bacterial cells replicate it.

   D) Both B and C are correct.

   E) A, B, and C are correct.

Answer: D
Skill: Knowledge

I.   *Transform bacteria with recombinant DNA molecule*
II.   *Cut the plasmid DNA using restriction enzymes*
III.   *Extract plasmid DNA from bacterial cells*
IV.   *Hydrogen–bond the plasmid DNA to nonplasmid DNA fragments*
V.   *Use ligase to seal plasmid DNA to nonplasmid DNA*

14) From the list above, which of the following is the most logical sequence of steps for splicing foreign DNA into a plasmid and inserting the plasmid into a bacterium?

   A) I, II, IV, III, V

   B) II, III, V, IV, I

   C) III, II, IV, V, I

   D) III, IV, V, I, II

   E) IV, V, I, II, III

Answer: C
Skill: Comprehension

15) Bacteria containing recombinant plasmids are often identified by which process?

   A) examining the cells with an electron microscope

   B) using radioactive tracers to locate the plasmids

   C) exposing the bacteria to an antibiotic that kills the cells lacking the plasmid

   D) removing the DNA of all cells in a culture to see which cells have plasmids

   E) producing antibodies specific for each bacterium containing a recombinant plasmid

Answer: C
Skill: Knowledge

Use the following information to answer the questions below.

A eukaryotic gene has "sticky ends" produced by the restriction endonuclease EcoRI. The gene is added to a mixture containing EcoRI and a bacterial plasmid that carries two genes, which make it resistant to ampicillin and tetracycline. The plasmid has one recognition site for EcoRI located in the tetracycline resistance gene. This mixture is incubated for several hours and then added to bacteria growing in nutrient broth. The bacteria are allowed to grow overnight and are streaked on a plate using a technique that produces isolated colonies that are clones of the original. Samples of these colonies are then grown in four different media: nutrient broth plus ampicillin, nutrient broth plus tetracycline, nutrient broth plus ampicillin and tetracycline, and nutrient broth containing no antibiotics.

16) The bacteria containing the engineered plasmid would grow in

A) the nutrient broth only.

B) the nutrient broth and the tetracycline broth only.

C) the nutrient broth, the ampicillin broth, and the tetracycline broth.

D) the ampicillin and tetracycline broth only.

E) the ampicillin broth and the nutrient broth.

Answer: E
Skill: Comprehension

17) The bacteria that contained the plasmid, but not the eukaryotic gene, would grow

A) in the nutrient broth plus ampicillin, but not in the broth containing tetracycline.

B) only in the broth containing both antibiotics.

C) in the broth containing tetracycline, but not in the broth containing ampicillin.

D) in all four types of broth.

E) only in the broth that contained no antibiotics.

Answer: D
Skill: Comprehension

18) Why was the gene inserted in the plasmid before it was mixed with the bacteria?

A) The plasmid acted as a vector to introduce the gene into the bacteria.

B) The plasmid contains control regions necessary for the replication of the gene.

C) The eukaryotic gene contains introns that must be removed by the plasmid.

D) Only A and B are correct.

E) A, B, and C are correct.

Answer: D
Skill: Comprehension

19) Bacteria that did not take up any plasmids would grow on which media?

A) the nutrient broth only

B) the nutrient broth and the tetracycline broth only

C) the nutrient broth and the ampicillin broth only

D) the tetracycline and ampicillin broth only

E) all four broths

Answer: A
Skill: Comprehension

20) All of the following statements about probes are true *except:*

A) They are single-stranded segments of DNA or RNA.

B) Shorter probes adhere to more fragments than do longer probes.

C) The probe must be labeled with a radioactive isotope or fluorescent tab.

D) They must be produced with the same restriction enzyme as the fragments.

E) In many cases, a probe from one organism can be used to locate a homologous DNA segment in another organism.

Answer: D
Skill: Comprehension

21) After being digested with a restriction enzyme, DNA fragments are separated by gel electrophoresis. Specific fragments are then identified through the use of a

A) plasmid.

B) restriction enzyme.

C) sticky end.

D) nucleic acid probe.

E) RFLP.

Answer: D
Skill: Knowledge

22) Andy Will has cloned a gene that he believes is important in conferring resistance to insects in a certain plant. He now wants to determine where in the genome that gene is physically located. He would *most* likely use which technique?

A) RFLP analysis

B) *in situ* hybridization

C) *in vivo* mutagenesis

D) DNA microarray assays

E) use of antisense nucleic acids

Answer: B
Skill: Comprehension

23) Probes are short, single–stranded DNA or RNA segments that are used to identify DNA fragments with a particular sequence. Before the probe can identify a specific restriction fragment, what must be done?

A) The fragments must be separated by electrophoresis.

B) The fragments must be treated with heat or chemicals to separate the strands of the double helix.

C) The probe must be hybridized with the fragment.

D) A and B only

E) A, B, and C

Answer: E
Skill: Knowledge

24) Which of the following is *least* related to the others?

A) denaturation

B) DNA ligase

C) sticky ends

D) restriction enzymes

E) cloning vector

Answer: A
Skill: Comprehension

25) Why is it difficult to get bacteria to express genes directly from eukaryotic DNA?

A) Eukaryotic genes are not transcribed in a single transcript.

B) Eukaryotic genes do not contain enhancer sequences.

C) Eukaryotic genes contain introns.

D) Eukaryotic genes lack controlling regions.

E) Eukaryotic genes may contain transposons.

Answer: C
Skill: Knowledge

26) The principal problem with inserting an unmodified mammalian gene into the bacterial chromosome, and then getting that gene expressed, is that

A) prokaryotes use a different genetic code from that of eukaryotes.

B) bacteria translate polycistronic messages only.

C) bacteria cannot remove eukaryotic introns.

D) bacterial RNA polymerase cannot make RNA complementary to mammalian DNA.

E) bacterial DNA is not found in a membrane–enclosed nucleus and is therefore incompatible with mammalian DNA.

Answer: C
Skill: Application

27) A gene that contains introns can be made shorter (but remain functional) for genetic engineering purposes by

   A) using RNA polymerase to transcribe the gene.

   B) using a restriction enzyme to cut the gene into shorter pieces.

   C) using reverse transcriptase to reconstruct the gene from its mRNA.

   D) using DNA polymerase to reconstruct the gene from its polypeptide product.

   E) using DNA ligase to put together fragments of the DNA that codes for a particular polypeptide.

Answer: C
Skill: Comprehension

28) Yeast cells are frequently used as hosts for cloning because

   A) they are easy to grow.

   B) they have multiple restriction sites.

   C) they have plasmids.

   D) A and B are correct.

   E) A and C are correct.

Answer: E
Skill: Knowledge

29) Specific DNA fragments of a genomic library are contained in

   A) recombinant plasmids of bacteria.

   B) recombinant viral DNA.

   C) eukaryotic chromosomes.

   D) A and B.

   E) A, B, and C.

Answer: D
Skill: Comprehension

30) The DNA of a cell is like a library. The books of a library are analogous to genes, and the sections of a library are analogous to chromosomes. Which of the following would *not* be a library activity analogous to a function of biotechnology?

   A) finding a particular book in the library

   B) moving a book from one library to another

   C) reading and understanding the contents of a book

   D) identifying a library by the books that it has

   E) returning books that had been checked out

Answer: E
Skill: Comprehension

31) The polymerase chain reaction is important because it allows us to

   A) insert eukaryotic genes into prokaryotic plasmids.

   B) incorporate genes into viruses.

   C) make DNA from RNA transcripts.

   D) make many copies of a targeted segment of DNA.

   E) insert regulatory sequences into eukaryotic genes.

Answer: D
Skill: Knowledge

32) The polymerase chain reaction (PCR) could be used to amplify DNA from which of the following?

   A) a fossil

   B) a fetal cell

   C) a virus

   D) B and C

   E) A, B, and C

Answer: E
Skill: Comprehension

33) Restriction fragments of DNA are separated from one another by which process?

A) filtering

B) centrifugation

C) gel electrophoresis

D) chromatography

E) electron microscopy

Answer: C
Skill: Knowledge

The following questions refer to the techniques, tools, or substances listed below. Answers may be used once, more than once, or not at all.

A. *restriction enzymes*
B. *gene cloning*
C. *DNA ligase*
D. *gel electrophoresis*
E. *reverse transcriptase*

34) produces multiple identical copies of a gene for basic research or for large-scale production of a gene product

Answer: B
Skill: Knowledge

35) enables one to create complementary DNA (cDNA) from mRNA; results in a smaller gene product (RNA processed; no introns) that is more easily translated by bacteria

Answer: E
Skill: Knowledge

36) separates molecules by movement due to size and electrical charge

Answer: D
Skill: Knowledge

37) seals the sticky ends of restriction fragments to make recombinant DNA

Answer: C
Skill: Knowledge

38) Which of the following procedures would produce RFLPs?

A) incubating a mixture of single-stranded DNA from two closely related species

B) incubating DNA nucleotides with DNA polymerase

C) incubating DNA with restriction enzymes

D) incubating RNA with DNA nucleotides and reverse transcriptase

E) incubating DNA fragments with "sticky ends" with ligase

Answer: C
Skill: Knowledge

Use the following information and Figure 20.2 to answer the following questions. The DNA profiles below represent four different individuals.

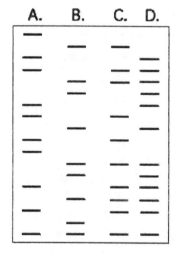

Figure 20.2

39) Which of the following statements is consistent with the results?

A) B is the child of A and C.

B) C is the child of A and B.

C) D is the child of B and C.

D) A is the child of B and C.

E) A is the child of C and D.

Answer: B
Skill: Application

40) Which of the following statements is most likely *true*?

A) D is the child of A and C.

B) D is the child of A and B.

C) D is the child of B and C.

D) A is the child of C and D.

E) B is the child of A and C.

Answer: B
Skill: Application

41) Which of the following are probably siblings?

A) A and B

B) A and C

C) A and D

D) C and D

E) B and D

Answer: D
Skill: Application

Use the following choices to answer the questions below. Each choice may be used once, more than once, or not at all.

A. *restriction enzyme*
B. *DNA ligase*
C. *reverse transcriptase*
D. *RNA polymerase*
E. *DNA polymerase*

42) Which enzyme permanently seals together DNA fragments that have complementary sticky ends?

Answer: B
Skill: Knowledge

43) Which enzyme is used to make complementary DNA (cDNA) from RNA?

Answer: C
Skill: Knowledge

44) Which enzyme is used to make multiple copies of genes in the polymerase chain reaction (PCR)?

Answer: E
Skill: Knowledge

45) Which enzyme is used to produce RFLPs?

Answer: A
Skill: Knowledge

46) Which enzyme cuts DNA molecules at specific locations?

Answer: A
Skill: Knowledge

47) DNA fragments from a gel are transferred to a membrane during the procedure called Southern blotting. The purpose of transferring the DNA from a gel to a membrane is to

A) permanently attach the DNA fragments to a substrate.

B) separate the two complementary DNA strands.

C) transfer only the DNA that is of interest.

D) analyze the RFLPs in the DNA.

E) separate out the PCRs.

Answer: A
Skill: Knowledge

48) The Southern blotting procedure enables the detection and analysis of DNA sequences. This means that

A) the existence of specific sequences can be determined.

B) the number of sequences can be determined.

C) the size of restriction fragments that contain the sequence can be determined.

D) the DNA of individuals and species can be compared.

E) all of the above are possible using the Southern blotting procedure.

Answer: E
Skill: Knowledge

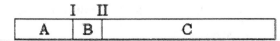

Figure 20.3

49) The segment of DNA shown in Figure 20.3 has restriction sites I and II, which create restriction fragments A, B, and C. Which of the gels produced by electrophoresis shown below would represent the separation and identity of these fragments?

A)

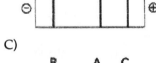

B)

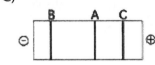

C)

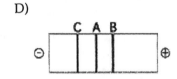

D)

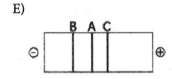

E)

Answer: B
Skill: Application

50) Surprisingly, the human genome contains fewer genes than expected. How, then, is the human genome more complex than that of other organisms?
   A) RNA transcripts of human genes are more likely to experiance alternative splicing.
   B) Post-translational processing adds diversity to the resulting polypeptides.
   C) Polypeptide domains are combined in a variety of ways.
   D) Different combinations of exons are used.
   E) All of the above are correct.

Answer: E
Skill: Comprehension

51) Which of the following is *least* related to the others?
   A) Southern blotting
   B) denaturation
   C) nucleic acid probe
   D) DNA microarray assays
   E) nucleic acid hybridization

Answer: D
Skill: Comprehension

52) Gene therapy
   A) has proven to be beneficial to HIV patients.
   B) involves replacement of a defective allele in sex cells.
   C) cannot be used to correct genetic disorders.
   D) has its greatest chance of success with bone marrow cells.
   E) is a widely accepted procedure.

Answer: D
Skill: Comprehension

53) Which of these is *not* one of the procedures used in Southern blotting?

   A) electrophoresis

   B) hybridization

   C) autoradiography

   D) restriction fragment preparation

   E) DNA microarray assay

   Answer: E
   Skill: Knowledge

54) Proteomics presents a particular challenge because

   A) the number of proteins in humans probably exceeds the number of genes.

   B) a cell's proteins differ with cell type.

   C) proteins are extremely varied in structure and chemical properties.

   D) A and B are true.

   E) A, B, and C are true.

   Answer: E
   Skill: Knowledge

55) Genetic engineering is being used by the pharmaceutical industry. Which of the following is *not* currently one of the uses?

   A) production of human insulin

   B) production of human growth hormone

   C) production of tissue plasminogen activator

   D) genetic modification of plants to produce vaccines

   E) creation of products that will remove poisons from the human body

   Answer: E
   Skill: Knowledge

56) A DNA profile is produced by

   A) treating selected segments of DNA with restriction enzymes.

   B) electrophoresis of restriction fragments.

   C) using a probe to locate specific nucleotide sequences.

   D) A and B.

   E) A, B, and C.

   Answer: E
   Skill: Application

57) Which of the following is *least* related to the others?

   A) restriction fragment length polymorphism (RFLP)

   B) chromosome walking

   C) simple tandem repeat (STR)

   D) polymerase chain reaction

   E) DNA fingerprint

   Answer: B
   Skill: Comprehension

58) Genetically engineered plants

   A) are more difficult to engineer than animals.

   B) include a transgenic rice plant that could help prevent vitamin A deficiency.

   C) are being rapidly developed, but traditional plant breeding programs are still the method used to develop new plants.

   D) are able to fix nitrogen themselves.

   E) are all monocots.

   Answer: B
   Skill: Knowledge

59) Scientists developed a set of guidelines to address the safety of DNA technology. Which of the following is one of the adopted safety measures?

A) Microorganisms used in recombinant DNA experiments are genetically crippled to ensure that they cannot survive outside of the laboratory.

B) Genetically modified organisms cannot be part of our food supply.

C) Transgenic plants are engineered so that the plant genes cannot hybridize.

D) Experiments involving HIV or other potentially dangerous viruses have been banned.

E) Recombinant plasmids cannot be replicated.

Answer: A
Skill: Knowledge

Media Activity Questions

1) What is the advantage of being able to clone the gene for human insulin?

   A) Human insulin is more variable than other sources of insulin, so cloning would provide a greater chance of obtaining a form that can be used by the diabetic's muscles.

   B) There are too few cows, pigs, and horses to provide an adequate supply of their insulin.

   C) Human insulin is less likely to provoke an allergic reaction than cow, pig, or horse insulin.

   D) Cow, pig, or horse insulin cannot keep a diabetic alive for more than three months.

   E) Using human insulin increases the probability that, in the future, the diabetic can be weaned from a dependence on insulin.

   Answer: C
   Topic: Web/CD Activity 20A

2) What is a major source of restriction enzymes?

   A) chief cells

   B) DNA technology

   C) parietal cells

   D) archaea

   E) bacteria

   Answer: E
   Topic: Web/CD Activity 20B

3) _____ is the process by which a bacterium takes up a plasmid from the surrounding solution.

   A) Transformation

   B) Transcription

   C) Transition

   D) Transduction

   E) Translation

   Answer: A
   Topic: Web/CD Activity 20C

4) Gel electrophoresis separates DNA molecules on the basis of

   A) the nucleotide sequence of their sticky ends.

   B) their nucleotide sequences.

   C) the amount of adenine they contain relative to the amount of thymine they contain.

   D) the amount of adenine they contain relative to the amount of guanine they contain.

   E) their lengths.

   Answer: E
   Topic: Web/CD Activity 20D

5) What is the designation for the short arm of a chromosome?

   A) l   B) p   C) q   D) r   E) s

   Answer: B
   Topic: Web/CD Activity 20F

Self-Quiz Questions

Answers to these questions also appear in the textbook.

1) Which of the following tools of recombinant DNA technology is *incorrectly* paired with its use?

   A) restriction enzyme—production of RFLPs

   B) DNA ligase—enzyme that cuts DNA, creating the sticky ends of restriction fragments

   C) DNA polymerase—used in a polymerase chain reaction to amplify sections of DNA

   D) reverse transcriptase—production of cDNA from mRNA

   E) electrophoresis—DNA sequencing

   Answer: B

2) Which of the following would *not* be true of cDNA produced using human brain tissue as the starting material?

   A) It could be amplified by the polymerase chain reaction.

   B) It could be used to create a complete genomic library.

   C) It is produced from mRNA using reverse transcriptase.

   D) It could be used as a probe to locate a gene of interest.

   E) It lacks the introns of the human genes and thus can probably be introduced into phage vectors.

   Answer: B

3) Plants are more readily manipulated by genetic engineering than are animals because

   A) plant genes do not contain introns.

   B) more vectors are available for transferring recombinant DNA into plant cells.

   C) a somatic plant cell can often give rise to a complete plant.

   D) genes can be inserted into plant cells by microinjection.

   E) plant cells have larger nuclei.

   Answer: C

4) A paleontologist has recovered a bit of tissue from the 400–year–old preserved skin of an extinct dodo (a bird). The researcher would like to compare DNA from the sample with DNA from living birds. Which of the following would be most useful for increasing the amount of dodo DNA available for testing?

   A) RFLP analysis

   B) polymerase chain reaction (PCR)

   C) electroporation

   D) gel electrophoresis

   E) Southern hybridization

   Answer: B

5) Expression of a cloned eukaryotic gene in a prokaryotic cell involves many difficulties. The use of mRNA and reverse transcriptase is part of a strategy to solve the problem of

   A) post-transcriptional processing.

   B) electroporation.

   C) post-translational processing.

   D) nucleic acid hybridization.

   E) restriction fragment ligation.

   Answer: A

6) DNA technology has many medical applications. Which of the following is *not yet* done routinely?

A) production of hormones for treating diabetes and dwarfism

B) production of viral subunits for vaccines

C) introduction of genetically engineered genes into human gametes

D) prenatal identification of genetic disease genes

E) genetic testing for carriers of harmful alleles

Answer: C

7) Which of the following has the largest genome size and the smallest number of genes per million base pairs?

A) *H. influenzae* (bacterium)

B) *S. cerevisiae* (yeast)

C) *A. thaliana* (plant)

D) *D. melanogaster* (fruit fly)

E) *H. sapiens* (human)

Answer: E

8) Which of the following sequences in double-stranded DNA is most likely to be recognized as a cutting site for a restriction enzyme?

A) AAGG
   TTCC

B) AGTC
   TCAG

C) GGCC
   CCGG

D) ACCA
   TGGT

E) AAAA
   TTTT

Answer: C

9) In recombinant DNA methods, the term *vector* can refer to

A) the enzyme that cuts DNA into restriction fragments.

B) the sticky end of a DNA fragment.

C) a RFLP marker.

D) a plasmid used to transfer DNA into a living cell.

E) a DNA probe used to identify a particular gene.

Answer: D

10) In its sequencing of the human genome, Celera carried out

A) linkage mapping of each chromosome.

B) extensive physical mapping of each chromosome, starting with large chromosomal fragments.

C) DNA sequencing of small fragments and then assembly of the fragments to determine overall nucleotide sequence.

D) A and B

E) A, B, and C

Answer: C

Chapter 21 The Genetic Basis of Development

1) Which of the following is involved in embryonic development?
   A) cell division
   B) cell differentiation
   C) morphogenesis
   D) A and B
   E) A, B, and C

   Answer: E
   Skill: Knowledge

2) "Becoming specialized in structure and function" is a definition of
   A) morphogenesis.
   B) development.
   C) induction.
   D) differentiation.
   E) pattern formation.

   Answer: D
   Skill: Knowledge

3) Without which of the following processes would all the others be impossible?
   A) differentiation
   B) morphogenesis
   C) cell division
   D) induction
   E) activation

   Answer: C
   Skill: Comprehension

4) One striking difference between development in plants and development in animals is the importance of cell _____ in animal embryos.
   A) division
   B) differentiation
   C) growth
   D) movement
   E) death

   Answer: D
   Skill: Knowledge

5) One striking difference between development in plants and development in animals is that in plant development
   A) growth and morphogenesis continue throughout the life of the plant.
   B) cell differentiation never stops.
   C) once a structure develops, it cannot reverse its path.
   D) haploid and diploid cells are equally important.
   E) chemical signals play a much greater role than in animal development.

   Answer: A
   Skill: Knowledge

6) A model organism for genetic analysis must meet certain criteria. Which of these is *not* one of the criteria?
   A) readily observable embryos
   B) short generation times
   C) relatively small genomes
   D) the ability to produce both egg and sperm
   E) knowledge of the organism

   Answer: D
   Skill: Knowledge

7) Of the following, which has *not* proven to be a useful model organism in the study of developmental genetics?
   A) humans
   B) *Drosophila*
   C) *Arabidopsis*
   D) *Caenorhabditis*
   E) mice

   Answer: A
   Skill: Knowledge

8) The nematode *Caenorhabditis elegans* is used as a model organism for genetic studies. One of the key advantages of using *Caenorhabditis elegans* for study is that

A) it is hermaphroditic, making it easy to detect recessive mutations.

B) it has a great variety of somatic cells.

C) its genome is as large as ours.

D) early stages of development proceed quickly.

E) morphogenesis and growth occur throughout life.

Answer: A
Skill: Knowledge

9) The process of cellular differentiation is a direct result of

A) differential gene expression.

B) morphogenesis.

C) cell division.

D) induction.

E) differences in cellular genomes.

Answer: A
Skill: Knowledge

10) The cloning of a plant from somatic cells is consistent with the view that

A) differentiated cells retain all the genes of the zygote.

B) genes are lost during differentiation.

C) the differentiated state is normally very unstable.

D) differentiated cells contain masked mRNA.

E) cells can be easily reprogrammed to differentiate and develop into another kind of cell.

Answer: A
Skill: Comprehension

11) The ability of a transplanted nucleus to support development

A) is inversely related to the age of the donor.

B) depends on the DNA base sequence.

C) only occurs in plants.

D) depends on the size of the genome.

E) depends on the nucleus not changing.

Answer: A
Skill: Knowledge

12) A cell that remains flexible in its developmental possibilities is said to be

A) differentiated.

B) determined.

C) totipotent.

D) genomically equivalent.

E) epigenic.

Answer: C
Skill: Knowledge

13) The cloning of "Dolly" was considered a major scientific breakthrough because

A) it showed that differentiated adult mammal cells can dedifferentiate.

B) it showed that cells can be arrested in the cell cycle.

C) it was the first time a surrogate mother was used successfully.

D) it was evidence that DNA methylation regulates gene expression.

E) it proved that the pattern of gene expression is controlled at transcription.

Answer: A
Skill: Knowledge

14) All of the following statements are true about stem cells *except:*

A) Stem cells can continually reproduce themselves.

B) Stem cells can differentiate into specialized cells.

C) Stem cells are found in bone marrow.

D) Stem cells are found in the adult human brain.

E) Stem cell DNA lacks introns.

Answer: E
Skill: Knowledge

15) The first evidence of differentiation is

A) cell division.

B) the occurrence of mRNAs for the production of tissue–specific proteins.

C) determination.

D) changes in the size and shape of the cell.

E) changes resulting from induction.

Answer: B
Skill: Knowledge

16) In most cases, differentiation is controlled at the level of

A) replication of the DNA.

B) nucleosome formation.

C) transcription.

D) translation.

E) post–translational activation of the proteins.

Answer: C
Skill: Comprehension

17) Which of the following serve as sources of developmental information?

A) cytoplasmic determinants such as mRNAs and proteins produced before fertilization

B) signal molecules produced by neighboring cells

C) tissue–specific proteins

D) A and B

E) A, B, and C

Answer: D
Skill: Comprehension

18) Which features of the unfertilized egg serve as sources of developmental information?

A) RNA molecules

B) proteins

C) gradients of small molecules such as calcium ions

D) A and B

E) A, B, and C

Answer: E
Skill: Comprehension

19) "The development of spatial organization in which the tissues and organs are all in their characteristic places" is a definition of

A) morphogenesis.

B) development.

C) induction.

D) differentiation.

E) pattern formation.

Answer: E
Skill: Knowledge

20) One difference between development in plants and development in animals involves pattern formation because
   A) pattern formation is continuous in plants and limited to early development in animals.
   B) pattern formation is continuous in animals and limited to early development in plants.
   C) pattern formation occurs in all parts of the plant, but is limited to specific locations in animals.
   D) pattern formation is limited to specific locations in plants, but occurs in all parts of animals.
   E) A and C are correct.

   Answer: A
   Skill: Knowledge

21) Your brother, Todd, has just purchased a new plastic model of an airplane. He removes it from the box and places all the parts on the table in approximately the positions they will finally be located when the model is put together. Todd's actions are analogous to which process in development?
   A) morphogenesis
   B) development
   C) induction
   D) differentiation
   E) pattern formation

   Answer: E
   Skill: Knowledge

22) A cell's location relative to the body axes in an animal embryo is determined by molecular clues that control pattern formation. Which of the following contribute to positional information in *Drosophila*?
   A) egg polarity genes
   B) tissue–specific proteins
   C) bicoid mRNA
   D) A and C only
   E) A, B, and C

   Answer: D
   Skill: Knowledge

23) Of the approximately 12,000 genes in *Drosophila*, what proportion are essential for embryonic development?
   A) 1% (about 120 genes)
   B) 2% (about 240 genes)
   C) 10% (about 1,200 genes)
   D) 50% (about 6,000 genes)
   E) 75% (about 9,000 genes)

   Answer: C
   Skill: Knowledge

24) The product of the *bicoid* gene in *Drosophila* provides essential information about
   A) the head–tail axis.
   B) the dorsal–ventral axis.
   C) the left–right axis.
   D) segmentation.
   E) lethal genes.

   Answer: A
   Skill: Knowledge

25) Suppose a mutation occurred in *Drosophila* in the region of DNA that codes for the protein called bicoid. What is most likely to happen during development?

   A) Two sets of limbs will form in a mirror–image arrangement.

   B) The polarity of the fertilized egg will be disrupted.

   C) The transcription of developmental genes will stop.

   D) The embryos will express their father's genotype.

   E) The fertilized egg will be bipolar.

   Answer: B
   Skill: Application

For the following questions, use the following responses:

   A. bicoid gene
   B. gap genes
   C. pair–rule genes
   D. segment–polarity genes
   E. homeotic genes

26) Which map out the basic subdivisions along the anterior–posterior axis of the *Drosophila* embryo?

   Answer: B
   Skill: Knowledge

27) Which define the modular pattern of segments?

   Answer: C
   Skill: Knowledge

28) Which sets the anterior–posterior polarity of the segment?

   Answer: D
   Skill: Knowledge

29) Which establishes the overall anterior–posterior axis of the embryo?

   Answer: A
   Skill: Knowledge

30) The failure of which of these would result in an embryo with only half the normal number of segments?

   Answer: C
   Skill: Comprehension

31) The failure of which of these would result in an embryo lacking groups of body segments?

   Answer: B
   Skill: Comprehension

32) The failure of which of these would result in an embryo with the normal number of segments, but having parts of some segments replaced by mirror–image repeats of other segments?

   Answer: D
   Skill: Comprehension

33) Which of these do all the others rely upon?

   Answer: A
   Skill: Comprehension

34) Generals map out an overall plan of a war. Colonels determine the plans for specific battles. Majors decide which units will perform each function, and captains determine which soldiers will have which jobs. Given this analogy, gap genes function like

   A) generals.

   B) colonels.

   C) majors.

   D) captains.

   E) soldiers.

   Answer: B
   Skill: Comprehension

35) The product of the *bicoid* gene in *Drosophila* could be considered a

A) tissue–specific protein.

B) cytoplasmic determinant.

C) morphogen.

D) B and C.

E) A, B, and C.

Answer: D
Skill: Comprehension

36) Given the function of the *bicoid* gene product, if the gene were cloned and large amounts of the product were injected into eggs, which of the following would be *true*?

A) The embryos would grow much larger.

B) The embryos would grow extra wings and legs.

C) The embryos would die and probably show no anterior development.

D) Anterior structures would form in the area of injection.

E) The embryos would develop normally.

Answer: D
Skill: Comprehension

37) What do gap genes, pair–rule genes, segment–polarity genes, and homeotic genes all have in common?

A) Their products act as transcription factors.

B) They have no counterparts in animals other than *Drosophila*.

C) Their products are all synthesized prior to fertilization.

D) They act independently of other positional information.

E) They apparently can be activated and inactivated at any time of the fly's life.

Answer: A
Skill: Comprehension

38) Which of the following is *least* related to the others?

A) cell division

B) morphogenesis

C) induction

D) differentiation

E) bacterial transformation

Answer: E
Skill: Comprehension

39) Which of the following is *least* related to the others?

A) gap genes

B) cyclin genes

C) pair–rule genes

D) segment–polarity genes

E) segmentation genes

Answer: B
Skill: Comprehension

40) Which of the following is *least* related to the others?

A) cytoplasmic determinants

B) morphogens

C) totipotent

D) induction

E) homeotic genes

Answer: C
Skill: Comprehension

41) All of the following are *true* concerning homeotic genes *except*:

   A) They are the primary inducer of frog morphogenesis.

   B) A DNA sequence of 180 nucleotides is common to all of the genes.

   C) They are translated into peptide sequences called homeodomains.

   D) The peptide gene product is a regulatory protein that controls transcription.

   E) A mutation may cause misplacement of body segments.

   Answer: A
   Skill: Comprehension

42) Which of the following statements concerning homeotic genes is *correct*?

   A) There is a sequence of 180 nucleotides common to all the genes.

   B) They are translated into homeodomains that function as transcription factors.

   C) They are egg-polarity genes that code for morphogens.

   D) Only A and B are correct.

   E) A, B, and C are correct.

   Answer: D
   Skill: Comprehension

43) The term *homeobox* refers to

   A) a group of genes that determine polarity during development.

   B) peptide sequences of 60 amino acids that turn other genes on or off.

   C) zones of polarizing activity commonly present during limb formation.

   D) a specific nucleotide sequence of some genes that regulate development.

   E) glycoproteins that assist cells during morphogenetic movements.

   Answer: D
   Skill: Knowledge

44) Why is a certain 180-nucleotide sequence in many developmental genes called a homeobox?

   A) because it reads the same forwards as backwards

   B) because it contains no introns

   C) because virtually the same sequence is found in every homeotic gene

   D) because when it was first cloned, it could only be inserted into a bacterial plasmid called "box"

   E) because it was first cloned by Dr. H. O. Meobox

   Answer: C
   Skill: Knowledge

45) A small, impermeable membrane is placed between the anchor cell and the other vulva precursor cells in a larva of *C. elegans*. What would you expect the result to be?

   A) The vulva would continue to develop normally.

   B) The vulva would not develop at all.

   C) The outer part of the vulva would develop, but the inner part would not.

   D) The inner part of the vulva would develop, but the outer part would not.

   E) Only the posterior part of the vulva would develop.

   Answer: B
   Skill: Comprehension

46) Which of the following statements is *false*?

A) Induction involves cells communicating with each other.

B) Induction usually involves transcriptional regulation.

C) Induction can play an essential role in the formation of complex organs.

D) Induction may involve stimulating cells to die as well as to divide and grow.

E) Induction signals are almost always small carbohydrates.

Answer: E
Skill: Knowledge

47) Which of the following is *least* related to the others?

A) pattern formation

B) maternal effect genes

C) positional information

D) apoptosis

E) egg-polarity genes

Answer: D
Skill: Comprehension

48) Which of the following might involve apoptosis?

A) Interactions between muscle cells and bone cells that guide the growth of the muscle to a specific location so it can attach to the bone.

B) Cells from the top of the mouth combine with cells from the base of the brain to form the pituitary.

C) Gonads begin as an undifferentiated organ that can form either an ovary or a testis. At a certain time, hormonal signals trigger the growth of some cells and the death of others to form an ovary or testis.

D) If part of the developing spinal chord in a frog embryo is transplanted to just under the skin of the back, it will stimulate development of an eye in that location.

E) As the bones of the spinal column form, they develop from blocks of undifferentiated tissue called somites.

Answer: C
Skill: Comprehension

49) In vertebrates, programmed cell death is essential for all of the following reasons *except*

A) normal development of the nervous system.

B) normal operation of the immune system.

C) normal morphogenesis of human feet.

D) normal removal of damaged cells.

E) normal triggering of the single-transduction pathways.

Answer: E
Skill: Knowledge

Media Activity Questions

1) To initiate a signal-transduction pathway, a signal binds to a receptor protein usually located in the
   A) cytosol.
   B) nucleus.
   C) plasma membrane.
   D) ER.
   E) cytoplasm.

   Answer: C
   Topic: Web/CD Activity 21C

2) Transcription factors attach to
   A) DNA.
   B) signal molecules.
   C) plasma membrane receptors.
   D) proteins.
   E) mRNA.

   Answer: A
   Topic: Web/CD Activity 21C

3) The _____ protein is responsible for the establishment of the anterior–posterior axis of a developing *Drosophila* embryo.
   A) bicoid
   B) homeodomain
   C) ced-3
   D) Hox
   E) anchor

   Answer: A
   Topic: Web/CD Activity 21D

4) Which of these is a type of egg–polarity gene?
   A) bicoid
   B) homeodomain
   C) ced-3
   D) Hox
   E) anchor

   Answer: A
   Topic: Web/CD Activity 21D

5) *Bicoid* protein is produced by
   A) the embryo.
   B) a sperm cell.
   C) nurse cells.
   D) the egg.
   E) the acrosome.

   Answer: C
   Topic: Web/CD Activity 21D

Self-Quiz Questions

Answers to these questions also appear in the textbook.

1) The establishment of the dorsal–ventral axis in a developing fruit fly embryo is a crucial aspect of

   A) pattern formation.

   B) transcriptional regulation.

   C) apoptosis.

   D) cell division.

   E) induction.

   Answer: A

2) The criteria for a good model organism for studying development would probably include all of the following *except*

   A) observable embryonic development.

   B) short generation time.

   C) a relatively small genome.

   D) preexisting knowledge of the organism's life history.

   E) abundant local populations for specimen collection.

   Answer: E

3) Totipotency is demonstrated when

   A) mutations in homeotic genes result in the development of misplaced appendages.

   B) a cell isolated from a plant leaf grows into a normal adult plant.

   C) an embryonic cell divides and differentiates.

   D) the replacement of the nucleus of an unfertilized egg with that of an intestinal cell converts the egg to an intestinal cell.

   E) segment-specific organs develop along the anterior–posterior axis of a *Drosophila* embryo.

   Answer: B

4) Cell differentiation always involves

   A) the production of tissue-specific proteins, such as muscle actin.

   B) the formation of a gastrula.

   C) the transcription of the *myo*D gene.

   D) the selective loss of certain genes from the genome.

   E) the cell's sensitivity to environmental cues such as light or heat.

   Answer: A

5) The development of *Drosophila* is somewhat unusual in that

   A) the early mitotic divisions proceed without cytokinesis.

   B) metamorphosis occurs during the larval stage rather than the pupal stage, as with other insects.

   C) homeotic genes are mutated.

   D) cell migration within the embryo does not occur.

   E) the initial cell divisions have lengthy G_1 phases.

   Answer: A

6) In *Drosophila*, which genes initiate a cascade of gene activation that includes all other genes in the list?

   A) homeotic genes

   B) gap genes

   C) pair-rule genes

   D) egg-polarity genes

   E) segment polarity genes

   Answer: D

7) Absence of *bicoid* mRNA from a *Drosophila* egg leads to the absence of anterior larval body parts and mirror–image duplication of posterior parts. This is evidence that the product of the *bicoid* gene

   A) is an inducer.

   B) contains a homeobox.

   C) is a morphogen.

   D) is a transcription factor.

   E) is a caspase.

   Answer: C

8) Homeotic genes

   A) encode transcription factors that control the expression of genes responsible for specific anatomical structures.

   B) are found only in *Drosophila* and other arthropods.

   C) specify the anterior–posterior axis for each fruit fly segment.

   D) create the basic subdivisions of the anterior–posterior axis of the fly embryo.

   E) are responsible for the programmed cell death occurring during morphogenesis.

   Answer: A

9) The embryonic development of *C. elegans* illustrates all of the following developmental concepts *except*:

   A) An inducer's effect can depend on its concentration gradient.

   B) The response of an induced cell involves the establishment of a unique pattern of gene activity.

   C) The signal–transduction pathways activated by inducers are unique to embryonic cells.

   D) Sequential inductions direct the formation of complex structures in the developing embryo.

   E) Inducers promote their effects via the activation or inactivation of genes that code for transcriptional regulators.

   Answer: C

10) Although quite different in structure, plants and animals share some basic similarities in their development, such as

   A) the importance of cell and tissue movements.

   B) the importance of selective cell enlargement.

   C) the importance of signals from the environment.

   D) the retention of meristematic tissues in the adult.

   E) master regulatory genes that encode DNA-binding proteins.

   Answer: E

Chapter 22   Descent with Modification: A Darwinian View of Life

1) What is the name of the person who devised a taxonomic system that used morphological (i.e., anatomical) features as the primary criteria for classifying organisms?
   A) Charles Darwin
   B) Alfred Wallace
   C) Carolus Linnaeus
   D) Charles Lyell
   E) Jean Baptiste Lamarck

   Answer: C
   Skill: Knowledge

2) Which statement is most consistent with the natural theology that was prevalent in Europe and America during Darwin's life?
   A) God is nature.
   B) God is all–natural.
   C) Nature reflects God's intelligent design.
   D) God can be discerned only through the study of nature.
   E) To love God is to love nature.

   Answer: C
   Skill: Comprehension

3) On which of the following did Linnaeus base his classification system?
   A) morphology and anatomy
   B) evolutionary history
   C) the fossil record
   D) only A and B are correct
   E) A, B, and C are correct

   Answer: A
   Skill: Knowledge

4) Catastrophism was Cuvier's attempt to explain
   A) evolution.
   B) the fossil record.
   C) uniformitarianism.
   D) the origin of new species.
   E) natural selection.

   Answer: B
   Skill: Knowledge

5) What was the prevailing notion prior to the time of Lyell and Darwin?
   A) The Earth is 6,000 years old and populations are unchanging.
   B) The Earth is 6,000 years old and populations gradually change.
   C) The Earth is millions of years old and populations rapidly change.
   D) The Earth is millions of years old and populations are unchanging.
   E) The Earth is millions of years old and populations gradually change.

   Answer: A
   Skill: Knowledge

6) During a study session about evolution, one of your fellow students remarks, "The giraffe stretched its neck while reaching for higher leaves; its offspring inherited longer necks as a result." Which statement most accurately corrects the student's misconception?

  A) Characteristics acquired during an organism's life are not passed on through genes.

  B) Spontaneous mutations can result in the appearance of new traits.

  C) Only favorable adaptations have survival value.

  D) Disuse of an organ may lead to its eventual disappearance.

  E) Overproduction of offspring leads to a struggle for survival.

Answer: A
Skill: Comprehension

7) The statement "Improving the intelligence of an adult through education will result in that adult's descendants being born with a greater native intelligence" is an example of

  A) Darwinism.

  B) Lamarckism.

  C) uniformitarianism.

  D) *scala naturae*.

  E) natural theology.

Answer: B
Skill: Application

8) Increased UV irradiation causes the skin of humans to become more darkly pigmented over a period of days. The notion that the offspring of such tanned individuals should consequently inherit darkened skin from their parents is consistent with the ideas of

  A) Charles Darwin.

  B) Carolus Linnaeus.

  C) Alfred Wallace.

  D) Jean Baptiste Lamarck.

  E) Charles Lyell.

Answer: D
Skill: Application

9) Darwin's mechanism of natural selection required long time spans in order to modify species. From whom did Darwin get the concept of the Earth's ancient age?

  A) Georges Cuvier

  B) Charles Lyell

  C) Alfred Wallace

  D) Thomas Malthus

  E) John Henslow

Answer: B
Skill: Knowledge

10) The naturalist who synthesized a concept of natural selection independently of Darwin was

  A) Charles Lyell.

  B) Gregor Mendel.

  C) Alfred Wallace.

  D) Rev. John Henslow.

  E) Thomas Malthus.

Answer: C
Skill: Knowledge

11) Linnaeus' concept of taxonomy is that the more closely two organisms resemble each other, the more closely related they are in a classification scheme. In evolutionary terms, the more closely related two organisms are, the

A) more similar their habitats are.

B) less similar their DNA sequences are.

C) more recently they shared a common ancestor.

D) less likely they are to be related to fossil forms.

E) more similar they are in size.

Answer: C
Skill: Comprehension

12) Darwin's mechanism of evolution differed from Lamarck's by proposing that

A) species are not fixed.

B) evolution leads to adaptation.

C) life on Earth has had a long evolutionary history.

D) life on Earth did not evolve abruptly but rather through a gradual process of minute changes.

E) inherent variations in the population are more important in evolution than variations acquired during individual lifetimes.

Answer: E
Skill: Knowledge

13) Natural selection is based on all of the following *except*

A) variation exists within populations.

B) the fittest individuals leave the most offspring.

C) there is differential reproductive success within populations.

D) populations tend to produce more individuals than the environment can support.

E) use or disuse of organs during one generation causes modifications of these same organs in subsequent generations.

Answer: E
Skill: Knowledge

14) All of the following statements are part of the Darwin–Wallace theory of natural selection *except*

A) heritable variations occur in natural populations.

B) characteristics that are acquired during the life of an individual are passed on to offspring.

C) organisms tend to increase in numbers at a rate more rapid than the environment can support.

D) on average, the best adapted individuals leave more offspring.

E) natural selection results from differential success in reproduction among members of a population.

Answer: B
Skill: Knowledge

15) Insects with mutations that prevent flight (e.g., the "vestigial wing" mutation in fruit flies) usually can't survive long in nature. But in four of the following environments, flightlessness could be selected for. Which environment should favor the survival of fruit flies that can actually fly?

   A) an island where stiff winds blow some flying insects out to sea, only to drown

   B) a swamp full of frogs that can see and catch flying insects better than crawling insects

   C) a forest full of bats that catch and eat insects while in flight

   D) a cage in which food cannot be reached by sole use of the legs

   E) a cage with slippery walls that insects can't climb and an electrified screen on top that electrocutes insects that touch it

Answer: D
Skill: Application

16) Darwin was able to formulate his theory of evolution based on several facts. Which of the following facts was unavailable to Darwin in the mid–nineteenth century?

   A) Most populations are stable in size.

   B) Individual organisms in a population are not alike.

   C) All populations have the potential to increase.

   D) Natural resources are limited.

   E) Characteristics are inherited as genes on chromosomes.

Answer: E
Skill: Knowledge

17) Which of the following represents an idea Darwin took from the writings of Thomas Malthus?

   A) All species are fixed in the form in which they are created.

   B) Populations tend to increase at a faster rate than their food supply increases.

   C) The Earth changed over the years through a series of catastrophic upheavals.

   D) The environment is responsible for natural selection.

   E) The Earth is more than 10,000 years old.

Answer: B
Skill: Knowledge

18) Darwin's and Lamarck's ideas regarding evolution both suggest that

   A) species are fixed.

   B) natural theology is an acceptable alternative explanation in cases where evolutionary explanations are not yet available.

   C) the environment creates favorable characteristics on demand.

   D) the main mechanism of evolution is natural selection.

   E) the interaction of organisms with their environment is important in the evolutionary process.

Answer: E
Skill: Knowledge

19) Which of the following elements of Darwinism is associated with Malthus?

A) Artificial selection improves plant and animal breeds.

B) Differential reproductive success is the cornerstone of natural selection.

C) The potential for population growth exceeds what the environment can support.

D) Species become better adapted to their local environments through natural selection.

E) Favorable variations accumulate in a population after many generations of natural selection.

Answer: C
Skill: Knowledge

20) A biologist studied a population of squirrels for 15 years. Over that time, the population was never fewer than 30 squirrels and never more than 45. Her data showed that over half of the squirrels born did not survive to reproduce, because of competition for food and predation. Suddenly, the population increased to 80. In a single generation, 90% of the squirrels that were born lived to reproduce. What inferences might you make about that population?

A) The amount of available food probably increased.

B) The number of predators probably decreased.

C) The young squirrels in the next generation will show greater levels of variation than in the previous generations because squirrels that would not have survived in the past are now surviving.

D) All three of these are reasonable inferences.

E) Only B and C are reasonable inferences.

Answer: D
Skill: Application

21) Which statement about natural selection is *most* correct?

A) Adaptations beneficial in one habitat should generally be beneficial in all other habitats as well.

B) Different species that together occupy the same habitat should adapt to that habitat by undergoing the same changes.

C) Adaptations beneficial in one era should generally be beneficial during all other eras as well.

D) Populations change over time as maladapted individuals pass fewer genes to subsequent generations than do well-adapted individuals.

E) Natural selection is the sole means by which populations can evolve.

Answer: D
Skill: Comprehension

22) Given a population that contains genetic variation, what is the correct sequence of the following events, under the influence of natural selection?

1. Differential reproduction occurs.
2. A new selective pressure occurs.
3. Allele frequencies within the population change.
4. Environmental change occurs.

A) 2, 4, 1, 3

B) 4, 2, 1, 3

C) 4, 1, 2, 3

D) 4, 2, 3, 1

E) 2, 4, 3, 1

Answer: B
Skill: Comprehension

23) All of the following statements are inferences of natural selection *except*

A) subsequent generations of a population should have greater proportions of individuals that possess favorable traits.

B) an individual organism undergoes evolution over the course of its lifetime.

C) often only a fraction of offspring survive because there is a struggle for limited resources.

D) individuals whose inherited characteristics best fit them to the environment should leave more offspring.

E) unequal reproductive success among its members leads a population to adapt over time.

Answer: B
Skill: Knowledge

24) Which of the following is the *best* example of humans undergoing evolution, understood as "descent with modification"?

A) reduction in coarseness of body hair over millennia

B) reduction in number of hairs on the head of a balding person

C) increased pigment production by the skin of a person who is exposed to increased UV radiation levels

D) increase in weight over an individual's lifetime

E) widening of the pupils of the eyes when one encounters dimly lit conditions

Answer: A
Skill: Comprehension

25) To observe natural selection's effects on a population, what must be true?

A) One must observe more than one generation of the population.

B) The population must contain genetic variation.

C) Members of the population must increase or decrease the use of some portion of their anatomy.

D) Only A and C are correct.

E) Only A and B are correct.

Answer: E
Skill: Comprehension

26) It should be *impossible* to observe natural selection occurring in a(n)

A) individual organism.

B) clone of (genetically identical) organisms.

C) species.

D) population.

E) Both A and B are correct answers.

Answer: E
Skill: Comprehension

27) Which statement best describes how the evolution of pesticide resistance occurs in a population of insects?

A) Individual members of the population slowly adapt to the presence of the chemical by striving to meet the new challenge.

B) All insects exposed to the insecticide begin to use a formerly silent gene to make a new enzyme that breaks down the insecticide molecules.

C) Insects observe the behavior of other insects that survive pesticide application, and adjust their own behaviors to copy those of the survivors.

D) A number of genetically resistant pesticide survivors reproduce. The next generation of insects contains more genes from the survivors than it does from those killed by the insecticide.

E) More than one of these is correct.

Answer: D
Skill: Comprehension

28) DDT was once considered a "silver bullet" that would permanently eradicate insect pests. Today, instead, DDT is largely useless against many insects. What would need to be true for pest eradication efforts to have been successful in the long run?

A) Larger doses of DDT would need to have been applied.

B) All habitats would need to have received applications of DDT at about the same time.

C) The frequency of DDT application would need to have been higher.

D) All individual insects would need to have possessed genomes that made them vulnerable to DDT.

Answer: D
Skill: Application

29) In a hypothetical environment, fishes called pike–cichlids are visual predators of algae–eating fish, i.e., they locate their prey by sight. If a population of algae eaters experiences predation pressure from pike–cichlids, then which of the following should *not* be observed in the algae–eater population over the course of many generations?

A) Coloration of the algae eaters may become drab.

B) The algae eaters may become nocturnal (active only at night).

C) Female algae eaters may become larger, bearing broods composed of more, and larger, young.

D) The algae eaters may become sexually mature at smaller overall body sizes.

E) The algae eaters may become faster swimmers.

Answer: C
Skill: Application

30) When chemicals are used to control unwanted organisms, then the wisest application strategy, in light of natural selection and assuming that chemicals generally have negative effects on the environment, is to apply

A) a large dose of a single chemical.

B) a small dose of a single chemical.

C) a moderate dose of a single chemical.

D) large doses of several different chemicals.

E) moderate doses of several different chemicals.

Answer: E
Skill: Application

31) Of the following anatomical structures, which is homologous to the wing of a bat? The

A) dorsal fin of a shark

B) tail of a kangaroo

C) wing of a butterfly

D) tail fin of a fish

E) arm of a human

Answer: E
Skill: Knowledge

32) If two modern organisms are *distantly* related in an evolutionary sense, then one should expect that

A) they ought to live in very different habitats.

B) they should share fewer homologous organs than two closely related organisms.

C) their chromosomes should be very similar.

D) they shared a common ancestor relatively recently.

E) they should be members of the same genus.

Answer: B
Skill: Application

33) Structures as different as human arms, bat wings, and dolphin flippers contain many of the same bones, these bones having developed from the same embryonic tissues. How do biologists interpret these similarities?

A) by identifying the bones as being homologous

B) by the principles of natural theology

C) by proposing that humans, bats, and dolphins share a common ancestor

D) Only A and C are correct.

E) A, B, and C are correct.

Answer: D
Skill: Comprehension

34) As adults, certain species of whales possess baleen instead of teeth. Baleen is used to filter the whales' diet of planktonic animals from seawater. As embryos, baleen whales possess teeth, which are later replaced by baleen. The teeth of embryonic baleen whales are evidence that

A) all whales are the descendants of terrestrial mammals.

B) baleen whale embryos pass through a stage when they resemble adult toothed whales.

C) baleen whales are descendants of toothed whales.

D) ontogeny recapitulates phylogeny.

E) among ancient whales, baleen evolved before teeth.

Answer: C
Skill: Application

35) Over evolutionary time, many cave–dwelling organisms have lost their eyes. Tapeworms have lost their digestive systems. Whales have lost their hind limbs. How can natural selection account for these losses?

A) Natural selection cannot account for losses, only for innovations.

B) by the principle of use and disuse

C) Under particular circumstances that persisted for long periods, each of these structures presented greater costs than benefits.

D) These organisms had the misfortune to experience harmful mutations, which caused the loss of these structures.

E) Both B and D are correct.

Answer: C
Skill: Comprehension

36) Which of the following pieces of evidence most strongly supports the common origin of all life on Earth? All organisms

A) require energy.

B) use essentially the same genetic code.

C) reproduce.

D) show heritable variation.

E) have undergone evolution.

Answer: B
Skill: Comprehension

37) Which kind of homology is the source of all other kinds of homology—making it, when available, the best criterion for determining evolutionary relationships? Homologous

A) protein sequences.

B) organs.

C) behavioral patterns.

D) gene sequences.

E) embryological patterns.

Answer: D
Skill: Comprehension

38) What would be the best technique for determining the evolutionary relationships among several closely related species, each of which still contains living members?

A) examining the fossil record

B) comparison of homologous structures

C) comparative embryology

D) comparative anatomy

E) DNA or RNA analysis

Answer: E
Skill: Application

39) Logically, which of these should cast the most doubt on the relationships depicted by an evolutionary tree?

A) None of the organisms depicted by the tree provided DNA samples for analysis.

B) Some of the organisms depicted by the tree had lived in different habitats.

C) The skeletal remains of the organisms depicted by the tree were incomplete (i.e., some bones were missing).

D) Transitional fossils had not been found.

E) DNA sequence evidence fully disagreed with morphological evidence.

Answer: E
Skill: Application

40) Ichthyosaurs were aquatic dinosaurs. Fossils show us that they had dorsal fins and tails just as fish do, even though their closest relatives were terrestrial reptiles that had neither dorsal fins nor aquatic tails. The dorsal fins and tails of ichthyosaurs and fish are

A) homologous.

B) examples of convergent evolution.

C) adaptations to a common environment.

D) Both A and C are correct.

E) Both B and C are correct.

Answer: E
Skill: Comprehension

41) One finds that organisms on islands are different from, but closely related to, similar forms found on the nearest continent. This is taken as evidence that

A) island forms and mainland forms descended from common ancestors.

B) common environments are inhabited by the same organisms.

C) the islands were originally part of the continent.

D) the island forms and mainland forms are converging.

E) island forms and mainland forms have identical gene pools.

Answer: A
Skill: Comprehension

42) Monkeys of South and Central America have prehensile tails, meaning that their tails can be used to grasp objects. The tails of African and Asian monkeys are not prehensile. Which discipline is most likely to provide an explanation for how this difference in tails came about?

A) natural theology

B) biogeography

C) physiology

D) biochemistry

E) botany

Answer: B
Skill: Application

43) Which of the following disciplines has contributed *least* to the modern body of physical evidence for evolution?

A) biogeography

B) comparative anatomy

C) molecular biology

D) taxonomy

E) paleontology

Answer: D
Skill: Comprehension

44) The theory of evolution is most accurately described as

A) an educated guess about how species originate.

B) one possible explanation, among several scientific alternatives, about how species have come into existence.

C) an opinion that some scientists hold about how living things change over time.

D) an overarching explanation, supported by much evidence, for how populations change over time.

E) an idea about how acquired characteristics are passed on to subsequent generations.

Answer: D
Skill: Knowledge

45) Human intestines are held in place by membranes called mesenteries. In bipedal humans, it would be logical for these mesenteries to be attached to the rib cage. Instead, they are attached to the backbone, as they are in quadrupedal mammals. Because of this arrangement, human mesenteries have a tendency to tear more often than mesenteries in other mammals, as frequently observed among truck drivers and jackhammer operators. The same evolutionary modification that causes increased susceptibility to torn mesenteries is responsible for

A) tonsillitis.

B) appendicitis.

C) back and knee problems.

D) susceptibility to HIV infection.

E) vision problems associated with advanced age.

Answer: C
Skill: Application

46) Which of the following statements gives the *least* support to the claim that the human appendix is a completely vestigial organ?

    A) The appendix can be surgically removed with no apparent ill effects.

    B) The appendix might have been larger in fossil hominids.

    C) The appendix can have a substantial amount of defensive lymphatic tissue in its walls.

    D) Individuals with a larger–than–average appendix leave fewer offspring than those with a below–average–sized appendix.

    E) In a million years, the human species might completely lack an appendix.

Answer: C
Skill: Comprehension

The graph below depicts four possible patterns for the abundance of 3TC–resistant HIV within an infected human over time.

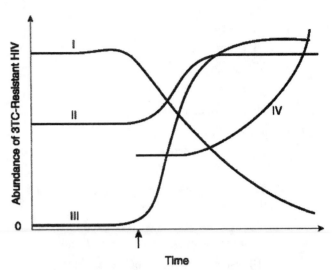

47) If 3TC resistance is costly for HIV, then which plot (I–IV) best represents the response of a strain of 3TC–resistant HIV over time, if 3TC administration begins at the time indicated by the arrow?

    A) I   B) II   C) III   D) IV

Answer: C
Skill: Application

Media Activity Questions

1) The Galápagos Islands are off the west coast of
   A) Brazil.
   B) Colombia.
   C) Canada.
   D) Ecuador.
   E) Portugal.

   Answer: D
   Topic: Web/CD Activity 22B

2) The primary purpose of the 1831 voyage of the *Beagle* was to
   A) provide Darwin with an excuse to get away from his domineering father.
   B) discover examples of divine creation.
   C) transport Darwin to the Galápagos Islands.
   D) discover how species change through time.
   E) survey the waters around the southern coast of South America.

   Answer: E
   Topic: Web/CD Activity 22D

3) What was Darwin's job on board the *Beagle*?
   A) ship's navigator
   B) ship's naturalist
   C) ship's captain
   D) ship's doctor
   E) ship's surveyor

   Answer: B
   Topic: Web/CD Activity 22D

4) Darwin's observations while with the *Beagle* led him to wonder why
   A) organisms looked as they did.
   B) God created so many species.
   C) there were so few finch species.
   D) marine tortoises lived so long.
   E) he agreed to go on the voyage.

   Answer: A
   Topic: Web/CD Activity 22D

5) What term is used to refer to structures that have a similar origin or ancestry even though they may be very different in appearance?
   A) convergent
   B) comparable
   C) analogous
   D) divergent
   E) homologous

   Answer: E
   Topic: Web/CD Activity 22F

Self-Quiz Questions

Answers to these questions also appear in the textbook.

1) The ideas of Hutton and Lyell that Darwin incorporated into his theory pertained to

   A) the age of Earth and gradual change.

   B) extinctions evident in the fossil record.

   C) adaptation of species to the environment.

   D) a hierarchical classification of organisms.

   E) the inheritance of acquired characteristics.

   Answer: A

2) Which of the following is *not* an observation or inference on which natural selection is based?

   A) There is heritable variation among individuals.

   B) Poorly adapted individuals never leave offspring.

   C) There is a struggle for limited resources, and only a fraction of offspring survive.

   D) Individuals whose inherited characteristics best fit them to the environment will generally leave more offspring.

   E) Organisms interact with their environments.

   Answer: B

3) Which of the following would provide the best information for distinguishing phylogenetic relationships between several species that are almost identical in anatomy?

   A) the fossil record

   B) homologous structures

   C) comparative anatomy

   D) comparative embryology

   E) molecular comparisons of DNA and amino acid sequences

   Answer: E

4) Which of the following observations helped Darwin shape his concept of descent with modification?

   A) Species diversity declined as distance from the equator increased.

   B) Fewer species were found living on islands than on the nearest continents.

   C) Birds could be found on islands more distant from the mainland than their maximum nonstop flight distance.

   D) South American temperate plants were more similar to the tropical plants of South America than to the temperate plants of Europe.

   E) Finches on the Galápagos fed on seeds, whereas finches on the South American mainland were insectivorous.

   Answer: D

5) Darwin synthesized information from several sources in developing his theory of evolution by natural selection. Which of the following did *not* influence his thinking?

   A) Linnaeus' hierarchical classification of species, which could imply evolutionary relationships

   B) Lyell's Principles of Geology, which described the gradualness and uniformity of geologic changes over long periods of time

   C) Mendel's paper describing the basic principles of inheritance

   D) examples of major changes in domesticated species produced by artificial selection

   E) the biogeographic distribution of species that he observed on the Galápagos Islands and during his journey around South America

   Answer: C

6) In science, the term *theory* generally applies to an idea that

A) is a speculation lacking supportive observations or experiments.

B) attempts to explain many related phenomena.

C) is synonymous with what biologists mean by a hypothesis.

D) is so widely accepted that it is considered a law of nature.

E) cannot be tested.

Answer: B

7) Within a few weeks of treatment with the drug 3TC, a patient's HIV population consists entirely of 3TC-resistant viruses. How can this result best be explained?

A) HIV has the ability to change its surface proteins and resist vaccines.

B) The patient must have become reinfected with 3TC-resistant viruses.

C) HIV began making drug-resistant versions of reverse transcriptase in response to the drug.

D) A few drug-resistant viruses were present at the start of treatment, and natural selection increased their frequency.

E) Some viruses developed drug resistance and then passed their resistant genes to all the patient's viruses.

Answer: D

8) The smallest biological unit that can evolve over time is

A) a cell.

B) an individual organism.

C) a population.

D) a species.

E) an ecosystem.

Answer: C

9) Which of the following ideas is common to *both* Darwin's *and* Lamarck's theories of evolution?

A) Adaptation results from differential reproductive success.

B) Evolution drives organisms to greater and greater complexity.

C) Evolutionary adaptation results from interactions between organisms and their environments.

D) Adaptation results from the use and disuse of anatomical structures.

E) The fossil record supports the view that species are fixed.

Answer: C

10) Which of the following pairs of structures is *least* likely to represent homology?

A) the wings of a bat and the forelimbs of a human

B) the hemoglobin of a baboon and the hemoglobin of a gorilla

C) the mitochondria of a plant and those of an animal

D) the bark of a tree and the protective covering of a lobster

E) the brain of a frog and the brain of a dog

Answer: D

Chapter 23   The Evolution of Populations

1) What is the most important missing evidence or observation in Darwin's theory of 1859?

A) the source of genetic variation

B) evidence of the overproduction of offspring

C) evidence that some organisms became extinct

D) observation that variation is common in populations

E) observation that competition exists in populations

Answer: A
Skill: Knowledge

2) Which of the following is the unit of evolution? In other words, which of the following can evolve in the Darwinian sense?

A) gene

B) chromosome

C) individual

D) population

E) species

Answer: D
Skill: Knowledge

3) What effect do sexual processes (meiosis and fertilization) have on the allelic frequencies in a population?

A) They tend to reduce the frequencies of deleterious alleles and increase the frequencies of advantageous ones.

B) They tend to increase the frequencies of deleterious alleles and decrease the frequencies of advantageous ones.

C) They tend to selectively combine favorable alleles into the same zygote but do not change allelic frequencies.

D) They tend to increase the frequency of new alleles and decrease the frequency of old ones.

E) They have no effect on allelic frequencies.

Answer: E
Skill: Knowledge

Use the following information to answer the questions below. A large population of laboratory animals has been allowed to breed randomly for a number of generations. After several generations, 49 percent of the animals display a recessive trait (aa), the same percentage as at the beginning of the breeding program. The rest of the animals show the dominant phenotype, with heterozygotes indistinguishable from the homozygous dominants.

4) What is the most reasonable conclusion that can be drawn from the fact that the frequency of the recessive trait (*aa*) has *not* changed over time?

A) The population is undergoing genetic drift.

B) The two phenotypes are about equally adaptive under laboratory conditions.

C) The genotype *AA* is lethal.

D) There has been a high rate of mutation of allele *A* to allele *a.*

E) There has been sexual selection favoring allele *a.*

Answer: B
Skill: Comprehension

5) What is the estimated frequency of allele *a* in the gene pool?

   A) 0.70

   B) 0.51

   C) 0.49

   D) 0.30

   E) 0.07

   Answer: A
   Skill: Application

6) What proportion of the population is probably heterozygous (*Aa*) for this trait?

   A) 0.51

   B) 0.42

   C) 0.21

   D) 0.09

   E) 0.07

   Answer: B
   Skill: Application

7) All of the following are criteria for maintaining a Hardy–Weinberg equilibrium involving two alleles *except*

   A) the frequency of all genotypes must be equal.

   B) there should be no natural selection.

   C) matings must be random.

   D) populations must be large.

   E) gene flow from other populations must be zero.

   Answer: A
   Skill: Comprehension

8) In a population that is in Hardy–Weinberg equilibrium, the frequency of the allele *a* is 0.3. What is the percentage of the population that is homozygous for this allele?

   A) 3

   B) 9

   C) 21

   D) 30

   E) 42

   Answer: B
   Skill: Application

9) In a population that is in Hardy–Weinberg equilibrium, the frequency of the allele *a* is 0.3. What is the percentage of the population that is heterozygous for this allele?

   A) 3

   B) 9

   C) 21

   D) 30

   E) 42

   Answer: E
   Skill: Application

10) In a Hardy–Weinberg population, the frequency of the *a* allele is 0.4. What is the frequency of individuals with *Aa* genotype?

   A) 0.16

   B) 0.20

   C) 0.48

   D) 0.60

   E) cannot tell from the information provided

   Answer: C
   Skill: Application

11) In a population with two alleles, *A* and *a*, the frequency of *a* is 0.6. What would be the frequency of heterozygotes if the population is in Hardy–Weinberg equilibrium?

A) 0.16

B) 0.36

C) 0.40

D) 0.48

E) 0.64

Answer: D
Skill: Application

12) Most copies of harmful recessive alleles in a population are carried by individuals that are

A) haploid.

B) polymorphic.

C) homozygous for the allele.

D) heterozygous for the allele.

E) afflicted with the disorder caused by the allele.

Answer: D
Skill: Knowledge

The following questions refer to this information: In the year 2500, five male space colonists and five female space colonists from Earth settle on an uninhabited Earthlike planet in the Andromeda galaxy. The colonists and their offspring randomly mate for generations. All ten of the original colonists had free ear lobes, and two are heterozygous for that trait. The allele for free ear lobes is dominant to the allele for attached ear lobes.

13) What is the allele frequency in the founding population?

A) 0.1 *a*, 0.9 *A*

B) 0.2 *a*, 0.8 *A*

C) 0.5 *a*, 0.5 *A*

D) 0.8 *a*, 0.2 *A*

E) 0.4 *a*, 0.6 *A*

Answer: A
Skill: Application

14) If one assumes that Hardy–Weinberg equilibrium applies to the population of colonists on this planet, about how many people will have attached ear lobes when the planet's population reaches 10,000?

A) 100

B) 400

C) 800

D) 1,000

E) 10,000

Answer: A
Skill: Application

15) If four of the original colonists died before they produced offspring, the ratios of genotypes could be quite different in the subsequent generations. This is an example of

A) diploidy.

B) gene flow.

C) genetic drift.

D) diversifying selection.

E) stabilizing selection.

Answer: C
Skill: Application

16) After many generations, the population on this planet has an unusually high frequency for the incidence of retinitis pigmentosa, relative to Earth's population. This is most likely due to

A) the founder effect.

B) sexual selection.

C) the inheritance of acquired characteristics.

D) mutations.

E) the bottleneck effect.

Answer: A
Skill: Application

17) In a population with two alleles, A and a, the frequency of A is 0.2. Organisms that are homozygous for A die before reaching sexual maturity. In five generations, what would be the frequency of individuals with aa genotypes?

A) less than 0.04

B) 0.04

C) 0.32

D) 0.64

E) greater than 0.64

Answer: E
Skill: Application

18) You sample a population of butterflies and find that 42% are heterozygous for a particular gene. What would be the frequency of the recessive allele in this population?

A) 0.09

B) 0.30

C) 0.49

D) 0.70

E) Allele frequency cannot be estimated from this information.

Answer: E
Skill: Application

Use the following information to answer the questions below. In a hypothetical population of 1,000 people, tests of blood type genes show that 160 have the genotype AA, 480 have the genotype AB, and 360 have the genotype BB.

19) What is the frequency of the A allele?

A) 0.001

B) 0.002

C) 0.100

D) 0.400

E) 0.600

Answer: D
Skill: Application

20) What is the frequency of the B allele?

A) 0.001

B) 0.002

C) 0.100

D) 0.400

E) 0.600

Answer: E
Skill: Application

21) What percentage of the population has type O blood?

A) 0

B) 10

C) 24

D) 48

E) 60

Answer: A
Skill: Application

22) If there are 4,000 children produced by this generation, how many would be expected to have AB blood under the conditions of Hardy–Weinberg equilibrium?

A) 960

B) 100

C) 1,920

D) 2,000

E) 2,400

Answer: C
Skill: Application

23) In peas, a gene controls flower color such that R = red and r = white. In an isolated pea patch, there were 36 red flowers and 64 white flowers. Assuming Hardy–Weinberg equilibrium, what is the value of q for this population?

A) 0.36

B) 0.60

C) 0.64

D) 0.75

E) 0.80

Answer: E
Skill: Application

24) Which of the following is *not* a requirement for maintenance of Hardy-Weinberg equilibrium?

A) an increasing mutation rate

B) random mating

C) large population size

D) no migration

E) no natural selection

Answer: A
Skill: Knowledge

The following questions utilize the following information: You are studying three populations of birds. Population 1 has ten birds, of which one is brown (a recessive trait) rather than red. Population 2 has 100 birds. In that population, ten of the birds are brown. Population 3 has 30 birds, and three of them are brown. Use the following options to answer the questions:

A. *Population 1*

B. *Population 2*

C. *Population 3*

D. *They are all the same.*

E. *It is impossible to tell from the information given.*

25) In which population is the frequency of the allele for brown feathers highest?

Answer: D
Skill: Application

26) In which population would it be *least* likely that an accident would significantly alter the frequency of the brown allele?

Answer: B
Skill: Application

27) Which population is *most* likely to be subject to the bottleneck effect?

Answer: A
Skill: Comprehension

28) If the frequency of a particular allele that is present in a small, isolated population of alpine plants should change due to a landslide that leaves an even smaller remnant of surviving plants, then what has occurred?

A) a bottleneck

B) genetic drift

C) microevolution

D) A and B only are correct.

E) A, B, and C are correct.

Answer: D
Skill: Comprehension

29) Natural selection is most closely related to

A) diploidy.

B) gene flow.

C) genetic drift.

D) assortative mating.

E) differential reproductive success.

Answer: E
Skill: Knowledge

30) In a large, sexually reproducing population, the frequency of an allele changes from 60% to 20%. From this change, one can most logically assume that, in this environment,

A) the allele is linked to a detrimental allele.

B) the allele mutates readily.

C) random processes have changed allelic frequencies.

D) there is no sexual selection.

E) the allele reduces fitness.

Answer: E
Skill: Comprehension

31) Through time, the movement of people on Earth has steadily increased. This has altered the course of human evolution by increasing

A) nonrandom reproduction.

B) geographical isolation.

C) genetic drift.

D) mutations.

E) gene flow.

Answer: E
Skill: Knowledge

32) Gene flow is a concept best used to describe an exchange between

A) species.

B) males and females.

C) populations.

D) individuals.

E) chromosomes.

Answer: C
Skill: Knowledge

33) All of the following important concepts of population genetics are due to random events or chance *except*

A) mutation.

B) the bottleneck effect.

C) the founder effect.

D) natural selection.

E) sexual recombination.

Answer: D
Skill: Knowledge

34) The probability of a mutation at a particular gene locus is _____ and the probability of a mutation in the genome of a particular individual is _____.

A) high ... low

B) low ... high

C) low ... low

D) high ... high

E) moderate ... moderate

Answer: B
Skill: Knowledge

35) Variations in populations can be demonstrated by studying which of the following?

A) morphological characteristics

B) proteins

C) DNA sequences

D) Both B and C are correct.

E) A, B, and C are correct.

Answer: E
Skill: Comprehension

36) The decrease in the size of plants on the slopes of mountains as altitudes increase is an example of

A) a cline.

B) a bottleneck.

C) relative fitness.

D) genetic drift.

E) speciation.

Answer: A
Skill: Knowledge

37) Which factor is the *most* important in producing the variability that occurs in each generation of humans?

A) diploidy

B) genetic recombination

C) genetic drift

D) nonrandom mating

E) natural selection

Answer: B
Skill: Comprehension

38) In modern terminology, diversity is understood to be a result of genetic variation. Sources of variation for evolution include all of the following *except*

A) mistakes in translation of structural genes.

B) mistakes in DNA replication.

C) translocations and mistakes in meiosis.

D) recombination at fertilization.

E) recombination by crossing over in meiosis.

Answer: A
Skill: Comprehension

39) Genetic recombination is a critical process in evolution. This statement is supported by the continuous existence of which of the following in evolving populations?

A) sexual reproduction

B) bacterial conjugation

C) exchange of chromosome regions in meiosis (crossing over)

D) Both A and C are correct.

E) A, B, and C are correct.

Answer: E
Skill: Comprehension

40) Changes to the nucleotide sequence within a gene can occur through which process(es)?

A) mutation

B) crossing over

C) independent assortment

D) Only A and B are correct.

E) A, B, and C are correct.

Answer: D
Skill: Comprehension

41) Which of the following is one important evolutionary feature of the diploid condition?

A) An extra set of genes facilitates the inheritance of characteristics acquired by the previous generation.

B) Recombination can only occur in diploid organisms.

C) DNA is more resistant to mutation in diploid cells than is the DNA of haploid cells.

D) Diploid organisms express less of their genetic variability than haploid organisms.

E) Diploid organisms are more likely to clone successfully than are haploid organisms.

Answer: D
Skill: Comprehension

42) You are maintaining a small population of fruit flies in the laboratory by transferring the flies to a new culture bottle after each generation. After several generations, you notice that the viability of the flies has decreased greatly. Recognizing that small population size is likely to be linked to decreased viability, the best way to reverse this trend is to

A) cross your flies with flies from another lab.

B) reduce the number of flies that you transfer at each generation.

C) transfer only the largest flies.

D) change the temperature at which you rear the flies.

E) shock the flies with a brief treatment of heat or cold to make them more hardy.

Answer: A
Skill: Application

The restriction enzymes of bacteria protect the bacteria from successful attack by bacteriophage, whose genomes can be degraded by the restriction enzymes. The bacterial genomes are not vulnerable to these restriction enzymes because bacterial DNA is methylated. This situation selects for bacteriophage whose genomes are also methylated. As new strains of resistant bacteriophage become more prevalent, this in turn selects for bacteria whose genomes are not methylated and whose restriction enzymes instead degrade methylated DNA.

43) Over the course of evolutionary time, what should occur?

A) Methylated DNA should become fixed in the gene pools of bacterial species.

B) Nonmethylated DNA should become fixed in the gene pools of bacteriophage.

C) Methylated DNA should become fixed in the gene pools of bacteriophage.

D) Methylated and nonmethylated strains should be maintained among both bacteria and bacteriophage, with ratios that vary over time.

E) Both A and B are correct.

Answer: D
Skill: Application

44) The outcome of the conflict between bacteria and bacteriophage at any point in time results from

A) frequency–dependent selection.

B) evolutionary imbalance.

C) heterozygote advantage.

D) neutral variation.

E) genetic variation being preserved by diploidy.

Answer: A
Skill: Comprehension

45) Which of the following chromosomal mutations can increase the mass of DNA present in an organism's genome, creating superfluous DNA that may undergo further changes to produce entirely new genes?
   A) transposition
   B) translocation
   C) inversion
   D) duplication
   E) crossing over

   Answer: D
   Skill: Knowledge

46) The Darwinian fitness of an individual is measured by
   A) the number of its offspring that survive to reproduce.
   B) the number of supergenes in the genotype.
   C) the number of mates it attracts.
   D) its physical strength.
   E) how long it lives.

   Answer: A
   Skill: Knowledge

47) When we say that one organism has a greater fitness than another organism, we specifically mean that it
   A) lives longer than others of its species.
   B) competes for resources more successfully than others of its species.
   C) mates more frequently than others of its species.
   D) utilizes resources more efficiently than other species occupying similar niches.
   E) leaves more viable offspring than others of its species.

   Answer: E
   Skill: Knowledge

48) What is the measure of Darwinian fitness in a population?
   A) longevity in a species
   B) survival under adverse conditions
   C) the number of fertile offspring
   D) strength, in a predator
   E) fleetness, in a prey animal

   Answer: C
   Skill: Knowledge

49) Which of the following statements best summarizes evolution as it is viewed today?
   A) It is goal directed.
   B) It represents the result of selection for acquired characteristics.
   C) It is synonymous with the process of gene flow.
   D) It is the descent of humans from the present-day great apes.
   E) It is the differential survival and reproduction of the most fit phenotypes.

   Answer: E
   Skill: Comprehension

Choose among the following options to answer the following questions. Each option may be used once, more than once, or not at all.

   A. *random selection*
   B. *directional selection*
   C. *stabilizing selection*
   D. *diversifying selection*
   E. *sexual selection*

50) An African butterfly species exists in two strikingly different color patterns.

   Answer: D
   Skill: Knowledge

51) Brightly colored peacocks mate more frequently than do drab peacocks.

   Answer: E
   Skill: Knowledge

52) Most Swiss starlings produce 4 to 5 eggs in each clutch.

Answer: C
Skill: Knowledge

53) Fossil evidence indicates that horses have gradually increased in size over geological time.

Answer: B
Skill: Application

54) The average birth weight for human babies is about 7 pounds.

Answer: C
Skill: Knowledge

55) A certain species of land snail exists as either a cream color or a solid brown color. Intermediate individuals are relatively rare.

Answer: D
Skill: Knowledge

56) Pathogenic bacteria found in many hospitals are antibiotic resistant.

Answer: B
Skill: Application

57) Cattle breeders have improved the quality of meat over the years by which process?
    A) artificial selection
    B) directional selection
    C) stabilizing selection
    D) Only A and B are correct.
    E) Only A and C are correct.

Answer: D
Skill: Comprehension

58) A balanced polymorphism exists through diversifying selection in seedcracker finches from Cameroon in which small- and large-billed birds specialize in cracking soft and hard seeds, respectively. If long-term climatic change resulted in all seeds becoming hard, what type of selection would then operate on the finch population?
    A) diversifying selection
    B) directional selection
    C) stabilizing selection
    D) sexual selection
    E) No selection would operate because the population is in Hardy-Weinberg equilibrium.

Answer: B
Skill: Application

59) *Cecropia* moths overwinter as pupae inside cocoons and emerge as adults ready to mate and lay eggs on host plants such as wild cherry the following spring. It is adaptative for eggs to be laid as soon as trees have leafed out and there is larval food available. *Cecropia* has a bimodal emergence curve. Most adults emerge in May and probably receive a selective advantage most years. But some adults do not emerge until later in the summer and, in years in which there are late frosts, they have the selective advantage. This bimodal emergence curve is likely maintained in the population by
    A) stabilizing selection.
    B) directional selection.
    C) diversifying selection.
    D) genetic drift.
    E) mutation.

Answer: C
Skill: Application

In a very large population, a quantitative trait has the following distribution pattern:

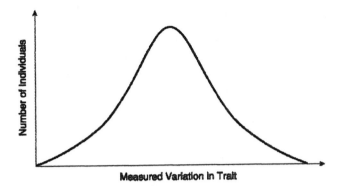

Figure 23.1

60) What is true of the trait whose frequency distribution in a large population appears above? It is undergoing

A) directional selection.

B) stabilizing selection.

C) diversifying selection.

D) sexual selection.

E) It is not possible to say, solely from the information above.

Answer: E
Skill: Comprehension

61) If the unimodal distribution shown above becomes a bimodal distribution over time, then

A) there must be some advantage to being heterozygous at all of the contributing gene loci.

B) a situation of balanced polymorphism may be produced.

C) directional selection is operating on this trait.

D) the twofold disadvantage of sex is the cause of the switch.

E) the trait must be neutral.

Answer: B
Skill: Comprehension

62) If the curve shifts to the left or to the right, and if there is no gene flow, and if the population size consequently increases over successive generations, then which of these is (are) probably occurring?
1. immigration or emigration
2. directional selection
3. adaptation
4. genetic drift
5. diversifying selection

A) 1 only

B) 4 only

C) 2 and 3

D) 4 and 5

E) 1, 2, and 3

Answer: C
Skill: Comprehension

63) Male satin bower birds adorn stations called bowers with parrot feathers, flowers, and other bizarre ornamentations in order to attract females. Females inspect the bowers and, if suitably impressed, allow males to mate with them, after which they go off to nest by themselves. The evolution of this behavior is best described as due to

A) survival of the fittest.

B) artificial selection.

C) sexual selection.

D) natural selection.

E) diversifying selection.

Answer: C
Skill: Comprehension

64) In many animal species, mature males are much larger than mature females. This size difference can be attributed to

A) males having a diet that is quantitatively or qualitatively better than that of females.

B) male hormones having a more positive effect on body size than female hormones have.

C) the operation of intrasexual selection.

D) females preferentially selecting larger males as mates.

E) all of the above.

Answer: E
Skill: Application

65) Which of the following is likely to have been produced by sexual selection?

A) a male lion's mane

B) bright colors of female flowers

C) the ability of desert animals to concentrate their urine

D) different sizes of male and female pine cones

E) camouflage coloration in animals

Answer: A
Skill: Knowledge

66) Female wasps, which are protected by the use of a painful stinger, often make their presence conspicuous by rapidly moving their usually long antennae. These wasps are often mimicked by flies with short antennae who give the appearance of rapidly moving long antennae by waving their forelegs in front of their bodies. Which of the following statements concerning this behavior is *not* consistent with current evolutionary theory?

A) Natural selection cannot fashion perfect organisms.

B) The behavior of the flies may be a compromise if their short antennae are adapted for other uses.

C) Variation in leg-waving behavior may have been present in ancestral populations and available for natural selection, while variation in antennal length may not have.

D) Given enough time, these flies will develop longer antennae and become perfect mimics.

E) Organisms are often locked into historical genetic constraints.

Answer: D
Skill: Comprehension

67) The same gene that causes various coat patterns in wild and domesticated cats also causes the cross–eyed condition in these cats, the cross–eyed condition being slightly maladaptive. In a hypothetical environment, the coat pattern that is associated with crossed eyes is highly adaptive, with the result that both the coat pattern and the cross–eyed condition increase in a feline population over time. Which statement is best supported by these observations?

A) Evolution is progressive and tends toward a more perfect population.

B) Phenotype is often the result of compromise.

C) Natural selection reduces the frequency of maladaptive genes in populations over the course of time.

D) Pleiotropy is generally maladaptive, and should become less common in future generations.

E) In all environments, coat pattern is a more important survival factor than is eye–muscle tone.

Answer: B
Skill: Comprehension

68) A proficient engineer can easily design skeletal structures that are more functional than those currently found in the forelimbs of such diverse mammals as horses, whales, and bats. That the actual forelimbs of these mammals do not seem to be optimally arranged is because

A) natural selection has not had sufficient time to create the optimal design in each case, but will do so given enough time.

B) natural selection operates in ways that are beyond the capability of the human mind to comprehend.

C) in many cases, phenotype is not merely determined by genotype, but by the environment as well.

D) though we may not consider the fit between the current skeletal arrangements and their functions excellent, we should not doubt that natural selection ultimately produces the best design.

E) natural selection is generally limited to modifying structures that were present in previous generations and in previous species.

Answer: E
Skill: Comprehension

Media Activity Questions

1) What is a mutation?

   A) a gene that causes a disease

   B) a random change in an organism's DNA

   C) a chance change in the gene pool of a small population

   D) the immigration of alleles into a gene pool

   E) the emigration of alleles out of a gene pool

   Answer: B
   Topic: Web/CD Activity 23A

2) What is the result of natural selection?

   A) a chance change in the gene pool of a small population

   B) the entry of alleles into a population due to immigration

   C) a change in the gene pool of a population due to differential reproductive success

   D) a change in allelic frequencies due to mutation

   E) the loss of alleles from a population due to emigration

   Answer: C
   Topic: Web/CD Activity 23A

3) What is genetic drift?

   A) chance changes in the gene pool of a small population

   B) the entry of alleles into a population due to immigration

   C) changes in the gene pool of a population that is due to differential reproductive success

   D) a change in allelic frequencies due to mutation

   E) the loss of alleles from a population due to emigration

   Answer: A
   Topic: Web/CD Activity 23A

4) In a cell in which $2n = 6$, the independent assortment of chromosomes during meiosis can by itself give rise to _____ genetically different gametes.

   A) two

   B) four

   C) six

   D) eight

   E) ten

   Answer: D
   Topic: Web/CD Activity 23B

5) In sexually reproducing organisms, the events of _____ do *not* contribute to an increase in genetic variation.

   A) prophase I

   B) random fertilization

   C) metaphase I

   D) interphase

   E) All of these events *do* contribute to an increase in genetic variation.

   Answer: D
   Topic: Web/CD Activity 23B

Self–Quiz Questions

Answers to these questions also appear in the textbook.

1) A gene pool consists of
   A) all the alleles exposed to natural selection.
   B) the total of all alleles present in a population.
   C) the entire genome of a reproducing individual.
   D) the frequencies of the alleles for a gene locus within a population.
   E) all the gametes in a population.

   Answer: B

2) In a population with two alleles for a particular locus, *B* and *b*, the allele frequency of *B* is 0.7. What would be the frequency of heterozygotes if the population were in Hardy–Weinberg equilibrium?
   A) 0.7
   B) 0.49
   C) 0.21
   D) 0.42
   E) 0.09

   Answer: D

3) In a population in Hardy–Weinberg equilibrium, 16% of the individuals show the recessive trait. What is the frequency of the dominant allele in the population?
   A) 0.84
   B) 0.36
   C) 0.6
   D) 0.4
   E) 0.48

   Answer: C

4) The average length of jackrabbit ears decreases the farther north the rabbits live. This variation is an example of
   A) a cline.
   B) discrete variation.
   C) polymorphism.
   D) genetic drift.
   E) diversifying selection.

   Answer: A

5) Which of the following is an example of polymorphism in humans?
   A) variation in height
   B) variation in intelligence
   C) the presence or absence of a widow's peak
   D) variation in the number of fingers
   E) variation in fingerprints

   Answer: C

6) Selection acts *directly* on
   A) phenotype.
   B) genotype.
   C) the entire genome.
   D) each allele.
   E) the entire gene pool.

   Answer: A

7) Male swallows with the longest tails were found to attract more mates than those with shorter tails. This observation is an example of

A) genetic drift, in which tail length increases as a result of small population size.

B) selection for sexual reproduction, through which high genetic variation is maintained within a population.

C) intersexual selection in which females are more likely to choose mates with long tails.

D) intrasexual selection in which males with the longest tails are most successful in fighting with other males over access to females.

E) directional selection in which longer tail length increases flying ability and thus ability to forage for food over longer distances.

Answer: C

8) Most of the variation we see in coat coloration and pattern in a population of wild mustangs in any generation is probably due to

A) new mutations that occurred in the preceding generation.

B) sexual recombination of alleles.

C) genetic drift due to the small size of the population.

D) geographic variation within the population.

E) environmental effects.

Answer: B

9) A founder event favors microevolution in the founding population mainly because

A) mutations are more common in a new environment.

B) a small founding population is subject to extensive sampling error in the composition of its gene pool.

C) the new environment is likely to be patchy, favoring diversifying selection.

D) gene flow increases.

E) members of a small population tend to migrate.

Answer: B

10) In a particular bird species, individuals with average–sized wings survive severe storms more successfully than other birds in the same population with longer or shorter wings. This illustrates

A) the founder effect.

B) stabilizing selection.

C) artificial selection.

D) gene flow.

E) diversifying selection.

Answer: B

Chapter 24   The Origin of Species

1) Which of the following applies to *both* anagenesis and cladogenesis?

A) branching

B) increased diversity

C) speciation

D) more species

E) adaptive radiation

Answer: C
Skill: Comprehension

2) What is true of speciation? It

A) occurs at such a slow pace that no one has ever observed the emergence of new species.

B) occurs only by the accumulation of genetic change over vast expanses of time.

C) must begin with the geographic isolation of a small, peripheral population.

D) proceeds at a uniform tempo across all taxa.

E) occurs via anagenesis or cladogenesis, but only the latter increases biodiversity.

Answer: E
Skill: Knowledge

3) Which of the following statements about species, as defined by the biological species concept, is (are) correct?

I. Biological species are defined by reproductive isolation.

II. Biological species are the model used for grouping extinct forms of life.

III. The biological species is the largest unit of population in which gene flow is possible.

A) I only

B) II only

C) I and III

D) II and III

E) I, II, and III

Answer: C
Skill: Comprehension

4) Which of the various species concepts separates species based on the degree of genetic exchange between gene pools?

A) pluralistic

B) ecological

C) biological

D) morphological

E) genealogical

Answer: C
Skill: Knowledge

5) Which of the following is *not* considered an intrinsic reproductive isolating mechanism?

A) sterile offspring

B) ecological isolation

C) geographic isolation

D) gametic incompatibility

E) timing of courtship display

Answer: C
Skill: Knowledge

6) Two closely related species can best remain distinct biological species by

   A) colonizing new habitats.

   B) convergent evolution.

   C) hybridization.

   D) geographic isolation from one another.

   E) reproductive isolation from one another.

   Answer: E
   Skill: Knowledge

7) The usual isolating mechanism keeping closely related species of birds reproductively isolated from each other is _____ isolation.

   A) ecological

   B) temporal

   C) behavioral

   D) mechanical

   E) gametic

   Answer: C
   Skill: Knowledge

8) Some species of *Anopheles* mosquito live in brackish water, some in running fresh water, and others in stagnant water. What type of reproductive barrier is most obviously separating these different species?

   A) habitat isolation

   B) temporal isolation

   C) behavioral isolation

   D) gametic isolation

   E) postzygotic isolation

   Answer: A
   Skill: Comprehension

Use the following options to answer the following questions. For each description of reproductive isolation, select the option that best describes it. Options may be used once, more than once, or not at all.

   A. *gametic*
   B. *temporal*
   C. *behavioral*
   D. *habitat*
   E. *mechanical*

9) two species of orchids with different floral anatomy

   Answer: E
   Skill: Application

10) two species of trout that breed in different seasons

   Answer: B
   Skill: Knowledge

11) two species of meadowlarks with different mating songs

   Answer: C
   Skill: Knowledge

12) Two species of garter snakes live in the same region, but one lives in water and the other lives on land.

   Answer: D
   Skill: Knowledge

13) Two species of pine shed their pollen at different times.

   Answer: B
   Skill: Knowledge

14) Mating fruit flies recognize the appearance, odor, tapping motions, and sounds of members of their own species, but not of other species.

   Answer: C
   Skill: Application

15) The scarlet oak is adapted to moist bottomland, whereas the black oak is adapted to dry upland soils.

Answer: D
Skill: Application

16) Dog breeders maintain the purity of breeds by keeping dogs of different breeds apart when they are in season. This kind of isolation is most similar to which of the following reproductive isolating mechanisms?
   A) reduced hybrid fertility
   B) hybrid breakdown
   C) mechanical isolation
   D) habitat isolation
   E) gametic isolation

Answer: D
Skill: Comprehension

The questions below are based on the following description:

In the forests of the southeastern United States can be found several closely related frog species of the genus, Rana. The species boundaries are maintained by reproductive isolating mechanisms. In each case, match the various descriptions of frogs below with the appropriate reproductive isolating mechanisms listed. There is only one correct response for each item, but some mechanisms may be used more than once; others not at all.

A) behavioral   B) gametic   C) habitat
D) temporal   E) mechanical

17) Males of one species sing only during rainy conditions; males of another species sing only when it is not raining.

Answer: A
Skill: Application

18) One species lives only in tree holes; another species lives only in streams.

Answer: C
Skill: Application

19) Females of one species choose mates based on song quality; females of another species choose mates on the basis of size.

Answer: A
Skill: Application

20) One species mates for two weeks in early April; another species mates for three weeks in early May.

Answer: D
Skill: Application

21) Males of one species are too small to perform amplexus (an action that stimulates ovulation) with females of all other species.

Answer: E
Skill: Application

22) Two species of frogs belonging to the same genus occasionally mate, but the offspring do not complete development. This is an example of
   A) the postzygotic barrier called hybrid inviability.
   B) the postzygotic barrier called hybrid breakdown.
   C) the prezygotic barrier called hybrid sterility.
   D) gametic isolation.
   E) adaptation.

Answer: A
Skill: Knowledge

23) If two species are able to interbreed but produce sterile hybrids, their species integrity is maintained by
   A) gametic isolation.
   B) a prezygotic barrier.
   C) hybrid inviability.
   D) a postzygotic barrier.
   E) mechanical isolation.

Answer: D
Skill: Knowledge

24) Which of the following reproductive isolating mechanisms is postzygotic?

A) habitat isolation

B) temporal isolation

C) hybrid sterility

D) behavioral isolation

E) gamete incompatibility

Answer: C
Skill: Knowledge

25) The reproductive barrier that maintains the species boundary between horses and donkeys is

A) mechanical isolation.

B) gametic isolation.

C) hybrid inviability.

D) hybrid sterility.

E) hybrid breakdown.

Answer: D
Skill: Knowledge

26) Theoretically, the production of sterile mules by interbreeding between female horses and male donkeys should

A) result in the extinction of one of the two parental species.

B) cause convergent evolution.

C) reinforce prezygotic isolating mechanisms between horses and donkeys.

D) weaken the intrinsic reproductive isolating mechanisms between horses and donkeys.

E) eventually result in the formation of a single species from the two parental species.

Answer: C
Skill: Comprehension

27) The biological species concept is inadequate for grouping

A) plants.

B) parasites.

C) asexual organisms.

D) endemic populations.

E) sympatric populations.

Answer: C
Skill: Knowledge

28) A biologist discovers two populations of wolf spiders whose members appear identical. Members of one population are found in the leaf litter deep within a woods. Members of the other population are found in the grass at the edge of the woods. The biologist decides to designate the members of the two populations as two separate species. Which species concept is this biologist most closely utilizing?

A) ecological

B) biological

C) morphological

D) pluralistic

E) genealogical

Answer: A
Skill: Application

29) The species concept used by Linnaeus was the _____ species concept.

A) biological

B) morphological

C) pluralistic

D) ecological

E) genealogical

Answer: B
Skill: Knowledge

30) You are confronted with a box of pinned (preserved) grasshoppers of various species that are undescribed (new to science). Your assignment is to separate them into what you think are species. The specimens have no information with them as to where or when they were collected. Which species concept will you have to use?

A) biological

B) genealogical

C) ecological

D) pluralistic

E) morphological

Answer: E
Skill: Application

31) Races of humans are unlikely to evolve extensive differences in the future for which of the following reasons?

I. The environment is unlikely to change.

II. Humans are essentially perfect.

III. The human races are incompletely isolated.

A) I only

B) III only

C) I and II only

D) II and III only

E) I, II, and III

Answer: B
Skill: Comprehension

32) A defining characteristic of allopatric speciation is

A) the appearance of new species in the midst of old ones.

B) asexually reproducing populations.

C) geographic isolation.

D) artificial selection.

E) large populations.

Answer: C
Skill: Knowledge

33) The formation of a land bridge between North and South America about three million years ago should have resulted in which of the following?

I. allopatry of marine populations that were previously sympatric

II. sympatry of marine populations that were previously allopatric

III. sympatry of terrestrial populations that were previously allopatric

A) I only

B) II only

C) III only

D) I and II

E) I and III

Answer: E
Skill: Application

34) All of the following statements about splinter populations, or peripheral isolates, are correct *except*

A) the gene pool may represent the extremes of genotypic and phenotypic clines.

B) many peripheral isolates have an increased likelihood of experiencing a founder effect.

C) life on the frontier is usually harsh for the peripheral isolates, and most become extinct.

D) they undergo speciation readily because they are large populations with immense gene pools.

E) the selective factors operating on peripheral isolates may be quite different from those operating on the parent population.

Answer: D
Skill: Comprehension

35) If two subspecies, A and B, are not considered separate species even though they cannot interbreed, then
   A) they are groups that are endemic to isolated geographic regions.
   B) they have eliminated postzygotic barriers but not prezygotic barriers.
   C) gene flow between A and B may exist through other related subspecies.
   D) gene flow has ceased and genetic isolation is complete.
   E) their diploid gametes are produced by nondisjunction.

   Answer: C
   Skill: Comprehension

36) All are correct statements about *Ensatina eshscholtzii*, the ring species of Californian salamanders, *except*
   A) hybridization among salamander populations in northern California occurs readily.
   B) originating in the north, the species has migrated southward along two fronts, one along the Coast Ranges, the other along the Sierra Nevada.
   C) comparing gene pools from coastal and from inland salamander populations that exist at the same latitude, one should find that the gene pools become more similar as one progresses southward.
   D) hybridization has not been observed among salamanders in the southernmost part of this ring species' range, where overlap can occur.
   E) California's Central Valley acts somewhat as a geographic barrier that prevents ready interbreeding between coastal and inland salamander populations.

   Answer: C
   Skill: Comprehension

37) The Hawaiian Islands are a great showcase of evolution because of intense
   A) ecological isolation and sympatric speciation.
   B) adaptive radiation and allopatric speciation.
   C) allopolyploidy and sympatric speciation.
   D) cross–specific mating and reinforcement.
   E) hybrid vigor and allopatric speciation.

   Answer: B
   Skill: Knowledge

38) All of the following have contributed to the diversity of organisms on the Hawaiian Archipelago *except* that
   A) the islands are distant from the mainland.
   B) multiple invasions have occurred.
   C) adaptive radiation has occurred.
   D) the islands are very young.
   E) environmental conditions differ from one island to the next.

   Answer: D
   Skill: Comprehension

39) The Galápagos Archipelago appeared about 2 million years ago, when submerged volcanoes (seamounts) rose above the ocean's surface. A single hypothetical colonization event introduced a species of finch to one island in the distant past. Today, several islands in the archipelago each contain unique species of finches. What must have happened following the initial colonization event to account for the current situation?
1. cladogenesis
2. anagenesis
3. allopatry
4. adaptive radiation

A) 1 and 3

B) 1 and 4

C) 2 and 3

D) 1, 3, and 4

E) 2, 3, and 4

Answer: D
Skill: Comprehension

40) A rapid method of speciation that has been important in the history of flowering plants is

A) genetic drift.

B) paedomorphosis.

C) a mutation in the gene controlling the timing of flowering.

D) behavioral isolation.

E) polyploidy.

Answer: E
Skill: Knowledge

41) Plant species A has a diploid number of 8. A new species, B, arises as an autopolyploid from A. The diploid number of B would probably be

A) 4.

B) 8.

C) 16.

D) 32.

E) 64.

Answer: C
Skill: Application

42) Autopolyploidy is a speciation process that begins with an event during

A) habitat selection.

B) copulation.

C) meiosis.

D) embryonic development.

E) hybridization.

Answer: C
Skill: Knowledge

43) Which of the following is a way that allopolyploidy can most directly cause speciation?

A) It can improve success in island habitats.

B) It can overcome hybrid sterility.

C) It can change the mating behavior of animals.

D) It can generate geographic barriers.

E) It can produce heterochrony.

Answer: B
Skill: Comprehension

44) A new plant species formed from the hybridization of a plant with a diploid number of 16 with a plant with a diploid number of 12 would probably have a gamete chromosome number of

A) 12.

B) 14.

C) 16.

D) 22.

E) 28.

Answer: B
Skill: Application

45) Plant species A has a diploid number of 28. Plant species B has a diploid number of 14. A new, sexually reproducing species C arises as an allopolyploid from hybridization of A and B. The diploid number of C would probably be

A) 14.

B) 21.

C) 28.

D) 42.

E) 63.

Answer: D
Skill: Application

46) The origin of a new plant species by hybridization coupled with nondisjunction is an example of

A) allopatric speciation.

B) sympatric speciation.

C) autopolyploidy.

D) heterochrony.

E) a ring species.

Answer: B
Skill: Comprehension

47) Two closely related populations of mice have been separated for a long period by a river. Climatic change causes the river to dry up, thereby bringing them back into contact in a zone of overlap. Which of the following is *not* a possible outcome when they meet?

A) They interbreed freely and produce fertile hybrid offspring.

B) They no longer attempt to interbreed.

C) They interbreed in the region of overlap, producing an inferior hybrid. Subsequent interbreeding between inferior hybrids produces progressively superior hybrids over several generations.

D) They remain separate in the extremes of their ranges but develop a hybrid zone in the area of overlap.

E) They interbreed in the region of overlap, but produce sterile offspring.

Answer: C
Skill: Comprehension

48) According to the concept of punctuated equilibrium, the "sudden" appearance of a new species in the fossil record means that

A) the species is now extinct.

B) speciation occurred instantaneously.

C) speciation occurred in one generation.

D) speciation occurred over many thousands of years.

E) the species will consequently have a relatively short existence, compared to other species.

Answer: D
Skill: Knowledge

49) According to the concept of punctuated equilibrium,

A) natural selection is unimportant as a mechanism of evolution.

B) given enough time, most existing species will branch gradually into new species.

C) a new species accumulates most of its unique features as it comes into existence.

D) evolution of new species features long periods during which changes are occurring, interspersed with short periods of equilibrium or stasis.

E) transitional fossils, intermediate between newer species and their parent species, should be abundant.

Answer: C
Skill: Comprehension

50) Which of the following is a *correct* statement about the concept of punctuated equilibrium?

A) It explains variation in the tempo of speciation.

B) It contradicts much of the evidence for evolution.

C) It explains gradual changes in the fossil record.

D) It applies equally to all taxa.

E) It argues against the possibility of morphological stasis.

Answer: A
Skill: Comprehension

51) Which of the following would be a position held by a punctuationalist?

A) A new species forms most of its unique features as it comes into existence and then changes little for the duration of its existence.

B) One should expect to find many transitional fossils left by organisms in the process of forming new species.

C) Given enough time, most existing species will gradually evolve into new species.

D) Natural selection is unimportant as a mechanism of evolution.

E) Most speciation is anagenic.

Answer: A
Skill: Knowledge

52) Which of the following statements about speciation is *correct*?

A) The goal of natural selection is speciation.

B) When reunited, two allopatric populations will not interbreed.

C) Natural selection chooses the reproductive barriers for populations.

D) Prezygotic reproductive barriers usually evolve before postzygotic barriers.

E) Speciation is an example of macroevolution.

Answer: E
Skill: Knowledge

53) Which of the following would be an example of macroevolution?

A) populations of peppered moths in England shifting from a predominantly white form that was cryptic on lichen-covered tree trunks to a black, melanistic form that was less visible on darkened, soot-covered tree trunks following the pollution-producing Industrial Revolution

B) evolution of polymorphism in *Papilio dardanus*, with each morph mimicking a different protected butterfly

C) evolution of modern man, *Homo sapiens*, from australopithecine ancestors

D) evolution of insecticide resistance in populations of insect pests treated through the years with DDT

E) evolution of antibiotic resistance in bacteria

Answer: C
Skill: Application

54) Which of the following is *not* an idea or fact consistent with the model of punctuated equilibrium?

A) "Although each species must have passed through numerous transitional stages, it is probable that the periods during which each underwent development, though many and long as measured in years, have been short in comparison with the periods during which each remained in an unchanged condition." — Charles Darwin

B) Species undergo most of their morphological modifications as they first bud from parent species, then change little.

C) Transitional forms between taxa are relatively rare in the fossil record.

D) When new species are rapidly evolving, they are often doing so in small, isolated populations.

E) Macroevolution is simply microevolution spread across vast expanses of time.

Answer: E
Skill: Comprehension

The following questions are based on the observation that several dozen different proteins comprise the prokaryotic flagellum and its attachment to the prokaryotic cell wall, producing an incredibly complex structure.

55) If the complex protein assemblage of the prokaryotic flagellum arose by the same general processes by which the complex eyes of advanced mollusks (such as squids) arose, then
   A) natural selection cannot account for the rise of the prokaryotic flagellum.
   B) ancestral versions of this protein assemblage were either less functional, or had different functions, than modern prokaryotic flagella.
   C) science should accept the conclusion that neither of these structures could have arisen by evolution.
   D) we can conclude that both of these structures must have arisen through the direct action of an intelligent "designer."
   E) more than one of these is correct.

Answer: B
Skill: Comprehension

56) If the prokaryotic flagellum developed from assemblages of proteins that originally were *not* involved with cell motility but, instead, with some other function, then the modern prokaryotic flagellum is an example of a(n)
   A) vestigial organ.
   B) adoption.
   C) exaptation.
   D) homogeneous organ.
   E) allometric organ.

Answer: C
Skill: Comprehension

57) There are some who propose that because science cannot currently outline the specific sequence of events involved in the evolution of the vertebrate eye, the vertebrate eye cannot be a product of evolution. The logic of this statement is most similar to that displayed in which of the following situations?
   A) A murdered body is found, but because there is no suspect and no murder weapon, there cannot have been a murder.
   B) Common sense indicates that the Earth is unmoving, but scientific evidence supports the claim that the Earth moves.
   C) It used to be thought that blood ebbed and flowed in blood vessels, but then capillaries were discovered and Harvey's cyclical view of blood flow was accepted as a better model.
   D) If true human bones were discovered in rocks of the same age in which true dinosaur bones are encased, then the theory of evolution would be seriously challenged.
   E) If it is the citric acid in lemon juice that prevents sliced avocadoes from turning brown when coated with lemon juice, then the acetic acid in vinegar should have the same effect.

Answer: A
Skill: Application

58) An explanation for the evolution of insect wings suggests that wings began as lateral extensions of the body that were used as heat dissipaters for thermoregulation. Later, when they had become sufficiently large, these extensions became useful for gliding through the air and selection later refined them as flight-producing wings. If this hypothesis is correct, insect wings could best be described as

A) adaptations.

B) mutations.

C) exaptations.

D) isolating mechanisms.

E) examples of natural selection's predictive ability.

Answer: C
Skill: Application

59) If one organ is an exaptation of another organ, then what must be true of these two organs?

A) They are both vestigial organs.

B) They are homologous organs.

C) They are undergoing convergent evolution.

D) They are found together in the same hybrid species.

E) They have the same function.

Answer: B
Skill: Comprehension

60) Ants occur in various morphological forms, such as workers and soldiers, called castes. The larval stage that produces a worker can produce a soldier if it is fed more food and grows larger. The head capsule and associated mandibles increase in size to a greater extent than the rest of the body to produce the soldier form. This is a good example of

A) allometric growth.

B) paedomorphosis.

C) homeotic gene expression.

D) heterochrony.

E) exaptation.

Answer: A
Skill: Comprehension

61) The changing facial features of a maturing child are an example of

A) phylogeny.

B) exaptation.

C) allometric growth.

D) nondisjunction.

E) homologies.

Answer: C
Skill: Knowledge

62) Which of the following is the most likely mechanism of macroevolution?

A) a change in a regulatory gene, which has a major and adaptive impact on morphology

B) a point mutation deep within an intron

C) DNA–DNA hybridization

D) gene flow

E) genetic drift involving a trait that seems to exhibit neutral variation

Answer: A
Skill: Comprehension

63) Bagworm moth caterpillars feed on evergreens and carry a silken case or bag around with them in which they eventually pupate. Adult female bagworm moths are larviform; they lack the wings and other structures of the adult male and instead retain the appearance of a caterpillar even though they are sexually mature and can lay eggs within the bag. This is a good example of

A) anagenesis.

B) paedomorphosis.

C) sympatric speciation.

D) adaptive radiation.

E) changes in homeotic genes.

Answer: B
Skill: Comprehension

64) Which of the following terms best describes the process in which organisms reach sexual maturity while retaining some juvenile characteristics?

A) homeotic gene expression

B) allometric growth

C) cladogenesis

D) paedomorphosis

E) sexual selection

Answer: D
Skill: Knowledge

65) Paedomorphosis is the result of

A) gradualism.

B) heterochromatin.

C) autopolyploidy.

D) paleontology.

E) heterochrony.

Answer: E
Skill: Knowledge

66) Rat pups can be described as "cute," much as baby mice are cute. As rat pups mature, however, growth of their snouts and tails outpaces growth of the rest of their bodies, producing adult features that are not considered "cute" by most humans. But if sexually mature female rats prefer to mate with mutant males that possess snouts and tails with juvenile proportions, then which of these terms is (are) appropriately applied to this situation?

A) sexual selection

B) paedomorphosis

C) allometric growth

D) Only B and C apply.

E) A, B, and C are correct.

Answer: E
Skill: Comprehension

67) A hypothetical mutation in a squirrel population produces organisms with eight legs rather than four. Further, these mutant squirrels survive, successfully invade new habitats, and eventually give rise through evolution to a new class of vertebrates. The initial event giving rise to extra legs would be a good example of

A) punctuated equilibrium.

B) species selection.

C) cladogenesis.

D) changes in homeotic genes.

E) allometry.

Answer: D
Skill: Comprehension

68) Many species of snakes lay eggs, but in the forests of northern Minnesota with short growing seasons, only live–bearing snake species are present. This trend toward species that perform live birth is an example of

A) natural selection.

B) sexual selection.

C) species selection.

D) goal direction in evolution.

E) directed selection.

Answer: C
Skill: Comprehension

69) Which of the following best describes our current understanding of the role of natural selection in evolutionary theory?

A) Natural selection has been discarded as an important concept in evolution.

B) Changes in gene pools due to natural selection are now seen to be unimportant.

C) Microevolution has replaced natural selection as an organizing concept.

D) Natural selection is able to explain virtually all changes in gene pools.

E) Natural selection produces adaptations that are essential to the survival of populations in changing environments.

Answer: E
Skill: Comprehension

70) In the 4–5 million years that the hominid lineage has been diverging from its common ancestor with the apes, dozens of hominid species have arisen, often with several species coexisting in time and space. As recently as 30,000 years ago, *Homo sapiens* coexisted with *Homo neanderthalensis*. Both species had large brains and advanced intellects. That these traits belonged to both species is most easily explained by

A) species selection.

B) uniformitarianism.

C) extreme coincidence.

D) sexual selection.

E) All but C are correct.

Answer: A
Skill: Comprehension

71) In a hypothetical situation, a certain species of flea feeds only on pronghorn antelopes. In rangelands of the western United States, pronghorns and cattle often associate together. If it should happen that some of these fleas develop a strong preference, instead, for cattle blood and mate only with fleas that, likewise, prefer cattle blood, it is possible that over time _____ will occur.

1. reproductive isolation
2. sympatry
3. habitat isolation
4. prezygotic barriers
5. cladogenesis

A) 1 only

B) 2 and 3

C) 1, 2, and 3

D) 1, 2, 3, and 5

E) 1 through 5

Answer: E
Skill: Comprehension

72) The existence of evolutionary trends, such as toward larger body sizes among horse species, is evidence that

A) a larger volume–to–surface area ratio is beneficial to all mammals.

B) an unseen guiding force is at work.

C) evolution always tends toward increased complexity or increased size.

D) in particular environments, similar adaptations can be beneficial in more than one species.

E) evolution generally progresses toward some predetermined goal.

Answer: D
Skill: Comprehension

73) All of the following statements about macroevolution are correct *except*

A) long, stable periods have been interrupted by brief intervals of extensive species extinction.

B) most evolutionary trends appear to be the result of gradual change in an unbranched lineage.

C) major adaptive radiations have often followed the evolution of novel features.

D) major adaptive radiations have often followed the opening of niches by mass extinctions.

E) differential speciation may be a driving force behind macroevolution.

Answer: B
Skill: Comprehension

74) All of the following have played important roles in causing macroevolution, *except*

A) chance mutations and natural selection.

B) homeotic gene expression and heterochrony.

C) taxonomy and molecular systematics.

D) extinction and adaptive radiation.

E) allometry and paedomorphosis.

Answer: C
Skill: Comprehension

Media Activity Questions

1) What is macroevolution?

   A) evolution as it occurs on a large scale

   B) it is a synonym for "stabilizing selection"

   C) population-level changes in gene frequencies

   D) a uniform change in the rate and pattern of evolution

   E) change on the subspecies level

   Answer: A
   Topic: Web/CD Activity 24A

2) The skulls of human and chimpanzee fetuses

   A) provide evidence that humans evolved from chimpanzees.

   B) are very similar.

   C) are identical.

   D) differ in the tissues of which they are composed.

   E) provide evidence that humans and chimpanzees could not have a common ancestor.

   Answer: B
   Topic: Web/CD Activity 24B

3) "Allometric" growth refers to

   A) the retention of juvenile characteristics in the adult.

   B) growth in height.

   C) large genetic changes.

   D) the variation in growth rate of various parts of the body.

   E) growth in girth.

   Answer: D
   Topic: Web/CD Activity 24B

4) What accounts for the differences between the skulls of adult chimpanzees and adult humans?

   A) large genetic differences

   B) the fact that chimpanzees and humans do not share a common ancestor

   C) a magnification of the differences seen in their fetal skulls

   D) similar developmental timetables

   E) variations in allometric growth patterns

   Answer: E
   Topic: Web/CD Activity 24B

5) The fetal skulls of chimpanzees and humans both have

   A) massive jaws.

   B) heavy brow ridges.

   C) small jaws.

   D) sharp angular skulls.

   E) three eyes.

   Answer: C
   Topic: Web/CD Activity 24B

Self–Quiz Questions

Answers to these questions also appear in the textbook.

1) Most of biological diversity has probably arisen by
   A) anagenesis.
   B) cladogenesis.
   C) phyletic evolution.
   D) hybridization.
   E) sympatric speciation.

   Answer: B

2) The *largest* unit in which gene flow is possible is a
   A) population.
   B) species.
   C) genus.
   D) subspecies.
   E) phylum.

   Answer: B

3) Bird guides once listed the myrtle warbler and Audubon's warbler as distinct species, but applying the biological species concept, recent books show them as eastern and western forms of a single species, the yellow–rumped warbler. Experts must have found that the two kinds of warblers
   A) live in the same areas.
   B) successfully interbreed in nature.
   C) look enough alike to be considered one species.
   D) are reproductively isolated from each other.
   E) are allopatric.

   Answer: B

4) Among allopatric species of *Anopheles* mosquito, some live in brackish water, some in running fresh water, and others in stagnant water. What type of reproductive barrier is most obviously separating these different species?
   A) habitat isolation
   B) temporal isolation
   C) behavioral isolation
   D) gametic isolation
   E) postzygotic barriers

   Answer: A

5) A genetic change that caused a certain *Hox* gene to be expressed along the tip of a vertebrate limb bud instead of further back made possible the evolution of the tetrapod limb. This type of change is illustrative of
   A) heterochrony, a change in the timing of developmental events.
   B) allopolyploidy, an increase in chromosome number.
   C) paedomorphosis, or retention of ancestral juvenile structures in an adult organism.
   D) a change in a homeotic developmental gene that altered the spatial organization of body parts.
   E) allopatric speciation.

   Answer: D

6) According to advocates of the punctuated equilibrium model,

A) natural selection is unimportant as a mechanism of evolution.

B) given enough time, most existing species will branch gradually into new species.

C) a new species accumulates most of its unique features as it comes into existence, then changes little for the rest of its duration as a species.

D) most evolution is anagenic.

E) speciation is usually due to a single mutation.

Answer: C

7) Which of the following species concepts identifies species based on their shared genetic histories and thus unique genetic markers?

A) biological

B) ecological

C) genealogical

D) morphological

E) pluralistic

Answer: C

8) Which of the following factors would *not* contribute to allopatric speciation?

A) A population becomes geographically isolated from the parent population.

B) The separated population is small, and genetic drift occurs.

C) The isolated population is exposed to different selection pressures than the ancestral population.

D) Gene flow between the two populations is minimal or does not occur.

E) The different environments of the two populations create different mutations.

Answer: E

9) Plant species A has a diploid number of 12. Plant species B has a diploid number of 16. A new species, C, arises as an allopolyploid from hybridization of A and B. The diploid number of C would probably be

A) 12.

B) 14.

C) 16.

D) 28.

E) 56.

Answer: D

10) The speciation episode described in question 9 is most likely a case of

A) allopatric speciation.

B) sympatric speciation.

C) speciation based on sexual selection.

D) adaptive radiation.

E) anagenic speciation.

Answer: B

Chapter 25   Phylogeny and Systematics

1) Which combination of the following species characteristics would cause the greatest likelihood of fossilization in sedimentary rock?
   I. aquatic
   II. tropical
   III. hard body parts
   IV. presence of organic material
   V. flight
   VI. long duration as a species

   A) I, III, and VI
   B) I, II, and VI
   C) III only
   D) II and VI
   E) II, IV, and V

   Answer: A
   Skill: Comprehension

2) Which of the following should *not* be considered fossils?

   A) All of the below are properly considered fossils.
   B) dinosaur footprints preserved in rocks
   C) insects enclosed in amber
   D) mammoths frozen in arctic ice
   E) ancient pollen grains in lake sediments

   Answer: A
   Skill: Knowledge

3) Peat bogs can have pHs as low as 3.8. Animals classified as fossils have been exhumed from such bogs with most of their bodies intact (except bones), and with DNA still present. What probably accounts for the persistence of the fleshy parts of these animals while in peat bogs? The peat bogs

   A) lack carbon dioxide.
   B) lack the temperatures necessary for decomposition.
   C) harbor relatively few bacteria.
   D) are not acidic.
   E) are not moist enough for complete decomposition.

   Answer: C
   Skill: Comprehension

4) The best index fossils for assigning relative ages to different strata are those of

   A) dinosaurs.
   B) flightless birds.
   C) widespread, shelled marine organisms.
   D) soft–bodied invertebrates.
   E) bacteria.

   Answer: C
   Skill: Knowledge

5) Which of the following can be used to determine the absolute age of fossils?

   A) index fossils
   B) racemization
   C) cladistics
   D) sedimentary strata
   E) the half–life of isotopes

   Answer: E
   Skill: Knowledge

6) If the half-life of carbon-14 is about 5,730 years, then a fossil that has one-eighth the normal proportion of carbon-14 to carbon-12 is probably _____ years old.
A) 1,400
B) 2,800
C) 11,200
D) 16,800
E) 22,400

Answer: D
Skill: Application

7) Theoretically, how can absolute dates be determined by radiometric means? By measuring
A) the accumulation of the daughter isotope.
B) the loss of parental radioisotopes.
C) the loss of the daughter isotope.
D) all three of these.
E) only A and B.

Answer: E
Skill: Comprehension

8) How many half-lives should have elapsed if 12.5% of the parental radioisotope remains in a fossil at the time of analysis?
A) one
B) two
C) three
D) four
E) five

Answer: C
Skill: Application

9) Racemization of amino acids might be a useful technique for dating all of the following *except*
A) a mammoth frozen in arctic ice.
B) remains of humans exhumed from peat bogs.
C) an insect preserved in amber.
D) petrified trees.
E) leaf films pressed between layers of shale.

Answer: D
Skill: Comprehension

10) A biologist discovers two new species of organisms, one in Africa and one in South America. The organisms resemble one another closely. Which type of evidence would probably be *least* useful in determining whether these organisms are closely related or are the products of convergent evolution?
A) the history and timing of continental drift
B) a comparison of DNA from the two species
C) the fossil record of the two species
D) analysis of the behavior of the two species
E) comparative embryology

Answer: D
Skill: Application

11) All of the following are usual methods for dating fossils *except*
A) molecular clocks.
B) carbon-14.
C) uranium-238.
D) L- and D-amino acids.
E) superposition of sedimentary rock.

Answer: A
Skill: Knowledge

12) The fossil record of a hypothetical taxon is likely to be incomplete if
    A) members of the taxon lacked hard parts.
    B) the taxon evolved according to the model of punctuated equilibrium.
    C) the taxon featured a relatively small number of individuals during its existence.
    D) Only A and C are correct.
    E) A, B, and C are true.

    Answer: E
    Skill: Comprehension

13) If two continental land masses converge and are united during continental drift, then the collision should bring about
    A) a net loss of intertidal zone and coastal habitat.
    B) the extinction of species adapted to intertidal and coastal habitats.
    C) an overall increase in the surface area located in the continental interior.
    D) an increase in climatic extremes in the interior of the new supercontinent.
    E) all of the above.

    Answer: E
    Skill: Comprehension

14) Active tectonic subduction zones are characterized by
    1. trenches.
    2. earthquakes.
    3. volcanoes.
    A) 1 only
    B) 2 only
    C) 3 only
    D) 2 and 3
    E) all of these

    Answer: E
    Skill: Knowledge

15) Which of the following can best be explained by continental drift?
    A) The relative age of fossils.
    B) The scarcity of eutherian (placental) mammals in Australia.
    C) The Chicxulub crater.
    D) The evolution of aquatic reptiles, such as ichthyosaurs.
    E) The Cretaceous extinctions of 65 million years ago.

    Answer: B
    Skill: Comprehension

16) A major evolutionary episode that corresponded in time most closely with the formation of Pangaea was the
    A) origin of humans.
    B) Cambrian explosion.
    C) Permian extinctions.
    D) Pleistocene ice ages.
    E) Cretaceous extinctions.

    Answer: C
    Skill: Knowledge

17) If a fossil is limited to undisturbed geological strata shallower than the iridium layer, then it
    A) existed more recently than the reptiles known as dinosaurs.
    B) should be embedded in volcanic ash.
    C) became extinct during the Cretaceous era.
    D) was abundant on Earth at the time of the Chicxulub impact.
    E) is more than 65 million years old.

    Answer: A
    Skill: Comprehension

18) A randomly selected group of organisms from a taxonomic family should show more genetic variation than a randomly selected group from a

A) class.

B) genus.

C) kingdom.

D) order.

E) phylum.

Answer: B
Skill: Comprehension

19) The correct sequence from the most to the least comprehensive of the taxonomic levels listed here is

A) family, phylum, class, kingdom, order, species, and genus.

B) kingdom, phylum, class, order, family, genus, and species.

C) kingdom, phylum, order, class, family, genus, and species.

D) phylum, kingdom, order, class, species, family, and genus.

E) phylum, family, class, order, kingdom, genus, and species.

Answer: B
Skill: Knowledge

20) The common house fly belongs to all of the following taxa. Assuming you had access to textbooks or other scientific literature, knowing which of the following should provide you with the greatest amount of detailed information about this organism?

A) order Diptera

B) family Muscidae

C) genus *Musca*

D) class Hexapoda

E) phylum Arthropoda

Answer: C
Skill: Application

Use Figure 25.1 to answer the following questions.

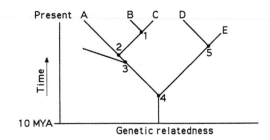

Figure 25.1

21) A common ancestor for species C and E could be at position number

A) 1.

B) 2.

C) 3.

D) 4.

E) 5.

Answer: D
Skill: Application

22) The two extant species that are most closely related to each other are

A) A and B.

B) B and D.

C) C and B.

D) D and E.

E) E and A.

Answer: C
Skill: Application

23) Which species is extinct?

A) A

B) B

C) C

D) D

E) E

Answer: E
Skill: Application

24) Which extinct species should be the best candidate to serve as the outgroup for the clade whose common ancestor occurs at position number two?

A) A

B) B

C) C

D) D

E) E

Answer: D
Skill: Application

25) If this evolutionary tree turns out to be a faulty depiction of relatedness because the common ancestor at position number four never existed, and if all of the other species depicted here continue to be placed in the same genus, then

A) this genus is unacceptable, according to cladistics.

B) this genus is still accurate, but only if the genealogical species concept is applied.

C) this genus includes species whose similarities may be due to analogies rather than to homologies.

D) all three of these are correct.

E) only A and C are correct.

Answer: E
Skill: Application

26) If this evolutionary tree is an accurate depiction of relatedness, then which of the following should be *correct*?

1. The entire tree depicts anagenesis.
2. If all species depicted here make up a taxon, this taxon is monophyletic.
3. The last common ancestor of species B and C occurred more recently than the last common ancestor of species D and E.
4. Species A is the ancestor of both species B and C.
5. The species present at position number three is ancestral to three extant species.

A) 2 only

B) 1 and 3

C) 3 and 4

D) 2, 3, and 4

E) 2, 3, and 5

Answer: E
Skill: Application

The following questions refer to the hypothetical patterns of taxonomic hierarchy shown in Figure 25.2.

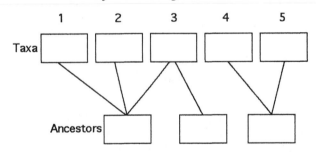

Figure 25.2

27) Which of the following numbers could represent monophyletic taxa?

A) 2 only

B) 4 only

C) 5 only

D) 1, 2, and 3

E) 1, 2, 4, and 5

Answer: E
Skill: Application

28) If this figure is an accurate depiction of relatedness, then which taxon is unacceptable, based on cladistics?

A) 1   B) 2   C) 3   D) 4   E) 5

Answer: C
Skill: Application

29) All are true of pure cladograms *except*

A) each branch point represents a point in absolute time.

B) organisms represented at the base of such cladograms are ancestral to those represented at higher levels.

C) the more branch points that occur between two taxa, the more divergent their DNA sequences should be.

D) the common ancestor represented by the highest branch point existed more recently in time than the common ancestors represented at lower branch points.

E) the more branch points there are, the more instances of cladogenesis are represented.

Answer: A
Skill: Comprehension

30) Upon their discovery by Europeans, koalas were classified as bears (Ursidae). Later, it became apparent that koalas are not bears, but marsupial mammals of the family Phasolarctidae. For as long as the koalas were classified as bears, what was true of the family Ursidae?

A) It was actually polyphyletic.

B) Its classification had a better basis in fact than the current one.

C) Its classification was more in line with molecular evidence than the current one.

D) all three of these

E) only B and C

Answer: A
Skill: Comprehension

31) The ostrich and the emu look very similar and live in similar habitats, although they are not very closely related. This is an example of

A) divergent evolution.

B) convergent evolution.

C) exaptation.

D) adaptive radiation.

E) sympatric speciation.

Answer: B
Skill: Comprehension

32) The vertebrate eye and the eye of squids are similar in structure and function. Which of the following accounts for most of this similarity?

A) cladogenesis

B) convergent evolution

C) the iridium anomaly

D) hybridization

E) balanced polymorphism

Answer: B
Skill: Knowledge

The questions below refer to the following terms. Each term may be used once, more than once, or not at all.

A. nonadaptive
B. analogous
C. homologous
D. vestigial
E. monophyletic

33) shared derived characters

Answer: C
Skill: Knowledge

34) shared primitive characters

Answer: C
Skill: Knowledge

35) a taxon, all of whose members have the same common ancestor

Answer: E
Skill: Knowledge

36) human hand and lobster claw

Answer: B
Skill: Knowledge

37) whale flipper and horse foreleg

Answer: C
Skill: Knowledge

38) the term that is most appropriately associated with the term *clade*

Answer: E
Skill: Knowledge

39) Some DNA–DNA hybridization data place the giant panda in the bear family (Ursidae), but place the lesser panda in the raccoon family (Procyonidae). The similarity of body morphology of these two animals must therefore be due to

A) inheritance of acquired characteristics.

B) sexual selection.

C) inheritance of shared derived characters.

D) convergent evolution.

E) possession of shared primitive characters.

Answer: D
Skill: Comprehension

40) When using a cladistic approach to systematics, which of the following is considered most important for classification?

A) shared primitive characters

B) analogous primitive characters

C) shared derived characters

D) the degree of evolutionary divergence

E) overall phenotypic similarity

Answer: C
Skill: Comprehension

41) Which technique provides the most important information for determining whether a particular character is a shared derived character or a shared primitive character?

A) a molecular clock

B) outgroup comparison

C) radiometric dating

D) amino acid sequencing

E) radioactive labeling

Answer: B
Skill: Knowledge

42) Nucleic acid sequences that undergo few changes over the course of evolutionary time are said to be *conserved*. Conserved nucleic acids should

A) be found in the most crucial portions of proteins.

B) include all mitochondrial DNA.

C) be abundant in ribosomes.

D) be proportionately more common in eukaryotic introns than in eukaryotic exons.

E) comprise a larger proportion of pre–mRNA (immature mRNA) than of mature mRNA.

Answer: C
Skill: Comprehension

The following questions refer to the information below.

A researcher compared the nucleotide sequences of a homologous gene from five different species of mammals. The sequence homology between each species' version of the gene and the human gene are presented as a percentage of similarity.

Species	Percentage
Chimpanzee	99.7
Orangutan	98.6
Baboon	97.2
Rhesus Monkey	96.9
Rabbit	93.7

43) What probably explains the inclusion of rabbits in this research?

   A) Their short generation time provides a ready source of DNA.

   B) They possess all of the shared derived characters as do the other species listed.

   C) They are the closest known relatives of rhesus monkeys.

   D) They are being used as the outgroup.

   E) They are the most recent common ancestor of the Primates.

   Answer: D
   Skill: Comprehension

44) What conclusion can be validly drawn from these data?

   A) Humans and other primates evolved from rabbits.

   B) All organisms have similar DNA.

   C) Among the organisms listed, humans shared a common ancestor most recently with chimpanzees.

   D) Humans evolved from chimpanzees.

   E) Both A and D are correct.

   Answer: C
   Skill: Application

45) Which technology was most important in directly providing these data?

   A) restriction fragment length analysis

   B) amino acid sequencing

   C) electrophoresis

   D) Polymerase Chain Reaction

   E) automated DNA sequencing

   Answer: E
   Skill: Comprehension

46) A technique used in molecular systematics relies on the comparison of the respiratory enzyme, cytochrome *c,* from different animals. This technique can be referred to as

   A) DNA–DNA hybridization.

   B) restriction mapping.

   C) electron transport.

   D) protein comparison.

   E) translation.

   Answer: D
   Skill: Knowledge

47) Typically, mutations that modify the active site of an enzyme are more likely to be harmful than mutations that affect other parts of the enzyme. A hypothetical enzyme consists of four domains (A–D), and the amino acid sequences of these four domains have been determined in five closely related species. Given the proportion of amino acid homologies among the five species at each of the four domains, which domain probably contains the active site?

Domain	Percentage of Homologous Amino Acids
A	32%
B	8%
C	78%
D	45%

   A) A   B) B   C) C   D) D

   Answer: C
   Skill: Application

48) When sufficient heat is applied, double-stranded DNA denatures into two single-stranded molecules as the heat breaks all of the hydrogen bonds. In an experiment, molecules of single-stranded DNA from species X are separately hybridized with putatively homologous single-stranded DNA molecules from five species (A–E). The hybridized DNAs are then heated, and the temperature at which complete denaturation occurs is recorded. Based on the data below, which species is probably most closely related to species X?

Species	Temperature at which Hybridized DNA Denatures
A	30°C
B	85°C
C	74°C
D	60°C
E	61°C

A) A

B) B

C) C

D) D

E) E

Answer: B
Skill: Application

49) The lakes of northern Minnesota contain many similar species of damselflies of the genus *Enallagma* that have apparently undergone speciation from ancestral stock since the last glacial retreat about 10,000 years ago. Which of the following techniques should be most useful in sorting out evolutionary relationships among these species? Sequencing of

A) nucleoid DNA.

B) mitochondrial DNA.

C) nuclear DNA.

D) ribosomal RNA.

E) amino acids in proteins.

Answer: B
Skill: Comprehension

50) Which of the following technologies can be used to determine the evolutionary relationship between horses and zebras?

A) All of the techniques below might prove useful.

B) DNA–DNA hybridization

C) analysis of amino acid differences in homologous proteins

D) restriction mapping of DNA

E) analysis of DNA from recent fossils

Answer: A
Skill: Application

51) A researcher who constructs cladograms based on evidence from molecular systematics will construct such cladograms based on similarities in

A) morphology.

B) the pattern of embryological development.

C) biochemical pathways.

D) habitat and lifestyle choices.

E) mutations to homologous genes.

Answer: E
Skill: Comprehension

52) The four-chambered hearts of birds and the four-chambered hearts of mammals evolved independently of each other. If one were unaware of this independence, then one might logically assume that

A) the common ancestor of birds and mammals had a three-chambered heart.

B) birds and mammals are more distantly related than is actually the case.

C) early mammals possessed feathers.

D) the common ancestor of birds and mammals had a four-chambered heart.

E) birds and mammals should be placed in the same class.

Answer: D
Skill: Comprehension

53) In using the average mutation rate of a gene as a molecular clock, which of the following would act to make the clock *underestimate* the true amount of time that had elapsed since two related species diverged from their common ancestor? A mutation

A) to the second base of a nucleotide codon.

B) to the first base of a nucleotide codon.

C) that returns a mutated nucleotide to its original state.

D) that substitutes a different amino acid in place of the original amino acid.

E) three of these would produce the same underestimation.

Answer: C
Skill: Comprehension

54) Assuming that the various mutations described below occur within the same gene, and that each kind of mutation has an equal likelihood of occurrence, which situation should require the longest span of time?

A) one, four–base deletion

B) two, two–base deletions

C) one, one–base addition and one, three–base addition

D) one, three–base deletion and one, one–base deletion

E) four, one–base deletions

Answer: E
Skill: Comprehension

55) Which statement represents the best explanation for the observation that the nuclear DNA of wolves and domestic dogs has a very high degree of homology?

A) Dogs and wolves have very similar morphologies.

B) Dogs and wolves belong to the same genus.

C) Dogs and wolves are both members of the family Canidae.

D) Dogs and wolves shared a common ancestor relatively recently.

E) Convergent evolution has occurred.

Answer: D
Skill: Comprehension

56) Phylogenetic hypotheses (such as those represented by cladograms) are strongest when

A) they are based on amino acid sequences from homologous proteins.

B) each clade in the cladogram is defined by a single derived character.

C) they are supported by more than one kind of evidence (such as when fossil evidence corroborates molecular evidence).

D) they are accepted by the foremost authorities in the field.

E) they are based on a single putatively homologous DNA sequence.

Answer: C
Skill: Comprehension

57) If both the evidence from molecular systematics and the "phylogenetic fuse" hypothesis are correct in proposing that early mammalian orders originated about 100 million years ago, then what probably kept the numbers of these early mammals low until about 60 million years ago, when they become more abundant in the fossil record?

A) a physical environment that was unsuitable for mammals

B) competition from birds, which also had four-chambered hearts

C) the dominance of well-adapted reptiles until the Cretaceous extinctions

D) the breakup of Pangaea

E) the Chicxulub impact

Answer: C
Skill: Comprehension

58) Some claim that the birds should continue to be placed in a class (Aves) separate from the Reptilia, despite evidence from molecular systematics indicating a close relationship between birds and crocodiles. Their claim is based on the extent of the adaptations that birds have undergone for flight. The logic of their claim is most similar to that found in which statement?

A) Dolphins should be classified as fish because of their streamlined bodies and dorsal fins.

B) Humans should be placed in their own order because no other member of the order Primates features so many modifications for bipedalism.

C) Koalas (Australian marsupials that feed on Eucalyptus leaves) should be placed in a new family because they are so similar in appearance to true (eutherian) bears.

D) Convergent evolution has made the cacti of the New World and the euphorbs of the Old World so alike in appearance that they ought to be placed together in the same taxon.

E) Pterodactyls are an extinct group of reptiles that were well-adapted for flight and, thus, were the first birds.

Answer: B
Skill: Comprehension

59) If birds are "glorified reptiles," with their many adaptations for flight obscuring the homologies that would otherwise reveal their true identity as reptiles, then one should expect that

A) a careful study of adult reptiles would reveal more birdlike traits.

B) a careful study of adult birds would reveal more reptilelike traits.

C) the embryos of birds should be far more similar to the embryos of reptiles than adult birds are to adult reptiles.

D) all egg-laying vertebrates should actually be classified as reptiles.

E) both A and B are correct.

Answer: C
Skill: Comprehension

Media Activity Questions

1) The Grand Canyon was formed by the _____ River.

A) Missouri

B) Arizona

C) Colorado

D) Mississippi

E) Columbia

Answer: C
Topic: Web/CD Activity 25A

2) The four geologic eras are directly subdivided into

A) eons.

B) periods.

C) plates.

D) sub-eras.

E) epochs.

Answer: B
Topic: Web/CD Activity 25B

3) _____ first appeared during the Precambrian era.

A) Mammals

B) Reptiles

C) Amphibians

D) Cyanobacteria

E) Dinosaurs

Answer: D
Topic: Web/CD Activity 25B

4) The Paleozoic era began approximately _____ million years ago.

A) 4,600

B) 570

C) 245

D) 65

E) 25

Answer: B
Topic: Web/CD Activity 25B

5) _____ were the dominant plant life during the early Mesozoic era.

A) Mosses

B) Gymnosperms

C) Angiosperms

D) Horsetails

E) Ferns

Answer: B
Topic: Web/CD Activity 25B

Self–Quiz Questions

Answers to these questions also appear in the textbook.

1) A paleontologist estimates that when a particular rock formed, it contained 12 mg of the radioactive isotope potassium–40. The rock now contains 3 mg of potassium–40. The half–life of potassium–40 is 1.3 billion years. About how old is the rock?

A) 0.4 billion years

B) 0.3 billion years

C) 1.3 billion years

D) 2.6 billion years

E) 5.2 billion years

Answer: D

2) If humans and pandas belong to the same class, then they must also belong to the same

A) order.

B) phylum.

C) family.

D) genus.

E) species.

Answer: B

3) In the case of comparing birds to other vertebrates, having four appendages is

A) a shared primitive character.

B) a shared derived character.

C) a character useful for distinguishing the birds from other vertebrates.

D) an example of analogy rather than homology.

E) a character useful for sorting the avian (bird) class into orders.

Answer: A

4) The animals and plants of India are almost completely different from the species in nearby Southeast Asia. Why might this be true?

A) They have become separated by convergent evolution.

B) The climates of the two regions are completely different.

C) India is in the process of separating from the rest of Asia.

D) Life in India was wiped out by ancient volcanic eruptions.

E) India was a separate continent until relatively recently.

Answer: E

5) How would one apply the principle of parsimony to the construction of a phylogenetic tree?

A) Choose the tree in which the branch points are based on as few shared derived characters as possible.

B) Choose the tree in which the branch points are based on as many shared derived characters as possible.

C) Base phylogenetic trees only on the fossil record, as this provides the simplest explanation for evolution.

D) Choose the tree that represents the fewest evolutionary changes, either in DNA sequence comparisons or morphological characters.

E) Choose the tree with the fewest branch points and thus the fewest taxa.

Answer: D

6) What would be the best source of data for determining the order of divergence of the various lineages of protists?

   A) fossils from the Precambrian era

   B) morphological characters that are shared and derived

   C) amino acid sequences of their various chlorophyll molecules

   D) DNA sequences for mitochondrial genes

   E) DNA sequences for ribosomal RNA

   Answer: E

7) If you were using cladistic analysis to build a phylogenetic tree of cats, which of the following would be the best choice for an outgroup?

   A) lion

   B) domestic cat

   C) wolf

   D) leopard

   E) tiger

   Answer: C

8) Which of the following would be most useful for constructing a phylogenetic tree emphasizing evolutionary branchings among several fish species?

   A) several analogous characteristics shared by all the fishes

   B) single homologous characteristic shared by all the fishes

   C) the total degree of morphological similarity among various fish species

   D) several characteristics thought to have evolved after different fishes diverged from one another

   E) a single characteristic that is different in all the fishes

   Answer: D

9) Molecular clocks indicate that most modern mammalian orders originated about 100 million years ago, whereas fossil evidence dates the origin of these orders about 60 million years ago. What explanation does the phylogenetic fuse hypothesis offer for this discrepancy?

   A) Molecular clocks have not been shown to be reliable for anything more than giving the sequence of divergence.

   B) The radiometric method of dating fossils has a large margin of error, so these time estimates are actually quite close.

   C) Mammals did not become abundant and widespread enough to appear in the fossil record until after the extinction of the dinosaurs.

   D) The genes that were used in the molecular clock comparison did not have a consistent rate of evolution, but must have evolved more rapidly during the early adaptive radiation of mammals.

   E) When in doubt, always trust the fossil record over molecular comparisons, because DNA sequence comparisons cannot account for homologous segments that do not align properly.

   Answer: C

10) The recent estimate that HIV-1 M first jumped from chimpanzees to humans in the 1930s is based on

A) the first clinical evidence of AIDS recorded in local village records in Africa.

B) a molecular clock that plotted changes in sequences of an HIV gene sampled from patients over the past 20 years and then projected backward to an estimated origin.

C) a comparison of homologous genes in HIV found in chimpanzees and in humans.

D) a parsimonious explanation of the evolutionary relationships among the various strains of the virus found in humans.

E) the recent discovery of HIV in a blood sample saved from that period.

Answer: B

Chapter 26   Early Earth and the Origin of Life

1) What is the strongest evidence that protobionts may have formed spontaneously?
   A) The discovery of ribozymes, showing that prebiotic RNA molecules may have been autocatalytic.
   B) The relative ease with which liposomes can be synthesized in laboratories.
   C) The fossil record found in the stromatolites.
   D) The abiotic synthesis of polymers.
   E) The production of organic compounds within a laboratory apparatus simulating conditions on early Earth.

   Answer: B
   Skill: Comprehension

2) Current theories of prebiotic evolution are based on evidence for all of the following *except* the abiotic
   A) production of small organic molecules.
   B) polymerization of amino acids.
   C) replication of oligopeptides.
   D) origin of DNA–protein interactions.
   E) production of liposomes.

   Answer: D
   Skill: Knowledge

3) The first genetic material was most likely a(n)
   A) DNA polymer.
   B) DNA oligonucleotide.
   C) RNA polymer.
   D) protein.
   E) protein enzyme.

   Answer: C
   Skill: Knowledge

Use the following information to answer the questions below. According to the Miller–Urey experimental results, chemical evolution leading up to and including the formation of living matter is believed to have occurred during the early history of Earth. Below are four pairs of events that might have occurred during this period. Judge the relative time of each of these pairs of events according to the key below.

   A. Event I occurred before Event II.
   B. Event II occurred before Event I.
   C. Events I and II occurred simultaneously.

4) Event I: nitrogen oxides and carbon dioxide in the atmosphere
   Event II: free oxygen in the atmosphere

   Answer: A
   Skill: Comprehension

5) Event I: formation of photosynthetic organisms
   Event II: formation of heterotrophic organisms

   Answer: B
   Skill: Comprehension

6) Event I: formation of amino acids
   Event II: formation of enzymes

   Answer: A
   Skill: Comprehension

7) Event I: atmosphere of water, methane, and ammonia
   Event II: reducing atmosphere

   Answer: C
   Skill: Comprehension

8) Approximately how far does the fossil record extend back in time?

   A) 6,000 years

   B) 3,500,000 years

   C) 6,000,000 years

   D) 3,500,000,000 years

   E) 5,000,000,000,000 years

   Answer: D
   Skill: Knowledge

9) Which gas was probably *least* abundant in Earth's early atmosphere?

   A) O_2

   B) CO

   C) CH_4

   D) H_2O

   E) NH_3

   Answer: A
   Skill: Knowledge

10) In his laboratory simulation of the early Earth, Miller observed the abiotic synthesis of

   A) amino acids.

   B) complex organic polymers.

   C) DNA.

   D) liposomes.

   E) nucleoli.

   Answer: A
   Skill: Knowledge

11) Which of the following factors was *most* important in the origin of life on Earth?

   A) natural selection acting on molecules and protobionts

   B) competition for oxygen

   C) low levels of solar energy

   D) biotic synthesis of organic molecules

   E) low–intensity electrical discharges in the upper atmosphere

   Answer: A
   Skill: Comprehension

12) Which of the following has not yet been synthesized in laboratory experiments studying the origin of life?

   A) lipids

   B) liposomes with selectively permeable membranes

   C) oligopeptides and other oligomers

   D) protobionts that use DNA to program protein synthesis

   E) amino acids

   Answer: D
   Skill: Comprehension

13) What condition would have made the primitive atmosphere of Earth more conducive to the origin of life than the modern atmosphere of Earth? The primitive atmosphere

   A) had a layer of ozone that shielded the first fragile cells.

   B) removed electrons that impeded the formation of protobionts.

   C) may have been a reducing one that facilitated the formation of complex substances from simple molecules.

   D) had more oxygen than the modern atmosphere, and thus it successfully sustained the first living organisms.

   E) had less free energy than the modern atmosphere, and thus newly formed organisms were less likely to be destroyed.

   Answer: C
   Skill: Comprehension

14) A key role that clay may have played in the origin of life is the tendency for clay to

A) plug gaps in membranous bilayers so that electrical differences could be maintained across them.

B) assemble into liposome membranes.

C) generate life through spontaneous processes.

D) provide a catalytic surface for the polymerization of organic monomers.

E) remain suspended in solution.

Answer: D
Skill: Comprehension

15) In what way were conditions on early Earth different from those on modern Earth?

A) The early Earth had no water.

B) The early Earth was intensely bombarded by large space debris.

C) The early Earth had an oxidizing atmosphere.

D) Less ultraviolet radiation penetrated the early atmosphere.

E) The early atmosphere had significant quantities of ozone.

Answer: B
Skill: Knowledge

16) Which of the following is the *correct* sequence of events in the origin of life?
    I. Formation of protobionts
    II. Synthesis of organic monomers
    III. Synthesis of organic polymers

A) I, II, III

B) I, III, II

C) II, III, I

D) III, I, II

E) III, II, I

Answer: C
Skill: Comprehension

17) Which of the following statements about the origin of genetic material is most probably *correct*? The first genes were

A) DNA produced by reverse transcriptase from abiotically produced RNA.

B) DNA molecules whose information was transcribed to RNA and later translated in polypeptides.

C) autocatalytic RNA molecules bound to clay surfaces.

D) RNA produced by autocatalytic, proteinaceous enzymes called ribozymes.

E) protobionts produced by dehydration syntheses of nucleic acids.

Answer: C
Skill: Comprehension

The questions below refer to the following scientists.

A. Pasteur
B. Cech
C. Oparin and Haldane
D. Miller
E. Whittaker

18) discovered ribozymes

Answer: B
Skill: Knowledge

19) demonstrated experimentally that microorganisms do not arise abiogenetically

Answer: A
Skill: Knowledge

20) synthesized organic monomers in an apparatus designed to simulate early Earth's conditions

Answer: D
Skill: Knowledge

21) proposed the five-kingdom classification system

Answer: E
Skill: Knowledge

22) proposed that the spontaneous synthesis of complex molecules could not occur today because oxygen attacks chemical bonds, extracting electrons

Answer: C
Skill: Knowledge

The questions below refer to the following list, which uses the five-kingdom classification system.

1. *Plantae*
2. *Fungi*
3. *Animalia*
4. *Protista*
5. *Monera*

23) Which obsolete kingdom includes prokaryotic organisms?

A) 1   B) 2   C) 3   D) 4   E) 5

Answer: E
Skill: Knowledge

24) Which kingdom was most intimately associated with the earliest land plants, both functionally and anatomically?

A) 1   B) 2   C) 3   D) 4   E) 5

Answer: B
Skill: Knowledge

25) Which kingdom has recently been replaced with two domains?

A) 1   B) 2   C) 3   D) 4   E) 5

Answer: E
Skill: Knowledge

26) Which eukaryotic kingdom is polyphyletic and, therefore, obsolete?

A) 1   B) 2   C) 3   D) 4   E) 5

Answer: D
Skill: Knowledge

27) Which kingdoms include free-living photosynthetic organisms?

A) 1 and 5 only

B) 2 and 4 only

C) 1, 2, and 5 only

D) 1, 4, and 5 only

E) 1, 2, 3, 4, and 5

Answer: D
Skill: Knowledge

28) What probably accounts for the switch to DNA-based genetic systems during the evolution of life on Earth?

A) DNA is chemically more stable and replicates with fewer errors (mutations) than RNA.

B) Only DNA can replicate during cell division.

C) RNA is too involved with translation of proteins and cannot provide multiple functions.

D) DNA forms the rod-shaped chromosomes necessary for cell division.

E) Replication of RNA occurs too quickly.

Answer: A
Skill: Knowledge

29) In an experiment, zinc and RNA nucleotides are placed in a test tube. If a short RNA molecule is added to the test tube, what happens?

A) RNA becomes autocatalytic and replicates portions of itself.

B) RNA degrades into nucleotides.

C) An autocatalytic protein, amino adenosine triacid ester (AATE), is produced.

D) A protein enzyme is formed that assists RNA in replication.

E) DNA is formed.

Answer: A
Skill: Knowledge

30) What characteristic would all protobionts have had in common?

A) the ability to synthesize enzymes

B) a boundary membrane

C) RNA genes

D) a nucleus

E) the ability to replicate RNA

Answer: B
Skill: Comprehension

31) Although absolute distinctions between the "most evolved" protobiont and the first living cell are fuzzy, all scientists agree that one major difference is that protobionts could *not*

A) possess a selectively permeable membrane boundary.

B) perform osmosis.

C) grow in size.

D) perform controlled, precise reproduction.

E) absorb compounds from the external environment.

Answer: D
Skill: Comprehension

32) High temperatures, the presence of metal ions such as zinc, and the presence of a substrate such as clay all directly facilitate the laboratory formation of

A) amino acids.

B) organic polymers.

C) lipid bilayers.

D) cells.

E) liposomes.

Answer: B
Skill: Knowledge

33) Which of the following is the strongest evidence that prokaryotes evolved before eukaryotes?

A) the primitive structure of plants

B) meteorites that have struck the Earth

C) abiotic experiments that constructed liposomes in the laboratory

D) Liposomes look like prokaryotic cells.

E) The oldest fossilized cells resemble prokaryotes.

Answer: E
Skill: Comprehension

34) How could RNA have become involved in the mechanism for protein translation?

A) Only ribozymes were available as catalysts.

B) RNA replication is enhanced if proteins are produced.

C) Natural selection acted against autocatalyic protein formation.

D) DNA was not available for protein translation.

E) Natural selection favored RNA molecules that synthesized proteins, which enhanced the replication of more of the same RNA.

Answer: E
Skill: Comprehension

35) Life on Earth today comes only from preexisting life. How could life have evolved from "nonlife" about 3.8 billion years ago?

A) Environmental conditions were very different when life evolved.

B) The early environment of Earth was an oxidizing one that destroyed organic molecules and prevented evolution.

C) The numerous meteors and volcanoes produced organic molecules in large numbers.

D) Nobody knows; there is no evidence and there are no testable hypotheses.

E) In interstellar gas clouds, where the vacuum of space induced redox reactions among organic chemicals.

Answer: A
Skill: Comprehension

36) When considering the possibility of an extraterrestrial origin of life, all of the following provide valid evidence *except*

A) apparent bacteria–like structures recovered from a Martian meteorite.

B) evidence of water on Mars.

C) evidence of water on one of Jupiter's moons.

D) organic molecules found in meteorites.

E) impact craters on Earth's surface.

Answer: E
Skill: Comprehension

37) RNA molecules can be both self–replicating and catalytic. This probably means that

A) RNA was the first hereditary information.

B) protobionts had an RNA membrane.

C) RNA could make energy.

D) free nucleotides would not have been necessary ingredients in the synthesis of new RNA molecules.

E) RNA is a polymer of amino acids.

Answer: A
Skill: Comprehension

38) The Miller experiments

A) proved how cells formed on the early Earth.

B) could not be repeated under present atmospheric conditions.

C) continue to stimulate debate about the origin of life on Earth.

D) were based on our precise knowledge of Earth's early atmosphere.

E) simulated an early Earth whose seas and atmosphere were oxidizing.

Answer: C
Skill: Comprehension

39) The production of oxygen by plant and bacterial photosynthesis

A) made life on land difficult.

B) is a relatively recent event.

C) made it easier to maintain reduced molecules.

D) made the Earth an oxidizing environment.

E) prevented the formation of an ozone layer.

Answer: D
Skill: Comprehension

40) The early atmosphere of the Earth probably contained all of the following molecules in large amounts *except*

A) H_2

B) CH_4

C) CO

D) NH_3

E) H_2O

Answer: C
Skill: Knowledge

41) What is (are) the drawback(s) associated with the hypothesized abiogenetic formation of organic monomers in early Earth's atmosphere?
1. the relatively short time between intense meteor bombardment and appearance of the first life forms
2. the lack of experimental evidence that organic monomers can form abiogenetically
3. uncertainty about which gases comprised early Earth's atmosphere

A) 1 only
B) 2 only
C) 3 only
D) 1 and 3
E) 2 and 3

Answer: D
Skill: Comprehension

42) Recent evidence indicates that the first major diversification of multicellular eukaryotes may have coincided in time with the

A) origin of eukaryotes.
B) switch to an oxidizing atmosphere.
C) melting that ended the "snowball Earth" period.
D) origin of multicellular organisms.
E) massive eruptions of deep-sea vents.

Answer: C
Skill: Knowledge

43) Whereas the initial oxygenation of Earth's seas and atmosphere was due to the origin of _____, a major increase in the rate of oxygenation may have subsequently coincided with the origin of _____.

A) archaea ... bacteria
B) green plants ... mitochondria
C) cyanobacteria ... chloroplasts
D) anaerobic archaea ... aerobic bacteria
E) cyanobacteria ... terrestrial plants and fungi

Answer: C
Skill: Knowledge

44) Which putative early Earth condition did Stanley Miller's experimental apparatus *not* attempt to simulate directly?

A) presence of water vapor
B) intense lightning storms
C) warm seas
D) intense UV bombardment
E) reducing atmosphere

Answer: D
Skill: Comprehension

45) Wave splash onto warm coastal rock or the ebb of tides may have been physical factors that resulted in the _____ on early Earth.

A) production of bilayered membranes
B) first genetic systems
C) polymerization of organic polymers
D) synthesis of organic monomers
E) early green plants forming terrestrial colonies

Answer: C
Skill: Knowledge

46) Which feature(s) generally characterized the animals that comprised the Precambrian fauna?
1. multicellularity
2. lack of hard parts
3. small size
4. presence of mitochondria

A) 1 only
B) 1 and 3
C) 1, 3, and 4
D) 2, 3, and 4
E) all of these

Answer: E
Skill: Comprehension

47) What kind of evidence has recently made it necessary to assign the prokaryotes to either of two different domains, rather than assigning all prokaryotes to the same kingdom?

A) molecular

B) behavioral

C) nutritional

D) anatomical

E) ecological

Answer: A
Skill: Knowledge

48) What important criterion was used in the late 1960s to distinguish between the three multicellular eukaryotic kingdoms of the five-kingdom classification system?

A) the number of cells present in individual organisms

B) the geological stratum in which fossils first appear

C) the nutritional modes they employ

D) the biogeographic province where each first appears

E) the features of their embryos

Answer: C
Skill: Knowledge

49) Which of these prokaryotes are most likely to be found in the immediate vicinity of active deep-sea vents?

A) cyanobacteria

B) archaea

C) aerobically respiring bacteria

D) bacteria adapted to being embedded in ice

E) N_2-fixing root nodule bacteria

Answer: B
Skill: Comprehension

50) As the number of kingdoms was increased beyond two, what was true of the kingdom Protista?

A) It was used to harbor all prokaryotes.

B) All photosynthetic organisms were assigned to it.

C) Viruses were assigned to this kingdom.

D) Unicellular organisms of all kinds were placed here.

E) It was used for organisms that did not fit clearly into any of the other, more well-defined kingdoms.

Answer: E
Skill: Comprehension

51) What is the correct sequence of these events, from earliest to most recent, in the evolution of life on Earth?

1. origin of mitochondria
2. origin of multicellular eukaryotes
3. origin of chloroplasts
4. origin of cyanobacteria
5. origin of fungal/plant symbioses

A) 4, 3, 2, 1, 5

B) 4, 1, 2, 3, 5

C) 4, 3, 1, 2, 5

D) 4, 3, 1, 5, 2

E) 3, 4, 1, 2, 5

Answer: C
Skill: Comprehension

52) The snowball Earth hypothesis provides a possible explanation for the

A) diversification of animals at the start of the Precambrian era.

B) oxygenation of Earth's seas and atmosphere.

C) colonization of land by plants and fungi.

D) origin of O_2-releasing photosynthesis.

E) existence of hydrothermal vents on the ocean floor.

Answer: A
Skill: Comprehension

53) What is the relationship between the snowball Earth hypothesis and the planet Mars?

A) The dislodging of a chunk of primeval Earth gave rise to Mars; this event coincided with Earth being pushed into an orbit farther from the Sun, causing Earth to cool.

B) Bacteria that originated on Mars contained ice–nucleation genes. Upon colonizing Earth, these same bacteria induced a major ice age.

C) Massive volcanic eruptions on Earth ejected bacteria–containing debris into space. Some of this debris made it to Mars; the rest created a global dust cloud that induced a kind of "nuclear winter" on Earth.

D) Volcanic eruptions on Mars spewed H_2O vapor into space where it condensed and then fell to Earth as snow.

E) There is no direct relationship between the snowball Earth hypothesis and the planet Mars.

Answer: E
Skill: Comprehension

54) Which of the following does *not* belong with the rest?

A) cyanobacteria

B) stromatolites

C) origin of O_2–releasing photosynthesis

D) unicellular eukaryotes

E) microbial mats

Answer: D
Skill: Comprehension

55) The synthesis of new DNA requires the prior existence of oligonucleotides to serve as primers. On Earth, these primers are small RNA molecules. This latter observation is evidence in support of the hypothesized existence of

A) snowball Earth.

B) an RNA world.

C) the abiogenetic production of organic monomers.

D) the delivery of organic matter to Earth aboard meteors and comets.

E) the endosymbiotic origin of mitochondria and chloroplasts.

Answer: B
Skill: Comprehension

56) The best classification system is that which most closely

A) unites organisms that possess similar morphologies.

B) conforms to traditional, Linnaean taxonomic practices.

C) reflects evolutionary history.

D) corroborates the classification scheme in use at the time of Charles Darwin.

E) reflects the basic separation of prokaryotes from eukaryotes.

Answer: C
Skill: Comprehension

Media Activity Questions

1) Which of these is arranged in the appropriate sequence from the earliest to the most recent?

A) origin of Earth, origin of prokaryotes, beginning of the accumulation of atmospheric oxygen, oldest eukaryotic cell fossils, origin of multicellular eukaryotes, colonization of land by plants and fungi, first humans

B) origin of Earth, origin of prokaryotes, oldest eukaryotic cell fossils, beginning of the accumulation of atmospheric oxygen, origin of multicellular eukaryotes, colonization of land by plants and fungi, first humans

C) origin of Earth, beginning of the accumulation of atmospheric oxygen, origin of prokaryotes, oldest eukaryotic cell fossils, origin of multicellular eukaryotes, colonization of land by plants and fungi, first humans

D) origin of Earth, origin of prokaryotes, oldest eukaryotic cell fossils, origin of multicellular organisms, colonization of land by plants and fungi, beginning of the accumulation of atmospheric oxygen, first humans

E) origin of prokaryotes, origin of Earth, beginning of the accumulation of atmospheric oxygen, oldest eukaryotic cell fossils, origin of multicellular eukaryotes, colonization of land by plants and fungi, first humans

Answer: A
Topic: Web/CD Activity 26A

2) Which of these events occurred during the Cenozoic?

A) origin of prokaryotes

B) beginning of the accumulation of atmospheric oxygen

C) origin of eukaryotes

D) first humans

E) colonization of land by plants

Answer: D
Topic: Web/CD Activity 26A

3) The prokaryotes that serve as the basis for the hydrothermal vent community seen in the video obtain their energy from

A) methane.

B) hydrogen sulfide.

C) hydrogen cyanide.

D) light.

E) water.

Answer: B
Topic: Web/CD Activity 26b

4) The Domain Eukarya includes all of the following kingdoms *except*

A) Animalia.

B) Plantae.

C) Monera.

D) Fungi.

E) all of these.

Answer: C
Topic: Web/CD Activity 26C

5) Which of these domains includes prokaryotic cells?

A) Protista

B) Eukarya

C) Monera

D) Archaea

E) Fungi

Answer: D
Topic: Web/CD Activity 26C

Self–Quiz Questions

Answers to these questions also appear in the textbook.

1) The *main* explanation for the lack of a continuing abiotic origin of life on Earth today is that

   A) there is not sufficient lightning to provide an energy source.

   B) our oxidizing atmosphere is not conducive to the spontaneous formation of complex molecules.

   C) much less visible light is reaching Earth to serve as an energy source.

   D) there are no molten surfaces on which weak solutions of organic molecules would polymerize.

   E) all habitable places are already filled.

   Answer: B

2) Which statement does *not* support the hypothesis that RNA functioned as the first genetic material of early protobionts?

   A) Short RNA sequences can self-assemble when combined with nucleotide monomers.

   B) Catalytic activity has been demonstrated for RNA in modern cells.

   C) Variations in base sequences produce molecules with variable stabilities in different environments.

   D) Modern cells use an RNA template when synthesizing proteins.

   E) In modern cells, RNA provides the template on which DNA nucleotides are assembled.

   Answer: E

3) Fossilized mats called stromatolites

   A) date from 3.5 billion years ago and contain fossils that resemble modern filamentous prokaryotes.

   B) formed around deep-sea vents and provide the first evidence of life on Earth.

   C) contain layers of iron oxide that provide evidence for the oxygenic photosynthesis of cyanobacteria around 2.7 billion years ago.

   D) provide evidence that plants moved onto land in the company of fungi around 500 million years ago.

   E) contain the first undisputed fossils of eukaryotes and date from 2.1 billion years ago.

   Answer: A

4) The oxygen revolution changed Earth's environment dramatically. Which of the following adaptations took advantage of this change?

   A) the evolution of chloroplasts when early protists engulfed photosynthetic cyanobacteria

   B) the persistence of some animal groups in anaerobic habitats

   C) the evolution of photosynthetic pigments that protected early algae from the corrosive effects of oxygen

   D) the evolution of cellular respiration, which used oxygen to help harvest energy from fuel molecules

   E) the evolution of multicellular eukaryotic colonies from symbiotic communities of prokaryotes

   Answer: D

5) The oldest known fossils of multicellular eukaryotes
   A) are dated by molecular clocks to be 1.5 billion years old.
   B) are corkscrew-shaped algae and date from 2.2 billion years ago.
   C) are filamentous algae that date from 1.2 billion years ago.
   D) are fossilized embryos that have been found in Chinese sediments 570 million years old.
   E) first appear in the fossil record in the late Precambrian after the thawing of snowball Earth.

   Answer: C

6) Competition among various protobionts may have led to evolutionary improvement only when
   A) they were first able to catalyze chemical reactions.
   B) some kind of heredity mechanism developed.
   C) they were able to grow and split in two.
   D) photosynthesis evolved.
   E) DNA first appeared.

   Answer: B

7) Which of the following represents a probable order in the biological history of Earth?
   A) metabolism before mitosis
   B) an oxidizing atmosphere followed by a reducing atmosphere
   C) eukaryotes before prokaryotes
   D) DNA genes before RNA genes
   E) animals before algae

   Answer: A

8) One current debate raises the issue that, rather than beginning in shallow pools, life could have begun
   A) on dry land.
   B) near deep-sea vents.
   C) from viruses.
   D) in northern Africa.
   E) when chunks that broke off from the moon bombarded Earth.

   Answer: B

9) Which of the following steps has *not* yet been accomplished by scientists studying the origin of life?
   A) abiotic synthesis of small RNA polymers
   B) abiotic synthesis of polypeptides
   C) formation of molecular aggregates with selectively permeable membranes
   D) formation of protobionts that use DNA to direct the polymerization of amino acids
   E) abiotic synthesis of organic monomers

   Answer: D

10) Current debates about the number and boundaries of the kingdoms of life center *mainly* on which groups of organisms?
   A) plants and animals
   B) plants and fungi
   C) prokaryotes and single-celled eukaryotes
   D) fungi and animals
   E) amphibians and reptiles

   Answer: C

Chapter 27 Prokaryotes and the Origins of Metabolic Diversity

1) Which of the following would most likely occur if all prokaryotes were suddenly to perish?
   A) All life would eventually perish due to disease.
   B) Many organisms would perish as nutrient recycling underwent dramatic reduction.
   C) All life would eventually perish because of increased global warming due to the greenhouse effect.
   D) Only the organisms that feed directly on prokaryotes would suffer any harmful effects.
   E) Very little change would occur because prokaryotes are not of significant ecological importance.

   Answer: B
   Skill: Comprehension

2) If all the bacteria on Earth suddenly disappeared, which of the following would be the most likely and most direct result?
   A) The number of organisms on Earth would decrease by 10–20%.
   B) Human populations would thrive in the absence of disease.
   C) There would be little change in Earth's ecosystems.
   D) Recycling of nutrients would be greatly reduced, at least initially.
   E) Earth's total photosynthesis would decline markedly.

   Answer: D
   Skill: Knowledge

3) Broad–spectrum antibiotics inhibit the growth of most intestinal bacteria. Consequently, a hospital patient who is receiving broad–spectrum antibiotics is most likely to become _____, assuming that nothing is done to counter the reduction of intestinal bacteria.
   A) unable to digest cellulose
   B) antibiotic resistant
   C) unable to fix nitrogen
   D) unable to synthesize peptidoglycan
   E) deficient in certain vitamins

   Answer: E
   Skill: Application

4) Which is the *least* accurate statement about the evolution of prokaryotes and the changing environment of Earth?
   A) Prokaryotes have interacted with the environment for more than 3.5 billion years.
   B) Although prokaryotes have a diverse morphology, they basically have the same metabolic pathways and products.
   C) Oxygen–producing photosynthesis favored the evolution of cells capable of performing aerobic respiration.
   D) Cyanobacteria evolved before aerobically respiring bacteria.
   E) Bacteria are among several kinds of organisms that recycle chemical elements in ecosystems.

   Answer: B
   Skill: Comprehension

5) In which of the following ways can prokaryotes be considered to be more successful on Earth than humans?

   A) Prokaryotes are much more numerous and have more biomass than humans.

   B) Prokaryotes occupy more diverse habitats than humans.

   C) Prokaryotes have survived on Earth for billions of years longer than humans have.

   D) Only B and C are correct.

   E) A, B, and C are correct.

   Answer: E
   Skill: Comprehension

6) Carl Woese of the University of Illinois and his collaborators identified two major branches of prokaryotic evolution. What was the basis for dividing prokaryotes into two domains?

   A) microscopic examination of staining characteristics

   B) metabolic characteristics such as the production of methane gas

   C) metabolic characteristics such as chemoautotrophy and photosynthesis

   D) molecular characteristics such as ribosomal RNA sequences

   E) ecological characteristics such as the ability to survive in extreme environments

   Answer: D
   Skill: Knowledge

7) What is the primary ecological role of prokaryotes?

   A) parasitizing eukaryotes, thus causing diseases

   B) the decomposition of organic matter

   C) metabolizing materials in extreme environments

   D) adding methane to the atmosphere

   E) serving as primary producers in terrestrial environments

   Answer: B
   Skill: Comprehension

8) Prokaryotic organisms have recently been divided into two domains, bacteria and archaea. This division is based primarily on

   A) differences in cell wall composition.

   B) kind of inhibitor amino acid for start of protein synthesis.

   C) presence or absence of introns.

   D) Only B and C are correct.

   E) A, B, and C are correct.

   Answer: E
   Skill: Knowledge

9) Though plants, fungi, and prokaryotes all have cell walls, we classify them in different taxonomic units. Which of these observations comes closest to explaining *why* these organisms are placed in different taxa?

   A) Some closely resemble animals, which lack cell walls.

   B) Their cell walls are constructed from very different biochemicals.

   C) Some have cell walls only for support.

   D) Some have cell walls only for protection from herbivores.

   E) Some have cell walls only to control osmotic balance.

   Answer: B
   Skill: Comprehension

10) Why do biologists now reject the use of a single kingdom Monera for all prokaryotic organisms?

A) Only eukaryotic organisms have membrane–enclosed organelles.

B) Molecular evidence shows that archaea and eukaryotes share a more recent common ancestor than archaea and bacteria.

C) Structural data show that bacteria are more closely related to eukaryotes and that archaea differ in a greater number of characteristics.

D) Only prokaryotic organisms show growth inhibition in the presence of antibiotics.

E) Only species of archaea lack the noncoding parts of genes (that is, introns).

Answer: B
Skill: Comprehension

11) The following statements about bacterial cell walls are all true *except* they

A) differ in molecular composition from plant cell walls.

B) prevent cells from bursting in hypoosmotic environments.

C) prevent cells from dying in hyperosmotic conditions.

D) are analogous to the cell walls of many protists, fungi, and plants.

E) provide the cell with a degree of physical protection from the environment.

Answer: C
Skill: Knowledge

12) Jams, jellies, preserves, honey, and other foodstuffs with a high–sugar content hardly ever become contaminated by bacteria, even when the food containers are left open at room temperature. This is because bacteria that encounter such an environment

A) undergo death by plasmolysis.

B) are unable to metabolize the glucose or fructose and thus starve to death.

C) undergo death by lysis.

D) suffocate once the lid is replaced.

E) are unable to swim through these thick and viscous materials.

Answer: A
Skill: Application

13) Mycoplasmas are bacteria that lack cell walls. On the basis of this structural anomaly, one should expect mycoplasmas to

A) be gram–negative.

B) be subject to lysis in hypoosmotic conditions.

C) lack a cell membrane as well.

D) undergo ready fossilization in sedimentary rock.

E) possess typical prokaryotic flagella.

Answer: B
Skill: Comprehension

14) The following statements are all true of the domain Archaea *except*

A) based on DNA analysis, archaea are probably more closely related to eukaryotes than they are to bacteria.

B) some archaeans can reduce CO_2 to methane.

C) archaean cell walls are composed of peptidoglycan.

D) some archaeans can inhabit solutions that are nearly 30% salt.

E) some archaeans are adapted to waters with temperatures above the boiling point.

Answer: C
Skill: Knowledge

15) The antibiotics known as *penicillins* inhibit the ability of certain bacteria to

A) form spores.

B) perform respiration.

C) replicate DNA.

D) synthesize proteins.

E) synthesize cell walls.

Answer: E
Skill: Knowledge

16) Which of the following statements is *correct* about gram–negative bacteria?

A) Penicillins are effective antibiotics to use against them.

B) They often possess an outer membrane containing toxic lipopolysaccharides.

C) On a cell–to–cell basis, they possess more DNA than do the cells of any taxonomically higher organism.

D) Their chromosomes are composed of DNA tightly wrapped around histone proteins.

E) Their cell walls are primarily composed of peptidoglycan.

Answer: B
Skill: Knowledge

17) In a hypothetical situation, the genes for sex pilus construction and for tetracycline resistance are located together on the same plasmid within a particular bacterium. If this bacterium performs conjugation involving a copy of this plasmid, then the result should be

A) a clone of daughter cells possessing the same plasmid.

B) the rapid spread of tetracycline resistance to other bacteria in that habitat.

C) that this bacterium will subsequently lose tetracycline resistance.

D) the production of endospores among the bacterium's progeny.

E) that this bacterium will temporarily possess a completely diploid genome.

Answer: B
Skill: Application

18) About half of all prokaryotes are capable of directional movement. The following statements are all true of such directional movement *except*

A) it may occur via flagellar action.

B) it may happen in response to Earth's magnetic field.

C) internal helical filaments with basal motors can drive this movement.

D) it should produce negative phototaxis in photosynthetic forms.

E) it may occur via gliding along a thread of "slime" secreted by filamentous forms.

Answer: D
Skill: Comprehension

19) In an aerobic prokaryotic cell, the molecules of the respiratory chain should be located in the

A) cytosol.

B) cristae.

C) cell wall.

D) plasma membrane.

E) mitochondrial matrix.

Answer: D
Skill: Comprehension

20) Which structure has been present in Earth's living organisms for the *least* amount of evolutionary time?

A) enzymes that catalyze glycolysis

B) photosystems I and II

C) cell walls

D) nuclei

E) genes composed of DNA

Answer: D
Skill: Comprehension

21) Which of the following is a *correct* statement about the genomes of prokaryotes?

A) Prokaryotic genomes are diploid throughout most of the cell cycle.

B) Prokaryotic chromosomes are sometimes called "genochromes."

C) Prokaryotic cells have multiple chromosomes packaged with a relatively large amount of protein.

D) Instead of a nucleus, prokaryotic cells have a "nucleoid" region.

E) Prokaryotic genomes are composed of circularized DNA (that is, DNA existing in the form of a circle).

Answer: D
Skill: Knowledge

22) If archaeans are more closely related to eukaryotes than to bacteria, then which of the following is it reasonable to propose?

A) Archaean DNA should have no introns.

B) Archaean genophores should have no protein bonded to them.

C) Archaean DNA should be single–stranded.

D) Archaean ribosomes should be larger than typical prokaryotic ribosomes.

E) Archaeans should lack cell walls.

Answer: D
Skill: Comprehension

23) Which of the following statements about prokaryotes is *correct*?

A) Bacterial cells conjugate to mutually exchange genetic material.

B) Their genetic material is confined within a nuclear envelope.

C) They divide by binary fission, without mitosis or meiosis.

D) The persistence of bacteria throughout evolutionary time is due to metabolic similarity.

E) Genetic variation in bacteria is not known to occur, nor should it occur because of their asexual mode of reproduction.

Answer: C
Skill: Comprehension

24) Prokaryotes have ribosomes different from those of eukaryotes. Because of this, which of the following is *true*?

A) Some selective antibiotics can block protein synthesis of bacteria without harming the eukaryotic host.

B) It is believed that eukaryotes did not evolve from prokaryotes.

C) Protein synthesis can occur at the same time as transcription in prokaryotes.

D) Some antibiotics can block the formation of cross-links in the peptidoglycan walls of bacteria.

E) Prokaryotes are able to use a much greater variety of molecules as food sources.

Answer: A
Skill: Knowledge

25) In regard to prokaryotic reproduction, which of the following is *true*?

A) Prokaryotes perform meiosis.

B) Prokaryotes feature syngamy as done by eukaryotes.

C) Prokaryotes have ways of exchanging some of their genes by conjugation, syngamy, and transduction.

D) Mutation is a primary source of variation in prokaryote populations.

E) Prokaryotes skip sexual life cycles because their life cycle is too short.

Answer: D
Skill: Comprehension

26) Most genetic variation in prokaryotes is introduced by which process?

A) meiosis.

B) mutations.

C) conjugation.

D) transformation.

E) transduction.

Answer: B
Skill: Knowledge

For the following questions, use the list below of types of bacterial metabolism. Pick the term that best matches the statement. Responses may be used once, more than once, or not at all.

A. *photoautotrophs*
B. *photoheterotrophs*
C. *chemoautotrophs*
D. *saprobic chemoheterotrophs*
E. *parasitic chemoheterotrophs*

27) responsible for many human diseases

Answer: E
Skill: Knowledge

28) cyanobacteria

Answer: A
Skill: Knowledge

29) use light energy to synthesize organic compounds from CO_2

Answer: A
Skill: Knowledge

30) obtain energy by oxidizing inorganic substances; energy that is used, in part, to fix CO_2

Answer: C
Skill: Knowledge

31) use light energy to generate ATP but do not release oxygen

Answer: B
Skill: Knowledge

32) responsible for high levels of O_2 in Earth's present atmosphere

Answer: A
Skill: Knowledge

33) Modes of obtaining nutrition, used by at least some bacteria, include all of the following *except*

A) chemoautotrophy.
B) photoautotrophy.
C) heteroautotrophy.
D) chemoheterotrophy.
E) photoheterotrophy.

108 Midterm Fall 03

Answer: C
Skill: Knowledge

For the following questions, refer to the categories of nutrition below. Each answer may be used once, more than once, or not at all.

A. saprobes
B. chemoheterotrophs
C. chemoautotrophs
D. photoautotrophs
E. photoheterotrophs

34) bacteria that oxidize NH_3 to NO_2

Answer: C
Skill: Knowledge

35) bacteria that oxidize sulfur to sulfate

Answer: C
Skill: Knowledge

36) bacteria that use light for energy and organic matter for a carbon source

Answer: E
Skill: Knowledge

37) bacteria that possess both photosystems I and II

Answer: D
Skill: Knowledge

38) bacteria that are known as methanogens

Answer: C
Skill: Knowledge

39) Which of the following statements is *true* of chemoautotrophs?

A) They use hydrogen sulfide as their hydrogen source for the photosynthesis of their organic compounds.
B) They "feed themselves" by obtaining energy from the chemical bonds of organic molecules.
C) They oxidize inorganic compounds to obtain energy to drive the synthesis of their organic compounds.
D) They live as decomposers of inorganic chemicals in organic litter.
E) They obtain their energy from oxidizing chemical compounds and get their carbon skeletons from organic compounds.

Answer: C
Skill: Comprehension

40) Of all the organisms, the prokaryotes have the greatest range of metabolic diversity. Among the prokaryotes listed below, which are currently the most important ecologically?

A) nitrogen fixers
B) obligate anaerobes
C) thermoacidophiles
D) chemoautotrophs
E) extreme halophiles

Answer: A
Skill: Comprehension

41) Nitrogen fixation cannot occur in the presence of oxygen. Which of the following represents the best adaptation for nitrogen-fixing cyanobacteria that produce oxygen as a by-product of their metabolism? They should

A) be unable to perform aerobic photosynthesis.

B) lose their ability to be photoautotrophs.

C) isolate nitrogen-fixation within cells that are protected from oxygen.

D) limit themselves to habitats where there is no oxygen.

E) limit themselves to habitats where there is no light.

Answer: C
Skill: Application

42) The following statements about prokaryotes are all correct *except*

A) the gradual accumulation of oxygen probably caused the extinction of many prokaryotes.

B) glycolysis probably evolved in prokaryotes to regenerate ATP in anaerobic environments.

C) early photosynthetic prokaryotes probably used pigments and light-powered photosystems to fix carbon dioxide.

D) the first prokaryotes were likely photoautotrophs that could utilize the abundant light energy and inorganic minerals of early Earth.

E) the gradual accumulation of oxygen favored the evolution of respiratory mechanisms that permitted certain organisms to either tolerate or capitalize on rising oxygen levels.

Answer: D
Skill: Comprehension

43) If the following events had left physical evidence of their occurrences, then which could indicate that Earth's environment was switching from a reducing one to an oxidizing one around 2.7 billion years ago?

A) precipitation of iron oxide

B) extinction of many anaerobic prokaryotes

C) evolution of antioxidant mechanisms

D) evolution of aerobic respiration

E) All of the above could provide evidence of the rise of an oxidizing environment.

Answer: E
Skill: Comprehension

44) The oxygen revolution probably began with the origin of which group of organisms?

A) plants

B) eukaryotes

C) prokaryotes

D) cyanobacteria

E) cellular respiration

Answer: D
Skill: Knowledge

45) If ancient prokaryotes had not evolved a way to use water as a source of electrons and protons, which of the following processes is *least* likely to have evolved later on?

A) enzyme catabolism

B) the Krebs cycle

C) protein synthesis

D) fermentation

E) glycolysis

Answer: B
Skill: Comprehension

46) Huge populations of filamentous cyanobacteria can form scums on the surfaces of certain lakes and ponds on calm summer afternoons. The cyanobacteria generally sink during the night. During the day, the cyanobacteria are most likely to be brought to the surface by accumulating _____, which the cyanobacteria are _____.

A) oxygen ... producing

B) nitrogen ... fixing

C) carbon dioxide ... fixing

D) oxygen ... using as an electron receptor

E) oxygen ... fixing

Answer: A
Skill: Application

47) In the following list of major metabolic pathways, which one must have evolved most recently?

A) glycolysis

B) oxidative phosphorylation

C) fermentation

D) O_2-producing photosynthesis

E) sulfur-producing photosynthesis

Answer: B
Skill: Comprehension

48) Coordination of two photosystems occurs during photosynthesis in

A) chemoautotrophic bacteria.

B) methanogens.

C) archaea surrounding deep-sea hydrothermal vents.

D) anaerobic bacteria.

E) cyanobacteria.

Answer: E
Skill: Knowledge

49) Archaeans are currently assigned to either one of two putative kingdoms, based on

A) the composition of their cell walls.

B) whether or not they possess cell walls.

C) the habitats they prefer.

D) nucleotide sequences of small-subunit ribosomal RNA.

E) whether their metabolisms produce methane or oxygen as a by-product.

Answer: D
Skill: Knowledge

50) Which of the following traits do archaea and bacteria share?
1. composition of the cell wall
2. glycolysis
3. lack of a nuclear envelope
4. identical rRNA sequences

A) 1 only

B) 3 only

C) 1 and 3

D) 2 and 3

E) 2 and 4

Answer: D
Skill: Comprehension

51) "By studying modern prokaryotic organisms, we can be absolutely certain of how metabolic pathways evolved." This statement is

A) true, because all the fossil evidence indicates that ancient prokaryotes were much like modern prokaryotes.

B) false, because we have no evidence of ancient metabolic pathways.

C) impossible to evaluate, because ancient prokaryotes are all dead.

D) false, because our understanding of early metabolic pathways must always be hypothetical.

E) true, because both ancient and modern prokaryotes have few enzymes.

Answer: D
Skill: Application

52) What do the archaeans used in primary sewage treatment and the archaeans that help cattle digest cellulose have in common?

A) They contribute to the greenhouse effect.

B) They live only at extremely low pHs.

C) They are nitrogen–fixers.

D) They possess both photosystems I and II.

E) They require extremely high temperatures for reproduction.

Answer: A
Skill: Comprehension

53) What is true of the archaea? They are

A) limited to extreme environments.

B) limited to aquatic environments.

C) the universal ancestors of all life on Earth.

D) abundant in marine environments.

E) morphologically indistinguishable from bacteria when observed with an electron microscope.

Answer: D
Skill: Knowledge

54) In a hypothetical situation, a bacterium lives on the surface of a leaf, where it obtains nutrition from the leaf's nonliving, waxy covering, and where it inhibits the growth of other microbes that damage the plant. If, and only if, this bacterium accidentally gains access to the inside of a leaf, it causes a fatal disease in the plant. Once the plant dies, the bacterium and its offspring decompose the plant. What is the correct sequence of ecological roles played by the bacterium in that situation?
1. saprobe
2. mutualist
3. commensal
4. parasite
5. primary producer

A) 1, 3, 4

B) 2, 3, 4

C) 1, 2, 4

D) 1, 2, 5

E) 1, 2, 3

Answer: C
Skill: Application

55) Symbiosis is common among prokaryotes and probably has been for billions of years. Which of the following does *not* represent a known prokaryotic symbiosis?

A) Some prokaryotes are pathogenic (cause illness).

B) Bacteria on skin and mucous membranes can control the abundance of pathogenic microbes by outcompeting these microbes.

C) Bacteria are required for the pollination of some plants.

D) Bacteria in the human intestine produce essential vitamins.

E) Nitrogen–fixing bacteria inhabit root nodules of leguminous plants.

Answer: C
Skill: Knowledge

56) In a practice known as *crop rotation*, farmers alternate a crop of legumes (plants, like beans, whose roots bear nodules containing *Rhizobium*) with a crop of nonlegumes. What is the benefit of this practice?

A) *Rhizobium* fixes nitrogen, and excess products of this process can fertilize the soil.

B) It prevents the farmer from being personally exposed to the same crop pathogens year after year.

C) It keeps the plants from getting too used to the bacteria in a particular variety of soil.

D) It keeps the plants from becoming pesticide resistant.

E) It keeps those bacteria that are plant pathogens from becoming pesticide resistant.

Answer: A
Skill: Application

57) A new pathogenic bacterium has been obtained from a number of individuals exhibiting the same symptoms, and it has been isolated and grown in pure culture. What additional steps, if any, are necessary to establish that this bacterium is the cause of the disease?

A) Sufficient data have been accumulated, and no further research need be done.

B) Gram stains must be applied, the appropriate exotoxins or endotoxins must be isolated, and their chemical structures must be analyzed.

C) The method of transfer of the infection must be identified, and the bacteria must be shown to infect a variety of different species.

D) Cultured bacteria must be introduced to uninfected organisms, cause the same symptoms, and then be isolated from these test organisms.

E) An antibody must be located, isolated, and shown to provide immunization against further infection by the bacteria.

Answer: D
Skill: Application

58) Foods can be preserved in many ways by slowing or preventing bacterial growth. Which of the following methods and materials would *not* substantially inhibit bacterial growth?

A) Refrigeration: Slows bacterial metabolism and growth.

B) Closing previously opened containers: Prevents more bacteria from entering.

C) Pickling: Creates a pH at which bacterial enzymes will not function.

D) Canning in heavy sugar syrup: Creates osmotic conditions that remove water from bacterial cells.

E) Irradiation: Kills bacteria by mutating their DNA.

Answer: B
Skill: Application

59) Many physicians administer antibiotics to patients at the first sign of any disease symptoms. Why can this practice cause more problems for these patients and for others not yet infected?

A) The antibiotic administered may not be effective for the particular type of bacterium.

B) Antibiotics may cause other side effects in patients.

C) Overuse of antibiotics can select for antibiotic-resistant strains of bacteria.

D) Particular patients may be allergic to the antibiotic.

E) Antibiotics may interfere with the ability to identify the bacteria present.

Answer: C
Skill: Comprehension

60) The following statements are all true of the prokaryotes *except* that they

A) are important decomposers in ecosystems.

B) have every mode of nutrition and metabolism, distributed among the various species.

C) can most accurately be classified using molecular techniques.

D) include some species that can use crude oil as a nutrition source.

E) All of the above are true of prokaryotes.

Answer: E
Skill: Knowledge

61) Which of the following compounds is the *most* common compound in the cell wells of gram-positive bacteria?

A) cellulose

B) lipopolysaccharide

C) lignin

D) peptidoglycan

E) capsule

Answer: D
Skill: Knowledge

The following questions refer to structures found in a gram-positive prokaryotic cell. Answers (A–E) may be used once, more than once, or not at all.

A. *endospore*
B. *genophore*
C. *flagellum*
D. *cell wall*
E. *capsule*

62) composed almost entirely of peptidoglycan

Answer: D
Skill: Knowledge

63) composed of at least 35 different proteins, requires ATP to function

Answer: C
Skill: Knowledge

64) Not present in all bacteria, this slimy material enables cells that possess it to resist the defenses of host organisms.

Answer: E
Skill: Knowledge

65) Not present in all bacteria, this structure enables those that possess it to revive after exposure to harsh conditions, such as boiling.

Answer: A
Skill: Knowledge

66) term used for the bacterial chromosome

Answer: B
Skill: Knowledge

67) an important source of endotoxin in gram-negative species

Answer: D
Skill: Knowledge

Media Activity Questions

1) Bacteria are propelled by
   A) flagella.
   B) ribosomes.
   C) cell walls.
   D) pili.
   E) nuclei.

   Answer: A
   Topic: Web/CD Activity 27A

2) Which structure is the outermost component of a bacterium?
   A) nucleoid region
   B) capsule
   C) cell wall
   D) ribosome
   E) plasma membrane

   Answer: B
   Topic: Web/CD Activity 27A

3) Within the domain Bacteria, chlamydias are most closely related to
   A) gram–positive bacteria.
   B) cyanobacteria.
   C) spirochetes.
   D) crenarchaeota.
   E) proteobacteria.

   Answer: C
   Topic: Web/CD Activity 27B

4) There are _____ subgroups within the domain Bacteria.
   A) one
   B) two
   C) three
   D) four
   E) five

   Answer: E
   Topic: Web/CD Activity 27B

5) There are _____ subgroups within the domain Archaea.
   A) one
   B) two
   C) three
   D) four
   E) five

   Answer: B
   Topic: Web/CD Activity 27B

Self–Quiz Questions

Answers to these questions also appear in the textbook.

1) Home canners pressure–cook vegetables as a precaution primarily against

   A) mycoplasmas.

   B) endospore–forming bacteria.

   C) enteric bacteria.

   D) cyanobacteria.

   E) actinomycetes.

   Answer: B

2) Photoautotrophs use

   A) light as an energy source and can use water or hydrogen sulfide as a source of electrons for producing organic compounds.

   B) light as an energy source and oxygen as an electron source.

   C) inorganic substances for energy and CO_2 as a carbon source.

   D) light to generate ATP but need organic molecules for a carbon source.

   E) light as an energy source and CO_2 to reduce organic nutrients.

   Answer: A

3) Which of the following statements about the domains of prokaryotes is *not* true?

   A) The lipid composition of the plasma membrane found in archaea is different from that of bacteria.

   B) Archaea and bacteria probably diverged very early in evolutionary history.

   C) Both archaea and bacteria have cell walls, but the walls of archaea lack peptidoglycan.

   D) Of the two groups, bacteria are more closely related to eukaryotes.

   E) Bacteria include the cyanobacteria.

   Answer: D

4) Several diverse branches of prokaryotes contain both photosynthetic and heterotrophic species. The most parsimonious interpretation of this observation is that

   A) photosynthesis evolved several times during prokaryotic history.

   B) all these lineages evolved from a primitive heterotrophic ancestor.

   C) all these lineages evolved from a photosynthetic ancestor, and some groups lost the ability to photosynthesize.

   D) photosynthesis evolved at the same time as aerobic respiration.

   E) glycolysis is the oldest metabolic pathway because it is present in all prokaryotic groups.

   Answer: C

5) Which of the following is *not* descriptive of the domain Archaea?

   A) It includes the taxa (kingdoms) Euryarchaeota and Crenarchaeota.

   B) It includes the methanogens, extreme halophiles, extreme thermophiles, and some marine groups.

   C) This domain is believed to include the universal ancestor of all life.

   D) It has characteristics in common with domain Bacteria (such as no nuclear envelope) and domain Eukarya (such as histone proteins associated with DNA) and characteristics it shares with neither (such as the ability to grow in harsh habitats).

   E) It is separated from domain Bacteria based on signature sequences and other molecular evidence of an early divergence between the two groups.

   Answer: C

6) Which of the following groups is mismatched with its members?

A) Proteobacteria—diverse gram-negative bacteria

B) Chlamydias—intracellular parasites

C) Spirochetes—helical heterotrophs

D) Gram-positive bacteria—diverse pathogens whose endotoxins are components of their outer membrane

E) Cyanobacteria—solitary and filamentous colonies exhibiting oxygenic photosynthesis

Answer: D

7) Which of the following statements about demonstrating the pathogenicity of a particular bacterial species is *not* true?

A) The bacteria must be capable of inducing the disease when transferred to an experimental host.

B) The bacteria isolated from a diseased host must be grown in pure culture.

C) The same bacteria must be present in each diseased host investigated.

D) The bacteria isolated from the experimental host must be capable of reinducing the disease when returned to the original host.

E) The bacteria must be identified in the artificially infected experimental host after the disease develops.

Answer: D

8) Penicillins function as antibiotics mainly by inhibiting the ability of some bacteria to

A) form spores.

B) replicate DNA.

C) normal cell walls.

D) produce functional ribosomes.

E) synthesize ATP.

Answer: C

9) Plantlike photosynthesis that releases O_2 occurs in the

A) cyanobacteria.

B) chlamydias.

C) archaea.

D) actinomycetes.

E) chemoautotrophic bacteria.

Answer: A

10) An example of bioremediation is

A) the use of prokaryotes to treat sewage or clean up oil spills.

B) the use of antibiotics produced by cultured prokaryotes.

C) the genetic engineering of bacteria to produce human proteins and useful chemical products.

D) the introduction of parasitic bacteria to kill other bacteria.

E) all of the above.

Answer: A

Chapter 28   The Origins of Eukaryotic Diversity

1) Biologists have discovered the kingdom Protista to be paraphyletic and therefore obsolete. Which of the following statements is consistent with this conclusion?
   A) Various combinations of prokaryote ancestors gave rise to different lineages of protists.
   B) Animals, plants, and fungi arose from different protistan ancestors.
   C) Multicellularity has evolved independently in different groups of protists.
   D) Chloroplasts in different eukaryotes are similar to different prokaryotes.
   E) Archaezoa are intermediate and should not be considered part of the Protista.

   Answer: A
   Skill: Comprehension

2) A unicellular, noncolonial, free-living protist is, by its very nature, most likely to be
   A) multinucleate.
   B) highly specialized.
   C) an exceedingly complex generalist.
   D) destined to become an endosymbiont.
   E) tremendously limited in structure and function, relative to other individual cells.

   Answer: C
   Skill: Comprehension

3) None of the following terms continue to have taxonomic significance *except*
   A) alga.
   B) protist.
   C) protozoan.
   D) moneran.
   E) Euglenozoa.

   Answer: E
   Skill: Knowledge

4) Which of the following statements are true about living phytoplanktonic organisms?
   1. They are important members of communities surrounding deep–sea hydrothermal vents.
   2. They are important primary producers in most aquatic food webs.
   3. They are important partners in maintaining oxygen in Earth's seas and atmosphere.
   4. They are most often found attached to underwater surfaces.
   5. They contain photosystems that are embedded within plastid membranes.

   A) 1 and 4
   B) 1, 2, and 4
   C) 2, 3, and 4
   D) 2, 3, and 5
   E) All of the statements are correct.

   Answer: D
   Skill: Comprehension

5) Protists are ecologically important in all of the following ecosystems *except*
   A) freshwater systems.
   B) marine phytoplankton.
   C) antarctic dry valleys.
   D) parasitic ones.
   E) pathogenic systems.

   Answer: C
   Skill: Knowledge

6) In what ways are all protists alike? They are all
   A) multicellular.
   B) photosynthetic.
   C) marine.
   D) nonparasitic.
   E) eukaryotic.

   Answer: E
   Skill: Knowledge

7) The small size and simple construction of prokaryotes imposes limits on the

A) number of simultaneous metabolic activities and the number of genes present.

B) type of habitat they occupy and the frequency of reproduction that can occur.

C) number of cells that can be associated in organized colonies.

D) ability to reproduce.

E) type of reproduction and the number of offspring that can be produced.

Answer: A
Skill: Comprehension

8) The multiple, complex organelles of eukaryotic cells probably arose by

A) serial endosymbiosis.

B) competition for engulfing organelles in the environment.

C) specialization of existing membranes.

D) Both A and C are correct.

E) A, B, and C are correct.

Answer: D
Skill: Comprehension

9) The strongest evidence for the endosymbiotic origin of eukaryotic organelles is the similarity between extant prokaryotes and

A) nuclei and chloroplasts.

B) mitochondria and chloroplasts.

C) cilia and mitochondria.

D) ribosomes and nuclei.

E) ribosomes and cilia.

Answer: B
Skill: Knowledge

10) All of the following *might* have arisen by endosymbiosis *except*

A) basal bodies and centrioles.

B) endoplasmic reticulum.

C) mitochondria.

D) cilia and flagella.

E) chloroplasts.

Answer: B
Skill: Comprehension

11) If certain organelles of modern eukaryotes were derived from endosymbioses involving what were once free–living prokaryotes, then what ought to have been true of the ancestral prokaryote that served as host?

A) It lacked a cell wall.

B) It possessed an endomembrane system.

C) It was heterotrophic.

D) Only A and C are correct.

E) A, B, and C are correct.

Answer: E
Skill: Comprehension

12) According to the endosymbiotic theory of the origin of eukaryotic cells, how did mitochondria originate?

A) from infoldings of the plasma membrane, coupled with mutations of genes for oxygen–using metabolism

B) from engulfed, originally free–living prokaryotes

C) by tertiary endosymbioses

D) from the nuclear envelope folding outward and forming mitochondrial membranes

E) when a protoeukaryote becomes symbiotic with a protobiont

Answer: B
Skill: Knowledge

13) If eukaryotic cells had first evolved in an environment much lower in O_2 than was actually the case, how might eukaryotes be different today? They would

A) all be unicellular.

B) be unable to photosynthesize.

C) be more motile.

D) lack ribosomes.

E) lack mitochondria.

Answer: E
Skill: Application

14) The endoplasmic reticulum and Golgi apparatus are very similar among the groups of alga–like protists, but chloroplasts differ significantly and appear to be related to different prokaryotes. What do these facts imply about the evolution of the endomembrane system of eukaryotic cells?

A) The Golgi apparatus evolved before the endomembrane system.

B) Endomembrane systems evolved before chloroplasts.

C) Endomembrane systems evolved from symbiotic prokaryotes.

D) Endomembrane systems evolved after chloroplasts.

E) Chloroplasts evolved before the endoplasmic reticulum.

Answer: B
Skill: Application

15) All eukaryotic cells have the following structures *except*

A) plastids.

B) ribosomes.

C) a plasma membrane.

D) one or more chromosomes.

E) organelles of the endomembrane system.

Answer: A
Skill: Knowledge

16) Evidence for an endosymbiotic origin of chloroplasts and mitochondria includes which of the following?

A) Both have circular DNA.

B) Both have prokaryote–like ribosomes.

C) Both have histone proteins associated with DNA.

D) Only A and B are correct.

E) A, B, and C are correct.

Answer: D
Skill: Knowledge

17) The following statements are all consistent with the hypothesis that chloroplasts and mitochondria originated as prokaryotic endosymbionts *except* that they

A) are roughly the same size as bacteria.

B) can be cultured on agar since they make all their own proteins.

C) contain circular DNA molecules not associated with histones.

D) have membranes that are similar to those found in the plasma membranes of prokaryotes.

E) have ribosomes that are similar to those of bacteria.

Answer: B
Skill: Comprehension

18) Which of the following characteristics of chloroplasts and mitochondria are more similar to prokaryote cells than to eukaryote cells?

A) enzymes and transport systems of inner membranes

B) DNA associated with histone proteins

C) single, circular chromosome

D) Only A and C are correct.

E) A, B, and C are correct.

Answer: D
Skill: Knowledge

19) Of the following characteristics of plants and animals, which is *not* evidence for the endosymbiotic origin of mitochondria and/or chloroplasts? Both mitochondria and chloroplasts

A) have double membranes.

B) have ribosomes that are similar to prokaryotic ribosomes.

C) have some of the genes necessary for their own construction.

D) can do energy transformations.

E) contain circular DNA molecules.

Answer: D
Skill: Comprehension

20) Which organisms represent the common ancestor of all plastids found in photosynthetic eukaryotes?

A) autotrophic euglenoids

B) diatoms

C) dinoflagellates

D) red algae

E) cyanobacteria

Answer: E
Skill: Knowledge

21) If endosymbiosis has resulted in eukaryotic cytoplasm that is "chimeric," then the process that later made the endosymbionts lose their self–sufficiency over evolutionary time has resulted in chimeric

A) cell walls.

B) cytoskeletons.

C) endomembrane systems.

D) nuclear genes.

E) flagella.

Answer: D
Skill: Comprehension

22) Molecular systematists claim that some of the protist taxa that currently lack mitochondria are descended from protists that formerly contained mitochondria. They can make this claim with some certainty, based on the observation that

A) some protists lacking mitochondria have mitochondrial genes in their nuclear genomes.

B) many endosymbioses have been documented among extant organisms.

C) many protists contain chloroplasts.

D) some plastids are surrounded by as many as three membranes.

E) SSU–rRNA sequences of mitochondrial ribosomes are more similar to those of alpha–proteobacteria than to eukaryotic ribosomes.

Answer: A
Skill: Comprehension

23) The chloroplasts of modern plants are thought to have been derived according to which sequence?

A) cyanobacteria → green algae → green plants

B) cyanobacteria → green algae → fungi → green plants

C) red algae → brown algae → green algae → green plants

D) red algae → cyanobacteria → green plants

E) cyanobacteria → red algae → green algae → green plants

Answer: A
Skill: Knowledge

24) The evolution of eukaryotes from prokaryotes probably

A) occurred many times.

B) involved symbiosis on many occasions.

C) allowed the formation of both complexity and multicellularity.

D) Both B and C are correct.

E) A, B, and C are all correct.

Answer: E
Skill: Comprehension

25) The goal in classifying organisms should be to create categories that reflect the evolutionary histories of organisms. What system would be best to use?

A) a three–kingdom classification system

B) a five–kingdom classification system

C) an eight–kingdom classification system

D) a system that uses as many kingdoms as necessary to be accurate

E) a system that returns to that used by Linnaeus

Answer: D
Skill: Comprehension

26) The nuclear genes that existed in the ancestral prokaryote immediately *before* any endosymbioses occurred were

A) pure and uncontaminated, because gene transfers had not yet occurred.

B) composed of archaean genes.

C) composed of bacterial genes.

D) those of "LUCA"––the Last Universal Common Ancestor.

E) a mixture of bacterial and archaean genes.

Answer: E
Skill: Knowledge

27) The current state of "protistan" taxonomy is an example of which feature of good scientific practice? The need to

A) suspend judgment until enough evidence is available to make an informed decision.

B) base conclusions on controlled, repeatable experiments.

C) be willing to change, or drop, one's hypotheses when the data warrant it.

D) avoid sampling techniques that can introduce bias.

E) Both A and C are correct.

Answer: E
Skill: Application

28) A biologist finds a new unicellular organism that possesses an endoplasmic reticulum, a simple cytoskeleton, and two small nuclei that are each surrounded by a membrane. The organism has neither mitochondria nor chloroplasts. This organism most probably is a(n)

A) apicomplexan.

B) diplomonad.

C) ciliate.

D) prokaryote.

E) *Chlamydomonas*.

Answer: B
Skill: Knowledge

29) Each of the following groups includes many planktonic species *except*

A) kinetoplastids.

B) golden algae.

C) diatoms.

D) dinoflagellates.

E) actinopods.

Answer: A
Skill: Knowledge

30) A mixotrophic protist loses its plastids but continues to survive. Which of the following best accounts for its continued survival?

    A) It relies on photosystems that float freely in its cytosol.

    B) It must have gained extra mitochondria when it lost its plastids.

    C) It engulfs organic material by phagocytosis.

    D) It has an endospore.

    E) It is protected by a siliceous case.

Answer: C
Skill: Comprehension

31) Organisms classified as Euglenozoa have previously been classified as Protozoa, Protista, plants, and animals. Why the confusion?

    A) Like Protozoa, they are unicellular.

    B) Like animals, many are heterotrophic.

    C) Like plants, many are photosynthetic.

    D) Like most protists, they don't fit neatly into other categories.

    E) All of the above have caused confusion about the evolutionary relationships of Euglenozoa.

Answer: E
Skill: Comprehension

32) Which of the following cause red tides?

    A) red algae (Rhodophyta)

    B) dinoflagellates

    C) diatoms

    D) Only A and C are correct.

    E) A, B, and C are correct.

Answer: B
Skill: Knowledge

33) Which of the following is mismatched?

    A) Apicomplexa; internal parasites

    B) golden algae; planktonic producers

    C) euglenozoa; unicellular flagellates

    D) ciliates; red-tide organisms

    E) Rhizopoda; ingestive heterotrophs

Answer: D
Skill: Knowledge

34) The following statements about the dinoflagellates are true *except*

    A) they possess two unequal flagella.

    B) some cause red tides.

    C) they are unicellular.

    D) they have chlorophyll.

    E) their fossil remains form limestone deposits.

Answer: E
Skill: Knowledge

35) Which group within the Alveolata includes a group of organisms that are important in ocean food webs, cause red tides that kill many fish, can be carnivorous, and help build coral reefs?

    A) ciliates

    B) apicomplexans

    C) dinoflagellates

    D) euglenoids

    E) There is not a group of organisms that encompasses all of these characteristics.

Answer: C
Skill: Knowledge

36) Which of the following *correctly* pairs a protist with one of its characteristics?

    A) Kinetoplastids; slender pseudopodia

    B) Rhizopoda; flagellated stages

    C) Apicomplexa; all parasitic

    D) Actinopoda; calcium carbonate shell

    E) Foraminifera; abundant in soils

Answer: C
Skill: Knowledge

37) The following statements concerning protists are all true *except*

A) all Protista are eukaryotic organisms; many are unicellular or colonial.

B) the organism that causes malaria is transmitted to humans by the bite of the tsetse fly.

C) all apicomplexans (sporozoans) are parasitic.

D) all Mycetozoa have an amoeboid stage that is followed by a sedentary stage during which spores are produced.

E) those Euglenozoa that have a pigment system have one that is similar to that of green algae and higher land plants.

Answer: B
Skill: Knowledge

38) In which group would you find organisms with the most complex cell structure?

A) ciliates

B) Archaezoa

C) Euglenozoa

D) brown algae

E) diplomonads

Answer: A
Skill: Knowledge

39) You are given an unknown organism to identify. It is unicellular and heterotrophic. It is motile, using many short extensions of the cytoplasm, each featuring the 9+2 pattern. It has well-developed organelles and three nuclei, one large and two small. This organism is most likely to be a member of which taxon?

A) rhizopods

B) actinopods

C) ciliates

D) kinetoplastids

E) water molds

Answer: C
Skill: Application

40) The following are all characteristic of ciliates *except* that

A) they use cilia as locomotory or feeding structures.

B) they are very complex cells.

C) they segregate macronuclear chromosomes by mitosis.

D) most live as solitary cells in fresh water.

E) they have two or more nuclei.

Answer: C
Skill: Knowledge

41) Which process results in genetic recombination but is separate from reproduction in *Paramecium*?

A) budding

B) meiotic division

C) mitotic division

D) conjugation

E) fission

Answer: D
Skill: Knowledge

42) The following are all characteristic of the water molds (Oomycota) *except*

A) hyphae.

B) flagellated zoospores.

C) a nutritional mode that can result in the decomposition of dead organic matter.

D) large egg cells.

E) feeding plasmodium.

Answer: E
Skill: Comprehension

43) Why is the filamentous body form of the slime and water molds considered a case of convergent evolution with the hyphae of fungi?

A) Fungi are closely related to the slime and water molds.

B) Body shape reflects ancestor–descendant relationships among organisms.

C) Filamentous shape is an adaptation for a nutritional mode as a decomposer.

D) Hyphae and filaments are necessary for locomotion in both groups.

E) Filamentous body shape is evolutionarily primitive for all eukaryotes.

Answer: C
Skill: Application

44) The Irish potato famine was caused by an organism that belongs to what group?

A) bacterium

B) stramenopilan

C) foraminiferan

D) apicomplexan

E) virus

Answer: B
Skill: Knowledge

45) A certain unicellular eukaryote has a siliceous (glasslike) shell and autotrophic nutrition. It is most likely a(n)

A) dinoflagellate.

B) diatom.

C) amoeba.

D) foraminiferan.

E) slime mold.

Answer: B
Skill: Knowledge

46) The largest seaweeds belong to which group?

A) Cyanobacteria

B) Rhodophyta (red algae)

C) Chlorophyta (green algae)

D) Phaeophyta (brown algae)

E) Euglenozoa

Answer: D
Skill: Knowledge

47) The organisms we call "seaweeds"

A) belong to a variety of kingdoms.

B) provide refuge and breeding grounds for many marine fishes.

C) are mostly found near coastlines.

D) Only A and B are correct.

E) A, B, and C are correct.

Answer: E
Skill: Comprehension

48) *Sargassum* is a large seaweed that floats freely on the surface of the Sargasso Sea, located in the mid–North Altlantic Ocean several hundred miles from the nearest continental landmass. On the basis of this description, one should expect these algae to lack

A) thalli.

B) stipes.

C) blades.

D) holdfasts.

E) gel-forming polysaccharides.

Answer: D
Skill: Application

49) Why are red algae red?

A) They live in warm coastal waters.

B) They possess pigments that reflect and transmit red light.

C) They use red light for photosynthesis.

D) They lack chlorophyll.

E) They contain the water-soluble pigment anthocyanin.

Answer: B
Skill: Comprehension

50) The chloroplast structure and biochemistry of the red algae are most like which of the following organisms?

A) Chrysophyta (golden algae)

B) Cyanobacteria

C) dinoflagellates

D) Chlorophyta (green algae)

E) Phaeophyta (brown algae)

Answer: B
Skill: Knowledge

51) A biologist discovers an alga that is marine, multicellular, lives in fairly deep water, and has phycoerythrin. It probably belongs to which group?

A) Rhodophyta (red algae)

B) Phaeophyta (brown algae)

C) Chlorophyta (green algae)

D) dinoflagellates

E) Chrysophyta (golden algae)

Answer: A
Skill: Application

52) Members of the Chlorophyta (green algae) often differ from members of Plantae in that some chlorophytans

A) are heterotrophs.

B) are unicellular.

C) have chlorophyll *a*.

D) store carbohydrates as starch.

E) have cellulose cell walls.

Answer: B
Skill: Comprehension

53) Which taxonomic group containing eukaryotic organisms is believed to be ancestral to the plant kingdom?

A) Chrysophyta (golden algae)

B) Actinopoda

C) Foraminifera

D) Apicomplexa

E) Chlorophyta (green algae)

Answer: E
Skill: Knowledge

54) Which of the following includes unicellular, colonial, and multicellular members?

A) Chlorophyta (green algae)

B) Rhizopoda

C) euglenoids

D) Phaeophyta (brown algae)

E) Both A and C are correct.

Answer: A
Skill: Knowledge

55) Which of the following produces the dense glassy ooze of the deep-ocean floor?

A) rhizopods

B) dinoflagellates

C) actinopods

D) ciliates

E) sporozoans

Answer: C
Skill: Knowledge

56) A snail-like, coiled, porous shell of calcium carbonate is characteristic of which group?

A) diatoms

B) foraminiferans

C) heliozoans

D) rhizopods

E) ciliates

Answer: B
Skill: Knowledge

57) What provides the best rationale for *not* classifying the slime molds as fungi? Their

　　A) SSU–rRNA sequences

　　B) nutritional modes

　　C) choice of habitats

　　D) morphologies

　　E) reproductive methods

　　Answer: A
　　Skill: Comprehension

58) Which dichotomous pair of alternatives is highlighted by the life cycle of the cellular slime molds, like *Dictyostelium*?

　　A) prokaryotic versus eukaryotic

　　B) plant versus animal

　　C) unicellular versus multicellular

　　D) archaean versus archaezoan

　　E) autotroph versus heterotroph

　　Answer: C
　　Skill: Comprehension

For the following questions, refer to Figure 28.1, which represents a hypothetical eukaryotic cell that is the result of serial endosymbioses involving its mitochondria, one of which is pictured. Labeled arrows (A–E) indicate various membranes in this cell. Responses may be used once, more than once, or not at all.

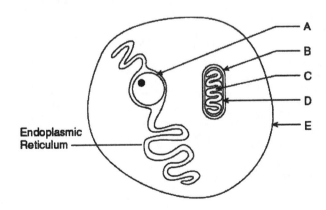

Figure 28.1

59) This membrane is homologous to the plasma membrane of the ancestral, aerobically respiring bacterium.

　　Answer: C
　　Skill: Application

60) This membrane is homologous to an ancestral host plasma membrane and was derived from the primary (first) endosymbiotic event.

　　Answer: D
　　Skill: Application

61) This membrane is homologous to an ancestral host plasma membrane and was derived from the secondary endosymbiotic event.

　　Answer: B
　　Skill: Application

62) Which one of the mitochondrial membranes should bear the strongest similarity to the plasma membrane of the current host cell?

　　Answer: B
　　Skill: Application

63) Invaginations of which membrane are most likely to have given rise to this cell's endomembrane system?

　　Answer: E
　　Skill: Application

64) Because of gene transfer, which membrane most immediately surrounds the gene for ATP synthase?

　　Answer: A
　　Skill: Application

Media Activity Questions

1) Which of these groups is named for its members' yellow and brown carotene and xanthophyll photosynthetic pigments?

    A) golden algae

    B) chlorophytes

    C) dinoflagellates

    D) diatoms

    E) brown algae

    Answer: A
    Topic: Web/CD Activity 28A

2) Which group of stramenophiles lacks chloroplasts?

    A) plants

    B) brown algae

    C) golden algae

    D) diatoms

    E) water molds

    Answer: E
    Topic: Web/CD Activity 28A

3) Organisms classified as _____ are responsible for red tides and toxins that are deadly to fishes and humans.

    A) brown algae

    B) red algae

    C) chlorophytes

    D) dinoflagellates

    E) charophyceans

    Answer: D
    Topic: Web/CD Activity 28A

4) Which of these groups includes multicellular organisms?

    A) choanoflagellates

    B) diatoms

    C) trichomonads

    D) diplomonads

    E) kinetoplastids

    Answer: A
    Topic: Web/CD Activity 28A

5) Which of these groups consists of organisms that are all flagellated, having some members that are autotrophic and others that are heterotrophic?

    A) dinoflagellates

    B) plasmodial slime molds

    C) euglenoids

    D) apicomplexans

    E) fungi

    Answer: C
    Topic: Web/CD Activity 28A

Self-Quiz Questions

Answers to these questions also appear in the textbook.

1) The hypothesis that life's three taxonomic domains originated from a community of gene-swapping prokaryotes is based mainly on

   A) comparisons of SSU–rRNA nucleotide sequences.

   B) evidence of gene transfer from plastids to mitochondria.

   C) the appearance of photosynthetic organisms in diverse prokaryotic and protist lineages.

   D) the presence of bacterial genes in the genomes of eukaryotes and modern archaeans.

   E) new fossil evidence.

   Answer: D

2) Which of the following organisms are *incorrectly* paired with their description?

   A) rhizopods—naked and shelled amoebas

   B) actinopods—planktonic with slender, raylike axopodia

   C) forams—flagellated algae, free-living or symbiotic

   D) apicomplexans—parasites with complex life cycles

   E) diplomonads—protists lacking mitochondria

   Answer: C

3) Which of the following algal groups is *mismatched* with its description?

   A) Dinoflagellates—glassy, two–part shells

   B) Green algae—closest relative of green plants

   C) Red algae—has no flagellated stages in life cycle

   D) Brown algae—includes the largest seaweeds

   E) Diatoms—examples of stramenopiles

   Answer: A

4) Plastids that are surrounded by more than two membranes are evidence of

   A) evolution from mitochondria.

   B) phagocytosis of algal cells by another autotrophic algae, after which their plastids fused.

   C) origin of the plastids from archaea.

   D) secondary endosymbiosis of an algal protist by a heterotrophic protist, which left the new endosymbiont wrapped in a vacuole membrane.

   E) budding of the plastids from the nuclear envelope.

   Answer: D

5) Biologists suspect that endosymbiosis gave rise to mitochondria before plastids because

   A) the products of photosynthesis could not be metabolized without mitochondrial enzymes.

   B) almost all eukaryotes have mitochondria, while only autotrophic eukaryotes have plastids.

   C) mitochondrial DNA is less similar to prokaryotic DNA than is the DNA from plastids.

   D) without mitochondrial CO_2 production, photosynthesis could not occur.

   E) plastids utilize their own ribosomes, while mitochondrial proteins are synthesized in the cytosol.

   Answer: B

6) Which of the following characteristics supports molecular evidence for combining the dinoflagellates, apicomplexans, and ciliates in the monophyletic clade Alveolata?

A) Their flagella or cilia are organized with the 9 + 2 microtubular ultrastructure.

B) All are pathogenic.

C) All are found exclusively in freshwater or marine habitats.

D) All possess mitochondria.

E) The three groups have small membrane–bound alveoli under their cell surfaces.

Answer: E

7) Which of the following is an *incorrect* statement about the possible endosymbiotic origins of plastids and mitochondria?

A) They are the appropriate size to be descendants of bacteria.

B) They contain their own genome and produce all their own proteins.

C) They contain circular DNA molecules.

D) Their membranes have enzymes and transport systems that resemble those found in the plasma membranes of prokaryotes.

E) Their ribosomes are more similar to those of bacteria than to those of eukaryotes.

Answer: B

8) The organism that contributed to the Irish potato famine is

A) an actinopod.

B) a ciliate.

C) an oomycote.

D) a plasmodial slime mold.

E) a cellular slime mold.

Answer: C

9) You find a colorful, weblike, amoeboid mass on a rotting log. After a dry period, you note stalked fruiting bodies growing up from this multinucleate mass. What is the probable identity of this organism?

A) euglenoid

B) plasmodial slime mold

C) cellular slime mold

D) foram

E) water mold

Answer: B

10) Which of the following groups probably represents the earliest branch in the evolution of eukaryotes?

A) archaea

B) diplomonads

C) fungi

D) amoebas

E) diatoms

Answer: B

Chapter 29   Plant Diversity I: How Plants Colonized Land

1) Bryophytes have all of the following characteristics *except*

A) multicellularity.

B) specialized cells and tissues.

C) lignified vascular tissue.

D) a protected, stationary egg cell.

E) a reduced, dependent sporophyte.

Answer: C
Skill: Knowledge

2) One of the major distinctions between plants and the green algae is that

A) only green algae have flagellated, swimming sperm.

B) embryos are not retained within parental tissues in green algae.

C) meiosis proceeds at a faster pace in green algae than in plants.

D) chlorophyll pigments in green algae are different from those in plants.

E) only plants form a cell plate during cytokinesis.

Answer: B
Skill: Comprehension

3) Arrange these adaptations to terrestrial existence in the order in which they first appeared during the evolution of land plants:
1. seeds
2. vascular tissues
3. apical meristems
4. flowers

A) 3, 2, 4, 1

B) 2, 3, 4, 1

C) 2, 4, 1, 3

D) 2, 3, 1, 4

E) 3, 2, 1, 4

Answer: E
Skill: Comprehension

4) The most recent common ancestors of all land plants were most likely similar to modern-day members of which group?

A) Cyanobacteria

B) Rhodophyta (red algae)

C) Charophycea

D) Phaeophyta (brown algae)

E) Chrysophyta (golden algae)

Answer: C
Skill: Knowledge

5) Which of the following characteristics, if observed in an unidentified green plant, would make it *unlikely* to be a charophycean?

A) phragmoplast

B) peroxisome

C) apical meristem

D) chlorophylls *a* and *b*

E) rosette cellulose–synthesizing complex

Answer: C
Skill: Knowledge

6) Which kind of plant tissue should lack phragmoplasts?

A) bryophyte tissues

B) diploid tissues

C) spore–producing tissues

D) tissues performing nuclear division without intervening cytokineses

E) fern gametophyte tissues

Answer: D
Skill: Application

7) A number of characteristics are very similar between green algae and members of the kingdom Plantae. Of the following, which characteristic does *not* provide evidence for an evolutionarily close relationship between these two groups (that is, which is *not* a shared derived character)?

A) alternation of generations

B) chloroplast structure

C) cell plate formation during cytokinesis

D) sperm cell structure

E) ribosomal RNA base sequences

Answer: A
Skill: Comprehension

8) Which of the following is a *true* statement about plant reproduction?

A) "Embryophytes" are small because they are in an early developmental stage.

B) Both male and female primitive plants produce gametangia.

C) Gametangia protect gametes from excess water.

D) Eggs and sperm of primitive plants swim toward one another.

E) It is limited to asexual reproduction in primitive plants.

Answer: B
Skill: Comprehension

9) In the life cycles of all land plants, there is true alternation of generations. Consequently,

A) haploid sporophytes make haploid spores.

B) gametophytes produce spores that develop into gametes.

C) sporophytes and gametophytes are typically similar in appearance.

D) meiosis in sporophytes produces haploid spores.

E) in plants, either the gametophyte or the sporophyte is unicellular.

Answer: D
Skill: Comprehension

10) Some green algae exhibit alternation of generations. All land plants exhibit alternation of generations. No charophyceans exhibit alternation of generations. Keeping in mind the recent evidence from molecular systematics, the correct interpretation of these observations is that

A) charophyceans are not related to either green algae or land plants.

B) plants evolved alternation of generations independently of green algae.

C) alternation of generations cannot be beneficial to charophyceans.

D) land plants evolved directly from the green algae that perform alternation of generations.

Answer: B
Skill: Knowledge

11) Whereas the zygotes of charophyceans may remain within maternal tissues during their initial development, one should *not* expect to observe

A) any nutrients from maternal tissues being used by the zygotes.

B) specialized placental transfer cells surounding the zygotes.

C) the zygotes undergoing nuclear division.

D) mitochondria in the maternal tissues, or in the tissues of the zygotes.

E) the zygotes avoid digestion by enzymes from maternal lysosomes.

Answer: B
Skill: Comprehension

12) Which putative taxon is essentially equivalent to the "embryophytes"?

A) Viridiplantae

B) Plantae

C) Pteridophyta

D) Streptophyta

E) Charophycea

Answer: B
Skill: Comprehension

13) Plant spores give rise directly to

A) sporophytes.

B) gametes.

C) gametophytes.

D) zygotes.

E) seeds.

Answer: C
Skill: Knowledge

14) Peptidoglycan is to the structural integrity of bacteria as _____ is to the structural integrity of plant spores.

A) lignin

B) cellulose

C) starch

D) tannin

E) sporopollenin

Answer: E
Skill: Application

15) Which of the following statements is true of archegonia?

A) They are the sites where male gametes are produced.

B) They may temporarily contain sporophyte embryos.

C) They are the same things as sporangia.

D) They are the ancestral versions of animal gonads.

E) They are asexual reproductive structures.

Answer: B
Skill: Comprehension

16) Of the following list, flagellated (swimming) sperm are generally present in which groups?

1. Lycophyta
2. Bryophyta
3. Angiospermae
4. Chlorophyta
5. Pterophyta

A) 1, 2, 3

B) 1, 2, 4, 5

C) 1, 3, 4, 5

D) 2, 3, 5

E) 2, 3, 4, 5

Answer: B
Skill: Knowledge

17) Assuming that they all belong to the same plant, arrange the following structures from smallest to largest (or from most inclusive to least inclusive):

1. antheridia
2. sperm cells
3. gametophytes
4. gametangia

A) 1, 4, 3, 2

B) 3, 1, 2, 4

C) 3, 4, 2, 1

D) 3, 4, 1, 2

E) 4, 3, 1, 2

Answer: D
Skill: Comprehension

18) The following are all common to both charophyceans and land plants *except*

A) sporopollenin.

B) lignin.

C) chlorophyll *a*.

D) cellulose.

E) Both B and C are correct.

Answer: B
Skill: Comprehension

19) The leaflike appendages of moss gametophytes may be one- to two–cell–layers thick. Consequently, which of these is *least* likely to be found associated with such appendages?

A) cuticle

B) rosette cellulose–synthesizing complexes

C) stomata

D) peroxisomes

E) phenolics

Answer: C
Skill: Application

20) Which of the following was *not* a problem for the first land plants?

A) sources of water

B) sperm transfer

C) desiccation

D) animal predation

E) support against gravity

Answer: D
Skill: Comprehension

21) The following are all defining characteristics of land plants *except*

A) a cellulose cell wall.

B) vascular tissue.

C) chlorophylls *a* and *b*.

D) being photosynthetic autotrophs.

E) being eukaryotic.

Answer: B
Skill: Comprehension

22) Which of the following is *not* an important structural chemical at some stage in a plant's life?

A) sporopollenin

B) waxes

C) lignin

D) cuticle made of protein

E) cellulose

Answer: D
Skill: Comprehension

23) The following are all adaptations to life on land *except*

A) rosette cellulose–synthesizing complexes.

B) cuticles.

C) tracheids.

D) reduced gametophyte generation.

E) seeds.

Answer: A
Skill: Comprehension

24) Which of the following is *not* a secondary compound of embryophytes?

A) adenosine triphosphate

B) alkaloids

C) terpenes

D) tannins

E) flavonoids

Answer: A
Skill: Knowledge

For each numbered challenge posed by life on land, choose the adaptation below that best meets the challenge.

A. *nonflagellated sperm*
B. *tracheids and phloem*
C. *secondary compounds*
D. *cuticle*
E. *alternation of generation*

25) protection against predators

Answer: C
Skill: Knowledge

26) protection against desiccation

Answer: D
Skill: Knowledge

27) support against gravity

Answer: B
Skill: Knowledge

28) transport of water, minerals and nutrients

Answer: B
Skill: Knowledge

29) reproduction away from water

Answer: A
Skill: Knowledge

30) Why are charophyceans considered *not* to have alternation of generations during their life cycle?

A) The haploid stage is not dependent on the diploid stage.

B) The diploid stage is not dependent on the haploid stage.

C) The zygote is diploid but is surrounded by nonreproductive cells.

D) The diploid stage is only unicellular.

E) The haploid stage is dominant.

Answer: D
Skill: Knowledge

31) The following characteristics all helped seedless plants evolve to be adapted to land *except*

A) a dominant gametophyte.

B) vascular tissue.

C) a waxy cuticle.

D) stomata.

E) a branched sporophyte.

Answer: A
Skill: Comprehension

32) The following are all true about the life cycle of mosses *except*

A) external water is required for fertilization.

B) flagellated sperm are produced.

C) antheridia and archegonia are produced by gametophytes.

D) gametes are directly produced by meiosis.

E) gametophytes arise from the protonema.

Answer: D
Skill: Comprehension

33) Beginning with the germination of a moss spore, what is the sequence of structures that develop after germination?
1. embryo
2. gametes
3. sporangium
4. protonema
5. gametophore

A) 4, 1, 3, 5, 2

B) 4, 3, 5, 2, 1

C) 4, 5, 2, 1, 3

D) 3, 4, 5, 2, 1

E) 3, 1, 4, 5, 2

Answer: C
Skill: Comprehension

34) In which of the following does the sporophyte depend on the gametophyte for nutrition?

A) fern

B) moss

C) horsetail (*Equisetum*)

D) Both A and C are correct.

E) A, B, and C are correct.

Answer: B
Skill: Knowledge

35) A botanist discovers a new species of plant in a tropical rain forest. After observing its anatomy and life cycle, the following characteristics are noted: flagellated sperm, xylem with tracheids, separate gametophyte and sporophyte phases, and no seeds. This plant is probably most closely related to

A) mosses.

B) *Chara*.

C) ferns.

D) liverworts.

E) flowering plants.

Answer: C
Skill: Application

36) Bryophytes may feature all of the following at some time during their existence *except*

A) microphylls.

B) rhizoids.

C) archegonia.

D) sporangia.

E) conducting tissues.

Answer: A
Skill: Knowledge

37) Two, small, poorly drained lakes lie close to each other in a boreal forest. The basins of both lakes are composed of the same geologic substratum. One lake is surrounded by a dense *Sphagnum* mat; the other is not. Compared with the pond without *Sphagnum*, the pond surrounded by the moss should have

A) a lower pH.

B) lower numbers of bacteria.

C) reduced rates of decomposition.

D) Only B and C are correct.

E) A, B, and C are correct.

Answer: E
Skill: Application

38) Bryophytes never formed forests (mats maybe, but no forests) because

A) they possess flagellated sperms.

B) not all are heterosporous.

C) they lack lignified vascular tissue.

D) they have no adaptations to prevent desiccation.

E) the sporophyte is too weak.

Answer: C
Skill: Comprehension

39) A major change that occurred in the evolution of plants from their algal ancestors was the origin of a branched sporophyte. What advantage would branched sporophytes provide in this stage of the life cycle?

A) increased gamete production

B) increased spore production

C) increased potential for independence of the diploid stage from the haploid stage

D) increased fertilization rate

E) increased size of the diploid stage

Answer: B
Skill: Knowledge

40) Sporophylls can be found in which of the following?

A) mosses

B) liverworts

C) hornworts

D) pteridophytes

E) charophyceans

Answer: D
Skill: Knowledge

41) Working from deep geologic strata toward shallow geologic strata, what is the sequence in which fossils of these groups should make their first appearance?
1. charophyceans
2. single–celled green algae
3. hornworts
4. plants with a dominant sporophyte

A) 1, 3, 2, 4

B) 3, 1, 2, 4

C) 2, 1, 3, 4

D) 3, 2, 4, 1

E) 2, 4, 1, 3

Answer: C
Skill: Application

42) The sori of ferns are analogous to which structures?

A) spores of bryophytes

B) capsules of moss sporophytes

C) gametangia of hornwort gametophytes

D) protonemata of moss gametophytes

E) strobili of horsetail sporophytes

Answer: B
Skill: Comprehension

43) Which of the following types of plants would *not* have been present in the forests that became today's coal deposits?

A) horsetails (*Equisetum*)

B) lycophytes

C) pine trees

D) tree ferns

E) *Cooksonia*

Answer: C
Skill: Comprehension

44) If a fern gametophyte is a hermaphrodite (that is, has both male and female gametangia on the same plant), then it

A) belongs to a species that is homosporous.

B) belongs to a species that has combined sporophyte and gametophyte generations into one, individual organism.

C) will perform meiosis to produce megaspores.

D) has antheridia and archegonia combined into a single sex organ.

E) is a mutant, because fern gametophytes are always either male or female.

Answer: A
Skill: Comprehension

The following questions are based on this description: A biology student hiking in a boreal forest happens upon an erect, 15–cm–tall plant that bears a pineconelike structure at its tallest point. Upon examination, the cone seems to be covered with a brownish dust and, when disturbed, emits a cloud of this dust. A pocket magnifying glass reveals the dust to be composed of tiny spheres with high–oil content.

45) This student has probably found a(n)

A) immature pine tree.

B) moss sporophyte.

C) fern sporophyte.

D) horsetail gametophyte.

E) club moss sporophyte.

Answer: E
Skill: Application

46) Besides oil, what other chemical should be detected in substantial amounts upon chemical analysis of these small spheres?

A) sporopollenins

B) phenolics

C) waxes

D) lignins

E) terpenes

Answer: A
Skill: Application

47) Closer observation reveals that these small spheres are produced upon tiny extensions of the stem, each of which helps compose the pineconelike structure. Library research (or referring to a good biology textbook) would reveal that the conelike structures are called _____, whereas the small, spore–producing extensions of the stem are called _____.

A) pinecones ... scales

B) sori ... sporangia

C) strobili ... sporophylls

D) sporophylls ... sporangia

E) sporangia ... strobili

Answer: C
Skill: Application

48) To which taxon does this organism seem to belong?

A) Pteridophyta

B) Lycophyta

C) Bryophyta

D) Both A and B are corect.

E) A, B, and C are correct.

Answer: D
Skill: Application

49) A dissection of the interior of the stem should reveal

A) vascular tissues.

B) cuticle.

C) gametangia.

D) that it is composed of only a single, long cell.

E) a relatively high proportion of dead, water-filled cells.

Answer: A
Skill: Application

50) Assuming that they all belong to the same plant, arrange the following structures from smallest to largest (or from most inclusive to least inclusive).

1. spores
2. sporophylls
3. sporophytes
4. sporangia

A) 2, 4, 3, 1

B) 2, 3, 4, 1

C) 3, 1, 4, 2

D) 3, 4, 2, 1

E) 3, 2, 4, 1

Answer: E
Skill: Comprehension

51) All of the following caused botanists to (incorrectly) identify *Psilotum* as the most primitive living land plant *except*

A) a dominant sporophyte generation.

B) absence of roots.

C) absence of leaves.

D) comparisons of DNA sequences.

E) its resemblance to *Cooksonia*.

Answer: D
Skill: Comprehension

52) Which of the following is *true* of seedless vascular plants?

A) The few seedless vascular plants still living are larger and rare.

B) Whole forests were dominated by large, vascular seedless plants.

C) They produce many spores, which are really the same as seeds.

D) Seedless vascular plants are all homosporous.

E) None of the above are true. Vascular plants never form seeds.

Answer: B
Skill: Comprehension

53) If you were building a large, log structure during the Carboniferous period, which plant type(s) would be suitable sources of logs?

A) ferns and epiphytes

B) horsetails and ferns

C) lycophytes and *Cooksonia*

D) horsetails and lycophytes

Answer: D
Skill: Application

Media Activity Questions

1) The first plants arose during the _____ era.

   A) Tertiary

   B) Precambrian

   C) Cenozoic

   D) Mesozoic

   E) Paleozoic

   Answer: E
   Topic: Web/CD Activity 29A

2) Which characteristic is shared by algae and seed plants?

   A) pollen

   B) cuticle

   C) vascular tissue

   D) cell walls

   E) stomata

   Answer: D
   Topic: Web/CD Activity 29B

3) Gametophytes are

   A) the inconspicuous generation of the moss life cycle.

   B) diploid.

   C) triploid.

   D) sporophytes.

   E) haploid.

   Answer: E
   Topic: Web/CD Activity 29C

4) In ferns, sori are clusters of _____ cells.

   A) triploid

   B) sporophyte

   C) diploid

   D) tetraploid

   E) haploid

   Answer: E
   Topic: Web/CD Activity 29D

5) In ferns, the _____ stage is _____ on the _____ stage.

   A) gametophyte ... not dependent ... sporophyte

   B) gametophyte ... dependent ... gametophyte

   C) gametophyte ... dependent ... protonema

   D) sporophyte ... dependent ... protonema

   E) sporophyte ... dependent ... gametophyte

   Answer: A
   Topic: Web/CD Activity 29D

Self-Quiz Questions

Answers to these questions also appear in the textbook.

1) Which of the following characteristics of plants is absent in their closest relatives, the charophycean algae?

   A) chlorophyll *b*

   B) cellulose in cell walls

   C) alternation of multicellular generations

   D) sexual reproduction

   E) formation of a cell plate during cytokinesis

   Answer: C

2) All bryophytes (mosses, liverworts, and hornworts) share certain characteristics. These are

   A) reproductive cells in gametangia; embryos.

   B) branched sporophytes.

   C) vascular tissues, true leaves, and a waxy cuticle.

   D) seeds.

   E) lignified walls.

   Answer: A

3) Which of the following is *not* common to all phyla of vascular plants?

   A) the development of seeds

   B) alternation of generations

   C) dominance of the diploid generation

   D) xylem and phloem

   E) the addition of lignin to cell walls

   Answer: A

4) A heterosporous plant is one that

   A) produces a gametophyte that bears both antheridia and archegonia.

   B) produces microspores and megaspores, which give rise to male and female gametophytes.

   C) produces spores all year long instead of during just one season.

   D) produces two kinds of spores, one asexually by mitosis and the other sexually by meiosis.

   E) reproduces only sexually.

   Answer: B

5) During the Carboniferous period, the dominant plants, which later formed the great coal beds, were mainly

   A) giant lycophytes, horsetails, and ferns.

   B) conifers.

   C) angiosperms.

   D) charophyceans.

   E) early seed plants.

   Answer: A

6) A land plant that produces flagellated sperm and has a diploid-dominant generation is most likely a

   A) fern.

   B) moss.

   C) liverwort.

   D) charophycean.

   E) hornwort.

   Answer: A

For each of the following structures or life cycle stages, indicate whether the cells are haploid or diploid in chromosome number.

7) The body of a charophycean

   Answer: Haploid

8) The nonreproductive cells that line the
   gametangia of a moss

   Answer: Haploid

9) The cells that make up the stalk of a moss
   sporophyte

   Answer: Diploid

10) The spores produced by the sporophyte of
    a fern

    Answer: Haploid

Chapter 30　Plant Diversity II: The Evolution of Seed Plants

1) The following are all *true* concerning the sporophyte or gametophyte generations in flowering plants *except*
   A) the flower is composed of gametophyte tissue only.
   B) the sporophyte generation is dominant.
   C) the sporophyte generation is what we see when observing a plant.
   D) unlike ferns, the gametophyte generation is not photosynthetic.
   E) the gametophyte generation consists of relatively few cells within the flower.

   Answer: A
   Skill: Comprehension

2) Which of the following is an ongoing trend in the evolution of land plants?
   A) a decrease in the size of the leaf
   B) the reduction of the gametophyte phase of the life cycle
   C) the elimination of sperm cells or sperm nuclei
   D) avoiding being eaten by dinosaurs
   E) the replacement of roots by rhizomes

   Answer: B
   Skill: Comprehension

3) The following cellular structures are all found in cells of angiosperm or gymnosperm gametophytes *except*
   A) haploid nuclei.
   B) mitochondria.
   C) cell walls.
   D) chloroplasts.
   E) endomembrane system.

   Answer: D
   Skill: Comprehension

4) Plants with a dominant sporophyte are successful on land partly because
   A) having no stomata, they lose less water.
   B) they all disperse by means of seeds.
   C) diploid plants are more protected from the effects of mutation than are haploid plants.
   D) their gametophytes are all parasitic on the sporophytes.
   E) eggs and sperm need not be produced.

   Answer: C
   Skill: Knowledge

5) The following are all advantages of seeds for survival *except*
   A) a choice of germination location.
   B) dispersal.
   C) dormancy.
   D) a nutrient supply for the embryo.
   E) desiccation resistance.

   Answer: A
   Skill: Comprehension

6) The following plant structures are all adaptations specifically for a terrestrial environment *except*
   A) roots.
   B) xylem.
   C) cell walls.
   D) waxy cuticle.
   E) seeds.

   Answer: C
   Skill: Comprehension

7) In addition to seeds, which of the following characteristics are unique to the seed–producing plants?

   A) a haploid gametophyte retained within tissues of the diploid sporophyte

   B) lignin present in cell walls

   C) pollen

   D) Both A and C are correct.

   E) A, B, and C are correct.

   Answer: D
   Skill: Knowledge

The following questions refer to the generalized life cycle for plants shown in Figure 30.1. Each number within a circle or square represents a specific plant or plant part, and each number over an arrow represents either meiosis, mitosis, or fertilization.

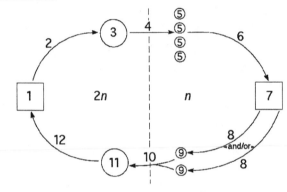

Figure 30.1

8) A moss gametophyte is represented by

   A) 1.

   B) 3.

   C) 5.

   D) 7.

   E) 11.

   Answer: D
   Skill: Comprehension

9) Which number represents the embryo sac of an angiosperm flower?

   A) 1

   B) 3

   C) 7

   D) 9

   E) 11

   Answer: C
   Skill: Comprehension

10) Meiosis is represented by

   A) 2 only.

   B) 3 only.

   C) 4 only.

   D) 8 only.

   E) both 4 and 8.

   Answer: C
   Skill: Comprehension

11) Which number is a megaspore mother cell?

   A) 1

   B) 3

   C) 5

   D) 7

   E) 11

   Answer: B
   Skill: Comprehension

12) In seed plants, which structure/material is properly considered part of a pollen grain?

   A) sporophyll

   B) male gametophyte

   C) sporopollenin

   D) stigma

   E) Both B and C contribute to the structure of the pollen grain.

   Answer: E
   Skill: Comprehension

13) In terms of alternation generations, the pollen grains of seed-producing plants are equivalent to a

A) moss sporophyte.

B) moss gametophyte bearing both male and female gametangia.

C) fern sporophyte.

D) hermaphroditic fern gametophyte.

E) fern gametophyte that will bear only antheridia.

Answer: E
Skill: Comprehension

14) Conifers are noted for all of the following *except*

A) size.

B) longevity.

C) utility to humans.

D) great diversity of species.

E) success in cold climates.

Answer: D
Skill: Knowledge

Use the following choices to identify the phrases for the questions below. Responses may be used once, more than once, or not at all.

A. *Bryophyta*
B. *Pterophyta*
C. *Coniferophyta*
D. *Anthophyta*
E. *Hepatophyta*

15) dominant sporophyte, small free-living gametophyte, swimming sperm

Answer: B
Skill: Knowledge

16) nonmotile sperm, both wind- and insect-pollinated

Answer: D
Skill: Knowledge

17) endosperm, xylem vessels, and fruit

Answer: D
Skill: Knowledge

18) no true vascular tissues, sporophyte dependent upon gametophyte, small leaflike appendages

Answer: A
Skill: Knowledge

19) needlelike leaves, "naked" seeds, nonmotile sperm

Answer: C
Skill: Knowledge

20) Gymnosperms differ from ferns in that gymnosperms

A) produce seeds.

B) have macrophylls.

C) have pollen.

D) Both A and C are correct.

E) A, B, and C are correct.

Answer: D
Skill: Knowledge

21) What is the main way that pine trees disperse their offspring? They use

A) fruits that are eaten by animals.

B) spores.

C) squirrels to bury cones.

D) wind-blown seeds.

E) flagellated sperm swimming through water.

Answer: D
Skill: Comprehension

22) The following statements all correctly describe portions of the pine life cycle *except*

A) female gametophytes have archegonia.

B) seeds are produced in ovulate cones.

C) meiosis occurs in sporangia.

D) pollen grains are male gametophytes.

E) pollination and fertilization are the same process.

Answer: E
Skill: Comprehension

23) Which of the following terms is equivalent to fertilization?

A) spore dispersal

B) fruit formation

C) pollination

D) fusion of gametes

E) meiosis

Answer: D
Skill: Comprehension

24) The following statements are all true of the pine life cycle *except*

A) cones are short stems with spore-bearing, leaflike structures.

B) the pine tree is a sporophyte.

C) male and female gametophytes come together for fertilization.

D) pollen grains are very different from pine male gametophytes.

E) pine trees have a simpler vascular tissue than flowering plants.

Answer: D
Skill: Comprehension

25) Which of the following statements are *true*?

A) A female pinecone is a short stem with spore-bearing appendages.

B) A male pinecone is a short stem with spore-bearing appendages.

C) A flower is a short stem with spore-bearing appendages.

D) Only A and C are true.

E) A, B, and C are true.

Answer: E
Skill: Comprehension

26) Within a gymnosperm megasporangium, what is the correct sequence in which the following should appear, assuming that fertilization occurs?
1. sporophyte embryo
2. female gametophyte
3. egg cell
4. megaspore

A) 4, 3, 2, 1

B) 4, 2, 3, 1

C) 4, 1, 2, 3

D) 1, 4, 3, 2

E) 1, 4, 2, 3

Answer: B
Skill: Comprehension

27) Which of the following are *true* of the food reserves of a conifer seed? They are

A) the result of double fertilization.

B) triploid.

C) called endosperm.

D) derived from gametophyte tissue.

E) Both C and D are true.

Answer: D
Skill: Comprehension

28) Arrange the following structures, which can be found on male pine trees, from the largest structure to the smallest structure (or from most inclusive to least inclusive).

1. sporophyte
2. microspores
3. microsporangia
4. pollen cone
5. pollen nuclei

A) 1, 4, 3, 2, 5
B) 1, 4, 2, 3, 5
C) 1, 2, 3, 5, 4
D) 4, 1, 2, 3, 5
E) 4, 3, 2, 5, 1

Answer: A
Skill: Comprehension

29) The following statements are all true of the monocots *except*

A) they are currently thought to be polyphyletic.
B) the veins of their leaves are parallel to each other.
C) they, along with the eudicots, *Amborella*, and water lilies, are currently placed in the phylum Anthophyta.
D) they possess a single seed leaf.
E) there are no exceptions among the statements listed above.

Answer: A
Skill: Knowledge

30) Which function is, at least partly, performed by cells that are no longer alive?

A) stomatal opening and closing in angiosperms
B) water transport in angiosperms
C) water transport in gymnosperms
D) structural support in gymnosperms
E) transport of sugars in gymnosperms

Answer: B
Skill: Comprehension

31) Which of the following most closely represents the male gametophyte of seed–bearing plants?

A) ovule
B) microspore mother cell
C) pollen grain
D) embryo sac
E) fertilized egg

Answer: C
Skill: Knowledge

32) Pistils and stamens are

A) sporophyte plants in their own right.
B) gametophyte plants in their own right.
C) gametes.
D) spores.
E) modified sporophylls.

Answer: E
Skill: Comprehension

33) The following statements are all true of angiosperm carpels *except* they

A) are features of the sporophyte generation.
B) consist of stigma, style, and ovary.
C) are structures that directly produce female gametes.
D) surround and nourish the female gametophyte.
E) consist of highly modified sporophylls.

Answer: C
Skill: Comprehension

34) A hypothetical angiosperm opens its flowers only at night. The flowers are dusky brown and emit a putrid odor. The pollinator is most likely to be which organism?

A) nectar–eating hummingbird

B) nectar–eating bee

C) pollen–eating moth

D) fruit–eating bat

E) detritivorous (scavenging) animal

Answer: E
Skill: Application

35) How have fruits contributed to the success of angiosperms?

A) by nourishing the plants that make them

B) by facilitating dispersal of seeds by wind and animals

C) by attracting insects to the pollen inside

D) by producing sperm and eggs inside a protective coat

E) by producing triploid cells via double fertilization

Answer: B
Skill: Comprehension

36) In flowering plants, meiosis occurs specifically in the

A) megaspore mother cells.

B) microspore mother cells.

C) endosperm.

D) Only A and B are correct.

E) A, B, and C are correct.

Answer: D
Skill: Comprehension

37) Which structure(s) is (are) part of the sporophyte generation of an angiosperm?

1. ovule
2. ovary
3. egg
4. pollen sac
5. embryo sac

A) 1

B) 1, 4

C) 1, 2, 3

D) 1, 2, 4

E) 1, 2, 5

Answer: D
Skill: Comprehension

38) Arrange the following structures from largest to smallest, assuming that they belong to two generations of the same angiosperm.

1. ovary
2. ovule
3. egg
4. carpel
5. embryo sac

A) 4, 2, 1, 5, 3

B) 4, 5, 2, 1, 3

C) 5, 4, 3, 1, 2

D) 5, 1, 4, 2, 3

E) 4, 1, 2, 5, 3

Answer: E
Skill: Comprehension

39) Which structure(s) must pass through the micropyle for successful fertilization to occur in angiosperms?

A) only one sperm nucleus

B) both sperm nuclei

C) the pollen tube

D) only A and C

E) only B and C

Answer: E
Skill: Comprehension

40) Which of the following *incorrectly* pairs a sporophyte embryo with its food source?

A) pine embryo; female gametophyte tissue

B) grass embryo; endosperm tissue in seed

C) moss embryo; female sporophyte tissue

D) fern embryo; photosynthetic gametophyte

Answer: C
Skill: Comprehension

41) Which trait(s) is (are) shared by most modern gymnosperms and angiosperms?
1. wind can serve as a pollinating agent
2. vessel elements
3. microscopic gametophytes
4. sterile sporophylls, modified to attract pollinators
5. endosperm

A) 1

B) 1, 3

C) 1, 2, 3

D) 1, 3, 5

E) 2, 4, 5

Answer: B
Skill: Comprehension

42) One of the major benefits of double fertilization in angiosperms is to

A) decrease the potential for mutation by insulating the embryo with other cells.

B) increase the number of fertilization events and offspring produced.

C) promote diversity in flower shape and color.

D) coordinate developmental timing between the embryo and its food stores.

E) emphasize embryonic survival by increasing embryo size.

Answer: D
Skill: Knowledge

43) Which of the following flower parts develops into a seed?

A) ovule

B) ovary

C) fruit

D) style

E) stamen

Answer: A
Skill: Knowledge

44) Which of the following flower parts develops into a fruit?

A) stigma

B) style

C) ovule

D) ovary

E) receptacle

Answer: D
Skill: Knowledge

45) Double fertilization means that angiosperms

A) are the only plants that can produce dizygotic twins.

B) have embryos that are triploid.

C) have two sperm nuclei, both of which unite with nuclei of the female gametophyte.

D) have two sperm nuclei, which simultaneously fertilize the single egg.

E) Both B and D are true.

Answer: C
Skill: Comprehension

46) Which of the following are *not* found in angiosperms?

A) vessel elements

B) triploid endosperm

C) fruit

D) flagellated sperm

E) carpels

Answer: D
Skill: Comprehension

47) Which part of the female gametophyte contributes to the formation of endosperm upon successful fertilization?

A) egg
B) synergids
C) antipodal cells
D) polar nuclei

Answer: D
Skill: Knowledge

48) Angiosperms are the most successful terrestrial plants. This success is due to all of the following *except*

A) animal pollination.
B) reduced gametophytes.
C) fruits enclosing seeds.
D) xylem with vessels.
E) sperm cells with flagella.

Answer: E
Skill: Comprehension

49) The following are all characteristic of angiosperms *except*

A) coevolution with animal pollinators.
B) double internal fertilization.
C) free–living gametophytes.
D) pistils.
E) fruit.

Answer: C
Skill: Knowledge

50) A botanist discovers a new species of plant with a dominant sporophyte, chlorophyll *a* and *b*, and a cell wall made of cellulose. In assigning this plant to a division, all of the following would provide useful information *except* whether or not the plant has

A) endosperm.
B) seeds.
C) flagellated sperm.
D) flowers.
E) starch.

Answer: E
Skill: Application

51) The following are all valid arguments for preserving tropical forests *except*

A) people in the tropics do not need to increase agricultural output.
B) many organisms are becoming extinct.
C) plants that are possible sources of medicines are being lost.
D) plants that could be developed into new crops are being lost.
E) clearing land for agriculture results in soil destruction.

Answer: A
Skill: Knowledge

52) Assume that a botanist was visiting a tropical region for the purpose of discovering plants with medicinal properties. All of the following might be ways of identifying potentially useful plants *except*

A) observing which plants sick animals seek out.
B) observing which plants are the most used food plants.
C) observing which plants animals do not eat.
D) collecting plants and subjecting them to chemical analysis.
E) asking local people which plants they use as medicine.

Answer: B
Skill: Application

53) Agricultural modifications of plants have progressed to the point that a number of cultivated plant species probably could not survive in the wild. Why is this so?
    A) Environmental conditions have changed since the plants evolved.
    B) Seeds can be obtained only from seed banks in agricultural countries.
    C) Cultivated plants are more vulnerable to human–caused pollution and disasters.
    D) Special conditions not found in nature are needed for their growth and reproduction.
    E) Their seeds cannot be dispersed without agricultural machinery.

Answer: D
Skill: Comprehension

For the following questions, match the various structures of seed plants with the proper sex and generation (A–D) that most directly produces them.

    A. *male gametophyte*
    B. *female gametophyte*
    C. *male sporophyte*
    D. *female sporophyte*

54) scale of ovulate pine cone

Answer: D
Skill: Comprehension

55) seed coat of pine nut

Answer: D
Skill: Comprehension

56) pollen grain

Answer: A
Skill: Comprehension

57) egg cell in the embryo sac

Answer: B
Skill: Comprehension

58) fruit

Answer: D
Skill: Comprehension

59) pollen sac

Answer: C
Skill: Comprehension

For the following questions, match the adaptations of the various fruits below with the most likely means used by the fruit to disperse the seeds contained within the fruit (A–E).
    A. *animal skin, fur, or feathers*
    B. *animal digestive tract*
    C. *water currents*
    D. *gravity and terrain*
    E. *air currents*

60) sticky, mucoid covering

Answer: A
Skill: Application

61) made of material high in calories

Answer: B
Skill: Application

62) covered with spines or hooks

Answer: A
Skill: Application

63) covered with low–density material

Answer: C
Skill: Application

64) spheroidal shape

Answer: D
Skill: Application

65) bearing a broad, thin membranous structure

Answer: E
Skill: Application

66) bearing light, fibrous plumes or puffs

Answer: E
Skill: Application

Media Activity Questions

1) In the pine life cycle the female gametophyte is produced by the

   A) microsporangium.

   B) megaspore.

   C) integument.

   D) microspore.

   E) antheridium.

   Answer: B
   Topic: Web/CD Activity 30A

2) In pines a pollen cone contains

   A) ovules.

   B) integuments.

   C) archegonia.

   D) microsporangia.

   E) megasporangia.

   Answer: D
   Topic: Web/CD Activity 30A

3) Flowers are made of modified

   A) roots.

   B) stems.

   C) leaves.

   D) ovules.

   E) shoots.

   Answer: C
   Topic: Web/CD Activity 30B

4) What process occurs in the ovary that initiates the development of female gametophytes?

   A) Fertilization

   B) Meiosis

   C) Mitosis

   D) Pollination

   E) Germination

   Answer: B
   Topic: Web/CD Activity 30B

5) Angiosperms are _____ plants.

   A) cone–bearing

   B) avascular

   C) naked seed

   D) seedless

   E) flowering

   Answer: E
   Topic: Web/CD Activity 30B

Self-Quiz Questions

Answers to these questions also appear in the textbook.

1) Where would you find a megasporangium in an angiosperm?

   A) at the base of a sporophyll in an ovulate cone

   B) producing a megaspore within the archegonium of the female gametophyte

   C) enclosed in the stigma of a flower

   D) within an ovule contained within an ovary of a flower

   E) packed into pollen sacs within the anthers found on a stamen

   Answer: D

2) What is a fruit?

   A) a mature ovary

   B) a thickened style

   C) an enlarged ovule

   D) a modified root

   E) a mature female gametophyte

   Answer: A

3) Which angiosperm cell is *incorrectly* paired with its chromosome count (n or $2n$)?

   A) egg cell—n

   B) megaspore—$2n$

   C) microspore—n

   D) zygote—$2n$

   E) sperm—n

   Answer: B

4) Plant diversity is greatest in

   A) tropical forests.

   B) deserts.

   C) salt marshes.

   D) temperate forests.

   E) farmlands.

   Answer: A

5) Evidence that *Amborella* may represent the only survivor of the oldest branch of the angiosperm lineage comes from

   A) the fossil record.

   B) the lack of flowers in this primitive plant.

   C) the lack of vessels in its xylem tissue.

   D) molecular systematics.

   E) Both C and D provide evidence for the early divergence of its ancestors.

   Answer: E

6) Gymnosperms and angiosperms have the following in common *except*

   A) seeds.

   B) pollen.

   C) vascular tissue.

   D) ovaries.

   E) ovules.

   Answer: D

In the following cladogram, match the derived characters (see Chapter 25) with the correct branch points.

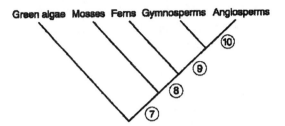

7) label 7

    A) flowers

    B) embryos

    C) seeds

    D) vascular tissues

    Answer: B

8) label 8

    A) flowers

    B) embryos

    C) seeds

    D) vascular tissues

    Answer: D

9) label 9

    A) flowers

    B) embryos

    C) seeds

    D) vascular tissues

    Answer: C

10) label 10

    A) flowers

    B) embryos

    C) seeds

    D) vascular tissues

    Answer: A

Chapter 31   Fungi

1) Which of the following do all fungi have in common?
   A) meiosis in basidia
   B) coenocytic hyphae
   C) sexual life cycle
   D) absorption of nutrients
   E) symbioses with algae

   Answer: D
   Skill: Knowledge

2) What is a characteristic of all fungi?
   A) heterotrophic nutrition
   B) saprobic lifestyle
   C) multicellularity
   D) dikaryotic hyphae
   E) parasitism

   Answer: A
   Skill: Knowledge

3) What is true of all fungi? They are
   A) eukaryotic, heterotrophic plants.
   B) eukaryotic, parasitic plants.
   C) saprobic plants.
   D) eukaryotic heterotrophs with cell walls.
   E) saprobic heterotrophs.

   Answer: D
   Skill: Knowledge

4) Fungi are all of the following *except*
   A) predators.
   B) decomposers.
   C) symbionts.
   D) absorptive heterotrophs.
   E) autotrophs.

   Answer: E
   Skill: Comprehension

5) If all saprobic fungi in an environment were to suddenly die, then which group of organisms should, as a whole, benefit?
   A) plants
   B) protists
   C) prokaryotes
   D) animals
   E) mutualistic fungi

   Answer: C
   Skill: Comprehension

6) When a mycelium grows into an unexploited source of dead organic matter, what is most likely to appear within the food source soon thereafter?
   A) haustoria
   B) soredia
   C) exoenzymes
   D) increased oxygen levels
   E) larger bacterial populations

   Answer: C
   Skill: Comprehension

7) Chemicals, secreted by soil fungi, that inhibit the growth of bacteria are known as
   A) antibodies.
   B) aflatoxins.
   C) hallucinogens.
   D) antigens.
   E) antibiotics.

   Answer: E
   Skill: Knowledge

8) The following are all characteristic of hyphate fungi (that is, fungi featuring hyphae) *except*

A) they acquire their nutrients by absorption.

B) their body plan is a netlike mass of filaments called a mycelium.

C) their cell walls consist mainly of cellulose microfibrils.

D) they may be saprobes, parasites, or mutualistic symbionts.

E) the nuclei of the mycelia are typically haploid.

Answer: C
Skill: Knowledge

9) The primary role of the mushroom's underground mycelium is

A) absorbing nutrients.

B) anchoring.

C) sexual reproduction.

D) asexual reproduction.

E) protection.

Answer: A
Skill: Comprehension

10) What do fungi and arthropods have in common?

A) Both groups are commonly coenocytic.

B) The haploid state is dominant in both groups.

C) Both groups are predominantly saprobic in nutrition.

D) Both groups use chitin for the construction of protective coats.

E) Both groups have cell walls.

Answer: D
Skill: Comprehension

11) In septate fungi, what structures allow cytoplasmic streaming to distribute needed nutrients, synthesized compounds, and organelles throughout the hyphae?

A) chitinous layers in cell walls

B) pores in septal walls

C) complex microtubular cytoskeletons

D) two nuclei

E) tight junctions that form in septal walls between cells

Answer: B
Skill: Comprehension

12) What accounts for the extremely fast growth of a fungal mycelium?

A) a rapid distribution of synthesized proteins by cytoplasmic streaming

B) their lack of motility that requires rapid spread of hyphae

C) a long tubular body shape

D) the readily available nutrients from their predatory mode of nutrition

E) a dikaryotic condition that supplies greater amounts of proteins and nutrients

Answer: A
Skill: Knowledge

13) The vegetative (nutritionally active) bodies of *most* fungi are

A) composed of hyphae.

B) referred to as a mycelium.

C) usually underground.

D) Only A and B

E) A, B, and C

Answer: E
Skill: Comprehension

14) *Coenocytic* refers to fungi (and other organisms) whose tissues are not clearly divided into cells. The above statement is

A) true and describes all fungi.

B) true but restricts the movement of fungal mycelia.

C) true but refers to only some fungi.

D) true but only for parasitic fungi.

E) false.

Answer: C
Skill: Comprehension

15) Consider two hyphae having equal dimensions: one from a septate species and the other from a coenocytic species. What should be true of the coenocytic species, relative to the septate species? It should have

A) fewer nuclei.

B) more pores.

C) less chitin.

D) less cytoplasm.

E) reduced cytoplasmic streaming.

Answer: C
Skill: Application

16) In fungi, karyogamy does not immediately follow plasmogamy, which

A) means that sexual reproduction can occur in specialized structures.

B) results in more genetic variation during sexual reproduction.

C) allows fungi to reproduce asexually most of the time.

D) creates dikaryotic cells.

E) is strong support for the claim that fungi are not truly eukaryotic.

Answer: D
Skill: Comprehension

17) Cytokinesis is to nuclear division as _____ is to karyogamy.

A) syngamy

B) plasmogamy

C) gametogenesis

D) endosymbiosis

E) parasitism

Answer: B
Skill: Comprehension

The questions below refer to the following phyla. Each term may be used once, more than once, or not at all.

A. *Zygomycota*
B. *Ascomycota*
C. *Basidiomycota*
D. *Deuteromycota*
E. *Chytridiomycota*

18) This phylum contains organisms that most closely resemble the common ancestor of fungi and animals.

Answer: E
Skill: Knowledge

19) This phylum consists of fungi having coenocytic hyphae with asexual spores that develop in aerial sporangia.

Answer: A
Skill: Knowledge

20) The members of this phylum produce two kinds of haploid spores, one kind being asexually produced conidia.

Answer: B
Skill: Knowledge

21) This phylum contains the mushrooms, shelf fungi, puffballs, and stinkhorns.

Answer: C
Skill: Knowledge

22) This phylum (which is not a true phylum) is characterized by the lack of an observed sexual phase in its members' life cycles.

Answer: D
Skill: Knowledge

23) Which of these structures is most likely to be a component of both chytrid and animal cells?

A) chloroplasts

B) 9 + 2 pattern of microtubules in flagella

C) cell walls composed of chitin

D) heterokaryons

E) haustoria

Answer: B
Skill: Comprehension

24) Concerning mode of sexual reproduction, chytrids are most similar to which plants?

A) ferns

B) conifers

C) eudicots

D) monocots

E) gnetophytes

Answer: A
Skill: Comprehension

25) The sporangia of bread molds are

A) asexual structures that produce haploid spores.

B) asexual structures that produce diploid spores.

C) sexual structures that produce haploid spores.

D) sexual structures that produce diploid spores.

E) vegetative structures with no role in reproduction.

Answer: A
Skill: Knowledge

26) The gray-black filamentous mycelium growing on bread is most likely what kind of organism?

A) chytridiomycete

B) ascomycete

C) basidiomycete

D) deuteromycete

E) zygomycete

Answer: E
Skill: Knowledge

27) Considered at the taxonomic level of the kingdom, which of the following constitutes a monophyletic combination?

A) mosses and zygomycetes

B) chytrids and fungi

C) algae and ascomycetes

D) chytrids and slime molds

E) mosses and fungi

Answer: B
Skill: Comprehension

28) The sac fungi (ascomycetes) get their name from which aspect of their life cycle?

A) vegetative growth form

B) asexual spore production

C) sexual structures

D) shape of the spore

E) type of vegetative mycelium

Answer: C
Skill: Knowledge

29) You are given an organism to identify. It has a fruiting body that contains many "sacs" with eight haploid spores lined up in a row. What kind of a fungus is it most likely to be?

A) zygomycete

B) ascomycete

C) deuteromycete

D) chytridiomycete

E) basidiomycete

Answer: B
Skill: Application

30) Which of these fungal structures is associated with asexual reproduction?

A) zygospore

B) basidium

C) conidium

D) ascus

E) antheridium

Answer: C
Skill: Knowledge

31) Mushrooms and toadstools are classified as

A) basidiomycetes.

B) ascomycetes.

C) deuteromycetes.

D) zygomycetes.

E) chytridiomycetes.

Answer: A
Skill: Knowledge

32) Arrange the following from largest to smallest, assuming that they all come from the same fungus.
1. basidiocarp
2. basidium
3. basidiospore
4. hypha
5. gill

A) 1, 5, 4, 2, 3

B) 5, 1, 4, 2, 3

C) 5, 1, 4, 3, 2

D) 5, 1, 3, 2, 4

E) 1, 5, 4, 3, 2

Answer: A
Skill: Comprehension

33) Mushrooms with gills, typically available in supermarkets, have meiotically produced spores located in or on _____ and belong to the phylum _____.

A) asci ... Basidiomycota

B) hyphae ... Zygomycota

C) basidia ... Basidiomycota

D) asci ... Ascomycota

E) hyphae ... Ascomycota

Answer: C
Skill: Knowledge

34) A fungal spore germinates, giving rise to a mycelium that grows outward into the soil surrounding the site where the spore originally landed. What process best accounts for the observation that, upon reaching sexual maturity, this fungus produces a nearly circular fairy ring despite the fact that organic nutrients are not evenly distributed in the soil?

A) karyogamy

B) plasmogamy

C) alternation of generations

D) fermentation

E) cytoplasmic streaming

Answer: E
Skill: Application

35) Which of the following are *true* of deuteromycetes?

A) They are the second of five fungal phyla to have evolved.

B) They represent the phylum in which all the fungal components of lichens are classified.

C) They are fungi whose forms of sexual reproduction, if they exist, have not been characterized.

D) They are the group that includes molds, yeasts, and lichens.

E) They include the fungi considered imperfect because they lack hyphae.

Answer: C
Skill: Knowledge

The questions below refer to the following information: A biologist is trying to classify a new organism on the basis of the following characteristics: funguslike in appearance, reproduces asexually by conidia, has no apparent sexual phase, and parasitizes woody plants.

36) If asked for advice, to which group would you assign this new species?

 A) Deuteromycota

 B) Zygomycota

 C) Ascomycota

 D) Basidiomycota

 E) Chytridiomycota

Answer: A
Skill: Application

37) Both *Penicillium* and *Aspergillus* produce asexual spores at the tips of the

 A) asci.

 B) antheridia.

 C) rhizoids.

 D) gametangia.

 E) conidiophores.

Answer: E
Skill: Knowledge

38) Which of the following cannot be assigned to any one kind of morphology (that is, unicellular or hyphate) or to any one fungal taxon?

 A) yeasts

 B) chytrids

 C) club fungi

 D) bread molds

 E) ergot fungi

Answer: A
Skill: Comprehension

39) Lichens are symbiotic associations of fungi and

 A) mosses.

 B) cyanobacteria.

 C) green algae.

 D) Both A and B are correct.

 E) Both B and C are correct.

Answer: E
Skill: Knowledge

40) Lichens sometimes reproduce asexually using

 A) aseptate fungal hyphae located within algal cells.

 B) the fruiting bodies of fungi.

 C) flagellated, conjoined spores of both the fungus and alga.

 D) specialized conidiophores.

 E) small clusters of fungal hyphae surrounding algal cells.

Answer: E
Skill: Knowledge

41) The symbiotic associations called mycorrhizae are considered

 A) parasitic.

 B) mutualistic.

 C) commensal.

 D) harmful to the plant partner.

 E) the beginning stages of the formation of lichens.

Answer: B
Skill: Knowledge

42) If there were no mycorrhizae, then which of the following would be *true*?

A) There would be fewer infectious diseases.

B) We wouldn't have any antibiotics.

C) There would be no mushrooms for pizza.

D) Most vascular plants would be stunted in their growth.

E) Cheeses like blue cheese or Roquefort would not exist.

Answer: D
Skill: Comprehension

43) Why do biologists who study lichens sometimes refer to the symbiotic relationship between fungus and alga as *controlled parasitism*?

A) Together, the fungus and alga may parasitize and kill other living organisms, such as plants.

B) Each contributes to the maintenance of the other.

C) Fungal haustoria may kill algal cells, but at a pace slow enough not to destroy all the algae present.

D) Algal cells die at a faster rate than fungal cells.

E) Fungal cells reproduce slower than the algae, thus becoming enclosed and unable to grow.

Answer: C
Skill: Comprehension

44) Which of the following *best* describes the physical relationship of the partners involved in lichens?

A) Fungal cells are enclosed within algal cells.

B) Lichen cells are enclosed within fungal cells.

C) Algal cells are surrounded by fungal hyphae.

D) The fungi grow on rocks and trees and are covered by algae.

E) Algal cells and fungal cells mix together without any apparent structure.

Answer: C
Skill: Knowledge

45) If haustoria were to appear within the photosynthetic partner of a lichen and if the growth rate of the photosynthetic partner consequently slowed substantially, then this would support the claim that

A) algae and cyanobacteria are autotrophic.

B) lichens are not purely mutualistic relationships.

C) algae require maximal contact with the fungal partner in order to grow at optimal rates.

D) fungi get all of the nutrition they need via the "leakiness" of photosynthetic partners.

E) soredia are asexual reproductive structures combining both the fungal and photosynthetic partners.

Answer: B
Skill: Application

46) How are the vascular plants that are involved in mycorrhizae and the algae that are involved in lichens alike?

   A) They provide organic nutrients to fungal partners.

   B) They secrete acids that keep the fungal partner from growing too quickly.

   C) They are in intimate associations with chytrids.

   D) They are digested by fungal exoenzymes while still alive.

   E) They contain endosymbiotic fungi.

   Answer: A
   Skill: Comprehension

47) When pathogenic fungi are found growing on the roots of grape vines, grape farmers sometimes respond by covering the ground around their vines with plastic sheeting and pumping a gaseous fungicide into the soil. An important concern of viticulturists who engage in this practice should be that the

   A) fungicide doesn't also kill the native yeasts residing on the surfaces of the grapes.

   B) fungicide isn't also harmful to insect pests.

   C) lichens growing on the vines' branches are not harmed.

   D) fungicide doesn't also kill mycorrhizae.

   E) sheeting is transparent so that photosynthesis can continue.

   Answer: D
   Skill: Application

48) The terms below all refer to symbiotic relationships that occur in fungi *except*

   A) pathogens.

   B) mycoses.

   C) spore production.

   D) lichens.

   E) mycorrhizae.

   Answer: C
   Skill: Knowledge

49) The following conditions are all caused by a fungus *except*

   A) AIDS.

   B) athlete's foot.

   C) histoplasmosis.

   D) candidiasis (*Candida* infection).

   E) coccidiodomycosis.

   Answer: A
   Skill: Knowledge

50) Fossil fungi date back to the origin and early evolution of plants. What combination of environmental change and morphological change is similar in the evolution of both fungi and plants?

   A) presence of "coal forests" and change in mode of nutrition

   B) periods of drought and presence of filamentous body shape

   C) predominance of swamps and presence of cellulose in cell walls

   D) colonization of land and loss of flagellated cells

   E) continental drift and mode of spore dispersal

   Answer: D
   Skill: Comprehension

51) Which of the following characteristics is *not* shared by both chytrids and other kinds of fungi?

   A) presence of hyphae

   B) flagellated zoospores

   C) absorptive mode of nutrition

   D) chitinous cell walls

   E) amino acid base sequences of some enzymes

   Answer: B
   Skill: Knowledge

52) Which of the following terms is *not* properly associated with fungi?

   A) decomposers

   B) sexual and asexual spores

   C) ecological importance

   D) polyphyletic

   E) absorptive nutrition

   Answer: D
   Skill: Knowledge

53) Fungi grow on which of the following?

   A) on exposed, barren rock surfaces

   B) in seawater

   C) within the living roots of vascular plants

   D) only A and B

   E) A, B, and C

   Answer: E
   Skill: Knowledge

54) Fungi are beneficial to agriculture in all of the following ways *except* they

   A) recycle nutrients that are tied up in dead organic matter.

   B) increase the ability of most vascular plants to absorb water and minerals from the soil.

   C) contribute to the initial stages of soil formation from rock.

   D) form mycoses on leaves and stems.

   E) may harbor photosynthetic partners that add nitrogenous compounds to the soil.

   Answer: D
   Skill: Comprehension

Media Activity Questions

1) Fungi are
   A) photoautotrophs.
   B) triploid.
   C) prokaryotic.
   D) heterotrophs.
   E) chemoautotrophs.

   Answer: D
   Topic: Web/CD Activity 31A

2) Fungal mycelia are composed of
   A) gills.
   B) hyphae.
   C) spores.
   D) cellulose.
   E) heterocysts.

   Answer: B
   Topic: Web/CD Activity 31A

3) The fusion of hyphae is called
   A) binary fusion.
   B) heterokaryosis.
   C) plasmogamy.
   D) dikaryosis.
   E) karyogamy.

   Answer: C
   Topic: Web/CD Activity 31B

4) A zygosporangium is
   A) homokaryotic.
   B) heterokaryotic.
   C) haploid.
   D) diploid.
   E) triploid.

   Answer: B
   Topic: Web/CD Activity 31B

5) Technically, a mushroom is a(n)
   A) mold.
   B) ascospore.
   C) ascocarp.
   D) basidiospore.
   E) basidiocarp.

   Answer: E
   Topic: Web/CD Activity 31B

Self–Quiz Questions

Answers to these questions also appear in the textbook.

1) *All* fungi share which one of the following characteristics?

   A) symbiotic

   B) heterotrophic

   C) flagellated

   D) pathogenic

   E) saprobic

   Answer: B

2) Which feature seen in chytrids supports the hypothesis that they represent the most primitive fungi?

   A) the absence of chitin within the cell wall

   B) coenocytic hyphae

   C) flagellated spores

   D) formation of resistant zygosporangia

   E) all representatives are parasitic

   Answer: C

3) Which of the following cells or structures are associated with *asexual* reproduction in fungi?

   A) ascospores

   B) basidiospores

   C) conidia

   D) zygosporangia

   E) ascogonia

   Answer: C

4) Which of the following is an example of an opportunistic pathogen that can cause a mycosis?

   A) *Claviceps pururea*, which produces ergots on rye that can cause serious symptoms in humans if milled into flour

   B) *Ophiostoma ulmi*, which causes Dutch elm disease

   C) the ascomycetes that cause ringworm

   D) *Candida albicans*, which causes vaginal yeast infections

   E) the mold *Penicillium*, an ascomycete that is now grown in liquid culture to produce antibiotics

   Answer: D

5) The adaptive advantage associated with the filamentous nature of the mycelium is primarily related to

   A) the ability to form haustoria and parasitize other organisms.

   B) avoiding sexual reproduction until environmental change occurs.

   C) the potential to inhabit almost all terrestrial habitats.

   D) the increased probability of contact between different mating types.

   E) an extensive surface area well suited for absorptive nutrition.

   Answer: E

6) Sporangia on erect hyphae that produce asexual spores are characteristic of

   A) Ascomycota.

   B) Basidiomycota.

   C) Ascocarps.

   D) Zygomycota.

   E) lichens.

   Answer: D

7) The basidiomycetes differ from other fungal phyla in that they
   A) have no known sexual reproduction stage.
   B) have long-lived dikaryotic mycelia.
   C) produce resistant sporangia that are initially heterokaryotic before karyogamy and meiosis occur.
   D) have members that are mutualistic partners with algae in lichens.
   E) form eight spores that line up in a sac in the order they were formed in meiosis, allowing geneticists to study genetic recombination.

   Answer: B

8) Which of the following is the best description of a mold?
   A) a deuteromycete, or imperfect fungus, which has no known sexual stage
   B) a coenocytic, rapidly growing mycelium
   C) mycorrhizae that envelope plant roots and reproduce without forming spores
   D) unicellular fungi that grow rapidly in liquid or moist habitats
   E) the fast-growing mycelia of any asexually reproducing fungus

   Answer: E

9) The photosynthetic symbiont of a lichen is most commonly a(n)
   A) moss.
   B) green alga.
   C) red alga.
   D) ascomycete.
   E) small vascular plant.

   Answer: B

10) The closest relatives of fungi are probably
   A) animals.
   B) vascular plants.
   C) mosses.
   D) brown algae.
   E) slime molds.

   Answer: A

Chapter 32   Introduction to Animal Evolution

1) The following are all generally observed among animals *except*

A) nervous and muscle tissue.

B) unique types of intercellular junctions such as tight and gap junctions.

C) autotrophic nutrition.

D) sexual reproduction.

E) multicellularity.

Answer: C
Skill: Knowledge

2) Which of the following terms or structures are *not* associated with animal cells?

A) eukaryotic

B) cell wall

C) desmosomes

D) zygote

E) blastula

Answer: B
Skill: Knowledge

3) Both animals and fungi are completely heterotrophic. What distinguishes animal heterotrophy from fungal heterotrophy is that only animals derive their nutrition

A) from organic matter.

B) by preying upon animals.

C) by ingesting it.

D) by consuming living, rather than dead, prey.

E) by using enzymes to digest their food.

Answer: C
Skill: Comprehension

4) The larvae of some insects are merely small versions of the adult, whereas the larvae of certain other insects look radically different from adults, eat different foods, and may even live in different environments. What condition should most directly favor the evolution of the more radical kind of metamorphosis?

A) limited resources

B) increasing oxygen content of the biosphere

C) the evolution of meiosis

D) volcanoes in the environment

E) the felt need to introduce variety into the species

Answer: A
Skill: Application

5) Assuming that all of the following events occur, what is the correct sequence in which the following processes occur during the development of an individual animal?
1. gastrulation
2. metamorphosis
3. fertilization
4. cleavage

A) 4, 3, 2, 1

B) 4, 3, 1, 2

C) 3, 2, 4, 1

D) 3, 4, 2, 1

E) 3, 4, 1, 2

Answer: E
Skill: Comprehension

6) According to the evidence collected so far, the animal kingdom is

A) monophyletic.

B) paraphyletic.

C) polyphyletic.

D) euphyletic.

E) multiphyletic.

Answer: A
Skill: Knowledge

7) The common ancestor of all animals was probably a

A) bacterium.

B) prokaryote.

C) plant.

D) fungus.

E) protist.

Answer: E
Skill: Knowledge

8) Which of the following statements concerning animal taxonomy is *true*?

1. Animals are more closely related to plants than to fungi.
2. All animal clades based on body plan have been found to be incorrect.
3. Kingdom Animalia is monophyletic.
4. Only animals reproduce by sexual means.
5. Animals are thought to have evolved from flagellated protists similar to modern choanoflagellates.

A) 5

B) 1, 3

C) 2, 4

D) 3, 5

E) 3, 4, 5

Answer: D
Skill: Knowledge

9) Which of the following is *not* consistent with distinguishing an animal from other life forms?

A) multicellular, autotrophic, eukaryote

B) structural proteins such as collagen

C) impulse conduction and movement

D) regulatory genes called *Hox* genes

E) sexual reproduction

Answer: A
Skill: Knowledge

10) Which of the following statements is *true*?

A) The rapid movements of Venus's flytraps, bladderworts, and sensitive plants (*Mimosa pudica*) are the result of primitive nervous conduction.

B) The movement of a fungal mycelium through organically rich soil is the result of cytoplasmic streaming.

C) The dispersal of spores from fungi, such as *Pilobolus*, is explained by the existence of mesodermally derived smooth muscle filaments.

D) Sunflower blossoms generally follow the motion of the sun in the sky by detecting stimuli using their nervous receptors.

E) The amoeboid motion observed in certain protists is the result of neuromuscular interactions within pseudopodia.

Answer: B
Skill: Comprehension

11) The number of legs an insect has, or the number of vertebrae in a vertebrate's vertebral column, or the number of joints in a digit (such as a finger), are all strongly influenced by _____ genes.

A) haploid

B) introns within

C) heterotic

D) heterogeneous

E) homeotic

Answer: E
Skill: Knowledge

12) Rank the following, from most inclusive to least inclusive.
1. chromosome
2. *Hox* gene
3. genome
4. homeobox

A) 1, 3, 2, 4
B) 1, 3, 4, 2
C) 3, 1, 2, 4
D) 3, 1, 4, 2
E) 1, 4, 3, 2

Answer: C
Skill: Comprehension

13) Among the following, the organism with the greatest number of *Hox* genes should be a(n)

A) earthworm.
B) horse.
C) sponge.
D) jellyfish.
E) flatworm.

Answer: B
Skill: Application

14) What should animals as diverse as corals and monkeys have in common?

A) body cavity between body wall and digestive system
B) number of embryonic tissue layers
C) type of body symmetry
D) presence of *Hox* genes
E) degree of cephalization

Answer: D
Skill: Comprehension

15) The most ancient branch point in animal phylogeny is that between having

A) radial or bilateral symmetry.
B) a well–defined head or no head.
C) diploblastic or triploblastic embryos.
D) true tissues or no tissues.
E) a body cavity or no body cavity.

Answer: D
Skill: Comprehension

16) If a multicellular animal lacks true tissues, then it should be classified among the

A) eumetazoa.
B) metazoa.
C) protozoa.
D) parazoa.
E) hydrozoa.

Answer: D
Skill: Knowledge

17) The major branches of eumetazoa are the radiata and the bilateria. These names refer to what characteristic of these animals?

A) size
B) body symmetry
C) embryonic cleavage
D) types of appendages
E) presence or absence of a nucleus in their cells

Answer: B
Skill: Knowledge

18) Organisms showing radial symmetry would likely

A) be good swimmers.
B) have rapid escape behavior.
C) move from place to place relatively slowly, if at all.
D) be able to fly.
E) have many fins.

Answer: C
Skill: Comprehension

19) During metamorphosis, echinoderms undergo a transformation from motile larvae to a fairly sedentary (and sometimes sessile) existence as adults. What should be true of adults, though *not* of larvae? Adults should

A) be diploblastic.

B) appear to possess radial symmetry.

C) lack mesodermally derived tissues.

D) lack a body cavity.

E) Two of these are true.

Answer: B
Skill: Comprehension

20) Cephalization is primarily

A) a result of adaptation to dark environments.

B) an adaptation to the method of reproduction.

C) due to the fate of the blastopore.

D) the result of the type of digestive system.

E) an adaptation to movement.

Answer: E
Skill: Comprehension

21) Cephalization is generally associated with all of the following *except*

A) bilateral symmetry.

B) concentration of sensory structures at the anterior end.

C) a brain.

D) a longitudinal nerve cord.

E) a sessile existence.

Answer: E
Skill: Comprehension

22) Which of the following is an *incorrect* association of an animal germ layer with the tissues or organs to which it gives rise?

A) ectoderm—outer covering

B) endoderm—internal lining of digestive tract

C) mesoderm—nervous system

D) mesoderm—muscle

E) endoderm—internal linings of liver and lungs

Answer: C
Skill: Knowledge

23) You are trying to indentify an organism. It is an animal but it contains *no* muscle tissue. It is *not* diploblastic. It must be a

A) flatworm.

B) jellyfish.

C) comb jelly.

D) sponge.

E) nematode.

Answer: D
Skill: Application

24) You have before you an unknown organism, which you examine carefully. Which of the following would convince you it is *not* an acoelomate?

A) It responds to food by moving towards it.

B) It is triploblastic.

C) It has bilateral symmetry.

D) It possesses sensory structures at the anterior end.

E) It exudes a fluid when you make an incision through the body wall.

Answer: E
Skill: Comprehension

(Figure 32.1 appears on page 417.)

Figure 32.1 shows a chart of the animal kingdom set up as a modified phylogenetic tree. Use the diagram to answer the following questions.

25) A pseudocoelom is characteristic of which of the following groups?
   A) I
   B) II
   C) III
   D) IV
   E) V

   Answer: D
   Skill: Knowledge

26) One opening to the digestive tract is characteristic of which of the following groups?
   A) I only
   B) III only
   C) IV only
   D) V only
   E) I and V

   Answer: E
   Skill: Knowledge

27) Which group is triploblastic and acoelomate?
   A) I
   B) II
   C) III
   D) IV
   E) V

   Answer: E
   Skill: Knowledge

28) Which group contains diploblastic organisms?
   A) I
   B) II
   C) III
   D) IV
   E) V

   Answer: A
   Skill: Knowledge

29) Which group includes both ecdysozoans and lophotrochozoans?
   A) I
   B) II
   C) III
   D) IV
   E) V

   Answer: C
   Skill: Knowledge

30) Which of the following is an important distinction between a coelomate animal and a pseudocoelomate animal? Coelomates
   A) have a body cavity, whereas pseudocoelomates have a solid body.
   B) contain tissues derived from mesoderm, whereas pseudocoelomates have no such tissue.
   C) have a body cavity completely lined by mesodermal tissue, whereas a pseudocoelomate's body cavity does not.
   D) have a complete digestive system with mouth and anus, whereas pseudocoelomates have a digestive tract with only one opening.
   E) have a gut that lacks suspension within the body cavity, whereas pseudocoelomates have mesenteries that hold the digestive system in place.

   Answer: C
   Skill: Comprehension

31) Which of the following is *not* a function that can be served by a fluid-filled body cavity?

A) It can serve as a storage compartment for food.

B) It helps prevent internal injury by cushioning internal organs.

C) It enables organs to grow and move independently of the outer body wall.

D) It can act as a hydrostatic skeleton.

E) All of the above are correct.

Answer: A
Skill: Comprehension

32) The following are all protostomes *except*

A) mollusks.

B) echinoderms.

C) segmented worms.

D) insects.

E) spiders.

Answer: B
Skill: Knowledge

33) An animal that swims rapidly in search of prey that it captures using visual senses is likely to be all of the following *except*

A) bilaterally symmetric.

B) coelomate.

C) deuterostomate.

D) diploblastic.

E) cephalized.

Answer: D
Skill: Comprehension

34) Which of the following organisms are deuterostomes?

A) mollusks

B) annelids

C) echinoderms

D) chordates

E) Both C and D are deuterostomes.

Answer: E
Skill: Knowledge

35) The blastopore is a structure that is evident in the

A) zygote.

B) blastula.

C) eight-cell stage.

D) gastrula.

E) egg and sperm.

Answer: D
Skill: Knowledge

36) The blastopore denotes the presence of an endoderm-lined tube in the developing embryo, a tube that is known as the

A) archenteron.

B) blastula.

C) coelom.

D) germ layer.

E) blastocoel.

Answer: A
Skill: Comprehension

37) Which of the following is descriptive of protostomes?

A) spiral and indeterminate cleavage, coelom forms as split in solid mass of mesoderm

B) spiral and determinate cleavage, blastopore becomes mouth, schizocoelous development

C) spiral and determinate cleavage, enterocoelous development

D) radial and determinate cleavage, enterocoelous development, blastopore becomes anus

E) radial and determinate cleavage, blastopore becomes mouth, schizocoelous development

Answer: B
Skill: Knowledge

38) Which of the following characteristics correctly applies to protosome development?

A) radial cleavage

B) determinate cleavage

C) enterocoelous

D) blastopore becomes the anus

E) archenteron absent

Answer: B
Skill: Knowledge

39) Protostome characteristics include all of the following *except*

A) a mouth that develops from the blastopore.

B) schizocoelous development.

C) spiral cleavage.

D) indeterminate cleavage.

E) solid masses of mesodermal tisue that splits to form the body cavity.

Answer: D
Skill: Comprehension

40) Rank the following, from most inclusive to least inclusive.
1. coelomate
2. protostome
3. bilateria
4. eumetazoa
5. triploblastic

A) 4, 2, 3, 5, 1

B) 4, 3, 5, 1, 2

C) 3, 5, 4, 1, 2

D) 3, 4, 5, 1, 2

E) 4, 5, 3, 2, 1

Answer: B
Skill: Comprehension

41) Recent evidence from molecular systematics is showing what to be true about the relationship between grades and clades?

A) They are one and the same.

B) There is no relationship.

C) Many, but not all, grades have a basis in phylogeny.

D) Grades have their basis in and flow from clades.

E) Each branch point on a cladogram is associated with the evolution of a new grade.

Answer: C
Skill: Comprehension

42) To date, analyses of sequences of which homologous genes have provided the evidence behind the recent realignment of clades in the phylogenetic tree of the animals?
1. genes that cause trochophore larvae to be produced
2. *Hox* genes
3. genes that cause a second opening to develop in the archenteron
4. SSU–rRNA genes
5. genes that code for lophophores

A) 1

B) 1, 5

C) 2, 4

D) 2, 3, 4

E) 1, 3, 4, 5

Answer: C
Skill: Comprehension

43) Recent evidence from molecular systematics indicates that the protostome clade seems to

A) be monophyletic.

B) be polyphyletic.

C) be euphyletic.

D) consist of two different clades.

E) Both B and D are true.

Answer: E
Skill: Comprehension

44) What is characteristic of all ecdysozoans?

A) the deuterostome condition

B) some kind of exoskeleton, or hard outer covering

C) a pseudocoelom

D) agile, speedy, and powerful locomotion

E) the diploblastic condition

Answer: B
Skill: Knowledge

45) Recent evidence from molecular systematics has shown which body plan–based grade to have no real bearing on animal phylogeny?

A) presence or absence of tissues

B) number of embryonic tissue layers

C) indeterminate embryonic development

D) presence, absence, or type of body cavity

E) presence of ecdysis

Answer: D
Skill: Comprehension

46) What kind of data should probably have the greatest impact on animal taxonomy in the coming decades?

A) fossil evidence

B) comparative morphology of living species

C) nucleotide sequences of homologous genes

D) similarities in metabolic pathways

E) the number and size of chromosomes within nuclei

Answer: C
Skill: Comprehension

47) Phylogenetic trees are best described as

A) true and inerrant statements about evolutionary relationships.

B) hypothetical portrayals of evolutionary relationships.

C) the most accurate possible representations of genetic relationships among taxa.

D) theories of evolution.

E) the closest things to absolute certainty that modern systematists can produce.

Answer: B
Skill: Comprehension

48) Generally, when referring to phylogenetic trees, all of the following belong *except*

A) unchanging.

B) probationary.

C) falsifiable.

D) hypothetical.

E) based on evidence.

Answer: A
Skill: Knowledge

49) If each of the following traits evolved only once during animal evolution, then which traits were probably possessed by the most recent common ancestor of the Deuterostomia, Ecdysozoa, and Lophotrochozoa?
1. indeterminate development
2. exoskeleton
3. triploblastic
4. cephalization
5. segmentation

A) 1, 2

B) 1, 2, 5

C) 1, 3, 4

D) 3, 4, 5

E) all of these

Answer: D
Skill: Comprehension

50) Almost all of the major animal body plans we see today appeared in the fossil record over 500 million years ago at the beginning of the

A) Cambrian period.

B) Ediacaran period.

C) Burgess period.

D) Carboniferous period.

E) Cretaceous period.

Answer: A
Skill: Knowledge

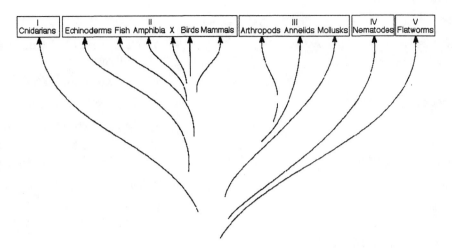

Figure 32.1

Media Activity Questions

1) Which phylum is characterized by the absence of true tissues?

   A) Cnidaria

   B) Nematoda

   C) Porifera

   D) Echinodermata

   E) Platyhelminthes

   Answer: C
   Topic: Web/CD Activity 32A

2) The characteristic of cnidarians that distinguishes them from other animal phyla is

   A) the presence of a body cavity.

   B) their three germ layers.

   C) their true tissues.

   D) radial symmetry.

   E) a coelomate structure.

   Answer: D
   Topic: Web/CD Activity 32A

3) Platyhelminths differ from cnidarians in that platyhelminths have _____, which cnidarians don't have.

   A) a mouth that develops from the blastopore

   B) true tissues

   C) three germ layers

   D) an anus that develops from the blastopore

   E) a coelom formed from the splitting of the mesoderm

   Answer: C
   Topic: Web/CD Activity 32A

4) Which of these is *not* true of an echinoderm?

   A) They are eumetazoans.

   B) They are diploblastic.

   C) They are deuterostomes.

   D) They exhibit bilateral symmetry at some stage of their life cycle.

   E) They are coelomates.

   Answer: B
   Topic: Web/CD Activity 32A

5) Mollusks differ from nematodes in that mollusks have _____, which nematodes lack.

   A) bilateral symmetry

   B) three germ layers

   C) a body cavity formed from cell masses

   D) true tissues

   E) a body cavity enclosed by mesoderm

   Answer: E
   Topic: Web/CD Activity 32A

Self-Quiz Questions

Answers to these questions also appear in the textbook.

1) The distinction between the parazoans and eumetazoans is based mainly on the absence versus the presence of

   A) body cavities.

   B) a complete digestive tract.

   C) true tissues.

   D) a circulatory system.

   E) mesoderm.

   Answer: C

2) As a group, acoelomates are characterized by

   A) the absence of a brain.

   B) the absence of mesoderm.

   C) deuterostome development.

   D) a coelom that is not completely lined with mesoderm.

   E) a solid body without a cavity surrounding internal organs.

   Answer: E

3) What is the main basis for placing the arthropods and nematodes in the Ecdysozoa?

   A) Animals in both groups are segmented.

   B) Animals in both groups undergo ecdysis.

   C) They both have radial, determinate cleavage, and their embryonic development is similar.

   D) The fossil record has revealed a common ancestor to these two phyla.

   E) Their SSU-rRNA sequences are quite similar, and these sequences differ from those of the lophotrochozoans and deuterostomes.

   Answer: E

4) How does the molecular-based phylogenetic tree differ from the grade-based tree?

   A) placement of the acoelomates and pseudocoelomates within the Protostomia

   B) division of the protostomes into clades Lophotrochozoa and Ecdysozoa

   C) grouping of arthropods and annelids (both segmented animals) in Ecdysozoa and assignment of mollusks to Lophotrochozoa

   D) Both A and B are correct.

   E) A, B, and C are correct.

   Answer: D

5) Bilateral symmetry in the animal kingdom is best correlated with

   A) an ability to sense equally in all directions.

   B) the presence of a skeleton.

   C) motility and active predation and escape.

   D) development of a true coelom.

   E) adaptation to terrestrial environments.

   Answer: C

6) A direct consequence of indeterminate cleavage is

   A) formation of the archenteron.

   B) the ability of cells isolated from the early embryo to develop into viable individuals.

   C) the arrangement of cleavage planes perpendicular to the egg's vertical axis.

   D) the unpredictable formation of either a schizocoelous or enterocoelous body cavity.

   E) a mouth that forms in association with the blastopore.

   Answer: B

7) Which of the following was the *least* likely factor in the Cambrian explosion?

A) the emergence of predator–prey relationships between animals

B) the accumulation of diverse adaptations such as shells and different modes of locomotion

C) the movement of animals onto land

D) the evolution of *Hox* genes that controlled development

E) the accumulation of sufficient atmospheric oxygen to support the more active metabolism of mobile animals

Answer: C

8) Among the characteristics unique to animals is

A) gastrulation.

B) multicellularity.

C) sexual reproduction.

D) flagellated sperm.

E) heterotrophic nutrition.

Answer: A

9) Which of the following combinations of phylum and description is *incorrect*?

A) Echinodermata—branch bilateria, coelom from archenteron

B) Nematoda—roundworms, pseudocoelomate

C) Cnidaria—radial symmetry, diploblastic

D) Platyhelminthes—flatworms, acoelomate

E) Porifera—coelomate, mouth from blastopore

Answer: E

10) Which of the following subdivisions of the animal kingdom encompasses all the others in the list?

A) protostomes

B) bilateria

C) pseudocoelomates

D) coelomates

E) deuterostomes

Answer: B

Chapter 33   Invertebrates

1) The cells in a sponge responsible for trapping food particles from circulating water are called
   A) amoebocytes.
   B) choanocytes.
   C) mesophyl cells.
   D) pore cells (porocytes).
   E) osculocytes.

   Answer: B
   Skill: Knowledge

2) A radially symmetrical animal that has two embryonic germ layers belongs to which phylum?
   A) Porifera (parazoa)
   B) Cnidaria
   C) Platyhelminthes
   D) Aschelminthes
   E) Echinodermata

   Answer: B
   Skill: Knowledge

3) All of the following are characteristics of the phylum Cnidaria *except*
   A) a gastrovascular cavity.
   B) a polyp stage.
   C) a medusa stage.
   D) cnidocytes.
   E) a pseudocoelom.

   Answer: E
   Skill: Knowledge

4) Which of the following are *not* found in sponges?
   A) oscula
   B) spongocoels
   C) cnidocytes
   D) spicules
   E) amoebocytes

   Answer: C
   Skill: Knowledge

5) Muscles and nerves in their simplest forms occur in the
   A) sponges.
   B) cnidarians.
   C) nematodes.
   D) flatworms.
   E) ribbon worms.

   Answer: B
   Skill: Knowledge

6) The best way to describe the brain of a sea anemone would be as
   A) a thick ring around the mouth.
   B) a series of ganglia at the base of the tentacles.
   C) a pair of ganglia at the anterior end.
   D) a single ganglion in the body wall.
   E) nonexistent.

   Answer: E
   Skill: Comprehension

7) Which of the following is a *correct* statement about the members of the phylum Cnidaria? They
   A) are not capable of locomotion because they lack contractile tissue.
   B) are primarily filter feeders.
   C) come in two body forms: mobile polyps and sessile medusae.
   D) have a hydrostatic skeleton.
   E) are the simplest organisms with a complete gut (two openings).

   Answer: D
   Skill: Comprehension

8) Which class of the phylum Cnidaria occurs *only* as a polyp?
   A) Hydrozoa
   B) Scyphozoa
   C) Anthozoa
   D) A and C
   E) A, B, and C

   Answer: C
   Skill: Knowledge

9) Which class of the phylum Cnidaria includes the animals called jellies?
   A) Hydrozoa
   B) Scyphozoa
   C) Anthozoa
   D) A and C
   E) A, B, and C

   Answer: B
   Skill: Knowledge

10) Corals are most closely related to which group?
    A) jellies
    B) freshwater hydras
    C) sea anemones
    D) sponges
    E) comb jellies

    Answer: C
    Skill: Comprehension

11) The cnidoyctes of the Cnidaria are analogous to the _____ of the Ctenophora.
    A) colloblasts
    B) choanocytes
    C) flame cells
    D) tentacles
    E) amoebocytes

    Answer: A
    Skill: Comprehension

12) In the phylum Platyhelminthes, which of the following classes is (are) mostly nonparasitic?
    A) Turbellaria
    B) Trematoda
    C) Cestoidea
    D) B and C
    E) A, B, and C

    Answer: A
    Skill: Knowledge

13) Which characteristic is shared by cnidarians and flatworms?
    A) B and D below
    B) flame cells
    C) radial symmetry
    D) a gut with a single opening
    E) dorsoventrally flattened bodies

    Answer: D
    Skill: Knowledge

14) In a small stream, you pick up a rock and observe many small wormlike organisms crawling on its undersurface. You decide that they belong to the Platyhelminthes. To which *class* do they belong?
    A) Cestoidea   B) Monogenea
    C) Turbellaria   D) Trematoda

    Answer: C
    Skill: Application

15) One method of reducing the incidence of blood flukes in a human population would be to
    A) reduce the mosquito population.
    B) reduce the freshwater snail population.
    C) purify all drinking water.
    D) ensure that all meat is properly cooked.
    E) carefully wash all raw fruits and vegetables.

    Answer: B
    Skill: Comprehension

16) In the phylum Platyhelminthes, which of the following classes is (are) mostly parasitic?

A) Turbellaria

B) Trematoda

C) Cestoidea

D) B and C

E) A, B, and C

Answer: D
Skill: Knowledge

17) The larvae of many common human tapeworms are usually found

A) encysted in human muscle.

B) encysted in the muscle of an animal such as a cow or pig.

C) in the abdominal blood vessels of humans.

D) in the human intestine.

E) in the intestines of cows and pigs.

Answer: B
Skill: Knowledge

18) All of the following statements about the method of feeding in the Cestoidea are true *except:*

A) They lack a digestive tract.

B) They subsist on undigested food.

C) As adults, they live in a digestive tract.

D) They are parasites.

E) They absorb nutrients across the walls of their body.

Answer: B
Skill: Comprehension

19) All of the following characterize the phylum Rotifera *except*

A) a complete digestive tract.

B) a crown of cilia at the anterior end that seems to rotate.

C) parthenogenic reproduction.

D) life stages resistant to desiccation.

E) relatively large size.

Answer: E
Skill: Knowledge

20) A lophophore is used by bryozoans, phoronids, and brachiopods

A) for locomotion.

B) as a larval stage.

C) for feeding.

D) for sensory reception.

E) as a skeletal system.

Answer: C
Skill: Knowledge

21) The proboscis of a ribbon worm (phylum Nemertea) is operated hydraulically by a fluid–filled sac. This sac is thought by some biologists to be homologous to what protostome structure?

A) coelom

B) pseudocoelom

C) digestive tract

D) blastopore

E) heart

Answer: A
Skill: Knowledge

22) While sampling marine plankton, a student encounters large numbers of eggs in her samples. She rears some of the eggs in the laboratory for further study and finds that the blastopore becomes the mouth in a complete digestive system. The embryo develops into a trochophore larva and eventually has a coelom and open circulation. These eggs belonged to a(n)

A) annelid.

B) echinoderm.

C) mollusk.

D) nemertean.

E) arthropod.

Answer: C
Skill: Application

23) Which molluscan class includes members that undergo embryonic torsion?

A) Polyplacophora

B) Bivalvia

C) Cephalopoda

D) Gastropoda

E) All molluscan classes have this characteristic.

Answer: D
Skill: Knowledge

24) A terrestrial mollusk without a shell belongs to which class?

A) Gastropoda

B) Polyplacophora

C) Bivalvia

D) Cephalopoda

E) Arthropoda

Answer: A
Skill: Application

25) Which molluscan class includes clams?

A) Polyplacophora

B) Bivalvia

C) Cephalopoda

D) Gastropoda

E) None of the above; clams are not mollusks.

Answer: B
Skill: Knowledge

26) A radula is *not* present in

A) Gastropoda.

B) Polyplacophora.

C) Bivalvia.

D) any of the classes above.

E) either A or B above.

Answer: C
Skill: Knowledge

27) While snorkeling, a student observes an active marine animal that has a series of muscular tentacles bearing suckers associated with its head. There is no evidence of segmentation, but a pair of large, well-developed eyes is evident. The student is observing an animal belonging to the class

A) Gastropoda.

B) Cephalopoda.

C) Polyplacophora.

D) Polychaeta.

E) Bivalvia.

Answer: B
Skill: Application

28) Which molluscan class includes the most "intelligent" invertebrates?

A) Polyplacophora

B) Bivalvia

C) Cephalopoda

D) Gastropoda

E) Both B and C are equally "intelligent."

Answer: C
Skill: Knowledge

29) Annelids are abundant and successful organisms characterized accurately by all of the following *except*

A) a hydrostatic skeleton.

B) segmentation.

C) a complete digestive system.

D) some parasitic forms.

E) a cuticle made of chitin.

Answer: E
Skill: Knowledge

Use the following choices to answer the questions below. Each choice may be used once, more than once, or not at all.

A. Oligochaeta
B. Polychaeta
C. Hirudinea
D. two of the above
E. all of the above

30) have parapodia

Answer: B
Skill: Knowledge

31) parasitic feeding

Answer: C
Skill: Knowledge

32) segmented

Answer: E
Skill: Knowledge

33) agriculturally important

Answer: A
Skill: Knowledge

34) mostly marine

Answer: B
Skill: Knowledge

35) medically important

Answer: C
Skill: Knowledge

36) All of the following correctly characterize nematodes *except* that they

A) play an important role in decomposition.

B) have both circular and longitudinal muscles.

C) have a pseudocoelom.

D) have a complete digestive system.

E) are often parasitic.

Answer: B
Skill: Knowledge

37) Humans can acquire trichinosis by

A) having sexual contact with an infected partner.

B) eating undercooked pork.

C) inhaling the eggs of worms.

D) eating undercooked beef.

E) being bitten by tsetse flies.

Answer: B
Skill: Knowledge

38) An arthropod has all the following characteristics *except*

A) protostome development.

B) bilateral symmetry.

C) a pseudocoelom.

D) three embryonic germ layers.

E) true tissues.

Answer: C
Skill: Knowledge

39) All of the following are characteristics of arthropods *except*

A) an exoskeleton.

B) numerous species.

C) jointed appendages.

D) a diversity of gas exchange structures.

E) a dorsal nerve cord.

Answer: E
Skill: Knowledge

40) Among the invertebrates, arthropods are unique in possessing

A) a notochord.

B) ventral nerve cords.

C) open circulation.

D) jointed appendages.

E) segmented bodies.

Answer: D
Skill: Knowledge

For the following questions, match the phrases with the choices below. Each choice may be used once, more than once, or not at all.

A. Cnidaria
B. Annelida
C. Mollusca
D. Arthropoda
E. Echinodermata

41) protostomes that have an open circulatory system and an exoskeleton of chitin

Answer: D
Skill: Knowledge

42) deuterostomes that have an internal skeleton

Answer: E
Skill: Knowledge

43) protostomes that have a closed circulatory system and true segmentation

Answer: B
Skill: Knowledge

44) The presence or absence of mandibles can be used to distinguish between

A) insects and centipedes.

B) insects and crustaceans.

C) insects and millipedes.

D) insects and spiders.

E) centipedes and millipedes.

Answer: D
Skill: Knowledge

45) A shared derived characteristic for the arthropod subgroup Chelicerata would be the presence of

A) chelicerae.

B) an open circulatory system.

C) an exoskeleton.

D) chewing mandibles.

E) paired, segmented appendages.

Answer: A
Skill: Comprehension

46) Spiders, insects, crustaceans, and centipedes are all arthropods. If one accepts the Uniramia as a valid taxon, then which of these four kinds of organisms are most closely related?

A) spiders and insects

B) insects and crustaceans

C) crustaceans and centipedes

D) centipedes and insects

E) spiders and crustaceans

Answer: D
Skill: Comprehension

47) You find a small animal with eight legs crawling up your bedroom wall. Closer examination will reveal that this animal has

A) antennae.

B) no antennae.

C) chelicera.

D) A and C.

E) B and C.

Answer: E
Skill: Comprehension

48) Which of the following members of the class Arachnida are primarily parasitic?

A) spiders

B) scorpions

C) ticks and mites

D) trilobites

E) eurypterids

Answer: C
Skill: Knowledge

49) While working in your garden, you uncover an animal with many legs, mostly as two pairs per segment. The animal is probably a

A) millipede.

B) caterpillar.

C) centipede.

D) polychaete worm.

E) sow bug.

Answer: A
Skill: Application

50) Which of the following characteristics most likely explains why insects are so successful?

A) hemocoel

B) wings

C) jointed appendages

D) chewing mandibles

E) internal fertilization

Answer: B
Skill: Comprehension

51) A species of terrestrial animal is discovered with the following characteristics: exoskeleton; tracheal system for gas exchange; modified segmentation. A knowledgeable zoologist would predict that its adults probably also would have

A) eight legs.

B) a water vascular system.

C) a sessile lifestyle.

D) wings.

E) parapodia.

Answer: D
Skill: Application

52) The possession of two pairs of antennae will distinguish

A) spiders from insects.

B) crustaceans from insects.

C) millipedes from centipedes.

D) millipedes from insects.

E) insects from centipedes.

Answer: B
Skill: Knowledge

53) Which of the following is a characteristic of adult echinoderms?

A) secondary radial symmetry

B) spiral cleavage

C) incomplete digestive system

D) external skeleton

E) a lophophore

Answer: A
Skill: Knowledge

Answer the following questions with the choices below. Each choice may be used once, more than once, or not at all.

A. class Crinoidea (sea lilies)
B. class Asteroidea (sea stars)
C. class Ophiuroidea (brittle stars)
D. class Echinoidea (sea urchins and sand dollars)
E. class Holothuroidea (sea cucumbers)

54) They can evert their stomach through their mouth to feed.

Answer: B
Skill: Knowledge

55) They have distinct central disks and long, flexible arms.

Answer: C
Skill: Knowledge

56) They are elongated in the oral–aboral axis.

Answer: E
Skill: Knowledge

57) Their mouth is directed upward.

Answer: A
Skill: Knowledge

58) They have long, movable spines.

Answer: D
Skill: Knowledge

59) All of the following animal groups have evolved terrestrial life forms *except*

A) Mollusca.
B) Crustacea.
C) Echinodermata.
D) Arthropoda.
E) Vertebrata.

Answer: C
Skill: Knowledge

Below is a proposed phylogeny for major clades of the animal kingdom, with several of the lineages labeled (A–E). Responses may be used once, more than once, or not at all.

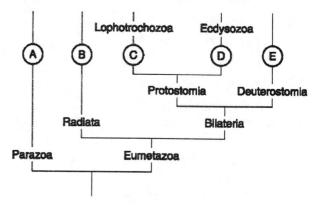

Figure 33.1

60) Which clade is known to possess cells that are similar in form and function to free–living protists thought to resemble the common ancestor of all animals?

A) A
B) B
C) C
D) D
E) E

Answer: A
Skill: Comprehension

61) Which is the diploblastic clade?

A) A
B) B
C) C
D) D
E) E

Answer: B
Skill: Comprehension

62) The ancestors of which clades possessed a true coelom?

A) A and B only

B) C and D only

C) C, D, and E

D) B, C, D, and E

E) all of these

Answer: C
Skill: Comprehension

63) The members of which clade have *no* regular body symmetry?

A) A

B) B

C) C

D) D

E) E

Answer: A
Skill: Comprehension

64) Which clades include both aquatic and terrestrial species?

A) C only

B) D only

C) E only

D) C and D

E) C, D, and E

Answer: E
Skill: Comprehension

65) To which clade do arthropods belong?

A) A

B) B

C) C

D) D

E) E

Answer: D
Skill: Comprehension

66) In which clade(s) do(does) the blastopore develop into the mouth?

A) C only

B) D only

C) E only

D) C and D

E) C, D, and E

Answer: D
Skill: Comprehension

67) Which clade(s) possess(es) species whose members display at least some degree of segmentation?

A) A only

B) B only

C) C and D

D) C, D, and E

E) all of these

Answer: D
Skill: Comprehension

68) To which clade do humans belong?

A) A

B) B

C) C

D) D

E) E

Answer: E
Skill: Comprehension

Media Activity Questions

1) Sponges are classified in the phylum
   A) Nematoda.
   B) Chordata.
   C) Cnidaria.
   D) Porifera.
   E) Platyhelminthes.

   Answer: D
   Topic: Web/CD Activity 33A

2) Which of these is true of flatworms?
   A) They have a body cavity.
   B) They have an exoskeleton composed of chitin.
   C) They are terrestrial organisms.
   D) They have a brain.
   E) They have a circulatory system.

   Answer: D
   Topic: Web/CD Activity 33A

3) Earthworms move by
   A) flying.
   B) running.
   C) swimming.
   D) hopping.
   E) creeping and burrowing.

   Answer: E
   Topic: Web/CD Activity 33A

4) Which of these features is a characteristic of grasshoppers?
   A) a gastrovascular cavity
   B) book lungs
   C) an exoskeleton
   D) a closed circulatory system
   E) nephridia

   Answer: C
   Topic: Web/CD Activity 33A

5) Which of these features is a characteristic of dogs?
   A) nephridia
   B) two tissue layers
   C) no body cavity
   D) segmentation
   E) an open circulatory system

   Answer: D
   Topic: Web/CD Activity 33A

Self-Quiz Questions

Answers to these questions also appear in the textbook.

1) Which two clades branch from the earliest Eumetazoan ancestor?

    A) Parazoa and Bilateria

    B) Parazoa and Radiata

    C) Radiata and Bilateria

    D) Protostomia and Deuterostomia

    E) Lophotrochozoa and Ecdysozoa

    Answer: C

2) Choose the phylum characterized by animals that have segmented bodies.

    A) Cnidaria

    B) Platyhelminthes

    C) Porifera

    D) Arthropoda

    E) Mollusca

    Answer: D

3) The water vascular system of echinoderms

    A) functions as a circulatory system that distributes nutrients to body cells.

    B) functions in locomotion, feeding, and gas exchange.

    C) is bilateral in organization, even though the adult animal has radial anatomy.

    D) moves water through the animal's body for suspension feeding.

    E) is analogous to the hydrostatic skeleton of annelids.

    Answer: B

4) Water movement through a sponge would follow what path?

    A) porocyte → spongocoel → osculum

    B) blastopore → gastrovascular cavity → protostome

    C) choanocyte → mesohyl → spongocoel

    D) porocyte → choanocyte → mesohyl

    E) colloblast → coelom → porocyte

    Answer: A

5) Although a diverse group, all cnidarians are characterized by

    A) a gastrovascular cavity.

    B) an alteration between a medusa and a polyp stage.

    C) some degree of cephalization.

    D) muscle tissue of mesodermal origin.

    E) the complete absence of asexual reproduction.

    Answer: A

6) A land snail, a clam, and an octopus all share

    A) a mantle.

    B) a radula.

    C) gills.

    D) embryonic torsion.

    E) distinct cephalization.

    Answer: A

7) Which of the following is *not* a characteristic of most members of the phylum Annelida?

    A) hydrostatic skeleton

    B) segmentation

    C) metanephridia

    D) pseudocoelom

    E) closed circulatory system

    Answer: D

8) Which of the following is *not* true of the chelicerates?

   A) They have antennae.

   B) Their body is divided into a cephalothorax and an abdomen.

   C) The horseshoe crab is one surviving marine member.

   D) They include ticks, scorpions, and spiders.

   E) Their anterior appendages are modified as pincers or fangs.

   Answer: A

9) Which of the following combinations of phylum and description is *incorrect*?

   A) Echinodermata—bilateral and radial symmetry, coelom from archenteron

   B) Nematoda—roundworms, pseudocoelomate

   C) Cnidaria—radial symmetry, polyp and medusa body forms

   D) Platyhelminthes—flatworms, gastrovascular cavity, acoelomate

   E) Porifera—gastrovascular cavity, coelom present

   Answer: E

10) Which of the following characteristics is probably *most* responsible for the incredible diversification of insects on land?

   A) segmentation

   B) exoskeleton

   C) tracheal system

   D) metamorphosis

   E) flight

   Answer: E

Chapter 34   Vertebrate Evolution and Diversity

1) Which of the following is *not* a shared characteristic of all chordates?

   A) pharyngeal slits

   B) post–anal tail

   C) notochord

   D) dorsal, hollow nerve cord

   E) four–chambered heart

   Answer: E
   Skill: Knowledge

2) What is one characteristic that separates chordates from all other animals?

   A) true coelom

   B) hollow dorsal nerve cord

   C) blastopore, which becomes the anus

   D) bilateral symmetry

   E) segmentation

   Answer: B
   Skill: Knowledge

3) Which of these are characteristics of all members of the Vertebrata during at least a portion of their development as individuals?

   A) a dorsal hollow nerve cord

   B) pharyngeal slits

   C) post–anal tail

   D) A and B only

   E) A, B, and C

   Answer: E
   Skill: Knowledge

4) Pharyngeal gill slits appear to have functioned first as

   A) the opening to the digestive system or mouth.

   B) suspension–feeding devices.

   C) components of the jaw.

   D) gill slits for respiration.

   E) portions of the inner ear.

   Answer: B
   Skill: Knowledge

5) Which of the following statements would be *least* acceptable to most zoologists?

   A) Modern cephalochordates are contemporaries of vertebrates, not their ancestors.

   B) The first fossils resembling cephalochordates appeared in the fossil record at least 550 million years ago.

   C) Recent work in molecular systematics supports the hypothesis that cephalochordates are the most recent common ancestor of all vertebrates.

   D) The modern cephalochordates are the immediate ancestors of the vertebrates.

   E) Cephalochordates display the same method of swimming as do fishes.

   Answer: D
   Skill: Comprehension

6) How does the study of urochordates and cephalochordates provide clues to the origin of vertebrates?

A) It proves the hypothesis that chordate segmentation evolved independently of segmentation in annelids and arthropods.

B) The ample supply of fossil evidence enables biologists to retrace the origin of urochordates and cephalochordates.

C) Molecular studies indicate that cephalochordates and vertebrates evolved from a common sessile ancestor by adaptative radiation.

D) It supports the idea that a small number of genes may regulate development and thus influence evolution.

E) It indicates that chordate characteristics are present in both the larval and adult forms of urochordates and cephalochordates.

Answer: D
Skill: Comprehension

7) Which chordate group is postulated to be *most* like the earliest chordates in appearance?

A) Cephalochordata

B) adult Urochordata

C) Amphibia

D) Reptilia

E) Chondrichthyes

Answer: A
Skill: Knowledge

8) Which of the following structures is (are) characteristic of vertebrates?

A) open circulation

B) pharyngeal slits

C) dorsal, hollow nerve cord

D) B and C

E) A, B, and C

Answer: D
Skill: Knowledge

9) A new species of aquatic chordate is discovered that closely resembles an ancient form. It has the following characteristics: external "armor" of bony plates; no paired fins; and a suspension–feeding mode of nutrition. In addition to these characteristics, it will probably have which of the following characteristics?

A) legs

B) no jaws

C) an amniotic egg

D) metamorphosis

E) endothermy

Answer: B
Skill: Application

10) In which class did jaws first occur?

A) Agnatha

B) Chondrichthyes

C) Osteichthyes

D) Ostracodermi

E) Placodermi

Answer: E
Skill: Knowledge

11) The jaws of vertebrates were derived by the modification of

A) scales of the lower lip.

B) one or more gill arches.

C) one or more gill slits.

D) one or more of the bones of the cranium.

E) one or more of the vertebrae.

Answer: B
Skill: Knowledge

For the following questions, match the characteristic or description with the class. Each choice may be used once, more than once, or not at all.

A. Amphibia
B. Aves
C. Chondrichthyes
D. Mammalia
E. Reptilia

12) most members have a cartilaginous endoskeleton

Answer: C
Skill: Knowledge

13) internal fertilization, amniotic egg, skin that resists drying, evolved in late Carboniferous

Answer: E
Skill: Knowledge

14) three major groups: egg-laying, pouched, and placental

Answer: D
Skill: Knowledge

15) includes salamanders, frogs, and toads

Answer: A
Skill: Knowledge

16) includes snakes, turtles, and lizards

Answer: E
Skill: Knowledge

17) What is a distinctive feature of the class Chondrichthyes?

A) an amniotic egg
B) unpaired fins
C) an acute sense of vision that includes the ability to distinguish colors
D) a cartilaginous endoskeleton
E) lack of jaws

Answer: D
Skill: Knowledge

18) Which one of the following has a two-chambered heart?

A) Osteichthyes
B) Amphibia
C) Reptilia
D) Aves
E) Mammalia

Answer: A
Skill: Knowledge

19) Which of these statements is a noted similarity between sharks and fishes?

A) The skin is typically covered by flattened bony scales.
B) They are able to exchange gases while stationary.
C) They are highly maneuverable due to their flexibility.
D) They have a lateral line that is sensitive to changes in water pressure.
E) A swim bladder helps control buoyancy.

Answer: D
Skill: Comprehension

20) Bony fishes (Osteichthyes) originally evolved

A) in response to a crisis that wiped out the Chondrichthyes.
B) directly from lampreys and hagfish.
C) early in the Cambrian.
D) directly from cephalochordates.
E) in freshwater environments.

Answer: E
Skill: Knowledge

21) What are the most abundant and diverse vertebrates?

A) bony fishes

B) birds

C) amphibians

D) reptiles

E) mammals

Answer: A
Skill: Knowledge

22) The class Osteichthyes is characterized by

A) a bony endoskeleton, operculum, and swim bladder.

B) a cartilaginous endoskeleton.

C) an amniotic egg.

D) teeth that are replaced regularly.

E) a three–chambered heart and lateral line system.

Answer: A
Skill: Knowledge

23) The swim bladder of modern bony fishes

A) was probably modified from simple lungs of freshwater fishes.

B) developed into lungs in saltwater fishes.

C) first appeared in sharks.

D) provides buoyancy but at a high energy cost.

E) Both C and D are correct.

Answer: A
Skill: Knowledge

24) The lobe–finned fishes appear to have given rise directly to

A) sharks.

B) amphibians.

C) stem reptiles.

D) freshwater ray–finned fishes.

E) placoderms.

Answer: B
Skill: Knowledge

25) The amniote egg first evolved in which of the following groups?

A) fish

B) birds

C) reptiles

D) amphibians

E) egg–laying mammals (monotremes)

Answer: C
Skill: Knowledge

26) In which vertebrates is fertilization exclusively internal?

A) Chondricthyes, Osteichthyes, and Mammalia

B) Amphibia, Mammalia, and Aves

C) Chondrichthyes, Osteichthyes, and Reptilia

D) Reptilia, Aves, and Mammalia

E) Mammalia, Aves, and Amphibia

Answer: D
Skill: Knowledge

27) Why do many reptiles thrive in desert environments?

A) Their bright coloration distracts enemies.

B) A large number of prey and a limited number of predators are available in the desert.

C) Their cartilaginous endoskeleton provides needed flexibility.

D) The protein keratin helps prevent dehydration.

E) They have an acute sense of sight.

Answer: D
Skill: Comprehension

28) Which of these is *not* considered an amniote?

A) amphibians

B) reptiles

C) birds

D) mammals

Answer: A
Skill: Knowledge

29) Why is the amniotic egg considered an important evolutionary breakthrough? It

A) has a shell that increases gas exchange.

B) allows incubation of eggs in a terrestrial environment.

C) prolongs embryonic development.

D) provides insulation to conserve heat energy.

E) permits internal fertilization to be replaced by external fertilization.

Answer: B
Skill: Comprehension

30) Why is the term *cold–blooded not* very appropriate for reptiles?

A) The keratinized skin of reptiles serves to insulate and conserve heat.

B) The scales of reptiles serve to dissipate excess body heat by reradiation to the environment.

C) Reptiles regulate body temperature by using various mechanisms such as behavioral adaptations.

D) Reptiles swallow large prey whole to provide enough food to generate body heat.

Answer: C
Skill: Comprehension

31) Which of the following is the era known as the "age of reptiles"?

A) Cenozoic

B) Mesozoic

C) Paleozoic

D) Precambrian

E) Cambrian

Answer: B
Skill: Knowledge

The next questions refer to Figure 34.1.

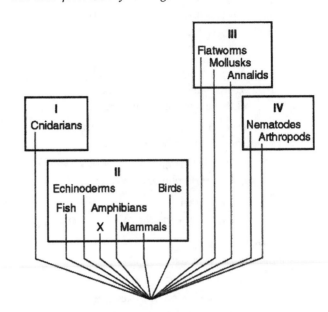

Figure 34.1

32) Which of the following is a *correct* description of the class represented by X?

A) endotherms; skin covered with feathers; embryo enclosed in protective membranes and a shell

B) endotherms; skin usually covered with hair; young nourished with milk secreted by the mother

C) ectotherms; skin usually covered with scales; embryo enclosed in protective membranes and a shell

D) ectotherms; naked skin; embryo not protected by membranes or a shell

E) ectotherms; bony skeleton; breathe by means of gills; usually have an air bladder

Answer: C
Skill: Application

33) Excluding the echinoderms, all the animals in group II have which of the following characteristics in common?

A) protostome embryo; coelom; radial symmetry; dorsal nerve cord

B) protostome embryo; no coelom; bilateral symmetry; ventral nerve cord

C) deuterostome embryo; coelom; bilateral symmetry; dorsal nerve cord

D) deuterostome embryo; pseudocoelom; asymmetry; ventral nerve cord

E) deuterostome embryo; no coelom; radial symmetry; dorsal nerve cord

Answer: C
Skill: Comprehension

34) Given the inclusion of birds as a separate entity in group II, what can be said about the taxonomic viewpoint represented by this phylogeny? It reflects the viewpoint of a

A) "lumper."

B) "splitter."

C) fixist, like Linnaeus.

D) catastrophist, like Cuvier.

E) supporter of punctuated equilibrium.

Answer: B
Skill: Comprehension

35) All organisms in group II *except* _____ are thought to share a common ancestor that possessed many of the same characteristics as the modern lancelet.

A) echinoderms

B) fish

C) amphibians

D) birds

E) mammals

Answer: A
Skill: Comprehension

36) What is true of the various terms that have been assembled together in group II? They are

A) all phyla.

B) all classes.

C) a mixture of phyla and classes.

D) a mixture of phyla, classes, and nontaxonomic terms.

E) a mixture of phyla, classes, nontaxonomic terms, and, if the lumpers get their way, of subclasses.

Answer: E
Skill: Comprehension

37) If bird DNA is more similar to crocodile DNA than turtle DNA is to crocodile DNA, then

A) birds should be included among the reptiles.

B) turtles and birds should be excluded from the reptiles.

C) the reptiles should be replaced by several new classes.

D) Each of the above represents a possible solution for taxonomists in the classification of amniotes.

Answer: D
Skill: Application

38) Which of these characteristics greatly added to vertebrate success in relatively dry environments?

A) the amniotic egg

B) the ability to maintain a constant body temperature

C) two pairs of appendages

D) claws

E) a four-chambered heart

Answer: A
Skill: Knowledge

39) From which of the following groups are snakes most likely descended?

 A) dinosaurs

 B) plesiosaurs

 C) lizards

 D) crocodiles

 E) synapsids

 Answer: C
 Skill: Knowledge

40) When did dinosaurs and pterosaurs become extinct?

 A) Cretaceous "crisis"

 B) Permian extinctions

 C) Devonian "disaster"

 D) Phanerozoic eon

 E) Hadeon eon

 Answer: A
 Skill: Knowledge

41) Which of the following are the only modern animals that may have descended directly from dinosaurs?

 A) lizards

 B) crocodiles

 C) snakes

 D) birds

 E) mammals

 Answer: D
 Skill: Knowledge

42) Examination of the fossils of *Archaeopteryx* reveals that, in common with modern birds, it had

 A) a long tail containing vertebrae.

 B) feathers.

 C) teeth.

 D) both A and B.

 E) A, B, and C.

 Answer: B
 Skill: Knowledge

43) What is the single unique characteristic that distinguishes modern birds from other modern animals?

 A) a hinged jaw

 B) feathers

 C) an amniotic egg

 D) a superb sense of sight

 E) a gizzard

 Answer: B
 Skill: Knowledge

44) Why is the discovery of the fossil *Archaeopteryx* significant? It supports the

 A) phylogenetic relatedness of birds and reptiles.

 B) contention that birds are much older than we originally thought.

 C) claim that mammals and dinosaurs coexisted.

 D) idea that the first birds were ratites.

 E) hypothesis that birds once had teeth.

 Answer: A
 Skill: Comprehension

45) Which of the following structures are possessed by birds only?

 A) enlarged pectoral muscles and a four-chambered heart

 B) light bones and a four-chambered heart

 C) feathers and carinate sternum

 D) a short tail and mammary glands

 E) a large brain and endothermy

 Answer: C
 Skill: Knowledge

46) Structures that are made of keratin include which of the following?
   I.   avian feathers
   II. reptilian scales
   III. mammalian hair
   A) I only
   B) III only
   C) I and II
   D) II and III
   E) I, II, and III
   Answer: E
   Skill: Knowledge

47) A sheet of muscle called the diaphragm is found in modern
   A) birds.
   B) mammals.
   C) reptiles.
   D) A and B.
   E) A, B, and C.
   Answer: D
   Skill: Knowledge

48) Which sequence of evolutionary relationships is consistent with the fossil record?
   A) reptiles → amphibians → birds → fishes
   B) reptiles → birds → fishes → amphibians
   C) fishes → amphibians → reptiles → birds
   D) fishes → birds → reptiles → amphibians
   E) reptiles → birds → amphibians → fishes
   Answer: C
   Skill: Comprehension

49) Which of the following statements about mammalian evolution is *correct*?
   A) Mammals evolved from reptilian stocks even earlier than birds.
   B) The first mammals were large predators like the saber-toothed tigers.
   C) Mammals did not coexist with the dominant dinosaurs.
   D) The early mammals were most similar to small, bipedal, ratite birds.
   E) Mammals evolved from the marsupials during the Pleistocene epoch.
   Answer: A
   Skill: Comprehension

The following questions refer to the phylogenetic tree shown in Figure 34.2.

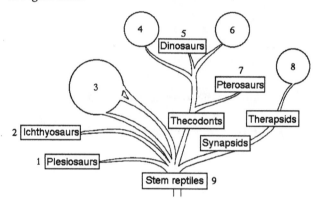

Figure 34.2

50) The organisms represented by 8 most likely are
   A) birds.
   B) all mammals.
   C) flying reptiles.
   D) modern reptiles.
   E) all mammals except humans.
   Answer: B
   Skill: Comprehension

51) Which organisms are represented by 6?

A) birds

B) all mammals

C) flying reptiles

D) modern reptiles

E) all mammals except humans

Answer: A
Skill: Comprehension

52) Which pair of numbers represents extinct reptiles that had returned to an aquatic life?

A) 1 and 2

B) 3 and 4

C) 5 and 7

D) 6 and 8

E) 7 and 9

Answer: A
Skill: Comprehension

53) Which pair of numbers most likely represents modern reptiles?

A) 1 and 2

B) 3 and 4

C) 5 and 7

D) 6 and 8

E) 7 and 9

Answer: B
Skill: Comprehension

54) Whose forelimbs are analogous to those of carinate birds and chiropterans?

A) 1   B) 2   C) 3   D) 7   E) 9

Answer: D
Skill: Comprehension

55) Whose DNA would have had the most sequence homologies with the early amphibians?

A) 5   B) 6   C) 7   D) 8   E) 9

Answer: E
Skill: Comprehension

56) Which pair of numbers includes modern endotherms?

A) 3 and 4

B) 4 and 5

C) 6 and 8

D) 3 and 8

E) 6 and 7

Answer: C
Skill: Comprehension

57) Differentiation of teeth is greatest in

A) sharks.

B) bony fishes.

C) amphibians.

D) reptiles.

E) mammals.

Answer: E
Skill: Knowledge

58) Which is *not* characteristic of all mammals?

A) a four-chambered heart that prevents mixing of oxygenated and deoxygenated blood

B) give birth to live young (viviparous)

C) have hair during at least some period of their life

D) have glands to produce milk to nourish their offspring

E) have a diaphragm to assist in ventilating the lungs

Answer: B
Skill: Knowledge

59) Which of these would a paleontologist be most likely to do in order to determine whether a fossil represents a reptile or a mammal?

A) Look for the presence of milk-producing glands.

B) Look for the mammalian characteristics of a four-chambered heart and a diaphragm.

C) Because animals are eutherians, look for evidence of a placenta.

D) Use molecular analysis to look for the protein keratin.

E) Examine the teeth.

Answer: E
Skill: Comprehension

60) Which of the following classifications would *not* apply to both dogs and humans?

A) class Mammalia

B) order Primata

C) phylum Chordata

D) kingdom Animalia

E) subphylum Vertebrata

Answer: B
Skill: Comprehension

61) Which of these is *not* a trend in primate evolution?

A) enhanced depth perception

B) well-developed claws for clinging to trees

C) a shoulder joint adapted to brachiation

D) reduction of the number of young to a single birth at one time

E) a long period of parental care of offspring

Answer: B
Skill: Knowledge

62) How are primates different from all other mammals?

A) placental embryonic development

B) hairy bodies

C) naked faces

D) ability to produce milk

E) opposable thumbs in many species

Answer: E
Skill: Comprehension

63) The adaptation to arboreal life by early human ancestors can explain, at least in part, all of the following human characteristics *except*

A) limber shoulder joints.

B) dexterous hands with opposable thumbs.

C) excellent eye-hand coordination.

D) enhanced depth perception.

E) reduced body hair.

Answer: E
Skill: Comprehension

64) Which of the following statements about human evolution is *correct*?

A) Modern humans are the only human species to have evolved on Earth.

B) Human ancestors were virtually identical to chimpanzees.

C) Human evolution occurred by anagenic change within an unbranched lineage.

D) The upright posture and enlarged brain of humans evolved simultaneously.

E) Fossil evidence indicates that early anthropoids were arboreal, were cat-sized, and lived about 35–45 million years ago.

Answer: E
Skill: Comprehension

65) All of the following are reptilian characteristics *except*

A) ectothermy.

B) brachiation.

C) amniote egg.

D) keratinized skin.

E) conical teeth that are relatively uniform in size.

Answer: B
Skill: Knowledge

66) Humans and apes are presently classified in the same category at all of the following levels *except*

A) class.

B) genus.

C) kingdom.

D) order.

E) phylum.

Answer: B
Skill: Comprehension

67) Which of the following are *not* considered apes?

A) gibbons

B) gorillas

C) rhesus monkeys

D) orangutans

E) chimpanzees

Answer: C
Skill: Knowledge

68) The most primitive hominid

A) may have hunted dinosaurs.

B) lived 1.2 million years ago.

C) closely resembled a chimpanzee.

D) walked on two legs.

E) had a relatively large brain.

Answer: D
Skill: Comprehension

69) With which of the following statements would a biologist be *most* inclined to agree?

A) Humans and apes represent divergent lines of evolution from a common ancestor.

B) Humans evolved from New World monkeys.

C) Humans have stopped evolving and now represent the pinnacle of evolution.

D) Apes evolved from humans.

E) Humans and apes are the result of disruptive selection in a species of gorilla.

Answer: A
Skill: Knowledge

70) The major and dramatic alteration of hominid anatomy was primarily the result of

A) an upright stance.

B) enlargement of the brain.

C) protracted postnatal development of offspring.

D) the development of speech.

E) the adoption of tool use.

Answer: A
Skill: Knowledge

71) Which of these statements about human evolution is *true*?

A) The ancestors of *Homo sapiens* were chimpanzees and other apes.

B) Human evolution has proceeded in an orderly fashion from an ancestral anthropoid to *Homo sapiens*.

C) The evolution of upright posture and enlarged brain occurred simultaneously.

D) Different features have evolved at different rates.

E) Mitochondrial DNA analysis indicates that modern humans are genetically very similar to Neanderthals.

Answer: D
Skill: Comprehension

72) Rank the following in terms of body size differences that are attributed to sexual dimorphism, from most dimorphic to least dimorphic.
1. *Homo sapiens*
2. Chimpanzees and bonobos
3. *Australopithecus afarensis*
4. Gorillas

A) 1, 2, 3, 4
B) 1, 3, 2, 4
C) 3, 2, 4, 1
D) 4, 2, 3, 1
E) 4, 3, 2, 1

Answer: E
Skill: Comprehension

73) Based on current evidence, which of the following statements *best* describes the evolution of humans?

A) Humans evolved from the chimpanzee.
B) Humans evolved in a single, orderly series of stages in which each stage became more advanced than its predecessor.
C) The various characteristics that we associate with humans evolved in unison over long periods of time.
D) Humans and apes diverged from a common ancestor about 5–7 million years ago.
E) Humans are more closely related to gorillas than to chimpanzees.

Answer: D
Skill: Knowledge

74) All of the following are true of *Homo erectus* *except*

A) fossils are limited to Africa.
B) on average, it had a larger brain than *Homo habilis*.
C) it had a level of sexual dimorphism similar to that of modern humans.
D) it was able to use tools.
E) it evolved after the rise of *Homo habilis*.

Answer: A
Skill: Knowledge

75) Why is it thought that the Neanderthals contributed little to the gene pool of modern humanity?

A) Recent studies of human and Neanderthal DNA show significant differences in base sequences.
B) The fossils found in the Neander Valley were a hoax and the "Neanderthals" never really existed.
C) Neanderthals had degenerated brain capacity and thus could not have contributed to human ancestry.
D) There is no evidence that Neanderthals were capable of walking upright or using tools.
E) Humans, the "naked apes," have nothing in common with the Neanderthals, the "hairy apes."

Answer: A
Skill: Comprehension

76) Which data provide the strongest support for the multiregional hypothesis concerning the evolution of modern humans?

A) The observation that Y chromosome sequences among modern human males lack significant amounts of divergence.
B) The observation that mtDNA sequences among modern humans lack significant amounts of divergence.
C) The lack of transitional fossils intermediate in morphology between European Neanderthals and European Cro-Magnons.
D) The possible existence of fossils intermediate in morphology between Asian *Homo erectus* and modern Asians.

Answer: D
Skill: Comprehension

Media Activity Questions

1) Collectively, jawless fish are referred to as

A) hagfish.

B) agnathans.

C) cephalochordates.

D) lampreys.

E) urochordates.

Answer: B
Topic: Web/CD Activity 34A

2) Tetrapods evolved from

A) reptiles.

B) sharks and rays.

C) tunicates.

D) bony fishes.

E) amphibians.

Answer: D
Topic: Web/CD Activity 34A

3) Which of these primates is a prosimian?

A) lemur

B) spider monkey

C) baboon

D) chimpanzee

E) gorilla

Answer: A
Topic: Web/CD Activity 34B

4) Which of these is an Old World monkey?

A) spider monkey

B) loris

C) baboon

D) human

E) chimpanzee

Answer: C
Topic: Web/CD Activity 34B

5) Which of these hominids evolved earliest?

A) *Australopithecus*

B) *Homo erectus*

C) *Ardipithecus*

D) *Homo habilis*

E) *Homo sapiens*

Answer: C
Topic: Web/CD Activity 34C

Self-Quiz Questions

Answers to these questions also appear in the textbook.

1) Vertebrates and tunicates may seem as different as two animal groups can be, yet they share
   A) jaws adapted for feeding.
   B) a high degree of cephalization.
   C) the formation of structures from the neural crest.
   D) an endoskeleton that includes a cranium.
   E) the presence of a notochord; a dorsal, hollow nerve cord; and pharyngeal slits.

   Answer: E

2) Some 530-million-year-old Chinese fossils resemble lancelets but have a more elaborate brain and a brain case (cranium). These fossils may represent
   A) the first chordate.
   B) a "missing link" between the urochordates and cephalochordates.
   C) an early vertebrate.
   D) a primitive bony fish.
   E) a non-tetrapod gnathostome.

   Answer: C

3) In addition to skeletal differences, cartilaginous fishes can be distinguished from bony fishes
   A) by the presence in bony fishes of a cranium.
   B) by the presence in bony fishes of a lateral line.
   C) by the presence in cartilaginous fishes of unpaired fins.
   D) by the absence in cartilaginous fishes of a swim bladder.
   E) by the absence in cartilaginous fishes of paired sensory organs.

   Answer: D

4) Mammals and extant birds share all of the following characteristics *except*
   A) endothermy.
   B) descent from reptiles.
   C) a dorsal, hollow nerve cord.
   D) teeth specialized for diverse diets.
   E) the ability of some species to fly.

   Answer: D

5) If you were to observe a monkey in a zoo, which characteristic would indicate a New World origin for that monkey species?
   A) distinct "seat pads"
   B) eyes close together on the front of the skull
   C) use of the tail to hang from a tree limb
   D) occasional bipedal walking
   E) downward orientation of the nostrils

   Answer: C

6) Which of the following could be considered to be the first tetrapod?
   A) sturdy-finned, shallow-water lungfishes whose appendages had skeletal supports similar to those of terrestrial vertebrates
   B) armored, jawed placoderms that had two sets of paired appendages
   C) early ray-finned fishes that developed bony skeletal supports in their paired fins
   D) salamanders of the order Urodela that had legs supported by a bony skeleton but moved with the same side-to-side bending typical of fishes
   E) an early terrestrial caecilian line whose legless condition had evolved secondarily

   Answer: A

7) Unlike eutherian (placental) mammals, both monotremes and marsupials

A) lack nipples.

B) have some embryonic development outside the mother's uterus.

C) lay eggs.

D) are found in Australia and Africa.

E) include only insectivores and herbivores.

Answer: B

8) Which of the following is *not* thought to be ancestral to humans?

A) a reptile

B) a bony fish

C) a primate

D) an amphibian

E) a bird

Answer: E

9) As humans diverged from other primates, which of the following most likely appeared first?

A) the development of technology

B) language

C) an erect stance

D) toolmaking

E) an enlarged brain

Answer: C

10) The multiregional and replacement hypotheses for the origin of modern humans agree that

A) *Homo erectus* had an African origin.

B) modern *Homo sapiens* originated only in Africa.

C) Neanderthals are the ancestors of modern humans in Europe.

D) Australopithecines migrated out of Africa.

E) North America had the first population of modern humans.

Answer: A

Chapter 35   Plant Structure and Growth

1) A friend has discovered a new plant and brings it to you to classify. The plant has the following characteristics: a fibrous root system; no petioles; parallel leaf veins; thick, lignified cell walls; and a vascular cambium. Which of the following best describes the new plant?

A) herbaceous dicot

B) woody dicot

C) woody monocot

D) herbaceous monocot

E) woody annual

Answer: C
Skill: Application

2) Most of the water and minerals taken up from the soil by a plant are absorbed by

A) taproots.

B) root hairs.

C) the thick parts of the roots near the base of the stem.

D) storage roots.

E) sections of the root that have secondary xylem.

Answer: B
Skill: Knowledge

3) An evolutionary adaptation that increases exposure of a plant to light in a dense forest is

A) closing of the stomates.

B) lateral buds.

C) apical dominance.

D) absence of petioles.

E) intercalary meristems.

Answer: C
Skill: Knowledge

4) A person working with plants may remove apical dominance by doing which of the following?

A) pruning

B) deep watering of the roots

C) fertilizing

D) transplanting

E) feeding the plants nutrients

Answer: A
Skill: Comprehension

The following question is based on parts of a growing primary root.

I.   root cap
II.   zone of elongation
III. zone of cell division
IV. zone of cell maturation
V.   apical meristem

5) Which of the following is the *correct* sequence from the growing tips of the root upward?

A) I, II, V, III, IV

B) III, V, I, II, IV

C) II, IV, I, V, III

D) IV, II, III, I, V

E) I, V, III, II, IV

Answer: E
Skill: Knowledge

6) What effect does "pinching back" a houseplant have on the plant?

A) increases apical dominance

B) inhibits the growth of lateral buds

C) produces a plant that will grow taller

D) produces a plant that will grow fuller

E) increases the flow of auxin down the shoot

Answer: D
Skill: Comprehension

7) Land plants are composed of all the following tissue types *except*

A) mesoderm.

B) epidermal.

C) meristematic.

D) vascular.

E) ground tissue.

Answer: A
Skill: Knowledge

8) Plant vascular tissue includes all of the following cell types *except*

A) vessel elements.

B) sieve cells.

C) tracheids.

D) companion cells.

E) cambium cells.

Answer: E
Skill: Knowledge

9) Which functional plant cells lack a nucleus?

A) xylem only

B) sieve–tube cell only

C) companion cells only

D) both companion and parenchyma cells

E) both xylem and sieve–tube cells

Answer: E
Skill: Knowledge

The questions below use the following answers. Each answer may be used once, more than once, or not at all.

A. *parenchyma*
B. *collenchyma*
C. *sclerenchyma*
D. *tracheids*
E. *sieve-tube cells*

10) long, thin, tapered cells with lignified cell walls that function in support and permit water flow through pits

Answer: D
Skill: Knowledge

11) living cells that lack nuclei and ribosomes; they transport sucrose and other organic nutrients

Answer: E
Skill: Knowledge

12) the least specialized plant cells, which serve general metabolic, synthetic, and storage functions

Answer: A
Skill: Knowledge

13) cells with unevenly thickened primary walls that support young parts of the plant

Answer: B
Skill: Knowledge

14) mature cells without protoplasts but with thick, lignified secondary walls that may form fibers

Answer: C
Skill: Knowledge

15) What is the largest organelle in most mature living plant cells?

A) chloroplast

B) nucleus

C) central vacuole

D) dictyosome (Golgi apparatus)

E) mitochondrion

Answer: C
Skill: Knowledge

16) Which of the following is *not* a characteristic of parenchyma cells?

A) thin primary walls

B) flexible primary walls

C) lack of specialization

D) lack of secondary walls

E) little metabolism and synthesis

Answer: E
Skill: Knowledge

17) Which of the following tissues is *incorrectly* matched with its characteristics?

 A) collenchyma—uniformly thick–walled supportive tissue

 B) epidermis—protective outer covering of plant body

 C) sclerenchyma—heavily lignified secondary walls

 D) meristematic tissue—undifferentiated tissue capable of cell division

 E) parenchyma—thin–walled, loosely packed, unspecialized cells

Answer: A
Skill: Knowledge

18) The fiber cells of plants are a type of

 A) parenchyma.

 B) sclerenchyma.

 C) collenchyma.

 D) meristematic cell.

 E) xylem cell.

Answer: B
Skill: Knowledge

19) The best word to describe the growth of plants in general is

 A) perennial.

 B) weedy.

 C) indeterminate.

 D) derivative.

 E) primary.

Answer: C
Skill: Comprehension

20) What is one result of an organism having meristems?

 A) a rapid change from juvenile to adult state

 B) a seasonal change in leaf morphology

 C) a rapid change from a vegetative state to a reproductive state

 D) indeterminate, life–long growth

 E) production of a fixed number of segments during growth

Answer: D
Skill: Comprehension

21) Which of the following are primary meristems?

 A) procambium

 B) protoderm

 C) ground meristem

 D) Only A and C are primary meristems.

 E) A, B, and C are primary meristems.

Answer: E
Skill: Knowledge

22) All of the following are primary meristems of a plant *except*

 A) epidermis only.

 B) protoderm only.

 C) ground meristem only.

 D) procambium only.

 E) both procambium and protoderm.

Answer: A
Skill: Knowledge

23) From which tissue does primary phloem in the root develop?

 A) protoderm

 B) endoderm

 C) procambium

 D) ground tissue

 E) vascular cambium

Answer: C
Skill: Knowledge

24) The vascular bundle in the shape of a single central cylinder in a root is called the

A) cortex.

B) stele.

C) endodermis.

D) periderm.

E) pith.

Answer: B
Skill: Knowledge

25) Which of the following is *incorrectly* paired with its structure and function?

A) sclerenchyma—supporting cells with thick secondary walls

B) periderm—protective coat of woody stems and roots

C) pericycle—waterproof ring of cells surrounding central stele in roots

D) mesophyll—parenchyma cells functioning in photosynthesis in leaves

E) ground meristem—primary meristem that produces ground tissue system

Answer: C
Skill: Knowledge

26) All of the following are derived from ground meristem *except*

A) collenchyma.

B) sclerenchyma.

C) parenchyma.

D) sclereids.

E) phloem.

Answer: E
Skill: Knowledge

The following questions are based on the drawing of root or stem cross sections shown in Figure 35.1.

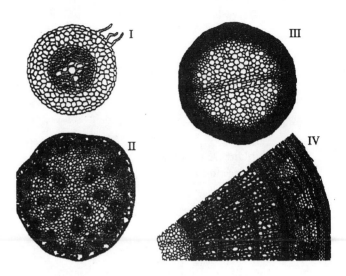

Figure 35.1

27) Endodermis is present in

A) I only.

B) II only.

C) III only.

D) IV only.

E) both I and III.

Answer: A
Skill: Comprehension

28) A woody dicot is represented by

A) I only.

B) II only.

C) III only.

D) IV only.

E) both I and III.

Answer: D
Skill: Comprehension

29) A monocot stem is represented by
   A) I only.
   B) II only.
   C) III only.
   D) IV only.
   E) both I and III.

   Answer: B
   Skill: Comprehension

30) A plant that is at least three years old is represented by
   A) I only.
   B) II only.
   C) III only.
   D) IV only.
   E) both I and III.

   Answer: D
   Skill: Comprehension

31) In a root, the ground meristem differentiates and forms the
   A) epidermis only.
   B) cork cambium only.
   C) cortex only.
   D) procambium only.
   E) epidermis and procambium.

   Answer: C
   Skill: Comprehension

32) Which of the following root tissues gives rise to secondary roots?
   A) endodermis
   B) phloem
   C) cortex
   D) epidermis
   E) pericycle

   Answer: E
   Skill: Knowledge

33) One important difference between the anatomy of roots and the anatomy of leaves is that
   A) only leaves have phloem and only roots have xylem.
   B) the cells of roots have cell walls that are lacking in leaf cells.
   C) a waxy cuticle covers leaves but is absent in roots.
   D) vascular tissue is found in roots but is absent from leaves.
   E) leaves have epidermal tissue but roots do not.

   Answer: C
   Skill: Comprehension

34) You are studying a plant from the arid southwestern United States. Which of the following adaptations is *least* likely to have evolved in response to water shortages?
   A) closing the stomata during the hottest time of the day
   B) development of large leaf surfaces to absorb water
   C) formation of a fibrous root system spread over a large area
   D) mycorrhizae associated with the root system
   E) a thick waxy cuticle on the epidermis

   Answer: B
   Skill: Application

35) Which of the following is *not* a fundamental difference between monocot and dicot morphology and anatomy? Monocots have _____, while dicots have _____.
   A) one cotyledon; two cotyledons
   B) parallel veins; net veins
   C) fibrous roots; taproots
   D) vascular bundles in a ring; vascular bundles scattered throughout the stem

   Answer: D
   Skill: Knowledge

36) The photosynthetic cells in the interior of a leaf are what kind of cells?

A) parenchyma

B) collenchyma

C) sclerenchyma

D) phloem

E) endodermis

Answer: A
Skill: Knowledge

37) A student examining leaf cross sections under a microscope finds many loosely packed cells with relatively thin cell walls. The cells have numerous chloroplasts. What cells are these?

A) parenchyma

B) xylem

C) endodermis

D) collenchyma

E) sclerenchyma

Answer: A
Skill: Application

38) Pores on the leaf surface that function in gas exchange are called

A) hairs.

B) xylem cells.

C) phloem cells.

D) stomata.

E) sclereids.

Answer: D
Skill: Knowledge

39) Which of the following is a *true* statement about growth in plants?

A) Only primary growth is localized at meristems.

B) Some plants lack secondary growth.

C) Only stems have secondary growth.

D) Only secondary growth produces reproductive structures.

E) Monocots have only primary growth and dicots have only secondary growth.

Answer: B
Skill: Comprehension

40) All of the following cell types are correctly matched with their functions *except*

A) mesophyll—photosynthesis.

B) guard cell—regulation of transpiration.

C) sieve-tube cell—translocation.

D) vessel element—water transport.

E) companion cell—formation of secondary xylem and phloem.

Answer: E
Skill: Comprehension

41) As a youngster, you drive a nail in the trunk of a young tree that is 3 meters tall. The nail is about 1.5 meters from the ground. Fifteen years later, you return and discover the tree has grown to a height of 30 meters. The nail is now _____ meters above the ground.

A) 0.5

B) 1.5

C) 3.0

D) 15.0

E) 28.5

Answer: B
Skill: Application

42) Which of the following is *true* about secondary growth in plants?

   A) Flowers may have secondary growth.

   B) Secondary growth is a common feature of eudicot leaves.

   C) Secondary growth is produced by both the vascular cambium and the cork cambium.

   D) Primary growth and secondary growth alternate in the life cycle of a plant.

   E) Plants with secondary growth are typically the smallest ones in an ecosystem.

   Answer: C
   Skill: Knowledge

43) What tissue makes up most of the wood of a tree?

   A) primary xylem

   B) secondary xylem

   C) secondary phloem

   D) mesophyll cells

   E) vascular cambium

   Answer: B
   Skill: Knowledge

44) The vascular system of a three-year-old dicot stem consists of

   A) 3 rings of xylem and 3 of phloem.

   B) 2 rings of xylem and 2 of phloem.

   C) 2 rings of xylem and 1 of phloem.

   D) 2 rings of xylem and 3 of phloem.

   E) 3 rings of xylem and 1 of phloem.

   Answer: E
   Skill: Comprehension

45) If you were able to walk into an opening cut into the center of a large redwood tree, when you exit from the middle of the trunk (stem) outward, you would cross, in order,

   A) the annual rings, phloem, and bark.

   B) the newest xylem, oldest phloem, and periderm.

   C) the vascular cambium, oldest xylem, and newest xylem.

   D) the secondary xylem, secondary phloem, and vascular cambium.

   E) the summer wood, bark, and phloem.

   Answer: A
   Skill: Application

46) Which of the following is *true* of bark?

   A) It is composed of phloem plus periderm.

   B) It is associated with annuals but not perennials.

   C) It is formed by the apical meristems.

   D) It has no identifiable function in trees.

   E) It forms annual rings in deciduous trees.

   Answer: A
   Skill: Knowledge

47) Which of the following are components of bark?

   A) secondary phloem

   B) cork

   C) cork cambium

   D) A and B only are components of bark.

   E) A, B, and C are components of bark.

   Answer: E
   Skill: Knowledge

48) George Washington completely removed the bark from around the base of a cherry tree but was stopped by his father before cutting the tree down. It was noticed that the leaves retained their normal appearance for several weeks, but that the tree eventually died. The tissue(s) that George left functional was (were) the

A) phloem.

B) xylem.

C) cork cambium.

D) cortex.

E) companion and sieve cells.

Answer: B
Skill: Application

49) Additional vascular tissue produced as secondary growth in a root originates from which cells?

A) vascular cambium

B) apical meristem

C) endodermis

D) phloem

E) xylem

Answer: A
Skill: Comprehension

50) A leaf primordium is initiatied as a small mound of tissue on the flank of a dome–shaped shoot apical meristem. The earliest physical evidence of the site of a newly forming leaf primordium would be

A) development of chloroplasts in a surface cell of the shoot apical meristem.

B) cell division in the shoot apical meristem with the newly forming walls perpendicular to the surface of the meristem.

C) pre-prophase bands parallel to the surface of the meristem in subsurface cells of the shoot apical meristem.

D) elongation of epidermal cells perpendicular to the surface of the shoot apical meristem.

E) formation of stomata in the epidermal layer of the shoot apical meristem.

Answer: C
Skill: Comprehension

51) A short branch was cut into three segments as shown in Figure 35.2 to root some cuttings. Roots will form at which position(s)?

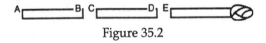

Figure 35.2

A) A only

B) A and B

C) A, B, and C

D) A, C, and E

E) A, B, C, D, and E

Answer: D
Skill: Application

52) While studying the plant *Arabidopsis*, a botanist finds that an RNA probe produces colored spots in the sepals of the plant. From this information, which information can be inferred?

   A) The differently colored plants will attract different pollinating insects.

   B) The RNA probe is transported only to certain tissues.

   C) The colored regions were caused by mutations that took place in the sepals.

   D) The RNA probe is specific to a gene active in sepals.

   E) More research needs to be done on the sepals of *Arabidopsis*.

   Answer: D
   Skill: Application

53) Before differentiation can begin during the processes of plant cell and tissue culture, parenchyma cells from the source tissue must

   A) differentiate into procambium.

   B) undergo dedifferentiation.

   C) increase the number of chromosomes in their nuclei.

   D) enzymatically digest their primary cell walls.

   E) establish a new polarity in their cytoplasm.

   Answer: B
   Skill: Comprehension

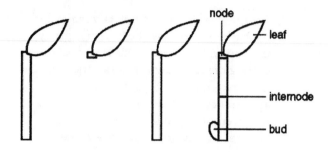

Figure 35.3
Sectors of corn plants

54) Each of the patterns indicated in Figure 35.3 above occurred as a sector during clonal analysis of several corn plants. Based on this data, a growth module in corn must consist of

   A) a leaf only.

   B) a leaf and its associated node.

   C) a leaf, its associated node, and the internode below.

   D) a leaf, its associated node, the internode below, and the bud below the leaf.

   E) a leaf and its associated node and axillary bud, and the internode below the leaf.

   Answer: D
   Skill: Comprehension

55) Silver–dollar eucalyptus has rounded juvenile leaves but lance–shaped mature leaves. A plant propagator wants to produce more plants of the juvenile form, but has only a single older plant. Where should the cuttings come from?

A) only the terminal stem containing the main shoot apical meristem because this is the most recently formed tissue of the shoot

B) the youngest, most recently formed lateral branches because they are the most immature branches

C) older, more basal branches because they were formed during the juvenile growth phase

D) either A or B

E) none of the above. As soon as a plant becomes mature, all of the branches will be mature.

Answer: C
Skill: Application

56) A feeding insect destroys only the very central portion of a developing flower bud. Which of the following statements is most likely to be true?

A) None of the "A," "B," or "C" floral organ identifying genes will "turn on" as floral development proceeds.

B) Petals formed subsequent to the insect attack will be disfigured.

C) Stamens formed subsequent to the insect attack will be sterile.

D) Carpels will not form in the developing flower.

E) Only the "A" floral organ identifying gene will be affected.

Answer: D
Skill: Comprehension

Media Activity Questions

1) In dicot stems the vascular bundles are usually arranged

   A) in parallel lines.

   B) complexly.

   C) in multiples of three.

   D) in a ring.

   E) in multiples of four.

   Answer: D
   Topic: Web/CD Activity 35A

2) In monocot stems the vascular bundles are usually arranged

   A) in parallel lines.

   B) complexly.

   C) in multiples of three.

   D) in a ring.

   E) in multiples of four.

   Answer: B
   Topic: Web/CD Activity 35A

3) Chloroplasts are found in

   A) xylem.

   B) cuticle.

   C) spongy parenchyma.

   D) stomata.

   E) phloem.

   Answer: C
   Topic: Web/CD Activity 35A

4) Most monocots do not

   A) have chloroplasts.

   B) exhibit primary growth.

   C) exhibit secondary growth.

   D) have vascular tissue.

   E) have stems.

   Answer: C
   Topic: Web/CD Activity 35A and 35B

5) _____ provide cells for primary growth.

   A) Lateral meristems

   B) Apical meristems

   C) Vascular cambium

   D) Cork cambium

   E) Xylem

   Answer: B
   Topic: Web/CD Activity 35B

Self-Quiz Questions

Answers to these questions also appear in the textbook.

1) Which structure is *incorrectly* paired with its tissue system?
   - A) root hair—dermal tissue
   - B) palisade parenchyma—ground tissue
   - C) guard cell—dermal tissue
   - D) companion cell—ground tissue
   - E) tracheid—vascular tissue

   Answer: D

2) A vessel cell would likely lose its protoplast in which zone of growth in a root?
   - A) zone of cell division
   - B) zone of elongation
   - C) zone of maturation
   - D) root cap
   - E) quiescent center

   Answer: C

3) Wood consists of
   - A) bark.
   - B) periderm.
   - C) secondary xylem.
   - D) secondary phloem.
   - E) cork.

   Answer: C

4) Which of the following is *not* part of an older tree's bark?
   - A) cork
   - B) cork cambium
   - C) lenticels
   - D) secondary xylem
   - E) secondary phloem

   Answer: D

5) The phase change of an apical meristem from the juvenile to mature vegetative phase is often signaled by
   - A) a change in the morphology of the leaves that are produced.
   - B) the initiation of secondary growth.
   - C) the transcription of different organ-identity genes within primordia on the flanks of the shoot tip.
   - D) a change in the orientation of both the preprophase bands and cortical microtubules within dividing cells of the lateral meristems.
   - E) the activation of floral meristem identity genes.

   Answer: A

6) A tree will eventually die if it is girdled, meaning that a ringlike cut has been made all the way around the trunk to a depth just below the bark. The cause of death is mainly
   - A) destruction of the procambium.
   - B) destruction of axillary buds.
   - C) the killing of bark cells.
   - D) destruction of the cork cambium, phloem, and vascular cambium.
   - E) destruction of the plant's ability to continue primary growth.

   Answer: D

7) Which of the following cell types is least likely to have a secondary wall?
   - A) sclerenchyma cell
   - B) parenchyma cell
   - C) fiber cell
   - D) tracheid
   - E) sclereid

   Answer: B

8) _____ is to primary xylem as vascular cambium is to _____.

A) Primary phloem; secondary xylem

B) Tracheid; vessel cell

C) Procambium; secondary xylem

D) Apical meristem; lateral meristem

E) Stele; primary phloem

Answer: C

9) The type of mature cell that a particular embryonic plant cell will become appears to be determined mainly by

A) the selective loss of genes.

B) the cell's final position in a developing organ.

C) the cell's pattern of migration.

D) the cell's age.

E) the cell's particular meristematic lineage.

Answer: B

10) Based on the hypothesis presented in Figures 21.20 and 35.36 in your textbook, predict the floral morphology of a mutant lacking activity of the B genes.

A) carpel–petal–petal–carpel

B) petal–petal–petal–petal

C) sepal–sepal–carpel–carpel

D) sepal–carpel–carpel–sepal

E) carpel–carpel–carpel–carpel

Answer: C

Chapter 36   Transport in Plants

1) Which of the following would be *least* likely to affect osmosis in plants?

A) proton pumps in the membrane

B) a difference in solute concentrations

C) receptor proteins in the membrane

D) aquaporins

E) water potential

Answer: C
Skill: Comprehension

2) Active transport involves all of the following *except*

A) slow movement through the lipid bilayer of a membrane.

B) pumping of solutes across the membrane.

C) hydrolysis of ATP.

D) transport of solute against a concentration gradient.

E) a specific transport protein in the membrane.

Answer: A
Skill: Comprehension

3) Like many plant processes, transport of various materials in plants at the cellular level nearly always requires all of the following *except*

A) a proton gradient.

B) ATP.

C) specific membrane proteins.

D) active transport.

E) xylem.

Answer: C
Skill: Comprehension

4) Which of the following is *not* a function of the plasma membrane proton pump?

A) hydrolyzes ATP

B) produces a proton gradient

C) generates a membrane potential

D) equalizes the charge on each side of a membrane

E) stores potential energy on one side of a membrane

Answer: D
Skill: Comprehension

5) A unifying principle of cellular energetics is

A) active transport.

B) chemiosmosis.

C) ATP hydrolysis.

D) water potential.

E) source–sink relationships.

Answer: B
Skill: Knowledge

6) Which of the following is an example of osmosis?

A) flow of water out of a cell

B) pumping of water into a cell

C) flow of water between cells

D) Both A and B are true of osmosis.

E) Both A and C are true of osmosis.

Answer: E
Skill: Comprehension

7) The amount and direction of movement of water in plants can *always* be predicted by measuring

 A) air pressure.

 B) rainfall.

 C) proton gradients.

 D) dissolved solutes.

 E) water potential (Ψ).

Answer: E
Skill: Comprehension

8) Which of the following is *true* concerning the water potential of a plant cell?

 A) It is higher than that of air.

 B) It is equal to zero when the cell is in pure water and is turgid.

 C) It is equal to 0.23 MPa.

 D) It becomes higher when K^+ ions are actively moved into the cell.

 E) It becomes lower after the uptake of water by osmosis.

Answer: B
Skill: Knowledge

9) Your laboratory partner has an open beaker of pure water. By definition, the water potential (Ψ) of this water is

 A) not meaningful, because it is an open beaker and not plant tissue.

 B) a negative number set by the volume of the beaker.

 C) a positive number set by the volume of the beaker.

 D) equal to the atmospheric pressure.

 E) zero.

Answer: E
Skill: Comprehension

10) The main mechanism(s) determining the direction of short–distance transport within a potato tuber is (are)

 A) diffusion due to concentration differences and bulk flow due to pressure differences.

 B) pressure flow through the phloem.

 C) active transport due to the hydrolysis of ATP and ion transport into the tuber cells.

 D) determined by the structure and function of the tonoplast of the tuber cells.

 E) not affected by temperature and pressure.

Answer: A
Skill: Comprehension

11) Which of the following would have an effect on water potential (Ψ) in plants?

 A) air pressure

 B) water–attracting matrices

 C) dissolved solutes

 D) A and C only would have an effect.

 E) A, B, and C would have an effect.

Answer: E
Skill: Comprehension

12) If $\Psi_P = 0.3$ MPa and $\Psi_S = -0.45$ MPa, the resulting Ψ is

 A) +0.75 MPa.

 B) –0.75 MPa.

 C) –0.15 MPa.

 D) +0.15 MPa.

 E) impossible to calculate with this information.

Answer: C
Skill: Application

13) The value for Ψ in root tissue was found to be –0.15 MPa. If you take the root tissue and place it in a 0.1 M solution of sucrose (Ψ = –0.23), net water flow would

A) be from the tissue into the sucrose solution.

B) be from the sucrose solution into the tissue.

C) be in both directions and the concentrations would remain equal.

D) occur only as ATP was hydrolyzed in the tissue.

E) be impossible to determine from the values given here.

Answer: A
Skill: Application

14) Compared to a cell with few aquaporins in its membrane, a cell containing many aquaporins will

A) have a faster rate of osmosis.

B) have a lower water potential.

C) have a higher water potential.

D) have a faster rate of active transport.

E) be less turgid.

Answer: A
Skill: Application

15) Some botanists argue that the entire plant should be considered as a single unit rather than a composite of many individual cells. Which of the following cellular structures *cannot* be used to argue this view?

A) cell wall

B) cell membrane

C) cytosol

D) tonoplast

E) symplast

Answer: D
Skill: Comprehension

16) Which of the following is a structure that might suggest that plants are a single unit rather than many individual cells?

A) apoplast

B) stomata

C) root hairs

D) mycorrhizae

E) plasmodesmata

Answer: E
Skill: Comprehension

17) All of the following statements about xylem are correct *except:*

A) Xylem conducts material upward.

B) Xylem conduction occurs within dead cells.

C) Xylem transports mainly sugars and amino acids.

D) Xylem has a lower water potential than the soil does.

E) No energy input from the plant is required for xylem transport.

Answer: C
Skill: Knowledge

18) Which of the following would likely *not* contribute to the surface area available for water absorption from the soil by a plant root system?

A) root hairs

B) endodermis

C) mycorrhizae

D) fungi associated with the roots

E) fibrous arrangement of the roots

Answer: B
Skill: Comprehension

19) Root hairs are most important to a plant because they

A) anchor a plant in the soil.

B) store starches.

C) increase the surface area for absorption.

D) provide a habitat for nitrogen-fixing bacteria.

E) contain xylem tissue.

Answer: C
Skill: Knowledge

20) Plants use proton pumps to do which of the following?

A) establish ATP gradients

B) acquire minerals from the soil

C) pressurize xylem transport

D) eliminate excess electrons

E) Both A and D are correct.

Answer: B
Skill: Comprehension

21) In plant roots, the Casparian strip is *correctly* described by which of the following?

A) It is located in the walls between endodermal cells and cortex cells.

B) It provides energy for the active transport of minerals into the stele from the cortex.

C) It ensures that all minerals are absorbed from the soil in equal amounts.

D) It ensures that all water and dissolved substances must pass through a cell before entering the stele.

E) It provides increased surface area for the absorption of mineral nutrients.

Answer: D
Skill: Comprehension

22) All of the following describe an important transport mechanism in plants *except*

A) cohesion–tension–transpiration.

B) osmosis.

C) endodermis Casparian strip.

D) active transport.

E) bulk flow from source to sink.

Answer: C
Skill: Comprehension

23) Water entering the stele of the root from the cortex must pass through the

A) Casparian strip.

B) phloem.

C) endodermal cytoplasm.

D) epidermis.

E) xylem.

Answer: C
Skill: Comprehension

24) A water molecule could move all the way through a plant from soil to root to leaf to air and pass through a living cell only once. This living cell would be a part of which structure?

A) the Casparian strip

B) a guard cell

C) the root epidermis

D) the endodermis

E) the root cortex

Answer: D
Skill: Comprehension

25) The following factors may sometimes play a role in the movement of sap through xylem. Which one depends upon the direct expenditure of ATP by the plant?

A) capillarity of water within the xylem

B) evaporation of water from leaves

C) cohesion among water molecules

D) concentration of ions in the symplast

E) bulk flow of water in the root apoplast

Answer: D
Skill: Knowledge

26) Which of the following factors that sometimes play a role in the rise of sap in the xylem depends on the expenditure of energy by the plant?
   A) secretion of ions into the stele of the root
   B) cohesion of water molecules due to hydrogen bonding
   C) transpiration of water from the leaves
   D) adhesion of water to xylem tracheids and vessels
   E) diffusion of water into the root hairs

Answer: A
Skill: Comprehension

27) What is the main cause of guttation in plants?
   A) root pressure
   B) transpiration
   C) pressure flow in phloem
   D) plant injury
   E) condensation of atmospheric water

Answer: A
Skill: Knowledge

28) One is most likely to see guttation in small plants when the
   A) transpiration rates are high.
   B) root pressure exceeds transpiration pull.
   C) preceding evening was hot, windy, and dry.
   D) water potential in the stele of the root is high.
   E) roots are not absorbing minerals from the soil.

Answer: B
Skill: Knowledge

29) Most of the water within xylem vessels moves toward the top of a tree as a result of
   A) active transport of ions into the stele.
   B) atmospheric pressure on roots.
   C) evaporation of water through stoma.
   D) the force of root pressure.
   E) osmosis in the root.

Answer: C
Skill: Knowledge

30) In which plant cell or tissue would the pressure component of water potential most often be negative?
   A) leaf mesophyll cell
   B) stem xylem
   C) stem phloem
   D) root cortex cell
   E) root epidermis

Answer: B
Skill: Comprehension

31) Water potential is generally most negative in which of the following parts of a plant?
   A) mesophyll cells of the leaf
   B) xylem vessels in leaves
   C) xylem vessels in roots
   D) cells of the root cortex
   E) root hairs

Answer: A
Skill: Comprehension

32) Which of the following has the *lowest* (most negative) water potential?
   A) soil
   B) root xylem
   C) trunk xylem
   D) leaf cell walls
   E) leaf air spaces

Answer: E
Skill: Comprehension

33) Which of the following is responsible for the cohesion of water molecules?

A) hydrogen bonds between the oxygen atoms of a water molecule and cellulose in a vessel cell

B) covalent bonds between the hydrogen atoms of two adjacent water molecules

C) hydrogen bonds between the oxygen atom of one water molecule and a hydrogen atom of another water molecule

D) covalent bonds between the oxygen atom of one water molecule and a hydrogen atom of another water molecule

E) Cohesion has nothing to do with the bonding but is the result of the tight packing of the water molecules in the xylem column.

Answer: C
Skill: Comprehension

34) Transpiration in plants requires all of the following *except*

A) adhesion of water molecules to cellulose.

B) cohesion between water molecules.

C) evaporation of water molecules.

D) active transport through xylem cells.

E) transport through tracheids.

Answer: D
Skill: Comprehension

35) Which of the following statements about transport in plants is *false*?

A) Weak bonding between water molecules and the walls of xylem vessels or tracheids helps support the columns of water in the xylem.

B) Hydrogen bonding between water molecules, which results in the high cohesion of the water, is essential for the rise of water in tall trees.

C) Although some angiosperm plants develop considerable root pressure, this is not sufficient to raise water to the tops of tall trees.

D) Most plant physiologists now agree that the pull from the top of the plant resulting from transpiration is sufficient, when combined with the cohesion of water, to explain the rise of water in the xylem in even the tallest trees.

E) Gymnosperms can sometimes develop especially high root pressure, which may account for the rise of water in tall pine trees without transpiration pull.

Answer: E
Skill: Comprehension

36) Active transport would be *least* important in the normal functioning of which of the following plant tissue types?

A) leaf transfer cells

B) stem xylem

C) root endodermis

D) leaf mesophyll

E) root phloem

Answer: B
Skill: Comprehension

37) Which of the following statements is *false* concerning the xylem?

A) Xylem tracheids and vessels fulfill their vital function only after their death.

B) The cell walls of the tracheids are greatly strengthened with cellulose fibrils forming thickened rings or spirals.

C) Water molecules are transpired from the cells of the leaves and replaced by water molecules in the xylem pulled up from the roots due to the cohesion of water molecules.

D) Movement of materials is by mass flow; materials move owing to a turgor pressure gradient from "source" to "sink."

E) In the morning, sap in the xylem begins to move first in the twigs of the upper portion of the tree, and later in the lower trunk.

Answer: D
Skill: Comprehension

38) What provides the energy for water transport upward in the xylem?

A) ATP

B) sucrose

C) the sun

D) proton gradients

E) cohesion

Answer: C
Skill: Comprehension

39) Water rises in plants primarily by the cohesion-tension model. All of the following are *true* about this model *except*:

A) Water loss (transpiration) is the driving force for water movement.

B) The "tension" of this model represents the excitability of the xylem cells.

C) Cohesion represents the tendency for water molecules to stick together by hydrogen bonds.

D) The physical forces in the capillary-sized xylem cells make it easier to overcome gravity.

E) The water potential of the air is more negative than the xylem.

Answer: B
Skill: Comprehension

40) Assume that a particular chemical interferes with the establishment and maintenance of proton gradients across the membranes of plant cells. All of the following processes would be directly affected by this chemical *except*

A) photosynthesis.

B) phloem loading.

C) xylem transport.

D) cellular respiration.

E) stomatal opening.

Answer: C
Skill: Application

41) Guard cells do which of the following?

A) protect the endodermis

B) accumulate K^+ ions and close the stomates

C) contain chloroplasts that import K^+ ions directly into the cells

D) guard against mineral loss through the stomates

E) help balance the photosynthesis–transpiration compromise

Answer: E
Skill: Knowledge

42) All of the following normally enter the plant through the roots *except*

A) carbon dioxide.

B) nitrogen.

C) potassium.

D) water.

E) calcium.

Answer: A
Skill: Comprehension

43) Photosynthesis begins to decline when leaves wilt because

A) flaccid cells are incapable of photosynthesis.

B) CO_2 accumulates in the leaves and inhibits photosynthesis.

C) there is insufficient water for photolysis during light reactions.

D) stomata close, preventing CO_2 entry into the leaf.

E) the chlorophyll of flaccid cells cannot absorb light.

Answer: D
Skill: Application

44) The water lost during transpiration is an unfortunate side effect of the plant's exchange of gases. However, the plant derives some benefit from this water loss in the form of

A) evaporative cooling.

B) mineral transport.

C) increased turgor.

D) A and B.

E) A, B, and C.

Answer: D
Skill: Knowledge

45) Ignoring all other factors, what kind of day would result in the fastest delivery of water and minerals to the leaves of a tree?

A) cool, dry day

B) warm, dry day

C) warm, humid day

D) cool, humid day

E) very hot, dry, windy day

Answer: B
Skill: Comprehension

46) If the guard cells and surrounding epidermal cells in a plant are deficient in potassium ions, all of the following would occur *except*

A) photosynthesis would decrease.

B) roots would take up less water.

C) phloem transport rates would decrease.

D) leaf temperatures would decrease.

E) stomata would be closed.

Answer: D
Skill: Application

47) The opening of stomates is thought to involve

A) an increase in the osmotic concentration of the guard cells.

B) a decrease in the osmotic concentration of the stoma.

C) active transport of water out of the guard cells.

D) decreased turgor pressure in guard cells.

E) movement of K^+ out of guard cells.

Answer: A
Skill: Knowledge

48) Which of the following experimental procedures would most likely reduce transpiration while allowing the normal growth of a plant?

A) subjecting the leaves of the plant to a partial vacuum

B) increasing the level of carbon dioxide around the plant

C) putting the plant in drier soil

D) decreasing the relative humidity around the plant

E) injecting potassium ions into the guard cells of the plant

Answer: B
Skill: Application

49) All of the following are adaptations that help reduce water loss from a plant *except*

A) transpiration.

B) sunken stomates.

C) C_4 photosynthesis.

D) small, thick leaves.

E) crassulacean acid metabolism.

Answer: A
Skill: Knowledge

50) Which of the following best explains why no tall trees seem to be CAM plants?

A) They would be unable to move water and minerals to the top of the plant during the day.

B) They would be unable to supply sufficient sucrose for active transport of minerals into the roots during the day or night.

C) Transpiration occurs only at night, and this would cause a highly negative Ψ in the roots of a tall plant during the day.

D) Since the stomates are closed in the leaves, the Casparian strip is closed in the endodermis of the root.

E) With the stomates open at night, the transpiration rate would limit plant height.

Answer: A
Skill: Application

51) As the biologist for the New Mexico state agriculture department, it is your job to look for plants that have evolved structures with a selective advantage in dry, hot conditions. Which of the following adaptations would be *least* likely to meet your objective?

A) CAM plants that grow rapidly

B) small, thick leaves with stomates on the lower surface

C) a thick cuticle on fleshy leaves

D) large, fleshy stems with the ability to carry out photosynthesis

E) plants that do not produce abscisic acid and have a short, thick tap root

Answer: E
Skill: Application

52) Phloem transport of sucrose can be described as going from "source to sink." Which of the following would *not* normally function as a sink?

A) growing leaf

B) growing root

C) storage organ in summer

D) mature leaf

E) shoot tip

Answer: D
Skill: Comprehension

53) Which of the following is a *correct* statement about sugar movement in phloem?

A) Diffusion can account for the observed rates of transport.

B) Movement can occur both upward and downward in the plant.

C) Sugar is translocated from sinks to sources.

D) Only phloem cells with nuclei can perform sugar movement.

E) Sugar transport does not require energy.

Answer: B
Skill: Knowledge

54) Phloem transport is described as being from source to sink. Which of the following would most accurately complete this statement about phloem transport as applied to most plants in the late spring? Phloem transports 1. _____ from the 2. _____ source to the 3. _____ sink.

A) 1. amino acids; 2. root; 3. mycorrhizae

B) 1. sugars; 2. leaf; 3. apical meristem

C) 1. nucleic acids; 2. flower; 3. root

D) 1. proteins; 2. root; 3. leaf

E) 1. sugars; 2. stem; 3. root

Answer: B
Skill: Comprehension

55) Arrange the following five events in an order that explains the mass flow of materials in the phloem.
1. Water diffuses into the sieve elements.
2. Leaf cells produce sugar by photosynthesis.
3. Solutes are actively transported into sieve elements.
4. Sugar is transported from cell to cell in the leaf.
5. Sugar moves down the stem.

A) 2, 1, 4, 3, 5

B) 1, 2, 3, 4, 5

C) 2, 4, 3, 1, 5

D) 4, 2, 1, 3, 5

E) 2, 4, 1, 3, 5

Answer: C
Skill: Comprehension

56) Water flows into the source end of a sieve tube because

A) sucrose has diffused into the sieve tube, making it hypertonic.

B) sucrose has been actively transported into the sieve tube, making it hypertonic.

C) water pressure outside the sieve tube forces in water.

D) the companion cell of a sieve tube actively pumps in water.

E) sucrose has been dumped from the sieve tube by active transport.

Answer: B
Skill: Comprehension

57) Which one of the following statements about transport of nutrients in phloem is *false*?

A) Solute particles can be actively transported into phloem at the source.

B) Companion cells control the rate and direction of movement of phloem sap.

C) Differences in osmotic concentration at the source and sink cause a hydrostatic pressure gradient to be formed.

D) A sink is that part of the plant where a particular solute is consumed or stored.

E) A sink may be located anywhere in the plant.

Answer: B
Skill: Knowledge

58) According to the pressure–flow hypothesis of phloem transport,

A) solute moves from a high concentration in the "source" to a lower concentration in the "sink."

B) water is actively transported into the "source" region of the phloem to create the turgor pressure needed.

C) the combination of a high turgor pressure in the "source" and transpiration water loss from the "sink" moves solutes through phloem conduits.

D) the formation of starch from sugar in the "sink" increases the osmotic concentration.

E) the pressure in the phloem of a root is normally greater than the pressure in the phloem of a leaf.

Answer: A
Skill: Application

59) According to the pressure–flow model of translocation in plants, sieve tubes near photosynthetic cells are sites of

A) relatively high hydrostatic pressure.

B) relatively low hydrostatic pressure.

C) relatively high concentrations of organic nutrients.

D) active pumping of sucrose out of the sieve tube.

E) A and C.

Answer: E
Skill: Comprehension

60) Plants do not have a circulatory system like that of some animals. If a given water molecule did "circulate" (that is, go from one point in a plant to another and back), it would require the activity of

A) only the xylem.

B) only the phloem.

C) only the endodermis.

D) both the xylem and the endodermis.

E) both the xylem and the phloem.

Answer: E
Skill: Application

61) In the pressure–flow hypothesis of translocation, what causes the pressure?

A) root pressure

B) the osmotic uptake of water by sieve tubes at the source

C) the accumulation of minerals and water by the stele in the root

D) the osmotic uptake of water by the sieve tubes of the sink

E) hydrostatic pressure in xylem vessels

Answer: B
Skill: Comprehension

Media Activity Questions

1) Water and minerals are transported upward from the roots by
   A) cork cambium.
   B) phloem.
   C) cork.
   D) xylem.
   E) vascular cambium.

   Answer: D
   Topic: Web/CD Activity 36A

2) _____ increase the surface area of roots.
   A) Symplasts
   B) Apoplasts
   C) Mycorrhizae
   D) Root hairs
   E) Root hairs and mycorrhizae

   Answer: E
   Topic: Web/CD Activity 36A

3) Water and ions can move from cell to cell through
   A) plasmodesmata.
   B) gap junctions.
   C) desmosomes.
   D) tight junctions.
   E) intercalated disks.

   Answer: A
   Topic: Web/CD Activity 36A

4) The transport of phloem sap is called
   A) transduction.
   B) translocation.
   C) transformation.
   D) transmogrification.
   E) transpiration.

   Answer: B
   Topic: Web/CD Activity 36B

5) In plants, the _____ is an example of a sugar source.
   A) amyloplast
   B) onion bulb
   C) tuber
   D) taproot
   E) leaf

   Answer: E
   Topic: Web/CD Activity 36B

Self-Quiz Questions

Answers to these questions also appear in the textbook.

1) Which of the following would *not* contribute to water uptake by a plant cell?

   A) an increase in the water potential (Ψ) of the surrounding solution

   B) a decrease in pressure on the cell exerted by the wall

   C) the uptake of solutes by the cell

   D) a decrease in (Ψ) of the cytoplasm

   E) an increase in tension on the surrounding solution

   Answer: E

2) Stomata open when guard cells

   A) sense an increase in CO_2 in the air spaces of the leaf.

   B) flop open because of a decrease in turgor pressure.

   C) become more turgid because of an influx of K^+, followed by the osmotic entry of water.

   D) close aquaporins, preventing uptake of water.

   E) accumulate water by active transport.

   Answer: C

3) Which of the following is *not* part of the transpiration–cohesion–tension mechanism for the ascent of xylem sap?

   A) the loss of water from the mesophyll cells, which initiates a pull of water molecules from neighboring cells

   B) the transfer of transpirational pull from one water molecule to the next owing to the cohesion caused by hydrogen bonds

   C) the hydrophilic walls of the narrow tracheids and xylem vessels that help maintain the column of water against the force of gravity

   D) the active pumping of water into the xylem of roots

   E) the reduction of water potential in the surface film of mesophyll cells due to transpiration

   Answer: D

4) Which of the following does *not* appear to involve active transport across membranes?

   A) the movement of mineral nutrients from the apoplast to the symplast

   B) the movement of sugar from mesophyll cells into sieve-tube members in corn

   C) the movement of sugar from one sieve-tube member to the next

   D) K^+ uptake by guard cells during stomatal opening

   E) the movement of mineral nutrients into cells of the root cortex

   Answer: C

5) The movement of sap from a sugar source to a sugar sink

A) occurs through the apoplast of sieve-tube members.

B) may translocate sugars from the breakdown of stored starch in a root up to developing shoots.

C) is similar to the flow of xylem sap in depending on tension, or negative pressure.

D) depends on the active pumping of water into sieve tubes at the source end.

E) results mainly from diffusion.

Answer: B

6) The productivity of a crop declines when leaves begin to wilt mainly because

A) the chlorophyll of wilting leaves decomposes.

B) flaccid mesophyll cells are incapable of photosynthesis.

C) stomata close, preventing CO_2 from entering the leaf.

D) photolysis, the water-splitting step of photosynthesis, cannot occur when there is a water deficiency.

E) an accumulation of CO_2 in the leaf inhibits the enzymes required for photosynthesis.

Answer: C

7) Imagine cutting a live twig from a tree and examining the cut surface of the twig with a magnifying glass. You locate the vascular tissue and observe a growing droplet of fluid exuding from the cut surface. This fluid is probably

A) phloem sap.

B) xylem sap.

C) guttation fluid.

D) fluid of the transpiration stream.

E) cell sap from the broken vacuoles of cells.

Answer: A

8) Which structure or compartment is *not* part of the plant's apoplast?

A) the lumen of a xylem vessel

B) the lumen of a sieve tube

C) the cell wall of a mesophyll cell

D) the cell wall of a transfer cell

E) the cell wall of a root hair

Answer: B

9) Which of the following is *not* an adaptation that enhances the uptake of water and minerals by roots?

A) mycorrhizae, the symbiotic associations of roots and fungi

B) root hairs, which increase surface area near root tips

C) selective uptake of minerals by xylem vessels

D) selective uptake of minerals by cortical cells

E) plasmodesmata, which facilitate symplastic transport from the cortex into the stele

Answer: C

10) A plant cell with a solute potential of –0.65 MPa maintains a constant volume when bathed in a solution that has a solute potential of –0.3 MPa and is in an open container. What do we know about the cell?

A) The cell has a pressure potential of +0.65 MPa.

B) The cell has a water potential of –0.65 MPa.

C) The cell has a pressure potential of +0.35 MPa.

D) The cell has a pressure potential of +0.3 MPa.

E) The cell has a water potential of 0 MPa.

Answer: C

Chapter 37   Plant Nutrition

1) There are several properties of a soil in which typical plants would grow well. Of the following, which would be the *least* conducive to plant growth?

A) abundant humus

B) numerous soil organisms

C) high clay content

D) high porosity

E) high cation exchange capacity

Answer: C
Skill: Knowledge

2) Which of the following describes the fate of most of the water taken up by a plant?

A) It is used as a solvent.

B) It is used as a hydrogen source in photosynthesis.

C) It is lost during transpiration.

D) It makes cell elongation possible.

E) It is used to keep cells turgid.

Answer: C
Skill: Knowledge

3) The greatest proportion of the water taken up by plants is

A) split during photosynthesis.

B) lost through stomata during transpiration.

C) absorbed by central vacuoles during cell elongation.

D) returned to the soil by roots.

E) stored in the xylem.

Answer: B
Skill: Knowledge

4) Organic molecules make up what percentage of the dry weight of a plant?

A) 6%

B) 17%

C) 67%

D) 81%

E) 96%

Answer: E
Skill: Knowledge

5) You are conducting an experiment on plant growth. You take a plant fresh from the soil and it weighs 5 kg. Then you dry the plant overnight and determine the dry weight to be 1 kg. Of this dry weight, how much would you expect to be made up of inorganic minerals?

A) 50 grams

B) 500 grams

C) 1 kg

D) 4 kg

E) 5 kg

Answer: A
Skill: Application

For the following questions, match the element with its immediate source and use in typical terrestrial plants.

Source	*Use*
A. soil solution	*nucleic acids and proteins*
B. soil solution	*most or all organic molecules*
C. air	*nucleic acids and proteins*
D. air	*most or all organic molecules*
E. air and soil solution	*most or all organic molecules*

6) carbon

Answer: D
Skill: Comprehension

7) hydrogen

Answer: B
Skill: Comprehension

8) oxygen

Answer: E
Skill: Comprehension

9) nitrogen

Answer: A
Skill: Comprehension

10) Which two elements make up more than 90% of the dry weight of plants?
   A) carbon and nitrogen
   B) oxygen and hydrogen
   C) nitrogen and oxygen
   D) oxygen and carbon
   E) carbon and potassium

Answer: D
Skill: Comprehension

11) The bulk of a plant's dry weight is derived from
   A) soil minerals.
   B) CO_2.
   C) the hydrogen from H_2O.
   D) the oxygen from H_2O.
   E) the uptake of organic nutrients from the soil.

Answer: B
Skill: Comprehension

12) Plant growth and development depend primarily on three main components: _____, _____, and _____.
   A) nitrogen; carbon; oxygen
   B) potassium; carbon; oxygen
   C) oxygen; carbon; hydrogen
   D) phosphorus; nitrogen; oxygen
   E) sulfur; nitrogen; phosphorus

Answer: C
Skill: Application

13) A growing plant exhibits chlorosis of the leaves of the entire plant. The chlorosis is probably due to a deficiency of which of the following macronutrients?
   A) carbon
   B) oxygen
   C) nitrogen
   D) calcium
   E) hydrogen

Answer: C
Skill: Comprehension

14) Which of the following elements is *incorrectly* paired with its function in a plant?
   A) nitrogen—component of nucleic acids, proteins, hormones, coenzymes
   B) magnesium—component of chlorophyll; activates many enzymes
   C) phosphorus—component of nucleic acids, phospholipids, ATP, several coenzymes
   D) potassium—cofactor functional in protein synthesis; osmosis; operation of stomata
   E) sulfur—component of DNA; activates some enzymes

Answer: E
Skill: Application

15) In the nutrition of a plant, which element is classified as a macronutrient?
   A) zinc
   B) chlorine
   C) calcium
   D) molybdenum
   E) manganese

Answer: C
Skill: Knowledge

For the following questions, match the element to its major function in plants. Use each choice only once.

Function
A. component of lignin-biosynthetic enzymes
B. component of DNA and RNA
C. active in chlorophyll formation
D. active in amino acid formation
E. formation and stability of cell walls

16) zinc

Answer: C
Skill: Knowledge

17) nitrogen

Answer: B
Skill: Knowledge

18) copper

Answer: A
Skill: Knowledge

19) calcium

Answer: E
Skill: Knowledge

20) manganese

Answer: D
Skill: Knowledge

21) Which of the following best describes the general role of micronutrients in plants?
   A) They are cofactors in enzyme reactions.
   B) They are necessary for essential regulatory functions.
   C) They prevent chlorosis.
   D) They are components of nucleic acids.
   E) They are necessary for the formation of cell walls.

Answer: A
Skill: Knowledge

22) All of the following are elements that plants need in very small amounts (micronutrients) *except*
   A) hydrogen.
   B) iron.
   C) chlorine.
   D) copper.
   E) zinc.

Answer: A
Skill: Comprehension

23) Which of the following is *not* true of micronutrients in plants?
   A) They are the elements required in relatively small amounts.
   B) They are required for a plant to grow from a seed and complete its life cycle.
   C) They generally help in catalytic functions in the plant.
   D) They are the essential elements of small size and molecular weight.
   E) Overdoses of them can be toxic.

Answer: D
Skill: Application

24) What is meant by the term *chlorosis*?
   A) the uptake of the micronutrient chlorine by a plant
   B) the formation of chlorophyll within the thylakoid membranes of a plant
   C) the yellowing of leaves due to decreased chlorophyll production
   D) a contamination of glassware in hydroponic culture
   E) release of negatively charged minerals such as chloride from clay particles in soil

Answer: C
Skill: Knowledge

25) If an African violet has chlorosis, which of the following elements might be a useful addition to the soil?

A) chlorine

B) chlorophyll

C) copper

D) iodine

E) magnesium

Answer: E
Skill: Application

26) The factor most limiting to algal growth in open ocean is

A) inadequate light exposure.

B) lack of nitrogen–fixing bacteria.

C) a deficit of dissolved iron and other minerals.

D) low concentrations of CO_2.

E) excessive wave action.

Answer: C
Skill: Knowledge

27) What soil(s) is (are) the most fertile?

A) humus only

B) loam only

C) silt only

D) clay only

E) both humus and loam

Answer: E
Skill: Knowledge

Figure 37.1 shows the results of a study to determine the effect of soil air spaces on plant growth. Use these data to answer the following questions.

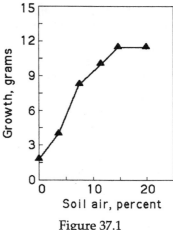

Figure 37.1

28) The best conclusion from the data in Figure 37.1 is that the plant

A) grows best without air in the soil.

B) grows fastest in 5 to 10% air.

C) grows best in air levels above 15%.

D) does not respond differently to different levels of air in the soil.

E) would grow to 24 grams in 40% air.

Answer: C
Skill: Application

29) The best explanation for the shape of this growth response curve is that

A) the plant requires air in the soil for photosynthesis.

B) the roots are able to absorb more nitrogen (N_2) in high levels of air.

C) most of the decrease in weight at low air levels is due to transpiration from the leaves.

D) increased soil air produces more root mass in the soil but does not affect the top stems and leaves.

E) the roots require oxygen for respiration and growth.

Answer: E
Skill: Comprehension

30) Overwatering a plant will kill it. Why?

A) Water does not have all the necessary minerals a plant needs to grow.

B) Water neutralizes the pH of the soil.

C) The roots cannot get air.

D) Water will attract parasites.

E) Water will form hydrogen bonds with the root of the cell wall.

Answer: C
Skill: Comprehension

31) What should be added to soil to prevent minerals from leaching away?

A) humus

B) sand

C) mycorrhizae

D) nitrogen

E) silt

Answer: A
Skill: Knowledge

32) Which soil mineral is most likely to be leached away due to a hard rain?

A) Na^+

B) K^+

C) CA^{++}

D) NO_3^-

E) H^+

Answer: D
Skill: Comprehension

33) Which of the following did *not* contribute to the dust bowl in the American southwest during the 1930s?

A) overgrazing by cattle

B) cutting of mature trees

C) plowing of native grasses

D) planting of field crops

E) lack of soil moisture

Answer: B
Skill: Knowledge

34) The N–P–K percentages on a package of fertilizer refer to the

A) total protein content of the three major ingredients of the fertilizer.

B) percentages of manure collected from different types of animals.

C) relative percentages of organic and inorganic nutrients in the fertilizer.

D) percentages of three important mineral nutrients.

E) proportions of three different nitrogen sources.

Answer: D
Skill: Knowledge

35) A soil well suited for the growth of most plants would have all of the following properties *except*

A) abundant humus.

B) air spaces.

C) good drainage.

D) high cation exchange capacity.

E) a high pH.

Answer: E
Skill: Knowledge

In west Texas, cotton has become an important crop in the last three decades. However, in this hot, dry part of the country there is little rainfall, so farmers irrigate their cotton fields. They must also regularly fertilize the cotton fields because the soil is very sandy. Figure 37.2 shows the record of annual productivity (measured in kilograms of cotton per hectare of land) since 1960 in a west Texas cotton field. Use these data to answer the following questions.

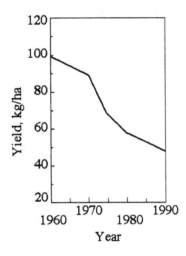

Figure 37.2

36) Based on the information provided above, what is the most likely cause of the decline in productivity?

A) The farmer used the wrong kind of fertilizer.

B) The cotton is developing a resistance to the fertilizer and to irrigation water.

C) Water has accumulated in the soil due to irrigation.

D) The soil has become hyperosmotic to the roots due to salination.

E) The rate of photosynthesis has declined due to irrigation.

Answer: D
Skill: Application

37) If you were the county agriculture agent, what would be the best advice you could give the farmer who owns the field under study in Figure 37.2?

A) Plant a variety of cotton that requires less water and can tolerate salinity.

B) Continue to fertilize, but stop irrigating and rely on rainfall.

C) Continue to irrigate, but stop fertilizing and rely on organic nutrients in the soil.

D) Continue to fertilize and irrigate, but add the nitrogen–fixing bacteria *Rhizobium* to the irrigation water until the productivity increases.

E) Add acid to the soil and increase its cation exchange capabilities so more nutrients are retained in the soil.

Answer: A
Skill: Application

38) A young farmer purchases some land in a relatively arid area and is interested in earning a reasonable profit for many years. Which of the following strategies would best allow such a goal to be achieved?

A) establishing an extensive irrigation system

B) using plenty of the best fertilizers

C) finding a way to sell all parts of crop plants

D) selecting crops adapted to arid areas

E) converting hillsides into fields

Answer: D
Skill: Application

39) A farming commitment embracing a variety of methods that are conservation-minded, environmentally safe, and profitable is called

A) hydroponics.

B) nitrogen fixation.

C) responsible irrigation.

D) genetic engineering.

E) sustainable agriculture.

Answer: E
Skill: Knowledge

40) An early use of indicator plants (plants that tolerate high levels of heavy metals in the soil) was to locate potential profitable areas to mine for those minerals. A current use for such plants is

A) to help locate suitable sites for toxic waste storage.

B) bioremediation to help clean up mine spoils.

C) to minimize soil erosion in arid lands.

D) nitrogen fixation by symbiotic bacteria in root nodules.

E) all of the above.

Answer: B
Skill: Knowledge

41) Why is nitrogen fixation such an important process?

A) Nitrogen fixation can only be done by certain prokaryotes.

B) Fixed nitrogen is most often the limiting factor in plant growth.

C) Nitrogen fixation is very expensive in terms of metabolic energy.

D) Nitrogen fixers are sometimes symbiotic with legumes.

E) Nitrogen-fixing capacity can be genetically engineered.

Answer: B
Skill: Comprehension

42) In what way do nitrogen compounds differ from other minerals needed by plants?

A) Only nitrogen can be lost from the soil.

B) Only nitrogen requires the action of bacteria to be made available to plants.

C) Only nitrogen is needed for protein synthesis.

D) Only nitrogen is held by cation exchange capacity in the soil.

E) Only nitrogen can be absorbed by root hairs.

Answer: B
Skill: Knowledge

43) Most crop plants acquire their nitrogen mainly in the form of

A) NH_3

B) N_2

C) CN_2H_2

D) NO_3-

E) amino acids absorbed from the soil

Answer: D
Skill: Comprehension

44) The enzyme nitrogenase reduces atmospheric nitrogen to form

A) N_2

B) NH_3

C) NO_2

D) NO^-

E) NH^-

Answer: B
Skill: Comprehension

45) In a root nodule, the gene coding for nitrogenase

A) is inactivated by leghemoglobin.

B) is absent in active bacteroids.

C) is found in the cells of the pericycle.

D) protects the nodule from nitrogen.

E) is part of the *Rhizobium* chromosome.

Answer: E
Skill: Knowledge

46) The most efficient way to increase essential amino acids in crop plants for human consumption is to
   A) breed for higher yield of deficient amino acids.
   B) increase the amount of fertilizer used on fields.
   C) use 20–20–20 fertilizer instead of 20–5–5 fertilizer.
   D) engineer nitrogen–fixing nodules into crop plants lacking them.
   E) increase irrigation of nitrogen–fixing crops.

   Answer: A
   Skill: Knowledge

47) Among important crop plants, nitrogen-fixing root nodules are most commonly an attribute of
   A) corn.
   B) legumes.
   C) wheat.
   D) members of the potato family.
   E) cabbage and other members of the brassica family.

   Answer: B
   Skill: Knowledge

48) If a legume is infected with *Rhizobium*, what is the probable effect on the plant?
   A) It gets chlorosis.
   B) It dies.
   C) It desiccates.
   D) It obtains nitrogen from nitrogen fixation.
   E) It contributes water to the soil.

   Answer: D
   Skill: Comprehension

49) You are weeding your garden when you accidently expose some roots. You notice swellings (root nodules) on the roots. Most likely your plant
   A) suffers from a mineral deficiency.
   B) is infected with a parasite.
   C) is benefiting from a mutualistic bacterium.
   D) is developing offshoots from the root.
   E) is where insect pupa are developing.

   Answer: C
   Skill: Comprehension

50) The enzyme nitrogenase is inhibited by oxygen. Which one of the following adaptations has evolved in response to this inhibition?
   A) leghemoglobin
   B) root nodules
   C) water ferns
   D) carbohydrate transfer from hosts
   E) bacteroids

   Answer: A
   Skill: Knowledge

51) Which of the following is a *true* statement about nitrogen fixation in root nodules?
   A) The plant contributes the nitrogenase enzyme.
   B) The process is relatively inexpensive in terms of ATP costs.
   C) Leghemoglobin helps maintain a low O_2 concentration within the nodule.
   D) The process tends to deplete nitrogen compounds in the soil.
   E) The bacteria of the nodule are autotrophic.

   Answer: C
   Skill: Comprehension

52) The function of a root nodule's leghemoglobin is to

A) extract macronutrients from the soil.

B) regulate the supply of oxygen to *Rhizobium*.

C) promote ion exchange in the soil.

D) form a mutualistic relationship with insects.

E) supply the legume with fixed nitrogen.

Answer: B
Skill: Comprehension

53) How do legume plant roots communicate with *Rhizobium* bacteria?

A) Flavenoids from *Rhizobium* create "nods."

B) Plants activate early nodulin genes.

C) *Rhizobium* secretes infection threads.

D) Flavenoids trigger gene–regulating proteins in bacterium.

E) Both A and C are correct.

Answer: D
Skill: Knowledge

54) A woodlot was sprayed with a fungicide. What would be the most serious effect of such spraying?

A) a decrease in food for animals that eat mushrooms

B) a decrease in rates of wood decay

C) a decrease in tree growth due to the death of mycorrhizae

D) an increase in the number of decomposing bacteria

E) There would be no serious results.

Answer: C
Skill: Application

55) What is the mutualistic association between roots and fungi called?

A) nitrogen fixation

B) *Rhizobium* infection

C) mycorrhizae

D) parasitism

E) root hair enhancement

Answer: C
Skill: Knowledge

56) Hyphae form a covering over roots. Altogether, these hyphae create a large surface area that helps to do which of the following?

A) aid in absorbing minerals and ions

B) maintain cell shape

C) increase cellular respiration

D) anchor a plant

E) protect the roots from ultraviolet light

Answer: A
Skill: Application

57) Which of the following is a primary difference between ectomycorrhizae and endomycorrhizae?

A) Endomycorrhizae have thicker, shorter hyphae than ectomycorrhizae.

B) Endomycorrhizae, but not ectomycorrhizae, form a dense sheath over the surface of the root.

C) Ectomycorrhize do not penetrate root cells, while endomycorrhizae grow into invaginations of the root cell membranes.

D) There are no significant differences between ectomycorrhizae and endomycorrhizae.

Answer: C
Skill: Knowledge

58) All of the statements below are false *except:*

A) The first nodulin genes are the same ones that are activated in ectomycorrhizae.

B) Cytokinins applied to legume root cells activate early nodulin genes.

C) *Rhizobium* Nod factor secretions are related to compounds that make fungi cell walls.

D) Legumes evolved 400 million years ago.

E) Mutations in nodulin genes promote development of root nodules but not mycorrhizae.

Answer: A
Skill: Knowledge

59) On an evolutionary scale, mycorrhizae

A) have only existed for a short time.

B) were not involved in the adaptation of plants to land.

C) have only been found in a few species.

D) helped plants survive as they adapted to land.

E) first evolved in aquatic fungi.

Answer: D
Skill: Knowledge

60) Dwarf mistletoe grows on many of the pine trees in the Rockies. Although the mistletoe is green, it is probably not sufficiently active in photosynthesis to produce all the sugar it needs. The mistletoe also produces haustoria. Thus, dwarf mistletoe growing on pine trees is best classified as

A) an epiphyte.

B) a nitrogen–fixing legume.

C) a carnivorous plant.

D) a symbiotic plant.

E) a parasite.

Answer: E
Skill: Application

61) What are epiphytes?

A) aerial vines common in tropical regions

B) haustoria for anchoring to host plants and obtaining xylem sap

C) plants that live in poor soil and digest insects to obtain nitrogen

D) plants that grow on other plants but do not obtain nutrients from their hosts

E) plants that have a symbiotic relationship with roots

Answer: D
Skill: Knowledge

62) Carnivorous plants have evolved mechanisms that trap and digest small animals. The products of this digestion are used to supplement the plant's supply of

A) energy.

B) carbohydrates.

C) lipids and steroids.

D) minerals.

E) water.

Answer: D
Skill: Knowledge

Media Activity Questions

1) Soil particles tend to
   A) repel positively charged ions.
   B) attract negatively charged ions.
   C) be uncharged.
   D) have a negative charge.
   E) have a positive charge.

   Answer: D
   Topic: Web/CD Activity 37A

2) Roots expend ATP to pump _____ ions from the root to the soil and by doing so displace mineral ions bound to soil particles.
   A) CO_3^{2-}
   B) H^+
   C) He
   D) Mg^{2+}
   E) Ca^{2+}

   Answer: B
   Topic: Web/CD Activity 37A

3) Which of these duplicates the effects of cation exchange making soil less fertile?
   A) fermentation
   B) acid precipitation
   C) photorespiration
   D) photosynthesis
   E) autolysis

   Answer: B
   Topic: Web/CD Activity 37A

4) _____ includes the incorporation of nitrogen into the body of a plant.
   A) Nitrification
   B) Assimilation
   C) Ammonification
   D) Denitrification
   E) Nitrogen fixation

   Answer: B
   Topic: Web/CD Activity 37B

5) _____ is the production of ammonium ions.
   A) Nitrification
   B) Assimilation
   C) Ammonification
   D) Denitrification
   E) Reconstitution

   Answer: C
   Topic: Web/CD Activity 37B

Self-Quiz Questions

Answers to these questions also appear in the textbook.

1) Most of the mass of organic material of a plant comes from
   A) water.
   B) carbon dioxide.
   C) soil minerals.
   D) atmospheric oxygen.
   E) nitrogen.

   Answer: B

2) Micronutrients are needed in very small amounts because
   A) most of them are mobile in the plant.
   B) most function as cofactors of enzymes.
   C) most are supplied in large enough quantities in seeds.
   D) they play only a minor role in the health of the plant.
   E) only the growing regions of the plants require them.

   Answer: B

3) Two groups of tomatoes were grown under laboratory conditions, one with humus added to the soil and one a control without the humus. The leaves of the plants grown without humus were yellowish (less green) than those of the plants growing in humus–enriched soil. The best explanation for this difference is that
   A) the healthy plants used the food in the decomposing leaves of the humus for energy to make chlorophyll.
   B) the humus made the soil more loosely packed, so the plants' roots grew with less resistance.
   C) the humus contained minerals such as magnesium and iron, needed for the synthesis of chlorophyll.
   D) the heat released by the decomposing leaves of the humus caused more rapid growth and chlorophyll synthesis.
   E) the plants absorbed chlorophyll from the humus.

   Answer: C

4) We would expect the greatest difference in size and general appearance between two groups of plants of the same species, one group with mycorrhizae and one without, in an environment
   A) where nitrogen–fixing bacteria are abundant.
   B) that has soil with poor drainage.
   C) that has hot summers and cold winters.
   D) in which the soil is relatively deficient in mineral nutrients.
   E) that is near a body of water, such as a pond or river.

   Answer: D

5) A mineral deficiency is likely to affect older leaves more than younger leaves if

A) the mineral is a micronutrient.

B) the mineral is very mobile within the plant.

C) the mineral is required for chlorophyll synthesis.

D) the deficiency persists for a long time.

E) the older leaves are in direct sunlight.

Answer: B

6) Carnivorous adaptations of plants mainly compensate for soil that has a relatively low content of

A) potassium.

B) nitrogen.

C) calcium.

D) water.

E) phosphate.

Answer: B

7) Based on our retrospective view, the most reasonable conclusion to draw from van Helmont's famous experiment on the growth of a willow tree is that

A) the tree increased in mass mainly by producing its own matter.

B) the increase in the mass of the tree could not be accounted for by the consumption of soil.

C) most of the increase in the mass of the tree was due to the uptake of O_2.

D) soil simply provides physical support for the tree without providing nutrients.

E) trees do not require water to grow.

Answer: B

8) It is valid to consider water a plant nutrient because

A) plants die without a water source.

B) cell elongation depends mainly on the osmotic absorption of water by cells.

C) hydrogen atoms from water molecules are incorporated into organic molecules.

D) transpiration depends on a continuous supply of water to leaves.

E) most of a plant's mass of organic compounds is derived from water.

Answer: C

9) The specific relationship between a legume and its symbiotic *Rhizobium* species probably depends on

A) each legume having a specific set of early nodulin genes.

B) each *Rhizobium* species having a form of nitrogenase that only works in the appropriate legume host.

C) each legume being found where the soil has only the *Rhizobium* specific to that legume.

D) specific recognition between the chemical signals and signal receptors of the *Rhizobium* and legume species.

E) destruction of all incompatible *Rhizobium* species by enzymes secreted from the legume's roots.

Answer: D

10) Mycorrhizae enhance plant nutrition mainly by

A) absorbing water and minerals through the fungal hyphae.

B) providing sugar to the root cells, which have no chloroplasts of their own.

C) converting atmospheric nitrogen to ammonia.

D) enabling the roots to parasitize neighboring plants.

E) stimulating the development of root hairs.

Answer: A

Chapter 38   Plant Reproduction and Biotechnology

1) The products of meiosis in plants are always which of the following?

 A) spores

 B) eggs

 C) sperm

 D) seeds

 E) Both B and C are correct.

Answer: A
Skill: Knowledge

2) Which of the following is the *correct* sequence during alternation of generations in a flowering plant?

 A) sporophyte-meiosis-gametophyte-gametes-fertilization-diploid zygote

 B) sporophyte-mitosis-gametophyte-meiosis-sporophyte

 C) haploid gametophyte-gametes-meiosis-fertilization-diploid sporophyte

 D) sporophyte-spores-meiosis-gametophyte-gametes

 E) haploid sporophyte-spores-fertilization-diploid gametophyte

Answer: A
Skill: Comprehension

3) Which of the following is *true* in plants?

 A) Meiosis occurs in gametophytes to produce gametes.

 B) Meiosis occurs in sporophytes to produce spores.

 C) The gametophyte is the dominant generation in flowering plants.

 D) Plants exist continually as either sporophytes or gametophytes.

 E) Male gametophytes and female gametophytes are the same structure.

Answer: B
Skill: Knowledge

4) All of the following are features that can account for the evolutionary success of angiosperms *except*

 A) a triploid endosperm.

 B) an ovary that becomes a fruit.

 C) animal pollination.

 D) a reduced sporophyte phase.

 E) double fertilization.

Answer: D
Skill: Knowledge

5) Based on studies of plant evolution, which flower part is *not* a modified leaf?

 A) stamen

 B) carpel

 C) petal

 D) sepal

 E) receptacle

Answer: E
Skill: Knowledge

6) All of the following floral parts are directly involved in pollination or fertilization *except* the

 A) stigma.

 B) anther.

 C) sepal.

 D) carpel.

 E) style.

Answer: C
Skill: Knowledge

A. stamen
B. stigma
C. embryo sac
D. sepal
E. coleoptile

7) the sheath covering the embryonic shoot in a monocot

Answer: E
Skill: Knowledge

8) flower part modified as a male reproductive structure

Answer: A
Skill: Knowledge

9) the outer modified leaf of a flower

Answer: D
Skill: Knowledge

10) the female gametophyte of angiosperms

Answer: C
Skill: Knowledge

11) the sticky top of a carpel

Answer: B
Skill: Knowledge

12) Which of the following is the *correct* order of floral organs from the outside to the inside of a complete flower?
   A) petals-sepals-stamens-carpels
   B) sepals-stamens-petals-carpels
   C) spores-gametes-zygote-embryo
   D) sepals-petals-stamens-carpels
   E) male gametophyte-female gametophyte-sepals-petals

Answer: D
Skill: Comprehension

13) All of the following are primary functions of flowers *except*
   A) pollen production.
   B) photosynthesis.
   C) meiosis.
   D) egg production.
   E) sexual reproduction.

Answer: B
Skill: Knowledge

14) Meiosis occurs within all of the following flower parts *except* the
   A) ovule.
   B) style.
   C) megasporangium.
   D) anther.
   E) ovary.

Answer: B
Skill: Comprehension

15) A perfect flower is *correctly* described as a flower that
   A) has no sepals.
   B) has fused carpels.
   C) is on a dioecious plant.
   D) has no endosperm.
   E) has both stamens and carpels.

Answer: E
Skill: Knowledge

16) Carpellate flowers
   A) are perfect.
   B) are complete.
   C) produce pollen.
   D) are found only on dioecious plants.
   E) develop into fruits.

Answer: E
Skill: Comprehension

17) Which of the following types of plants is *not* able to self-pollinate?

   A) dioecious

   B) monoecious

   C) complete

   D) wind–pollinated

   E) insect–pollinated

   Answer: A
   Skill: Knowledge

18) In flowering plants, pollen is released from the

   A) anther.

   B) stigma.

   C) carpel.

   D) sepal.

   E) pollen tube.

   Answer: A
   Skill: Knowledge

19) In the life cycle of an angiosperm, which of the following stages is diploid?

   A) megaspore only

   B) generative nucleus of a pollen grain only

   C) polar nuclei of the embryo sac only

   D) microsporocyte only

   E) both megaspore and microsporocyte

   Answer: D
   Skill: Comprehension

20) In flowering plants, meiosis occurs specifically in the

   A) megasporocyte only.

   B) microsporocyte only.

   C) endosperm only.

   D) pollen tube only.

   E) megasporocyte and microsporocyte.

   Answer: E
   Skill: Comprehension

21) Which of the following is a *correct* sequence of processes that takes place when a flowering plant reproduces?

   A) meiosis–fertilization–ovulation–germination

   B) fertilization–meiosis–nuclear fusion–formation of embryo and endosperm

   C) meiosis–pollination–nuclear fusion–formation of embryo and endosperm

   D) growth of pollen tube–pollination–germination–fertilization

   E) meiosis–mitosis–nuclear fusion–pollen

   Answer: C
   Skill: Application

22) Which of these is *incorrectly* paired with its life cycle generation?

   A) anther–gametophyte

   B) pollen–gametophyte

   C) embryo sac–gametophyte

   D) pistil–sporophyte

   E) embryo–sporophyte

   Answer: A
   Skill: Knowledge

23) Which of the following is the *correct* sequence of events in a pollen sac?

   A) sporangia–meiosis–two haploid cells–meiosis–two pollen grains per cell

   B) pollen grain–meiosis–two generative cells–two tube cells per pollen grain

   C) two haploid cells–meiosis–generative cell–tube cell–fertilization–pollen grain

   D) pollen grain–mitosis–microspores–meiosis–generative cell plus tube cell

   E) microsporocyte–meiosis–microspores–mitosis–two haploid cells per pollen grain

   Answer: E
   Skill: Comprehension

24) Which of the following occurs in an angiosperm ovule?

A) An antheridium forms from the megasporophyte.

B) A megaspore mother cell undergoes meiosis.

C) The egg nucleus is usually diploid.

D) The fusion nucleus develops into the embryo.

E) The endosperm surrounds the megaspore mother cell.

Answer: B
Skill: Knowledge

25) Where and by which process are sperm produced in plants?

A) meiosis in pollen grains

B) meiosis in anthers

C) mitosis in male gametophytes

D) mitosis in the micropyle

E) mitosis in the embryo sac

Answer: C
Skill: Knowledge

26) In which of the following pairs are the two terms truly equivalent?

A) ovule—egg

B) embryo sac—female gametophyte

C) endosperm—male gametophyte

D) seed—zygote

E) microspore—pollen grain

Answer: B
Skill: Comprehension

27) The male gametophyte of flowering plants is the

A) ovule.

B) microsporocyte.

C) pollen grain.

D) embryo sac.

E) stamen.

Answer: C
Skill: Knowledge

28) In flowering plants, a mature male gametophyte contains

A) two haploid gametes and a diploid pollen grain.

B) a generative cell and a tube cell.

C) two sperm nuclei and one tube cell nucleus.

D) two haploid microspores per gametophyte.

E) a haploid nucleus and a diploid pollen wall.

Answer: C
Skill: Knowledge

29) Within the female gametophyte, three mitotic divisions of the megaspore produce

A) three antipodal cells, two polar nuclei, one egg, and two synergids.

B) the triple fusion nucleus.

C) three pollen grains.

D) two antipodals, two polar nuclei, two eggs, and two synergids.

E) a tube nucleus, a generative cell, and a sperm cell.

Answer: A
Skill: Knowledge

30) The largest cell(s) of the typical angiosperm embryo sac is (are) the

A) egg cell.

B) antipodals.

C) synergids.

D) central cell.

E) microsporocyte.

Answer: D
Skill: Comprehension

The following questions refer to the diagram of an embryo sac of an angiosperm.

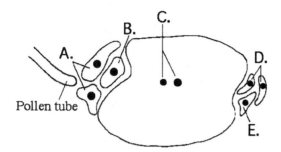

Figure 38.1

31) Which cell(s) after fertilization, give(s) rise to the embryo plant?

Answer: B
Skill: Knowledge

32) Which cell(s) become(s) the triploid endosperm?

Answer: C
Skill: Knowledge

33) Which cell(s) guide(s) the pollen tube to the egg cell?

Answer: A
Skill: Knowledge

34) What is the relationship between pollination and fertilization in flowering plants?

A) Fertilization precedes pollination.

B) Pollination easily occurs between plants of different species.

C) Pollen is formed within megasporangia so that male and female gametes are near each other.

D) Pollination brings gametophytes together so that fertilization can occur.

E) If fertilization occurs, pollination is unnecessary.

Answer: D
Skill: Comprehension

35) Recent research has shown that pollination requires that carpels recognize pollen grains as "self or nonself." For self–incompatibility, the system requires

A) rejection of nonself cells.

B) the rejection of self.

C) carpel incompatibility with the egg cells.

D) that the flowers be incomplete.

E) the union of genetically identical sperm and egg cells.

Answer: B
Skill: Comprehension

36) Genetic incompatibility does *not* affect the

A) attraction of a suitable insect pollinator.

B) germination of the pollen on the stigma.

C) growth of the pollen tube in the style.

D) membrane permeability of cells.

E) different individuals of the same species.

Answer: A
Skill: Comprehension

37) You are studying a plant from the Amazon that shows strong self–incompatibility. To characterize this reproductive mechanism, you would look for

A) ribonuclease (RNase) activity in stigma cells.

B) RNA in the plants.

C) pollen grains with very thick walls.

D) carpels that cannot produce eggs by meiosis.

E) systems of wind, but not insect, pollination.

Answer: A
Skill: Application

38) As flowers develop, all of the following transitions occur *except* that

A) the microspores become pollen grains.

B) the ovary becomes a fruit.

C) the petals are discarded.

D) the tube nucleus becomes a sperm nucleus.

E) the ovules become seeds.

Answer: D
Skill: Comprehension

39) In the life cycle of an angiosperm, double fertilization refers to

A) fertilization of the egg by sperm nuclei from two different pollen grains.

B) fertilization of the egg by two sperm nuclei released from a single pollen tube.

C) a pollen tube releasing two sperm nuclei, one fertilizing the egg and the other combining with the two polar nuclei.

D) fertilization of two different eggs within the embryo sac.

E) fertilization of two eggs within the archegonium.

Answer: C
Skill: Comprehension

40) How many sperm nuclei are needed for the double fertilization of angiosperms?

A) 1 (for the egg)

B) 2 (1 for the egg, 1 for the polar nuclei)

C) 4 (2 for each embryo sac)

D) 5 (1 for the egg, 2 for each of the polar nuclei)

E) 3 (2 for the egg, 1 for the polar nuclei, thus making a $3n$ nucleus)

Answer: B
Skill: Knowledge

41) A unique feature of fertilization in angiosperms is that

A) one sperm fertilizes the egg; another combines with the polar nuclei.

B) the sperm may be carried by the wind to the female organ.

C) a pollen tube carries a sperm nucleus into the female gametophyte.

D) a chemical attractant guides the sperm toward the egg.

E) the sperm cells have flagella for locomotion.

Answer: A
Skill: Comprehension

42) Which of the following is *not* an advantage of an extended gametophyte generation in plants?

A) Male gametophytes can travel more easily within spore walls.

B) The protection of female gametophytes within ovules keeps them from drying out.

C) The independence from the need for swimming sperm makes life on land easier.

D) Female gametophytes develop egg cells, which are fertilized within an ovule that will become a seed.

E) A modified triploid tissue called an endosperm forms a protective seed coat.

Answer: E
Skill: Comprehension

43) What is the result of double fertilization in angiosperms?

A) The endosperm develops into a diploid nutrient tissue.

B) A triploid zygote is formed.

C) Both a diploid embryo and triploid endosperm are formed.

D) Two embryos develop in every seed.

E) The fertilized antipodals develop into the seed coat.

Answer: C
Skill: Comprehension

44) All of the following statements regarding the endosperm are true *except:*

A) It may be absorbed by the cotyledons in the seeds of eudicots.

B) It is a triploid tissue.

C) It is digested by enzymes in monocot seeds following hydration.

D) It develops from the fertilized egg.

E) It is rich in nutrients, which it provides to the embryo.

Answer: D
Skill: Comprehension

45) In angiosperms, the terminal cell divides to become the

A) suspensor only.

B) proembryo only.

C) cotyledons only.

D) suspensor and the proembryo.

E) proembryo and the cotyledons.

Answer: E
Skill: Comprehension

46) Which of the following statements is *correct* about the basal cell in a zygote?

A) It develops into the root of the embryo.

B) It forms the suspensor that anchors the embryo.

C) It results from the fertilization of the polar nuclei by a sperm nucleus.

D) It divides to form the cotyledons.

E) It forms the proembryo.

Answer: B
Skill: Knowledge

47) The radicle of a plant embryo gives rise to which structure(s)?

A) leaves

B) cotyledons

C) root

D) stem

E) shoot

Answer: C
Skill: Knowledge

48) The embryonic root is the

A) plumule.

B) hypocotyl.

C) epicotyl.

D) radicle.

E) shoot.

Answer: D
Skill: Knowledge

49) Which of the following "vegetables" is technically a fruit?

A) potato

B) lettuce

C) broccoli

D) celery

E) green beans

Answer: E
Skill: Comprehension

50) Which of these structures is unique to the seed of a monocot?

   A) cotyledon
   B) endosperm
   C) coleoptile
   D) radicle
   E) seed coat

   Answer: C
   Skill: Knowledge

51) All of the following statements about fruits are true *except:*

   A) Fruits form from microsporangia and integuments.
   B) All normal fruits have seeds inside them.
   C) Green beans, corn, tomatoes, and wheat are all fruits.
   D) Fruits aid in the dispersal of seeds.
   E) During fruit development, the wall of the ovary becomes the pericarp.

   Answer: A
   Skill: Knowledge

52) Fruits develop from

   A) microsporangia.
   B) receptacles.
   C) fertilized eggs.
   D) ovaries.
   E) ovules.

   Answer: D
   Skill: Knowledge

53) Which of the following is *not* an advantage of producing seeds?

   A) Seeds can undergo periods of dormancy.
   B) Seeds germinate irregularly so that they can survive periods of adverse conditions.
   C) Seeds germinate immediately so that natural populations are maintained.
   D) Seeds often have hard walls that deter seed-eating animals.
   E) Seeds and their fruits are a means of seed dispersal.

   Answer: C
   Skill: Knowledge

54) The first step in the germination of a seed is usually

   A) pollination.
   B) fertilization.
   C) imbibition of water.
   D) hydrolysis of starch and other food reserves.
   E) emergence of the radicle.

   Answer: C
   Skill: Knowledge

55) When seeds germinate, the radicle emerges before the shoot. This allows the seedling to quickly do what?

   A) obtain a dependable water supply
   B) mobilize stored carbohydrates
   C) protect the emerging coleoptile
   D) avoid etiolation
   E) initiate photosynthesis

   Answer: A
   Skill: Comprehension

56) All of the following are true of the hypocotyl hook *except:*

A) It is the first structure to emerge from a eudicot seed.

B) It pulls the cotyledons up through the soil.

C) It straightens when exposed to light.

D) It becomes very long in an etiolated seedling.

E) It is the region just below the cotyledons.

Answer: A
Skill: Knowledge

57) In plants, which of the following could be an advantage of sexual reproduction as opposed to asexual reproduction?

A) genetic variation

B) mitosis

C) stable populations

D) rapid population increase

E) greater longevity

Answer: A
Skill: Comprehension

58) A disadvantage of monoculture is that

A) the whole crop ripens at one time.

B) genetic uniformity makes a crop vulnerable to a new pest or disease.

C) it predominantly uses vegetative propagation.

D) most grain crops self–pollinate.

E) it allows for the cultivation of large areas of land.

Answer: B
Skill: Comprehension

59) Vegetative reproduction

A) involves both meiosis and mitosis to produce haploid and diploid cells.

B) produces vegetables.

C) involves meiosis only.

D) can lead to genetically altered forms of the species.

E) produces clones.

Answer: E
Skill: Knowledge

60) Which of the following is a *true* statement about clonal reproduction in plants?

A) Clones of plants do *not* occur naturally.

B) Cloning, although recently reported for animals, has not been demonstrated in plants.

C) Making cuttings of ornamental plants is a form of fragmentation.

D) Reproduction of plants by cloning may be either sexual or asexual.

E) Viable seeds can only be produced by sexual reproduction.

Answer: C
Skill: Application

61) Which of the following statements about an apomictic seed is *incorrect*?

A) The seed coat is diploid tissue derived from the ovule of a flower.

B) The embryo is a diploid tissue derived from fertilization of a haploid egg by a haploid sperm.

C) Cotyledons are the primary food storage tissue of the embryo.

D) A diploid embryo is contained within the seed.

E) The embryo of the seed is a clone.

Answer: B
Skill: Comprehension

62) All of the following could be considered advantages of asexual reproduction in plants *except*

 A) success in a stable environment.

 B) increased agricultural productivity.

 C) cloning an exceptional plant.

 D) production of artificial seeds.

 E) adaptation to change.

Answer: E
Skill: Comprehension

63) Under which conditions would asexual plants have the greatest advantage over sexual plants?

 A) an environment that varies on a regular, predictable basis

 B) an environment with irregular fluctuations of conditions

 C) a relatively constant environment with infrequent disturbances

 D) a fire-maintained ecosystem

 E) an environment with many seed predators

Answer: C
Skill: Knowledge

64) Which of the following statements is *true* of protoplast fusion?

 A) It occurs when the second sperm nucleus fuses with the polar nuclei in the embryo sac.

 B) It can be used to form new plant varieties by combining genomes from two plants.

 C) It is used to develop gene banks to preserve genetic variability.

 D) It is the method of test–tube cloning that produces whole plants from explants.

 E) It occurs within a callus that is developing in tissue culture.

Answer: B
Skill: Knowledge

65) Which of the following statements is *correct* about protoplast fusion?

 A) It is used to develop gene banks to maintain genetic variability.

 B) It is the method of test–tube cloning thousands of copies.

 C) It can be used to form new plant species.

 D) It occurs within a callus.

 E) It requires that the cell wall remain intact during the fusion process.

Answer: C
Skill: Knowledge

66) Conventional breeding required almost 20 years to introduce the recessive "opaque–2" genes into maize. Which of the following statements is *false*?

 A) All of the characteristics found in the original "opaque–2" mutant plant were desirable.

 B) Modern maize varieties containing "opaque–2" are genetically modified.

 C) None of the F_1 progeny from a cross of an "opaque–2" mutant and a "normal" maize plant will express the "opaque–2" character.

 D) It takes three growing seasons to determine which F_1 progeny have a recessive parental trait when one parent is the recessive mutant and the other is wild-type.

 E) Both C and D are false.

Answer: A
Skill: Comprehension

67) Which of the following statements is *true*?
Transgenic plants

A) can be produced only by genetic engineering.

B) contain genes from more than one species.

C) require intermediate species for the transgenic plant to be produced.

D) require many years to be produced.

E) A and D are correct statements.

Answer: B
Skill: Comprehension

68) The most immediate potential benefits of introducing genetically modified crops include

A) increasing the amount of land suitable for agriculture.

B) overcoming genetic incompatibility.

C) increasing the frequency of self–pollination.

D) increasing crop yield.

E) both B and C.

Answer: D
Skill: Knowledge

69) Which of the following is *not* a scientific concern relating to creating genetically modified crops?

A) Herbicide resistance may spread to weedy species.

B) Insect pests may more rapidly evolve resistance to toxins.

C) Nontarget species may be affected.

D) The monetary costs of producing genetically modified plants are significantly greater than traditional breeding techniques.

E) Genetically modified plants may lead to unknown risks to human health.

Answer: D
Skill: Comprehension

Media Activity Questions

1) Flowers are made of modified
   A) roots.
   B) stems.
   C) leaves.
   D) ovules.
   E) shoots.

   Answer: C
   Topic: Web/CD Activity 38A

2) Flowers usually contain
   A) either petals or sepals.
   B) either ovaries or ovules.
   C) either carpels or stamens.
   D) both male and female reproductive structures.
   E) either male or female reproductive structures.

   Answer: D
   Topic: Web/CD Activity 38A

3) Angiosperms are _____ plants.
   A) cone-bearing
   B) avascular
   C) naked seed
   D) seedless
   E) flowering

   Answer: E
   Topic: Web/CD Activity 38A

4) _____ is the first event in seed formation.
   A) Formation of a zygote
   B) Pollination
   C) Formation of endosperm
   D) Fertilization
   E) Growth of the pollen tube

   Answer: B
   Topic: Web/CD Activity 38B

5) Endosperm is
   A) haploid.
   B) diploid.
   C) triploid.
   D) tetraploid.
   E) dikaryotic.

   Answer: C
   Topic: Web/CD Activity 38B

Self–Quiz Questions

Answers to these questions also appear in the textbook.

1) Which of the following would *definitely* be a unisexual flower? A flower that
   A) is also incomplete.
   B) lacks sepals.
   C) is self–compatible.
   D) is staminate.
   E) cannot self–pollinate.

   Answer: D

2) Germinated pollen grain is to _____ as _____ is to female gametophyte.
   A) male gametophyte; embryo sac
   B) embryo sac; ovule
   C) ovule; sporophyte
   D) anther; seed
   E) petal; sepal

   Answer: A

3) A seed develops from
   A) an ovum.
   B) a pollen grain.
   C) an ovule.
   D) an ovary.
   E) an embryo.

   Answer: C

4) A fruit is a (an)
   A) mature ovary.
   B) mature ovule.
   C) seed plus its integuments.
   D) fused carpel.
   E) enlarged embryo sac.

   Answer: A

5) Which of the following conditions is needed by almost all seeds to break dormancy?
   A) exposure to light
   B) imbibition
   C) abrasion of the seed coat
   D) exposure to cold temperatures
   E) covering of fertile soil

   Answer: B

6) A plant that is self–incompatible has a genotype of S_5S_9 for the S–locus. It receives pollen from a plant that is S_3S_9. Which of the following is most likely to occur?
   A) All of the pollen will germinate, forming pollen tubes.
   B) None of the pollen will germinate.
   C) About half of the pollen will germinate.
   D) Fertilization will occur in about half of the flowers of the pollinated plant.
   E) Pollen from the S_3S_9 plant will secrete ribonuclease that destroys epidermal cells of the S_5S_9 stigma.

   Answer: C

7) Plant biotechnologists use protoplast fusion mainly to
   A) culture plant cells in vitro.
   B) asexually propagate desirable plant varieties.
   C) introduce bacterial genes into a plant genome.
   D) study the early events following the fertilization of egg and sperm.
   E) produce new hybrid species.

   Answer: E

8) The basal cell formed from the first division of a plant zygote will eventually develop into

A) the suspensor that anchors the embryo and transfers nutrients.

B) the proembryo, in which develop the procambium, protoderm, and ground meristem.

C) the endosperm that nourishes the developing embryo.

D) the root apex of the embryo.

E) two cotyledons in dicots, but only one cotyledon in monocots.

Answer: A

9) The introduction of genes that code for *Bt* toxin from *Bacillus thuringiensis* into cotton, maize, and potatoes has raised concerns because

A) these crops have been shown to be toxic to humans.

B) pollen from these crops has been shown to harm monarch butterfly larvae in laboratory experiments.

C) if these genes "escape" to related weed species, herbicides will not be able to control their growth.

D) this bacterium is a pathogen of humans.

E) the toxin reduces the nutrional quality of crops.

Answer: B

10) "Golden Rice" is a transgenic variety that

A) is resistant to various herbicides and thus rice fields can be weeded with those herbicides.

B) is resistant to a virus that commonly attacks rice fields.

C) includes bacterial genes that produce a toxin that reduces damage from insect pests.

D) produces much larger, golden grains that increase crop yields.

E) contains daffodil genes that increase the vitamin A content of the rice.

Answer: E

Chapter 39   Plant Responses to Internal and External Signals

1) The step(s) between a plant's perception of a change in the environment and the plant's response to that change is best called

A) a mutation.

B) hormone production.

C) pH change.

D) signal transduction.

E) an "all-or-none" response.

Answer: D
Skill: Knowledge

2) All of the following may function in signal transduction in plants *except*

A) calcium ions.

B) nonrandom mutations.

C) receptor proteins.

D) phytochrome.

E) second messengers.

Answer: B
Skill: Knowledge

3) What is the function of calmodulin in a signal-transduction pathway?

A) to receive the stimulus and activate the second messenger in the transduction step

B) to induce the selective activation of genes

C) to be a membrane-bound hormone receptor that causes an influx of Ca^{2+}

D) to form a complex with Ca^{2+} and activate specific molecules

E) to induce rapid responses such as stomatal closing or cell elongation

Answer: D
Skill: Knowledge

4) Many recent discoveries about the function of plant hormones are due to

A) the frequent use of brassinosteroids.

B) our increased knowledge of development using *Arabidopsis*.

C) better analysis of signal-transduction pathways using mutant plants.

D) more precise use of molecular biology techniques.

E) B, C, and D.

Answer: E
Skill: Comprehension

5) Charles and Francis Darwin concluded from their experiments on phototropism by oat seedlings that the part of the seedling that detects the direction of light is

A) the tip of the coleoptile.

B) the part of the coleoptile that bends during the response.

C) the root tip.

D) the cotyledon.

E) phytochrome.

Answer: A
Skill: Knowledge

6) Plants growing in a partially dark environment will grow toward light. This is called phototropism. What do we know about how the plant "knows" how to do this? Choose the *incorrect* process.

A) It is caused by a chemical signal.

B) One chemical involved is auxin.

C) Auxin causes a growth increase on one side of the stem.

D) Auxin causes a decrease in growth on the light side of the stem.

E) Removing the apical meristem prevents phototropism.

Answer: D
Skill: Comprehension

7) Which of these conclusions is supported by the research of both Went and the Darwins on shoot responses to light?

A) When shoots are exposed to light, a chemical substance migrates toward the light.

B) Agar contains a chemical substance that mimics a plant hormone.

C) A chemical substance involved in shoot bending is produced in shoot tips.

D) Once shoot tips have been cut, normal growth cannot be induced.

E) Light stimulates the synthesis of a plant hormone that responds to light.

Answer: C
Skill: Comprehension

8) We know from the experiments of the past that plants bend toward light because

A) they need sunlight energy for photosynthesis.

B) the sun stimulates stem growth.

C) cell expansion is greater on the dark side of the stem.

D) auxin is inactive on the dark side of the stem.

E) phytochrome stimulates florigen formation.

Answer: C
Skill: Comprehension

9) Which of the following is *not* presently considered a major mechanism whereby hormones control plant development?

A) affecting cell respiration via regulation of the Krebs cycle

B) affecting cell division via the cell cycle

C) affecting cell elongation through acid growth

D) affecting cell differentiation through altered gene activity

E) mediating short–term physiological responses to environmental stimuli

Answer: A
Skill: Knowledge

10) Evidence for phototropism due to the asymmetric distribution of auxin moving down the stem

A) has not been found in eudicots such as sunflower and radish.

B) has been found in all monocots and most eudicots.

C) has been shown to involve only IAA stimulation of cell elongation on the dark side of the stem.

D) can be demonstrated with unilateral red light, but not blue light.

E) is now thought by most plant scientists *not* to involve the shoot tip.

Answer: A
Skill: Knowledge

11) Vines in tropical rain forests must grow toward large trees before being able to grow toward the sun. To reach a large tree, the most useful kind of growth movement for a tropical vine would be approximately the *opposite* of

A) positive thigmotropism.

B) positive phototropism.

C) positive gravitropism.

D) sleep movements.

E) circadian rhythms.

Answer: B
Skill: Application

12) Plant hormones can be characterized by all of the following *except* that they

A) may act by altering gene expression.

B) have a multiplicity of effects.

C) function independently of other hormones.

D) control plant growth and development.

E) affect division, elongation, and differentiation of cells.

Answer: C
Skill: Knowledge

13) Plant hormones produce their effects by

  A) altering the expression of genes.

  B) modifying the permeability of the plasma membrane.

  C) modifying the structure of the nuclear envelope membrane.

  D) both A and B.

  E) both B and C.

Answer: D
Skill: Comprehension

14) Why might animal hormones function differently from plant hormones?

  A) Animals move rapidly away from negative stimuli and most plants don't.

  B) Plant cells have a cell wall that blocks passage of many hormones.

  C) Plants must have more precise timing of their reproductive activities.

  D) Plants are much more variable in their morphology and development than animals.

  E) Both A and D are correct.

Answer: E
Skill: Comprehension

15) Which of the following is the only known naturally occurring auxin?

  A) 2, 4–D

  B) IAA

  C) GA

  D) ABA

  E) TCA

Answer: B
Skill: Knowledge

16) Which of the following is a significant difference between plant and animal hormones?

  A) Animal cells usually respond to single hormones, while plant hormones often cause activities dependent on the ratios of two or more hormones.

  B) Animal hormones travel in circulatory systems, and thus have relatively the same concentrations throughout the body, while the concentration of a plant hormone depends on where it is produced and how fast it travels, and thus has varying concentrations throughout the plant body.

  C) Plant hormones usually control growth, development, and responses to environmental stimuli, while animal hormones are more often responsible for maintaining homeostasis.

  D) A and C are significant differences.

  E) A, B, and C are significant differences.

Answer: E
Skill: Comprehension

17) Why is it so difficult to study the actions of plant hormones?

  A) They often interact to produce an effect.

  B) They are found in small quantities in the plant.

  C) We probably have not discovered all of them.

  D) They sometimes cause different responses in different plants.

  E) All of the above make the study of plant hormones difficult.

Answer: E
Skill: Comprehension

18) Plant hormones can have different effects at different concentrations. This is why
   A) some plants are long–day plants and others are short–day plants.
   B) signal-transduction pathways in plants are different from those in animals.
   C) plant genes recognize pathogen genes.
   D) auxin can stimulate cell elongation in apical meristems, yet will inhibit the growth of axillary buds.
   E) they really don't fit the definition of "hormone."

   Answer: D
   Skill: Knowledge

19) Which plant hormones might be used to enhance stem elongation and fruit growth?
   A) brassinosteroids and oligosaccharides
   B) auxins and gibberellins
   C) abscisic acid and phytochrome
   D) ethylene and cytokinins
   E) phytochrome and flowering hormone

   Answer: B
   Skill: Knowledge

For the following questions, match the hormone with the classic description of that hormone. Each choice may be used once, more than once, or not at all.

   A. *auxin*
   B. *cytokinin*
   C. *gibberellin*
   D. *ethylene*
   E. *abscisic acid*

20) inhibits growth; closes stomata during water stress

   Answer: E
   Skill: Knowledge

21) stimulates cell division by influencing the synthesis or activation of proteins required for mitosis

   Answer: B
   Skill: Knowledge

22) acts by increasing the plasticity of the cell wall

   Answer: A
   Skill: Knowledge

23) a gas that hastens fruit ripening

   Answer: D
   Skill: Knowledge

24) promotes internode elongation; promotes germination of certain seeds

   Answer: C
   Skill: Knowledge

25) Which of the following has *not* been established as an aspect of auxin's role in cell elongation?
   A) Auxin instigates a loosening of cell wall fibers.
   B) Auxin increases the quantity of cytoplasm in the cell.
   C) Through auxin activity, vacuoles increase in size.
   D) Auxin activity permits an increase in turgor pressure.
   E) Auxin stimulates proton pumps.

   Answer: B
   Skill: Comprehension

26) According to the acid growth hypothesis, auxin works by

A) dissolving sieve plates, permitting more rapid transport of nutrients.

B) dissolving the cell membranes temporarily, permitting cells that were on the verge of dividing to divide more rapidly.

C) changing the pH within the cell, which would permit the electron transport chain to operate more efficiently.

D) allowing the affected cell walls to stretch.

E) greatly increasing the rate of deposition of cell wall material.

Answer: D
Skill: Comprehension

27) Which of the following hormones would be most useful in causing the rooting of plant cuttings?

A) oligosaccharins

B) abscisic acid

C) cytokinins

D) gibberellins

E) auxins

Answer: E
Skill: Application

28) Which plant hormone(s) is (are) most closely associated with cell division?

A) ethylene

B) cytokinin

C) abscisic acid

D) phytochrome

E) brassinosteroids

Answer: B
Skill: Knowledge

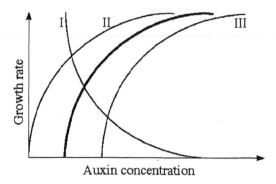

Figure 39.1

29) The heavy line in Figure 39.1 illustrates the relationship between auxin concentration and cell growth in stem tissues. If the same range of concentrations was applied to lateral buds, what curve would probably be produced?

A) I only

B) II only

C) III only

D) II and III

E) either I or III

Answer: A
Skill: Application

30) The application of which of the following hormones would be a logical first choice in an attempt to produce normal growth in mutant dwarf plants?

A) indoleacetic acid

B) cytokinin

C) gibberellin

D) abscisic acid

E) ethylene

Answer: C
Skill: Knowledge

Refer to Figure 39.2 to answer the following questions.

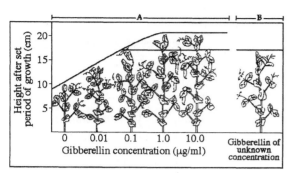

Figure 39.2

31) The results of this experiment shown on the left of the graph (area A) may be used

 A) to show that these plants can live without gibberellin.

 B) to show that gibberellin is necessary in positive gravitropism.

 C) to show that taller plants with more gibberellin produce fruit (pods).

 D) to show a correlation between plant height and gibberellin concentration.

 E) to study phytoalexins in plants.

Answer: D
Skill: Comprehension

32) This experiment suggests that the unknown amount of GA in the experimental plant (B) is approximately

 A) zero.

 B) 0.01 μg/ml.

 C) 0.1 μg/ml.

 D) 1.0 μg/ml.

 E) equal to the amount of gibberellin in the shortest plant.

Answer: C
Skill: Application

33) One effect of gibberellins is to stimulate cereal seeds to produce

 A) RuBP carboxylase.

 B) lipids.

 C) abscisic acid.

 D) starch.

 E) amylase.

Answer: E
Skill: Knowledge

34) In attempting to make a seed break dormancy, one could logically treat it with

 A) IAA.

 B) 2, 4-D.

 C) CO_2.

 D) gibberellins.

 E) abscisic acid.

Answer: D
Skill: Knowledge

Use the following answers in your responses to the questions below. Each one may be used once, more than once, or not at all.

 A. auxin
 B. cytokinins
 C. gibberellins
 D. abscisic acid
 E. ethylene

35) Growing a plant in space under conditions of microgravity is most likely to affect the activity of which hormone?

Answer: A
Skill: Application

36) Which hormone has been shown to trigger a rapid plant response to a sudden decrease in humidity?

Answer: D
Skill: Knowledge

37) A botanist is unable to germinate the seeds of a wild plant. This is most likely due to the action of which hormone?

Answer: D
Skill: Knowledge

38) While responses to plant hormones are normally slow, which of the following hormones has been shown to be involved in the rapid opening and closing of stomata?
   A) auxin
   B) cytokinin
   C) ethylene
   D) abscisic acid
   E) gibberellin

Answer: D
Skill: Knowledge

39) Ethylene, as an example of a plant hormone, may have multiple effects on a plant, depending on all of the following *except* the
   A) site of action within the plant.
   B) developmental stage of the plant.
   C) concentration of ethylene.
   D) altered chemical structure of ethylene from a gas to a liquid.
   E) readiness of cell membrane receptors for the ethylene.

Answer: D
Skill: Comprehension

40) If you were shipping green bananas to a supermarket in Boston, which of the following chemicals would you want to eliminate from the plants' environment?
   A) CO_2
   B) cytokinins
   C) ethylene
   D) auxin
   E) gibberellic acids

Answer: C
Skill: Application

41) Which of the following is currently the most powerful tool for research on plant hormones?
   A) comparisons of photoperiodic responses
   B) comparing tropisms and turgor movements
   C) subjecting plants to unusual stresses
   D) the study of phytochrome
   E) analysis of mutant plants

Answer: E
Skill: Knowledge

42) We tend to think of plants as immobile when, in fact, they can move in many ways. All of the below are movements plants can accomplish *except*
   A) growth movements up or down in response to gravity.
   B) folding and unfolding of leaves using muscle–like tissues.
   C) growth movements toward or away from light.
   D) changes in plant growth form in response to wind or touch.
   E) rapid responses using action potentials similar to those found in the nervous tissue of animals.

Answer: B
Skill: Comprehension

43) Auxin is responsible for many plant growth responses, including all of the following *except*
   A) phototropism.
   B) formation of adventitious roots.
   C) apical dominance.
   D) detection of photoperiod.
   E) cell elongation.

Answer: D
Skill: Knowledge

44) Incandescent light bulbs, which have high output of red light, are *least* effective in promoting

 A) photosynthesis.

 B) seed germination.

 C) phototropism.

 D) flowering.

 E) entrainment of circadian rhythms.

Answer: C
Skill: Application

45) Both red and blue light are involved with

 A) stem elongation.

 B) photoperiodism.

 C) positive phototropism.

 D) tracking seasons.

 E) all of the above.

Answer: A
Skill: Knowledge

46) In legumes, it has been shown that "sleep" movements are correlated with

 A) positive thigmotropisms.

 B) rhythmic opening and closing of K^+ channels in motor cell membranes.

 C) senescence (the aging process in plants).

 D) flowering and fruit development.

 E) ABA-stimulated closing of guard cells caused by loss of K^+.

Answer: B
Skill: Knowledge

47) Biological clocks cause organisms to perform daily activities on a regular basis. Which of the following is a *false* statement about this kind of "circadian rhythm"?

 A) It may have the same signal-transduction pathway in all organisms.

 B) It must be reset on a daily basis.

 C) It may help to cause photoperiodic responses.

 D) It is independent of day and night length.

 E) The exact mechanism of biological clocks remains unknown.

Answer: D
Skill: Knowledge

48) The biological clock controlling circadian rhythms must ultimately

 A) depend on environmental cues.

 B) affect gene transcription.

 C) stabilize on a 24-hour cycle.

 D) speed up or slow down with increasing or decreasing temperature.

 E) do all of the above.

Answer: B
Skill: Comprehension

49) Plants often use changes in day length (photoperiod) to trigger events such as dormancy and flowering. It is logical that plants have evolved this mechanism because photoperiod changes

 A) are more predictable than air temperature changes.

 B) alter the amount of energy available to the plant.

 C) are modified by soil temperature changes.

 D) can reset the biological clock.

 E) are correlated with moisture availability.

Answer: A
Skill: Application

50) If the range of a species of plants expands to a higher latitude, which of the following processes is the most *likely* to be modified by natural selection?
   A) circadian rhythm
   B) photoperiodic response
   C) phototropic response
   D) biological clock
   E) thigmomorphogenesis

Answer: B
Skill: Application

51) In nature, poinsettias bloom in early March. Research has shown that these plants are triggered to flower three months before they actually bloom. The trigger is the length of the light–dark cycle. In order to get poinsettias to bloom in December, florists change the length of the light–dark cycle in September. Given the information and clues above, which of the following is *false*?
   A) Poinsettias are short–day plants.
   B) Poinsettias require a light period shorter than some maximum.
   C) Poinsettias require a longer dark period than is available in September.
   D) The dark period can be interrupted without affecting flowering.
   E) Poinsettias will flower even if there are brief periods of dark during the daytime.

Answer: D
Skill: Application

52) A botanist exposed two groups of plants (of the same species) to two photoperiods, one with 14 hours of light and 10 hours of dark and the other with 10 hours of light and 14 hours of dark. Under the first set of conditions, the plants flowered, but they failed to flower under the second set of conditions. Which of the following conclusions would be consistent with these results?
   A) The critical night length is 14 hours.
   B) The plants are short–day plants.
   C) The critical day length is 10 hours.
   D) The plants can convert phytochrome to florigen.
   E) The plants flower in the spring.

Answer: E
Skill: Application

53) In order to flower, what does a short–day plant need?
   A) a burst of red light in the middle of the night
   B) a burst of far–red light in the middle of the night
   C) a day that is longer than a certain length
   D) a night that is longer than a certain length
   E) a higher ratio of P_r:P_{fr}

Answer: D
Skill: Comprehension

54) If a short–day plant has a critical night length of 15 hours, then which of the following 24–hour cycles will prevent flowering?

A) 8 hours light / 16 hours dark

B) 4 hours light / 20 hours dark

C) 6 hours light / 2 hours dark / light flash / 16 hours dark

D) 8 hours light / 8 hours dark / light flash / 8 hours dark

E) 2 hours light / 20 hours dark / 2 hours light

Answer: D
Skill: Comprehension

55) A long–day plant will flower if

A) the duration of continuous light exceeds a critical length.

B) the duration of continuous light is less than a critical length.

C) the duration of continuous darkness exceeds a critical length.

D) the duration of continuous darkness is less than a critical length.

E) it is kept in continuous far-red light.

Answer: D
Skill: Knowledge

56) Plants that have their flowering inhibited by being exposed to bright lights at night are

A) day-neutral plants.

B) short-night plants.

C) devoid of phytochrome.

D) short-day plants.

E) long-day plants.

Answer: D
Skill: Comprehension

57) Suppose there is a large deciduous ornamental tree on your campus and the city places a very bright street light right next to it on a tall pole. A botanist on the faculty complains to the city council and asks them to remove the light. Most likely the botanist is concerned because the light

A) will alter the photosynthetic rate of the tree and keep it growing at night.

B) may cause the stomates to close because of increased ABA synthesis. This could starve the tree for CO_2 and it could die.

C) may change the photoperiod and cause the tree to retain its leaves during the winter. This could cause dehydration and loss of the tree.

D) will cause the tree to bend toward the light on the pole and it could fall.

E) will stimulate ethylene production, premature senescence, and early death of the tree.

Answer: C
Skill: Application

58) If you take a short–day plant and put it in a lab under conditions where it will flower (long nights and short days), but interrupt its day period with a few minutes of darkness, what will happen?

A) It will flower.

B) It will not flower.

C) It will die.

D) It will lose its ability to photosynthesize.

E) It will form new shoots from the axillary buds.

Answer: A
Skill: Comprehension

59) There is some experimental evidence that a hypothetical flowering hormone may be produced by

A) flowers.

B) leaves.

C) roots.

D) seeds.

E) floral buds.

Answer: B
Skill: Knowledge

60) What do results of research on gravitropic responses of roots and stems show?

A) Different tissues have the same response to auxin.

B) The effect of a plant hormone can depend on the tissue.

C) Some responses of plants require no hormones at all.

D) Light is required for the gravitropic response.

E) Cytokinin can only function in the presence of auxin.

Answer: B
Skill: Comprehension

61) A botanist discovers a plant that lacks the ability to form starch grains in root cells, yet the roots still grow downward. This evidence refutes the long–standing hypothesis that

A) falling statoliths trigger gravitropism.

B) starch accumulation triggers the negative phototropic response of roots.

C) starch grains block the acid growth response in roots.

D) starch is converted to auxin, which causes the downward bending in roots.

E) starch and downward movement are necessary for thigmotropism.

Answer: A
Skill: Application

62) If a plant is mechanically stimulated, it will grow shorter, thicker stems. This response is

A) the result of ethylene production.

B) caused by an increase in turgor.

C) an adaptation to windy environments.

D) Only A and C are correct.

E) A, B, and C are correct.

Answer: D
Skill: Knowledge

63) You are part of a desert plant research team trying to discover crops that will be productive in arid climates. You discover a plant that produces a guard cell hormone under water deficit conditions. Most likely the hormone is

A) ABA.

B) GA.

C) IAA.

D) 2, 4–D.

E) salicylic acid.

Answer: A
Skill: Knowledge

64) If you wanted to genetically engineer a plant to be more resistant to drought, increasing amounts of which of the following hormones might be a good first attempt?

A) abscisic acid

B) brassinosteroids

C) gibberellins

D) cytokinins

E) auxin

Answer: A
Skill: Application

65) Plant cells begin synthesizing large quantities of heat-shock proteins

A) after the induction of chaperone proteins.

B) in response to the lack of CO_2 following the closing of stomates by ethylene.

C) when desert plants are quickly removed from high temperatures.

D) when they are subjected to moist heat (steam) followed by electrical shock.

E) when the air is above 40°C around species from temperate regions.

Answer: E
Skill: Knowledge

66) Most scientists agree that global warming has begun; thus it is important to know how plants will respond to heat stress. Which of the following is an immediate short-term response of plants to heat stress?

A) the production of heat-shock carbohydrates unique to each plant

B) the production of heat-shock proteins like those of other organisms

C) the opening of stomata to increase evaporational heat loss

D) their evolution into more xerophytic plants

E) all of the above

Answer: B
Skill: Knowledge

67) In extremely cold regions, woody species may survive freezing temperatures by

A) emptying water from the vacuoles to prevent freezing.

B) decreasing the numbers of phospholipids in cell membranes.

C) decreasing the fluidity of all cellular membranes.

D) producing canavanine as a natural antifreeze.

E) increasing specific solute concentrations inside cells to allow supercooling.

Answer: E
Skill: Knowledge

68) All of the following are responses of plants to cold stress *except*

A) the production of a specific solute "plant antifreeze" that reduces water loss.

B) excluding ice crystals from the interior walls.

C) conversion of the fluid mosaic cell membrane to a solid mosaic one.

D) an alteration of membrane lipids so that the membranes remain flexible.

E) increasing the proportion of unsaturated fatty acids in the membranes.

Answer: C
Skill: Comprehension

69) In general, which of the following is *not* a plant response to herbivores?

A) domestication, so that humans can protect the plant

B) attracting predatory animals, such as parasitoid wasps

C) chemical defenses, such as toxic compounds

D) physical defenses, such as thorns

E) production of volatile molecules

Answer: A
Skill: Knowledge

70) In order for a plant to initiate chemical responses to herbivory

A) the plant must be directly attacked by an herbivore.

B) volatile "signal" compounds mut be perceived.

C) gene–for–gene recognition must occur.

D) phytoalexins must be released.

E) all of the above must happen.

Answer: B
Skill: Comprehension

71) Plants are affected by an array of pathogens. Which of the following is *not* a plant defense against disease?

A) cells near the point of infection killing themselves to prevent the spread of the infection

B) production of chemicals that kill pathogens

C) acquiring gene–for–gene recognition that allows specific proteins to interact so that the plant can produce defenses against the pathogen

D) a waxy cuticle that pathogens have trouble penetrating

E) All of the above are correct.

Answer: E
Skill: Comprehension

72) A pathogenic fungus invades a plant. The infected plant produces _____ in response to the attack.

A) antisense RNA

B) phytoalexins

C) phytochrome

D) statoliths

E) thickened cellulose microfibrils in the cell wall

Answer: B
Skill: Knowledge

73) Which of the following plant responses does *not* create a physical barrier to the spread of pathogenic microorganisms?

A) lignification of cell walls in the area of infection

B) localized cell death

C) production of antimicrobial molecules

D) proliferation of cross–linkages in cell wall molecules

E) All of the above are physical barriers.

Answer: C
Skill: Comprehension

74) The transduction pathway that activates systemic acquired resistance in plants is initially signaled by

A) antisense RNA.

B) P_{fr} phytochrome.

C) salicylic acid.

D) abscisic acid.

E) red, but not far-red, light.

Answer: C
Skill: Knowledge

75) Which of the below are examples/parts of plants' systemic acquired resistance against infection?

A) the hypersensitive response

B) aspirin

C) alarm hormones

D) tropisms

E) phytoalexins

Answer: C
Skill: Knowledge

Media Activity Questions

1) Leaves that survive the winter tend to be

   A) small and narrow.

   B) broad and flat.

   C) large and narrow.

   D) thick and round.

   E) flat and square.

   Answer: A
   Topic: Web/CD Activity 39A

2) In leaf abscission, the abscission layer forms where the

   A) petiole joins the root.

   B) petiole joins the stem.

   C) axillary bud joins the stem.

   D) root joins the stem.

   E) scab joins the root.

   Answer: B
   Topic: Web/CD Activity 39A

3) The formation of an abscission layer may trap sugars in the _____ of palisade cells.

   A) vacuole

   B) amyloplast

   C) mitochondrion

   D) peroxisome

   E) chloroplast

   Answer: A
   Topic: Web/CD Activity 39A

4) What is the specific term that refers to seasonal changes in the relative lengths of night and day?

   A) photoperiod

   B) circadian rhythm

   C) chemotaxis

   D) gravitropism

   E) phototaxis

   Answer: A
   Topic: Web/CD Activity 39B

5) A plant with a critical minimum day length of 14 hours and flowers in summer is a

   A) long-day plant.

   B) short-night plant.

   C) short-day plant.

   D) neutral-day plant.

   E) neutral-night plant.

   Answer: A
   Topic: Web/CD Activity 39B

Self-Quiz Questions

Answers to these questions also appear in the textbook.

1) Which of the following plant hormones is incorrectly paired with its function?

   A) auxin—promotes stem growth through cell elongation

   B) cytokinins—initiate programmed cell death

   C) gibberellins—stimulate seed germination

   D) abscisic acid—promotes seed dormancy

   E) ethylene—inhibits cell elongation

   Answer: B

2) Which of the following is *not* a typical component of a signal-transduction pathway such as the one involved in producing the greening response?

   A) G-proteins acting as transcription factors that activate specific genes

   B) activation of enzymes that produce second messengers such as cGMP

   C) activation of a G-protein by an activated receptor protein

   D) protein kinase cascades

   E) phosphorylation of transcription factors

   Answer: A

3) Buds and sprouts often form on tree stumps. Which of the following hormones would you expect to stimulate their formation?

   A) auxin

   B) cytokinins

   C) abscisic acid

   D) ethylene

   E) gibberellins

   Answer: B

4) Which of the following is *not* part of the acid-growth hypothesis?

   A) Auxin stimulates proton pumps in cell membranes.

   B) Lowered pH results in the breakage of cross-links between cellulose microfibrils.

   C) The wall fabric becomes looser (more plastic).

   D) Auxin-activated proton pumps stimulate cell division in meristems.

   E) The turgor pressure of the cell exceeds the restraining pressure of the loosened cell wall, and the cell takes up water and elongates.

   Answer: D

5) The signal for flowering could be released earlier than normal in a long-day plant experimentally exposed to flashes of

   A) far-red light during the night.

   B) red light during the night.

   C) red light followed by far-red light during the night.

   D) far-red light during the day.

   E) red light during the day.

   Answer: B

6) How might a plant respond to *severe* heat stress?

A) orient leaves toward the sun to increase evaporative cooling

B) produce ethylene that kills some cortex cells and creates air tubes for ventilation

C) produce salicylic acid that initiates a systemic acquired resistance response

D) increase the proportion of unsaturated fatty acids in cell membranes to reduce their fluidity

E) produce heat-shock proteins that may protect the plant's proteins from denaturing

Answer: E

7) If a long-day plant has a critical night length of 9 hours, which of the following 24-hour cycles would prevent flowering?

A) 16 hours light/8 hours dark

B) 14 hours light/10 hours dark

C) 15.5 hours light/8.5 hours dark

D) 4 hours light/8 hours dark/4 hours light/8 hours dark

E) 8 hours light/8 hours dark/light flash/8 hours dark

Answer: B

8) The probable role of salicylic acid in systemic acquired resistance of plants is to

A) destroy pathogens directly.

B) activate plant defenses throughout the plant before infection spreads.

C) close stomata, thus preventing the entry of pathogens.

D) activate heat-shock proteins.

E) sacrifice infected tissues by hydrolyzing cells.

Answer: B

9) Auxin triggers the acidification of cell walls that results in rapid growth, but also stimulates sustained, long-term cell elongation. What best explains how auxin brings about this dual growth response?

A) Auxin binds to different receptors in different cells.

B) Different concentrations of auxin have different effects.

C) Auxin causes second messengers to activate both proton pumps and certain genes.

D) The dual effects are due to two different auxins.

E) Other antagonistic hormones modify auxin's effects.

Answer: C

10) The subscripts in the following choices indicate specific *Avr* and *R* genes in pathogens and plant cells. Uppercase letters indicate dominant alleles, while lowercase symbolizes recessive alleles. In which of the situations would the pathogen be avirulent?

A) Avr_D—R_d

B) Avr_E—R_G

C) Avr_M—R_M

D) Avr_g—R_g

E) Avr_e—R_E

Answer: C

Chapter 40   An Introduction to Animal Structure and Function

1) In herbivores, the observation that "form fits function" is best characterized by
   A) canine teeth for cutting grasses and leaves.
   B) an intestinal tract with a long cecum for digesting plant material.
   C) a shorter small intestine than carnivores.
   D) a small–diameter large intestine that slows peristalsis.
   E) both A and B are correct.

   Answer: B
   Skill: Comprehension

2) Cells are to tissues as tissues are to
   A) organs.
   B) membranes.
   C) organ systems.
   D) organelles.
   E) organisms.

   Answer: A
   Skill: Knowledge

3) In a typical multicellular animal, the circulatory system interacts with various specialized surfaces in order to exchange materials with the exterior environment. Which of the following is *not* an example of such an exchange surface?
   A) lung
   B) muscle
   C) skin
   D) intestine
   E) kidney

   Answer: B
   Skill: Comprehension

4) The epithelium best adapted for a body surface subject to abrasion is
   A) simple squamous.
   B) simple cuboidal.
   C) simple columnar.
   D) stratified columnar.
   E) stratified squamous.

   Answer: E
   Skill: Knowledge

5) Which of the following tissues lines the kidney ducts?
   A) connective
   B) smooth muscle
   C) nervous
   D) epithelial
   E) adipose

   Answer: D
   Skill: Knowledge

6) "Stratified columnar" is a description which might apply to what type of animal tissue?
   A) connective
   B) striated muscle
   C) nerve
   D) epithelial
   E) bone

   Answer: D
   Skill: Knowledge

7) What is stratified cuboidal epithelium composed of?

A) several layers of boxlike cells

B) a hierarchical arrangement of flat cells

C) a tight layer of square cells attached to a basement membrane

D) an irregularly arranged layer of pillarlike cells

E) a layer of ciliated, mucus–secreting cells

Answer: A
Skill: Knowledge

8) A malfunction in this glandular epithelium could adversely affect body metabolism.

A) thyroid gland

B) sebaceous gland

C) salivary gland

D) bulbourethral gland

E) exocrine gland

Answer: A
Skill: Application

9) Which statement best links the group of tissues known as connective tissue? A connective tissue will have

A) an extracellular matrix containing fibers.

B) a supporting material such as chondroitin sulfate.

C) an epithelial origin.

D) relatively few cells and a large amount of extracellular matrix.

E) both A and B.

Answer: D
Skill: Application

10) Which of the following fibers is responsible for the resistant property of tendons?

A) elastin fibers

B) fibrin fibers

C) collagenous fibers

D) reticular fibers

E) spindle fibers

Answer: C
Skill: Comprehension

11) If you gently twist your ear lobe it does not remain distorted because it contains

A) collagen fibers.

B) elastin fibers.

C) reticular fibers.

D) adipose tissue.

E) loose connective tissue.

Answer: B
Skill:

12) What do fibroblasts secret?

A) fats

B) chondrin

C) interstitial fluids

D) calcium phosphate for bone

E) proteins for connective fibers

Answer: E
Skill: Knowledge

13) An extended low-fat diet will have the most significant effect on which of the following?

A) muscle mass

B) glucose utilization

C) basal metabolic rate (BMR)

D) standard metabolic rate (SMR)

E) energy reserves

Answer: E
Skill: Application

14) What joins muscles to bones?

    A) ligaments

    B) tendons

    C) loose connective tissue

    D) Haversian systems

    E) spindle fibers

Answer: B
Skill: Knowledge

15) Cartilage is an example of which of the following types of tissue?

    A) connective

    B) reproductive

    C) nervous

    D) epithelial

    E) adipose

Answer: A
Skill: Knowledge

16) What holds bones together at joints?

    A) cartilage

    B) Haversian systems

    C) loose connective tissue

    D) tendons

    E) ligaments

Answer: E
Skill: Knowledge

17) Why is bone different from other tissues?

    A) It lacks a blood supply.

    B) It lacks a nerve supply.

    C) It lacks an extracellular matrix.

    D) It is a nonliving structure.

    E) Its cells are in an extracellular secretion.

Answer: E
Skill: Application

The following questions refer to the diagram shown in Figure 40.1.

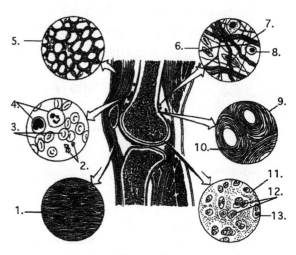

Figure 40.1

18) Which of the following numbers represents a tissue found in tendons?

    A) 1

    B) 5

    C) 6

    D) 9

    E) 13

Answer: A
Skill: Comprehension

19) Which of the following numbers represents a tissue rich in hydroxyapatite?

    A) 1

    B) 5

    C) 6

    D) 9

    E) 13

Answer: D
Skill: Comprehension

20) Which of the following numbers represents a tissue rich in fat?

A) 1

B) 5

C) 6

D) 9

E) 13

Answer: B
Skill: Comprehension

21) Which of the following numbers represents chondrocytes?

A) 3

B) 4

C) 8

D) 10

E) 12

Answer: E
Skill: Comprehension

22) Which of the following numbers represents the location of osteocytes?

A) 2

B) 3

C) 8

D) 10

E) 12

Answer: D
Skill: Comprehension

23) Matrices of connective tissue include all of the following *except*

A) chondroitin sulfate of cartilage.

B) actin and myosin of muscle.

C) plasma of blood.

D) hydroxyapatite of bone.

E) More than one of the above is correct.

Answer: B
Skill: Knowledge

24) The functional unit of nervous tissue is the

A) cell body.

B) neuron.

C) axon.

D) dendrite.

E) brain.

Answer: B
Skill: Knowledge

25) Which of the following traits is characteristic of *all* types of muscle tissue?

A) intercalated discs that allow cells to communicate

B) striated banding pattern seen under the microscope

C) cells that lengthen when appropriately stimulated

D) a response that can be consciously controlled

E) cells that contain actin and myosin

Answer: E
Skill: Knowledge

26) Skeletal muscle are

A) smooth and involuntary.

B) smooth and unbranched.

C) striated and voluntary.

D) smooth and voluntary.

E) striated and branched.

Answer: C
Skill: Knowledge

27) Cardiac muscle is

A) striated and branched.

B) striated and unbranched.

C) smooth and voluntary.

D) striated and voluntary.

E) smooth and involuntary.

Answer: A
Skill: Knowledge

28) The type of muscle tissue that is associated with internal organs, except the heart, is referred to as

A) skeletal.

B) cardiac.

C) striated.

D) intercalated.

E) smooth.

Answer: E
Skill: Knowledge

29) Which type of muscle is responsible for moving food along the digestive tract?

A) cardiac

B) smooth

C) voluntary

D) striated

E) skeletal

Answer: B
Skill: Comprehension

30) Which of the following layers of the stomach is best described as being composed primarily of epithelial tissue?

A) mucosa

B) submucosa

C) muscularis

D) serosa

E) mesenteries

Answer: A
Skill: Knowledge

31) In mammals, the diaphragm separates the abdominal cavity from the

A) coelom.

B) pharynx.

C) thoracic cavity.

D) gastrovascular cavity.

E) oral cavity.

Answer: C
Skill: Knowledge

32) Which choice could be used as a theoretical example of convergence between humans and aquatic animals?

A) a speed swimmer wearing a wet suit to reduce friction while in the water

B) a diver using an air tank to sustain a longer dive time

C) an aquatic mammal nursing its young

D) the appearance of hair on a whale

E) the aquatic mammal having eyes centered on the front of the head

Answer: A
Skill: Application

33) Regardless of their size, the one thing that is common to all animals is

A) an external body surface that is dry.

B) a basic body plan that resembles a two-layered sac.

C) the use of homeostatic mechanisms to control their internal environment.

D) the use of positive and negative feedback cycles to regulate body water content.

E) having cells surrounded by an aqueous medium.

Answer: E
Skill: Application

34) Which of the following is a problem that had to be solved as animals increased in size?

I.   decreasing surface-to-volume ratio
II. reproducing in aqueous environments
III. the increasing tendency for larger bodies to be more variable

A) I only

B) II only

C) III only

D) I and III only

E) I, II, and III

Answer: A
Skill: Comprehension

35) An increase in which of the following parameters is most important in the evolution of specialized exchange surfaces such as the linings of the lungs or intestines?

A) surface area

B) thickness

C) number of cell layers

D) metabolic rate of its component cells

E) volume of its component cells

Answer: A
Skill: Comprehension

36) What is the common functional significance of the many cells making up such seemingly different structures as the lining of the air sacs in the lungs and the wavy lining of the human intestine?

A) increased oxygen demand from their metabolic activity

B) increased exchange surface provided by their membranes

C) greater numbers of cell organelles contained within their cytoplasm

D) greater protection due to increased cellular mass

E) lowered basal metabolic rate due to cooperation between cells

Answer: B
Skill: Comprehension

37) Which of the following is true of interstitial fluid?

A) It forms the extracellular matrix of connective tissue.

B) It is the internal environment found in animal cells.

C) It is composed of blood.

D) It provides for the exchange of materials between blood and cells.

E) It is found inside the small intestine.

Answer: D
Skill: Knowledge

38) Why must multicellular organisms keep their cells awash in an "internal pond"?

A) Negative feedback will only operate in interstitial fluids.

B) All cells need an aqueous medium for the exchange of nutrients, gases, and wastes.

C) The cells of multicellular organisms tend to lose water because of osmosis.

D) The cells of multicellular organisms tend to accumulate wastes, a consequence of diffusion.

E) This phenomenon only occurs in aquatic organisms because terrestrial organisms have adapted to life in dry environments.

Answer: B
Skill: Knowledge

39) The body's automatic tendency to maintain a constant internal environment is termed

A) negative feedback.

B) physiologic control.

C) homeostasis.

D) static equilibrium.

E) organ system function.

Answer: C
Skill: Knowledge

40) Which example best describes a homeostatic control system?

A) The core body temperature of a runner is allowed to gradually rise from 37°C to 45°C.

B) The kidneys excrete salt into the urine when dietary salt levels rise.

C) A blood cell shrinks when placed in a solution of salt and water.

D) The blood pressure increases in response to an increase in blood volume.

E) Motility in the digestive tract increases following a meal.

Answer: B
Skill: Application

41) Which of the following is the best example of an effector's response in negative feedback?

A) an increase in body temperature resulting from shivering

B) an increase in body temperature resulting from exercise

C) an increase in body temperature resulting from exposure to the sun

D) an increase in body temperature resulting from fever

E) a decrease in body temperature resulting from shock

Answer: A
Skill: Comprehension

42) Which of the following is an example of positive feedback?

A) An increase in blood sugar concentration increases the amount of the hormone that stores sugar as glycogen.

B) A decrease in blood sugar concentration increases the amount of the hormone that converts glycogen to glucose.

C) An infant's suckling at the mother's breast increases the amount of the hormone that induces the release of milk from the mammary glands.

D) An increase in calcium concentration increases the amount of the hormone that stores calcium in bone.

E) A decrease in calcium concentration increases the amount of the hormone that releases calcium from bone.

Answer: C
Skill: Comprehension

43) How does positive feedback differ from negative feedback?

A) Positive feedback benefits the organism, whereas negative feedback is detrimental.

B) In positive feedback, the effector's response is in the same direction as the initiating stimulus rather than opposite to it.

C) In positive feedback, the effector increases some parameter (such as temperature), whereas in negative feedback it decreases.

D) Positive feedback systems have effectors, whereas negative feedback systems utilize receptors.

E) Positive feedback systems have control centers that are lacking in negative feedback systems.

Answer: B
Skill: Comprehension

44) Consider a husband and wife sharing a bed, with each one having an electric blanket. Their controls become switched. When the husband feels cold, he turns up the control. This warms up his spouse, who turns down her control. This chills the husband, who turns up his control even more. The process continues. For both the wife and the husband, this would be an example of

A) negative feedback.

B) positive feedback.

C) homeostasis.

D) regulated change.

E) integrated control.

Answer: B
Skill: Comprehension

45) Which common event most closely resembles negative feedback?

A) The water shuts off when the float rises in the tank of a toilet.

B) The chlorine level of swimming pool decreases when the chlorinator is turned off.

C) The flame size on a gas stove changes when the gas is turned off.

D) There is a continual buildup of moisture in a basement with a dehumidifier running.

E) There is a decrease in water pressure when the faucet is slowly turned off.

Answer: A
Skill: Application

46) Which choice offers the best time to measure basal metabolic rate?

A) a baby at rest prior to its first meal of the day

B) a baby at rest that has just had its first meal of the day

C) a child that has only eaten a sugar-free meal

D) a child that has only drunk diet soda all day

E) an adult watching TV after dinner

Answer: A
Skill: Application

47) Which statement about standard metabolic rate (SMR) and basal metabolic rate (BMR) is correct?

A) SMR measures energy use during exercise and BMR is measured at rest.

B) SMR is a measure of metabolic rate in endotherms and BMR is a measure of metabolic rate in ectotherms.

C) The measurement of both BMR and SMR is temperature dependent.

D) Human females actually have a higher BMR and a lower SMR than males.

E) Both SMR and BMR are measured in a resting, fasting, nonstressed state.

Answer: E
Skill: Application

48) Which of the following is an important distinction between the measurement of basal metabolic rate (BMR) and standard metabolic rate (SMR)?

A) An animal must be fasting for the measurement of SMR.

B) BMRs are performed only on ectothermic animals.

C) An organism must be actively exercising for the measurement of BMR.

D) SMRs must be determined at a specific temperature.

E) The BMR for a particular animal is usually lower than that animal's SMR.

Answer: D
Skill: Comprehension

49) Which of the following characteristics of blood best explains its classification as connective tissue?

A) Its cells are widely dispersed and surrounded by a fluid.

B) It contains more than one type of cell.

C) It is contained in vessels that "connect" different parts of an organism's body.

D) Its cells can move from place to place.

E) It is found within all the organs of the body.

Answer: A
Skill: Knowledge

50) Which of the following measurements would be the *least* reliable indicator of an animal's metabolic rate?

A) the amount of ATP produced within its cells

B) the amount of heat it generates

C) the amount of oxygen it inspires

D) the amount of carbon dioxide it expires

E) the amount of water it drinks

Answer: E
Skill: Comprehension

51) Which is the most significant single factor in preventing you from being able to run for a full 24 hours without stopping?

A) the changes in blood pressure that accompany extended periods of exercise

B) the circadian rhythm of the sleep–wake cycle

C) the basal metabolic rate exceeding the amount of ATP available

D) the lack of sustainable levels of cellular respiration

E) the type of muscle fibers

Answer: D
Skill: Application

52) Consider an ectotherm and an endotherm of equal body size. The ectotherm is more likely to survive an extended period of food deprivation than the endotherm because

A) the ectotherm is sustained by a higher basal metabolic rate.

B) the ectotherm will expend less energy/kg body weight than the endotherm.

C) the ectotherm will invest little to no energy in temperature regulation.

D) actually, assuming equal size, the ectotherm and the endotherm will have the same energy expenditures.

E) both B and C are correct.

Answer: E
Skill: Application

53) Which of the following ideas is *not* consistent with our understanding of animal structure?

A) The environment imposes similar problems on all animals.

B) The evolution of structure in an animal is influenced by its environment.

C) All but the simplest animals demonstrate the same hierarchical levels of organization.

D) Different animals contain fundamentally different categories of tissues.

E) Short–term adjustments to environmental changes are mediated by physiological organ systems.

Answer: D
Skill: Comprehension

Media Activity Questions

1) Epithelial tissues are characterized as such because they

   A) transmit impulses.

   B) cause body movements.

   C) cover both external and internal body surfaces.

   D) sense stimuli.

   E) form a framework that supports the body.

   Answer: C
   Topic: Web/CD Activity 40B

2) Which of these is a type of connective tissue?

   A) bone

   B) muscle

   C) axons

   D) striated muscle

   E) the interior lining of the mouth

   Answer: A
   Topic: Web/CD Activity 40C

3) Which of these cells is a functional component of the nervous system?

   A) leukocyte

   B) neuron

   C) adipocyte

   D) squamous

   E) chondrocyte

   Answer: B
   Topic: Web/CD Activity 40D

4) Which muscle tissue is responsible for voluntary movement?

   A) cardiac muscle only

   B) skeletal muscle only

   C) smooth muscle only

   D) cardiac and smooth muscle

   E) skeletal and smooth muscle

   Answer: B
   Topic: Web/CD Activity 40E

5) Which of these is an example of positive feedback?

   A) sweating when hot

   B) labor pains increasing in frequency and intensity

   C) drinking when thirsty

   D) shivering when cold

   E) eating when hungry

   Answer: B
   Topic: Web/CD Activity 40D

Self-Quiz Questions

Answers to these questions also appear in the textbook.

1) Consider the energy budgets for a human, an elephant, a penguin, a mouse, and a python. The _____ would have the highest total annual energy expenditure, and the _____ would have the highest energy expenditure per unit mass.

   A) elephant; mouse

   B) elephant; human

   C) human; penguin

   D) mouse; python

   E) penguin; mouse

   Answer: A

2) Which of the following structures or substances is *incorrectly* paired with a tissue?

   A) osteon—bone

   B) platelets—blood

   C) fibroblasts—skeletal muscle

   D) chondroitin sulfate—cartilage

   E) basement membrane—epithelium

   Answer: C

3) For which of the following animals would the percent of its energy budget spent for homeostatic control be the largest?

   A) an amoeba in a freshwater pond

   B) a marine jellyfish

   C) a snake in a temperate forest

   D) a desert insect

   E) an arctic bird

   Answer: E

4) The involuntary muscles that cause the wavelike contractions pushing food along our intestine are

   A) striated muscles.

   B) cardiac muscles.

   C) skeletal muscles.

   D) smooth muscles.

   E) intercalated muscles.

   Answer: D

5) Which of the following is *not* considered to be a tissue?

   A) cartilage

   B) the mucous membrane lining the stomach

   C) blood

   D) the brain

   E) cardiac muscle

   Answer: D

6) Which of the following statements about bioenergetics is *true*?

   A) Every animal has a specific metabolic rate that does not change.

   B) A BMR can be determined only at a specific temperature.

   C) Endotherms are warmed by metabolic heat.

   D) An SMR is best measured just after an ectotherm has eaten.

   E) Ectotherms and endotherms use the same basic energy "strategy."

   Answer: C

7) Compared to a smaller cell, a larger cell of the same shape has

A) less surface area.

B) less surface area per unit of volume.

C) the same surface–to–volume ratio.

D) a smaller average distance between its mitochondria and the external source of oxygen.

E) a smaller cytoplasm–to–nucleus ratio.

Answer: B

8) Which of the following vertebrate organ systems does *not* open directly to the external environment?

A) digestive system

B) circulatory system

C) excretory system

D) respiratory system

E) reproductive system

Answer: B

9) Most of our cells are surrounded by

A) blood.

B) basement membranes.

C) interstitial fluid.

D) pure water.

E) air.

Answer: C

10) Which of the following physiological responses is an example of *positive* feedback?

A) An increase in the concentration of glucose in the blood stimulates the pancreas to secrete insulin, a hormone that lowers blood glucose concentration.

B) A high concentration of carbon dioxide in the blood causes deeper, more rapid breathing, which expels carbon dioxide.

C) Stimulation of a nerve cell causes sodium ions to leak into the cell, and the sodium influx triggers the inward leaking of even more sodium.

D) The body's production of red blood cells, which transport oxygen from the lungs to other organs, is stimulated by a low concentration of oxygen.

E) The pituitary gland secretes a hormone called TSH, which stimulates the thyroid gland to secrete another hormone called thyroxine; a high concentration of thyroxine suppresses the pituitary's secretion of TSH.

Answer: C

Chapter 41 Animal Nutrition

1) The body is capable of catabolizing many substances as sources of energy. Which of the following could be used as a source of energy but would be the last utilized for this purpose?
   A) fat in adipose tissue
   B) glucose in the blood
   C) protein in muscle cells
   D) glycogen in muscle cells
   E) calcium phosphate in bone

   Answer: C
   Skill: Comprehension

2) Some nutrients are considered "essential" in the diets of certain animals because
   A) only those animals use the nutrients.
   B) they are subunits of important polymers.
   C) they cannot be manufactured by the organism.
   D) they are necessary coenzymes.
   E) only some foods contain them.

   Answer: C
   Skill: Knowledge

3) Which of the following is *not* one of the four classes of essential nutrients?
   A) essential sugars
   B) essential amino acids
   C) essential fatty acids
   D) essential vitamins
   E) essential minerals

   Answer: A
   Skill: Knowledge

4) Animals require certain basic amino acids in their diet. An amino acid that is referred to as nonessential would be best described as one that
   A) can be made from other substances.
   B) is not used by the organism in biosynthesis.
   C) must be ingested in the diet.
   D) is less important than an essential amino acid.
   E) is not found in many proteins.

   Answer: A
   Skill: Comprehension

5) What are essential amino acids?
   A) those that are absent in fruits and vegetables
   B) the only amino acids found in human proteins
   C) those amino acids that are generally more abundant in vegetables than in meat
   D) one class of vitamins that is indispensable for neurological development
   E) molecules that are not synthesized by most animals

   Answer: E
   Skill: Knowledge

6) All of the following statements about nutritional disorders are correct *except:*
   A) Rickets is caused by a vitamin C deficiency.
   B) Weak bones are caused by a calcium deficiency.
   C) Obesity is caused by overnourishment.
   D) Beriberi is caused by a vitamin B_1 deficiency.
   E) Lack of iodine in the diet affects metabolic rate.

   Answer: A
   Skill: Knowledge

7) Which of the following vitamins is *incorrectly* associated with its use?

A) vitamin C = synthesis of connective tissue

B) vitamin A = incorporation into the visual pigment of the eye

C) vitamin D = calcium absorption and bone formation

D) vitamin E = protection of membrane phospholipids from oxidation

E) vitamin K = production of red blood cells

Answer: E
Skill: Knowledge

8) Which of the following is an example of a fat-soluble vitamin?

A) vitamin A

B) vitamin B_{12}

C) vitamin C

D) iodine

E) biotin

Answer: A
Skill: Knowledge

9) Because they accumulate in the body, excess ingestion of which of the following can have toxic effects?

A) fat-soluble vitamins

B) water-soluble vitamins

C) calcium and phosphorus

D) proteins

E) sugars

Answer: A
Skill: Knowledge

10) Which of the following minerals is *incorrectly* associated with its use in animals?

A) calcium—construction and maintenance of bone

B) magnesium—cofactor in enzymes that split ATP

C) iron—regulation of metabolic rate

D) phosphorus—ingredient of nucleic acids

E) sodium—important in nerve function

Answer: C
Skill: Knowledge

11) In a variation of the game "Twenty Questions," you are asked whether the animal being thought of is a suspension feeder or not. Which of the following questions could *not* provide you with any useful information?

A) Is it aquatic?

B) Does it have teeth?

C) Is it bigger than your biology book?

D) Does it have claws?

E) Does it have tentacles?

Answer: C
Skill: Application

12) Which of the following terms could be applied to any organism with a digestive system?

A) heterotroph

B) autotroph

C) herbivore

D) omnivore

E) bulk feeder

Answer: A
Skill: Comprehension

13) The ticks you might find attached to your dog are best described as

A) substrate feeders.

B) bulk feeders.

C) suspension feeders.

D) deposit feeders.

E) fluid feeders.

Answer: E
Skill: Comprehension

14) During the process of digestion, fats are broken down when fatty acids are detached from glycerol and proteins are degraded when amino acids are separated from each other. What do these two processes have in common?

A) Both processes can be catalyzed by the same enzyme.

B) Both processes occur intracellularly in most organisms.

C) Both involve the addition of a water molecule to break bonds.

D) Both require the presence of hydrochloric acid to lower pH.

E) Both require ATP as an energy source.

Answer: C
Skill: Comprehension

15) Which of the following digestive processes requires enzymes?

A) ingestion

B) peristalsis

C) absorption

D) hydrolysis

E) elimination

Answer: D
Skill: Comprehension

16) To actually enter the body, a substance must cross a cell membrane. During which stage of food processing does this first happen?

A) ingestion

B) digestion

C) hydrolysis

D) absorption

E) elimination

Answer: D
Skill: Comprehension

17) The process of intracellular digestion is usually preceded by

A) hydrolysis.

B) endocytosis.

C) absorption.

D) elimination.

E) secretion.

Answer: B
Skill: Comprehension

18) Which of these animals has a gastrovascular cavity?

A) bird

B) hydra

C) mammal

D) insect

E) annelid

Answer: B
Skill: Knowledge

19) Increasing surface area facilitates which of the following digestive processes?

A) hydrolysis

B) absorption

C) ingestion

D) elimination

E) both A and B

Answer: E
Skill: Comprehension

20) Which of the following is an advantage of a complete digestive system over a gastrovascular cavity?

A) Extracellular digestion is not needed.

B) Specialized regions are possible.

C) Digestive enzymes can be more specific.

D) Extensive branching is possible.

E) Intracellular digestion is easier.

Answer: B
Skill: Comprehension

21) Digestive systems are not needed by

A) heterotrophs.

B) autotrophs.

C) herbivores.

D) omnivores.

E) carnivores.

Answer: B
Skill: Comprehension

22) What is peristalsis?

A) a process of fat emulsification in the small intestine

B) voluntary control of the rectal sphincters regulating defecation

C) the transport of nutrients to the liver through the hepatic portal vein

D) loss of appetite, fatigue, dehydration, and nervous disorders

E) smooth muscle contractions that move food through the alimentary canal

Answer: E
Skill: Knowledge

23) After ingestion, the first type of macromolecule to be enzymatically attacked in the human digestive system is

A) protein.

B) carbohydrate.

C) fat.

D) nucleic acid.

E) glucose.

Answer: B
Skill: Comprehension

24) What is the substrate of salivary amylase?

A) protein

B) starch

C) sucrose

D) glucose

E) maltose

Answer: B
Skill: Knowledge

25) Which of the following is *true* of the mammalian digestive system?

A) All foods begin their enzymatic digestion in the mouth.

B) After leaving the oral cavity, the bolus enters the larynx.

C) The epiglottis prevents food from entering the trachea.

D) Enzyme production continues in the esophagus.

E) The trachea leads to the esophagus and then to the stomach.

Answer: C
Skill: Knowledge

26) A digestive juice with a pH of 2 probably came from the

A) mouth.

B) stomach.

C) pancreas.

D) esophagus.

E) small intestine.

Answer: B
Skill: Comprehension

27) Which of the following is a *correct* statement about pepsin?

A) It is manufactured by the pancreas.

B) It helps stabilize fat–water emulsions.

C) It splits maltose into monosaccharides.

D) It is activated by the action of HCl on pepsinogen.

E) It is denatured and rendered inactive in solutions with low pH.

Answer: D
Skill: Knowledge

28) Without functioning parietal cells an individual would

A) not be able to initiate protein digestion in the stomach.

B) not be able to intiate mechanical digestion in the stomach.

C) only be able to digest fat in the stomach.

D) not be able to produce pepsinogen.

E) not be able to initiate digestion in the small intestine.

Answer: A
Skill: Comprehension

29) Most enzymatic hydrolysis of the macromolecules in food occurs in the

A) small intestine.

B) large intestine.

C) stomach.

D) liver.

E) mouth.

Answer: A
Skill: Knowledge

30) Most nutrients are absorbed across the epithelium of the

A) colon.

B) stomach.

C) esophagus.

D) small intestine.

E) large intestine.

Answer: D
Skill: Knowledge

31) A structure that produces no digestive secretions of any kind is the

A) duodenum.

B) pancreas.

C) salivary gland.

D) gallbladder.

E) liver.

Answer: D
Skill: Knowledge

32) Which of the following is a *correct* statement about bile salts?

A) They are enzymes.

B) They are manufactured by the pancreas.

C) They help stabilize fat–water emulsions.

D) They increase the efficiency of pepsin action.

E) They are normally an ingredient of gastric juice.

Answer: C
Skill: Knowledge

33) Which of the following is an enzyme produced by two entirely different accessory glands?

A) pepsin

B) trypsin

C) aminopeptidase

D) lactase

E) amylase

Answer: E
Skill: Knowledge

34) Which of the following terms could be used accurately to describe absorbed nutrients?

A) macromolecules

B) polymers

C) monomers

D) enzymes

E) peptides

Answer: C
Skill: Comprehension

35) Which of the following enzymes has the lowest pH optimum?

A) amylase

B) pepsin

C) lipase

D) trypsin

E) sucrase

Answer: B
Skill: Comprehension

36) Which of the following enzymes is most similar in mode of action to carboxypeptidase?

A) amylase

B) aminopeptidase

C) pepsin

D) lipase

E) trypsin

Answer: B
Skill: Comprehension

37) If you were to "design" an animal but could provide it with only one protein–digesting enzyme, which of the following would you choose so that the animal could absorb the maximum number of amino acids?

A) trypsin

B) pepsin

C) a dipeptidase

D) enteropeptidase

E) carboxypeptidase

Answer: E
Skill: Application

38) The source of trypsinogen and chymotrypsinogen is the

A) pancreas.

B) appendix.

C) gallbladder.

D) mouth.

E) liver.

Answer: A
Skill: Knowledge

39) Which of the following is a *correct* statement about trypsin, chymotrypsin, and carboxypeptidase?

A) They are manufactured by the liver.

B) They are all forms of the enzyme lipase.

C) They hydrolyze starch into disaccharides.

D) They are denatured and rendered inactive by sucrase.

E) They are activated in the small intestine by the action of enteropeptidase.

Answer: E
Skill: Knowledge

The following questions refer to the digestive system structures in Figure 41.1.

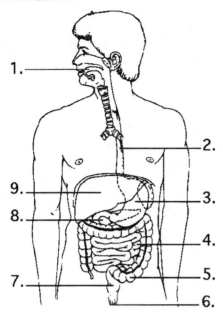

Figure 41.1

40) Agents that help emulsify fats are produced by

A) 1   B) 2   C) 3   D) 8   E) 9

Answer: E
Skill: Knowledge

41) Where does the digestion of carbohydrates occur?

A) 1 and 3
B) 1 and 4
C) 3 and 4
D) 4 and 5
E) 5 and 7

Answer: B
Skill: Knowledge

42) Where are the enzymes maltase, sucrase, and lactase produced?

A) 1
B) 3
C) 4
D) 8
E) 10

Answer: C
Skill: Knowledge

43) Where does the digestion of fats occur?

A) 3 only
B) 4 only
C) 1 and 4
D) 3 and 4
E) 1, 3, and 4

Answer: B
Skill: Knowledge

44) Where does the reabsorption of most of the water used in digestion occur?

A) 4   B) 5   C) 6   D) 7   E) 8

Answer: A
Skill: Knowledge

45) All of the following statements about digestion are correct *except*:

A) Digestion is catalyzed by enzymes.
B) Digestion cleaves nucleic acids into nucleotides.
C) Digestion cleaves fats into glycerol and fatty acids.
D) During digestion the essential macromolecules are directly absorbed.
E) During digestion polysaccharides and disaccharides are split into simple sugars.

Answer: D
Skill: Comprehension

The following questions refer to the substances below. From the list, match the term that best fits each of the following descriptions. Each term may be used once, more than once, or not at all.

    A. *nucleases*
    B. *chylomicrons*
    C. *lipoproteins*
    D. *lysine and leucine*
    E. *thiamine and niacin*

46) essential amino acids

    Answer: D
    Skill: Knowledge

47) water–soluble vitamins

    Answer: E
    Skill: Knowledge

48) fat globules transported by exocytosis into the lacteals of the microvilli

    Answer: B
    Skill: Knowledge

49) How does the digestion and absorption of fat differ from that of carbohydrates?

    A) Processing of fat does not require any digestive enzymes, whereas the processing of carbohydrates does.

    B) Fat absorption occurs in the stomach, whereas carbohydrates are absorbed from the small intestine.

    C) Carbohydrates need to be emulsified before they can be digested, whereas fats do not.

    D) Most absorbed fat first enters the lymphatic system, whereas carbohydrates directly enter the blood.

    E) Fat must be worked on by bacteria in the large intestine before it can be absorbed, which is not the case for carbohydrates.

    Answer: D
    Skill: Comprehension

50) All of the following are nutritional monomers that can be absorbed into the blood *except*

    A) sucrose.

    B) glucose.

    C) fatty acids.

    D) amino acids.

    E) nucleotides.

    Answer: A
    Skill: Comprehension

51) Blood sugar concentration is likely to vary *most* in which of these blood vessels?

    A) the abdominal artery

    B) the coronary arteries

    C) the pulmonary veins

    D) the hepatic portal vein

    E) the hepatic vein, which drains the liver

    Answer: D
    Skill: Comprehension

52) A hormone produced by the epithelial lining of the stomach is

    A) secretin.

    B) chymotrypsin.

    C) cholecystokinin.

    D) enterogastrone.

    E) gastrin.

    Answer: E
    Skill: Knowledge

53) Which of the following glandular secretions involved in digestion would be most likely to be released initially as inactive precursors?

    A) protein–digesting enzymes

    B) fat–solubilizing bile salts

    C) acid–neutralizing bicarbonate

    D) carbohydrate–digesting enzymes

    E) hormones such as gastrin

    Answer: A
    Skill: Comprehension

54) Secretin

    A) stimulates the release of alkaline products by the pancreas.

    B) stimulates the gastric glands.

    C) is released by the salivary glands.

    D) decreases the stomach's churning activity.

    E) stimulates the release of digestive enzymes.

Answer: A
Skill: Knowledge

The following questions refer to the substances below. From the list, match the term that best fits each of the following descriptions. Each term may be used once, more than once, or not at all.

    A. *pepsin*
    B. *secretin*
    C. *gastrin*
    D. *enterogastrone*
    E. *cholecystokinin*

55) produced by the stomach lining

Answer: C
Skill: Knowledge

56) stimulates the gallbladder to release bile

Answer: E
Skill: Knowledge

57) released by the duodenum in response to the acidic pH of chyme

Answer: B
Skill: Knowledge

58) peristalsis inhibitor that is released in response to a chyme rich in fats

Answer: D
Skill: Knowledge

59) Hormones that affect the pancreas include

    A) gastrin.

    B) enterogastrone.

    C) CCK.

    D) secretin.

    E) both C and D.

Answer: E
Skill: Knowledge

60) In humans, about 7 liters of fluid are secreted each day into the intestinal tract. Which of the following does *not* secrete fluid?

    A) salivary glands

    B) stomach

    C) liver

    D) pancreas

    E) large intestine

Answer: E
Skill: Comprehension

61) In general, herbivorous mammals have teeth modified for

    A) cutting.

    B) ripping.

    C) grinding.

    D) splitting.

    E) piercing.

Answer: C
Skill: Knowledge

62) In which group of animals would you expect to find a relatively long cecum?

    A) carnivores

    B) herbivores

    C) autotrophs

    D) heterotrophs

    E) humans

Answer: B
Skill: Comprehension

63) While working in the rain forest of Peru, you discover a monkey that only eats paddle tree leaves. You might also expect this animal to have

A) pointed incisors and pointed canines.

B) a smaller stomach than a carnivore.

C) a gallbladder to aid in digestion.

D) a shorter alimentary canal relative to its body size.

E) a well-developed cecum.

Answer: E
Skill: Comprehension

64) All of the following are adaptations to an herbivorous diet *except*

A) broad, flat teeth.

B) a rumen.

C) ingestion of feces.

D) bile salts.

E) amylase.

Answer: D
Skill: Comprehension

65) Cows are able to survive on a diet consisting almost entirely of cellulose because

A) cows are autotrophic.

B) the cow, like the rabbit, reingests its feces.

C) cows can manufacture all 15 amino acids out of sugars in the liver.

D) the cow's saliva has enzymes capable of digesting cellulose.

E) cows have cellulose-digesting, symbiotic microorganisms in their rumens.

Answer: E
Skill: Comprehension

Media Activity Questions

1) When digested, carbohydrates are broken down into

   A) fatty acids.

   B) monosaccharides.

   C) glycerols.

   D) nucleotides.

   E) amino acids.

   Answer: B
   Topic: Web/CD Activity 41A

2) When digested, nucleic acids are broken down into

   A) fatty acids.

   B) monosaccharides.

   C) glycerols.

   D) nucleotides.

   E) amino acids.

   Answer: D
   Topic: Web/CD Activity 41A

3) Which of these hormones triggers the secretion of gastric juice?

   A) pepsin

   B) CCK

   C) carboxypeptidase

   D) gastrin

   E) secretin

   Answer: D
   Topic: Web/CD Activity 41B

4) The stomach releases its acid contents to the small intestine. In the small intestine this acidity is neutralized by

   A) hydrochloric acid.

   B) sodium hydroxide.

   C) potassium hydroxide.

   D) ammonia.

   E) bicarbonate.

   Answer: E
   Topic: Web/CD Activity 41B

5) Diets rich in fat release enterogastrones that inhibit

   A) gastric secretion.

   B) stomach peristalsis.

   C) pancreatic secretion.

   D) esophageal peristalsis.

   E) intestinal secretion.

   Answer: B
   Topic: Web/CD Activity 41B

Self-Quiz Questions

Answers to these questions also appear in the textbook.

1) Which of the following animals is *incorrectly* paired with its feeding mechanism?
   A) lion—substrate-feeder
   B) baleen whale—suspension-feeder
   C) aphid—fluid-feeder
   D) earthworm—deposit-feeder
   E) snake—bulk-feeder

   Answer: A

2) The mammalian trachea and esophagus both open into the
   A) large intestine.
   B) stomach.
   C) pharynx.
   D) rectum.
   E) epiglottis.

   Answer: C

3) Our oral cavity, with its dentition, is most functionally analogous to an earthworm's
   A) intestine.
   B) pharynx.
   C) gizzard.
   D) stomach.
   E) anus.

   Answer: C

4) Which of the following enzymes has the lowest pH optimum?
   A) salivary amylase
   B) trypsin
   C) pepsin
   D) pancreatic amylase
   E) pancreatic lipase

   Answer: C

5) After surgical removal of an infected gallbladder, a person must be especially careful to restrict his or her dietary intake of
   A) starch.
   B) protein.
   C) sugar.
   D) fat.
   E) water.

   Answer: D

6) Enteropeptidase, a hormone secreted by the small intestine, has which of the following actions?
   A) inhibits bile secretion
   B) inhibits duodenal secretion
   C) activates pancreatic enzymes
   D) inhibits peristalsis in the stomach
   E) increases the pH of chyme

   Answer: C

7) Individuals whose diet consists primarily of corn would likely become
   A) obese.
   B) anorexic.
   C) overnourished.
   D) undernourished.
   E) malnourished.

   Answer: E

8) Which of the following organs is *incorrectly* paired with its function?
   A) stomach—protein digestion
   B) oral cavity—starch digestion
   C) large intestine—bile production
   D) small intestine—nutrient absorption
   E) pancreas—enzyme production

   Answer: C

9) If you were to jog a mile a few hours after lunch, which stored fuel would you probably tap?

A) muscle proteins

B) muscle and liver glycogen

C) fat stored in the liver

D) fats stored in adipose tissue

E) blood proteins

Answer: B

10) The symbiotic microbes that help nourish a ruminant live mainly in specialized regions of the

A) large intestine.

B) liver.

C) small intestine.

D) pharynx.

E) stomach.

Answer: E

Chapter 42 Circulation and Gas Exchange

1) Tapeworms are in class Cestoda, which is one type of flatworm. The tapeworm lacks a gastrovascular cavity and a circulatory system, yet it manages to survive very well in the host's intestinal tract. Which response best applies?

A) The diffusion of nutrients is not a limiting factor to survival.

B) Parasites do not need a gastrovascular cavity.

C) Peristaltic movements in the host's intestinal tract replace the need for a gastrovascular cavity in the worm.

D) Peristaltic movements in the host's intestinal tract replace the need for a circulatory system in the worm.

E) Since the nutrients are being predigested by enzymes present in the host's intestinal tract, there is no need for a gastrovascular cavity.

Answer: A
Skill: Comprehension

2) Which is a *correct* statement concerning the insect circulatory system?

A) Circulating fluid bathes tissues directly.

B) Blood is always contained in a system of tubes called tracheae.

C) Blood transports oxygen and nutrients to all the tissues.

D) There is no heart, or pump.

E) There is no blood, or circulating fluid.

Answer: A
Skill: Comprehension

3) Organisms in which a circulating body fluid is distinct from the fluid that directly surrounds the body's cells are likely to have

A) an open circulatory system.

B) a closed circulatory system.

C) a gastrovascular cavity.

D) gills.

E) hemolymph.

Answer: B
Skill: Comprehension

4) Which of the following blood components would interfere with the functioning of an open circulatory system but *not* a closed one?

A) electrolytes

B) water

C) red blood cells

D) amino acids

E) antibodies

Answer: C
Skill: Comprehension

5) If the amount of interstitial fluid surrounding the capillary beds of the lungs were to increase significantly, it would be expected that

A) the amount of carbon dioxide entering the lungs from the blood would increase.

B) the amount of oxygen entering the circulation from the lungs would increase.

C) the amount of oxygen entering the circulation from the lungs would decrease.

D) the pressure would cause the capillary beds to burst.

E) you could not make a prediction based on this information.

Answer: C
Skill: Comprehension

6) Three–chambered hearts generally consist of which of the following numbers of atria and ventricles?

A) one atrium; one ventricle

B) two atria; one ventricle

C) three atria; no ventricles

D) no atria; three ventricles

E) one atrium; two ventricles

Answer: B
Skill: Knowledge

7) In which animal does blood flow from the pulmocutaneous circulation to the heart before circulating through the rest of the body?

A) annelid

B) mollusk

C) fish

D) frog

E) insect

Answer: D
Skill: Knowledge

8) Which of the following are the only vertebrates in which blood flows directly from respiratory organs to body tissues without first returning to the heart?

A) amphibians

B) birds

C) fishes

D) mammals

E) reptiles

Answer: C
Skill: Comprehension

9) To adjust blood pressure independently in the capillaries of the gas–exchange surface and in the capillaries of the general body circulation, an organism would need

A) an open circulatory system.

B) a hemocoel.

C) a lymphatic system.

D) a two–chambered heart.

E) a four–chambered heart.

Answer: E
Skill: Comprehension

10) A red blood cell is in an artery in the left arm of a human. How many capillary beds must this cell pass through before it is returned to the left ventricle of the heart?

A) one

B) two

C) three

D) four

E) five

Answer: B
Skill: Application

11) Through how many capillary beds must a red blood cell of a human travel if it takes the shortest possible route from the right ventricle to the right atrium?

A) one

B) two

C) three

D) four

E) five

Answer: B
Skill: Comprehension

Refer to the diagram of the human heart in Figure 42.1 to answer the following questions.

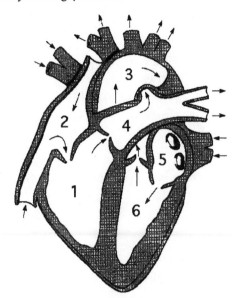

Figure 42.1

12) Chambers or vessels that carry oxygenated blood include which of the following?

A) 1 and 2 only

B) 3 and 4 only

C) 5 and 6 only

D) 1, 2, and 4

E) 3, 5, and 6

Answer: E
Skill: Knowledge

13) Blood is carried directly to the lungs from which of the following?

A) 2   B) 3   C) 4   D) 5   E) 6

Answer: C
Skill: Knowledge

14) The *correct* sequence of blood flow, beginning at the pulmonary artery and passing through the systematic circulation, is

A) 2-1-4-systematic-3-6-5.

B) 3-6-5-systematic-4-1-2.

C) 4-5-6-3-systematic-2-1.

D) 4-6-3-systematic-2-1-5.

E) 5-6-3-systematic-2-1-4-3.

Answer: C
Skill: Knowledge

15) Which of the following sequences does *not* indicate a *direct* pathway that blood might follow in mammalian circulation?

A) left ventricle → aorta

B) right ventricle → pulmonary vein

C) pulmonary vein → left atrium

D) vena cava → right atrium

E) right ventricle → pulmonary artery

Answer: B
Skill: Knowledge

16) A patient has a blood pressure of 120/75, a pulse rate of 40 beats/min, a stroke volume of 70 ml/beat, and a respiratory rate of 25 breaths/min. This person's cardiac output per minute will be

A) 500 ml.

B) 1000 ml.

C) 1750 ml.

D) 2800 ml.

E) 4800 ml.

Answer: D
Skill: Application

17) The sinoatrial node in humans
   A) delays transmission in the cardiac conduction system after the pacemaker has fired.
   B) is the valve between the left atrium and the left ventricle.
   C) is found in the lymphatic system.
   D) is the heart's pacemaker.
   E) monitors blood pressure in the aorta.

   Answer: D
   Skill: Knowledge

18) If the atrioventricular node could be surgically removed from the heart without disrupting signal transmission to the Purkinje fibers, what would be the effect?
   A) No apparent effect on heart activity would be observed.
   B) The heart rate would be decreased.
   C) Only the ventricles would contract.
   D) Only the atria would contract.
   E) Atria and ventricles would contract at about the same time.

   Answer: E
   Skill: Comprehension

19) A nonfunctional SA node would
   A) have no adverse effects on heart contraction.
   B) cause the heart to stop beating in an autorhythmic fashion.
   C) result in a block in ventricular contractions.
   D) cause no effects because hormones will take over regulation of the heart beat.
   E) have no significant effect on stroke volume.

   Answer: E
   Skill: Comprehension

20) Where is the velocity of blood flow the lowest?
   A) the aorta
   B) arteries
   C) arterioles
   D) capillaries
   E) veins

   Answer: D
   Skill: Knowledge

21) Average blood pressure is lowest in which structure?
   A) the aorta
   B) arteries
   C) arterioles
   D) capillaries
   E) vena cavae

   Answer: E
   Skill: Knowledge

22) Which of the following is *correct* for a blood pressure of 130/80?
   I.   The systolic pressure is 130.
   II. The diastolic pressure is 80.
   III. The blood pressure during heart contraction is 80.

   A) I only
   B) III only
   C) I and II only
   D) II and III only
   E) I, II, and III

   Answer: C
   Skill: Comprehension

23) What can be expected to happen to the blood pressure of a healthy individual during inhalation?
  A) The systolic pressure would rise and the diastolic pressure would decrease.
  B) The extra pressure exerted by the inflating lungs will increase blood pressure.
  C) There will be a transient decrease in blood pressure.
  D) Blood pressure will initially increase and then immediately decrease.
  E) Nothing will happen in healthy individuals.

Answer: C
Skill: Comprehension

24) What is the reason that fluid is forced out of systemic capillaries at the arteriolar end?
  A) The osmotic pressure of the interstitial fluid is greater than that of the blood.
  B) The hydrostatic pressure of the blood is less than that of the interstitial fluid.
  C) The hydrostatic pressure of the blood is greater than the osmotic pressure of the interstitial fluid.
  D) The osmotic pressure of the interstitial fluid is greater than the hydrostatic pressure of the blood.
  E) The osmotic pressure of the blood is greater than the hydrostatic pressure of the interstitial fluid.

Answer: C
Skill: Comprehension

25) If, during protein starvation, the osmotic pressure on the venous side of capillary beds drops below the hydrostatic pressure, then
  A) hemoglobin will not release oxygen.
  B) fluids will tend to accumulate in tissues.
  C) the pH of the interstitial fluids will increase.
  D) most carbon dioxide will be bound to hemoglobin and carried away from tissues.
  E) plasma proteins will escape through the endothelium of the capillaries.

Answer: B
Skill: Application

26) If a person were suffering from edema, which of the following conditions would reduce it?
  A) decreased plasma protein production by the liver
  B) a prolonged starvation diet
  C) an obstruction in the lymphatic system
  D) lower blood pressure
  E) enlarged clefts between capillary endothelial cells due to damage or inflammation

Answer: D
Skill: Comprehension

27) What would be the long-term effect if the lymphatic vessels associated with a capillary bed were to become blocked?
  A) More fluid will enter the venous capillaries.
  B) Blood pressure in the capillary bed will increase.
  C) Fluid will accumulate in the interstitium.
  D) Fewer proteins will leak into the interstitium from the blood.
  E) Nothing will happen.

Answer: C
Skill: Comprehension

28) Human plasma proteins include which of the following?
   I. fibrinogen
   II. hemoglobin
   III. immunoglobulin
   A) I only
   B) II only
   C) I and III only
   D) II and III only
   E) I, II, and III

   Answer: C
   Skill: Knowledge

29) Cyanide acts as a mitochondrial poison by blocking the final step in the electron transport chain. What will happen to human red blood cells if they are placed in an isotonic solution of cyanide?
   A) The cell shape will be maintained but the mitochondria will be poisoned.
   B) The cells will lyse as the cyanide concentration increases inside the cell.
   C) As a protective mechanism, the cells will switch to anaerobic metabolism.
   D) The cells will not be able to carry oxygen.
   E) The cells will be unaffected.

   Answer: E
   Skill: Comprehension

30) The meshwork that forms the fabric of a blood clot mostly consists of which protein?
   A) fibrinogen
   B) fibrin
   C) thrombin
   D) prothrombin
   E) collagen

   Answer: B
   Skill: Knowledge

31) Plasma proteins in humans have many functions. Which of the following is *not* one of these functions?
   A) maintenance of blood osmotic pressure
   B) transport of water–insoluble lipids
   C) blood clotting
   D) immune responses
   E) oxygen transport

   Answer: E
   Skill: Knowledge

32) Which of the following is *not* a normal event in the process of blood clotting?
   A) production of erythropoietin
   B) conversion of fibrinogen to fibrin
   C) activation of prothrombin to thrombin
   D) adhesion of platelets
   E) clotting factor release by clumped platelets

   Answer: A
   Skill: Knowledge

For the following questions, refer to the following conditions. Each term may be used once, more than once, or not at all.

   A. *atherosclerosis*
   B. *arteriosclerosis*
   C. *hypertension*
   D. *heart murmur*
   E. *cardiovascular thrombus*

33) high blood pressure

   Answer: C
   Skill: Knowledge

34) defect in one or more of the valves of the heart

   Answer: D
   Skill: Knowledge

35) calcification of plaques lining the inner walls of arteries

   Answer: B
   Skill: Knowledge

36) plaque formation by infiltration of lipids into arterial smooth muscles

Answer: A
Skill: Knowledge

For the following questions, refer to the following answers. Each answer can be used once, more than once, or not at all.

A. *low–density lipoproteins*
B. *immunoglobulins*
C. *erythropoietin*
D. *epinephrine*
E. *platelets*

37) speeds up heart rate

Answer: D
Skill: Knowledge

38) part of the formed elements of the blood

Answer: E
Skill: Knowledge

39) stimulates the production of red blood cells

Answer: C
Skill: Knowledge

40) an early participant in the clotting process

Answer: E
Skill: Knowledge

41) At an atmopheric pressure of 870 mm Hg, what is the contribution of oxygen?

A) 100 mm Hg

B) 127 mm Hg

C) 151 mm Hg

D) 182 mm Hg

E) 219 mm Hg

Answer: D
Skill: Application

42) Which of the following features do all gas exchange systems have in common?

A) The exchange surfaces are moist.

B) They are enclosed within ribs.

C) They are maintained at a constant temperature.

D) They are exposed to air.

E) They are found only in animals.

Answer: A
Skill: Comprehension

43) All of the following respiratory surfaces are associated with capillary beds *except* the

A) gills of fishes.

B) alveoli of lungs.

C) tracheae of insects.

D) skin of earthworms.

E) skin of frogs.

Answer: C
Skill: Comprehension

44) All of the following are reasons why gas exchange is more difficult for aquatic animals than it is for terrestrial animals *except*:

A) Water is denser than air.

B) Water contains much less O_2 than air per unit volume.

C) Gills have less surface area than lungs.

D) Water is harder to pump than air.

E) Exchanging gases with water causes substantial heat loss.

Answer: C
Skill: Comprehension

45) Which of the following is an example of countercurrent flow?

A) the flow of water across the gills of a fish and the flow of blood within those gills

B) the flow of blood in the dorsal vessel of an insect and the flow of air within its tracheae

C) the flow of air within the primary bronchi of a human and the flow of blood within the pulmonary veins

D) the flow of water across the skin of a frog and the flow of blood within the ventricle of its heart

E) the flow of fluid out of the arterial end of a capillary and the flow of fluid back into the venous end of that same capillary

Answer: A
Skill: Comprehension

46) Countercurrent exchange in the fish gill helps to maximize

A) endocytosis.

B) blood pressure.

C) diffusion.

D) active transport.

E) osmosis.

Answer: C
Skill: Comprehension

47) The phenomenon that increases the gas exchange efficiency of fish gills is the

A) countercurrent exchange mechanism.

B) largest tidal volume of all vertebrates.

C) high degree of oxygen saturation in water.

D) back-and-forth movement of water that maximizes oxygen uptake.

E) large blood flow velocity and pressure found in some fish species.

Answer: A
Skill: Knowledge

48) Which one of the following statements about gills operating in water is *false*?

A) Water can support the delicate gill features.

B) Most fish actively pump water over their gills.

C) Keeping membranes moist is no problem.

D) Water carries more oxygen than air and therefore makes gills more efficient than lungs.

E) Gills have evolved many times in aquatic animals.

Answer: D
Skill: Comprehension

49) Tracheal systems for gas exchange are found in which organism?

A) crustacean

B) earthworm

C) insect

D) jellyfish

E) vertebrate

Answer: C
Skill: Knowledge

50) Where do air-breathing insects carry out gas exchange?

A) in specialized external gills

B) in specialized internal gills

C) in the alveoli of their lungs

D) across the membranes of cells

E) across the thin cuticular exoskeleton

Answer: D
Skill: Knowledge

51) What is the primary effect that an oil spill would probably have on frogs?

   A) They will die because the toxins will build up in their blood.

   B) They will die because they will not be able to respire across their skin.

   C) They will survive by remaining hidden beneath the water.

   D) They will survive because they have a natural secretion that will repel the oil.

   E) Survival or death will be dependent upon the genetic makeup of each individual frog.

   Answer: B
   Skill: Comprehension

52) Air rushes into the lungs of humans during inspiration because

   A) the volume of the thoracic cavity increases.

   B) pressure in the alveoli increases.

   C) the diaphragm contracts and pushes upward on the chest cavity.

   D) pulmonary muscles contract and pull on the outer surface of the lungs.

   E) smooth muscle lining the trachea, bronchi, and bronchioles contracts and causes their volume to increase.

   Answer: A
   Skill: Comprehension

53) Which of the following occurs with the exhalation of air from human lungs?

   A) The volume of the thoracic cavity decreases.

   B) The residual volume of the lungs decreases.

   C) The diaphragm contracts.

   D) The epiglottis closes.

   E) The rib cage expands.

   Answer: A
   Skill: Comprehension

54) A "smoker's cough" often develops

   A) because the lungs are expelling a higher concentration of carbon dioxide.

   B) in response to damage to the cilia of the trachea.

   C) because the epiglottis does not function properly.

   D) because the glottis becomes inflamed.

   E) because the parabronchi have become blocked by the buildup of cigarette tar.

   Answer: B
   Skill: Application

55) If a molecule of CO_2 released into the blood in your left toe travels out of your nose, it must pass through all of the following structures *except* the

   A) right atrium.

   B) pulmonary vein.

   C) alveolus.

   D) trachea.

   E) right ventricle.

   Answer: B
   Skill: Application

56) Which of the following lung volumes would be different in a person at rest compared to that person exercising?

   A) tidal volume

   B) vital capacity

   C) residual volume

   D) total lung capacity

   E) All of the above would be different.

   Answer: A
   Skill: Comprehension

57) Tidal volume in respiration is analogous to what measurement in cardiac physiology?

A) cardiac output

B) heart rate

C) stroke volume

D) systolic pressure

E) diastolic pressure

Answer: C
Skill: Comprehension

58) A person with a tidal volume of 450 ml, a vital capacity of 4000 ml, and a residual volume of 1000 ml would have a potential total lung capacity of

A) 1450 ml.

B) 4000 ml.

C) 4450 ml.

D) 5000 ml.

E) 5450 ml.

Answer: D
Skill: Application

59) Air flows in only one direction through the lungs of which animals?

A) frogs

B) birds

C) mammals

D) crocodiles

E) flying insects

Answer: B
Skill: Comprehension

60) The blood level of which gas is *most* important in controlling human respiration rate?

A) nitric acid

B) nitrogen

C) oxygen

D) carbon dioxide

E) carbon monoxide

Answer: D
Skill: Knowledge

61) Breathing is usually regulated by

A) erythropoietin levels in the blood.

B) the concentration of red blood cells.

C) hemoglobin levels in the blood.

D) CO_2 and O_2 concentration and pH–level sensors.

E) the lungs and the larynx.

Answer: D
Skill: Comprehension

62) At sea level, atmospheric pressure is 760 mm Hg. Oxygen gas is approximately 20% of the total gases in the atmosphere. What is the partial pressure of oxygen?

A) 0.2 mm Hg

B) 20.0 mm Hg

C) 76.0 mm Hg

D) 152.0 mm Hg

E) 508.0 mm Hg

Answer: D
Skill: Comprehension

63) At the summit of a high mountain, the atmospheric pressure is 380 mm Hg. If the atmosphere is still composed of 21% oxygen, what is the partial pressure of oxygen at this altitude?

A) 0 mm Hg

B) 80 mm Hg

C) 160 mm Hg

D) 380 mm Hg

E) 760 mm Hg

Answer: B
Skill: Application

64) Most of the carbon dioxide carried by the blood in humans is carried as

A) bicarbonate ions in the plasma.

B) CO_2 attached to hemoglobin.

C) carbonic acid in the erythrocytes.

D) CO_2 dissolved in the plasma.

E) bicarbonate attached to hemoglobin.

Answer: A
Skill: Knowledge

65) Hydrogen ions produced in human red blood cells are prevented from significantly lowering pH by combining with

A) hemoglobin.

B) plasma proteins.

C) carbon dioxide.

D) carbonic acid.

E) plasma buffers.

Answer: A
Skill: Knowledge

66) Which one of these statements about lungs is *false*?

A) Gas exchange takes place across moist membranes.

B) The gases move across the exchange membranes by diffusion.

C) The total exchange surface area is relatively large.

D) The lining of the alveoli is only one cell thick.

E) The concentration of CO_2 is higher in the air than in the alveolar capillaries.

Answer: E
Skill: Comprehension

The following questions refer to the data shown below. Blood entering a vertebrate's capillary bed was measured for the pressures exerted by various factors.

	Arterial End of Capillary Bed	Venous End of Capillary Bed
Hydrostatic pressure	8 mm Hg	14 mm Hg
Osmotic pressure	26 mm Hg	26 mm Hg
PO₂	100 mm Hg	42 mm Hg
PCO₂	40 mm Hg	46 mm Hg

67) For this capillary bed, which of the following statements is *correct*?

A) The pH is lower on the arterial side than on the venous side.

B) Oxygen is taken up by the erythrocytes within the capillaries.

C) The osmotic pressure remains constant due to carbon dioxide compensation.

D) The hydrostatic pressure declines from the arterial side to the venous side because oxygen is lost.

E) Fluids will leave the capillaries on the arterial side of the bed and re-enter on the venous side.

Answer: E
Skill: Application

68) The site of this capillary bed could be all of the following *except* the

A) pancreas.

B) muscle tissue.

C) medulla.

D) alveoli.

E) kidneys.

Answer: D
Skill: Comprehension

69) Which of the following is *false* concerning the hemoglobin molecule?

A) It contains amino acids.

B) It contains iron.

C) It is composed of four polypeptide chains.

D) It can bind four O_2 molecules.

E) It is found in humans only.

Answer: E
Skill: Knowledge

70) Which of the following are characteristics of *both* hemoglobin and hemocyanin?

A) found within blood cells

B) red in color

C) contain the element iron

D) transport oxygen

E) occur in mammals

Answer: D
Skill: Knowledge

71) The Bohr effect on the oxygen–hemoglobin dissociation curve is produced by changes in

A) the partial pressure of oxygen.

B) the partial pressure of carbon dioxide.

C) hemoglobin concentration.

D) temperature.

E) pH.

Answer: E
Skill: Knowledge

Media Activity Questions

1) Blood flows from the right atrium to the right ventricle through the

   A) semilunar valve.

   B) left atrium.

   C) pulmonary capillaries.

   D) atrioventricular valve.

   E) aorta.

   Answer: D
   Topic: Web/CD Activity 42A

2) Blood pumped from the right ventricle passes through the capillaries of the _____ before entering the left atrium.

   A) abdominal organs

   B) forelimbs

   C) hind limbs

   D) head

   E) lungs

   Answer: E
   Topic: Web/CD Activity 42B

3) Which of these carries the most highly oxygenated blood?

   A) right atrium

   B) anterior vena cava

   C) posterior vena cava

   D) pulmonary arteries

   E) pulmonary veins

   Answer: E
   Topic: Web/CD Activity 42C

4) The _____ is a passageway shared by both food and air.

   A) alveoli

   B) trachea

   C) pharynx

   D) larynx

   E) nasal cavity

   Answer: C
   Topic: Web/CD Activity 42D

5) In the capillaries of the head, oxygen released from hemoglobin first diffuses into the

   A) blood plasma.

   B) pulmonary veins.

   C) pulmonary arteries.

   D) interstitial fluid.

   E) alveoli.

   Answer: A
   Topic: Web/CD Activity 42E

Self-Quiz Questions

1) Which of the following respiratory systems is *not* closely associated with a blood supply?

   A) vertebrate lungs

   B) fish gills

   C) tracheal systems of insects

   D) the outer skin of an earthworm

   E) the parapodia of a polychaete worm

   Answer: C

2) Blood returning to the mammalian heart in a pulmonary vein will drain first into the

   A) vena cava.

   B) left atrium.

   C) right atrium.

   D) left ventricle.

   E) right ventricle.

   Answer: B

3) Pulse is a direct measure of

   A) blood pressure.

   B) stroke volume.

   C) cardiac output.

   D) heart rate.

   E) breathing rate.

   Answer: D

4) When you hold your breath, which of the following blood gas changes first leads to the urge to breathe?

   A) rising O_2

   B) falling O_2

   C) rising CO_2

   D) falling CO_2

   E) rising CO_2 and falling O_2

   Answer: C

5) In negative-pressure breathing, inhalation results from

   A) forcing air from the throat down into the lungs.

   B) contracting the diaphragm.

   C) relaxing the muscles of the rib cage.

   D) using muscles of the lungs to expand the alveoli.

   E) contracting the abdominal muscles.

   Answer: B

6) The conversion of fibrinogen to fibrin

   A) occurs when fibrinogen is released from broken platelets.

   B) occurs within red blood cells.

   C) is linked to hypertension and may damage artery walls.

   D) is likely to occur too often in an individual with hemophilia.

   E) is the final step of a clotting process that involves multiple clotting factors.

   Answer: E

7) A decrease in the pH of human blood caused by exercise would

   A) decrease breathing rate.

   B) increase heart rate.

   C) decrease the amount of O_2 unloaded from hemoglobin.

   D) decrease cardiac output.

   E) decrease CO_2 binding to hemoglobin.

   Answer: B

8) Compared to the interstitial fluid that bathes active muscle cells, blood reaching these cells in arteries has a

A) higher P_{O_2}.

B) higher P_{CO_2}.

C) greater bicarbonate concentration.

D) lower pH.

E) lower osmotic pressure.

Answer: A

9) Which of the following reactions prevails in red blood cells traveling through pulmonary capillaries? (Hb = hemoglobin)

A) $Hb + 4 O_2 \rightarrow Hb(O_2)_4$

B) $Hb(O_2)_4 \rightarrow Hb + 4 O_2$

C) $CO_2 + H_2O \rightarrow H_2CO_3$

D) $H_2CO_3 \rightarrow H^1 + HCO_3^-$

E) $Hb + 4 CO_2 \rightarrow Hb(CO_2)_4$

Answer: A

10) The relationship between blood pressure (*bp*), cardiac output (*co*), and peripheral resistance (*pr*) can be expressed as $bp = co \times pr$. All of the following changes would result in an increase in blood pressure *except*

A) increase in the stroke volume.

B) increase in the heart rate.

C) increase in the duration of ventricular diastole.

D) contraction of the arteriolar smooth muscle.

E) reduction in arteriolar diameter.

Answer: C

Chapter 43   The Body's Defenses

1) In mammalian defenses against invading pathogens, all of these are considered nonspecific defense mechanisms *except*

A) the immune system.

B) the skin.

C) mucous membranes.

D) the inflammatory response.

E) antimicrobial proteins.

Answer: A
Skill: Knowledge

2) Physical barriers to invasion by other organisms

A) include the skin and the mucous membranes.

B) are difficult for bacteria and viruses to penetrate.

C) may work in conjunction with secretions like tears, perspiration, and mucus.

D) Only A and C are correct.

E) A, B, and C are correct.

Answer: E
Skill: Knowledge

3) One feature that the eye and the respiratory tract share is

A) the mucous membranes that cover their surface.

B) their role in the secondary immune response.

C) the release of slightly acidic secretions.

D) the production of lysozyme.

E) the formation of similar antibodies.

Answer: D
Skill: Comprehension

4) After preparing barbequed chicken, you came down with salmonella poisoning. Why?

A) The microbe survived the acidic environment of the stomach and resisted lysosomal degradation in macrophages.

B) The chemotactic messengers released by the salmonella bacterium did not attract sufficient neutrophils to entirely destroy the infection.

C) There was a delay in selection of the population of eosinophils that recognize and are responsible for fighting these bacterial infections.

D) The bacterium released chemical messengers that make it resistant to phagocytosis.

E) The combination of foods eaten at the meal reduced the pH of the stomach sufficiently that the bacterium was not destoyed.

Answer: A
Skill: Comprehension

5) The lymphatic system involves which of the following organs?

A) spleen and lymph nodes

B) adenoids and tonsils

C) appendix and special portions of the small intestine

D) Only A and B are correct.

E) A, B, and C are correct.

Answer: E
Skill: Knowledge

6) In the inflammatory response, the absence of which of the following would prevent all the others from happening?

   A) dilation of arterioles

   B) increased permeability of blood vessels

   C) increased population of phagocytes in the area

   D) release of histamine

   E) leakage of plasma to the affected area

   Answer: D
   Skill: Comprehension

7) The main effect of histamine is to

   A) destroy white blood cells.

   B) dilate blood vessels.

   C) decrease blood flow.

   D) phagocytize pathogens.

   E) attract T cells.

   Answer: B
   Skill: Knowledge

8) An alarm substance that triggers an inflammatory reaction is

   A) thyroxine.

   B) adrenaline.

   C) immunoglobulin.

   D) histamine.

   E) pyrogen.

   Answer: D
   Skill: Knowledge

9) Inflammatory responses may include all of the following *except*

   A) clotting proteins sealing off a localized area.

   B) increased activity of phagocytes in an inflamed area.

   C) reduced permeability of blood vessels to conserve plasma.

   D) release of substances to increase the blood supply to an inflamed area.

   E) release of substances to stimulate the release of white blood cells from bone marrow.

   Answer: C
   Skill: Comprehension

10) Each indication below is a clinical characteristic of inflammation *except*

   A) decreased temperature.

   B) edema.

   C) redness.

   D) pain.

   E) increased blood flow.

   Answer: A
   Skill: Knowledge

11) What is complement?

   A) a hormone from the thymus

   B) a form of interferon

   C) a set of antigens

   D) a specialized white blood cell

   E) a group of proteins

   Answer: E
   Skill: Knowledge

12) All of the following are correct statements about nonspecific defenses *except:*

A) They include inflammatory responses.

B) They include physical and chemical barriers.

C) They must be primed by the presence of antigen.

D) They may involve the formation of membrane attack complexes.

E) Macrophages and natural killer cells are participants in the process.

Answer: C
Skill: Comprehension

13) What are antigens?

A) proteins found in the blood that cause foreign blood cells to clump

B) proteins embedded in B cell membranes

C) proteins that consist of two light and two heavy polypeptide chains

D) antibody-generating foreign macromolecules

E) Both A and C are correct.

Answer: D
Skill: Knowledge

14) Jenner successfully used cowpox virus as a vaccine against a different virus that causes smallpox. Why was he successful even though he used viruses of different kinds?

A) All of the below are true.

B) The immune system responds nonspecifically to antigens.

C) The cowpox virus made antibodies in response to the presence of smallpox.

D) Cowpox and smallpox are antibodies with similar immunizing properties.

E) There are some antigenic determinants common to both pox viruses.

Answer: E
Skill: Application

15) The clonal selection theory implies that

A) related people have similar immune responses.

B) antigens activate specific lymphocytes.

C) only certain cells can produce interferon.

D) memory cells are present at birth.

E) the body selects which antigens it will respond to.

Answer: B
Skill: Comprehension

16) The clonal selection theory is an explanation for

A) how a single type of stem cell can produce both red blood cells and white blood cells.

B) how antibody proteins can be molded to fit antigens after the antigen interacts with an antibody-producing type of cell.

C) how an antigen can provoke development of very few cells to result in production of high levels of specific antibodies.

D) how HIV can disrupt the immune system.

E) how macrophages can recognize specific T cells and B cells.

Answer: C
Skill: Comprehension

17) What are plasma cells?

A) immature forms of T cells

B) cells that produce few antibodies

C) the effector cells of humoral immunity

D) the cells that are responsible for immunological memory

E) the cells that are responsible for the phagocytosis of foreign organisms

Answer: C
Skill: Knowledge

18) The following events occur when a mammalian immune system first encounters a pathogen. Place them in correct sequence, and then choose the answer that indicates that sequence.
 I.   Pathogen is destroyed.
 II. Lymphocytes secrete antibodies.
 III. Antigenic determinants from pathogen bind to antigen receptors on lymphocytes.
 IV. Lymphocytes specific to antigenic determinants from pathogen become numerous.
 V.   Only memory cells remain.

 A) I, III, II, IV, V
 B) III, II, I, V, IV
 C) II, I, IV, III, V
 D) IV, II, III, I, V
 E) III, IV, II, I, V

 Answer: E
 Skill: Comprehension

Use the graph in Figure 43.1 to answer the following questions.

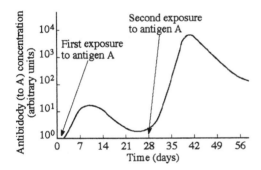

Figure 43.1

19) When would B cells produce effector cells?
 A) between 0 and 7 days
 B) between 7 and 14 days
 C) between 28 and 35 days
 D) Both A and B are correct.
 E) Both A and C are correct.

 Answer: A
 Skill: Application

20) When would memory cells proliferate?
 A) between 0 and 7 days
 B) between 7 and 14 days
 C) between 28 and 35 days
 D) between 35 and 42 days
 E) Both A and C are correct.

 Answer: E
 Skill: Application

21) When would you find antibodies being produced?
 A) between 3 and 7 days
 B) between 14 and 21 days
 C) between 28 and 35 days
 D) Both B and C are correct.
 E) Both A and C are correct.

 Answer: E
 Skill: Application

22) Which of the following cell types is responsible for initiating a secondary immune response?
 A) memory cells
 B) macrophages
 C) stem cells
 D) B cells
 E) T cells

 Answer: A
 Skill: Knowledge

23) Which of the following is true of both T cells and B cells?
 A) They produce effector cells against specific pathogens.
 B) They are produced from stem cells of the bone marrow.
 C) They can attack and destroy invading pathogens.
 D) Both A and B are true.
 E) A, B, and C are all true.

 Answer: D
 Skill: Comprehension

24) If a person's bone marrow were destroyed by radiation, which of the following cells could *not* be produced?

  A) B cells

  B) T cells

  C) erythrocytes

  D) neutrophils

  E) All of the above could not be produced.

Answer: E
Skill: Application

25) The T in T lymphocytes stands for

  A) thymus.

  B) trigger.

  C) threshold.

  D) toxic.

  E) thyroid.

Answer: A
Skill: Knowledge

26) All of the following statements about lymphocytes are true *except:*

  A) They are contained only within the lymphatic vessels and nodes.

  B) They may mature in either bone marrow or the thymus gland.

  C) All cells differentiate only from pluripotent stem cells.

  D) They originate from the liver of a developing fetus.

  E) All cells are produced in bone marrow.

Answer: A
Skill: Knowledge

27) The MHC (major histocompatibility complex) is important in

  A) distinguishing self from nonself.

  B) recognizing parasitic pathogens.

  C) identifying bacterial pathogens.

  D) identifying abnormal cells.

  E) Both A and D are correct.

Answer: E
Skill: Comprehension

The following questions refer to the diagram in Figure 43.2.

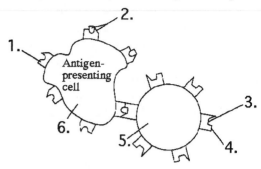

Figure 43.2

28) The cell represented by number 5 is a

  A) B cell.

  B) T cell.

  C) mast cell.

  D) macrophage.

  E) plasma cell.

Answer: B
Skill: Knowledge

29) The MHC binding site is represented by

  A) 1.

  B) 2.

  C) 3.

  D) 4.

  E) 6.

Answer: C
Skill: Knowledge

30) The MHC protein is represented by

  A) 1.

  B) 2.

  C) 3.

  D) 4.

  E) 6.

Answer: A
Skill: Knowledge

31) The "self and nonself" complex is represented by

A) 1.

B) 2.

C) 3.

D) 4.

E) 6.

Answer: B
Skill: Comprehension

32) Which of the following participates in both the specific and nonspecific defense systems of the body?

A) pyrogens

B) complement

C) macrophages

D) B cells

E) Both B and C are correct.

Answer: E
Skill: Comprehension

33) What is the single most important event establishing a primary immune response?

A) the presentation of viral protein complexed to MHC I

B) the lyses of virally infected cell by cytotoxic T cells

C) the phagocytosis of microbes by antigen-presenting cells

D) the recognition of self versus foreign

E) apoptosis of virally infected cells

Answer: D
Skill: Application

34) Which of the following types of cells is *not* involved in *both* antibody-mediated immunity and cell-mediated immunity?

A) pathogenic cells

B) plasma cells

C) helper T cells

D) macrophages

E) memory cells

Answer: B
Skill: Comprehension

35) Which of the following statements about humoral immunity is *correct*?

A) It primarily defends against fungi and protozoa.

B) It is responsible for transplant tissue rejection.

C) It protects the body against cells that become cancerous.

D) It is mounted by lymphocytes that have matured in the bone marrow.

E) It primarily defends against bacteria and viruses that have already infected cells.

Answer: D
Skill: Comprehension

36) What attracts helper T cells to macrophages?

A) lymphotoxins

B) antibodies

C) interferons

D) interleukins

E) antigens

Answer: D
Skill: Knowledge

37) Which of the following is an example of positive feedback in the immune system?

A) Memory cells proliferate and produce antibodies.

B) Cytotoxic cells release substances that attract macrophages.

C) Cells release a cytokine that stimulates these cells to divide and release more of the cytokine.

D) Large antigens with many repeating antigenic determinant sites can stimulate B cells without the aid of T cells.

E) Both A and B are examples of positive feedback in the immune system.

Answer: C
Skill: Comprehension

38) Each of the items below is a response of helper T cells once they are stimulated *except*

A) enlarging in size.

B) dividing by mitosis.

C) producing memory cells.

D) releasing interleukin–1.

E) releasing interleukin–2.

Answer: D
Skill: Comprehension

39) Which of the following are types of T cells that participate in the immune response system?

A) CD4, CD8, and helper cells

B) cytotoxic and helper cells

C) plasma, antigen–presenting, and memory cells

D) lymphocytes, macrophages, and coelomocytes

E) interleukin–1, interleukin–2, and interferon

Answer: B
Skill: Knowledge

40) Which of the following would be *most* beneficial in treating an individual who has been bitten by a poisonous snake that has a fast-acting toxin?

A) vaccination with a weakened form of the toxin

B) injection of antibodies to the toxin

C) injection of interleukin–1

D) injection of interleukin–2

E) injection of interferon

Answer: B
Skill: Application

41) The function of CD4 and CD8 is to assist T cells in

A) enhancing secretion of proteins such as interferon.

B) activating B cells and other T cells.

C) binding of the MHC–antigen complex.

D) recognition of self cells.

E) secretion of antibodies specific for each antigen.

Answer: C
Skill: Knowledge

For the questions below, match the following answers with the phrase that best describes them. Each answer may be used once, more than once, or not at all.

A. *cytotoxic T cells*
B. *delayed sensitivity T cells*
C. *helper T cells*
D. *suppressor T cells*
E. *B cells*

42) form plasma cells that give rise to antibodies

Answer: E
Skill: Knowledge

43) release cytokines, which activate B cells

Answer: C
Skill: Knowledge

44) release perforin, which causes target cells to lose their cytoplasm

Answer: A
Skill: Knowledge

45) cooperate with macrophages to enable the production of antibodies by effector cells

Answer: C
Skill: Knowledge

46) Which of the following is (are) *not* involved in the activation and functioning of cytotoxic T cells?

   A) interleukins

   B) antigen–presenting cells

   C) class I MHC molecules

   D) T cell surface protein CD4

   E) perforin

   Answer: D
   Skill: Comprehension

47) Cell–mediated immunity is mostly the function of

   A) T cells.

   B) B cells.

   C) erythrocytes.

   D) complement cells.

   E) cytotoxic cells.

   Answer: A
   Skill: Knowledge

48) Which of the following defensive actions would be part of the body's third, or most advanced, line of defense?

   A) lysozyme production

   B) phagocytosis by neutrophils

   C) antibody production by plasma cells

   D) histamine release by basophils

   E) action of natural killer cells

   Answer: C
   Skill: Knowledge

49) A patient can produce antibodies against some bacterial pathogens, but he does not produce antibodies against viral infections. This is probably due to a disorder in which cells of the immune system?

   A) B cells

   B) plasma cells

   C) cytotoxic cells

   D) T cells

   E) macrophages

   Answer: D
   Skill: Application

50) Why can normal immune responses be described as polyclonal?

   A) Blood contains many different antibodies to many different antigens.

   B) Construction of a hybridoma requires multiple types of cells.

   C) Multiple immunoglobulins are produced from descendants of a single B cell.

   D) Diverse antibodies are produced for different epitopes of a specific antigen.

   E) Macrophages, T cells, and B cells all are involved in normal immune response.

   Answer: D
   Skill: Comprehension

51) Antibodies of the different classes IgM, IgG, IgA, IgD, and IgE differ from each other in

   A) the way they are produced.

   B) the way they interact with the antigen.

   C) the type of cell that produces them.

   D) the antigenic determinants that they recognize.

   E) the number of carbohydrate subunits they have.

   Answer: B
   Skill: Comprehension

52) Which of the following are necessary to produce monoclonal antibodies?

A) fibroblasts

B) plasma cells

C) myeloma cells

D) macrophages

E) Both B and C are necessary.

Answer: E
Skill: Comprehension

53) Which of the following is *not* a part of an antibody molecule?

A) the epitope

B) the constant or C regions

C) the variable or V regions

D) the light chains

E) the heavy chains

Answer: A
Skill: Knowledge

54) When antibodies attack antigens, clumping of the affected cells generally occurs. This is best explained by

A) the shape of the antibody with at least two binding regions.

B) disulfide bridges between the antigens.

C) complement that makes the affected cells sticky.

D) bonds between class I and class II MHC molecules.

E) denaturation of the antibodies.

Answer: A
Skill: Comprehension

55) All of the following statements about antibodies are true *except:*

A) Antibodies are immunoglobulin proteins.

B) Antibodies bind with foreign cells and destroy them.

C) The structure of antibodies includes both a constant and a variable region.

D) Antibodies act as signals to blood complement proteins or phagocytes.

E) Plasma B cells are responsible for the production of antibodies.

Answer: B
Skill: Comprehension

The next questions refer to the following substances.

1. blood complement proteins
2. interleukin–1
3. interleukin–2
4. antibodies
5. perforin

56) Which substance is secreted by antigen–presenting cells?

A) 1   B) 2   C) 3   D) 4   E) 5

Answer: B
Skill: Knowledge

57) Which substances are used in the immune system to kill targeted, infected cells?

A) 1 and 5

B) 2 and 3

C) 4 and 5

D) 1 and 4

E) 1, 4, and 5

Answer: A
Skill: Knowledge

58) Which substance(s) may act to stimulate the proliferation of T cells?

A) 1 and 4

B) 1 only

C) 2 and 3

D) 3 only

E) 5 only

Answer: D
Skill: Knowledge

59) Which substance(s) is (are) used by cytotoxic T cells to lyse and kill infected cells?

A) 1 and 4

B) 1 only

C) 2 and 3

D) 3 only

E) 5 only

Answer: E
Skill: Knowledge

60) Which substance(s) activate(s) T cells?

A) 1 and 4

B) 1 only

C) 2 and 3

D) 3 only

E) 5 only

Answer: C
Skill: Knowledge

61) In order to investigate the immune system of an invertebrate animal, a scientist grafts a section of epidermis from one earthworm to another. What would you expect to happen?

A) Invertebrates do not have immune responses, so the graft will be accepted.

B) The graft will be recognized as nonself and rejected.

C) This graft will be accepted, but a second graft would be rejected.

D) Amoeboid coelomocytes may be activated against the foreign tissue.

E) Both B and D would happen.

Answer: D
Skill: Application

62) Naturally acquired passive immunity would involve the

A) injection of vaccine.

B) ingestion of interferon.

C) placental transfer of antibodies.

D) absorption of pathogens through mucous membranes.

E) injection of antibodies.

Answer: C
Skill: Comprehension

The questions below refer to the following list. Match the term that best fits each of the following descriptions. Each term may be used once, more than once, or not at all.

A. *clonal selection*
B. *opsonization*
C. *complement system*
D. *passive immunity*
E. *vaccination*

63) coating of foreign cells by proteins to attract macrophages

Answer: B
Skill: Knowledge

64) protection by antibodies that cross the placenta from mother to fetus

Answer: D
Skill: Knowledge

65) part of both specific and nonspecific defense mechanisms

Answer: C
Skill: Knowledge

66) process in which an attenuated pathogen is used to stimulate the body to produce antibodies against the pathogen

Answer: E
Skill: Knowledge

67) Prevention of a disease by the injection of an antiserum containing gamma globulins is an example of
   A) active immunity.
   B) passive immunity.
   C) cell–mediated immunity.
   D) clonal selection.
   E) autoimmunity.

Answer: B
Skill: Knowledge

68) A major difference between active and passive immunity is that active immunity requires
   A) acquisition and activation of antibodies.
   B) proliferation of lymphocytes in bone marrow.
   C) transfer of antibodies from the mother across the placenta.
   D) direct exposure to a living or simulated disease organism.
   E) secretion of interleukins from macrophages.

Answer: D
Skill: Comprehension

69) The major concern for an individual with type A blood who receives type B blood would be
   A) the antibodies in the serum of the donor.
   B) the antibodies in the serum of the recipient.
   C) the anti–A antibodies produced by the donor.
   D) the production of memory cells that will ocur in the recipient.
   E) antibodies in both the donor's and recipient's serum.

Answer: B
Skill: Comprehension

70) A transfusion of type A blood given to a person who has type O blood would result in
   A) the recipient's B antigens reacting with the donated anti–B antibodies.
   B) the recipient's anti–A antibodies clumping the donated red blood cells.
   C) the recipient's anti–A and anti–O antibodies reacting with the donated red blood cells if the donor was a heterozygote (Ai) for blood type.
   D) no reaction because type O is a universal donor.
   E) no reaction because the O–type individual does not have antibodies.

Answer: B
Skill: Comprehension

	Case 1	Case 2	Case 3
Mother	Rh⁻	Rh⁻	Rh⁺
Fetus	Rh⁺	Rh⁻	Rh⁻

71) In which of the cases could the mother exhibit an anti–Rh–factor reaction to the developing fetus?

   A) case 1 only

   B) case 3 only

   C) cases 1 and 2 only

   D) cases 1, 2, and 3

   E) It cannot be determined from the data given.

   Answer: A
   Skill: Application

72) In which of the cases would the mother *not* exhibit an anti–Rh–factor reaction to the developing fetus?

   A) case 1 only

   B) case 3 only

   C) cases 2 and 3 only

   D) cases 1, 2, and 3

   E) It cannot be determined from the data given.

   Answer: C
   Skill: Application

73) In which of the cases would the precaution likely be taken to give the mother anti–Rh antibodies before delivering her baby?

   A) case 1 only

   B) case 3 only

   C) cases 1 and 2 only

   D) cases 1, 2, and 3

   E) It cannot be determined from the data given.

   Answer: A
   Skill: Application

74) There is usually no concern if the mother's blood type is different from that of the developing fetus unless the Rh factor is involved. This is because

   A) antibodies against the Rh factor have a much greater impact on antigens compared to those involving the ABO blood groups.

   B) fetal blood cells can cross the placenta.

   C) maternal blood cells can cross the placenta.

   D) maternal Rh antibodies can cross the placenta, while those against the ABO blood groups cannot.

   E) maternal Rh antibodies cannot cross the placenta, while those against the ABO blood groups can.

   Answer: D
   Skill: Comprehension

75) An immune response to a tissue graft will differ from an immune response to a bacterium because

   A) MHC molecules on the graft may reject the host tissues.

   B) the tissue graft, unlike the bacterium, is isolated from the circulation and will not enter into an immune response.

   C) a response to the graft will involve T cells and a response to the bacterium will not.

   D) the bacterium can escape the immune system by replicating inside normal body cells.

   E) the graft will stimulate an autoimmune response in the recipient.

   Answer: A
   Skill: Comprehension

76) Which of the following could prevent the appearance of the symptoms of an allergy attack?

A) blocking the attachment of the IgE antibodies to the mast cells

B) blocking the antigenic determinants of the IgM antibodies

C) reducing the number of T helper cells in the body

D) Only A and B are correct.

E) Only B and C are correct.

Answer: A
Skill: Application

77) A patient reports severe symptoms of watery, itchy eyes and sneezing after being given a flower bouquet as a birthday gift. A reasonable initial treatment would involve the use of

A) a vaccine.

B) complement.

C) sterile pollen.

D) antihistamines.

E) monoclonal antibodies.

Answer: D
Skill: Application

78) All of the following are usually considered disorders of the immune system *except*

A) AIDS.

B) SCID.

C) lupus erythematosus.

D) allergic anaphylaxis.

E) MHC–induced transplant rejection.

Answer: E
Skill: Comprehension

79) A person suffering from AIDS would be unlikely to suffer from which of the following diseases?

A) cancer

B) rheumatoid arthritis

C) hepatitis

D) tuberculosis

E) influenza

Answer: B
Skill: Application

80) HIV is ultimately a fatal disease. Which choice could be used as an analogy to describe how HIV affects the body?

A) bypassing a light switch so that electricity is constantly flowing to a light

B) rebooting a computer after getting a program error message

C) snipping the wires coming from a car battery so that no electricity flows to the car components

D) an elevator stopping at the floor of which the button has been pushed

E) changing the color of your house to match the color of your car

Answer: C
Skill: Comprehension

Media Activity Questions

1) _____ play a role in both humoral and cell–mediated immune responses.

   A) Helper T cells

   B) Macrophages

   C) Plasma cells

   D) Cytotoxic T cells

   E) B cells

   Answer: A
   Topic: Web/CD Activity 43A

2) Foreign _____ are recognized by the immune system.

   A) monosaccharides

   B) aunts

   C) antidotes

   D) inert substances

   E) antigens

   Answer: E
   Topic: Web/CD Activity 43A

3) The secretion of _____ by helper T cells activates other immune system cells.

   A) interleukin–1

   B) interleukin–2

   C) antibodies

   D) complements

   E) nitric oxide

   Answer: B
   Topic: Web/CD Activity 43A

4) Which of these cells secretes antibodies?

   A) helper T cells

   B) macrophages

   C) bacterial cells

   D) plasma cells

   E) cytotoxic T cells

   Answer: D
   Topic: Web/CD Activity 43A

5) HIV is responsible for

   A) PKU.

   B) TB.

   C) SIDS.

   D) CPR.

   E) AIDS.

   Answer: E
   Topic: Web/CD Activity 43B

Self-Quiz Questions

Answers to these questions also appear in the textbook.

1) An Rh-positive baby is born to an Rh-negative mother. The mother is treated with antibodies specific for the Rh factor in order to
   A) protect her from an inappropriate immune response.
   B) prevent her from generating memory B cells specific for the Rh factor.
   C) protect her future Rh-positive babies.
   D) induce an immune response to Rh antibodies.
   E) both B and C.

   Answer: E

2) Which of the following results in long-term immunity?
   A) the passage of maternal antibodies to her developing fetus
   B) the inflammatory response to a splinter
   C) the administration of serum obtained from people immune to rabies
   D) the administration of the chicken pox vaccine
   E) the passage of maternal antibodies to her nursing infant

   Answer: D

3) Which of the following is *not* part of the body's nonspecific defense system?
   A) natural killer (NK) cells
   B) inflammation
   C) phagocytosis by neutrophils
   D) phagocytosis by macrophages
   E) antibodies

   Answer: E

4) Which of the following molecules is *incorrectly* paired with a source?
   A) lysozyme—tears
   B) interferons—virus-infected cells
   C) interleukin-1—macrophages
   D) perforins—cytotoxic T cells
   E) immunoglobulins—helper T cells

   Answer: E

5) HIV targets include all of the following *except*
   A) macrophages.
   B) cytotoxic T cells.
   C) helper T cells.
   D) cells bearing CD4 and fusin.
   E) cells bearing CD4 and CCR5.

   Answer: B

6) Which of the following best describes the difference in the way B cells and cytotoxic T cells respond to invaders?
   A) B cells confer active immunity; cytotoxic T cells confer passive immunity.
   B) B cells kill viruses directly; cytotoxic T cells kill virus-infected cells.
   C) B cells secrete antibodies against a virus; cytotoxic T cells kill virus-infected cells.
   D) B cells accomplish cell-mediated immunity; cytotoxic T cells accomplish humoral immunity.
   E) B cells respond the first time the invader is present; cytotoxic T cells respond subsequent times.

   Answer: C

7) Which of the following is a characteristic of the early stages of local inflammation?

A) precapillary arteriole constriction

B) fever

C) attack by cytotoxic T cells

D) release of histamine

E) antibody–complement––mediated lysis of microbes

Answer: D

8) An epitope associates with which part of an antibody?

A) the antibody–binding site

B) the heavy–chain constant regions only

C) the variable regions of a heavy chain and light chain combined

D) the light–chain constant regions only

E) the antibody tail

Answer: C

9) Which of the following is *not* true about helper T cells?

A) They function in both cell–mediated and humoral immune responses.

B) They recognize polysaccharide fragments presented by class II MHC molecules.

C) They bear surface CD4 molecules.

D) They are subject to infection by HIV.

E) When activated, they secrete IL–2 and other cytokines.

Answer: B

10) Indicate whether each of the following choices is descriptive of a B cell (B), cytotoxic T cell (T_C), helper T cell (T_H), or macrophage (M). A single feature may be descriptive of more than one type of cell.

A) develops into an antibody–secreting plasma cell

B) is phagocytic

C) bears antigen receptors called immunoglobulins

D) bears the surface molecule CD4

E) bears the surface molecule CD8

F) is an important component of nonspecific responses

G) produces cytokines such as interleukin-2 that boost both humoral and cell-mediated responses

H) mediates specific recognition of and response to a particular antigen

I) bears surface TCR and CD3

J) kills virus–infected cells

Answer: A) B
B) M
C) B
D) T_H
E) T_C
F) M
G) T_H
H) B, T_C, T_H
I) T_C, T_H
J) T_C

Chapter 44   Regulating the Internal Environment

1) A marine sea star was mistakenly placed in freshwater and it died. What is the most likely explanation for its death?
   A) The sea star was stressed and needed more time to adapt to new conditions.
   B) The sea star is hypertonic to the freshwater, and it could not osmoregulate.
   C) The osmoregulatory system of the sea star could not handle the change in ionic content presented by the freshwater.
   D) The contractile vacuoles used to regulate water content ruptured in the freshwater.
   E) The water was not a factor; the sea star simply died.

Answer: B
Skill: Comprehension

2) Terrestrial animals mainly exchange heat with the environment by all of the following physical processes *except*
   A) conduction.
   B) convection.
   C) evaporation.
   D) illumination.
   E) radiation.

Answer: D
Skill: Knowledge

3) Of the mechanisms by which organisms exchange heat with their surroundings, which one results in *only* loss of heat from the organism?
   A) conduction
   B) convection
   C) radiation
   D) evaporation
   E) metabolism

Answer: D
Skill: Comprehension

4) When is a snake more or less active? Why?
   A) A snake is less active in winter because the food supply is decreased.
   B) A snake is less active in winter because it does not need to avoid predators.
   C) A snake is more active in summer because that is the period for mating.
   D) A snake is more active in summer because it can gain body heat by conduction.
   E) A snake is more active in summer as a result of being disturbed by other animals.

Answer: D
Skill: Comprehension

5) Which organism is ectothermic and has little behavorial ability to adjust its body temperature?
   A) lizard
   B) sea star
   C) tuna fish
   D) hummingbird
   E) winter moth

Answer: B
Skill: Application

6) Which of these vertebrates are endotherms?
   A) cartilaginous fishes
   B) bony fishes
   C) amphibians
   D) reptiles
   E) birds

Answer: E
Skill: Knowledge

7) All of the following are mechanisms of thermoregulation in terrestrial mammals *except*

A) changing the rate of evaporative loss of heat.

B) changing the rate of metabolic heat production.

C) changing the rate of heat exchange by anhydrobiosis.

D) changing the rate of heat loss by vasodilation and vasoconstriction.

E) relocating to cool areas when too hot or to warm areas when too cold.

Answer: C
Skill: Comprehension

8) A normally healthy athlete training on a hot, humid day collapses and later dies. What is the most likely explanation?

A) The athlete was ectothermic, resulting in an unusually high level of metabolism to sustain this level of exercise.

B) The training conditions resulted in the athlete losing a large amount of water via perspiration.

C) The athlete had a high level of aerobic metabolism.

D) The athlete's core body temperature soared out of control.

E) The athlete was just out of shape.

Answer: D
Skill: Comprehension

9) Which of the following assertions about regulation of body temperature is *correct*?

A) Most animals are endotherms.

B) Endothermy involves production of heat through metabolism.

C) Ectothermic animals are cold-blooded.

D) Mammals are always ectothermic.

E) Insects are always ectothermic.

Answer: B
Skill: Comprehension

10) You are shoveling snow in the middle of a snowstorm and all of a sudden you begin to shiver. Why?

A) The flow of heat to the environment is exceeding metabolic heat production.

B) Shivering increases heat production to closer match the heat loss.

C) Shivering acts as a reflex action stimulated by the sight of snow.

D) Only A and B are correct.

E) A, B, and C are correct.

Answer: D
Skill: Comprehension

11) Most terrestrial animals dissipate excess heat by

A) countercurrent exchange.

B) acclimation.

C) vasoconstriction.

D) hibernation.

E) evaporation.

Answer: E
Skill: Knowledge

12) Which of the following organisms controls its body temperature by behavior *only*?

A) green frog

B) bumblebee

C) bluefin tuna

D) house sparrow

E) gray wolf

Answer: A
Skill: Knowledge

13) Amphibians and land–dwelling invertebrates have what in common?

A) They are ectothermic organisms.

B) They use behavoral adaptations to maintain body temperature.

C) When on land, most have a net loss across a moist body surface.

D) When in water, they are mainly thermoconformers.

E) Invertebrates have nothing in common when it comes to regulating body temperature.

Answer: A
Skill: Comprehension

14) Where is the thermostat of vertebrates located?

A) medulla oblongata

B) thyroid gland

C) hypothalamus

D) subcutaneous layer of the skin

E) liver

Answer: C
Skill: Knowledge

15) All of the following are aspects of temperature acclimation *except:*

A) Cells may increase the production of certain enzymes.

B) Cells may produce enzymes with different temperature optima.

C) Organisms may adjust some of the mechanisms that control internal temperature.

D) Cell membranes may change their proportions of saturated and unsaturated fats.

E) Organisms with countercurrent circulation adaptations have difficulty with thermoregulation.

Answer: E
Skill: Comprehension

16) Which of the following mechanisms helps you to thermoregulate in the hot summer months?

A) Chemical messengers from the anterior pituitary gland reduce metabolic heat production.

B) Your cells will produce cryoprotectants to reduce heat stress.

C) Vasoconstriction of the blood vessels supplying the skin.

D) Relying on nonshivering thermogenesis to regulate body temperature.

E) Insulating power is lost through a reduction in body fat.

Answer: E
Skill: Comprehension

Match the terms to the following questions. Each term may be used once, more than once, or not at all.

A. ectothermy
B. micturition
C. evaporation
D. torpor
E. thermogenesis

17) hibernation

Answer: D
Skill: Knowledge

18) aestivation

Answer: D
Skill: Knowledge

19) absorbance of heat from the surroundings

Answer: A
Skill: Knowledge

20) process that occurs in the brown fat of some mammals

Answer: E
Skill: Knowledge

21) The digestion and utilization of which nutrient creates the greatest need for osmoregulation by the kidneys?

A) protein

B) starch

C) fat

D) oil

E) cellulose

Answer: A
Skill: Comprehension

A.

B.

$$H_2N-\overset{\overset{\displaystyle O}{\|}}{C}-NH_2$$

C.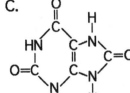

D.

$$H_2N^+-\overset{\overset{\displaystyle H}{|}}{\underset{\underset{\underset{CH_3\ \ CH_3}{|}}{CH}}{C}}-\overset{\overset{\displaystyle O}{\diagup}}{\underset{O^-}{C\diagdown}}$$

E.

CH₂OH

Figure 44.1

22) Which of the molecules shown in Figure 44.1 represents urea?

A) A

B) B

C) C

D) D

E) E

Answer: B
Skill: Knowledge

23) Urea is produced in the

A) liver from NH_3 and CO_2.

B) liver from glycogen.

C) kidneys from glucose.

D) kidneys from glycerol and fatty acids.

E) bladder from uric acid and H_2O.

Answer: A
Skill: Knowledge

24) Which of the following is true of urea? It is

A) insoluble in water.

B) more toxic to human cells than ammonia.

C) the primary nitrogenous waste product of humans.

D) the primary nitrogenous waste product of most birds.

E) the primary nitrogenous waste product of most aquatic invertebrates.

Answer: C
Skill: Knowledge

25) Important functions of the liver include all of the following *except*

A) storage of glycogen.

B) secretion of urea.

C) production of plasma proteins.

D) removal of glucose from the blood.

E) detoxification of chemical poisons in the blood.

Answer: B
Skill: Comprehension

26) The advantage of excreting wastes as urea rather than ammonia is that

A) urea can be exchanged for Na$^+$.

B) urea is less toxic than ammonia.

C) urea requires less water for excretion than ammonia.

D) urea does not affect the osmolar gradient.

E) Both B and C are advantages.

Answer: E
Skill: Knowledge

27) The main nitrogenous waste excreted by birds is

A) ammonia.

B) nitrate.

C) nitrite.

D) urea.

E) uric acid.

Answer: E
Skill: Knowledge

28) Which of the following is a nitrogenous waste that requires hardly any water for its excretion?

A) amino acid

B) urea

C) uric acid

D) ammonia

E) nitrogen gas

Answer: C
Skill: Knowledge

29) Organisms categorized as osmoconformers are most likely

A) terrestrial.

B) marine.

C) amphibious.

D) found in freshwater streams.

E) found in freshwater lakes.

Answer: B
Skill: Knowledge

30) The body fluids of an osmoconformer would be _____ with its _____ environment.

A) hypertonic; freshwater

B) isotonic; freshwater

C) hypertonic; saltwater

D) isotonic; saltwater

E) hypotonic; saltwater

Answer: D
Skill: Comprehension

31) Compared to the seawater around them, most marine invertebrates are *correctly* described as which of the following?
I.   hypertonic
II. hypotonic
III. isotonic

A) I only

B) II only

C) III only

D) I and III only

E) II and III only

Answer: C
Skill: Comprehension

32) It is possible for an animal to be classified as an osmoconformer at the same time as it regulates its extracellular environment. Why?

A) An animal can be an osmoconformer if the extracellular ionic content balances the osmolarity of the external.

B) An animal that has kidneys can produce urine that is hypotonic, isotonic, or hypertonic to the environment.

C) An animal may take on or lose water to balance extracellular and external osmolarity.

D) An animal with contractile vacuoles has a way to expel excess water, preventing it from being hypertonic to its environment.

E) Both A and C offer explanations.

Answer: E
Skill: Comprehension

33) Which feature of osmoregulation do both marine and freshwater bony fish have?

A) loss of water through gills

B) gain of salt through gills

C) large volume of urine

D) no drinking

E) gain of water through food

Answer: E
Skill: Comprehension

34) Compared to the seawater around them, most marine bony fishes are *correctly* described by which of the following?

I.   hypertonic

II. hypotonic

III. isotonic

A) I only

B) II only

C) III only

D) I and III only

E) II and III only

Answer: B
Skill: Comprehension

35) Contractile vacuoles most likely would be found in protists

A) in a marine environment.

B) that are internal parasites.

C) that are osmoregulators.

D) that are osmoconformers.

E) that are hypoosmotic to their environment.

Answer: C
Skill: Knowledge

36) In addition to their role in gas exchange, fish gills are also directly involved in

A) digestion.

B) osmoregulation.

C) thermoregulation.

D) the excretion of uric acid.

E) the release of atrial natriuretic proteins.

Answer: B
Skill: Comprehension

37) All of the following represent adaptations by terrestrial animals to drying conditions *except*

A) anhydrobiosis.

B) salt glands.

C) efficient kidneys.

D) impervious surfaces.

E) increased thirst.

Answer: B
Skill: Comprehension

38) What is the process called by which materials are returned to the blood from the nephron fluid?

A) filtration

B) ultrafiltration

C) reabsorption

D) secretion

E) active transport

Answer: C
Skill: Knowledge

39) Protonephridia are excretory structures found in

A) flatworms.

B) earthworms.

C) insects.

D) jellyfish.

E) vertebrates.

Answer: A
Skill: Knowledge

40) Malpighian tubules are excretory organs found in
   A) earthworms.
   B) flatworms.
   C) insects.
   D) jellyfish.
   E) vertebrates.

   Answer: C
   Skill: Knowledge

41) Which of the following mechanisms for osmoregulation/nitrogen removal is *incorrectly* paired with its animal?
   A) nephridium—annelid
   B) Malpighian tubule—insect
   C) kidney—frog
   D) flame cell—roundworm
   E) direct cellular exchange—marine invertebrate

   Answer: D
   Skill: Knowledge

42) The functional unit of the kidney is called the
   A) cortex.
   B) vasa recta.
   C) nephron.
   D) bladder.
   E) glomerulus.

   Answer: C
   Skill: Knowledge

43) Which of the following excretory systems is partly based on the filtration of fluid under high hydrostatic pressure?
   A) flame cell system of flatworms
   B) protonephridia of rotifers
   C) metanephridia of annelids
   D) Malpighian tubules of insects
   E) nephrons of vertebrates

   Answer: E
   Skill: Knowledge

44) Which of the following statements about the transfer of fluid from the glomerulus to Bowman's capsule is *correct*?
   A) It results from active transport.
   B) It transfers large molecules as easily as small ones.
   C) It is very selective as to which small molecules are transferred.
   D) It is mainly a consequence of blood pressure force-filtering the fluid.
   E) It usually includes the transfer of red blood cells to the nephron tubule.

   Answer: D
   Skill: Comprehension

45) A biologist discovers a new species of organism adapted to living in a deep underground cavern that provides no source of free water. The organism is eyeless and covered by fur, and it has a four-chambered heart with a closed circulatory system. What excretory system modifications might the biologist expect to find?
   A) very long Malpighian tubules
   B) very short Malpighian tubules
   C) metanephridia with a large number of nephridiopores
   D) kidneys with long juxtamedullary nephrons
   E) kidneys with only cortical nephrons

   Answer: C
   Skill: Application

46) Which part of the vertebrate nephron consists of capillaries?
   A) glomerulus
   B) loop of Henle
   C) distal tubule
   D) Bowman's capsule
   E) collecting tubule

   Answer: A
   Skill: Comprehension

47) Which of the following normally contains blood?

A) vasa recta

B) Bowman's capsule

C) loop of Henle

D) proximal tubule

E) collecting duct

Answer: A
Skill: Knowledge

Refer to Figure 44.2, a diagram of a renal tubule, to answer the following questions.

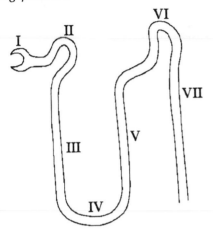

Figure 44.2

48) In which region would filtration occur?

A) I

B) III

C) IV

D) V

E) VII

Answer: A
Skill: Knowledge

49) In which region would urine become more concentrated?

A) I

B) III

C) IV

D) V

E) VII

Answer: E
Skill: Knowledge

50) Adjustment of the pH of urine to keep it from becoming too acidic is accomplished by synthesis and secretion of what substance by cells of the proximal tubule?

A) bicarbonate

B) salt

C) glucose

D) ammonia

E) HCl

Answer: D
Skill: Knowledge

For the following questions, refer to the following structures. Each structure name may be used once, more than once, or not at all.

A. loop of Henle
B. collecting duct
C. Bowman's capsule
D. proximal convoluted tubule
E. glomerulus

51) passes urine to the renal pelvis

Answer: B
Skill: Knowledge

52) increases the reabsorption of Na$^+$ when stimulated by aldosterone

Answer: E
Skill: Knowledge

53) possesses specialized cells called podocytes

Answer: C
Skill: Knowledge

54) possesses a specialized epithelial lining called a brush border

Answer: D
Skill: Knowledge

55) descends deep into the renal medulla only in juxtamedullary nephrons

Answer: A
Skill: Knowledge

56) All of the following are functions of the mammalian kidney *except*

A) water reabsorption.

B) filtration of blood.

C) excretion of nitrogenous waste.

D) regulation of salt balance in the blood.

E) production of urea as a waste product of protein catabolism.

Answer: E
Skill: Knowledge

57) Which of the following is *not* true concerning transport epithelia involved in water balance?

A) One surface of the epithelium faces the outside environment directly or indirectly.

B) The epithelium is a semipermeable barrier.

C) The surface area is small to prevent excessive water loss.

D) The epithelium regulates the movement of solute.

E) Cells are joined by tight junctions.

Answer: C
Skill: Comprehension

58) Which of the following processes of osmoregulation by the kidney is the *least* selective?

A) salt pumping to control osmolarity

B) H^+ ion pumping to control pH

C) reabsorption

D) filtration

E) secretion

Answer: D
Skill: Comprehension

59) A toxin that specifically blocks active transport in the loop of Henle might result in

A) a decrease in the interstitial concentration of NaCl.

B) a decrease in the filtrate concentration ability of the kidney.

C) an increase in the amount of interstitial urea to maintain interstitial osmolarity.

D) a decrease in the volume of hypertonic urine produced by the kidney.

E) All of the above are possibilities.

Answer: E
Skill: Comprehension

60) Humans can produce urine that is *correctly* described as being which of the following?
I.   hypertonic to body fluids
II. isotonic to body fluids
III. hypotonic to body fluids

A) I only

B) II only

C) III only

D) I and II only

E) I, II, and III

Answer: E
Skill: Comprehension

61) Proper functioning of the human kidney requires considerable active transport of sodium in the kidney tubules. If these active transport mechanisms were to stop completely, how would urine production be affected?

A) No urine would be produced.

B) A less–than–normal volume of hypotonic urine would be produced.

C) A greater–than–normal volume of isotonic urine would be produced.

D) A greater–than–normal volume of hypertonic urine would be produced.

E) A less–than–normal volume of isotontic urine would be produced.

Answer: C
Skill: Comprehension

62) Which of the following mechanisms would account for increased urine production as a result of drinking alcoholic beverages?

A) increased aldosterone production

B) increased blood pressure

C) decreased amount of antidiuretic hormone

D) the proximal tubule reabsorbing more water

E) the osmoregulator cells of the brain increasing their activity

Answer: C
Skill: Knowledge

63) In a laboratory experiment, one group of people consumes an amount of pure water, a second group an equal amount of beer, and a third group an equal amount of concentrated salt solution that is hypertonic to their blood. Their urine production is monitored for several hours. At the end of the measurement period, which group will have produced the greatest volume of urine and which group the least?

A) beer the most, salt solution the least

B) salt solution the most, water the least

C) water the most, beer the least

D) beer the most, water the least

E) There will be no significant difference.

Answer: A
Skill: Application

64) Which of the following activities would initiate an osmoregulatory adjustment brought about primarily through the renin-angiotensin-aldosterone system?

A) not drinking any fluids for a day or two

B) spending several hours mowing the lawn on a hot day

C) eating a bag of potato chips

D) eating a pizza with green olives and pepperoni

E) drinking several glasses of water

Answer: B
Skill: Application

65) Hormones involved in the production of urine include all of the following *except*

A) aldosterone.

B) angiotensin.

C) ADH.

D) atrial natriuretic factor.

E) secretin.

Answer: E
Skill: Knowledge

66) Which of the following substances is *incorrectly* matched with its producer?

A) antiotensinogen—liver

B) ADH—hypothalamus

C) renin—juxtaglomerular apparatus

D) aldosterone—kidney

E) atrial natriuretic factor— heart

Answer: D
Skill: Comprehension

Media Activity Questions

1) After being formed in a kidney, urine collects in the renal pelvis and drains directly into the _____ to reach the urinary bladder.

   A) bile duct

   B) urethra

   C) ductus venosus

   D) ureter

   E) aorta

   Answer: D
   Topic: Web/CD Activity 44A

2) The _____ is the functional unit of kidneys.

   A) T cell

   B) neuron

   C) villus

   D) alveolus

   E) nephron

   Answer: E
   Topic: Web/CD Activity 44A

3) Which of these is *not* a component of the filtrate that moves from the glomerulus to Bowman's capsule?

   A) urea

   B) water

   C) sodium chloride

   D) glucose

   E) blood cells

   Answer: E
   Topic: Web/CD Activity 44B

4) The high solute concentration of the interstitial fluid surrounding the medulla promotes the

   A) diffusion of glucose from the filtrate into the interstitial fluid.

   B) diffusion of glucose from the interstitial fluid into the filtrate.

   C) diffusion of sodium chloride from the filtrate into the interstitial fluid.

   D) osmosis of water from the filtrate into the interstitial fluid.

   E) osmosis of water from the interstitial fluid into the filtrate.

   Answer: D
   Topic: Web/CD Activity 44B

5) ADH is secreted by the

   A) thymus.

   B) adrenal glands.

   C) pancreas.

   D) pituitary gland.

   E) thyroid gland.

   Answer: D
   Topic: Web/CD Activity 44C

Self-Quiz Questions

Answers to these questions also appear in the textbook.

1) *Unlike* an earthworm's metanephridia, a mammalian nephron

   A) is intimately associated with a capillary network.

   B) forms urine by changing the composition of fluid inside the tubule.

   C) functions in both osmoregulation and the excretion of nitrogenous wastes.

   D) processes blood instead of coelomic fluid.

   E) has a transport epithelium.

   Answer: D

2) The majority of water and salt filtered into Bowman's capsule is reabsorbed by

   A) the transport epithelia of the proximal tubule.

   B) diffusion from the descending limb of the loop of Henle into the hyperosmotic interstitial fluid of the medulla.

   C) active transport across the transport epithelium of the thick upper segment of the ascending limb of the loop of Henle.

   D) selective secretion and diffusion across the distal tubule.

   E) diffusion from the collecting duct into the increasing osmotic gradient of the renal medulla.

   Answer: A

3) The high osmolarity of the renal medulla is maintained by all of the following *except*

   A) diffusion of salt from the ascending limb of the loop of Henle.

   B) active transport of salt from the upper region of the ascending limb.

   C) the spatial arrangement of juxtamedullary nephrons.

   D) diffusion of urea from the collecting duct.

   E) diffusion of salt from the descending limb of the loop of Henle.

   Answer: E

4) Select the pair in which the nitrogenous waste is incorrectly matched with the benefit of its excretion.

   A) urea—low toxicity relative to ammonia

   B) uric acid—can be stored as a precipitate

   C) ammonia—very soluble in water

   D) uric acid—minimal loss of water when excreted

   E) urea—very insoluble in water

   Answer: E

5) Which of the following is *not* a mechanism for reducing the rate of heat exchange between an animal and its environment?

   A) feathers or fur

   B) vasoconstriction

   C) nonshivering thermogenesis

   D) countercurrent heat exchanger

   E) blubber or fat layer

   Answer: C

6) An animal's inputs of energy and materials would exceed its outputs

A) if the animal is an endotherm, which must always take in more energy because of its high metabolic rate.

B) if it is actively foraging for food.

C) if it is hibernating.

D) if it is growing and increasing its biomass.

E) never—homeostasis makes these energy and material budgets always balance.

Answer: D

7) Which of the following correctly describes a case of osmoregulation?

A) body fluids that are isoosmotic with the external environment

B) discharge of excess water in a hypoosmotic environment

C) expenditure of energy to convert ammonia to less toxic wastes

D) excretion of salt in a hypoosmotic environment

E) secretion of drugs and reabsorption of nutrients by the proximal tubule

Answer: B

8) Which process in the nephron is *least* selective?

A) secretion

B) reabsorption

C) active transport

D) filtration

E) salt pumping by the loop of Henle

Answer: D

9) You are studying a large tropical reptile that has a high and quite constant body temperature. How would you determine whether this animal is an endotherm or an ectotherm?

A) You know from its high and constant body temperature that it must be an endotherm.

B) You know that it is an ectotherm because it is not a bird or mammal.

C) You subject this reptile to various temperatures in the lab and find that its body temperature and metabolic rate changes with the ambient temperature. You conclude that it is an ectotherm.

D) You note that its environment has a high and constant temperature. Because its body temperature matches the environmental temperature, you conclude that it is an ectotherm.

E) You measure the metabolic rate of the reptile, and, because it is higher than that of a related species that lives in temperate forests, you conclude that this reptile is an endotherm and its relative is an ectotherm.

Answer: C

10) The vertebrate liver functions in all of the following regulatory processes *except*

A) osmoregulation by variable excretion of salts.

B) maintenance of blood sugar concentration.

C) detoxification of harmful substances.

D) production of nitrogenous wastes.

E) caloric storage in the form of glycogen.

Answer: A

Chapter 45   Chemical Signals in Animals

1) All of the following statements about hormones are correct *except*:
   A) They are produced by endocrine glands.
   B) They are modified amino acids, peptides, or steroid molecules.
   C) They are carried by the circulatory system.
   D) They are used to communicate between different organisms.
   E) They elicit specific biological responses from target cells.

   Answer: D
   Skill: Comprehension

2) Hormones are able to control homeostasis because
   A) they are not produced by exocrine glands.
   B) they are subject to negative feedback.
   C) they may be found in the lymphatic system.
   D) they are present at low concentrations.
   E) they are steroids.

   Answer: B
   Skill: Knowledge

3) An overdose of which hormone would result in the molting of insects?
   A) ecdysone
   B) juvenile hormone
   C) oxytocin
   D) brain hormone
   E) prothoracic hormone

   Answer: D
   Skill: Application

4) Which of the following hormonal changes would result in the molt of an insect from an immature stage to an adult?
   A) decrease in ecdysone, increase in juvenile hormone
   B) increase in ecdysone, decrease in juvenile hormone
   C) increase in both ecdysone and juvenile hormone
   D) decrease in both ecdysone and juvenile hormone
   E) None of these choices is correct because molting is controlled strictly by the nervous system.

   Answer: B
   Skill: Knowledge

5) What do nitrous oxide and epinephrine have in common?
   A) They both function as neurotransmitters.
   B) They both function as hormones.
   C) They are both involved in the "fight–or–flight" response.
   D) A and B are correct.
   E) A, B, and C are correct.

   Answer: D
   Skill: Comprehension

6) Prostaglandins are derived from
   A) sugars.
   B) fatty acids.
   C) steroids.
   D) amino acids.
   E) ammonia.

   Answer: B
   Skill: Knowledge

7) Substance X is secreted by one cell, travels a short distance through interstitial fluid, and produces an effect in a cell immediately adjacent to the original secreting cell. All of the following terms might fit this substance *except*

A) nitric oxide.

B) neurotransmitter.

C) prostaglandin.

D) pheromone.

E) growth factor.

Answer: D
Skill: Comprehension

8) Aspirin and ibuprofen affect the production of

A) hormones.

B) prostaglandins.

C) neurotransmitters.

D) histamine.

E) interleukins.

Answer: B
Skill: Knowledge

9) Based on their effects, which choice could be considered antagonists?

A) prostaglandin F and nitrous oxide

B) growth hormone and ecdysone

C) endocrine and exocrine glands

D) hormones and target cells

E) neurosecretory cells and neurotransmitters

Answer: A
Skill: Comprehension

10) A cell that contains membrane proteins enabling a hormone to selectively bind to its plasma membrane is called a(n)

A) secretory cell.

B) plasma cell.

C) endocrine cell.

D) target cell.

E) regulatory cell.

Answer: D
Skill: Knowledge

11) Only certain cells in the body are target cells for the steroid hormone aldosterone. Which of the following is the *best* explanation for why these are the only cells that respond to this hormone?

A) Only target cells are exposed to aldosterone.

B) Only target cells contain receptors for aldosterone.

C) Aldosterone is unable to enter nontarget cells.

D) Nontarget cells destroy aldosterone before it can produce its effect.

E) Nontarget cells convert aldosterone to a hormone to which they do respond.

Answer: B
Skill: Comprehension

12) A varying response to a common chemical messenger is possible because

A) various target cells have different genes.

B) each cell knows how it fits into the body's master plan.

C) various target cells differ in their receptors to the same hormone.

D) the circulatory system regulates responses to hormones by routing the hormones to specific targets.

E) the hormone is chemically altered in different ways as it travels through different branches of the circulatory system.

Answer: C
Skill: Comprehension

13) An enzyme cascade

   A) takes several days to occur.

   B) ends in steroid hormone release.

   C) increases the response to a hormone.

   D) activates the parathyroid gland.

   E) initiates regulation of the nervous system.

Answer: C
Skill: Knowledge

14) Frequently, very few molecules of a hormone are required to effect changes in a target cell. This is because

   A) hormones are lipid soluble and readily penetrate the membranes of the target cell.

   B) hormones are large molecules that persist for years and can repeatedly stimulate the same cell.

   C) the mechanism of hormonal action involves an enzyme cascade that amplifies the response to a hormone.

   D) the mechanism of hormonal action involves the rapid replication of the hormone within the target cell to quickly magnify the hormone's effect.

   E) the mechanism of hormonal action involves memory cells that have had prior contact with the hormone and immediately respond to its presence.

Answer: C
Skill: Knowledge

15) Two kinds of cells may respond differently to the same steroid hormone because

   A) they have different receptor proteins within the cell.

   B) they have different acceptor proteins on the chromatin.

   C) steroid hormones usually transmit signals that are antagonistic.

   D) the acceptor proteins are associated with different genes in the two kinds of cells.

   E) the hormone-receptor complex is transcribed and processed differently in the two kinds of cells.

Answer: D
Skill: Application

16) Hormone X produces its effect in its target cells via the cAMP second messenger system. If you expose a target cell to only a single molecule, which of the following will produce the greatest effect?

   A) a molecule of hormone X applied to the extracellular fluid surrounding the cell

   B) a molecule of hormone X injected into the cytoplasm of the cell

   C) a molecule of cAMP applied to the extracellular fluid surrounding the cell

   D) a molecule of cAMP injected into the cytoplasm of the cell

   E) a molecule of activated, cAMP-dependent protein kinase injected into the cytoplasm of the cell

Answer: A
Skill: Application

17) Which of the following statements about hormones is *correct*?

A) Steroid and peptide hormones produce different effects but use the same biochemical mechanisms.

B) Steroid and peptide hormones produce the same effects but differ in the mechanisms that produce the effects.

C) Steroid hormones affect the synthesis of proteins, whereas peptide hormones affect the activity of proteins already present in the cell.

D) Steroid hormones affect the activity of certain proteins within the cell, whereas peptide hormones directly affect the processing of mRNA.

E) Steroid hormones affect the synthesis of proteins to be exported from the cell, whereas peptide hormones affect the synthesis of proteins that remain in the cell.

Answer: C
Skill: Comprehension

18) Receptor molecules for chemical signals would *not* likely be found

A) in the nucleus of target cells.

B) in the interstitial fluid surrounding target cells.

C) in the cytoplasm of target cells.

D) in the cell membrane of target cells.

E) associated with the DNA of target cells.

Answer: B
Skill: Comprehension

19) Which of the following examples is *incorrectly* paired with its class?

A) histamine—local regulator

B) estrogen—steroid hormone

C) prostaglandin—peptide hormone

D) ecdysone—steroid hormone

E) neurotransmitter—local regulator

Answer: C
Skill: Comprehension

20) Which of the following is an endocrine gland?

A) parathyroid gland

B) salivary gland

C) sweat gland

D) sebaceous gland

E) gallbladder

Answer: A
Skill: Knowledge

The question below refers to the following information. In an experiment, rats' ovaries were removed immediately after impregnation and then the rats were divided into two groups. Treatments and results are summarized in the table below.

	Group 1	Group 2
Daily injections of progesterone (milligrams)	0.25	2.0
Percent of rats that carried fetuses to birth	0	100

21) The results most likely occurred because progesterone exerts an effect on the

A) general health of the rat.

B) size of the fetus.

C) maintenance of the uterus.

D) gestation period of rats.

E) number of eggs fertilized.

Answer: C
Skill: Application

22) Which of the following would you expect to occur if you found an extremely large thymus gland in an adult human?

A) an unusual immune system

B) a high metabolic rate

C) decreased size of the gonads

D) no "fight–or–flight" reaction

E) high levels of Ca^{2+} in the blood

Answer: A
Skill: Knowledge

23) What is the main target organ of ADH?

A) anterior pituitary

B) posterior pituitary

C) adrenal gland

D) bladder

E) kidney

Answer: E
Skill: Knowledge

24) The hypothalamus controls the anterior pituitary by means of

A) releasing factors.

B) second messengers.

C) third messengers.

D) antibodies.

E) pyrogens.

Answer: A
Skill: Knowledge

25) Which hormone is *not* a steroid?

A) androgen

B) cortisone

C) estrogen

D) insulin

E) testosterone

Answer: D
Skill: Knowledge

26) Oxytocin and ADH are produced by the

A) hypothalamus and stored in the neurohypophysis.

B) adenohypophysis and stored in the kidneys.

C) thymus and stored in the thyroid.

D) adrenal cortex.

E) gonads.

Answer: A
Skill: Knowledge

27) All of the following statements about endocrine glands are correct *except:*

A) The parathyroids regulate metabolic rate.

B) The thyroid participates in blood calcium regulation.

C) The pituitary participates in the regulation of the gonads.

D) The adrenal medulla produces "fight-or-flight" responses.

E) The pancreas helps to regulate blood sugar concentration.

Answer: A
Skill: Knowledge

28) Which of these hormones is a protein?

A) epinephrine

B) cortisone

C) estrogen

D) androgen

E) insulin

Answer: E
Skill: Knowledge

29) The hormones secreted by the adrenal cortex are

A) steroids.

B) polypeptides.

C) inorganic ions.

D) amino acids.

E) proteins.

Answer: A
Skill: Knowledge

The following questions refer to the list of hormones below. Each hormone may be used once, more than once, or not at all.

    A. *ecdysone*
    B. *glucagon*
    C. *thymosin*
    D. *oxytocin*
    E. *growth hormone*

30) secreted by the pancreas

    Answer: B
    Skill: Knowledge

31) signals the liver to produce somatomedins

    Answer: E
    Skill: Knowledge

32) stimulates the contraction of uterine muscle

    Answer: D
    Skill: Knowledge

33) secreted by the anterior lobe of the pituitary

    Answer: E
    Skill: Knowledge

34) steroid hormone that triggers molting in arthropods

    Answer: A
    Skill: Knowledge

35) The endocrine system and the nervous system are structurally related. Which of the following cells best illustrates this relationship?
    A) a neuron in the spinal cord
    B) a steroid–producing cell in the adrenal cortex
    C) a neurosecretory cell in the hypothalamus
    D) a brain cell in the cerebral cortex
    E) a cell in the pancreas that produces digestive enzymes

    Answer: C
    Skill: Comprehension

36) Which of the following hormone sequences is *correct*?
    A) LH → FSH → adrenal glands
    B) GnRH → FSH → ovaries
    C) CRH → ACTH → FSH → thyroid gland
    D) CRH → LH → testes
    E) GnRH → FSH → LH → pineal gland

    Answer: B
    Skill: Knowledge

37) Insect brain hormone is most analogous to which of the following in humans?
    A) insulin from the pancreas
    B) parathyroid hormone from the parathyroid gland
    C) ADH from the posterior pituitary
    D) releasing hormones from the hypothalamus
    E) androgens from the adrenal cortex

    Answer: D
    Skill: Comprehension

38) Which of the following endocrine structures is (are) *not* controlled by a tropic hormone from the anterior pituitary?
    A) pancreatic islet cells
    B) thyroid gland
    C) adrenal cortex
    D) ovaries
    E) testes

    Answer: A
    Skill: Knowledge

39) A short blood vessel connects two sets of capillaries lying in which of the following?
    A) hypothalamus and thalamus
    B) anterior pituitary and posterior pituitary
    C) hypothalamus and anterior pituitary
    D) posterior pituitary and thyroid gland
    E) anterior pituitary and adrenal gland

    Answer: C
    Skill: Knowledge

40) Hormones from the hypothalamus affect the release of all of the following *except*

A) prolactin.

B) oxytocin.

C) growth hormone.

D) thyroid–stimulating hormone.

E) adrenocorticotropic hormone.

Answer: B
Skill: Comprehension

41) All of the following statements about the hypothalamus are correct *except:*

A) It functions as an endocrine gland.

B) It is part of the central nervous system.

C) It is subject to feedback inhibition by certain hormones.

D) It secretes tropic hormones that act directly on the gonads.

E) Its neurosecretory cells terminate in the posterior pituitary.

Answer: D
Skill: Comprehension

42) Which of the following glands is controlled directly by the hypothalamus or central nervous system and *not* the anterior pituitary?

A) ovary

B) adrenal medulla

C) adrenal cortex

D) testis

E) thyroid

Answer: B
Skill: Knowledge

43) The secretion of hormone A causes an increase in activity X in an organism. If this mechanism works by positive feedback, which of the following statements represents that fact?

A) An increase in X produces an increase in A.

B) An increase in A produces an increase in X.

C) An increase in X produces a decrease in A.

D) A decrease in A produces an increase in X.

E) Both A and B are correct.

Answer: E
Skill: Comprehension

44) Tropic hormones from the anterior pituitary directly affect the release of which of the following?

A) parathyroid hormone

B) calcitonin

C) epinephrine

D) thyroxine

E) glucagon

Answer: D
Skill: Comprehension

45) Prolactin stimulates mammary gland growth and development in mammals and regulates salt and water balance in freshwater fish. Many scientists believe that this wide range of functions indicates that

A) prolactin is a nonspecific hormone.

B) prolactin has a unique mechanism for eliciting its effects.

C) prolactin is an ancient hormone.

D) prolactin is derived from two separate sources.

E) prolactin interacts with many different receptor molecules.

Answer: C
Skill: Knowledge

46) Melatonin has been implicated in all of the following *except*

A) skin pigmentation.

B) monitoring day length.

C) reproduction.

D) biological rhythms and clocks.

E) calcium deposition in bone.

Answer: E
Skill: Knowledge

47) Which of the following pairs of hormones do *not* have antagonistic effects?

A) insulin and glucagon

B) thyroid–releasing hormone and T_3 and T_4

C) parathyroid hormone and calcitonin

D) follicle–stimulating hormone and luteinizing hormone

E) aldosterone and atrial natriuretic factor

Answer: D
Skill: Knowledge

48) A goiter is associated with improper functioning of which gland(s)?

A) parathyroids

B) adrenal

C) thyroid

D) pancreas

E) ovaries and testes

Answer: C
Skill: Knowledge

49) Which hormone exerts antagonistic action to PTH (parathyroid hormone)?

A) thyroxine

B) epinephrine

C) growth hormone

D) calcitonin

E) glucagon

Answer: D
Skill: Comprehension

50) Which of the following glands shows both endocrine and exocrine activity?

A) pituitary

B) parathyroid

C) salivary

D) pancreas

E) adrenal

Answer: D
Skill: Knowledge

51) Alpha cells and beta cells can be found in the

A) liver.

B) pancreas.

C) hypothalamus.

D) endocrine control center.

E) pituitary gland.

Answer: B
Skill: Knowledge

52) Blood samples taken from an individual who had been fasting for 24 hours would have which of the following?

A) high levels of insulin

B) high levels of glucagon

C) low levels of insulin

D) low levels of glucagon

E) Both B and C would be present.

Answer: E
Skill: Application

53) Which of the following endocrine structures are derived from nervous tissue?

A) the thymus and thyroid glands

B) the ovaries and the testes

C) the liver and the pancreas

D) the anterior pituitary and the adrenal cortex

E) the posterior pituitary and the adrenal medulla

Answer: E
Skill: Knowledge

54) The endocrine system and the nervous system are chemically related. Which of the following substances *best* illustrates this relationship?

A) estrogen

B) calcitonin

C) norepinephrine

D) calcium

E) thymosin

Answer: C
Skill: Comprehension

55) All of the following endocrine disorders are correctly matched with the malfunctioning gland *except*

A) diabetes and pancreas.

B) giantism and pituitary.

C) cretinism and adrenal medulla.

D) tetany and parathyroid.

E) dwarfism and pituitary.

Answer: C
Skill: Knowledge

56) Which of the following statements about the adrenal gland is *correct*?

A) During stress, TSH stimulates the adrenal cortex and medulla to secrete acetylcholine.

B) During stress, the alpha cells of islets secrete insulin and simultaneously the beta cells of the islets secrete glucagon.

C) During stress, ACTH stimulates the adrenal cortex, and neurons to the sympathetic nervous system stimulate the adrenal medulla.

D) At all times, the anterior portion secretes ACTH while the posterior portion secretes oxytocin.

E) At all times, the adrenal gland monitors calcium levels in the blood and regulates calcium by secreting the two antagonistic hormones, epinephrine and norepinephrine.

Answer: C
Skill: Comprehension

57) Which of the following hormones is (are) secreted by the adrenal gland in response to stress and promote(s) the synthesis of glucose from noncarbohydrate substrates?

A) glucagon

B) glucocorticoids

C) epinephrine

D) thyroxine

E) ACTH

Answer: B
Skill: Knowledge

The questions below refer to the following list of hormones. Each hormone may be used once, more than once, or not at all.

A. androgens
B. estrogens
C. progestins
D. thymosin
E. melatonin

58) testosterone

Answer: A
Skill: Knowledge

59) estradiol

Answer: B
Skill: Knowledge

60) secreted by the pineal gland

Answer: E
Skill: Knowledge

61) stimulates the development and differentiation of T lymphocytes

Answer: D
Skill: Knowledge

Media Activity Questions

1) The correct sequence of events in the cell–signaling process is
   A) reception, cell response, transduction.
   B) transduction, reception, cell response.
   C) transduction, cell response, reception.
   D) reception, transduction, cell response.
   E) cell response, transduction, reception.

   Answer: D
   Topic: Web/CD Activity 45A

2) Which of these is a type of nonsteroid hormone?
   A) testosterone
   B) hormones derived from amino acids
   C) vitamin D
   D) hormones derived from cholesterol
   E) estrogen

   Answer: B
   Topic: Web/CD Activity 45B

3) A(n) _____ is an example of a signal molecule that can bind to an intracellular receptor and thereby cause a gene to be turned on or off.
   A) glyceride
   B) nucleic acid
   C) steroid
   D) protein
   E) carbohydrate

   Answer: C
   Topic: Web/CD Activity 45C

4) Which of these hormones is secreted by the pancreas?
   A) insulin
   B) melatonin
   C) estrogen
   D) prolactin
   E) calcitonin

   Answer: A
   Topic: Web/CD Activity 45D

5) Which of these hormones stimulates and maintains metabolic processes?
   A) calcitonin
   B) thyroxine
   C) thymosin
   D) oxytocin
   E) melatonin

   Answer: B
   Topic: Web/CD Activity 45D

Self–Quiz Questions

Answers to these questions also appear in the textbook.

1) Which of the following is *not* an accurate statement about hormones?

   A) Hormones are chemical messengers that travel to target cells through the circulatory system.

   B) Hormones often regulate homeostasis through antagonistic functions.

   C) Hormones of the same chemical class usually have the same function.

   D) Hormones are secreted by specialized cells usually located in endocrine glands.

   E) Hormones are often regulated through feedback loops.

   Answer: C

2) A distinctive feature of the mechanism of action of thyroid hormones and steroid hormones is that

   A) these hormones are regulated by feedback loops.

   B) target cells react more rapidly to these hormones than to local regulators.

   C) these hormones bind with specific receptor proteins on target–cell plasma membranes.

   D) these hormones bind to receptors inside cells.

   E) these hormones affect metabolism.

   Answer: D

3) The relationship between the insect hormones ecdysone and brain hormone

   A) is an example of the interaction between the endocrine and nervous systems.

   B) illustrates homeostasis achieved by positive feedback.

   C) demonstrates that peptide–derived hormones have more widespread effects than steroidal hormones.

   D) illustrates homeostasis maintained by antagonistic hormones.

   E) demonstrates competitive inhibition for the hormone receptor.

   Answer: A

4) Growth factors are local regulators that

   A) are produced by the anterior pituitary.

   B) are modified fatty acids that stimulate bone and cartilage growth.

   C) are found on the surface of cancer cells and stimulate abnormal cell division.

   D) are proteins that bind to cell surface receptors and stimulate target–cell growth and development.

   E) include histamines and interleukins and are necessary for cellular differentiation.

   Answer: D

5) Which of the following hormones is *incorrectly* paired with its action?

   A) oxytocin—stimulates uterine contractions during childbirth

   B) thyroxine—stimulates metabolic processes

   C) insulin—stimulates glycogen breakdown in the liver

   D) ACTH—stimulates the release of glucocorticoids by the adrenal cortex

   E) melatonin—affects biological rhythms, seasonal reproduction

   Answer: C

6) An example of antagonistic hormones controlling homeostasis is
   A) thyroxine and parathyroid hormone in calcium balance.
   B) insulin and glucagon in glucose metabolism.
   C) progestins and estrogens in sexual differentiation.
   D) epinephrine and norepinephrine in "fight-or-flight" responses.
   E) oxytocin and prolactin in milk production.

   Answer: B

7) Which of the following is *not* an example of the close structural and functional relationship between the nervous and endocrine systems?
   A) the secretion of hormones by neurosecretory cells
   B) the multiple functions of norepinephrine
   C) the stimulation of the adrenal medulla in the short-term response to stress
   D) the embryonic development of the posterior pituitary from the hypothalamus
   E) the alteration of gene expression by steroid hormones

   Answer: E

8) A portal vessel carries blood from the hypothalamus directly to the
   A) thyroid.
   B) pineal gland.
   C) anterior pituitary.
   D) posterior pituitary.
   E) thymus.

   Answer: C

9) Which of the following is the most likely explanation for hypothyroidism in a patient whose iodine level is normal?
   A) a disproportionate production of T_3 to T_4
   B) hyposecretion of TSH
   C) hypersecretion of TSH
   D) hypersecretion of MSH
   E) a decrease in the thyroid secretion of calcitonin

   Answer: B

10) The main target organs for tropic hormones are
   A) muscles.
   B) blood vessels.
   C) endocrine glands.
   D) kidneys.
   E) nerves.

   Answer: C

Chapter 46   Animal Reproduction

1) What do budding and gemmules have in common?
   A) Both are types of asexual reproduction.
   B) Both produce large numbers of offspring.
   C) Both occur in sponges.
   D) Both occur in cnidarians.
   E) A and B are correct.

   Answer: A
   Skill: Comprehension

2) Asexual reproduction in animals might involve
   A) fission and budding.
   B) fragmentation and gemmule production.
   C) regeneration.
   D) A and B only.
   E) A, B, and C.

   Answer: E
   Skill: Knowledge

3) Which of the following are possible advantages of asexual reproduction?
   A) It allows the species to endure periods of fluctuating or unstable environmental conditions.
   B) It enhances genetic variability in the species.
   C) It enables the species to rapidly colonize new regions.
   D) A and B only.
   E) A, B, and C.

   Answer: C
   Skill: Comprehension

4) Why do genetic mutations in asexual organisms lead to more evolutionary change than genetic mutations in sexual forms?
   A) The haploid mutations of asexual organisms are immediately expressed.
   B) Asexual organisms devote more time and energy to the process of reproduction.
   C) Sexual organisms can produce more offspring in a given time.
   D) More genetic variation is present in organisms that reproduce asexually.
   E) Asexual organisms have more dominant genes than organisms that reproduce sexually.

   Answer: A
   Skill: Comprehension

5) What are the advantages of asexual reproduction?
   A) It promotes genetic stability.
   B) It enhances the survival rates of parents.
   C) The limited number of offspring prevents overpopulation.
   D) It promotes geographic distribution of species.
   E) It allows animals to replace lost appendages.

   Answer: A
   Skill: Comprehension

6) Which of the following is a form of asexual reproduction?
   A) protandry
   B) protogyny
   C) hermaphroditism
   D) parthenogenesis
   E) anadromesis

   Answer: D
   Skill: Knowledge

7) You observe an organism with the following characteristics: parthenogenetic reproduction, internal development of embryos, presence of an amnion, lack of parental care of young. Of the following, the organism is probably a(an)

A) earthworm.

B) lizard.

C) bird.

D) frog.

E) mammal.

Answer: B
Skill: Application

8) Which animal would be *least* likely to be hermaphroditic?

A) barnacle

B) earthworm

C) tapeworm

D) lobster

E) liver fluke

Answer: D
Skill: Comprehension

9) Why is sexual reproduction important?

A) It allows animals to conserve resources and reproduce only during optimal conditions.

B) The resulting diverse phenotypes may enhance survival of a population in a changing environment.

C) It can result in numerous offspring in a short amount of time.

D) It enables isolated animals to colonize a habitat rapidly.

E) Both A and D are important.

Answer: B
Skill: Comprehension

10) Which of the following is *not* required for internal fertilization?

A) copulatory organ

B) sperm receptacle

C) behavioral interaction

D) internal development of the embryo

E) All of the above are necessary for internal fertilization.

Answer: D
Skill: Knowledge

11) Why is internal fertilization considered more advantageous than external fertilization?

A) Usually fewer offspring are produced, so ample food supply is available.

B) The time and energy devoted to reproduction is decreased.

C) The smaller number of offspring often receive a greater amount of parental protection.

D) The increased survival rate results in rapid population increases.

E) Usually a smaller number of genes are present, which promotes genetic stability.

Answer: C
Skill: Comprehension

12) Internal and external fertilization both

A) produce a zygote.

B) occur in vertebrates.

C) occur in eutherian animals.

D) A and B only are correct.

E) A and C only are correct.

Answer: D
Skill: Comprehension

13) Organisms that produce amniote eggs, in general
   A) have a higher embryo mortality rate than do those with unprotected embryos.
   B) invest most of their reproductive energy in the embryonic and early postnatal development of their offspring.
   C) invest more parenting energy than do placental animals.
   D) produce more gametes than do those animals with external fertilization and development.
   E) All of the above are correct.

Answer: B
Skill: Comprehension

14) Which of these is *not* a correct statement about reproduction in invertebrates?
   A) Many invertebrates have separate sexes.
   B) Many invertebrates utilize external fertilization.
   C) A few species split open to release gametes to the environment.
   D) Some invertebrates have structures that store sperm.
   E) Invertebrates do not engage in copulation.

Answer: E
Skill: Knowledge

15) A cloaca is an anatomical structure found in most vertebrates, which functions as
   A) a specialized sperm-transfer device produced by males.
   B) a common exit for the digestive, excretory, and reproductive systems.
   C) a region bordered by the labia minora and clitoris in females.
   D) a source of nutrients for developing sperm in the testes.
   E) a gland that secretes mucus to lubricate the vaginal opening.

Answer: B
Skill: Knowledge

16) Which of the following produce testosterone?
   A) sperm cells
   B) hypothalamus
   C) Leydig cells
   D) anterior pituitary
   E) seminiferous tubules

Answer: C
Skill: Knowledge

17) Suspending the testes in a scrotum outside the abdominal cavity in male mammals is functional because
   A) this arrangement is more attractive to females.
   B) lower temperatures promote normal maturation of sperm in seminiferous tubules.
   C) the scrotum serves as a shifting counterweight during running locomotion.
   D) lower temperatures enhance the release of secretions from the prostate gland.
   E) this arrangement assists sperm and semen to flow into the urethra.

Answer: B
Skill: Knowledge

18) After sperm cells are produced, they are mainly stored in the

A) urethra.

B) prostate.

C) epididymis.

D) seminal vesicles.

E) bulbourethral gland.

Answer: C
Skill: Knowledge

19) In men, the excretory and reproductive systems share which structure?

A) vas deferens

B) urinary bladder

C) seminal vesicle

D) urethra

E) ureter

Answer: D
Skill: Knowledge

20) Which of these does *not* contribute to the fluids that make up human semen?

A) bulbourethral glands

B) vas deferens

C) prostate gland

D) seminal vesicles

Answer: B
Skill: Knowledge

21) What effect would surgical removal of the seminal vesicles have on the human male reproductive system?

A) It would be sterile because sperm would not be produced.

B) It would be sterile because sperm would not be able to exit the body.

C) The failure rate for the withdrawal method of birth control would go down.

D) There would be a minimal loss in semen volume.

E) The sperm would lose their major nutrients.

Answer: E
Skill: Comprehension

22) What comprises human semen?

A) about 250 to 400 million sperm

B) sperm and secretions from the prostate and bulbourethral glands

C) sperm and secretions from the prostate gland, bulbourethral glands, and seminal vesicles

D) sperm and prostaglandins to narrow the opening of the uterus

E) sperm and anticoagulant enzymes

Answer: C
Skill: Knowledge

23) A major difference between the human male and female reproductive tracts is the

A) location of the gonads.

B) temperature at which gamete production can successfully occur.

C) fact that the scrotum houses testes and the ovaries are covered by a protective capsule.

D) A and B are correct answers.

E) A, B, and C are correct answers.

Answer: E
Skill: Comprehension

24) In humans, the egg is released from the ovary and enters the fallopian tube. How is this accomplished?
   A) The force of the follicular ejection propels the egg into the fallopian tube.
   B) The egg is drawn into the fallopian tube by the action of beating cilia located in the opening of the fallopian tube.
   C) The egg moves through a small tube that connects the ovary and the fallopian tube.
   D) The egg propels itself into the fallopian tube by the beating action of its flagellum.
   E) Peristalsis of ovarian muscles moves the egg into the fallopian tube.

   Answer: B
   Skill: Comprehension

25) What is the narrow opening or neck of the human uterus called?
   A) vagina
   B) cervix
   C) oviduct
   D) fallopian tube
   E) vas deferens

   Answer: B
   Skill: Knowledge

26) Which of the following male and female structures consist largely of erectile tissue and are richly supplied with nerve endings?
   A) penis and clitoris
   B) vas deferens and oviduct
   C) testes and ovaries
   D) seminiferous tubules and vagina
   E) fallopian tube and vas deferens

   Answer: A
   Skill: Comprehension

27) During the human sexual response, vasocongestion
   A) occurs in the clitoris, vagina, and penis.
   B) occurs in the testes.
   C) can cause vaginal lubrication.
   D) Only A and B are correct.
   E) A, B, and C are correct.

   Answer: E
   Skill: Knowledge

28) During sexual arousal, myotonia is to nipple as
   A) orgasm is to resolution.
   B) excitement is to plateau.
   C) estrogen is to the mammary glands.
   D) vasocongestion is to the penis.
   E) labia minora is to labia majora.

   Answer: D
   Skill: Comprehension

29) Where are human sperm cells produced?
   A) prostate gland
   B) vas deferens
   C) the seminiferous tubules of the testes
   D) epididymis
   E) Sertoli cells

   Answer: C
   Skill: Knowledge

30) The diploid chromosome number for humans is 46. How many chromatids will there be in a secondary spermatocyte?
   A) 23
   B) 46
   C) 69
   D) 92
   E) 184

   Answer: B
   Skill: Comprehension

31) Diploid cells include which of the following?

    A) spermatids

    B) spermatogonia

    C) mature sperm cells

    D) A and B only

    E) A, B, and C are diploid.

    Answer: B
    Skill: Comprehension

32) Which of these statements is *true* about human sperm cells?

    A) They are rich in nutrient material.

    B) They are liberated from the corpus luteum.

    C) They are less numerous than ova.

    D) They are highly motile.

    E) They have 46 chromosomes.

    Answer: D
    Skill: Knowledge

33) In vertebrate animals, spermatogenesis and oogenesis differ, in that

    A) oogenesis begins at the onset of sexual maturity.

    B) oogenesis produces four haploid cells, whereas spermatogenesis produces only one functional spermatozoon.

    C) oogenesis produces one functional ovum, whereas spermatogenesis produces four functional spermatozoa.

    D) spermatogenesis begins before birth.

    E) spermatogenesis is not complete until fertilization occurs.

    Answer: C
    Skill: Comprehension

34) In which of the following ways are mature human sperm and ova similar?

    A) They both have the same number of chromosomes.

    B) They are approximately the same size.

    C) They each have a flagellum that provides motility.

    D) They are produced from puberty until death.

    E) They are formed before birth.

    Answer: A
    Skill: Comprehension

35) All of the following statements about gametogenesis are true *except:*

    A) Spermatogenesis continues throughout the male's life; oogenesis stops at menopause.

    B) Oogenesis results in one ovum, while spermatogenesis results in millions of sperm.

    C) Spermatogenesis is a continuous, uninterrupted process; oogenesis undergoes long resting periods.

    D) The process of oogenesis is completed when the egg cell is penetrated by sperm.

    E) The primary spermatocyte is a haploid cell.

    Answer: E
    Skill: Comprehension

36) Which of these is a male primary sex characteristic?

    A) deepening of the voice

    B) facial and pubic hair

    C) increased muscle growth

    D) development of external reproductive structures

    Answer: D
    Skill: Knowledge

37) Which of these is a male secondary sex characteristic?

A) development of external reproductive structures

B) development of vasa efferentia and other ducts

C) sperm production

D) increased muscle growth

Answer: D
Skill: Knowledge

38) How do the estrous and menstrual cycles compare?

A) In menstrual cycles, endometrial bleeding occurs, while the endometrium is reabsorbed by the uterus in estrous cycles.

B) There are more pronounced behavioral changes during menstrual cycles than during estrous cycles.

C) There are stronger effects of season and climate on menstrual cycles.

D) Copulation can only occur during the period surrounding ovulation in both the estrous and menstrual cycles.

E) The length of both cycles averages 28 days.

Answer: A
Skill: Comprehension

39) What is the breakdown and discharge of the soft uterine tissues and the unfertilized egg called?

A) menstruation

B) lactation

C) fertilization

D) menopause

E) ovulation

Answer: A
Skill: Knowledge

40) Which of these best describes the menstrual cycle?

A) It refers specifically to changes that occur in the endometrium of the uterus.

B) The cycle length is 28 days and varies little from one woman to another.

C) It continues from puberty until death.

D) It begins with the follicular phase.

E) It is primarily regulated by follicle–stimulating hormone (FSH).

Answer: A
Skill: Comprehension

41) The secretory phase of the menstrual cycle

A) is associated with dropping levels of estrogen and progesterone.

B) is when the endometrium begins to degenerate and menstrual flow occurs.

C) corresponds with the luteal phase of the ovarian cycle.

D) corresponds with the follicular phase of the ovarian cycle.

E) is the beginning of the menstrual flow.

Answer: C
Skill: Comprehension

42) What are the three phases of the ovarian cycle?

A) embryo, fetus, and newborn

B) first, second, and third trimesters

C) menstrual, proliferative, and secretory

D) follicular, ovulatory, and luteal

E) zygote, cleavage, and blastocyst

Answer: D
Skill: Knowledge

43) There are five hormones regulating the human menstrual and ovarian cycles. Which of these structures secretes these hormones?

A) hypothalamus

B) pituitary

C) ovaries

D) Both B and C are correct.

E) A, B, and C are correct.

Answer: E
Skill: Knowledge

44) Inhibition of the release of GnRH from the hypothalamus will

A) stimulate production of estrogen and progesterone.

B) initiate ovulation.

C) inhibit secretion of gonadotropins from the pituitary.

D) stimulate secretion of LH and FSH.

E) initiate the flow phase of the menstrual cycle.

Answer: C
Skill: Comprehension

45) If the release of LH were inhibited in a human female, which of the following events would *not* occur?

A) release of FSH from the pituitary

B) maturation of a primary follicle and oocyte

C) ovulation of a secondary oocyte

D) release of GnRH from the hypothalamus

E) production of estrogen by follicle cells

Answer: C
Skill: Application

46) All of the following structures are correctly paired with their function *except*

A) seminiferous tubules—add fluid containing mucus, fructose, and prostaglandin to semen

B) scrotum—encases testes and holds them below the abdominal cavity

C) epididymis—stores sperm

D) prostate gland—adds alkaline secretions to semen

E) ovary—secretes estrogen and progesterone

Answer: A
Skill: Knowledge

47) One function of the corpus luteum is to

A) nourish and protect the egg cell.

B) produce prolactin in the alveoli.

C) produce progesterone and estrogen.

D) convert into a hormone–producing follicle after ovulation.

E) stimulate ovulation.

Answer: C
Skill: Knowledge

48) During the menstrual cycle, what is the main source of progesterone in females?

A) adrenal cortex

B) anterior pituitary

C) corpus luteum

D) developing follicle

E) placenta

Answer: C
Skill: Knowledge

For the following questions, choose the term from the list below that best fits each description. Each term may be used once, more than once, or not at all.

A. LH
B. FSH
C. ICSH
D. GnRH
E. estrogen

49) hormone that triggers ovulation

Answer: A
Skill: Knowledge

50) hormone secreted by the growing follicle

Answer: E
Skill: Knowledge

51) stimulates the corpus luteum in females

Answer: A
Skill: Knowledge

52) hypothalamic hormone that stimulates the secretion of gonadotropins by the anterior pituitary

Answer: D
Skill: Knowledge

53) the anterior pituitary hormone that stimulates the maturation of the follicle in the ovary during the beginning of the menstrual cycle

Answer: B
Skill: Knowledge

54) Which of the following hormones is *incorrectly* paired with its action?
   A) GnRH—controls release of FSH and LH
   B) estrogen—responsible for primary and secondary female sex characteristics
   C) human chorionic gonadotropin—maintains secretions from the corpus luteum
   D) luteinizing hormone—stimulates ovulation
   E) progesterone—stimulates follicles to develop

Answer: E
Skill: Knowledge

55) The hormone progesterone is produced
   A) by the pituitary and acts directly on the ovary.
   B) in the ovary and acts directly on the testes.
   C) in the ovary and acts directly on the uterus.
   D) in the pituitary and acts directly on the uterus.
   E) in the uterus and acts directly on the pituitary.

Answer: C
Skill: Knowledge

56) What happens if the hormone progesterone is not secreted in a human female?
   A) Secondary sex characteristics do not develop.
   B) The pituitary is stimulated to secrete gonadotropins.
   C) Uterine contractions begin stimulating childbirth.
   D) Enlargement of arteries supplying blood to the endometrium and growth of endometrial glands are inhibited.
   E) The ovary begins to form the corpus luteum.

Answer: D
Skill: Application

57) What causes menopause?

   A) The follicle supply is exhausted.

   B) There is a decline in production of estrogens by the ovaries.

   C) Temperature increases inhibit ova maturation.

   D) There is a lack of adequate blood supply to the ovaries.

   E) Oxytocin blocks the ovarian cycle.

   Answer: B
   Skill: Comprehension

58) For normal human fertilization to occur,

   A) many ova must be released.

   B) the uterus must be enlarged.

   C) only one sperm must penetrate the egg.

   D) secretion of pituitary FSH and LH must decrease.

   E) the secondary oocyte must implant in the uterus.

   Answer: C
   Skill: Comprehension

59) Fertilization of human eggs usually takes place in the

   A) ovary.

   B) uterus.

   C) vagina.

   D) oviduct.

   E) labia minora.

   Answer: D
   Skill: Knowledge

60) Which of the following structures is *incorrectly* paired with its function?

   A) epididymis—maturation and storage of sperm

   B) fallopian tube—site of normal embryonic implantation

   C) seminal vesicles—add sugar and mucus to semen

   D) placenta—maternal/fetal exchange organ; progesterone producing

   E) prostate gland—adds alkaline substances to semen

   Answer: B
   Skill: Knowledge

61) Why do physicians recommend that pregnant women drink milk, take vitamins, and avoid alcohol?

   A) It is important that a woman be as healthy as possible for normal childbirth to occur.

   B) It helps to maintain a healthy placental connection.

   C) These materials are exchanged between mother and fetus through the placenta.

   D) These nutrients help to ensure that the baby's gestation period lasts for the full term.

   E) These measures prevent abnormal blood clotting, atherosclerosis, and heart attacks from occurring.

   Answer: C
   Skill: Application

62) During human gestation, organogenesis occurs during the first trimester. What is the significance of this fact?

A) It allows for early detection of genetic disorders.

B) This may block progesterone production and thus cause a spontaneous abortion.

C) It may stimulate infant cardiovascular problems.

D) Radiation and drugs should be avoided, as the embryo is extremely sensitive to birth defects at this time.

E) It may compress the mother's abdominal organs, causing frequent urination and constipation.

Answer: D
Skill: Application

Choose the term from the list below that best fits each of the following descriptions. Each term may be used once, more than once, or not at all.

A. *luteinizing hormone (LH)*
B. *follicle-stimulating hormone (FSH)*
C. *progesterone*
D. *human chorionic gonadotropin (HCG)*
E. *gonadotropin-releasing hormone (GnRH)*

63) embryonic hormone that maintains progesterone and estrogen secretion by the corpus luteum through the first trimester of pregnancy

Answer: D
Skill: Knowledge

64) triggers ovulation of the secondary oocyte

Answer: A
Skill: Knowledge

65) hormone produced by the corpus luteum when stimulated by LH

Answer: C
Skill: Knowledge

66) hypothalamic hormone that triggers the secretion of FSH

Answer: E
Skill: Knowledge

67) Which substance can be detected in the urine of females and is a positive test for pregnancy?

A) progesterone

B) estrogen

C) follicle-stimulating hormone

D) human chorionic gonadotropin

E) hypothalamus releasing factors

Answer: D
Skill: Knowledge

For the following questions, choose the term from the list below that best fits each description.

A. *HCG*
B. *androgen*
C. *oxytocin*
D. *prolactin*
E. *progesterone*

68) secreted by the Leydig cells of the testes

Answer: B
Skill: Knowledge

69) participates in the regulation of labor contractions

Answer: C
Skill: Knowledge

70) initiates the growth of the placenta and enlargement of the uterus

Answer: E
Skill: Knowledge

71) secretion of LH from the pituitary inhibited by a high concentration of this hormone

Answer: E
Skill: Knowledge

72) required so that the corpus luteum can function through the first and part of the second trimesters of pregnancy

Answer: A
Skill: Knowledge

73) What would happen if a woman in the later stages of pregnancy were given a combination of estrogen and oxytocin?
   A) Oxytocin receptors would develop on uterine smooth muscle cells.
   B) Prostaglandins would be secreted from the placenta.
   C) Contractions of uterine muscles would begin.
   D) Only A and C are correct.
   E) A, B, and C are correct.

Answer: E
Skill: Application

74) Which of these is *not* a correct statement about human reproduction?
   A) The ability of a pregnant woman not to reject her "foreign" fetus may be due to the suppression of the immune response in her uterus.
   B) By the eighth week, organogenesis is complete and the embryo is referred to as a fetus.
   C) Lactation is the production and release of milk from the mammary glands.
   D) Parturition begins with conception and ends with gestation.
   E) Puberty is the onset of reproductive ability.

Answer: D
Skill: Comprehension

75) Why does the mother *not* reject the developing embryo as a foreign body?
   A) A protective layer prevents the embryo from contacting maternal tissue.
   B) A suppressor cell develops that blocks normal immune response.
   C) If the father's genes are similar to the mother's, no immune response occurs.
   D) A woman's immune system can be sensitized to her mate's antigens and thus prevent rejection.
   E) These are all possible hypotheses, but more research is needed for a definitive answer.

Answer: E
Skill: Comprehension

76) Which of the following birth control methods is *least* effective?
   A) diaphragm
   B) condom
   C) coitus interruptus
   D) vasectomy
   E) rhythm method

Answer: C
Skill: Knowledge

For the following questions, choose the description from the list below that best fits each term. Each description may be used once, more than once, or not at all.

A. *prevents release of mature eggs and/or sperm from the gonads*
B. *prevents fertilization by keeping sperm and egg physically separated by a barrier*
C. *prevents implantation of an embryo*
D. *prevents sperm from entering the urethra*
E. *prevents oocytes from traveling into the uterus*

77) birth control pill

Answer: A
Skill: Knowledge

78) intrauterine device

Answer: C
Skill: Knowledge

79) tubal ligation

Answer: E
Skill: Knowledge

80) vasectomy

Answer: D
Skill: Knowledge

81) diaphragm

Answer: B
Skill: Knowledge

82) Which of the following is the *least* reliable method of birth (conception) control?

A) birth control pills

B) intrauterine device

C) tubal ligation

D) coitus interruptus

E) diaphragm

Answer: D
Skill: Knowledge

83) Which of the following is a male method of contraception?

A) hysterectomy

B) IUD

C) condom

D) tubal ligation

E) circumcision

Answer: C
Skill: Knowledge

84) How do different contraceptive methods work?

A) prevent the release of sperm and eggs

B) keep sperm and eggs separated

C) prevent implantation of an embryo

D) A and B

E) A, B, and C

Answer: E
Skill: Comprehension

85) All of the following statements about the human reproductive system are correct *except:*

A) The most effective means of birth control are abstinence, sterilization, and the pill.

B) Males produce sperm continuously, whereas females ovulate according to a cycle.

C) Males produce 4 sperm but females produce 3 polar bodies.

D) The period of sexual activity in human females is called estrus.

E) Mammary glands occur in both females and males.

Answer: D
Skill: Comprehension

86) Intrauterine devices (IUDs) probably prevent pregnancy by preventing

A) ejaculation.

B) fertilization.

C) the release of gonadotropins.

D) implantation.

E) ovulation.

Answer: D
Skill: Knowledge

87) Which of these statements explains how birth control pills work?

A) A negative feedback system stops the release of GnRH, FSH, and LH.

B) They cause a woman's cervical mucus to change and block sperm from entering the uterus.

C) They cause spontaneous abortions.

D) They block progesterone, thus pregnancy cannot be maintained.

E) They prevent uterine implantation by irritating the endometrium.

Answer: A
Skill: Knowledge

88) The drug RU–486 functions by

   A) inhibiting release of gonadotropins from the pituitary.

   B) blocking progesterone receptors in the uterus.

   C) preventing release of the secondary oocyte from the ovary.

   D) A and B.

   E) A, B, and C.

   Answer: B
   Skill: Knowledge

89) Human fertility drugs increase the chance of multiple births, probably because they

   A) enhance implantation.

   B) stimulate follicle development.

   C) mimic progesterone.

   D) stimulate spermatogenesis.

   E) prevent parturition.

   Answer: B
   Skill: Comprehension

Media Activity Questions

1) Sperm develop in the
   A) urethra.
   B) testes.
   C) seminal vesicles.
   D) epididymis.
   E) ureter.

   Answer: B
   Topic: Web/CD Activity 46A

2) Hormones secreted by the _____ have ultimate control over the production of sperm and male sex hormones.

   A) thyroid
   B) parathyroid
   C) thalamus
   D) hypothalamus
   E) pancreas

   Answer: D
   Topic: Web/CD Activity 46A

3) _____ is the most important androgen secreted by the testes.

   A) Estrogen
   B) Prolactin
   C) Inhibin
   D) Progesterone
   E) Testosterone

   Answer: E
   Topic: Web/CD Activity 46A

4) Which of these is *not* a component of the female reproductive system?

   A) uterus
   B) ovaries
   C) epididymis
   D) oviducts
   E) vagina

   Answer: C
   Topic: Web/CD Activity 46B

5) Which hormone is responsible for shaping the development of the female reproductive system and for secondary female sex characteristics such as broad hips?

   A) progesterone
   B) inhibin
   C) thymosin
   D) testosterone
   E) estrogen

   Answer: E
   Topic: Web/CD Activity 46B

Self-Quiz Questions

Answers to these questions also appear in the textbook.

1) Which of the following characterizes parthenogenesis?

   A) An individual may change its sex during its lifetime.

   B) Specialized groups of cells may be released and grow into new individuals.

   C) An organism is first a male and then a female.

   D) An egg develops without being fertilized.

   E) Both members of a mating pair have male and female reproductive organs.

   Answer: D

2) Which of the following structures is *incorrectly* paired with its function?

   A) gonads—gamete-producing organs

   B) spermatheca—sperm-transferring organ found in male insects

   C) cloaca—common opening for reproductive, excretory, and digestive systems

   D) baculum—bone that stiffens the penis, found in some mammals

   E) endometrium—lining of the uterus; forms the maternal part of the placenta

   Answer: B

3) Which of the following male and female structures are *least* alike in function?

   A) seminiferous tubules—vagina

   B) Leydig cells of testes—follicle cells of ovaries

   C) testes—ovaries

   D) spermatogonia—oogonia

   E) vas deferens—oviduct

   Answer: A

4) A difference between estrous and menstrual cycles is that

   A) nonmammalian vertebrates have estrous cycles, whereas mammals have menstrual cycles.

   B) the endometrial lining is shed in menstrual cycles but reabsorbed in estrous cycles.

   C) estrous cycles occur more frequently than menstrual cycles.

   D) estrous cycles are not controlled by hormones.

   E) ovulation occurs before the endometrium thickens in estrous cycles.

   Answer: B

5) Peaks of LH and FSH production occur during the

   A) flow phase of the menstrual cycle.

   B) beginning of the follicular phase of the ovarian cycle.

   C) period surrounding ovulation.

   D) end of the luteal phase of the ovarian cycle.

   E) secretory phase of the menstrual cycle.

   Answer: C

6) In protandrous hermaphroditism

   A) some individuals may change from male to female.

   B) individuals fertilize themselves.

   C) males rather than females release pheromones.

   D) diploid ova are produced.

   E) the adult gonads are undifferentiated.

   Answer: A

7) During human gestation, organogenesis occurs

A) in the first trimester.

B) in the second trimester.

C) in the third trimester.

D) while the embryo is in the oviduct.

E) during the blastocyst stage.

Answer: A

8) Which pharmacological strategy is most likely to result in a successful male contraceptive?

A) block FSH receptors on spermatagonia

B) maintain high circulating concentrations of androgen

C) block testosterone receptors on Leydig cells

D) block androgen receptors within the hypothalamus

E) maintain high circulating concentrations of FSH

Answer: A

9) Fertilization of human eggs most often takes place in the

A) vagina.

B) ovary.

C) uterus.

D) oviduct (fallopian tube).

E) vas deferens.

Answer: D

10) In male mammals, the excretory and reproductive systems share the

A) testes.

B) urethra.

C) ureter.

D) vas deferens.

E) prostate.

Answer: B

Chapter 47   Animal Development

1) Which of the following is a function of the contents of the acrosome during fertilization?
   A) to block polyspermy
   B) to help propel the sperm
   C) to digest the exterior coats of the egg
   D) to nourish the mitochondria of the sperm
   E) to trigger the completion of meiosis by the sperm cell

   Answer: C
   Skill: Comprehension

2) Which of the following statements is (are) *true* concerning the vitelline layer of the sea urchin egg?
   A) It is outside the fertilization membrane.
   B) It releases calcium, which initiates the cortical reaction.
   C) It has receptor molecules that are specific for binding acrosomal proteins.
   D) Only A and B are correct.
   E) A, B, and C are correct.

   Answer: C
   Skill: Knowledge

3) The cortical reaction functions directly in the
   A) formation of a fertilization membrane.
   B) production of a fast block to polyspermy.
   C) release of hydrolytic enzymes from the sperm cell.
   D) generation of a nervelike impulse by the egg cell.
   E) fusion of egg and sperm nuclei.

   Answer: A
   Skill: Knowledge

4) What causes the "slow block" to polyspermy?
   A) a transient voltage change across the membrane
   B) the consumption of yolk protein
   C) the jelly coat blocking sperm penetration
   D) formation of the fertilization membrane
   E) inactivation of the sperm acrosome

   Answer: D
   Skill: Knowledge

5) Which of the following is *least* related to the others?
   A) slow block to polyspermy
   B) cortical granules
   C) cortical reaction
   D) bindin
   E) fertilization membrane

   Answer: D
   Skill: Comprehension

6) If an egg cell contained EDTA, a chemical that binds calcium and magnesium, what effect would this have on reproduction?
   A) The acrosomal reaction would be blocked.
   B) The fusion of sperm and egg nuclei would be blocked.
   C) The fast block to polyspermy would not occur.
   D) The fertilization envelope would not be formed.
   E) The zygote would not contain 46 chromosomes.

   Answer: D
   Skill: Comprehension

7) Which statement about egg developement is *true*?

   A) Eggs without a nucleus cannot initiate division.

   B) A second messenger system is activated following fertilization.

   C) The sperm and egg micronuclei have fused by the end of the cortical reaction.

   D) The contents of the cortical granules contribute to the fast block to polyspermy.

   E) The mRNA involved with early activation of the egg arises from the sperm nucleus.

   Answer: B
   Skill: Comprehension

8) Arrange the following stages of fertilization and early development into a proper sequence.
   I.   onset of new DNA synthesis
   II. cortical reaction
   III. first cell division
   IV. acrosomal reaction; plasma membrane depolarization
   V.   fusion of egg and sperm nuclei complete

   A) III, V, I, IV, II

   B) V, I, IV, II, III

   C) I, III, II, IV, V

   D) V, III, I, II, IV

   E) IV, II, V, I, III

   Answer: E
   Skill: Comprehension

9) All of the following statements about fertilization are correct *except*:

   A) It reinstates diploidy.

   B) It invaginates the blastula to form the gastrula.

   C) Egg cell depolarization initiates the cortical reaction.

   D) Gamete fusion depolarizes the egg cell membrane and sets up a fast block to polyspermy.

   E) A slow block to polyspermy occurs when cortical granules erect a fertilization membrane.

   Answer: B
   Skill: Knowledge

10) What part of the sperm first contacts the egg plasma membrane?

   A) the anterior plasma membrane

   B) the posterior plasma membrane

   C) the anterior acrosomal membrane

   D) the posterior acrosomal membrane

   E) the fertilization membrane

   Answer: D
   Skill: Knowledge

11) All of the following occur during early cleavage of an animal zygote *except*:

   A) The developing cell undergoes mitosis.

   B) The nuclear-to-cytoplasmic ratio of the cells increases.

   C) The ratio of surface area to volume of the cells increases.

   D) The embryo grows significantly in mass.

   E) The developing cell undergoes cytokinesis.

   Answer: D
   Skill: Application

12) How does the animal pole differ from the vegetal pole of a zygote?

A) The animal pole has a higher concentration of yolk.

B) The blastomere originates in the animal pole.

C) The posterior end of the embryo forms here.

D) The animal pole gives rise to the hemisphere with yellow yolk.

E) The polar bodies bud from this region.

Answer: E
Skill: Comprehension

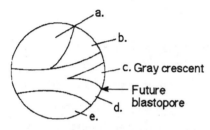

Figure 47.1

13) Which labeled area in the frog blastula diagram in Figure 47.1 forms opposite the point of sperm penetration?

Answer: c
Skill: Knowledge

14) Which of the following is *correct* about the yolk of the frog egg?

A) It prevents gastrulation.

B) It is concentrated at the animal pole.

C) It is homogeneously arranged in the egg.

D) It impedes the formation of a primitive streak.

E) It leads to unequal rates of cleavage for the animal pole compared to the vegetal pole.

Answer: E
Skill: Comprehension

15) You observe an embryo in which the initial cleavage divisions are radial and meroblastic, extraembryonic membranes develop, and a primitive streak is formed. How would you identify this organism, based on the information given?

A) invertebrate

B) fish or amphibian

C) reptile or bird

D) bird or mammal

E) mammal

Answer: D
Skill: Application

16) Meroblastic cleavage occurs in which of the following?
I.   sea urchins
II. humans
III. birds

A) I only

B) III only

C) I and II only

D) I and III only

E) II and III only

Answer: B
Skill: Knowledge

17) Which developmental sequence is *correct*?

A) cleavage, blastula, gastrula, and morula

B) cleavage, gastrula, morula, and blastula

C) cleavage, morula, blastula, and gastrula

D) gastrula, morula, blastula, and cleavage

E) morula, cleavage, gastrula, and blastula

Answer: C
Skill: Knowledge

18) What is the process called that involves the movement of cells into new relative positions in an embryo and results in the establishment of three tissue layers?

A) determination

B) cleavage

C) fertilization

D) induction

E) gastrulation

Answer: E
Skill: Knowledge

19) After gastrulation, the outer-to-inner sequence of tissue layers in a vertebrate is

A) endoderm, ectoderm, mesoderm.

B) mesoderm, endoderm, ectoderm.

C) ectoderm, mesoderm, endoderm.

D) ectoderm, endoderm, mesoderm.

E) endoderm, mesoderm, ectoderm.

Answer: C
Skill: Knowledge

20) If gastrulation did not occur,

A) cleavage would not occur in the zygote.

B) the embryonic germ layers would not form.

C) fertilization would be blocked.

D) the blastula would not be formed.

E) B and D would be the case.

Answer: B
Skill: Comprehension

21) Without the formulation of an ectoderm, we would lack

A) a nervous system.

B) a liver.

C) a pancreas.

D) a heart.

E) kidneys.

Answer: A
Skill: Comprehension

22) The archenteron of the developing frog eventually develops into which structure?

A) reproductive organs

B) the blastocoel

C) heart and lungs

D) digestive tract

E) brain and spinal cord

Answer: D
Skill: Knowledge

The following questions refer to the diagram of the embryo in Figure 47.2.

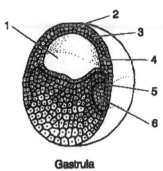

Gastrula
Figure 47.2

23) The embryo shown probably belongs to a

A) dog.

B) frog.

C) chick.

D) snake.

E) human.

Answer: B
Skill: Knowledge

24) Which of the following was the most recent developmental process that directly affected this embryo?

A) gastrulation

B) fertilization

C) blastula formation

D) morula formation

E) cleavage

Answer: A
Skill: Comprehension

25) Ectoderm, mesoderm, and endoderm are, respectively,

   A) 1, 2, and 6.

   B) 3, 4, and 5.

   C) 2, 3, and 4.

   D) 5, 6, and 3.

   E) 1, 2, and 6.

   Answer: C
   Skill: Application

26) Which of the following will form the lumen of the digestive tract?

   A) 1   B) 4   C) 5   D) 6   E) 7

   Answer: A
   Skill: Knowledge

27) The blastopore in this organism will become the

   A) anus.

   B) ears.

   C) eyes.

   D) nose.

   E) mouth.

   Answer: A
   Skill: Knowledge

28) In a frog embryo, gastrulation

   A) produces a blastocoel displaced into the animal hemisphere.

   B) occurs along the primitive streak in the animal hemisphere.

   C) is impossible because of the large amount of yolk in the ovum.

   D) proceeds by involution as cells roll over the dorsal lip of the blastopore.

   E) occurs within the inner cell mass that is embedded in the large amount of yolk.

   Answer: D
   Skill: Comprehension

The following questions refer to the diagram of an embryo in Figure 47.3. Match the word or statement to the lettered structures.

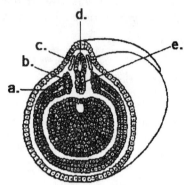

Figure 47.3

29) coelom

   Answer: a
   Skill: Knowledge

30) somites

   Answer: b
   Skill: Knowledge

31) notochord

   Answer: e
   Skill: Knowledge

32) gives rise to the muscles

   Answer: b
   Skill: Knowledge

33) gives rise to the brain and spinal cord

   Answer: d
   Skill: Knowledge

Figure 47.4

34) The drawing in Figure 47.4 is from what stage of amphibian development?

A) blastula

B) neurula

C) early gastrula

D) late gastrula

E) gray crescent stage

Answer: B
Skill: Knowledge

35) Which of the following is *least* related to the others?

A) cleavage

B) morula

C) neurulation

D) gastrulation

E) invagination

Answer: B
Skill: Comprehension

36) Which of the following is mismatched?

A) mesoderm—notochord

B) endoderm—lungs

C) ectoderm—liver

D) mesoderm—somites

E) ectoderm—eye

Answer: C
Skill: Knowledge

37) Which of the following is *least* related to the others?

A) ectoderm

B) mesoderm

C) archenteron

D) endoderm

E) notochord

Answer: C
Skill: Comprehension

Use the following information to answer the questions below. In a study of the development of frog embryos, several early gastrulas were stained with vital dyes. The location of the dyes after gastrulation was noted. The results are shown in the following table.

Tissue	Stain
Brain	red
Notochord	yellow
Liver	green
Lens of the eye	blue
Lining of the digestive tract	purple

38) Ectoderm would give rise to tissues containing which of the following colors?

A) yellow and purple

B) purple and green

C) green and red

D) red and blue

E) red and yellow

Answer: D
Skill: Comprehension

39) The mesoderm was probably stained with which color?

A) blue

B) yellow

C) red

D) purple

E) green

Answer: B
Skill: Comprehension

40) The endoderm was probably which color?

A) red and yellow

B) yellow and green

C) green and purple

D) blue and yellow

E) purple and red

Answer: C
Skill: Comprehension

41) Which of the following is *least* related to the others?

A) dorsal lip

B) archenteron

C) notochord

D) primitive streak

E) neural tube

Answer: B
Skill: Comprehension

42) Blastodisc is to blastula as

A) gastrulation is to mesoderm.

B) primitive streak is to blastopore.

C) blastocoel is to blastula.

D) meroblastic cleavage is to bird.

E) epiblast is to hypoblast.

Answer: B
Skill: Comprehension

43) Which of the following is *not* an extraembryonic membrane that develops from the embryos of reptiles, birds, and mammals?

A) chorion

B) yolk sac

C) egg shell

D) amnion

E) allantois

Answer: C
Skill: Knowledge

44) Which of the following is *least* related to the others?

A) zona pellucida

B) amnion

C) chorion

D) allantois

E) yolk sac

Answer: A
Skill: Comprehension

45) The *least* amount of yolk would be found in the egg of a

A) bird.

B) fish.

C) frog.

D) eutherian (placental) mammal.

E) terrestrial reptile.

Answer: D
Skill: Knowledge

46) A primitive streak forms during the early embryonic development of which of the following?

I. birds
II. frogs
III. humans

A) I only

B) II only

C) I and II only

D) I and III only

E) II and III only

Answer: D
Skill: Knowledge

47) Which structure in bird and mammalian embryos functions like the blastopore of frog embryos?

A) primitive streak

B) neural plate

C) archenteron

D) notochord

E) somites

Answer: A
Skill: Comprehension

48) Extraembryonic membranes develop in which of the following?

I.   mammals
II. birds
III. lizards

A) I only

B) II only

C) I and II only

D) II and III only

E) I, II, and III

Answer: E
Skill: Knowledge

49) At the time of implantation, the human embryo is called a(n)

A) blastocyst.

B) embryo.

C) fetus.

D) somite.

E) zygote.

Answer: A
Skill: Knowledge

50) The embryonic portion of the mammalian placenta comes from which of the following?

I.   inner cell mass
II. trophoblast
III. chorion

A) I only

B) II only

C) III only

D) I and II only

E) II and III only

Answer: E
Skill: Comprehension

51) In placental mammals, what is the major function of the yolk sac during development?

A) It transfers nutrients from the yolk to the embryo.

B) It differentiates into the placenta.

C) It becomes a fluid–filled sac that surrounds and protects the embryo.

D) It produces blood cells which then migrate into the embryo.

E) It stores waste products from the embryo until the placenta develops.

Answer: D
Skill: Knowledge

52) Which extraembryonic membrane of a chick embryo is a receptacle for uric acid wastes?

A) amnion

B) allantois

C) chorion

D) trophoblast

E) yolk sac

Answer: B
Skill: Knowledge

53) Thalidomide was a chemical prescribed as a sedative in the early 1960s. If taken by women in their first trimester of pregnancy, the children born had deformities of the arms and legs. What developmental process was affected by this drug?

A) early cleavage divisions

B) determination of the polarity of the zygote

C) differentiation of bone tissue

D) morphogenesis

E) organogenesis

Answer: D
Skill: Application

54) The term applied to a morphogenetic process whereby cells extend themselves, making the mass of cells narrower and longer, is

A) convergent extension.

B) induction.

C) elongational streaming.

D) bi-axial elongation.

E) blastomere formation.

Answer: A
Skill: Knowledge

55) Which of the following would probably have the *greatest* effect upon convergent extension?

A) stopping DNA synthesis

B) stopping mRNA synthesis

C) stopping translation

D) releasing an enzyme that digests glycoproteins

E) A, B, or C would all stop the process.

Answer: D
Skill: Comprehension

56) Which of the following is *least* related to the others?

A) fibronectin

B) adhesion molecules

C) cadherins

D) convergent extension

E) cleavage

Answer: A
Skill: Comprehension

57) The development of the experimental technique leading to fate maps was a serious blow to which idea?

A) preformationism

B) epigenesis

C) induction

D) morphogenesis

E) involution

Answer: A
Skill: Comprehension

58) Which of the following is *least* related to the others?

A) slow block to polyspermy

B) cortical granules

C) cortical reaction

D) bindin

E) fertilization membrane

Answer: D
Skill: Comprehension

59) If an amphibian zygote is manipulated so that the first cleavage plane does *not* divide the gray crescent, what is the expected fate of the two daughter cells?

A) The daughter cell with the entire gray crescent will die.

B) Both daughter cells will develop normally because amphibians are totipotent at this stage.

C) Only the daughter cell with the gray crescent will develop normally.

D) Both daughter cells will develop abnormally.

E) Both daughter cells will die immediately.

Answer: C
Skill: Comprehension

60) In humans, identical twins are possible because

A) of the heterozygeneous distribution of cytoplasmic determinants in unfertilized eggs.

B) of interactions between extraembryonic cells and the zygote nucleus.

C) of convergent extension.

D) the blastomeres are genetically the same.

E) the gray crescent divides the dorsal-ventral axis into new cells.

Answer: D
Skill: Comprehension

61) Hans Spemann has referred to which of the following structures as the primary organizer in the early development of amphibian embryos?

A) optic cup

B) notochord

C) neural tube

D) dorsal ectoderm

E) dorsal lip of the blastopore

Answer: E
Skill: Knowledge

62) In frogs, formation of the eye lens is induced by chemical signals from

A) ectodermal cells.

B) mesodermal cells.

C) endodermal cells.

D) A and B.

E) A, B, and C.

Answer: D
Skill: Comprehension

63) The shaping of an animal and its individual parts into a body form with specialized organs and tissues is called

A) pattern formation.

B) induction.

C) differentiation.

D) determination.

E) organogenesis.

Answer: A
Skill: Knowledge

64) Which mathematical situation has a parallel in embryonic limb development?

A) using X, Y, and Z coordinates to plot a graph

B) plotting a graph of an exponential growth curve

C) plotting a graph of a linear growth curve

D) using parallel lines to construct a parallelogram

E) $E = MC^2$

Answer: A
Skill: Comprehension

The following questions refer to the list of terms below. Each term may be used once, more than once, or not at all.

A. *homeodomains*
B. *morphogen*
C. *egg–polarity genes*
D. *zone of polarizing activity*
E. *cell adhesion molecules*

65) contribute to selective reaggregation of dissociated gastrula cells

Answer: E
Skill: Comprehension

66) assigns positional information along the anterior–posterior axis to developing avian limb buds

Answer: D
Skill: Comprehension

67) when translated, provide positional information for development of the body plan on the coarsest level

Answer: C
Skill: Comprehension

68) a substance such as retinoic acid that varies in concentration and therefore enables cells to resolve their position along a gradient

Answer: B
Skill: Comprehension

69) Which of the following is *not* involved in positional information for pattern formation?

A) apical ectodermal ridge

B) zone of polarizing activity

C) cadherins

D) fibroblast growth factors

E) sonic hedgehog

Answer: C
Skill: Knowledge

Media Activity Questions

1) Sea urchin embryos are fertilized

   A) within the male.

   B) within the female.

   C) externally.

   D) within the male and female.

   E) both externally and within the female.

   Answer: C
   Topic: Web/CD Activity 47A

2) Each cell in an early embryo is called a

   A) blastomere.

   B) blastocoel.

   C) gastrulomere.

   D) archenteron.

   E) blastopore.

   Answer: A
   Topic: Web/CD Activity 47A

3) In frogs, the blastopore develops into the

   A) digestive tract.

   B) mouth.

   C) brain.

   D) anus.

   E) archenteron.

   Answer: D
   Topic: Web/CD Activity 47B

4) What species of frog, a favorite of embryologists, is shown in the video?

   A) *Pan*

   B) *Xenopus*

   C) *Homo*

   D) *Rana*

   E) *Bufo*

   Answer: B
   Topic: Web/CD Activity 47B

5) During frog development, yolk–laden cells originate

   A) at the vegetal pole.

   B) at the animal pole.

   C) from ectoderm.

   D) from mesoderm.

   E) from endoderm.

   Answer: A
   Topic: Web/CD Activity 47B

Self-Quiz Questions

Answers to these questions also appear in the textbook.

1) The cortical reaction of sea urchin eggs functions directly in the
   A) formation of a fertilization envelope.
   B) production of a fast block to polyspermy.
   C) release of hydrolytic enzymes from the sperm cell.
   D) generation of an electrical impulse by the egg cell.
   E) fusion of egg and sperm nuclei.

   Answer: A

2) Which of the following is common to both avian and mammalian development?
   A) holoblastic cleavage
   B) epiblast and hypoblast
   C) trophoblast
   D) yolk plug
   E) gray crescent

   Answer: B

3) The archenteron develops into
   A) the mouth in protostomes.
   B) the blastocoel.
   C) the endoderm.
   D) the lumen of the digestive tract.
   E) the placenta.

   Answer: D

4) In a frog embryo, the blastocoel is
   A) completely obliterated by yolk platelets.
   B) lined with endoderm during gastrulation.
   C) located primarily in the animal hemisphere.
   D) the cavity that becomes the coelom.
   E) the cavity that later forms the archenteron.

   Answer: C

5) Amphibians, unlike reptiles, generally lay their eggs in water or moist places. This difference is related to the absence (in amphibians) versus the presence (in reptiles) of
   A) extraembryonic membranes.
   B) yolk.
   C) cleavage.
   D) gastrulation.
   E) development of the brain from ectoderm.

   Answer: A

6) In an amphibian embryo, a band of cells called the neural crest
   A) rolls up to form the neural tube.
   B) develops into the main sections of the brain.
   C) produces cells that migrate to form teeth, skull bones, and other structures in the embryo.
   D) has been shown by experiments to be the organizer region of the developing embryo.
   E) induces the formation of the notochord.

   Answer: C

7) Differences in the development of different cells in the early frog embryo (zygote to blastula) are due to
   A) the differences between meroblastic and holoblastic cleavage.
   B) the heterogeneous distribution of cytoplasmic determinants, such as proteins and mRNA.
   C) inductive interactions occurring between the developing cells.
   D) concentration gradients for regulatory molecules such as BMP-4.
   E) the position of the cells relative to the zone of polarizing activity (ZPA).

   Answer: B

8) During convergent extension
   A) cells on the opposite side of the embryo follow converging developmental pathways leading to bilateral symmetry.
   B) the cells of the neural folds adhere to one another to complete the neural tube.
   C) the cells of a tissue layer reorganize forming a narrowed elongated sheet.
   D) the dorsal-ventral axis is established.
   E) cell adhesion molecules are expressed, causing the eight blastomeres to adhere tightly to one another.

   Answer: C

9) In the early development of an amphibian embryo, an important "organizer" is the
   A) neural tube.
   B) notochord.
   C) archenteron roof.
   D) dorsal lip of the blastopore.
   E) dorsal ectoderm.

   Answer: D

10) The occurrence of genetically identical twins indicates that in humans
   A) only the zygote is totipotent.
   B) the progressive restriction of potency hypothesis does not apply.
   C) the first cleavage event must be transverse to the animal–vegetal axis of the zygote.
   D) cell divisions producing the earliest blastomeres do not result in an asymmetric distribution of cytoplasmic determinants.
   E) the primary organizer continues to function well past gastrulation.

   Answer: D

1) An organism that lacks integration centers
   A) cannot receive stimuli.
   B) will not have a nervous system.
   C) will not be able to interpret stimuli.
   D) can be expected to lack myelinated neurons.
   E) Both A and D are correct.

   Answer: C
   Skill: Comprehension

2) What do muscles, nerves, and glands have in common?
   A) They synapse with neurons.
   B) They are referred to as postsynaptic cells.
   C) They are target cells.
   D) A and B
   E) A, B, and C

   Answer: E
   Skill: Comprehension

3) Integration of simple responses to certain stimuli, such as the patellar reflex, is accomplished by which of the following?
   A) spinal cord
   B) hypothalamus
   C) corpus callosum
   D) cerebellum
   E) medulla

   Answer: A
   Skill: Knowledge

4) The general functions of the nervous system include which of the following?
   I.   integration
   II. motor output
   III. sensory input
   A) I only
   B) II only
   C) III only
   D) I and II only
   E) I, II, and III

   Answer: E
   Skill: Comprehension

5) A ganglion is a group of nerve cell bodies
   A) in the central nervous system.
   B) in the peripheral nervous system.
   C) anywhere in the nervous system.
   D) within the brain.
   E) within the spinal cord.

   Answer: B
   Skill: Knowledge

6) The blood–brain barrier
   A) is formed by tight junctions.
   B) is formed by oligodendrocytes.
   C) tightly regulates the intracellular environment of the CNS.
   D) uses chemical signals to communicate with the spinal cord.
   E) provides support to the brain tissue.

   Answer: A
   Skill: Comprehension

7) A squirrel chewing the insulation off an electrical wire is analogous to

A) Schwann cells failing to myelinate axons of the CNA.

B) the nodes of Ranvier in the PNS.

C) the depolarization of the unmyelinated axons.

D) the deterioration of the brain–blood barrier.

E) demyelination of the nervous system.

Answer: E
Skill: Comprehension

8) Which of the following statements is *false*?

A) All cells have a membrane potential.

B) Gray matter is the site of neuronal integration.

C) Astrocytes can communicate with nerve cells.

D) The outside of a cell is negative with respect to the inside of a cell.

E) Squid axons are a model system for nerve conductance.

Answer: D
Skill: Comprehension

9) If the concentration of potassium in the cytoplasm of a nerve cell with a resting membrane potential of –70 mV were elevated above normal, the new resting potential would

A) still be –70 mV.

B) be –69 mV or higher.

C) be –71 mV or lower.

D) be 0 mV.

E) reverse polarity.

Answer: B
Skill: Application

10) Neurons at rest are not at the equilibrium potential for K^+ because the cell membrane is

A) only permeable to K^+.

B) slightly permeable to Na^+.

C) not permeable to Na^+.

D) not permeable to K^+.

E) only permeable to Na^+.

Answer: B
Skill: Knowledge

11) If an otherwise normal nerve cell were made permeable to large negative ions, what would happen?

A) The membrane potential would not form.

B) Potassium would not leave the resting cell.

C) Sodium would not enter the resting cell.

D) The membrane potential would become positive.

E) The Na+/K+ pump would not function.

Answer: A
Skill: Comprehension

12) The sodium–potassium pump of neurons pumps

A) Na^+ and K^+ into the cell.

B) Na^+ and K^+ out of the cell.

C) Na^+ into the cell and K^+ out of the cell.

D) Na^+ out of the cell and K^+ into the cell.

E) Na^+ and K^+ into the cell and H^+ out of the cell through an antiport.

Answer: D
Skill: Knowledge

The questions below refer to the following information:
An unknown organism has been discovered. It contains long cells with excitable membranes that scientists suspect are used for rapid information transfer. The membrane of the cell is permeable only to ion X, which carries a negative charge. Active transport pumps in the membrane move X into the cell while simultaneously moving ion Y, also carrying a negative charge, out of the cell.

13) Which of the following is *true* about the establishment of the resting membrane potential in this cell?

   A) The resting potential of this cell will be zero.

   B) The resting potential of this cell will be negative.

   C) A negative resting potential is directly produced by the pump moving a negative charge into the cell.

   D) A negative resting potential is directly produced by the diffusion of Y^- into the cell.

   E) A positive resting potential is directly produced by the diffusion of X^- out of the cell.

Answer: E
Skill: Application

14) When neurotransmitter Z is released into the extracellular fluid in contact with a portion of the cell membrane, channels open that allow both X^- and Y^- through the membrane. Which of the following is *incorrect*?

   A) The magnitude of the potential will immediately increase.

   B) Y^- will diffuse into the cell.

   C) X^- will diffuse out of the cell.

   D) The membrane will depolarize.

   E) The channels are chemically gated.

Answer: A
Skill: Application

15) The threshold potential of a membrane

   A) is equal to about 35 mV.

   B) is equal to about 70 mV.

   C) opens voltage–sensitive gates that result in the rapid outflow of sodium ions.

   D) is the depolarization that is needed to generate an action potential.

   E) is a graded potential that is proportional to the strength of a stimulus.

Answer: D
Skill: Knowledge

16) Which of the following is a *correct* statement about a resting neuron?

   A) It is releasing lots of acetylcholine.

   B) The membrane is very leaky to sodium.

   C) The membrane is equally permeable to sodium and potassium.

   D) The membrane potential is more negative than the threshold potential.

   E) The concentration of sodium is greater inside the cell than outside.

Answer: D
Skill: Knowledge

17) A toxin that binds specifically to the voltage–gated sodium channels of axons would

   A) block all sodium movement.

   B) block repolarization.

   C) prevent the axon from reaching the threshold potential.

   D) not work on the giant squid axon.

   E) ultimately block sodium and potassium movement.

Answer: C
Skill: Comprehension

18) After an action potential, how is the resting potential restored?

   A) by the opening of sodium activation gates

   B) by the opening of voltage–sensitive potassium channels and the closing of sodium activation gates

   C) by an increase in the membrane's permeability to potassium and chloride ions

   D) by the delay in the action of the sodium–potassium pump

   E) by the refractory period in which the membrane is hyperpolarized

   Answer: B
   Skill: Knowledge

19) Repolarization of the membrane of a neuron after an action potential is a consequence of which of the following?
   I. Ca^{2+} gates opening
   II. Na^+ gates inactivating
   III. K^+ gates opening

   A) I only

   B) II only

   C) III only

   D) I and II only

   E) II and III only

   Answer: E
   Skill: Comprehension

20) In the sequence of permeability changes that depolarizes and then repolarizes the membrane of a neuron during an action potential, which of the following changes occurs first?

   A) Sodium gates open.

   B) The Na^+–K^+ pump shuts down.

   C) The Na^+–K^+ pump is activated.

   D) Potassium gates close.

   E) Potassium gates open.

   Answer: A
   Skill: Knowledge

For the following questions, refer to the graph of an action potential in Figure 48.1 and use the lettered line to indicate your answer.

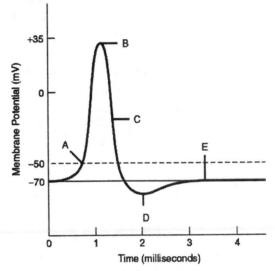

Figure 48.1

21) The membrane is unable to respond to any further stimulation, regardless of intensity.

   Answer: D
   Skill: Comprehension

22) The sodium gates open.

   Answer: A
   Skill: Comprehension

23) The threshold potential is reached.

   Answer: A
   Skill: Comprehension

24) Repolarization occurs, sodium gates close, and potassium gates reopen.

   Answer: C
   Skill: Comprehension

25) Action potentials are normally carried in one direction from the axon hillock to the axon terminals. By using an electronic probe, you experimentally depolarize the middle of the axon to threshold. What do you expect?

A) No action potential will be initiated.

B) An action potential will be initiated and proceed in the normal direction toward the axon terminal.

C) An action potential will be initiated and proceed back toward the axon hillock.

D) Two action potentials will be initiated, one going toward the axon terminal and one going back toward the hillock.

E) An action potential will be initiated, but it will die out before it reaches the axon terminal.

Answer: D
Skill: Application

26) All of the following statements about transmission along neurons are correct *except:*

A) The rate of transmission of a nerve impulse is directly related to the diameter of the axon.

B) The intensity of a stimulus is related to the frequency of the action potential.

C) The resting potential is maintained by differential ion permeabilities and the sodium–potassium pump.

D) Once initiated, local depolarizations stimulate a propagation of serial action potentials down the axon.

E) A stimulus that affects the membrane's permeability to ions can either depolarize or hyperpolarize the membrane.

Answer: B
Skill: Comprehension

27) Saltatory conduction is a term applied to conduction of impulses

A) across electrical synapses.

B) along the postsynaptic membrane from dendrite to axon hillock.

C) in two directions at the same time.

D) from one neuron to another.

E) along myelinated nerve fibers.

Answer: E
Skill: Knowledge

28) Which animal movement could be used to represent impulse conductance along a myelinated axon?

A) a person out on a power-walk

B) an earthworm moving along the surface of the ground

C) an amoeba extending pseudopodia

D) a moth moving toward a light

E) a frog leaping between lily pads

Answer: E
Skill: Comprehension

29) Synaptic vesicles discharge their contents by exocytosis at the

A) dendrite.

B) axon hillock.

C) nodes of Ranvier.

D) postsynaptic membrane.

E) presynaptic membrane.

Answer: E
Skill: Knowledge

30) Neurotransmitters are released from presynaptic axon terminals into the synaptic cleft by which of the following mechanisms?

A) osmosis

B) active transport

C) diffusion

D) endocytosis

E) exocytosis

Answer: E
Skill: Knowledge

31) Which of the following offers the best description of neural transmission across a mammalian synaptic gap?
 A) Neural impulses involve the flow of K^+ and Na^+ across the gap.
 B) Neural impulses travel across the gap as electrical currents.
 C) Neural impulses cause the release of chemicals that diffuse across the gap.
 D) Neural impulses travel across the gap in both directions.
 E) The calcium within the axons and dendrites of nerves adjacent to a synapse acts as the neurotransmitter.

Answer: C
Skill: Knowledge

32) Given the steps shown below, which of the following is the *correct* sequence for transmission at a chemical synapse?
 1. neurotransmitter binds with receptor
 2. sodium ions rush into neuron's cytoplasm
 3. action potential depolarizes the presynaptic membrane
 4. ion channel opens to allow particular ion to enter cell
 5. synaptic vesicles release neurotransmitter into the synaptic cleft
 A) 1, 2, 3, 4, 5
 B) 2, 3, 5, 4, 1
 C) 3, 2, 5, 1, 4
 D) 4, 3, 1, 2, 5
 E) 5, 1, 2, 4, 3

Answer: C
Skill: Comprehension

33) A drug might act as a stimulant of the somatic nervous system if it
 A) makes the membrane permanently impermeable to sodium.
 B) stimulates the activity of acetylcholinesterase in the synaptic cleft.
 C) increases the release of substances that cause the hyperpolarization of the neurons.
 D) increases the sensitivity of the postsynaptic membrane to acetylcholine.
 E) increases the sensitivity of the presynaptic membrane to acetylcholine.

Answer: D
Skill: Comprehension

34) One disadvantage to a nerve net is that it can conduct impulses in two directions from the point of the stimulus. The vertebrate system conducts in only one direction. This one-way conductance occurs
 A) as a result of the appearance of the nodes of Ranvier.
 B) as a result of voltage–gated sodium channels found in the vertebrate system.
 C) because vertebrate nerve cells have dendrites.
 D) because only the postsynaptic membranes can bind neurotransmitters.
 E) because the Na^+-K^+ pump moves ions in one direction.

Answer: D
Skill: Comprehension

35) An EPSP facilitates depolarization of the postsynaptic membrane by
   A) increasing the permeability of the membrane to Na^+.
   B) increasing the permeability of the membrane to K^+.
   C) insulating the hillock region of the axon.
   D) allowing Cl^- to enter the cell.
   E) stimulating the Na^+–K^+ pump.

   Answer: A
   Skill: Knowledge

36) The postsynaptic membrane of a nerve may be stimulated by certain neurotransmitters to permit the influx of negative chloride ions into the cell. This process will result in
   A) membrane depolarization.
   B) an action potential.
   C) the production of an IPSP.
   D) the production of an EPSP.
   E) the membrane becoming more positive.

   Answer: C
   Skill: Comprehension

37) During an IPSP, the postsynaptic membrane becomes more permeable to
   A) K^+.
   B) Na^+.
   C) Ca^{2+}.
   D) GABA.
   E) serotonin.

   Answer: A
   Skill: Knowledge

38) Neurotransmitters categorized as inhibitory would *not* be expected to
   A) bind to receptors.
   B) open K^+ channels.
   C) open Na^+ channels.
   D) open Cl^- channels.
   E) hyperpolarize the membrane.

   Answer: C
   Skill: Comprehension

39) A neurotransmitter can trigger different responses in postsynaptic cells due to the
   A) point of release.
   B) receptors present.
   C) concentration of neurotransmitter.
   D) receptor mode of action.
   E) Both B and D are correct responses.

   Answer: E
   Skill: Comprehension

The next questions refer to the following terms. Each term may be used once, more than once, or not at all.

   A. meninges
   B. telodendria
   C. axon hillocks
   D. myelin sheaths
   E. postsynaptic membranes

40) possess neurotransmitter receptors

   Answer: E
   Skill: Knowledge

41) usually the sites of the initial action potential in neurons

   Answer: C
   Skill: Knowledge

42) Which of the following statements is *true* regarding temporal summation?

A) The sum of simultaneously arriving neurotransmitters from different presynaptic nerve cells determines whether the postsynaptic cell fires.

B) Several action potentials arrive in fast succession without allowing the postsynaptic cell to return to its resting potential.

C) Several IPSPs arrive concurrently, bringing the presynaptic cell closer to its threshold.

D) Several postsynaptic cells fire at the same time when neurotransmitters are released from several synaptic terminals simultaneously.

E) The voltage spike of the action potential that is initiated is higher than normal.

Answer: B
Skill: Knowledge

43) A single inhibitory postsynaptic potential has a magnitude of 0.5 mV at the axon hillock and a single excitatory postsynaptic potential has a magnitude of 0.5 mV. What will be the membrane potential at the hillock after the spatial summation of 6 IPSPs and 2 EPSPs, if the initial membrane potential is –70 mV?

A) –72 mV

B) –71 mV

C) –70 mV

D) –69 mV

E) –68 mV

Answer: A
Skill: Application

44) Which statement could be applied to *both* the nervous system and the endocrine system?

A) They both use chemical signaling.

B) The final response depends upon the receptor mode of action.

C) Specific parts of both systems use chemical messengers produced by axons.

D) A and B only are true.

E) A, B, and C are true.

Answer: E
Skill: Comprehension

45) The major inhibitory neurotransmitter of the brain is

A) acetylcholine.

B) cholinesterase.

C) norepinephrine.

D) dopamine.

E) GABA.

Answer: E
Skill: Knowledge

46) Neurotransmitters affect postsynaptic cells by

A) signal–transduction pathways in the cells.

B) causing molecular changes in the cells.

C) affecting ion–channel proteins.

D) altering the permeability of the cells.

E) all of the above.

Answer: E
Skill: Knowledge

The questions below refer to the following choices of neurotransmitters. Each choice may be used once, more than once, or not at all.

A. acetylcholine
B. epinephrine
C. endorphin
D. serotonin
E. GABA

47) a neuropeptide that functions as a natural analgesic

Answer: C
Skill: Knowledge

48) an amino acid that operates at inhibitory synapses in the brain

Answer: E
Skill: Knowledge

49) The simplest nervous system can be described as all of the following *except*

A) present in cnidarians such as hydras.
B) radiating from a central nerve ring.
C) being a branching net of nerves throughout the body.
D) not having ganglia.
E) having electrical impulses traveling in both directions.

Answer: B
Skill: Knowledge

50) Centralization of the nervous system seems to be associated with the evolution of

A) a complete gut.
B) bilateral symmetry.
C) radial symmetry.
D) a closed circulatory system.
E) excitable membranes.

Answer: B
Skill: Knowledge

51) Which of the following statements is *true*?

A) NO is an example of neurotransmitter stored in presynaptic vesicles.
B) Learning does not appear to require a specific number of neurons.
C) Organisms with bilateral symmetry were first to have nerve nets.
D) Biogenic amines are derived from proteins.
E) Serotonin is a neurotransmitter synthesized from tyrosine.

Answer: B
Skill: Comprehension

52) Cerebrospinal fluid can be described as all of the following *except*

A) functioning to transport nutrients and hormones through the brain.
B) a product of the filtration of blood by the brain.
C) formed from layers of connective tissue.
D) functioning to cushion the brain.
E) filling cavities in the brain called ventricles.

Answer: C
Skill: Knowledge

53) The motor division of the PNS can be divided into

A) the brain and spinal cord.
B) the sympathetic and parasympathetic system.
C) the central nervous and sensory systems.
D) the somatic and autonomic systems.
E) muscles and glands.

Answer: D
Skill: Knowledge

54) What is the main neurotransmitter of the parasympathetic system?

A) acetylcholine

B) cholinesterase

C) epinephrine

D) adrenaline

E) dopamine

Answer: A
Skill: Knowledge

55) Which part of the vertebrate nervous system is most involved in preparation for the "fight–or–flight" response?

A) sympathetic

B) somatic

C) central

D) visceral

E) parasympathetic

Answer: A
Skill: Knowledge

56) Which of the following activities would be associated with the parasympathetic division of the nervous system?

A) resting and digesting

B) release of both acetylcholine and epinephrine

C) increased metabolic rate

D) "fight–or–flight" response

E) release of epinephrine only

Answer: A
Skill: Knowledge

57) Which of the following is *correct* about the telencephalon region of the brain?

A) It develops as the neural tube differentiates.

B) It develops from the midbrain.

C) It is the brain region most like that of ancestral vertebrates.

D) It gives rise to the cerebrum.

E) It divides further into the metencephalon and myelencephalon.

Answer: D
Skill: Comprehension

58) What controls the heart rate?

A) neocortex

B) medulla

C) thalamus

D) pituitary

E) cerebellum

Answer: B
Skill: Knowledge

59) Which area of the brain is most intimately associated with the unconscious control of respiration and circulation?

A) thalamus

B) cerebellum

C) medulla

D) corpus callosum

E) cerebrum

Answer: C
Skill: Knowledge

60) Which selection is *incorrectly* paired?

A) forebrain—diencephalon

B) forebrain—cerebrum

C) midbrain—brainstem

D) midbrain—cerebellum

E) pons—ventilation

Answer: D
Skill: Knowledge

61) As you read and answer the questions on this exam

   A) your alpha brain waves increase.

   B) your beta brain waves increase.

   C) your delta brain waves increase.

   D) the amount of serotonin being released increases.

   E) activity in the cerebellum has increased.

   Answer: B
   Skill: Comprehension

62) If an accident causes trauma to the hypothalamus

   A) sorting of sensory information might be affected.

   B) the primary center for motor information for the cerebellum might be affected.

   C) the production of CSF might be affected.

   D) regulation of body temperature might be affected.

   E) cognitive response might be affected.

   Answer: D
   Skill: Comprehension

63) Circadian rhythms in animals may regulate such processes as

   A) sleep cycles.

   B) hormone release.

   C) sex drive.

   D) sensitivity to external stimuli.

   E) all of the above.

   Answer: E
   Skill: Knowledge

64) What would you predict would happen if an individual were forced to remain in a cave in isolation for at least two months?

   A) Nothing would happen, with the exception that the person might be bored.

   B) Nervous activity in the thalamus will decrease.

   C) The superchiasmatic nuclei in the hypothalamus will stop functioning.

   D) It is likely that the person would think that it is night when it is actually day outside.

   E) B, C, and D would happen.

   Answer: D
   Skill: Comprehension

65) The motor cortex is part of which part of the nervous system?

   A) cerebrum

   B) cerebellum

   C) spinal cord

   D) midbrain

   E) medulla

   Answer: A
   Skill: Knowledge

For the next questions, choose the best answer from the following list. Each answer may be used once, more than once, or not at all.

   A. cerebrum
   B. cerebellum
   C. thalamus
   D. hypothalamus
   E. medulla oblongata

66) produces hormones that are secreted by the pituitary gland

   Answer: D
   Skill: Knowledge

67) coordinates muscle actions

   Answer: B
   Skill: Knowledge

68) regulates body temperature

Answer: D
Skill: Knowledge

69) contains regulatory centers for the respiratory and circulatory systems

Answer: E
Skill: Knowledge

70) contains regions that help regulate hunger and thirst

Answer: D
Skill: Knowledge

71) By comparing the size and degree of convolution of various vertebrate cerebral cortices, biologists would gain insight into the relative

A) size of the brain centers of taxonomic groups.

B) emotions and learning capabilities of vertebrate classes.

C) motor impulse complexities.

D) sophistication of behaviors possible.

E) sensory stimuli that regulate motor impulses.

Answer: D
Skill: Comprehension

72) What do Wernicke's and Broca's regions of the brain affect?

A) olfaction

B) vision

C) speech

D) memory

E) hearing

Answer: C
Skill: Comprehension

73) If you were writing an essay, which part of the brain would be most active?

A) temporal and frontal lobes

B) parietal lobe

C) Broca's area

D) Wernicke's area

E) occipital lobe

Answer: A
Skill: Comprehension

74) All of the following statements about the nervous system are correct *except:*

A) The three evolutionary changes in the vertebrate brain include increases in relative size, increases in compartmentalization of function, and decreases in cephalization.

B) The size of the primary motor and sensory areas of the cortex devoted to controlling each part of the body is proportional to the importance of that part of the body.

C) Human emotions are believed to originate from interactions between the cerebral cortex and the limbic system.

D) The localization of pain involves the somatosensory cortex.

E) The autonomic nervous system is subdivided into the parasympathetic and sympathetic nervous systems.

Answer: A
Skill: Comprehension

75) The establishment and expression of emotions involves the

A) frontal lobes and limbic system.

B) frontal lobes and parietal lobes.

C) parietal lobes and limbic system.

D) frontal and occipital lobes.

E) occipital lobes and limbic system.

Answer: A
Skill: Comprehension

Media Activity Questions

1) A motor neuron is insulated by
   A) dendrites.
   B) nodes of Ranvier.
   C) cell bodies.
   D) Schwann cells.
   E) axonal cells.

   Answer: D
   Topic: Web/CD Activity 48A

2) At rest, there is a higher concentration of _____ outside the neuron membrane than inside the neuron membrane.
   A) potassium ions
   B) phosphate ions
   C) sodium ions
   D) sulfate
   E) amino acids

   Answer: C
   Topic: Web/CD Activity 48B

3) After an impulse has passed along an axon, the balance of ions is ultimately restored by the _____ pump.
   A) sulfate–chloride
   B) potassium–sulfate
   C) chloride–potassium
   D) sodium–chloride
   E) sodium–potassium

   Answer: E
   Topic: Web/CD Activity 48B

4) Neurons communicate across junctions called
   A) tight junctions.
   B) desmosomes.
   C) gap junctions.
   D) synapses.
   E) intercalated disks.

   Answer: D
   Topic: Web/CD Activity 48C

5) A synapse usually conducts an impulse directly from the _____ of one neuron to the dendrite of another neuron.
   A) Nissl body
   B) cell body
   C) synaptic terminal
   D) myelin sheath
   E) dendrite

   Answer: C
   Topic: Web/CD Activity 48C

Self-Quiz Questions

Answers to these questions also appear in the textbook.

1) Which of the following occurs when a stimulus depolarizes a neuron's membrane?

   A) Na^+ diffuses out of the cell.

   B) The action potential approaches zero.

   C) The membrane potential changes from the resting potential to a voltage closer to the threshold potential.

   D) The depolarization is all or none.

   E) The inside of the cell becomes more negative in charge relative to the outside of the cell.

   Answer: C

2) Action potentials are usually propagated in only one direction along an axon because

   A) the nodes of Ranvier conduct only in one direction.

   B) the brief refractory period prevents opening of voltage-gated Na^+ channels.

   C) the axon hillock has a higher membrane potential than the tips of the axon.

   D) ions can flow along the axon only in one direction.

   E) both sodium and potassium voltage-gated channels open in one direction.

   Answer: B

3) The depolarization of the presynaptic membrane of an axon *directly* causes

   A) voltage-gated calcium channels in the membrane to open.

   B) synaptic vesicles to fuse with the membrane.

   C) an action potential in the postsynaptic cell.

   D) the opening of chemically sensitive gates that allow neurotransmitters to spill into the synaptic cleft.

   E) an EPSP or IPSP in the postsynaptic cell.

   Answer: A

4) What is the neocortex?

   A) a primitive brain region common to reptiles, birds, and mammals

   B) a region deep in the cortex that is associated with the formation of emotional memories

   C) a central part of the cortex that receives olfactory information

   D) an additional outer layer of neurons running along the cerebral cortex that is unique to mammals

   E) the association area of the frontal lobe that is involved in higher cognitive functions

   Answer: D

5) Which of the following provides evidence that emotional brain circuits form early during human development?

   A) Humans are more likely to be able to recall emotional memories from childhood than factual memories.

   B) Infants are able to understand language before they are able to speak.

   C) Emotional brain circuits involve more "primitive" parts of the brain that evolved before the neocortex develops.

   D) Young infants are able to bond to a caregiver and to express fear, distress, and anger.

   E) Individuals with damage to the amygdala no longer have autonomic responses to stressful stimuli.

   Answer: D

6) Which of the following structures or regions is *incorrectly* paired with its function?

   A) limbic system—the motor control of speech

   B) medulla oblongata—homeostatic control center

   C) cerebellum—coordination of movement and balance

   D) corpus callosum—band of fibers connecting left and right cerebral hemispheres

   E) hypothalamus—production of hormones and regulation of temperature, hunger, and thirst

   Answer: A

7) Receptor sites for neurotransmitters are located on the

   A) tips of axons.

   B) axon membranes in the regions of the nodes of Ranvier.

   C) postsynaptic membrane.

   D) membranes of synaptic vesicles.

   E) presynaptic membrane.

   Answer: C

8) All the following electrical changes of neurons are graded events *except*

   A) EPSPs.

   B) IPSPs.

   C) action potentials.

   D) depolarizations caused by stimuli.

   E) hyperpolarizations caused by stimuli.

   Answer: C

9) Of the following components of the nervous system, which is *most inclusive*?

   A) brain

   B) spinal cord

   C) central nervous system

   D) gray matter

   E) neuron

   Answer: C

10) Which of the following best describes what is known about how axons grow toward their proper target cell?

   A) Axons grow in a direct path, attracted by signal molecules that are released from the target cell.

   B) Cells along the growth path release signal molecules that either attract or repel the axon, and the interaction of CAMs on the growth cone and neighboring cells may provide tracks that guide axon growth.

   C) Nerve growth factor released by astrocytes stimulates neural progenitor cells to differentiate into neurons, whose axons then grow toward an increasing concentration of signal molecules.

   D) Axons produce growth-promoting proteins only in the growth cone, causing the axon to grow in an outward direction toward its target cell.

   E) Glia first migrate to the target cell, leaving a trail of CAMs along the path that the growth cone of the axon follows.

   Answer: B

Chapter 49   Sensory and Motor Mechanisms

1) Which of the following is a sensation and *not* a perception?

   A) the color blue as interpreted by the brain

   B) the nerve impulse caused by light hitting the back of the eye

   C) the smell of chocolate chip cookies baking

   D) the unique taste of broccoli with cheese

   E) the sound of a train passing through the city

   Answer: B
   Skill: Comprehension

2) Which of the following explains the perceptions we differentiate as taste and smell?

   A) the areas of the brain that receive each sensation

   B) the level of amplification of each stimulus

   C) the intensity of the action potential caused by each impulse

   D) the frequency of each impulse transmission

   E) the type of receptor receiving each signal

   Answer: A
   Skill: Knowledge

3) The ability of a receptor to absorb the energy of a stimulus is called what?

   A) integration

   B) transmission

   C) transduction

   D) reception

   E) amplification

   Answer: D
   Skill: Knowledge

4) An interoceptor would detect which of the following stimuli?

   A) a change from lying on one's back to lying on one's side

   B) a sudden drop in the temperature of a room

   C) contact as bodies are pushed into a subway car

   D) standing up quickly, causing a drop in blood pressure

   E) both A and D

   Answer: E
   Skill: Comprehension

The question below refers to the following information:

1. reception
2. transmission
3. transduction
4. perception
5. amplification

5) For the events above, which of the following is the *correct* sequence as it relates to being able to hear sound?

   A) 1, 2, 3, 4, 5

   B) 1, 5, 2, 3, 4

   C) 1, 3, 5, 2, 4

   D) 2, 3, 5, 1, 4

   E) 2, 1, 5, 3, 4

   Answer: A
   Skill: Application

6) People are not constantly aware of the rings, watches, or clothes that they may be wearing because of a phenomenon called

   A) sensory adaptation.

   B) fovea accommodation.

   C) rhodopsin bleaching.

   D) motor unit recruitment.

   E) receptor amplification.

   Answer: A
   Skill: Knowledge

7) Which of the following is a good example of sensory adaptation?

A) olfactory receptors ceasing to produce receptor potentials when triggered by perfume molecules

B) hair cells in the organ of Corti not responding to high-pitched sounds after prolonged exposure to high levels of sound at a concert

C) cones in the human eye failing to respond to light in the infrared range

D) hair cells in the utricle and saccule responding to a change in orientation of the head

E) rods in the human eye responding to mechanical stimulation from a blow to the eye so that a flash of light is perceived

Answer: A
Skill: Comprehension

8) Receptor cells have all of the following functions in common *except*

A) increased permeability to sodium and potassium ions.

B) conversion of stimulus energy to membrane potential.

C) strengthening of stimulus energy to the nervous system.

D) processing information through graded potentials.

E) conduction of impulses to the central nervous system.

Answer: A
Skill: Comprehension

9) Why do you feel cold if you go outside in the winter without wearing a coat?

A) Circulating levels of prostaglandins increase.

B) Nociceptors send signals to the cerebral cortex.

C) Thermoreceptors send signals to the cerebral cortex.

D) Thermoreceptors in the skin undergo accommodation, which increases their sensitivity.

E) Thermoreceptors send signals to the posterior hypothalamus.

Answer: E
Skill: Comprehension

10) Which of the following receptors is *incorrectly* paired with the type of energy it transduces?

A) mechanoreceptors—sound

B) electromagnetic receptors—magnetism

C) chemoreceptors—solute concentrations

D) thermoreceptors—heat

E) pain receptors—electricity

Answer: E
Skill: Knowledge

11) Compound eyes are very good for detecting motion because

A) they have multiple neurons.

B) they have multiple facets.

C) they are in a group referred to as the single-lens type of eyes.

D) visual information is decoded by more than one region of the brain.

E) they provide binocular vision.

Answer: B
Skill: Comprehension

12) What do planarians, insects, and humans have in common?

   A) photopigments, photoreceptors, and associated nerves

   B) the ability to detect light

   C) the ability to detect light and form an image

   D) both A and B

   E) A, B, and C

   Answer: A
   Skill: Comprehension

13) All of the following are *correct* statements about the vertebrate eye *except:*

   A) The vitreous humor regulates the amount of light entering the pupil.

   B) The transparent cornea is an extension of the sclera.

   C) The fovea is the center of the visual field and contains only cones.

   D) The ciliary muscle functions in accommodation.

   E) The retina lies just inside the choroid and contains the photoreceptor cells.

   Answer: A
   Skill: Comprehension

14) Focusing the eye by changing the shape of the lens is called

   A) zooming.

   B) refraction.

   C) conditioning.

   D) habituation.

   E) accommodation.

   Answer: E
   Skill: Knowledge

15) Which of the following receptors is *incorrectly* paired with its category?

   A) hair cell—mechanoreceptor

   B) muscle spindle—mechanoreceptor

   C) gustatory receptor—chemoreceptor

   D) rod—photoreceptor

   E) cone—deep-pressure receptor

   Answer: E
   Skill: Knowledge

16) Which of the following is a *correct* statement about the cells of the human retina?

   A) Cone cells can detect color and rod cells cannot.

   B) Cone cells are more sensitive to light than rod cells are.

   C) Cone cells, but not rod cells, have a visual pigment.

   D) Rod cells are most highly concentrated in the center of the retina.

   E) Rod cells require higher illumination for stimulation than do cone cells.

   Answer: A
   Skill: Knowledge

17) In the vertebrate eye, the material known as transducin is best categorized as a(n)

   A) visual pigment.

   B) G protein.

   C) second messenger.

   D) ion channel.

   E) receptor protein.

   Answer: B
   Skill: Knowledge

18) A vitamin A deficiency can result in

   A) blindness.

   B) decreased synthesis of transducin.

   C) decreased synthesis of opsin.

   D) an inactivation of sight–specific G protein.

   E) an inactivation of bipolar cells.

   Answer: A
   Skill: Comprehension

19) The axons of rods and cones synapse with

   A) ganglion cells.

   B) horizontal cells.

   C) amacrine cells.

   D) bipolar cells.

   E) lateral cells.

   Answer: D
   Skill: Knowledge

20) All of the following statements about vision are correct *except:*

   A) Perception of visual information takes place in the brain.

   B) Rods contain the light–absorbing molecule called rhodopsin.

   C) Rods are more light sensitive than cones and are responsible for night vision.

   D) All information from the left eye goes to the right visual cortex, and all information from the right eye goes to the left visual cortex.

   E) Color vision results from the presence of three subclasses of cones in the retina, each with its own type of opsin associated with retinal.

   Answer: D
   Skill: Comprehension

21) Which of the following structures is *last* encountered by sensory information during visual processing?

   A) ganglion cells

   B) bipolar cells

   C) primary visual cortex

   D) optic chiasma

   E) lateral geniculate nuclei

   Answer: C
   Skill: Knowledge

22) Hair cells of the organ of Corti are deflected when they brush against the

   A) basilar membrane.

   B) tympanic membrane.

   C) tectorial membrane.

   D) plasma membrane.

   E) ciliary body.

   Answer: C
   Skill: Knowledge

23) The perceived pitch of a sound depends partly on

   A) the amplitude of the sound waves.

   B) which bones of the middle ear move.

   C) which hair cells of the cochlea are stimulated.

   D) where particles settle in the semicircular canals.

   E) whether it is the round window or the oval window that vibrates.

   Answer: C
   Skill: Comprehension

24) Information carried by the optic nerve is perceived as "sight," whereas information carried by the auditory nerve is perceived as "sound." Which of the following statements best explains this?

A) The information is carried to different areas of the brain.

B) The structure of neurons in the optic nerve differs from that in the auditory nerve.

C) Light energy and sound waves are different from each other.

D) Different ions enter and leave the axons of the two different nerves.

E) Action potentials that carry visual information are of a different amplitude and frequency than those carrying sound information.

Answer: A
Skill: Comprehension

The following questions refer to the diagram of the ear (Figure 49.1).

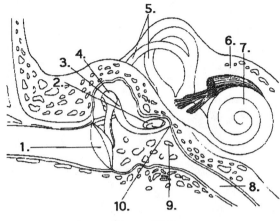

Figure 49.1

25) The number that represents the structure equalizing the pressure between the ear and the atmosphere is

A) 1.

B) 7.

C) 8.

D) 9.

E) 10.

Answer: C
Skill: Knowledge

26) The number that represents a structure that functions in balance and equilibrium is

A) 2.

B) 3.

C) 4.

D) 5.

E) 8.

Answer: D
Skill: Knowledge

27) The number that represents the stapes is
    A) 1.
    B) 2.
    C) 3.
    D) 4.
    E) 5.

    Answer: B
    Skill: Knowledge

28) The organ of Corti is located in the structure represented by number
    A) 3.
    B) 4.
    C) 5.
    D) 6.
    E) 7.

    Answer: E
    Skill: Knowledge

29) Hair cells are found in structures represented by numbers
    A) 1 and 2.
    B) 3 and 4.
    C) 5 and 7.
    D) 6 and 8.
    E) 9 and 10.

    Answer: C
    Skill: Knowledge

30) All of the following are correct statements about hearing and balance *except:*
    A) The semicircular canals respond to rotation of the head.
    B) Fish have inner ears that sense vibrations in the water.
    C) The volume of sound is a function of the size of the action potentials that reach the brain.
    D) In mammals, the tympanic membrane transmits sound to the three middle ear bones.
    E) In mammals, the middle ear bones transmit sound through the oval window to the coiled cochlea of the inner ear.

    Answer: C
    Skill: Knowledge

31) Hair cells can be found in all of the following locations *except*
    A) the statocysts of invertebrates.
    B) the lateral line system of fish.
    C) the retina of mammals.
    D) the organ of Corti in humans.
    E) the semicircular canals in mammals.

    Answer: C
    Skill: Knowledge

Figure 49.2

32) The structure diagrammed in Figure 49.2 is

A) a neuromast.

B) a statocyst.

C) a taste bud.

D) an ommatidium.

E) an olfactory bulb.

Answer: B
Skill: Knowledge

33) Which adaptation best accounts for the efficiency of the dolphin as it is adapted to movement through water?

A) its large oarlike flippers

B) the torpedo shape of its body

C) the blowhole located on the top of its head

D) the presence of a large powerful tail

E) none of these

Answer: B
Skill: Comprehension

34) Hydrostatic skeletons are normally used for movement by all of the following *except*

A) annelids.

B) cnidarians.

C) crustaceans.

D) nematodes.

E) flatworms.

Answer: C
Skill: Knowledge

35) What structural feature contributes most to the diverse adaptations for animal movement?

A) sensory system

B) skeletal system

C) muscular system

D) nervous system

E) both B and C

Answer: E
Skill: Comprehension

The following questions refer to Figure 49.3. Match each of the phrases with the letter of its structure in the figure.

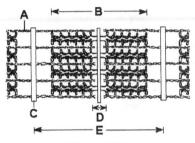

Figure 49.3

36) a sarcomere

Answer: E
Skill: Knowledge

37) consists only of myosin filaments

Answer: D
Skill: Knowledge

38) consists of both actin and myosin filaments

Answer: B
Skill: Knowledge

39) When an organism dies, its muscles remain in a contracted state termed rigor mortis for a brief period of time. Which of the following most directly contributes to this phenomenon?

A) no ATP to move cross-bridges

B) no ATP to break bonds between the thick and thin filaments

C) no calcium to bind to troponin

D) no oxygen supplied to muscle

E) no energy for the synthesis of actin and myosin

Answer: B
Skill: Application

40) Muscle cells are stimulated by neurotransmitters released from the tips of

A) T tubules.

B) motor cell axons.

C) sensory cell axons.

D) motor cell dendrites.

E) sensory cell dendrites.

Answer: B
Skill: Comprehension

41) Which of the following does *not* form part of the thin filaments of a muscle cell?

A) actin

B) troponin

C) tropomyosin

D) myosin

E) calcium-binding site

Answer: D
Skill: Knowledge

42) What is the role of calcium in muscle contractions?

A) to break the cross-bridges as a cofactor in the hydrolysis of ATP

B) to bind with troponin, changing its shape so that the actin filament is exposed

C) to transmit the action potential across the neuromuscular junction

D) to spread the action potential through the T tubules

E) to reestablish the polarization of the plasma's membrane following an action potential

Answer: B
Skill: Knowledge

43) During muscle contraction, the ion that leaks out of the sarcoplasmic reticulum and induces myofibrils to contract is

A) K^+.

B) Cl^-.

C) Na^+.

D) Ca^{2+}.

E) Mg^{2+}.

Answer: D
Skill: Knowledge

The question below refers to the following information.

1. *Tropomyosin shifts and unblocks the cross–bridge binding sites.*
2. *Calcium is released and binds to troponin.*
3. *Transverse tubules depolarize the sarcoplasmic reticulum.*
4. *The thin filaments are ratcheted across the thick filaments by the heads of the myosin molecules and ATP.*
5. *An action potential in a motor neuron causes the axon to release acetylcholine, which depolarizes the muscle cell membrane.*

44) For the events listed above, which of the following is the *correct* sequence for their occurrence during the excitation and contraction of a muscle cell?

A) 1, 2, 3, 4, 5

B) 2, 1, 3, 5, 4

C) 2, 3, 4, 1, 5

D) 5, 3, 1, 2, 4

E) 5, 3, 2, 1, 4

Answer: E
Skill: Application

45) Which of the following could you find in the lumen of a transverse tubule?

A) extracellular fluid

B) cytoplasm

C) actin

D) myosin

E) sarcomeres

Answer: A
Skill: Comprehension

46) A sustained muscle contraction due to a lack of relaxation between successive stimuli is called

A) tonus.

B) tetanus.

C) an all–or–none response.

D) fatigue.

E) a spasm.

Answer: B
Skill: Knowledge

47) The breast muscle of turkeys and chickens is usually referred to as light meat, whereas that of wild ducks and geese is described as dark meat. Which of the following is consistent with this observation?

A) Turkeys and chickens are not closely related to ducks and geese.

B) Turkeys and chickens do not use their breast muscle, whereas ducks and geese do.

C) Turkeys and chickens do not fly for sustained periods; ducks and geese do.

D) The muscles of these two groups of birds contain different filamentous proteins.

E) The darker body color of ducks and geese provides protective camouflage against predators.

Answer: C
Skill: Application

48) Which of the following are shared by skeletal, cardiac, and smooth muscle?

A) A bands and I bands

B) transverse tubules

C) gap junctions

D) motor units

E) thick and thin filaments

Answer: E
Skill: Comprehension

49) Which type of muscle is responsible for peristalsis along the digestive tract?

A) cardiac

B) smooth

C) skeletal

D) striated

E) voluntary

Answer: B
Skill: Knowledge

Media Activity Questions

1) An eye's photoreceptors are located on the
   A) cornea.
   B) choroid.
   C) iris.
   D) retina.
   E) sclera.

   Answer: D
   Topic: Web/CD Activity 49A

2) The _____ contains the muscles that regulate the size of the pupil.
   A) choroid
   B) retina
   C) cornea
   D) sclera
   E) iris

   Answer: E
   Topic: Web/CD Activity 49A

3) Which of these is a component of a human's axial skeleton?
   A) sternum
   B) carpal
   C) patella
   D) tibia
   E) ulna

   Answer: A
   Topic: Web/CD Activity 49B

4) Which of these levels of skeletal muscle organization includes the others?
   A) sarcomere
   B) thick filament
   C) thin filament
   D) Z line
   E) myofibril

   Answer: E
   Topic: Web/CD Activity 49C

5) What are the functional units of muscle contraction?
   A) thick filaments
   B) myofibrils
   C) Z lines
   D) thin filaments
   E) sarcomeres

   Answer: E
   Topic: Web/CD Activity 49D

Self-Quiz Questions

Answers to these questions also appear in the textbook.

1) Which of the following receptors is *incorrectly* paired with its category?

   A) hair cell—mechanoreceptor

   B) muscle spindle—mechanoreceptor

   C) taste receptor—chemoreceptor

   D) rod—electromagnetic receptor

   E) gustatory receptor—electromagnetic receptor

   Answer: E

2) Some sharks close their eyes just before they bite. Although they cannot see their prey, their bites are on target. Researchers have noted that sharks often misdirect their bites at metal objects, and they can find batteries buried under the sand of an aquarium. This evidence suggests that sharks keep track of their prey during the split second before they bite in the same way that

   A) a rattlesnake finds a mouse in its burrow.

   B) a male silkworm moth locates a mate.

   C) a bat can find moths in the dark.

   D) a platypus locates its prey in a muddy river.

   E) a flatworm avoids light places.

   Answer: D

3) Which of the following is an *incorrect* statement about the vertebrate eye?

   A) The vitreous humor regulates the amount of light entering the pupil.

   B) The transparent cornea is an extension of the sclera.

   C) The fovea is the center of the visual field and contains only cones.

   D) The ciliary muscle functions in accommodation.

   E) The retina lies just inside the choroid and contains the photoreceptor cells.

   Answer: A

4) The transduction of sound waves to action potentials takes place

   A) within the tectorial membrane as it is stimulated by the hair cells.

   B) when hair cells are bent against the tectorial membrane, causing them to depolarize and release neurotransmitter molecules that stimulate sensory neurons.

   C) as the basilar membrane becomes more permeable to sodium ions and depolarizes, initiating an action potential in a sensory neuron.

   D) as the basilar membrane vibrates at different frequencies in response to the varying volume of sounds.

   E) within the middle ear as the vibrations are amplified by the malleus, incus, and stapes.

   Answer: B

5) When light strikes the pigment rhodopsin in a rod cell, retinal dissociates from opsin, initiating a signal-transduction pathway that

   A) depolarizes the neighboring bipolar cells and initiates an action potential in a ganglion cell.

   B) depolarizes the rod cell, causing it to release the neurotransmitter glutamate, which excites bipolar cells.

   C) hyperpolarizes the rod cell, reducing its release of glutamate, which excites some bipolar cells and inhibits others.

   D) hyperpolarizes the rod cell, increasing its release of glutamate, which excites amacrine cells but inhibits horizontal cells.

   E) converts cGMP to GMP, opening sodium channels and hyperpolarizing the membrane, causing the rhodopsin to become bleached.

   Answer: C

6) Clams and lobsters both have exoskeletons, but lobsters have much greater mobility. Why?

A) Clams only have adductor muscles that hold the shell closed, whereas lobsters have both abductor and adductor muscles.

B) The paramyosin of clam muscles holds them in a low-energy state of contraction, whereas lobster muscles are very similar to vertebrate striated muscles.

C) Clams can only grow by adding to the outer edge of the shell, whereas lobsters molt and repeatedly replace their exoskeleton with a larger, more flexible one.

D) The lobster skeleton can actively contract, while the clam skeleton lacks its own contractile mechanism.

E) Lobsters have a jointed exoskeleton, allowing for the flexible movement of appendages and body parts at the joints.

Answer: E

7) The role of calcium in muscle contraction is

A) to break the cross-bridges as a cofactor in the hydrolysis of ATP.

B) to bind with troponin, changing its shape so that the myosin binding sites on the actin filament are exposed.

C) to transmit the action potential across the neuromuscular junction.

D) to spread the action potential through the T tubules.

E) to reestablish the polarization of the plasma membrane following an action potential.

Answer: B

8) Tetanus refers to

A) the partial sustained contraction of major supporting muscles.

B) the all-or-none contraction of a single muscle fiber.

C) a stronger contraction resulting from multiple motor unit summation.

D) the result of wave summation, which produces a smooth and sustained contraction of a muscle.

E) the state of muscle fatigue caused by the depletion of ATP and the accumulation of lactate.

Answer: D

9) Which of the following is a *true* statement about cardiac muscle cells?

A) They lack an orderly arrangement of actin and myosin filaments.

B) They have less extensive sarcoplasmic reticulum and thus contract more slowly than smooth muscle cells.

C) They are connected by intercalated discs, through which action potentials spread to all cells in the heart.

D) They have a resting potential more positive than an action potential threshold.

E) They contract only when stimulated by neurons.

Answer: C

10) Which of the following changes occurs when a skeletal muscle contracts?

A) The A bands shorten.

B) The I bands shorten.

C) The Z lines slide farther apart.

D) The thin filaments contract.

E) The thick filaments contract.

Answer: B

Chapter 50   An Introduction to Ecology and the Biosphere

1) Important abiotic factors in ecosystems include which of the following?
   I.   temperature
   II. water
   III. wind
   A) I only
   B) II only
   C) III only
   D) I and II only
   E) I, II, and III

Answer: E
Skill: Comprehension

2) All of the following statements about ecology are correct *except:*
   A) Ecologists may study populations and communities of organisms.
   B) Ecological studies may involve the use of models and computers.
   C) Ecology is a discipline that is independent from natural selection and evolutionary history.
   D) Ecology spans increasingly comprehensive levels of organization, from individuals to ecosystems.
   E) Ecology is the study of the interactions between biotic and abiotic aspects of the environment.

Answer: C
Skill: Comprehension

3) Which of the following levels of organization is arranged in the *correct* sequence from most to least inclusive?
   A) community, ecosystem, individual, population
   B) ecosystem, community, population, individual
   C) population, ecosystem, individual, community
   D) individual, population, community, ecosystem
   E) individual, community, population, ecosystem

Answer: B
Skill: Knowledge

4) Which of the following are important biotic factors that can affect the structure and organization of biological communities?
   A) precipitation, wind, temperature
   B) nutrient availability, soil pH, light intensity
   C) predation, competition, disease
   D) A and B only
   E) A, B, and C

Answer: C
Skill: Comprehension

5) Landscape ecology is best described as the study of
   A) the array of interacting species within a community.
   B) abiotic factors and the community of species that exist in a particular area.
   C) related arrays of ecosystems.
   D) physiological and behavioral ways in which organisms meet the challenges of their environment.
   E) the factors affecting the abundance of single species.

Answer: C
Skill: Comprehension

6) Ecology as a discipline directly deals with all of the following levels of biological organization *except*

A) population.

B) cellular.

C) organismal.

D) ecosystem.

E) community.

Answer: B
Skill: Comprehension

7) "How does the foraging of animals on tree seeds affect the distribution and abundance of the trees?" This question

A) is a valid ecological question.

B) is difficult to answer because a large experimental area would be required.

C) is difficult to answer because a long–term experiment would be required.

D) Both A and B are correct.

E) A, B, and C are correct.

Answer: E
Skill: Comprehension

8) You are working for the Environmental Protection Agency considering the effect of a potentially toxic chemical in drinking water. There is as yet no documented scientific evidence against the chemical, but many suspect it to be a health hazard. Using the Precautionary Principle, what would be a reasonable environmental policy?

A) Establish no regulations until there are conclusive scientific studies.

B) Set the acceptable levels conservatively low, and keep them there unless future studies show that they can be safely raised.

C) Set the acceptable levels at the highest levels encountered, and keep them there unless future studies demonstrate negative health effects.

D) Caution individuals to use their own judgment in deciding whether to drink water from a potentially contaminated area.

E) Establish a contingency fund to handle insurance claims in the event that the chemical turns out to produce negative health effects.

Answer: B
Skill: Application

9) All of the following would have a direct effect on the amount of precipitation in an area *except*

A) air circulation cells.

B) continental drift.

C) ocean currents.

D) mountain ranges.

E) evaporation from vegetation.

Answer: B
Skill: Comprehension

10) The biogeographic realms described by Darwin, Wallace, and others are associated with patterns of

A) continental drift.

B) precipitation and temperature.

C) rocks and soil.

D) climate.

E) light intensity.

Answer: A
Skill: Knowledge

11) Species transplants are one way of

A) determining the abundance of a species in a specified area.

B) determining the distribution of a species in a specified area.

C) developing mathematical models for distribution and abundance.

D) determining if dispersal is a key factor in limiting distribution.

E) consolidating a landscape into a single ecosystem.

Answer: C
Skill: Comprehension

12) Zebra mussel populations are growing explosively in the river systems of the central United States. The best explanation for this unchecked population growth is that

A) they muddy the water around them, making it difficult for their natural enemies to see them.

B) predators are too few to slow down population growth of the mussels.

C) they are better adapted to the environment than competing species.

D) they are feeding on a source of food that had previously been underutilized.

E) a mutation caused by pollution has increased their reproductive rate.

Answer: B
Skill: Comprehension

13) Introduced species

A) often fail to colonize the new area.

B) may become common enough to become pests.

C) can disrupt the balance of the natural species with which they become associated.

D) Both B and C are correct.

E) A, B, and C are all correct.

Answer: E
Skill: Comprehension

14) Which ecological unit or relationship is *least* related to abiotic factors?

A) community

B) ecosystem

C) population

D) species

E) symbiosis

Answer: E
Skill: Comprehension

15) Which of the following are *correct* statements about light in aquatic environments?

I. Water selectively reflects and absorbs certain wavelengths of light.

II. Photosynthetic organisms that live in deep water probably utilize red light.

III. Light intensity is an important abiotic factor in limiting the distribution of photosynthetic organisms.

A) I only

B) II only

C) I and III only

D) II and III only

E) I, II, and III

Answer: C
Skill: Comprehension

16) In an altitudinal gradient all of the following would change in the same way as in a latitudinal gradient *except*

  A) temperature.

  B) humidity.

  C) vegetation.

  D) day length.

  E) communities.

  Answer: D
  Skill: Comprehension

17) Probably the most important factor(s) affecting the distribution of biomes is (are)

  A) wind and water current patterns.

  B) species diversity.

  C) community succession.

  D) climate.

  E) day length and rainfall.

  Answer: D
  Skill: Knowledge

18) Which of the following abiotic factors has the greatest influence on the metabolic rates of plants and animals?

  A) water

  B) wind

  C) temperature

  D) rocks and soil

  E) disturbances

  Answer: C
  Skill: Comprehension

19) Which of the following statements best describes the effect of climate on biome distribution?

  A) Knowledge of annual temperature and precipitation is sufficient to predict which biome will be found in an area.

  B) Fluctuation of environmental variables is not important if areas have the same annual temperature and precipitation means.

  C) The distribution of biomes depends, in part, on the mean annual temperature and precipitation of an area.

  D) Temperate forests, coniferous forests, and grasslands all have the same mean annual temperatures and precipitation.

  E) Correlation of climate with biome distribution is sufficient to determine the cause of biome patterns.

  Answer: C
  Skill: Comprehension

20) As you travel toward the poles, _____ becomes the major factor in delimiting biomes. Near the equator, _____ is the major factor.

  A) wind ... photoperiod

  B) precipitation ... wind

  C) temperature ... precipitation

  D) photoperiod ... temperature

  E) sunlight intensity ... topography

  Answer: C
  Skill: Comprehension

21) Imagine some cosmic catastrophe that jolts Earth so that its axis is perpendicular to the orbital plane between Earth and the sun. The most obvious effect of this change would be

A) the elimination of tides.

B) an increase in the length of night.

C) an increase in the length of a year.

D) the elimination of the greenhouse effect and a cooling of the equator.

E) the elimination of seasonal variation.

Answer: E
Skill: Comprehension

22) Which of the following causes Earth's seasons?

A) global air circulation

B) global wind patterns

C) ocean currents

D) changes in Earth's distance from the sun

E) the tilt of Earth's axis

Answer: E
Skill: Comprehension

23) Which of the following events might you predict to occur if the tilt of Earth's axis relative to its plane of orbit was increased beyond 23.5 degrees?

A) Summers in the United States might become warmer.

B) Winters in Australia might become more severe.

C) Seasonal variation at the equator might decrease.

D) Both A and B are correct.

E) A, B, and C are all correct.

Answer: D
Skill: Comprehension

24) Generally speaking, deserts are located in places where air masses are usually

A) cold.

B) humid.

C) rising.

D) falling.

E) expanding.

Answer: D
Skill: Comprehension

25) Polar regions are cooler than the equator because

A) there is more ice at the poles.

B) sunlight strikes the poles at an oblique angle.

C) the poles are farther from the sun.

D) the poles have a thicker atmosphere.

E) the poles are permanently tilted away from the sun.

Answer: B
Skill: Comprehension

26) In mountainous areas of western North America, north-facing slopes (compared with south-facing slopes) would be expected to

A) receive more sunlight.

B) be warmer and drier.

C) support biological communities similar to those found at lower elevations and higher latitudes.

D) support biological communities similar to those found at higher elevations and higher latitudes.

E) Both B and C are true.

Answer: D
Skill: Comprehension

27) In temperate lakes, the surface water is replenished with nutrients during turnovers that occur in the
   A) fall and spring.
   B) fall and winter.
   C) spring and summer.
   D) summer and winter.
   E) summer and fall.

   Answer: A
   Skill: Comprehension

28) Which of the following is responsible for the summer and winter stratification of lakes?
   A) Water is densest at 4°C.
   B) Oxygen is most abundant in deeper waters.
   C) Winter ice sinks in the summer.
   D) Stratification is caused by a thermocline.
   E) Stratification always follows the fall and spring turnovers.

   Answer: A
   Skill: Comprehension

29) Which of the following environmental features might influence microclimates?
   A) All of the below might influence microclimates.
   B) a tree
   C) a fallen log
   D) a stone
   E) a discarded soft–drink can

   Answer: A
   Skill: Comprehension

30) Thorough mixing of water in temperate lakes during the spring and fall turnovers is made possible by which of the following?
   A) warm water layered at the top
   B) cold water layered at the bottom
   C) a pronounced thermocline under the surface
   D) changing water temperature profiles
   E) currents generated by nektonic animals

   Answer: D
   Skill: Knowledge

31) The speed with which plants extend their range northward following glacial retreat is best determined by
   A) whether there is simultaneous migration of herbivores.
   B) their tolerance to shade.
   C) their seed dispersal rate.
   D) their size.
   E) their growth rate.

   Answer: C
   Skill: Comprehension

32) Which of the following statements about aquatic ecosystems is *false*?
   A) The distribution of photosynthetic organisms is not limited by the quality and intensity of light in marine ecosystems.
   B) Many lakes in temperate regions are characterized by seasonal thermal stratification.
   C) Marine algae and photosynthetic bacteria produce a substantial portion of the biosphere's atmospheric oxygen.
   D) Many aquatic biomes exhibit pronounced vertical stratification of chemical variables.
   E) All of the statements above are true.

   Answer: A
   Skill: Knowledge

33) The benthic zone in an aquatic biome

   A) often supports communities of organisms that feed largely on detritus.

   B) is the site of most photosynthesis within the biome.

   C) is where one would most expect to find a thermocline.

   D) B and C only are correct.

   E) A, B, and C are correct.

Answer: A
Skill: Knowledge

34) Where would an ecologist find the most phytoplankton in a lake?

   A) profundal zone

   B) benthic zone

   C) limnetic zone

   D) oligotrophic zone

   E) aphotic zone

Answer: C
Skill: Comprehension

35) Which of the following is *not* true about estuaries?

   A) Estuaries are often bordered by mudflats and salt marshes.

   B) Estuaries contain waters of varying salinity.

   C) Estuaries support a variety of animal life that humans consume.

   D) Estuaries usually contain no or few producers.

   E) Estuaries support many semiaquatic species.

Answer: D
Skill: Knowledge

36) Nutrient-rich agricultural runoff into freshwater ecosystems

   A) is usually associated with a decrease in phytoplankton productivity.

   B) can result in "cultural eutrophication."

   C) often leads to increasingly oligotrophic lakes.

   D) often results in a dramatic reduction in the amount of detritus.

   E) will eventually increase the amount of available dissolved oxygen.

Answer: B
Skill: Comprehension

37) Where would you be most likely to find plants known as hydrophytes?

   A) desert

   B) temperate forest

   C) tropical rain forest

   D) bog

   E) tundra

Answer: D
Skill: Knowledge

38) Phytoplankton is most frequently found in which of the following zones?

   A) oligotrophic

   B) photic

   C) benthic

   D) abyssal

   E) aphotic

Answer: B
Skill: Knowledge

39) Coral animals

   A) are a diverse group of cnidarians.

   B) are predominantly photosynthetic, multicellular algae.

   C) excrete external, carbonaceous skeletons.

   D) Both A and C are correct answers.

   E) Both B and C are correct answers.

Answer: D
Skill: Knowledge

40) Coral reefs can be found on the southern east coast of the United States but not at similar latitudes on the southern west coast. Differences in which of the following most likely account for this?

A) sunlight

B) precipitation

C) day length

D) ocean currents

E) salinity

Answer: D
Skill: Comprehension

41) Which marine zone would have the lowest rates of primary productivity (photosynthesis)?

A) pelagic

B) abyssal

C) neritic

D) estuary

E) intertidal

Answer: B
Skill: Comprehension

42) If a meteor impact or volcanic eruption injected a lot of dust into the atmosphere and reduced sunlight reaching Earth's surface by 70% for one year, all of the following marine communities would be greatly affected *except* a

A) deep-sea vent community.

B) coral reef community.

C) benthic community.

D) pelagic community.

E) estuary community.

Answer: A
Skill: Comprehension

43) In which community would organisms most likely have evolved to respond to different photoperiods?

A) tropical forest

B) coral reef

C) savanna

D) temperate forest

E) abyssal

Answer: D
Skill: Knowledge

44) Two plant species live in the same biome but on different continents. Although these two are not at all closely related, they may appear quite similar as a result of

A) parallel evolution.

B) convergent evolution.

C) allopatric speciation.

D) introgression.

E) gene flow.

Answer: B
Skill: Knowledge

45) All of the following statements about biomes are correct *except:*

A) Biomes are major terrestrial communities.

B) Within biomes there may be extensive patchiness.

C) Climographs are often used to demonstrate climatic differences between biomes.

D) Temperature and precipitation account for most of the variation between biomes.

E) Biomes can be recognized as separate entities because they have sharp, well-defined boundaries.

Answer: E
Skill: Knowledge

46) An area in which different terrestrial biomes grade into each other is known as a(n)

A) littoral zone.

B) vertically stratified canopy.

C) ecotone.

D) abyssal zone.

E) cline.

Answer: C
Skill: Knowledge

47) Which of the following statements best describes the interaction between fire and ecosystems?

A) The chance of fire in a given ecosystem is highly predictable over the short term.

B) Many kinds of plants and plant communities have adapted to frequent fires.

C) The prevention of forest fires has allowed more productive and stable plant communities to develop.

D) Chaparral communities have evolved to the extent that they rarely burn.

E) Fire is unnatural in ecosystems and should be prevented.

Answer: B
Skill: Comprehension

48) Within any given type of terrestrial biome

A) species composition is typically uniform.

B) there is little or no vertical stratification.

C) periodic disturbance is rare.

D) A and B are true.

E) none of the above is true.

Answer: E
Skill: Knowledge

49) In the development of terrestrial biomes, which factor is most dependent on all the others?

A) the species of colonizing animals

B) prevailing temperature

C) prevailing rainfall

D) mineral nutrient availability

E) soil structure

Answer: A
Skill: Comprehension

50) Which of the following terrestrial biomes is (are) adapted to frequent fires?

A) savanna

B) chaparral

C) temperate grasslands

D) only A and B

E) A, B, and C

Answer: E
Skill: Knowledge

51) Fire suppression by humans

A) will always result in an increase in the number of species in a given biome.

B) can change the species composition within biological communities.

C) will result ultimately in sustainable production of increased amounts of wood for human use.

D) is necessary for the protection of threatened and endangered forest species.

E) Only C and D are correct.

Answer: B
Skill: Comprehension

52) Concerning the distribution of species, which of the following statements is *true*?

A) Most species have wide ranges.

B) Most species have small ranges.

C) Most plant species are widespread, while most animal species have small geographic ranges.

D) Most aquatic animal species are widespread, while most terrestrial animal species have small geographic ranges.

E) Biotic interactions such as symbiosis, predation, and competition limit the geographic range of species on a global scale.

Answer: B
Skill: Comprehension

53) Which biome is able to support many large animals despite receiving moderate amounts of rainfall?

A) tropical rain forest

B) temperate forest

C) chaparral

D) taiga

E) savanna

Answer: E
Skill: Knowledge

54) Tropical grasslands with scattered trees are also known as

A) taigas.

B) tundras.

C) savannas.

D) chaparrals.

E) temperate plains.

Answer: C
Skill: Knowledge

55) The growing season would generally be shortest in which of the following biomes?

A) savanna

B) deciduous forest

C) temperate grassland

D) tropical rain forest

E) taiga

Answer: E
Skill: Knowledge

56) Which type of biome would most likely occur in a climate with mild, rainy winters and hot, dry summers?

A) desert

B) taiga

C) temperate grassland

D) chaparral

E) savanna

Answer: D
Skill: Comprehension

Media Activity Questions

1) In Africa, DDT has been very successful in controlling the incidence of
   A) birth defects.
   B) trisomy 21.
   C) malaria.
   D) tuberculosis.
   E) pancreatic cancer.

   Answer: C
   Topic: Web/CD Activity 50A

2) Which of these is an abiotic component of an environment?
   A) dogs
   B) light
   C) cats
   D) bacteria
   E) classmates

   Answer: B
   Topic: Web/CD Activity 50B

3) Which of these abiotic factors is a major determinant of composition of the biotic communities that inhabit aquatic biomes?
   A) light
   B) water depth
   C) temperature
   D) oxygen content
   E) All of the above are major factors that affect the makeup of the biotic communities that inhabit aquatic biomes.

   Answer: E
   Topic: Web/CD Activity 50C

4) Which of these life zones is a component of a marine biome but *not* a component of a freshwater biome?
   A) aphotic zone
   B) intertidal zone
   C) photic zone
   D) benthic zone
   E) both the aphotic and benthic zones

   Answer: B
   Topic: Web/CD Activity 50C

5) Biomes are
   A) all of the populations of a particular species.
   B) recognized on the basis of the dominant animal life.
   C) a major type of ecosystem.
   D) unaffected by climatic factors.
   E) limited to aquatic regions.

   Answer: C
   Topic: Web/CD Activity 50D

Self–Quiz Questions

Answers to these questions also appear in the textbook.

1) Which of the following levels of study in ecology includes all other levels in the list?

   A) population

   B) organism

   C) landscape

   D) ecosystem

   E) community

   Answer: C

2) Which statement about dispersal is *incorrect*?

   A) Dispersal is a common component of the life cycles of plants and animals.

   B) Colonization of devastated areas after floods or volcanic eruptions depends on dispersal.

   C) Dispersal occurs only on an evolutionary time scale.

   D) Seeds are important dispersal stages in the life cycles of most flowering plants.

   E) The ability to disperse can limit the geographic distribution of a species.

   Answer: C

3) Which of the following biomes is *correctly* paired with the description of its climate?

   A) savanna—cool temperature, precipitation uniform during the year

   B) tundra—long summers, mild winters

   C) temperate deciduous forest—relatively short growing season, mild winters

   D) temperate grasslands—relatively warm winters, most rainfall in summer

   E) tropical forests—nearly constant photoperiod and temperature

   Answer: E

4) The oceans affect the biosphere in all of the following ways *except*

   A) producing a substantial amount of the biosphere's oxygen.

   B) removing carbon dioxide from the atmosphere.

   C) moderating the climate of terrestrial biomes.

   D) regulating the pH of freshwater biomes and terrestrial groundwater.

   E) being the source of most terrestrial rainfall.

   Answer: D

5) Which of the following is *correctly* paired with its description?

   A) neritic zone—shallow area over continental shelf

   B) benthic zone—surface water of shallow seas

   C) pelagic zone—seafloor

   D) aphotic zone—zone in which light penetrates

   E) intertidal zone—open water at the edge of the continental shelf

   Answer: A

6) Which of the following do all terrestrial biomes have in common?

   A) annual average rainfall in excess of 25 cm

   B) a distribution predicted almost entirely by rock and soil patterns

   C) clear boundaries between adjacent biomes

   D) vegetation demonstrating vertical stratification

   E) cold winter months

   Answer: D

7) The tree line on mountains illustrates the altitudinal limitation for the geographic ranges of trees. Which of the following observations or experiments would be *least* helpful for studying the causes for a particular tree line in the Rocky Mountains?

A) Analyze the growth rates of individual trees as they occur closer and closer to the tree line.

B) Transplant small seedlings above the tree line.

C) Determine the position of the tree line on south-facing slopes and north-facing slopes.

D) Sow seeds of trees in tundra areas above the tree line.

E) Measure the rate of photosynthesis for a random sample of tree seedlings in a laboratory greenhouse at sea level.

Answer: E

8) The growing season would generally be shortest in which biome?

A) tropical rain forest

B) savanna

C) taiga

D) temperate deciduous forest

E) temperate grassland

Answer: C

9) Imagine some cosmic catastrophe that jolts Earth so that it is no longer tilted. Instead, its axis is perpendicular to the line between the sun and Earth. The most predictable effect of this change would be

A) no more night and day.

B) a big change in the length of the year.

C) a cooling of the equator.

D) a loss of seasonal variations at northern and southern latitudes.

E) the elimination of ocean currents.

Answer: D

10) While climbing up mountains, one observes transitions in biological communities that are analogous to the changes one encounters

A) in biomes at different latitudes.

B) at different depths in the ocean.

C) in a community through different seasons.

D) in an ecosystem as it evolves over time.

E) traveling across the United States from east to west.

Answer: A

Chapter 51   Behavioral Biology

1) When, during a field trip, the instructor touched the body of a moth that was sitting on a tree trunk, the moth raised its forewings to reveal large eye–spots on its hind wings. The instructor asked the class why the moth lifted its wings. One student said that certain sensory receptors had fired and triggered a neuronal reflex culminating in the contraction of certain muscles. A second student responded that the behavior might frighten would–be predators. What can you say about the explanations of these two students?

A) The first response is correct, while the second is incorrect.

B) The first response answers a proximate question, while the second answers an ultimate question.

C) The first response is biological, while the second is philosophical.

D) The first explanation is testable as a scientific hypothesis, while the second is not.

E) Both explanations are reasonable and simply represent a difference of opinion.

Answer: B
Skill: Comprehension

Use the following information to answer the questions below. When a female cat comes into heat, she urinates more frequently and in a large number of places. Male cats from the neighborhood congregate near urine deposits and fight with each other.

2) Which of the following is a proximate cause of this behavior of increased urination?

A) It announces to the males that she is in heat.

B) Female cats that did this in the past attracted more males.

C) It is a result of hormonal changes associated with her reproductive cycle.

D) The female cat saw other cats doing it, and it worked for them.

E) In the past, when she did it, more males were attracted.

Answer: C
Skill: Comprehension

3) Which of the following would be an ultimate cause of the male cats' response to the female's urinating behavior?

A) The males have learned to recognize the specific odor of the urine of a female in heat.

B) By smelling the odor, various neurons in the males' brains are stimulated.

C) Male cats respond to the odor because it is a means of locating females in heat.

D) Male cats' hormones are triggered by the odor released by the female.

E) The odor serves as a releaser for the instinctive behavior of the males.

Answer: C
Skill: Comprehension

4) Which of the following is a behavioral pattern that results from a proximate cause?

A) A cat kills a mouse to obtain food.

B) A male sheep fights with another male because it helps it to improve its social position and find a mate.

C) A female bird lays its eggs because the amount of daylight is decreasing slightly each day.

D) A goose squats and freezes motionless because that helps it to escape a predator.

E) A cockroach runs into a crack in the wall and avoids being stepped on.

Answer: C
Skill: Comprehension

5) Which of the following is a behavioral pattern resulting from an ultimate cause?

A) A male robin attacks a red tennis ball because it is much like the breast of another male.

B) A male robin attacks a red tennis ball because it is spring and hormonal changes increase its aggression.

C) A male robin attacks a red tennis ball because a part of its brain is stimulated by objects that are red.

D) A male robin attacks a red tennis ball because several times in the past, red tennis balls have been thrown at it, and it has learned that they are dangerous.

E) A male robin attacks a red tennis ball because it confuses it with an encroaching male, and if it does not attack rival males it will lose its territory.

Answer: E
Skill: Comprehension

6) After eating a monarch butterfly and regurgitating, a bird will subsequently avoid orange and black butterflies. This is *not* an example of

A) associative learning.

B) operant conditioning.

C) innate behavior.

D) trial–and–error learning.

E) adaptive behavior.

Answer: C
Skill: Comprehension

7) In the territorial behavior of the stickleback fish, the red belly of one male elicits attack from another male by functioning as

A) a pheromone.

B) a sign stimulus.

C) a fixed action pattern.

D) a search image.

E) an imprint stimulus.

Answer: B
Skill: Knowledge

8) A cage with male mosquitoes in it has a small earphone placed on top, through which the sound of a female mosquito is played. All the males immediately fly to the earphone and thrust their abdomens through the fabric of the cage. Which of the following best describes this?

A) The males learn to associate the sound with a female and are thus attracted to it.

B) Copulation is a fixed action pattern, and the female flight sound is a sign stimulus that initiates it.

C) The sound from the earphone irritated the male mosquitoes, causing them to attempt to sting it.

D) The reproductive drive is so strong that when males are deprived of females, they will attempt to mate with anything that has even the slightest female characteristic.

E) Through classical conditioning, the male mosquitoes have associated the inappropriate stimulus from the earphone with the normal response of copulation.

Answer: B
Skill: Application

9) Mayflies laying eggs on roads instead of in water involves which of the following?

A) a defective behavioral gene

B) trial–and–error learning

C) misdirected response to a sign stimulus

D) natural behavioral variation in the mayfly population

E) insecticide poisoning

Answer: C
Skill: Knowledge

10) Which of the following statements is (are) *true* of fixed action patterns?

A) They are highly stereotyped, instinctive behaviors.

B) They are triggered by sign stimuli in the environment and, once begun, are continued to completion.

C) An inappropriate stimulus can sometimes trigger them.

D) Only A and B are correct.

E) A, B, and C are correct.

Answer: E
Skill: Knowledge

11) The proximate causes of behavior are interactions with the environment, but behavior is ultimately shaped by

A) hormones.

B) evolution.

C) sexuality.

D) pheromones.

E) the nervous system.

Answer: B
Skill: Comprehension

12) Which of the following is *least* related to the others?

A) fixed action pattern

B) pheromones

C) sign stimulus

D) hormones

E) optimal foraging

Answer: E
Skill: Comprehension

13) During a trip to the north woods, you discover a patch of blueberries. There are not very many of them, as it is a dry year, so you pick every one you find in order to have enough for pancakes the next morning. The next year you return to the same spot and find berries everywhere. Now you pick only the largest berries and only from the tops of the plants where they are easier to see. This is a good example of

A) cognitive thinking.

B) trial-and-error learning.

C) operant conditioning.

D) optimal foraging.

E) associative learning.

Answer: D
Skill: Comprehension

14) In the evolution of whelk-eating behavior in the crows studied by Zack, which of the following was being minimized by natural selection?

A) the average number of drops required to break the shell

B) the average height a bird flew to drop a shell

C) the average total energy used to break shells

D) the average size of the shells dropped by the birds

E) the average thickness of the shells dropped by the birds

Answer: C
Skill: Comprehension

15) Animals tend to maximize their energy intake-to-expenditure ratio. What is this behavior called?

A) agonistic behavior

B) optimal foraging

C) dominance hierarchies

D) animal cognition

E) territoriality

Answer: B
Skill: Comprehension

16) Feeding behavior that has a high energy intake-to-expenditure ratio is called

A) herbivory.

B) autotrophy.

C) heterotrophy.

D) search scavenging.

E) optimal foraging.

Answer: E
Skill: Knowledge

17) Optimal foraging involves all of the following *except*

A) maximizing energy gained by the forager.

B) minimizing energy expended by the forager.

C) securing essential nutrients for the forager.

D) minimizing the risk of predation on the forager.

E) maximizing the population size of the forager.

Answer: E
Skill: Comprehension

18) Learning to ignore unimportant stimuli is called

A) adapting.

B) spacing.

C) conditioning.

D) imprinting.

E) habituation.

Answer: E
Skill: Knowledge

19) Which of the following would you classify as habituation?

A) You enter a room and hear the motor of a fan. After a period of time, you are no longer aware of the sound of the fan motor.

B) You are driving your car and you hear a horn blow. You step on the brakes, but see that it is someone on a side street. So, you resume your previous speed.

C) You are sitting in a room and suddenly hear a steady beep–beep–beep. You look out the window and see a garbage truck backing up. A week later, you hear the same beep–beep–beep but don't bother to look out the window.

D) Both A and C are correct.

E) A, B, and C are correct.

Answer: D
Skill: Comprehension

20) Which of the following is *true* about imprinting?

A) It may be triggered by visual or chemical stimuli.

B) It happens to many adult animals, but not to their young.

C) It is a type of learning involving no innate behavior.

D) It occurs only in birds.

E) It causes behaviors that last for only a short time (the critical period).

Answer: A
Skill: Comprehension

21) A type of learning that can occur only during a brief period of early life and results in a behavior that is difficult to modify through later experiences is called

A) insight.

B) imprinting.

C) habituation.

D) operant conditioning.

E) trial–and–error learning.

Answer: B
Skill: Knowledge

22) *Mary had a little lamb*
     Its fleece was white as snow.
     And everywhere that Mary went
        The lamb was sure to go.

Which of the following statements is *correct* regarding Mary and her lamb?

A) Mary raised the lamb from shortly after birth.

B) The lamb had little contact with its mother.

C) The lamb will eventually outgrow this attachment.

D) Both A and B are correct.

E) A, B, and C are correct.

Answer: D
Skill: Application

23) You are watching some ducks. You see a male wood duck apparently courting a different species of duck, a female mallard. Which of the following statements is most likely to be *correct* concerning this behavior?

   A) The male wood duck was reared by a mallard female.

   B) The female mallard was reared by a female wood duck.

   C) The male will be unsuccessful and will eventually learn that he should court a female of his own species.

   D) The female will eventually give an appropriate response to the male, and the two will mate.

   E) Although the two will mate and produce offspring, the offspring will be so confused that they will never mate.

   Answer: A
   Skill: Application

24) Which of the following is *least* related to the others?

   A) fixed action pattern

   B) imprinting

   C) instinct

   D) taxis

   E) kinesis

   Answer: B
   Skill: Comprehension

25) Learning in which an associated stimulus may be used to elicit the same behavioral response as the original sign stimulus is called

   A) concept formation.

   B) trial and error.

   C) classical conditioning.

   D) operant conditioning.

   E) habituation.

   Answer: C
   Skill: Comprehension

26) Every morning at the same time John went into the den to feed his new tropical fish. After a few weeks John noticed that the fish would rise to the top of the tank as soon as he would enter the room. This is a good example of

   A) habituation.

   B) imprinting.

   C) classical conditioning.

   D) operant conditioning.

   E) maturation.

   Answer: C
   Skill: Comprehension

27) The type of learning that causes specially trained dogs to salivate when they hear bells is called

   A) insight.

   B) imprinting.

   C) habituation.

   D) classical conditioning.

   E) trial-and-error learning.

   Answer: D
   Skill: Knowledge

28) All of the following statements about learning and behavior are correct *except*:

   A) Operant conditioning involves associating a behavior with a reward or punishment.

   B) Associative learning involves linking one stimulus with another.

   C) Classical conditioning involves trial-and-error learning.

   D) Behavior can be modified by learning, but some apparent learning is due to maturation.

   E) Imprinting is a learned behavior with an innate component acquired during a sensitive period.

   Answer: C
   Skill: Comprehension

29) A dog learns that it will get a treat when it barks. Which of the following might you use to describe this behavior?
   A) The dog is displaying an instinctive fixed action pattern.
   B) The dog is performing a social behavior.
   C) The dog is trying to protect its territory.
   D) The dog has been classically conditioned.
   E) The dog's behavior is a result of operant conditioning.

Answer: E
Skill: Application

30) When a bag of potato chips is moved in the kitchen, a pet dog comes running. This usually results in the dog getting a potato chip. Which of the following is (are) involved here?
   A) fixed action patterns
   B) classical conditioning
   C) operant conditioning
   D) both B and C
   E) A, B, and C

Answer: D
Skill: Application

31) Which of the following is *least* related to the others?
   A) fixed action pattern
   B) imprinting
   C) operant conditioning
   D) classical conditioning
   E) habituation

Answer: A
Skill: Comprehension

Use the following terms to answer the questions below. Match the term that best fits each of the following descriptions of behavior. Each term may be used once, more than once, or not at all.

   A. *sign stimulus*
   B. *habituation*
   C. *imprinting*
   D. *classical conditioning*
   E. *operant conditioning*

32) Tits (chickadee–like birds) learned to peck through the paper tops of milk bottles left on doorsteps and drink the cream from the top.

Answer: E
Skill: Comprehension

33) Male insects attempt to mate with orchids but eventually stop responding to them.

Answer: B
Skill: Comprehension

34) A returning salmon goes back to its own home stream to spawn.

Answer: C
Skill: Comprehension

35) A stickleback fish will attack a model fish as long as the model has red color.

Answer: A
Skill: Comprehension

36) Parental protective behavior in turkeys is triggered by the cheeping sound produced by the young chicks.

Answer: A
Skill: Comprehension

37) Sparrows are receptive to learning songs only during a sensitive period.

Answer: C
Skill: Comprehension

38) Which of the following is *false* regarding play behavior?

A) It is usually performed by young animals.

B) It usually involves safe activities.

C) It may provide exercise.

D) It may provide practice.

E) It may be performed by adult animals.

Answer: B
Skill: Knowledge

39) The congregation of lice in a moist location due to greater activity in dry areas is an example of

A) taxis.

B) tropism.

C) kinesis.

D) cognition.

E) net reflex.

Answer: C
Skill: Comprehension

40) Which of the following is *least* related to the others?

A) agonistic behavior

B) cognitive maps

C) dominance hierarchy

D) ritual

E) territory

Answer: B
Skill: Comprehension

41) The central concept of sociobiology is that

A) human behavior is rigidly predetermined.

B) the behavior of an individual cannot be modified.

C) our behavior consists mainly of fixed action patterns.

D) most aspects of our social behavior have an evolutionary basis.

E) the social behavior of humans is homologous to the social behavior of honeybees.

Answer: D
Skill: Comprehension

42) Reconciliation behavior is likely to follow

A) conflict behavior between members of a permanent social group.

B) agonistic behavior between territorial males.

C) mating behavior between a male and a female.

D) ritualized behavior.

E) imprinting by young animals on a member of the wrong species.

Answer: A
Skill: Comprehension

The next questions refer to the following list of scientists.

A. E. O. Wilson
B. Jane Goodall
C. J. B. S. Haldane
D. Donald Griffin
E. William Hamilton

43) foremost proponent that many nonhuman animals have cognitive abilities

Answer: D
Skill: Knowledge

44) studied social behavior of insects on an evolutionary basis

Answer: A
Skill: Knowledge

45) developed the concept of inclusive fitness

Answer: E
Skill: Knowledge

46) Fred and Joe, two unrelated, mature male gorillas, encounter one another. Fred is courting a female. Fred grunts as Joe comes near. As Joe continues to advance, Fred begins drumming (pounding his chest) and bares his teeth. At this, Joe rolls on the ground on his back, then gets up and quickly leaves. This behavioral pattern is repeated several times during the mating season. Choose the most specific behavior described by this example.

A) agonistic behavior

B) territorial behavior

C) learned behavior

D) social behavior

E) fixed action pattern

Answer: A
Skill: Application

47) Which of the following is *not* associated with a species in which the female makes a greater contribution to rearing offspring than the male?

A) dominance hierarchies in males

B) polygyny

C) short courtship

D) females having multiple male partners

E) agonistic behavior

Answer: D
Skill: Comprehension

48) Which of the following is *not* a significant cost associated with mating?

A) energy expended in finding a mate

B) energy expended in ensuring that the mate is of the same species

C) resources allocated for producing gametes

D) loss of opportunity to do something other than mate

E) loss of genetic recombination associated with sex

Answer: E
Skill: Comprehension

49) All of the following statements about mating behavior are correct *except*:

A) Some aspects of courtship behavior may have evolved from agonistic interactions.

B) Courtship interactions ensure that the participating individuals are nonthreatening and of the proper species, sex, and physiological condition for mating.

C) The degree to which evolution affects mating relationships depends on the degree of prenatal and postnatal input the parents are required to make.

D) The mating relationship in most mammals is monogamous, to ensure the reproductive success of the pair.

E) Polygamous relationships most often involve a single male and many females, but in some species this is reversed.

Answer: D
Skill: Comprehension

50) Animal communication involves what type of sensory information?

A) visual

B) auditory

C) chemical

D) tactile

E) All of the above can be correct.

Answer: E
Skill: Comprehension

51) Which of the following groups of scientists is closely associated with ethology?

A) Watson, Crick, and Franklin

B) McClintock, Goodall, and Lyon

C) Fossey, Hershey, and Chase

D) von Frisch, Lorenz, and Tinbergen

E) Hardy, Weinberg, and Castle

Answer: D
Skill: Knowledge

52) A chemical produced by an animal that serves as a communication to another animal of the same species is called

A) a marker.

B) an inducer.

C) a pheromone.

D) an imprinter.

E) an agonistic chemical.

Answer: C
Skill: Knowledge

The next questions refer to the following list of scientists.

A. Karl von Frisch
B. Niko Tinbergen
C. Konrad Lorenz
D. B. F. Skinner
E. Ivan Pavlov

53) studied communication in bees

Answer: A
Skill: Knowledge

54) studied operant conditioning in rats

Answer: D
Skill: Knowledge

55) studied imprinting of greylag geese

Answer: C
Skill: Knowledge

56) Which of the following is *least* related to the others?

A) altruism

B) polygamy

C) monogamy

D) polygyny

E) polyandry

Answer: A
Skill: Comprehension

57) Modern behavioral concepts relate the cost of a behavior to its benefit. Under which relationship might a behavior be performed?

A) cost is greater than the benefit

B) cost is less than the benefit

C) cost is equal to the benefit

D) both A and C

E) both B and C

Answer: E
Skill: Comprehension

58) Which of the following is *not* a concept associated with sociobiology?

A) parental investment

B) inclusive fitness

C) associative learning

D) reciprocal altruism

E) kin selection

Answer: C
Skill: Comprehension

59) Which of the following does *not* have a coefficient of relatedness of 0.5?

A) a father to his daughter

B) a mother to her son

C) an uncle to his nephew

D) a brother to his brother

E) a sister to her brother

Answer: C
Skill: Comprehension

60) Animals that help other animals of the same species are expected to

A) have excess energy reserves.

B) be bigger and stronger than the other animals.

C) be genetically related to the other animals.

D) be male.

E) have defective genes controlling behavior.

Answer: C
Skill: Comprehension

61) The presence of altruistic behavior in animals is most likely due to kin selection, a theory that maintains that

A) aggression between sexes promotes the survival of the fittest individuals.

B) genes enhance survival of copies of themselves by directing organisms to assist others who share those genes.

C) companionship is advantageous to animals because in the future they can help each other.

D) critical thinking abilities are normal traits for animals and they have arisen, like other traits, through natural selection.

E) natural selection has generally favored the evolution of exaggerated aggressive and submissive behaviors to resolve conflict without grave harm to participants.

Answer: B
Skill: Comprehension

62) Which of the following statements is *correct* concerning the evolution of behavior?

A) Natural selection will favor behavior that enhances survival and reproduction.

B) An animal may show behavior that maximizes reproductive fitness.

C) If a behavior is less than optimal, it is not yet completely evolved and will eventually become optimal.

D) A and B are both correct.

E) A, B, and C are all correct.

Answer: D
Skill: Comprehension

Media Activity Question

1) The function of the waggle dance in bees is to

   A) indicate only the distance to food.

   B) indicate only the direction to food.

   C) indicate both the direction and the distance to a food source.

   D) attract mates.

   E) attract mates and indicate the direction and distance to food.

   Answer: C
   Topic: Web/CD Activity 51A

Self-Quiz Questions

Answers to these questions also appear in the textbook.

1) Bees can detect wavelengths of light that we cannot see and sense minute amounts of chemicals we cannot smell. But unlike many insects, bees cannot hear very well. Which of the following statements best fits in the perspective of behavioral ecology?

   A) Bees are too small to have functional ears.

   B) Hearing must not contribute much to a bee's fitness.

   C) If a bee could hear, its tiny brain would be swamped with information.

   D) This is an example of a proximate causation.

   E) If bees could hear, the noise of the hive would distract the bees from their work.

   Answer: B

2) The nature–versus–nurture controversy centers on

   A) the distinction between proximate and ultimate causes of behavior.

   B) the role of genes in learning.

   C) whether animals have conscious feelings or thoughts.

   D) the extent to which an animal's behavior is innate or learned.

   E) the importance of good parental care.

   Answer: D

3) According to the inequality known as Hamilton's rule ($rB > C$),

   A) natural selection could not favor altruism if the altruist loses its life.

   B) natural selection would favor altruistic acts when the benefit to the receiver, reduced by the coefficient of relatedness, exceeds the cost to the altruist.

   C) natural selection is more likely to favor altruistic acts when the beneficiary is an offspring than when it is a sibling.

   D) kin selection is a stronger selection factor than the individual reproductive success favored by natural selection.

   E) altruism must always be reciprocal.

   Answer: B

4) Female spotted sandpipers aggressively court males and then, after mating, leave the clutch for the male to incubate. This sequence may be repeated several times with different males until no available males remain, forcing the female to incubate her last clutch. All of the following terms describe this behavior *except*

   A) polygamy.

   B) polyandry.

   C) polygyny.

   D) promiscuity.

   E) parental investment.

   Answer: C

5) Which of the following is *least* likely to involve cognition?

    A) navigation of a sparrow during seasonal migration

    B) being aware of your neighbor's lawn care

    C) territoriality

    D) positive rheotaxis of a fish in a current

    E) optimal foraging

Answer: D

6) Which of the following is *not* true of agonistic behavior?

    A) It is most common among members of the same species.

    B) It may be used to establish and defend territories.

    C) It often involves symbolic conflict and often does not cause serious harm to either the winner or the loser in the encounter.

    D) It is a uniquely male behavior.

    E) It may be used to establish dominance hierarchies.

Answer: D

7) A researcher found that a region of the forebrain in canaries shrinks and regenerates each breeding season. This finding correlates with

    A) the plastic song stage and then the learning of a new, more elaborate song each year.

    B) the crystallization of its adult song from the subsong it developed when it first learned to sing.

    C) the sensitive period in which the male parent bonds with new offspring.

    D) the renewal of nest-building and mating activity each spring.

    E) the sensitive period in which canaries form a template of their species-specific song.

Answer: A

8) The core idea of sociobiology is that

    A) human behavior is rigidly predetermined by inheritance.

    B) humans cannot learn to alter their social behavior.

    C) many aspects of social behavior have an evolutionary basis.

    D) the social behavior of humans is comparable to that of bees.

    E) environment outweighs genes in human behavior.

Answer: C

9) Which of the following provides an example of habituation?

    A) Humpback whales migrating from Hawaii to Alaska are observed singing songs first identified in humpbacks migrating between Alaska and Baja California.

    B) Male sticklebacks attempt to attack any red-colored object near their tank.

    C) Adult brown pelicans are more successful at capturing fish than are juveniles.

    D) Female warblers incubate the eggs cowbirds deposit in their nests.

    E) Aquarium fish are initially startled by tapping on the aquarium glass but eventually ignore it.

Answer: E

10) A honeybee returning to the hive from a food source performs a waggle dance with the sun oriented straight to the left on the vertical surface. Most likely, this means that the food is located

    A) 90° left of the hive.

    B) 90° left of the line from the hive to the sun.

    C) in the opposite direction, straight to the right of the hive.

    D) above the hive and slightly to the left.

    E) very close to the hive.

Answer: B

Chapter 52   Population Biology

1) A population is *correctly* defined as having which of the following characteristics?
   I.   inhabiting the same general area
   II. individuals belonging to the same species
   III. possessing a constant and uniform density and dispersion

   A) I only
   B) III only
   C) I and II only
   D) II and III only
   E) I, II, and III

   Answer: C
   Skill: Knowledge

2) A biologist reported that a sample of ocean water had 5 million diatoms of the species *Coscinodiscus centralis* per cubic meter. What was the biologist measuring?

   A) density
   B) dispersion
   C) carrying capacity
   D) quadrats
   E) range

   Answer: A
   Skill: Knowledge

3) All of the following phrases could characterize a population *except*

   A) interacting individuals.
   B) dispersion.
   C) density.
   D) several species.
   E) boundaries.

   Answer: D
   Skill: Comprehension

4) To measure the population density of monarch butterflies occupying a particular park, 100 butterflies are captured, marked with a small dot on a wing, and then released. The next day, another 100 butterflies are captured, including the recapture of 20 marked butterflies. One would correctly estimate the population to be

   A) 200.
   B) 500.
   C) 1,000.
   D) 10,000.
   E) 900,000.

   Answer: B
   Skill: Application

5) The most common kind of dispersion in nature is

   A) clumped.
   B) random.
   C) uniform.
   D) indeterminate.
   E) dispersive.

   Answer: A
   Skill: Knowledge

6) How would the dispersion of humans in the United States best be described?

   A) dense
   B) clumped
   C) random
   D) intrinsic
   E) uniform

   Answer: B
   Skill: Comprehension

7) The pattern of dispersion for a certain species of kelp is clumped. The pattern of dispersion for a certain species of snail that lives only on this kelp would likely be

A) absolute.

B) clumped.

C) demographic.

D) random.

E) uniform.

Answer: B
Skill: Comprehension

8) Uniform spacing patterns in plants such as the creosote bush are most often associated with which of the following?

A) chance

B) patterns of high humidity

C) the random distribution of seeds

D) antagonistic interactions among individuals in the population

E) the concentration of resources within the population's range

Answer: D
Skill: Comprehension

9) Which of the following would be most likely to exhibit uniform dispersion?

A) red squirrels, which hide food and actively defend territories

B) cattails, which grow primarily at edges of lakes and streams

C) dwarf mistletoes, which parasitize particular species of forest trees

D) tassel-eared squirrels, which are nonterritorial

E) lake trout, which seek out deep water

Answer: A
Skill: Comprehension

10) A table listing such items as age, observed number of organisms alive each year, and life expectancy is known as a(an)

A) life table.

B) mortality table.

C) survivorship table.

D) rate table.

E) insurance table.

Answer: A
Skill: Knowledge

11) Life tables are useful in determining which of the following?

I. carrying capacity
II. mortality rates
III. the fate of a cohort of newborn organisms throughout their lives

A) I only

B) II only

C) III only

D) I and III only

E) II and III only

Answer: E
Skill: Comprehension

12) Which of the following statements about human birth and death rates in populations is *correct*?

A) Both death rates and birth rates are highest in 30-year-olds.

B) Both death rates and birth rates are highest in teenagers.

C) Death rates are highest in middle-aged adults, whereas the birth rates are highest in teenagers.

D) Death rates are highest in newborns and in the elderly, whereas birth rates are highest in 20-year-olds.

E) Death rates are highest in the elderly, whereas birth rates are highest in newborns.

Answer: D
Skill: Comprehension

Use the survivorship curves in Figure 52.1 to answer the following questions.

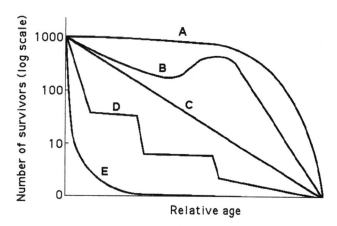

Figure 52.1

13) Which curve best describes survivorship in oysters?

Answer: E
Skill: Comprehension

14) Which curve best describes survivorship in elephants?

Answer: A
Skill: Comprehension

15) Which curve best describes survivorship in a marine crustacean that molts?

Answer: D
Skill: Comprehension

16) Which curve best describes survivorship in humans who live in developed nations?

Answer: A
Skill: Comprehension

17) Which curve is impossible?

Answer: B
Skill: Comprehension

18) Which curve best describes survivorship that is independent of age?

Answer: C
Skill: Comprehension

19) A demographer studying a population of a particular organism would be *least* likely to be engaged in which of the following?
   A) constructing a life table for the organism
   B) sampling the population and determining the sex ratio
   C) studying courtship behavior between males and females
   D) measuring birth and death rates
   E) estimating how long an individual of a given age will live

Answer: C
Skill: Comprehension

20) Life history strategies result from
   A) environmental pressures.
   B) natural selection.
   C) conscious choice.
   D) both A and B.
   E) A, B, and C.

Answer: D
Skill: Comprehension

21) Which of the following is a life history characteristic that would *not* be associated with big–bang reproduction?
   A) many gametes produced at reproductive maturity
   B) reproduction triggered by an unpredictable event
   C) death of the parent following reproduction
   D) repeated reproductive events over a long life span
   E) a life cycle that may require a number of years of maturing before reproduction

Answer: D
Skill: Comprehension

22) Natural selection has led to the evolution of diverse natural history strategies which have in common
   A) many offspring per reproductive episode.
   B) limitation by density–dependent limiting factors.
   C) adaptation to stable environments.
   D) maximum lifetime reproductive success.
   E) relatively large offspring.

   Answer: D
   Skill: Comprehension

23) Natural selection involves energetic trade–offs between or among life history traits such as
   A) number of offspring per reproductive episode.
   B) number of reproductive episodes per lifetime.
   C) age at first reproduction.
   D) A and C.
   E) A, B, and C.

   Answer: E
   Skill: Comprehension

24) A population of ground squirrels has an annual per capita birth rate of 0.06 and an annual per capita death rate of 0.02. Estimate the number of individuals added to (or lost from) a population of 1,000 individuals in one year.
   A) 120 individuals added
   B) 40 individuals added
   C) 20 individuals added
   D) 400 individuals added
   E) 20 individuals lost

   Answer: B
   Skill: Application

Use the following choices to answer the questions below. Each choice may be used once, more than once, or not at all.

A. $\dfrac{rN}{K}$

B. rN

C. $rN(K+N)$

D. $rN\dfrac{(K-N)}{K}$

E. $rN\dfrac{(N-K)}{K}$

25) Logistic growth of a population is represented by $dN/dt =$

   Answer: D
   Skill: Knowledge

26) Exponential growth of a population is represented by $dN/dt =$

   Answer: B
   Skill: Comprehension

27) Carrying capacity (K)
   A) is calculated as the product of annual per capita birth rate (r).
   B) remains constant in the presence of density–dependent population regulation.
   C) differs among species, but does not vary within a given species.
   D) is often determined by energy limitation.
   E) is always eventually reached in any population.

   Answer: D
   Skill: Knowledge

28) In the logistic equation $dN/dt = rN\dfrac{(K-N)}{K}$, r is a measure of the population's intrinsic rate of increase. It is determined by which of the following?

A) birth rate

B) death rate

C) density

D) both A and B

E) A, B, and C

Answer: D
Skill: Comprehension

29) As N approaches K for a certain population, which of the following is predicted by the logistic equation?

A) The growth rate will not change.

B) The growth rate will approach zero.

C) The population will show an Allee effect.

D) The population will increase exponentially.

E) The carrying capacity of the environment will increase.

Answer: B
Skill: Comprehension

30) Often the growth cycle of one population has an effect on the cycle of another—as moose populations increase, wolf populations also increase. Thus, if we are considering the logistic equation for the wolf population,

$$dN/dt = rN\frac{(K-N)}{K},$$

which of the factors accounts for the effect on the moose population?

A) r

B) N

C) rN

D) K

E) dt

Answer: D
Skill: Comprehension

31) Which of the following might be expected in the logistic model of population growth?

A) As N approaches K, b increases.

B) As N approaches K, r increases.

C) As N approaches K, d increases.

D) Both A and B are true.

E) Both B and C are true.

Answer: C
Skill: Comprehension

32) In models of sigmoidal (logistic) population growth,

A) population growth rate slows dramatically as N approaches K.

B) new individuals are added to the population most rapidly at intermediate population sizes.

C) density–dependent factors affect the rate of population growth.

D) all of the above are true.

E) A and C only are true.

Answer: D
Skill: Knowledge

33) The Allee effect is a phenomenon that occurs when population size

A) becomes too small.

B) becomes too large.

C) approaches carrying capacity.

D) exceeds carrying capacity.

E) More than one of the choices above is correct.

Answer: A
Skill: Knowledge

A   cohort
B. dispersion
C. Allee effect
D. iteroparous
E. semelparous

34) a density–dependent factor

   Answer: C
   Skill: Comprehension

35) Pacific salmon or annual plants

   Answer: E
   Skill: Knowledge

36) reproduce more than once in a lifetime

   Answer: D
   Skill: Knowledge

37) pattern of spacing for individuals within the boundaries of the population

   Answer: B
   Skill: Knowledge

38) A predator might be more likely to be spotted if a large number of prey are all together than it would be by a single prey animal.

   Answer: C
   Skill: Comprehension

39) All of the following statements about the logistic model of population growth are correct *except*:

   A) It fits an S–shaped curve.

   B) It incorporates the concept of carrying capacity.

   C) It describes population density shifts over time.

   D) It accurately predicts the growth of most populations.

   E) It predicts an eventual state in which birth rate equals death rate.

   Answer: D
   Skill: Comprehension

40) Which of the following is *true*?

   A) *K*–selection can be density independent.

   B) *r*–selection occurs in crowded environments.

   C) Different populations of the same species can exhibit either *K*– or *r*–selection.

   D) All populations of the same species are either *K*– or *r*–selected.

   E) *r*–selection tends to maximize population size, not the rate of increase in population size.

   Answer: D
   Skill: Knowledge

41) The life history traits favored by selection may vary with

   A) density–dependent selection.

   B) density–independent selection.

   C) the maximum size of a population.

   D) population density.

   E) the terms used in the logistic equation.

   Answer: D
   Skill: Comprehension

42) A species that is relatively *r*-selected might have all of the following characteristics *except*

A) a disturbed habitat.

B) small offspring.

C) parental care of offspring.

D) numerous offspring.

E) little homeostatic capability.

Answer: C
Skill: Comprehension

43) In which of the following habitats would you expect to find the largest number of *K*-selected individuals?

A) an abandoned field in Ohio

B) the sand dunes south of Lake Michigan

C) the rain forests of Brazil

D) south Florida after a hurricane

E) a newly emergent volcanic island

Answer: C
Skill: Application

44) All of the following characteristics are typical of an *r*-selected population *except*

A) it occurs in variable environments.

B) a high intrinsic rate of growth.

C) onset of reproduction at an early age.

D) extensive parental care of offspring.

E) it occurs in open habitats.

Answer: D
Skill: Comprehension

45) Which of the following characterizes relatively *K*-selected populations?

A) offspring with good chances of survival

B) many offspring per reproductive episode

C) small offspring

D) a high intrinsic rate of increase

E) early parental reproduction

Answer: A
Skill: Comprehension

46) Which of the following statements about the evolution of life histories is *correct*?

A) Stable environments with limited resources favor *r*-selected populations.

B) *K*-selected populations are most often found in environments where density-independent factors are important regulators of population size.

C) Most populations have both *r*- and *K*-selected characteristics that vary under different environmental conditions.

D) The reproductive efforts of *r*-selected populations are directed at producing just a few offspring with good competitive abilities.

E) *K*-selected populations rarely approach carrying capacity.

Answer: C
Skill: Comprehension

47) Unlimited population growth is often prevented when death rates increase as population density increases. This is an example of

A) *K*-selection.

B) *r*-selection.

C) positive feedback.

D) negative feedback.

E) the Allee effect.

Answer: D
Skill: Knowledge

48) Which of the following can contribute to density-dependent regulation of populations?

A) the accumulation of toxic wastes

B) intraspecific competition for nutrients

C) predation

D) all of the above

E) none of the above

Answer: D
Skill: Knowledge

49) Field observation suggests that populations of a particular species of herbivorous mammal undergo cyclic fluctuations in density at 3- to 5-year intervals. Which of the following represent (a) plausible explanation(s) of these cycles?

A) Periodic crowding affects the endocrine system, resulting in increased aggressiveness.

B) Increases in population density lead to increased rates of predation.

C) Increases in rates of herbivory lead to changes in the nutritive value of plants utilized as food.

D) All of the above are plausible explanations of population cycling.

E) Only B and C are plausible explanations of cycling in this population.

Answer: D
Skill: Comprehension

50) All of the following are correct statements about the regulation of populations *except:*

A) The logistic equation reflects the effect of density-dependent factors, which can ultimately stabilize populations around the carrying capacity.

B) Density-independent factors have an increasingly greater effect as a population's density increases.

C) High densities in a population may cause physiological changes that inhibit reproduction.

D) Because of the overlapping nature of population-regulating factors, it is often difficult to precisely determine their cause-and-effect relationships.

E) The occurrence of population cycles in some populations may be the result of crowding or lag times in the response to density-dependent factors.

Answer: B
Skill: Comprehension

51) In a mature forest of oak, maple, and hickory trees, a disease causes a reduction in the number of acorns produced by oak trees. Which of the following would *least* likely be a result of this?

A) There might be fewer squirrels because they feed on acorns.

B) There might be fewer mice and seed-eating birds because squirrels would eat more seeds and compete with the mice and birds.

C) There might be an increase in the number of hickory trees because the competition between hickory nuts and acorns for germination sites would be reduced or eliminated.

D) There might be fewer owls because they feed on baby squirrels, mice, and young seed-eating birds, whose populations would be reduced.

E) There might be a decrease in the number of maple seeds as the disease spreads to other trees in the forest.

Answer: E
Skill: Comprehension

52) Your friend comes to you with a problem. It seems his shrimp boats aren't catching nearly as much shrimp as they used to. He can't understand it because originally he caught all the shrimp he could handle. Each year, he added a new boat, and for a long time, each boat caught tons of shrimp. As he added more boats, there came a time when each boat caught a little less shrimp, and now, each boat is catching a lot less shrimp. Which of the following topics might help your friend understand the source of his problem?

A) density–dependent population regulation

B) logistic growth and intrinsic characteristics of population growth

C) density–independent population regulation

D) both A and B

E) A, B, and C

Answer: D
Skill: Comprehension

53) Consider several human populations of equal size and net reproductive rate, but different in age structure. The population that is likely to grow the most during the next 30 years is the one with the greatest fraction of people in which age range?

A) 50 to 60 years

B) 40 to 50 years

C) 30 to 40 years

D) 20 to 30 years

E) 10 to 20 years

Answer: E
Skill: Application

The following questions refer to Figure 52.2, which depicts the age structure of three populations.

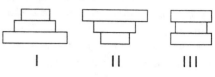

Figure 52.2

54) Which population is in the process of decreasing?

A) I only

B) II only

C) III only

D) I and II

E) II and III

Answer: B
Skill: Application

55) Which population appears to be stable?

A) I only

B) II only

C) III only

D) I and II

E) II and III

Answer: C
Skill: Application

56) Assuming these age structure diagrams describe human populations, in which population is unemployment likely to be most severe in the future?

A) I

B) II

C) III

D) No differences in the magnitude of future unemployment would be expected among these populations.

E) It is not possible to infer anything about future social conditions from age structure diagrams.

Answer: A
Skill: Application

57) Assuming these age structure diagrams describe human populations, which population is likely to experience zero population growth (ZPG)?

A) I only

B) II only

C) III only

D) I and II

E) II and III

Answer: C
Skill: Application

58) Which of the following is *not* used in calculating an ecological footprint?

A) arable land

B) pasture and forest lands

C) fossil energy land

D) demographically transitional land

E) built–up land

Answer: D
Skill: Knowledge

59) The unit(s) of measurement for an ecological footprint is (are)

A) weight of biomass per year.

B) number of species per ecosystem.

C) number of individuals per population.

D) number of people per continent.

E) area of land per person.

Answer: E
Skill: Comprehension

60) All of the following have contributed to the growth of the human population *except*

A) environmental degradation.

B) improved nutrition.

C) vaccines.

D) pesticides.

E) improved sanitation.

Answer: A
Skill: Knowledge

61) Which of the following is a density–independent factor limiting human population growth?

A) social pressure for birth control

B) earthquakes

C) plagues

D) famines

E) pollution

Answer: B
Skill: Comprehension

62) Which of the following variables is (are) important in contributing to the rapid growth of human populations?

A) the high percentage of young people

B) the average age to first give birth

C) carrying capacity of the environment

D) only A and B

E) A, B, and C

Answer: D
Skill: Comprehension

Media Activity Questions

1) The sample–plot method of determining the population density of a wild population would work best for organisms such as
   A) sharks.
   B) tuna.
   C) pine trees.
   D) mice.
   E) wolves.

   Answer: C
   Topic: Web/CD Activity 52A

2) A survivorship curve that involves producing very few offspring, each of which has a high probability of surviving to adulthood, is typical of
   A) sea stars.
   B) elephants.
   C) oysters.
   D) butterflies.
   E) mice.

   Answer: B
   Topic: Web/CD Activity 52B

3) A survivorship curve that involves producing large numbers of offspring, each with a very low probability of surviving to adulthood, is typical of
   A) humans.
   B) elephants.
   C) oysters.
   D) whales.
   E) cats.

   Answer: C
   Topic: Web/CD Activity 52B

4) In the 14th century, _____ was responsible for the death of more than one–third of the entire European population of humans.
   A) tuberculosis
   B) AIDS
   C) influenza
   D) bubonic plague
   E) pneumonia

   Answer: D
   Topic: Web/CD Activity 52C

5) If most of the individuals of a human population are in their prereproductive years, you would expect the population size to _____ after 20 years.
   A) stay the same
   B) increase
   C) decrease
   D) decrease and then stabilize
   E) decrease and then decrease more sharply

   Answer: B
   Topic: Web/CD Activity 52D

Self-Quiz Questions

Answers to these questions also appear in the textbook.

1) A uniform dispersion pattern for a population may indicate that
   A) the population is spreading out and increasing its range.
   B) resources are heterogeneously distributed.
   C) individuals of the population are competing for some resource, such as water and minerals for plants or nesting sites for animals.
   D) there is an absence of strong attractions or repulsions among individuals.
   E) the density of the population is low.

   Answer: C

2) A "cohort" in a human life table consists of
   A) people who are the same age.
   B) people who live in the same city.
   C) people of the same education level.
   D) people who have the same occupation.
   E) people who have the same number of children.

   Answer: A

3) The term $(K-N)/K$ influences dN/dt such that
   A) the increase in actual population numbers is greatest when N is small.
   B) as N approaches K, r, the intrinsic rate of increase, becomes smaller.
   C) when N equals K, population growth is zero.
   D) when K is small, the population begins growing exponentially.
   E) as N approaches K, the birth rate approaches zero.

   Answer: C

4) A population's carrying capacity is
   A) the number of individuals in that population.
   B) a constant that can be estimated for all populations.
   C) inversely related to r.
   D) the population size that can be supported by available resources for that species within the habitat.
   E) set at 8 billion for the human population.

   Answer: D

5) Which life history strategy would be favored by natural selection if survival of offspring is quite low and unpredictable?
   A) big-bang reproduction, or semelparity
   B) production of a large number of large eggs and a great deal of parental care
   C) repeated reproduction, or iteroparity
   D) very early age of first reproduction
   E) relatively late age of first reproduction

   Answer: C

6) In a mark–recapture study of a lake trout population, 40 fish were captured, marked, and released. In a second capture, 45 fish were captured; 9 of these were marked. What is the estimated number of individuals in the lake trout population?
   A) 90
   B) 200
   C) 360
   D) 800
   E) 1,800

   Answer: B

7) The population cycle of the snowshoe hare and its predator, the lynx, illustrates that

A) predators are the only factor controlling the size of prey populations.

B) the two species must have evolved in close contact because one cannot live without the other.

C) one should not conclude a cause–and–effect relationship when viewing population patterns without careful observation and experimentation.

D) both populations are controlled mainly by abiotic factors.

E) the hare population is *r*-selected, whereas the lynx population is *K*-selected.

Answer: C

8) The current size of the human population is closest to

A) 2 million.

B) 3 billion.

C) 4 billion.

D) 6 billion.

E) 10 billion.

Answer: D

9) All these descriptions are characteristic of human populations in industrialized countries *except*

A) relatively small family size.

B) several potential reproductions per lifetime.

C) *r*-selected life history.

D) Type I survivorship curve.

E) relatively even age structure.

Answer: C

10) According to the study of ecological footprints produced in 1997,

A) the carrying capacity of the world is 10 billion.

B) the carrying capacity of the world would be higher if all people became vegetarians.

C) the current demand on global resources by each industrialized country is well below the ecological capacity of those countries.

D) the United States has a larger ecological footprint than available ecological capacity of its own land.

E) a technological fix to expand the world's carrying capacity is not ecologically sound.

Answer: D

Chapter 53   Community Ecology

1) Which of the following statements is most consistent with F. E. Clements's interactive hypothesis?
   A) Species are distributed independently of other species.
   B) Communities lack discrete geographic boundaries.
   C) The community functions as an integrated unit.
   D) The composition of plant species seems to change on a continuum.
   E) The community is a chance assemblage of species.

Answer: C
Skill: Comprehension

2) All of the following statements about communities are correct *except:*
   A) Many plant species in communities seem to be independently distributed.
   B) Some animal species distributions within a community are linked to other species.
   C) The distribution of almost all organisms is probably affected to some extent by both abiotic gradients and interactions with other species.
   D) Ecologists refer to species richness as the number of species within a community.
   E) The trophic structure of a community describes abiotic factors such as rainfall and temperature affecting members of the community.

Answer: E
Skill: Comprehension

3) A biologist measures predation rates by crab spiders on flower–visiting insects in a particular field community and then experimentally removes as many of the spiders as she can. She discovers that predation rates remain the same but that the major predators shift from spiders to ambush bugs. Which of the following community structure models is most consistent with her findings?
   A) individualistic
   B) interactive
   C) rivet
   D) redundancy
   E) manipulative

Answer: D
Skill: Comprehension

4) Communities can be linked by which of the following?
   I.   predation
   II. systematics
   III. competition
   A) I only
   B) III only
   C) I and II only
   D) I and III only
   E) I, II, and III

Answer: D
Skill: Knowledge

5) Which of the following statements is consistent with the competitive exclusion principle?
    A) Bird species generally do not compete for nesting sites.
    B) The density of one competing species will have a positive impact on the population growth of the other competing species.
    C) Two species with the same fundamental niche will exclude other competing species.
    D) Even a slight reproductive advantage will eventually lead to the elimination of inferior species.
    E) Evolution tends to increase competition between related species.

Answer: D
Skill: Comprehension

6) All of the following act to increase species diversity *except*
    A) competitive exclusion.
    B) keystone predators.
    C) patchy environments.
    D) moderate disturbances.
    E) migration of populations.

Answer: A
Skill: Comprehension

7) According to the competitive exclusion principle, two species cannot continue to occupy the same
    A) habitat.
    B) niche.
    C) territory.
    D) range.
    E) biome.

Answer: B
Skill: Knowledge

Figure 53.1

8) The entire box shown in Figure 53.1 represents the niche of species A. Species A is biologically constrained from the striped area of its niche by species B. This is an example of
    A) dynamic stability.
    B) facilitation.
    C) commensalism.
    D) competitive exclusion.
    E) secondary succession.

Answer: D
Skill: Application

9) The sum total of an organism's interaction with the biotic and abiotic resources of its environment is called its
    A) habitat.
    B) logistic growth.
    C) biotic potential.
    D) microclimax.
    E) ecological niche.

Answer: E
Skill: Knowledge

10) A species of fish is found to require a certain temperature, a particular oxygen content of the water, a particular depth, and a rocky substrate on the bottom. These requirements are part of its
    A) dimensional profile.
    B) ecological niche.
    C) prime habitat.
    D) resource partition.
    E) home base.

Answer: B
Skill: Comprehension

11) Resource partitioning is best described by which of the following statements?

A) Competitive exclusion results in the success of the superior species.

B) Slight variations in niche allow similar species to coexist.

C) Two species can coevolve and share the same niche.

D) Species diversity is maintained by switching between prey species.

E) A climax community is reached when no new niches are available.

Answer: B
Skill: Knowledge

12) Two barnacles, *Balanus* and *Chthamalus*, can both survive on the lower rocks just above the low tide line on the Scottish coast, but only *Balanus* actually does so, with *Chthamalus* adopting a higher zone. Which of the following best accounts for this niche separation?

A) competitive exclusion

B) predation of *Chthamalus* by *Balanus*

C) cooperative displacement

D) primary succession

E) mutualism

Answer: A
Skill: Comprehension

13) Resource partitioning would be most likely to occur between

A) sympatric populations of a predator and its prey.

B) sympatric populations of species with similar ecological niches.

C) sympatric populations of a flowering plant and its specialized insect pollinator.

D) allopatric populations of the same animal species.

E) allopatric populations of species with similar ecological niches.

Answer: B
Skill: Comprehension

14) Dwarf mistletoes are flowering plants that grow on certain forest trees. They obtain nutrients and water from the vascular tissues of the trees. The trees derive no known benefits from the dwarf mistletoes. Which of the following best describes the interactions between dwarf mistletoes and trees?

A) mutualism

B) parasitism

C) commensalism

D) facilitation

E) competition

Answer: B
Skill: Comprehension

15) Which of the following is *not* an example of a plant defense against herbivory?

A) nicotine

B) cryptic coloration

C) spines

D) thorns

E) morphine

Answer: B
Skill: Comprehension

16) An insect that has evolved to resemble a plant twig will probably be able to avoid

A) parasitism.

B) symbiosis.

C) predation.

D) competition.

E) commensalism.

Answer: C
Skill: Comprehension

17) Which of the following is an example of cryptic coloration?

   A) bands on a coral snake

   B) brown color of tree bark

   C) markings of a viceroy butterfly

   D) colors of an insect-pollinated flower

   E) mottled coloring of peppered moths living in the unpolluted regions of England

   Answer: E
   Skill: Comprehension

18) Batesian mimicry systems involve all of the following *except*

   A) the models being noxious or disagreeable.

   B) the mimics having no defense mechanism.

   C) the ability of predators to "learn" characteristics of their prey.

   D) the models being cryptically colored.

   E) the models being easily recognized.

   Answer: D
   Skill: Comprehension

19) Which of the following is an example of Müllerian mimicry?

   A) two species of unpalatable butterfly that have the same color pattern

   B) a day-flying hawkmoth that looks like a wasp

   C) a katydid whose wings look like a dead leaf

   D) two species of rattlesnake that both rattle their tails

   E) two species of moths that have eye spots that make them look like owls

   Answer: A
   Skill: Comprehension

20) Which of the following is an example of Batesian mimicry?

   A) an insect that resembles a twig

   B) a butterfly that resembles a leaf

   C) a nonvenomous snake that looks like a venomous snake

   D) a fawn with fur coloring that camouflages it in the forest environment

   E) a snapping turtle that uses its tongue to mimic a worm, thus attracting fish

   Answer: C
   Skill: Comprehension

21) Which of the following is an example of warning coloration?

   A) stripes of a skunk

   B) eye color in humans

   C) green color of a plant

   D) colors of an insect-pollinated flower

   E) mottled coloring of peppered moths living in the unpolluted regions of England

   Answer: A
   Skill: Knowledge

22) All of the following describe possible results of competition between two species *except*

   A) competitive exclusion.

   B) warning coloration.

   C) resource partitioning.

   D) reduction in the population of one species.

   E) reduction in the populations of both species.

   Answer: B
   Skill: Comprehension

23) All of the following are terms that ecologists use to describe communities *except*

   A) species richness.

   B) species diversity.

   C) Batesian diversity.

   D) trophic structure.

   E) stability.

   Answer: C
   Skill: Comprehension

24) Two species of insects from different geographic areas display characteristic black and red stripes. Which of the following is *unlikely* to be related to this phenomenon?

   A) warning coloration

   B) convergent evolution

   C) common ancestry

   D) mimicry

   E) antipredator defense

   Answer: D
   Skill: Comprehension

25) A palatable fly that avoids predation by appearing to be a predaceous wasp is an example of a

   A) Batesian mimic.

   B) Batesian model.

   C) Müllerian mimic.

   D) Müllerian model.

   E) None of the above is correct.

   Answer: A
   Skill: Comprehension

26) Which of the following is *least* likely to kill the organism it feeds on?

   A) herbivore

   B) predator

   C) seed eater

   D) carnivore

   E) parasite

   Answer: E
   Skill: Comprehension

27) All of the following represent ways that animals defend themselves against predators *except*

   A) incorporating plant toxins into their tissues.

   B) cryptic coloration.

   C) mobbing.

   D) interspecific competition.

   E) hiding or fleeing.

   Answer: D
   Skill: Comprehension

28) Evidence shows that some grasses benefit from being grazed. Which of the following terms would best describe this plant–herbivore interaction?

   A) mutualism

   B) commensalism

   C) parasitism

   D) competition

   E) predation

   Answer: A
   Skill: Comprehension

29) Which of the following terms best describes the interaction between termites and the protozoans that feed in their gut?

   A) commensalism

   B) mutualism

   C) competitive exclusion

   D) ectoparasitism

   E) endoparasitism

   Answer: B
   Skill: Knowledge

30) Which of the following types of species interaction is *incorrectly* paired to its effects on the density of the two interacting populations?

 A) predation—one increases, one decreases

 B) parasitism—one increases, one decreases

 C) commensalism—both increase

 D) mutualism—both increase

 E) competition—both decrease

Answer: C
Skill: Comprehension

31) With a few exceptions, most of the food chains studied by ecologists have a maximum of how many links?

 A) two

 B) three

 C) five

 D) ten

 E) fifteen

Answer: C
Skill: Knowledge

32) Which of the following members of a marine food chain is most analogous to a grasshopper in a terrestrial food chain?

 A) phytoplankton

 B) zooplankton

 C) detritivore

 D) fish

 E) shark

Answer: B
Skill: Comprehension

33) Consider a field plot containing 200 kg of plant material. How many kg of carnivore production can be supported?

 A) 200

 B) 100

 C) 20

 D) 10

 E) 2

Answer: E
Skill: Application

34) The energetic hypothesis and dynamic stability hypothesis are explanations to account for

 A) plant defenses against herbivores.

 B) the length of food chains.

 C) the evolution of mutualism.

 D) resource partitioning.

 E) the competitive exclusion principle.

Answer: B
Skill: Knowledge

35) In a tide pool, 15 species of invertebrates were reduced to eight after one species was removed. The species removed was likely a(n)

 A) community facilitator.

 B) keystone predator.

 C) herbivore.

 D) resource partitioner.

 E) mutualistic organism.

Answer: B
Skill: Application

36) All of the following statements about community interactions are correct *except*:

A) Closely related species may be able to coexist if there is at least one significant difference in their niches.

B) Plants can defend themselves against herbivores by the production of compounds that are irritating or toxic.

C) Keystone predators reduce diversity in a community by holding down or wiping out prey populations.

D) Mutualism is an important biotic interaction that occurs in communities.

E) Some predators use mimicry to attract prey.

Answer: C
Skill: Comprehension

37) Elephants are not the most common species in African grasslands. The grasslands contain scattered woody plants, but they are kept in check by the uprooting activities of the elephants. Take away the elephants, and the grasslands convert to forests or to shrublands. The newly growing forests support fewer species than the previous grasslands. Elephants can be defined as what type of species in this community?

A) redundant

B) dominant

C) keystone

D) dominant and keystone

E) none of the above

Answer: C
Skill: Comprehension

38) Which of the following statements concerning the control of community structure is *not* true?

A) A bottom–up community is controlled by nutrients.

B) A top-down community is controlled by predators.

C) Increasing the biomass of vegetation in a bottom–up community will increase herbivores.

D) Increasing the biomass of vegetation in a bottom–up community will increase predators.

E) Increasing the number of predators in a top-down community will decrease the biomass of vegetation.

Answer: E
Skill: Comprehension

39) Which of the following is considered by ecologists a measure of the ability of a community either to resist change or to recover to its original state after change?

A) stability

B) succession

C) partitioning

D) productivity

E) competitive exclusion

Answer: A
Skill: Knowledge

40) According to the nonequilibrial model,

A) communities will remain in a state of equilibrium in the absence of human activities.

B) community structure remains constant in the absence of interspecific competition.

C) communities are assemblages of closely linked species that function as tightly integrated units.

D) interspecific interactions induce changes in community composition over time.

E) communities are constantly changing after being affected by disturbances.

Answer: E
Skill: Knowledge

41) Which of the following statements about the Yellowstone fires of 1988 is *not* true?

A) Secondary succession followed the fires.

B) The dominant lodgepole pines require fire to complete their normal life history.

C) Human environmental policy increased the severity of the fires.

D) It took years before new vegetation returned to the area.

E) Severe drought helped to trigger the fires.

Answer: D
Skill: Knowledge

42) Disturbances to biological communities

A) are frequently related to human activities.

B) can remove organisms and alter resource availability.

C) can create vacated ecological niches that other species can colonize.

D) All of the above are true.

E) A and B only are true.

Answer: D
Skill: Knowledge

43) What is it called when established species in a community make their environment more favorable for competitors than for later species?

A) coevolution

B) competitive exclusion

C) facilitation

D) inhibition

E) competitive replacement

Answer: C
Skill: Knowledge

44) When lichens grow on bare rock they may eventually accumulate enough organic material around them to supply the foothold for later rooted vegetation. These early pioneering lichens can be said to do what to the later arrivals?

A) tolerate

B) inhibit

C) facilitate

D) exclude

E) concentrate

Answer: C
Skill: Comprehension

45) In a particular case of secondary succession, three species of wild grass all invaded a field the first growing season after a farmer abandoned the field. By the second season, a single one of the wild grasses dominated the field. A possible factor in this succession was

A) equilibrium.

B) facilitation.

C) immigration.

D) inhibition.

E) mutualism.

Answer: D
Skill: Comprehension

The next questions refer to the following list of terms. Each term may be used once, more than once, or not at all.

A. parasitism
B. mutualism
C. inhibition
D. facilitation
E. commensalism

46) the relationship existing between ants and acacia trees

Answer: B
Skill: Knowledge

47) the relationship existing between cattle egrets and cattle

Answer: E
Skill: Knowledge

48) the relationship existing between legumes and nitrogen-fixing bacteria

Answer: B
Skill: Knowledge

49) successional event in which one organism makes the environment more suitable for another organism

Answer: D
Skill: Knowledge

50) the relationship between aphids and plants

Answer: A
Skill: Knowledge

51) Following clear–cutting of a deciduous forest several hundred years ago, the land was colonized by herbaceous species which, over time, were replaced largely by shrubs, then by forest trees. Assuming the growth of the shrubs and trees was enhanced by the soil–holding properties of the herbaceous plants, which of the following processes best describe the progression from herbaceous plants to forest trees?

A) primary succession; facilitation

B) primary succession; inhibition

C) primary succession; toleration

D) secondary succession; facilitation

E) secondary succession; inhibition

Answer: D
Skill: Comprehension

52) Which of the following statements about succession is *correct*?

A) Secondary succession occurs where no soil exists.

B) Primary succession occurs in areas where soil remains after a disturbance.

C) Secondary succession can occur where a disturbance has left soil intact.

D) Some cases of succession involve facilitation, a phenomenon in which species inhibit the growth of newcomers.

E) Through successional dynamics, most communities will eventually become more stable through time.

Answer: C
Skill: Comprehension

53) What does the species richness of a community refer to?

A) the number of food chains

B) the number of different species

C) the energy content of all species

D) the relative numbers of individuals in each species

E) the total number of all organisms

Answer: B
Skill: Knowledge

54) To measure biodiversity in a community you need to know

A) the number of species.

B) the relative abundance of each species.

C) the physical size of each species.

D) both A and B.

E) A, B, and C.

Answer: D
Skill: Knowledge

55) Species richness increases

A) as one travels north from the equator.

B) as one travels north from the South Pole.

C) on islands as island distance from the mainland increases.

D) as rates of evapotranspiration decrease.

E) as community size decreases.

Answer: B
Skill: Comprehension

56) In conservation biology, species–area curves for key taxa make it possible to predict

A) the size of an area that needs to be sampled.

B) the area that a keystone species will occupy.

C) whether or not a redundancy model will apply to a given area.

D) how the loss of a certain area of habitat is likely to affect biodiversity.

E) whether or not an area will reach equilibrium.

Answer: D
Skill: Knowledge

The following questions refer to the diagram in Figure 53.2 of five islands formed at about the same time near a particular mainland.

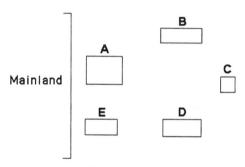

Figure 53.2

57) island with the greatest number of species

Answer: A
Skill: Application

58) island with the least number of species

Answer: C
Skill: Application

59) island with the lowest extinction rate

Answer: A
Skill: Application

60) island with the lowest immigration rate

Answer: C
Skill: Application

61) According to the theory of island biogeography, all of the following contribute to greater species diversity on an island *except*

A) a relatively recent formation of the island.

B) a shorter distance of the island from the mainland.

C) a bigger island.

D) a lower extinction rate on the island.

E) higher rates of migration to and from the island.

Answer: A
Skill: Comprehension

62) All of the following statements about the biogeographical aspects of diversity are correct *except:*

A) The patterns of continental drift are important considerations in the study of the past and present distributions of species.

B) The magnitude of photosynthesis is the factor that accounts for the major variations in species diversity over Earth's large areas.

C) Species richness on an island reaches an equilibrium point when immigration equals extinction.

D) A species may be limited to a particular range because it never dispersed beyond that range, or it dispersed but failed to survive in other locations.

E) Island biogeographical theory applies to the relatively short period of time when colonization is the important process determining species composition; over a longer time, actual speciation affects the composition.

Answer: B
Skill: Comprehension

Media Activity Questions

1) An owl and a hawk both eat mice. Which of these terms describes the relationship between a hawk and an owl?

   A) predation

   B) competition

   C) parasitism

   D) commensalism

   E) mutualism

   Answer: B
   Topic: Web/CD Activity 53A

2) Within an ecosystem, a tree is a

   A) secondary consumer.

   B) detritivore.

   C) tertiary consumer.

   D) primary consumer.

   E) producer.

   Answer: E
   Topic: Web/CD Activity 53B

3) When you eat lettuce, you are acting as a

   A) producer.

   B) primary consumer.

   C) secondary consumer.

   D) tertiary consumer.

   E) detritivore.

   Answer: B
   Topic: Web/CD Activity 53B

4) According to island biogeography, the farther an island is from the mainland, the

   A) smaller the island.

   B) larger the island.

   C) fewer the number of endemic species.

   D) lower the rate of colonization.

   E) higher the rate of colonization.

   Answer: D
   Topic: Web/CD Activity 53D

5) According to island biogeography, the larger an island, the

   A) less the species richness.

   B) greater the species richness.

   C) less the diversity of available habitats.

   D) farther it is from the nearest mainland.

   E) closer it is to the nearest mainland.

   Answer: B
   Topic: Web/CD Activity 53D

Self-Quiz Questions

Answers to these questions also appear in the textbook.

1) The concept of trophic structure of a community emphasizes the
   A) prevalent form of vegetation.
   B) keystone predator.
   C) feeding relationships within a community.
   D) effects of coevolution.
   E) species richness of the community.

   Answer: C

2) According to the concept of competitive exclusion,
   A) two species cannot coexist in the same habitat.
   B) extinction or emigration are the only possible results of competitive interactions.
   C) competition within a population results in the success of the best-adapted individuals.
   D) two species cannot share the exact same niche in a community.
   E) resource partitioning will allow a species to utilize all the resources of its niche.

   Answer: D

3) The effect of a keystone predator within a community may be to
   A) competitively exclude other predators from the community.
   B) maintain species diversity by preying on the prey species that is the dominant competitor.
   C) increase the relative abundance of other predators.
   D) encourage the coevolution of predator and prey adaptations.
   E) create nonequilibrium in species diversity.

   Answer: B

4) Food chains are relatively short in communities because
   A) two herbivore species may not feed on the same plant species.
   B) local extinction of one species dooms all the other species in a food web.
   C) energy is lost as it passes from one trophic level to the next higher level.
   D) very few predatory species have evolved.
   E) most plant species are inedible.

   Answer: C

5) According to the rivet model of community organization,
   A) two closely related species cannot coexist in the same community.
   B) extinction is rare in well-organized communities.
   C) species can be easily replaced if one should be driven extinct by human actions.
   D) all species in a natural community contribute to its integrity.
   E) communities are loosely structured groups of individualistic species with similar abiotic requirements.

   Answer: D

6) An example of cryptic coloration is the
   A) green color of a plant.
   B) bright markings of a poisonous tropical frog.
   C) stripes of a skunk.
   D) mottled coloring of moths that rest on lichens.
   E) bright colors of an insect-pollinated flower.

   Answer: D

7) An example of Müllerian mimicry is

A) a butterfly that resembles a leaf.

B) two poisonous frogs that resemble each other in coloration.

C) a minnow with spots that look like large eyes.

D) a beetle that resembles a scorpion.

E) a carnivorous fish with a wormlike tongue that lures prey.

Answer: B

8) Predation and parasitism are similar in that both can be characterized as

A) +/+ interactions.

B) +/- interactions.

C) +/0 interactions.

D) -/- interactions.

E) symbiotic interactions.

Answer: B

9) Which of the following is the best explanation for the finding that equatorial (tropical) regions have the greatest species richness?

A) the species–area curve that predicts high richness in large areas

B) a climate with high levels of solar radiation and water availability

C) the increased speed of speciation due to higher temperatures in the region

D) the inverse relationship between evapotranspiration and biodiversity

E) the greater immigration rate and lower extinction rate found on large tropical islands close to the mainland

Answer: B

10) According to the hypothesis of island biogeography, species richness would be greatest on an island that is

A) small and remote.

B) large and remote.

C) large and close to a mainland.

D) small and close to a mainland.

E) environmentally homogeneous.

Answer: C

1) A cow's herbivorous diet indicates that it
   is a(n)
   A) primary consumer.
   B) secondary consumer.
   C) decomposer.
   D) autotroph.
   E) producer.

   Answer: A
   Skill: Knowledge

2) Which of the following organisms fix
   nitrogen in aquatic ecosystems?
   A) cyanobacteria
   B) chemoautotrophs
   C) phytoplankton
   D) legumes
   E) fungi

   Answer: A
   Skill: Knowledge

3) Which of the following statements is (are)
   true?
   A) An ecosystem's trophic structure
      determines the rate at which energy
      cycles within the system.
   B) At any point in time, it is impossible
      for consumers to outnumber producers
      in an ecosystem.
   C) Chemoautotrophic prokaryotes near
      deep-sea vents are primary producers.
   D) There has been a well-documented
      increase in atmospheric carbon dioxide
      over the past several decades.
   E) Both C and D are true.

   Answer: E
   Skill: Knowledge

4) Production, consumption, and
   decomposition are important ecosystem
   processes. Organisms in which of the
   following taxa perform decomposition?
   A) bacteria
   B) vertebrates
   C) invertebrates
   D) A and C
   E) A, B, and C

   Answer: E
   Skill: Knowledge

5) Organisms in which of the following taxa
   are responsible for most of the conversion
   of organic materials into inorganic
   compounds that can be utilized in primary
   production?
   A) autotrophs
   B) bacteria
   C) fungi
   D) B and C
   E) A, B, and C

   Answer: D
   Skill: Knowledge

*Use Figure 54.1 to answer the following questions. Examine
this food web for a particular terrestrial ecosystem. Each
letter is a species. The arrows represent energy flow.*

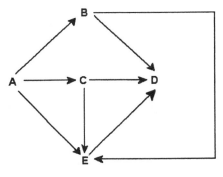

Figure 54.1

6) Which species is autotrophic?

   Answer: A
   Skill: Comprehension

7) Which species is most likely the decomposer?

Answer: E
Skill: Comprehension

8) A toxic pollutant would probably reach its highest concentration in which species?

Answer: D
Skill: Comprehension

9) Species C makes its predators sick. Which species is most likely to benefit from being a mimic of C?

Answer: B
Skill: Application

10) Excluding the decomposer, biomass would probably be smallest for which species?

Answer: D
Skill: Comprehension

11) The main decomposers in an ecosystem are
   A) fungi.
   B) plants.
   C) insects.
   D) prokaryotes.
   E) A and B.

Answer: E
Skill: Knowledge

12) The fundamental difference between materials and energy is that
   A) materials are cycled through ecosystems; energy is not.
   B) energy is cycled through ecosystems; materials are not.
   C) energy can be converted into materials; materials cannot be converted into energy.
   D) materials can be converted into energy; energy cannot be converted into materials.
   E) ecosystems are much more efficient in their transfer of energy than in their transfer of materials.

Answer: A
Skill: Comprehension

13) The concept that energy cannot cycle through an ecosystem is best explained by
   A) the law of conservation of energy.
   B) the second law of thermodynamics.
   C) the competitive exclusion principle.
   D) the Green World hypothesis.
   E) the principle of biomagnification.

Answer: B
Skill: Comprehension

14) Subtraction of which of the following will convert gross primary productivity into net primary productivity?
   A) the energy contained in the standing crop
   B) the energy used by heterotrophs in respiration
   C) the energy used by autotrophs in respiration
   D) the energy fixed by photosynthesis
   E) all solar energy

Answer: C
Skill: Comprehension

15) The difference between net and gross primary productivity would likely be greatest for

A) phytoplankton in the ocean.

B) corn plants in a farmer's field.

C) prairie grasses.

D) an oak tree in a forest.

E) sphagnum moss in a bog.

Answer: D
Skill: Comprehension

16) Which of these ecosystems accounts for the largest amount of Earth's primary productivity?

A) tundra

B) savanna

C) salt marsh

D) open ocean

E) tropical rain forest

Answer: D
Skill: Knowledge

17) The producers in ecosystems include which of the following?

I.   prokaryotes

II. algae

III. plants

A) I only

B) II only

C) III only

D) I and III only

E) I, II, and III

Answer: E
Skill: Knowledge

18) Which of these ecosystems has the highest primary productivity per square meter?

A) savanna

B) open ocean

C) boreal forest

D) tropical rain forest

E) temperate forest

Answer: D
Skill: Comprehension

19) The total biomass of photosynthetic autotrophs present in an ecosystem is known as the

A) gross primary productivity.

B) standing crop.

C) net primary productivity.

D) secondary productivity.

E) trophic efficiency.

Answer: B
Skill: Knowledge

20) Aquatic primary productivity is often limited by which of the following?

I.   light

II. nutrients

III. pressure

A) II only

B) III only

C) I and II only

D) II and III only

E) I, II, and III

Answer: C
Skill: Comprehension

21) The highest primary productivity occurs in the open ocean rather than other ecosystems. Why?

A) It contains greater concentrations of nutrients.

B) It receives a greater amount of solar energy per unit area.

C) It has the greatest total area.

D) It contains more species of organisms

E) Its producers are generally much smaller than its consumers.

Answer: C
Skill: Knowledge

22) Compared with the open ocean, marine life is especially abundant and diverse near the shore because
   A) the open ocean is too salty.
   B) the water is calmer near the shore.
   C) the water is warmer near the shore.
   D) there is less competition for light near the shore.
   E) inorganic nutrients are more plentiful near the shore.

Answer: E
Skill: Knowledge

23) The amount of chemical energy in consumers' food that is converted to their own new biomass is called the
   A) biomass.
   B) standing crop.
   C) biomagnification.
   D) primary production.
   E) secondary production.

Answer: E
Skill: Knowledge

24) Organisms in which of the following groups can be primary producers?
   A) cyanobacteria
   B) zooplankton
   C) flowering plants
   D) A and C
   E) A, B, and C

Answer: D
Skill: Knowledge

25) Aquatic ecosystems are *unlikely* to be limited by insufficient
   A) nitrogen.
   B) carbon.
   C) phosphorus.
   D) iron.
   E) More than one of the above is correct.

Answer: B
Skill: Comprehension

26) Trophic efficiency is
   A) the ratio of net secondary production to assimilation of primary production.
   B) the percentage of production transferred from one trophic level to the next.
   C) the ratio of net production at one trophic level to the net production at the level below, expressed as a percent.
   D) usually greater than production efficiencies.
   E) both B and C.

Answer: E
Skill: Comprehension

27) If you had a large quantity of excess grain and wanted to convert it into the greatest amount of animal biomass, to what would you feed it?
   A) chickens
   B) mice
   C) cattle
   D) carp (a type of fish)
   E) mealworms (larval insects)

Answer: E
Skill: Comprehension

28) Which of the following is primarily responsible for limiting the number of trophic levels in most ecosystems?
   A) Many primary and higher-order consumers are opportunistic feeders.
   B) Most predators require large home ranges.
   C) Nutrient cycles involve both abiotic and biotic components of ecosystems.
   D) Nutrient cycling rates tend to be limited by decomposition.
   E) Each energy transfer is less than 100% efficient.

Answer: E
Skill: Comprehension

29) In general, the total biomass in a terrestrial ecosystem will be greatest for which trophic level?

A) producers

B) herbivores

C) primary consumers

D) tertiary consumers

E) secondary consumers

Answer: A
Skill: Knowledge

30) Some aquatic ecosystems can have inverted biomass pyramids because

A) phytoplankton are much larger than zooplankton.

B) phytoplankton have a relatively short turnover time.

C) consumption of phytoplankton by zooplankton is so rapid that the standing crop of phytoplankton remains relatively low.

D) both B and C are true.

E) A, B, and C are true.

Answer: D
Skill: Knowledge

31) Which of the following terms actually encompasses all of the others?

A) heterotrophs

B) herbivores

C) carnivores

D) primary consumers

E) secondary consumers

Answer: A
Skill: Comprehension

Refer to Figure 54.2, a diagram of a food web, for the following questions. (Arrows represent energy flow and letters represent species.)

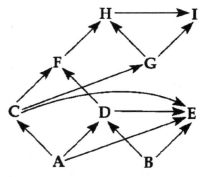

Figure 54.2

32) If this were a terrestrial food web, the combined biomass of C + D would probably be

A) greater than the biomass of A.

B) less than the biomass of H.

C) greater than the biomass of B.

D) less than the biomass of A + B.

E) less than the biomass of E.

Answer: D
Skill: Comprehension

33) If this were a marine food web, the smallest organism might be

A) A.

B) F.

C) C.

D) I.

E) E.

Answer: A
Skill: Application

34) Which species might be described as an omnivore?

A) F

B) B

C) I

D) D

E) E

Answer: E
Skill: Application

35) For most terrestrial ecosystems, pyramids of numbers, biomass, and energy are essentially the same: They have a broad base and a narrow top. The primary reason for this pattern is that

A) secondary consumers and top carnivores require less energy than producers.

B) at each step, energy is lost from the system as a result of keeping the organisms alive.

C) as materials pass through ecosystems, some of them are lost to the environment.

D) biomagnification of toxic materials limits the secondary consumers and top carnivores.

E) top carnivores and secondary consumers have a more general diet than primary producers.

Answer: B
Skill: Comprehension

36) Which of the following pyramids *cannot* possibly be inverted?

A) production

B) biomass

C) numbers

D) both A and B

E) A, B, and C

Answer: A
Skill: Comprehension

37) Which of the following situations is consistent with the Green World hypothesis?

A) Milkweed plants are eaten by monarch caterpillars.

B) Some gypsy moths cannot feed and die because others have defoliated the trees in the area.

C) Webworms cooperate with each other to build a protective silken structure around themselves.

D) A mild winter improves the survival rate of overwintering cutworms.

E) Grasshoppers in a corn field are killed by a viral infection.

Answer: E
Skill: Comprehension

The following questions refer to the organisms in a grassland ecosystem listed below. Each term may be used once, more than once, or not at all.

A. hawks
B. snakes
C. shrews
D. grasshoppers
E. grass

38) an autotroph

Answer: E
Skill: Comprehension

39) an herbivore

Answer: D
Skill: Comprehension

40) smallest biomass

Answer: A
Skill: Comprehension

41) tertiary consumer

Answer: B
Skill: Comprehension

42) probably the highest internal concentration of toxic pollutants

Answer: A
Skill: Comprehension

43) All of the following statements about energy flow are correct *except:*

A) Secondary productivity declines with each trophic level.

B) Only net primary productivity is available to consumers.

C) About 90% of the energy at one trophic level does not appear at the next.

D) Eating meat is probably the most efficient way of acquiring the energy of photosynthetic productivity.

E) Only about one-thousandth of the chemical energy fixed by photosynthesis actually reaches a tertiary–level consumer.

Answer: D
Skill: Comprehension

44) Many homeowners mow their lawns during the summer and collect the clippings, which are then hauled to the local landfill. Which of the following would comprise an alternative that would cause the least disturbance to local ecosystems?

A) Don't mow the lawn—have a sheep graze on it and put the sheep's feces into the landfill.

B) Collect the clippings and burn them.

C) Either collect the clippings and add them to a compost pile, or don't collect the clippings and let them decompose in the lawn.

D) Collect the clippings and wash them into the nearest storm sewer that feeds into the local lake.

E) Dig up the lawn and cover the yard with asphalt.

Answer: C
Skill: Comprehension

45) To recycle nutrients, the minimum an ecosystem must have is

A) producers.

B) producers and decomposers.

C) producers, primary consumers, and decomposers.

D) producers, primary consumers, secondary consumers, and decomposers.

E) producers, primary consumers, secondary consumers, top carnivores, and decomposers.

Answer: B
Skill: Comprehension

46) Nitrogen is available to plants only in the form of

A) ammonium.

B) nitrite.

C) nitrate.

D) A and C.

E) A, B, and C.

Answer: D
Skill: Knowledge

47) All organisms capable of fixing nitrogen belong to the group

A) Protista.

B) Archaea.

C) Fungi.

D) Plantae.

E) Animalia.

Answer: B
Skill: Knowledge

48) In the nitrogen cycle, the bacteria that replenish the atmosphere with N_2 are

A) *Rhizobium* bacteria.

B) nitrifying bacteria.

C) denitrifying bacteria.

D) methanogenic protozoans.

E) nitrogen–fixing bacteria.

Answer: C
Skill: Knowledge

49) How does phosphorus normally enter the atmosphere?
   A) respiration
   B) photosynthesis
   C) rock weathering
   D) geological uplifting (subduction and vulcanism)
   E) It does not enter the atmosphere in biologically significant amounts.

   Answer: E
   Skill: Knowledge

50) Which of the following statements is *correct* about biogeochemical cycling?
   A) The phosphorus cycle involves the rapid recycling of atmospheric phosphorus.
   B) The phosphorus cycle is a sedimentary cycle that involves the weathering of rocks.
   C) The carbon cycle is a localized cycle that primarily reflects the burning of fossil fuels.
   D) The carbon cycle has maintained a constant atmospheric concentration of CO_2 for the past million years.
   E) The nitrogen cycle involves movement of nitrogen in which very little of it is chemically altered by either the biotic or abiotic components of the ecosystem.

   Answer: B
   Skill: Knowledge

51) Long-term ecological research at the Hubbard Brook Experimental Forest indicates that
   A) intensive logging can dramatically increase levels of nitrate and calcium ions retained in the soil.
   B) the amount of nutrients leaving an intact forest ecosystem is controlled by the plants themselves.
   C) selective logging can actually increase species richness in deciduous forests.
   D) two of the above are true.
   E) all of the above are true.

   Answer: B
   Skill: Knowledge

52) Human-induced modifications of the nitrogen cycle can result in
   A) eutrophication of freshwater ecosystems.
   B) increased availability of fixed nitrogen to primary producers.
   C) accumulation of toxic levels of nitrates in groundwater.
   D) depletion of atmospheric ozone.
   E) all of the above.

   Answer: E
   Skill: Knowledge

53) The high levels of pesticides found in birds of prey is an example of
   A) eutrophication.
   B) predation.
   C) biological magnification.
   D) the Green World hypothesis.
   E) chemical cycling through an ecosystem.

   Answer: C
   Skill: Knowledge

54) If the flow of energy in an Arctic ecosystem goes through a simple food chain from seaweeds to fish to seals to polar bears, then which of the following is *true*?

A) Polar bears can provide more food for Eskimos than seals can.

B) The total energy content of the seaweeds is lower than that of the seals.

C) Polar bear meat probably contains the highest concentrations of fat–soluble toxins.

D) Seals are more numerous than fish.

E) The carnivores can provide more food for the Eskimos than the herbivores can.

Answer: C
Skill: Application

55) When levels of CO_2 are experimentally increased, C_3 plants generally respond with a greater increase in productivity than C_4 plants. This is because

A) C_3 plants are more efficient in their use of CO_2.

B) C_3 plants are able to obtain the same amount of CO_2 by keeping their stomata open for shorter periods of time.

C) C_4 plants don't use CO_2 as their source of carbon.

D) the rate of photosynthesis is limited more by CO_2 in C_3 plants than in C_4 plants.

E) both B and D are correct.

Answer: D
Skill: Comprehension

The following questions refer to the terms below. Each term may be used once, more than once, or not at all.

A. Green World hypothesis
B. turnover
C. biological magnification
D. greenhouse effect
E. cultural eutrophication

56) increased concentrations of CO_2 in the atmosphere

Answer: D
Skill: Comprehension

57) caused by excessive nutrient input into lakes

Answer: E
Skill: Comprehension

58) caused excessive levels of DDT in fish–eating birds

Answer: C
Skill: Comprehension

59) occurs at a high rate for nutrients in tropical rain forests

Answer: B
Skill: Comprehension

60) All of the following are likely results of land–clearing operations such as deforestation and agricultural activity *except*

A) destruction of plant and animal habitats.

B) erosion of soil due to increased water runoff.

C) leaching of minerals from the soil.

D) rapid eutrophication of streams and lakes.

E) decreased carbon dioxide in the atmosphere.

Answer: E
Skill: Comprehension

Media Activity Questions

1) Which of these terms applies to organisms that produce the organic molecules needed by all living things?

   A) producers

   B) primary consumers

   C) secondary consumers

   D) tertiary consumers

   E) detritivores

   Answer: A
   Topic: Web/CD Activity 54A

2) On Earth, most organic molecules are produced by

   A) photorespiration.

   B) photosynthesis.

   C) glycolysis.

   D) hydrolysis.

   E) cellular respiration.

   Answer: B
   Topic: Web/CD Activity 54B

3) Which of these processes removes carbon dioxide from the atmosphere?

   A) death

   B) decomposition

   C) burning

   D) cellular respiration

   E) photosynthesis

   Answer: E
   Topic: Web/CD Activity 54C

4) Denitrifying bacteria convert _____ to _____.

   A) ammonium ... nitrogen gas

   B) nitrates ... nitrogen gas

   C) nitrogen gas ... nitrates

   D) nitrogen gas ... ammonium

   E) nitrogen gas ... nitrites

   Answer: B
   Topic: Web/CD Activity 54D

5) Proteins are converted into ammonia by

   A) decomposers.

   B) tertiary consumers.

   C) secondary consumers.

   D) producers.

   E) primary consumers.

   Answer: A
   Topic: Web/CD Activity 54E

Self-Quiz Questions

Answers to these questions also appear in the textbook.

1) Which of the following organisms is *incorrectly* paired with its trophic level?

   A) cyanobacteria—primary producer

   B) grasshopper—primary consumer

   C) zooplankton—secondary consumer

   D) eagle—tertiary consumer

   E) fungi—detritivore

   Answer: C

2) One of the lessons from a pyramid of production is that

   A) only one-half of the energy in one trophic level is passed on to the next level.

   B) most of the energy from one trophic level is incorporated into the biomass of the next level.

   C) the energy lost as heat or lost in cellular respiration is 10% of the available energy of each trophic level.

   D) production efficiency is highest for primary consumers.

   E) eating grain-fed beef is an inefficient means of obtaining the energy trapped by photosynthesis.

   Answer: E

3) The role of decomposers in the nitrogen cycle is to

   A) fix N_2 into ammonia.

   B) release ammonia from organic compounds, thus returning it to the soil.

   C) denitrify ammonia, thus returning N_2 to the atmosphere.

   D) convert ammonia to nitrate, which can then be absorbed by plants.

   E) incorporate nitrogen into amino acids and organic compounds.

   Answer: B

4) The Hubbard Brook Experimental Forest study demonstrated all of the following *except* that

   A) most minerals were recycled within a forest ecosystem.

   B) mineral inflow and outflow within a natural watershed were nearly balanced.

   C) deforestation resulted in an increase in water runoff.

   D) the nitrate concentration in waters draining the deforested area became dangerously high.

   E) deforestation caused a large increase in the density of soil bacteria.

   Answer: E

5) The recent increase in atmospheric CO_2 concentration is mainly a result of an increase in

   A) primary production.

   B) the biosphere's biomass.

   C) the absorption of infrared radiation escaping from Earth.

   D) the burning of fossil fuels and wood.

   E) cellular respiration by the exploding human population.

   Answer: D

6) Which of the following is a result of biological magnification?

   A) Top-level predators may be most harmed by toxic environmental chemicals.

   B) DDT has spread throughout every ecosystem and is found in almost every organism.

   C) The greenhouse effect will be most significant at the poles.

   D) Energy is lost at each trophic level of a food chain.

   E) Many nutrients are being removed from agricultural lands and shunted into aquatic ecosystems.

   Answer: A

7) Which of these ecosystems has the lowest primary production per square meter?

   A) a salt marsh

   B) an open ocean

   C) a coral reef

   D) a grassland

   E) a tropical rain forest

   Answer: B

8) Quantities of mineral nutrients in soils of tropical rain forests are relatively low because

   A) the standing crop is small.

   B) microorganisms that recycle chemicals are not very abundant in tropical soils.

   C) the decomposition of organic refuse and reassimilation of chemicals by plants occur rapidly.

   D) nutrient cycles occur at a relatively slow rate in tropical soils.

   E) the high temperatures destroy the nutrients.

   Answer: C

9) Coastal water polluted with phosphate and nitrogenous compounds from duck farms showed detectable levels of phosphates but not nitrogen. In experiments, algae were grown in water samples that were controls or enriched with phosphate or ammonium. The greatest algal growth was observed in the nitrogen–enriched samples; phosphate–enriched and control samples both had similar growth. From these results, one could conclude that

   A) reducing the levels of phosphate in these waters will not help reduce phytoplankton production.

   B) adding nitrogen to these waters will help reduce eutrophication.

   C) the high levels of phosphates in the water are helping to control algal growth.

   D) nitrogen is the limiting nutrient in these waters.

   E) both A and D are reasonable conclusions.

   Answer: E

10) Which of the following contributes *most* to the rate of chemical cycling in an ecosystem?

   A) the rate of primary production

   B) the efficiency of secondary production

   C) the rate of decomposition

   D) the trophic efficiency of the ecosystem

   E) the location of available nutrients in inorganic or organic compartments

   Answer: C

Chapter 55   Conservation Biology

1) The total number of extant species is approximately
   A) 1,000 to 50,000.
   B) 50,000 to 150,000.
   C) 500,000 to 1,000,000.
   D) 10,000,000 to 80,000,000.
   E) 5–10 billion.

   Answer: D
   Skill: Knowledge

2) Which of the following most directly relates to the current biodiversity crisis?
   A) increased atmospheric carbon dioxide
   B) ozone depletion
   C) the rate of extinction
   D) introduced species
   E) zoned reserves

   Answer: D
   Skill: Comprehension

3) Which of the following terms includes all of the others?
   A) species diversity
   B) biodiversity
   C) genetic diversity
   D) ecosystem diversity

   Answer: B
   Skill: Knowledge

4) In order to better understand the extent of current extinctions it will be necessary to do which of the following?
   A) Monitor atmospheric carbon dioxide levels.
   B) Differentiate between plant extinction and animal extinction.
   C) Focus intensely on identifying more species of mammals and birds.
   D) Identify more of the yet unknown species of organisms on our planet.
   E) Use the average extinction rates of vertebrates as a baseline.

   Answer: D
   Skill: Comprehension

5) Estimates of current rates of extinction
   A) indicate that we have reached a state of unstable equilibrium in which speciation and extinction rates are approximately equal.
   B) suggest that one–half of all animal and plant species may be gone by the year 2100.
   C) indicate that rates may be 1,000 times higher than at any other time in the last 100,000 years.
   D) B and C only are true.
   E) A, B, and C are true.

   Answer: D
   Skill: Knowledge

6) The most accurate assessments of current extinction rates probably come from studies of

A) birds and mammals, because they are relatively well-known taxa.

B) marine invertebrates, because of their relatively long and complete fossil history.

C) insects, because they comprise the vast majority of extant multicellular organisms.

D) vascular plants, because they do not move around.

E) reptiles, because they are ectothermic and susceptible to population declines during frequent past glacial periods.

Answer: A
Skill: Knowledge

7) Which of the following would *not* qualify as an ecosystem service?

A) rain falling to Earth

B) blowfly larvae infesting a deer carcass

C) bees pollinating an apple tree

D) squirrels burying acorns

E) leaves falling on a forest floor

Answer: A
Skill: Comprehension

8) Which of the following is a valid conclusion about the outcome of Biosphere II?

A) Natural ecosystems are complex and not easily duplicated.

B) Humans cannot live in small spaces for an extended period of time.

C) Closed ecosystems must be made airtight.

D) Fragmented habitats can reduce species diversity.

E) Small populations are more likely to go extinct.

Answer: A
Skill: Comprehension

9) According to most conservation biologists, the single greatest threat to global biodiversity is

A) chemical pollution of water and air.

B) stratospheric ozone depletion.

C) insufficient recycling programs for nonrenewable resources.

D) alteration or destruction of the physical habitat.

E) global climate change resulting from a variety of human activities.

Answer: D
Skill: Knowledge

10) The Nile perch (*Lates niloticus*) is a good example of a(n)

A) introduced predator.

B) endangered endemic.

C) population sink.

D) threatened migratory species.

E) primary consumer.

Answer: A
Skill: Knowledge

11) Which of the following was *not* presented as an example of an introduced species?

A) red foxes in Australia

B) timber wolves in Minnesota

C) zebra mussels in the Great Lakes

D) kudzu in the southern United States

E) starlings in New York

Answer: B
Skill: Knowledge

12) Introduced species can have important effects on biological communities by

A) preying upon native species.

B) competing with native species for resources.

C) displacing native species.

D) reducing biodiversity.

E) doing all of the above.

Answer: E
Skill: Knowledge

13) Which of the following does *not* represent a potential threat to biodiversity?

A) importing a European insect into the United States to control an undesirable weed

B) building a new mall on a previously unoccupied piece of midwestern prairie.

C) letting previously used farmland go fallow and begin to fill with weeds and shrubs

D) harvesting all of the oysters from an oyster bed off the Atlantic coast

E) shooting wolves because they pose a threat to cattle farmers

Answer: C
Skill: Comprehension

14) All of the following apply to the concept of the extinction vortex *except:*

A) Populations of the species entering it are small.

B) The key factor driving the extinction vortex is intraspecific competition.

C) The genetic variation of the species' population decreases.

D) It is a concept developed by conservation biologists who adopt the "small population approach."

E) Interbreeding leads to smaller populations, which leads to more interbreeding, and so on.

Answer: B
Skill: Comprehension

15) Which of the following is a method of predicting the likelihood that a species will persist in a particular environment?

A) source–sink analysis

B) population viability analysis

C) minimum viable population size

D) population dynamic analysis

E) None of the above can predict whether a species will persist.

Answer: B
Skill: Knowledge

16) If the sex ratio in a population is significantly different from 50:50, then which of the following will always be *true*?

A) The population will enter the extinction vortex.

B) The genetic variation in the population will increase over time.

C) The genetic variation in the population will decrease over time.

D) The effective population size is greater than the actual population size.

E) The effective population size is less than the actual population size.

Answer: E
Skill: Comprehension

17) Which of the following statements related to genetic variation is *true*?

A) Genetic variation does not contribute to biodiversity.

B) Population size is always positively correlated with genetic variation.

C) Populations with low N_e are relatively susceptible to effects of bottlenecking and genetic drift.

D) Recent increases in population size of the northern sea elephant are probably related to high levels of genetic variation.

E) Cordgrass populations that live in salt marshes require great genetic variation to thrive.

Answer: C
Skill: Comprehension

18) Which of the following life history traits can potentially influence effective population size (N_e)?

   A) maturation age

   B) genetic relatedness among individuals in a population

   C) family size

   D) A and B only

   E) A, B, and C

   Answer: E
   Skill: Knowledge

19) The declining population approach to conservation strategies

   A) emphasizes the development of theories to understand the extinction process.

   B) emphasizes smallness of a population as the ultimate cause of extinction.

   C) emphasizes the environmental factors that cause a population decline.

   D) is proactive.

   E) Both C and D are true.

   Answer: E
   Skill: Comprehension

20) Conservation ecology often highlights the relationships among or between which of the following?

   A) science

   B) technology

   C) society

   D) A and C

   E) A, B, and C

   Answer: E
   Skill: Knowledge

21) A top predator that contributes to the maintenance of species diversity among its animal prey could be appropriately termed a

   A) keystone species.

   B) keystone mutualist.

   C) landscape species.

   D) primary consumer.

   E) none of the above.

   Answer: A
   Skill: Comprehension

22) Modern conservation science increasingly aims at

   A) protection of federally listed endangered species.

   B) lobbying for strict enforcement of the Endangered Species Act.

   C) sustaining biodiversity of entire ecosystems and communities.

   D) maintenance of all genetic diversity within all species.

   E) both A and B.

   Answer: C
   Skill: Knowledge

23) Which of the following would a landscape ecologist consider in designing a nature preserve?

   A) patterns of landscape use by humans

   B) human economic concerns

   C) possible edge effects related to human activities

   D) A and B only

   E) A , B, and C

   Answer: E
   Skill: Comprehension

24) Which of the following statements is *correct* about landscape ecology?

A) It is the application of ecological principles to the design and construction of sustainable lawns and gardens.

B) It is the application of ecological principles to the study of land–use patterns.

C) It focuses primarily on human–altered ecological systems.

D) It deals primarily with ecosystems in urban settings.

E) It deals with the study of the home ranges of various animals.

Answer: B
Skill: Knowledge

25) Which of the following statements is *false*?

A) Edges become more extensive with increased forest fragmentation.

B) Edges are features of human–altered habitats only.

C) Edges frequently have their own biological communities.

D) The proliferation of edge species can have a positive or negative effect on biodiversity.

E) The interface between a forest and an adjoining field would be considered an edge.

Answer: B
Skill: Comprehension

26) A movement corridor

A) is a path used by migratory animals when they move to their overwintering locales.

B) is the path most commonly used by an animal within its home range.

C) unites otherwise isolated patches of quality habitat for a species.

D) is always beneficial to a species.

E) is always some natural component of the environment.

Answer: C
Skill: Comprehension

27) Which of the following statements about movement corridors is *true*?

A) Corridors can be either strips or a series of clumps of quality habitat.

B) Corridors can be natural or constructed by humans.

C) Riparian habitats frequently serve as effective corridors.

D) A and C only are true.

E) A, B, and C are true.

Answer: E
Skill: Knowledge

28) Relatively small geographic areas with high concentrations of endemic species are known as

A) endemic sinks.

B) critical communities.

C) biodiversity hot spots.

D) endemic metapopulations.

E) bottlenecks.

Answer: C
Skill: Knowledge

29) Which of the following is (are) *true* for biodiversity hot spots for plants? They

A) have high concentrations of endemic species.

B) have large numbers of endangered and threatened species.

C) tend to be found in tropical forest and dry shrubland biomes.

D) make up a total of only 0.5% of the global land surface.

E) All of the above are true.

Answer: E
Skill: Knowledge

30) Which of the following nations has become a world leader in the establishment of zoned reserves?

A) Costa Rica

B) Canada

C) China

D) United States

E) Mexico

Answer: A
Skill: Knowledge

31) Human use of prokaryotic organisms to help detoxify a polluted wetland would be an example of

A) ecosystem augmentation.

B) keystone species introduction.

C) biological control.

D) bioremediation.

E) population viability analysis.

Answer: D
Skill: Knowledge

32) Which of the following is (are) related to the agenda of the Sustainable Biosphere Initiative?

A) defining what ecological studies are needed for conserving Earth's resources

B) maintaining productivity of man-made as well as natural ecosystems

C) understanding interactions between climate and ecological dynamics

D) resource management and development

E) all of the above

Answer: E
Skill: Comprehension

33) Conservation science includes which of the following?

A) ecology and evolution

B) physiology

C) molecular genetics

D) human social sciences and economics

E) All of the above are included within conservation science.

Answer: E
Skill: Knowledge

34) E. O. Wilson coined the term _____ for our innate appreciation of wild environments and living organisms.

A) bioremediation

B) bioethics

C) biophilia

D) biophobia

E) landscape ecology

Answer: C
Skill: Knowledge

Media Activity Questions

1) Biodiversity hot spots are recognized on the basis of the
   A) number of species present.
   B) number of endemic species.
   C) degree to which the species are threatened with extinction.
   D) numbers of species present and endemic species.
   E) all of the above.

   Answer: E
   Topic: Web/CD Activity 55A

2) Madagascar is an island in the _____ Ocean.
   A) North Atlantic
   B) South Atlantic
   C) Indian
   D) North Pacific
   E) South Pacific

   Answer: C
   Topic: Web/CD Activity 55A

3) Fire ants (*Solenopsis invicta*) are native to
   A) Australia.
   B) Southeast Asia.
   C) Africa.
   D) North America.
   E) South America.

   Answer: E
   Topic: Web/CD Activity 55B

4) Fire ants can spread naturally at a rate of up to _____ miles per year.
   A) 2
   B) 4
   C) 10
   D) 15
   E) 20

   Answer: C
   Topic: Web/CD Activity 55B

5) Carbon dioxide traps heat and warms the atmosphere. This is known as the _____ effect.
   A) warming
   B) summer
   C) carbon
   D) carbon dioxide
   E) greenhouse

   Answer: E
   Topic: Web/CD Activity 55C

Self-Quiz Questions

Answers to these questions also appear in the textbook.

1) Extinction is a natural phenomenon. It is estimated that 99% of all species that ever lived are now extinct. Why, then, do we say that we are now in a biodiversity crisis?

   A) Because of our biophilia, humans feel ethically responsible for protecting endangered species.

   B) Scientists have finally identified most of the species on Earth and are thus able to quantify the number of species becoming extinct.

   C) The current rate of extinction is as much as 1,000 times higher than at any time in the last 100,000 years.

   D) Humans have greater medical needs than at any previous time in history, and many potential medicinal compounds are being lost as plant species become extinct.

   E) Most biodiversity hot spots have been destroyed by recent ecological disasters.

   Answer: C

2) One level of the biodiversity crisis is the potential loss of ecosystems. The most likely serious consequence of a loss in ecosystem diversity would be the

   A) increase in global warming and thinning of the ozone layer.

   B) loss of ecosystem services on which humans depend.

   C) increase in the dominance of edge-adapted species.

   D) loss of a source of genetic diversity to preserve endangered species.

   E) loss of species for "bioprospecting."

   Answer: B

3) A population of strictly monogamous swans consists of 40 males and ten females. The effective population size (N_e) for this population is

   A) 50.

   B) 40.

   C) 32.

   D) 20.

   E) 10.

   Answer: C

4) Which of the following conditions is the *most* likely indicator of a population in an extinction vortex?

   A) The population is divided into smaller populations.

   B) The species is rare.

   C) The effective population size of the species is around 500.

   D) Genetic measurements indicate a continuing loss of genetic variation.

   E) All populations are connected by corridors.

   Answer: D

5) The application of ecological principles to return a degraded ecosystem to its natural state is specifically characteristic of

   A) population viability analysis.

   B) landscape ecology.

   C) conservation ecology.

   D) restoration ecology.

   E) resource conservation.

   Answer: D

6) What is the greatest threat to biodiversity?

A) overexploitation of commercially important species

B) introduced species that compete with or prey on native species

C) the high rate of destruction of tropical rain forests

D) disruption of trophic relationships as more and more prey species become extinct

E) human alteration, fragmentation, and destruction of terrestrial and aquatic habitats

Answer: E

7) Which of the following statements about the declining-population approach to conservation is *not* correct?

A) We need information on whether or not the population in question is in decline.

B) We need to do something quickly, even if we have no information, because conservation biology is a crisis discipline.

C) Several hypotheses about why the population is declining should be evaluated.

D) A proposed reason for the decline should be tested experimentally.

E) Humans may not be the cause of every population decline.

Answer: B

8) According to the small-population approach, what would be the best strategy for saving a population that is in an extinction vortex?

A) determining the minimum viable population size by taking into account the effective population size

B) establishing a nature reserve to protect its habitat

C) introducing individuals from other populations to increase genetic variation

D) determining and remedying the cause of its decline

E) reducing the population size of its predators and competitors

Answer: C

9) Which of the following statements about protected areas is *not* correct?

A) We now protect 25% of the land areas of the planet.

B) National parks are only one type of protected area.

C) Most protected areas are small in size.

D) Protected area management must be coordinated with management of lands outside the protected zone.

E) Biodiversity hot spots are important areas to protect.

Answer: A

10) What is the Sustainable Biosphere
Initiative?

A) a failed experiment that tried to create
an artificial, self-sufficient biosphere

B) a research agenda to study biodiversity
and support sustainable development

C) a conservation practice that sets up
zoned reserves surrounded by buffer
zones

D) the declining-population approach to
conservation that seeks to identify and
remedy causes of species' declines

E) a conservation program that uses
adaptive management to experiment
and learn while working with
disturbed ecosystems

Answer: C

NOTES

NOTES

NOTES

NOTES

NOTES

NOTES

NOTES

NOTES

NOTES

NOTES

NOTES

NOTES

NOTES

NOTES